The **PoP,** Rock, and **SOUL** Reader

# The PoP, ROCK, and SOUL Reader

## HISTORIES AND DEBATES

David Brackett

McGill University

New York     Oxford

OXFORD UNIVERSITY PRESS

2005

Oxford University Press

Oxford     New York
Auckland   Bangkok   Buenos Aires   Cape Town   Chennai
Dar es Salaam   Delhi   Hong Kong   Istanbul   Karachi   Kolkata
Kuala Lumpur   Madrid   Melbourne   Mexico City   Mumbai   Nairobi
São Paulo   Shanghai   Taipei   Tokyo   Toronto

Published by Oxford University Press, Inc.
198 Madison Avenue, New York, New York 10016
www.oup.com

Oxford is a registered trademark of Oxford University Press

**Library of Congress Cataloging-in-Publication Data**

Brackett, David.
   The pop, rock, and soul reader : histories and debates / David Brackett.
      p. cm.
   Includes bibliographical references and index.
   ISBN-13 978-0-19-512570-2    978-0-19-512571-9 (pbk.)
   ISBN 0-19-512570-3           0-19-15-512571-1 (pbk.)
      1. Popular music—History and criticism. 2. Popular music—Analysis, appreciation.   I.
Title.

ML3470.B75 2004
781.64'09—dc22                                                    2004041598

Text design by Cathleen Elliott

Printing number: 9 8 7 6 5 4 3 2

Printed in the United States of America
on acid-free paper

# CONTENTS

# PREFACE

*The music of a well-ordered age is calm and cheerful, and so is its govern-
ment. The music of a restive age is excited and fierce, and its government is per-
verted. The music of a decaying state is sentimental and sad and its government
is imperiled.*

— Lu Be We, ancient Chinese philosopher[1]

*It seems that music is used and produced [in one era] in the ritual in an attempt
to make people* forget *the general violence; in another, it is employed to make
people* believe *in the harmony of the world, that there is order in exchange and
legitimacy in commercial power; and finally, there is one in which it serves to
silence, by mass-producing a deafening, syncretic kind of music, and censoring
all other human noises.*

— Jacques Attali, contemporary French philosopher[2]

To some extent the genesis of this project can be blamed on my mother, who gave me a copy
of *The Rolling Stone Record Review* (a collection of reviews from *Rolling Stone* from the years
1967–70) when I was 13. I became aware of an ongoing world of criticism with its own set
of myths and assumptions about what was important in popular music. The contributors
to the *Record Review* took popular music seriously, wrote about it literately, and seemed to
share a sense of how the sound and style of popular music was bound up with contemporary social and political currents. I have continued to use that same, now-tattered paper-
back copy of the *Record Review* and its successor, *The Rolling Stone Record Review, Volume 2,*
as a reference volume for the subsequent 30 years, and two reviews from the first volume
(plus the epigraph by Lu Be We) made it into this book.

  As is true of many things that happen during puberty, reading the *Record Review* had an
impact that could not have been foreseen at the time. I subsequently morphed from music
fan and fledgling musician to music student to professional musician to music academic,
yet these early encounters with music criticism continued to exert a powerful fascination.

## The Book's Approach

In the course of teaching classes on the history of 20th- and 21st-century (mostly) U.S. popular music for several years, I began to ponder ways to explore the interconnection between
popular music, musical techniques, current events, and social identity in a way that would
make popular music as exciting and powerful for students as it had become for me. I

---

[1]*The Rolling Stone Record Review* by the Editors of *Rolling Stone* (New York: Pocket Books, 1971), i.

[2]Jacques Attali, *Noise: The Political Economy of Music,* trans. Brian Massumi (Minneapolis: University
Of Minnesota Press, 1985), 19.

wanted to find material that could address several particularly compelling questions: How did the musicians who made the music explain it? What did the music sound like? Who listened to it? Why did they listen to it? How did they react? What was the dominant impression made by the music to society at large? Why do some types of popular music still matter today?

### Readings Offer Breadth and Flexibility

Over time, it became clear to me that one of the best ways to focus attention on these questions and, in some cases, to suggest possible answers to them was to assign source readings. Source readings challenge readers to recreate the context in which the first expressions of excitement and arguments about value in various genres occurred. This engagement with the social context is a large part of the reason why source readings tend to stimulate critical thinking and lively discussions, as readers relive the controversies and conflicts that accompanied significant events in the history of popular music. The wealth of entries means that readers and instructors using this book can pick and choose readings to correspond to a variety of interests and emphases.

### Readings Provide Diverse Perspectives

A collection of source readings provides a different sense of history than do more conventional narrative histories, which tend to emphasize continuity. By contrast, the sense of history that emerges from an anthology of source readings is more disjunct in some respects, since different voices present authoritative versions of historical events that may compete or conflict with one another. This unresolved quality can be wonderfully stimulating. In this volume, for example, artists such as James Brown, Bob Dylan, the Beatles, and Jimi Hendrix can be seen through a prism of shifting perspectives consisting of critics writing at different times, as well as interviews and autobiographies of people involved in the creation of the music. This lack of resolution may also provide the impetus for classroom discussions.

### Commentary Provides an Overarching Historical Backdrop

This book is a hybrid of sorts, differing from most other anthologies in that it furnishes its own sense of linear history. In addition to the usual sort of material found in headnotes (introductions to the entries), I have provided historical background about different artists, eras, and genres. This was necessitated by several factors: First, the large social and stylistic distances between genres grouped within the larger rubric of "popular music" made transitions between some entries difficult. It didn't seem right, for example, to go from an entry discussing the aesthetic innovation and cultural importance of disco to entries discussing the different aesthetic and social context of punk, with only a headnote to function as a transition. Second, these transitional historical passages allowed me to discuss a broader range of sources than I could include in the book as entries, and they opened the book up to a wider range of uses.

### Organization Allows Broad Usage

The book is arranged chronologically by decades, with the first part of the book devoted to developments prior to the 1950s. Throughout this collection of source readings, I've woven in commentary that provides context preceding the articles and, on occasion, in the midst of them, thereby creating a hybrid text/reader. Thus the book can be used either as the main text for a course or as a supporting reader. In addition to courses on the history of 20th- and 21st-century popular music, the content applies to courses on American music, American studies, media studies, history, and sociology.

# The Selections

The documents in this collection may be grouped into two large categories; the first includes articles from general-interest magazines, music magazines, newspapers, and music industry publications, and the second is interviews and autobiographies of musicians and other participants in the music industry.

## *Journalism/Criticism*

Works of journalism and criticism convey reactions to important musical developments at the moment they began to receive public attention. The interest in these pieces—often written with a tight deadline in mind and with little thought for creating enduring historical narratives—comes from a palpable sense of excitement as the pieces respond to, for example, the appearance of a new genre, the reinterpretation of an old genre as it finds a new audience, or the impact of new technology on production and reception. Journalistic criticism is particularly useful in communicating a sense of unfolding events, since critics fill an important role, mediating between musicians, the music industry, and the audience.

Within the category of "criticism," I have included a variety of different types of writing about music, from articles and record reviews in magazines with a broad readership, to excerpts from underground "fanzines," to examples of "new journalism" in which the subjective impressions of the critic are highlighted. In deciding which pieces of criticism to select, I sought out examples of critics who have been historically influential, some of whom have played a role in the reception and meaning of the music itself. One of the clearest examples of this synergy between criticism, style, and meaning may be found in the debates that exploded in the late 1960s around rock aesthetics. These debates indicated a major shift in the reception of post–rock 'n' roll popular music and continue to illuminate debates that still rage whenever musicians and fans argue about their preferences. I also included accounts that are not particularly hip or influential in terms of popular music criticism, not in order to make fun of them or show how wrong the authors were, but because these articles are useful for conveying widespread attitudes about popular music at that time in a way that more specialized publications are not.

An interesting facet of working with journalistic sources is the variation in point of view and tone between different publications. This may be confusing for students because interpreting many of the entries often requires reading skills beyond those needed for gleaning facts from a standard textbook. The headnotes are intended to clarify some of the complicating factors: These include (to name only a few) the assumed readership of the publication, the ongoing dialogue with other critics in which the article might have been participating, and the larger issues in the music industry and/or society at large to which the article might have been alluding.

## *Interviews and Autobiographies*

I looked for statements by musicians that focused on their social and musical backgrounds and on aspects of their music that had the greatest influence on others. I concentrated on artists who had a significant historical impact even if they were not necessarily the most popular in statistical terms during the period in which they worked. I also sought the views of "backstage" figures who played an important role in the history of popular music—it was often the vision of these entrepreneurs, record producers, and engineers that led to the formation of new musical alliances and the redrawing of the stylistic map. While it may be true that many of the interviews and autobiographies display the kind of self-serving revisionism that comes with first-person re-creations of events long past, even in their idealized form these recollections can still provide a good starting point for discussions.

I do not attempt to include every important personage in popular music during the period covered here. Some figures, such as Nat "King" Cole, Frank Sinatra, and Bill Haley, while they do not have entries devoted specifically to them, are mentioned in articles, headnotes, or interviews with and autobiographies of others. These omissions are not intended as a slight or an indication of what I think is important so much as they may reflect the accessibility of primary materials that focus on these musicians. In the cases of certain genres, such as doo-wop or the girl groups, I had difficulty tracking down source materials that I found acceptable. In other cases, I simply ran out of time, luck, money, or some combination of the three. At any rate, I welcome suggestions for future editions.

## So What, Exactly, Constitutes Popular Music?

The organization of this book reflects my long-time interest in issues of genre. This interest arose out of attempts to synthesize my experiences as a musician and as an academically trained music scholar; in other words, I sought a point of articulation between music analysis—the formal or technical description of music—and the social meanings and functions of music. Focusing on genre provides an ideal theoretical framework for exploring such an interest, since genre may be understood as a way of categorizing popular music so as to create a connection among musical styles, producers, musicians, and consumers. Genres also underline how meaning circulates in a kind of "feedback loop" that binds musicians, fans, and critics. Thus no one source rooted in any one of these groups can act as the ultimate arbiter of musical significance. The focus on genre in this book resembles that of a book like Philip Ennis's *The Seventh Stream*: one that relies on a model of popular music as an assemblage of several (or, as in Ennis's case, seven) simultaneous streams, that cross, interweave, and diverge at different historical moments. Although one may quibble with what constitutes the boundaries of a stream at any given moment, the metaphor remains useful.

The main categorical or generic division, and one that occurs in every part of this book, is that between black popular music and white popular music. While there have certainly been moments of strong interconnection (the mid-1950s, for example), at other times these two large categories really do seem to exist in separate, although not necessarily equal, universes. This frequent sense of distance between musical categories, and my desire to contextualize the categories, is one of the driving forces behind what I referred to earlier as the "hybrid" nature of this anthology. The presence of these many streams is reflected in my title: I avoided calling this book *The Rock 'n' Roll Reader* or *The Rock Reader* precisely because those terms seem somewhat more limited to me, especially in that they are frequently understood as not including the full range of African American popular music since World War II. The usage of "rock," for example, sometimes refers to all popular music after 1955; at other times the term refers to popular music made by (mostly) white, (mostly) male musicians after 1965. Neither "rock 'n' roll" nor the twin usages of "rock" do justice to the rich range of genres that have dominated popular music of the past 50 years. Dave Marsh's notion of "rock and soul music" comes close to capturing the complex of styles discussed in this book and to granting recognition to the importance of African American musicians, although I felt it necessary to expand "rock" and "soul" further by adding "pop."[3]

One question that readers are bound to raise concerns the boundaries of popular music itself. While my title, *The Pop, Rock, and Soul Reader*, may project capaciousness in terms of styles and genres, I am sure that despite my best efforts, the issue of inclusiveness will inevitably arise. It is, of course, not possible to include everything (imagine how large a

---

[3]The phrase "rock and soul" comes from Dave Marsh, *The Heart of Rock and Soul: The 1001 Greatest Singles Ever Made* (New York: Da Capo Press, [1989] 1999).

book that would be!); nevertheless, I believe that the material presented here is diverse enough to encourage and enable the tracing of a variety of histories with different points of emphasis. The ability to refocus on a varying assortment of genres makes it possible to shift which dates, places, and personages seem important.

## A Note on Chronology and Sources

That this anthology provides a variety of routes through history by allowing the reader to pick and choose from among the entries also underscores the fuzziness of generic borders, in that our perceptions of these borders may shift, depending on which points of view we consider. By the same token, a genre's temporal boundaries may also appear to be imprecise if we view them from different perspectives; therefore, the histories of genres will not necessarily begin or end clearly on specific dates. Acknowledging the lack of a specific point of origin for genres, however, does not preclude the possibility that certain types of historical emphases within genres will correspond more strongly than others to the perceptions of a particular socially or culturally situated group. For example, from the point of view of the first wave of baby boomers who came of age as fans in the 1950s, 1955 may seem like an obvious date for the transformation of popular music. On the other hand, this date may seem less important to those who formed strong attachments to popular music in the 1990s or 1930s. That the book goes back to the 1920s suggests that the intrageneric dialogue that we now associate with rock 'n' roll had already started by the early decades of the 20th century.

Although I was tempted, I decided not to divide chapters by dates that create the appearance of a significant point of arrival (e.g., 1955, 1964, and 1977) in order to open the use of the book to those who disagree about when significant breaks occur. Even the division by decades does not provide an easy solution, however, since many artists who are presented here through autobiography or interview had careers that spanned several decades, and their thoughts were inflected by the period in which they were written down, a period that may have occurred long after the time of the musical events they are describing. This historical untidiness sometimes means that readings referring to a single genre are spread out over two or more chapters.

This book is also very much a history of the different types of mass media and trade publications about popular music since 1920. The surge of writing in the late 1960s significantly altered the landscape of popular music criticism, a development that is reflected in this book. Prior to the late 1960s, sources consisted of music industry publications, such as *Billboard* and *Variety;* magazines that catered to jazz aficionados, such as *Down Beat* and *Metronome;* the occasional feature piece in a general-interest magazine or newspaper; and the odd interview or musician's autobiography (although it is interesting to note that many of the interviews and autobiographies dealing with events from before 1960 were actually published after 1970, a phenomenon facilitated by the same boom that produced an abundance of new publications). Whereas the problem with finding suitable material pre-1967 was its scarcity, or the lack of variety in the type of sources, the surfeit of riches after 1967 creates the opposite problem of having too much material and too many choices.

In a few cases I have included pieces of a more scholarly hue that are particularly illuminating about an issue occurring close in time to the publication of the piece, thus putting these essays in a context similar to that of the journalistic work or the trade publications. These scholarly works, along with several intensely researched pieces that could easily pass for academic work even if their conventional assignation falls into the category of "journalism" or "trade publication," emphasize how hazy the line can be between the scholarly and the nonscholarly. However, while some of the criticism here displays the thorough research and analysis that many would associate with scholarly work, many of these pieces do not provide the type of sustained analysis found in scholarship, nor do they usually contain in-depth descriptions of musical style like those found in musicological studies. The work of critics may seem remarkably prescient or spectacularly wrongheaded after the fact, but it almost always tells us something about how people felt at the time the events were happening. Scholars, with the benefit of hindsight, are able to work backward from questions that interest them in the present, to shock, surprise, or comfort readers on the basis of how the authors perceive present-day attitudes toward their subjects. Although I am a musicologist, rather than a critic, I have emphasized criticism and trade publications far more than scholarship because criticism better served the goals of this book. An impressive expansion occurred in academic studies of popular music in the 1980s and 1990s that would require a separate volume were I to attempt to do it justice. For those hankering for a greater proportion of academic work, references are given throughout to direct readers toward relevant scholarship.

## Acknowledgments

Now for the second account of the origins of this book. In this version, the book began one fateful night several years ago when Soo Mee Kwon, then an assistant music editor at Oxford University Press (OUP), suggested that I might think about editing a "Rock and Roll Reader." I responded positively, assuming that it was the sort of project I could do in the course of other activities: preparing lectures, working on other research, or perhaps even reading the newspaper (two of these three assumptions proved to be correct). Little did I appreciate the extent of my naïveté. Despite the innocence with which I committed myself to this project, I thank Soo Mee for having the idea in the first place. In the wake of Soo Mee's departure from OUP, I had the pleasure of working with several of her successors at OUP: Jonathan Wiener, Ellen Welch, Maureen Buja, and (especially) Talia Krohn, who was an invaluable resource for me down the homestretch. I began this book with Maribeth Payne as editor, and her encouragement helped get the book off the ground. Since then, Peter Labella and finally, Jan Beatty steered the book to completion. I am grateful to all these folks for their patience in waiting for the most difficult "easy" project I have ever undertaken.

   Editing an anthology like this involves sifting through mountains of material, and I benefited enormously from the expertise of fellow popular music scholars. Thanks to Theo Cateforis, Susan Fast, Kevin Holm-Hudson, Tim Taylor, Steve Waksman, and Rob Walser, who either helped get me pointed in the right direction (sometimes even providing copies of hard-to-find articles) or who acted as sounding boards when I wandered into unfamiliar territory. Bernard Gendron's enthusiasm for the project and knowledge about primary sources helped me more than he'll ever know. Many of the connections with these scholars were made in the relaxed and collegial environs of meetings of the International Association for the Study of Popular Music (IASPM), a unique interdisciplinary organization to which I owe an enormous intellectual debt. The readers commissioned by OUP were thorough and knowledgeable. I'm sure the book is better for the suggestions of theirs that I managed to incorporate. Music and talk about music has always been a family affair, and I was lucky to have Stanley Brackett as a reader. As with virtually all my research projects, one of the best and most reliable sources of information, and one of my most diligent readers, is also in-house—a deep "thank you" goes to Buzz Brackett.

   I am also grateful to the following writers, whom I dealt with directly, for making it easy: George Csicsery, Robert Christgau, J. D. Considine, Caroline Coon, Jane Dark, Richard Goldstein, Greil Marcus, Simon Frith, Nelson George, George Lipsitz, Dave Marsh, Camille Paglia, Jon Pareles, Steve Perry, Ann Powers, Simon Reynolds, Dave Schulps, Greg Tate, and Eric Weisbard.

No anthologist is an island: I also profited from various forms of institutional support. I want to thank the dean's office of Harpur College (SUNY Binghamton) for research leave during spring 2001, which helped get the project jump-started after years of sporadic progress (even though they may have thought they were supporting another project) and for work-study help during the summer of 2002. Chris Dulgerian, a student of mine at Binghamton, helped me track down several articles. The helpful staff at the SUNY Binghamton library also played a crucial role; this book owes much to the staff at Interlibrary Loan. McGill University became my institutional home during the final phase of this project, and I want to thank McGill for an internal SSHRC grant that helped me complete the book and also to thank my new colleagues at McGill, Bill Caplin, Bruce Minorgan, Steven Heubner, who helped with the grant application.

Peter Winkler had been teaching large survey courses on popular music for years at SUNY Stony Brook when he helped me get started with my own course—thanks again, Peter. And I am grateful to my students and teaching assistants through the years in my Pop, Rock, and Soul Music course at SUNY Binghamton, who provided the laboratory where I developed a notion of how to teach large courses in popular music history.

I reserve my final expressions of gratitude for three people without whom this book would be unimaginable. First, Marion Brackett devoted much of the first year of her retirement to helping get the manuscript in shape. I owe a huge debt to her flying fingers. Second, my partner, Lisa Barg, participated in this project on virtually every level, from discussing which entries to include and how they might be edited, to reading the entire manuscript, to debating the overall philosophy of constructing such a book. I am truly fortunate to live with my best reader, who is also an endless source of support and intellectual inspiration. Last but not least, I must thank Sophie Barg Brackett, who arrived between chapters 3 and 4; the book might have been finished sooner without her, but my life would have been infinitely poorer had she not been around to help keep my priorities straight.

## A Note on the Text

There are two kinds of footnotes in this anthology: those I prepared myself and those that are being reprinted from the original source readings. I have indicated my notes with numbers and the others with symbols.

# 1. Technology, the Dawn of Modern Popular Music, and the "King of Jazz"

Prior to the 1920s, popular music in the United States mainly circulated as sheet music and in what we would now call live performance. A whole network of music publishers and theaters featuring musical productions developed in and around New York City, focused in the early years of the 20th century on 28th Street in Manhattan. This area, dubbed "Tin Pan Alley," later became the name for the style of music created there as well.[1]

The introduction of new technology in the 1920s for music consumers began a process that revolutionized the industry, leading to a shift from musical recreation, featuring performances of sheet music in the home, to an emphasis on listening to recordings or broadcast performances. Record players and discs had become standardized enough by this time to permit several companies to produce compatible equipment on a mass scale. Radio broadcasting of music developed during the decade to become a popular source of domestic entertainment.

The music industry developed a classification system that affected what types of music were recorded and how they were distributed. A "popular" category emerged, in contrast to "classical" or "serious" music, that catered primarily to bourgeois, white literate residents of urban areas. This category included music from dance bands (the music of which began to be called "jazz" during this decade), as well as recordings of solo singers that ranged in style from vaudeville (Al Jolson, Sophie Tucker), to "crooning" (Gene Austin, Rudy Vallee), to torch singing (Helen Morgan, Libby Holman).

While the story of jazz as an autonomous history is not the central concern of this book, a few moments during which jazz and popular music intersected do warrant inclusion. From the early 1920s through the

---

1. For introductions to the background and music of Tin Pan Alley, see the pertinent chapters in Charles Hamm, *Yesterdays: Popular Song in America* (New York: W. W. Norton, 1979); Alec Wilder, *American Popular Song: The Great Innovators, 1900–1950* (New York: Oxford University Press, 1972).

mid-1940s, the two categories were often synonymous. The decade of the 1920s is often referred to as the "Jazz Age"; however, the most popular music of the era—the music played by the high-society orchestras of Paul Whiteman (the "King of Jazz," 1890–1967) and Guy Lombardo, which is sometimes known as "syncopated dance music"—bears little resemblance to what contemporary listeners (or authors of jazz history books) would now recognize as jazz.[2] In the following excerpt from Whiteman's 1926 autobiography, the "King of Jazz" discusses his early recording career. Of particular interest is his discussion of the importance of keeping abreast of ever-changing dance fads and how the mysterious alchemy of the change in popular style occurs, fueled as it is by countless anonymous contributors. In his playful, self-deprecating writing style, Whiteman also describes the particular challenges of early, "acoustic" recording, and how changes in technology affected both the instrumentation heard on his recordings and the permanent makeup of his performing forces. Like many autobiographies by celebrity popular musicians, Whiteman and McBride assume an audience of fans who will associate the prose style with the public persona of the bandleader, which was, in this case, unassuming to say the least. Later denizens of dance music may be amused to hear of Whiteman's innovation in that area.

## ON WAX

### Paul Whiteman and Mary Margaret McBride

When our first records came down from the laboratories of the Victor Company for their initial "audition," a visitor exploded, "What the dickens?"

Then he listened to a few bars—he was an experienced listener—and demanded: "Who is it?"

The one step was dying a natural death and in that death was becoming apotheosized into the fox trot. But our first record was different from either. Perhaps dancers in America who are old enough will remember it. It was a twelve-inch disc, the first I think of the dance variety ever made that size, and there was a one step on one side of it arranged from the "Dance of the Hours." On the other, was the legally immortalized "Avalon" which gave occupation for a time to the copyright lawyers of two continents under the theory that it

---

2. But for surveys that do not exclude this music, see Gunther Schuller, *The Swing Era: The Development of Jazz, 1930–1945* (New York: Oxford University Press, 1989), 632–769; and Michael Campbell, *And the Beat Goes On: An Introduction to Popular Music in America, 1840 to Today* (New York: Schirmer Books, 1996). For an examination of the eclectic repertoires (which often included "syncopated dance music") of bands that were later canonized as jazz pioneers, see Jeffrey Magee, "Before Louis: When Fletcher Henderson Was the 'Paul Whiteman of the Race,'" *American Music*, 18, no. 4 (Winter 2000): 391–425.

*Source:* "On Wax," in Paul Whiteman and Mary Margaret McBride, *Jazz* (New York: J. H. Sears & Company, 1926), 223–31.

had been plagiarized from "La Tosca." This was one of the greatest fox trots of the late "glide" period.

The companion record was that masterpiece of dance composition "The Japanese Sandman," ranking with the earlier "Havanola," which Rudolph Gans had had scored by the composer and played by the St. Louis Symphony Orchestra as an example of American music. The even more popular "Whispering" was on the other side.

For years before we began to record, it had been necessary for almost all recording laboratories to change the instrumentation of nearly all orchestral pieces. Certain instruments, notably the double basses, which were then used, the horn, the tympani, and in lesser degree, other instruments, failed to yield satisfactory results. The double basses frequently were discarded and replaced by a single tuba. Modifications also in the placing of the orchestra were necessary in order to make the volume of tone from a large number of instruments converge upon a tiny diaphragm whose vibrating needle inscribed, upon a disc of wax, the mysterious grooves, which, retraced by a second needle attached to a second diaphragm, gave back the voices and accents of music.

So for all our labor and study, we had to go into the recording room and learn all over. One of the changes we made when we found that ordinary drums could not be put on the record was to use the banjo as a tune drum. The tympani and snare drum record, but the regular drum creates a muddy and fuzzed-up effect when other music is going, although solo drums make very good records. It was at this time that I tried out the banjo for the ground rhythm and discovered the possibilities of that small instrument which until then had been kept in the back and hardly heard at all. We also discovered that almost every instrument has a treacherous or bad note and that when the score calls for that note the instrument had better stop playing. An extreme dissonance would mean that the record would be blasted. For all our troubles, however, we were told that fewer changes had to be made in our scoring than in any dance records of the time. As a rule we made two records at a time, though once I believe we made nine in three days. Each record averages about an hour and a half or two hours, for there must first be a rehearsal and a test before the perfect record is passed upon by the company "hearing committee."

Recording is perhaps the most difficult task in the day's work—or the lifetime's. A slip may pass unnoticed in concert, whether across the footlights or over the radio, and even if noticed, it may be forgiven, since living flesh and sensitive will cannot always achieve mechanical perfection. But a slip in a record after a time becomes the most audible thing in it. Everything else will be neglected to wait for the slip and to call the attention of someone else uninstructed in music to a great artist's false note. So every composition has to be recorded until it is perfect. If things go fine from the first, well and good; but if, from the three records of each number usually made, there is none which will quite pass the exacting standards of the committee, there must be another afternoon of making and remaking. Every faculty of the artist, emotional as well as physical, must be expended in producing a perfect result.

In late recording practice, with highly improved methods of capturing sound and with new scientific principles, it has grown more and more practicable to record large bodies of instruments without losing volume, without having a large quantity of tone dilute and diffuse itself before reaching the actual path of the recording apparatus.

In the laboratory, as we worked, the possibilities of the orchestra began to loom large and the original plan with a single player for each type of instrument began to expand. The saxophone, for instance, had always had a shadow or understudy. A third saxophone now was added and in time the orchestra developed the full Wagnerian quartette of instruments in this group. The one trumpet was reinforced by a second and the now popular combination "straight" and "comedy" trumpets came into existence. The banjo instead of just marking time began to make new excursions into the realms of rhythm and the fox trot began to change without, however, disturbing the pedestrian order of things.

Not all these changes took place, of course, in the laboratory. Most of the rehearsing and discussing and rescoring was done in consultations outside—consultations not always free of the heat of argument. The actual business of recording is a star chamber matter but it is no violation of a secret to admit that some of our early records were spoiled by men swearing softly at themselves before they learned the new adroitness which the delicate mechanism of the recording room required.

The records of our orchestra that I have liked particularly are fox trots like the "Song of India," with its burst of two part harmony, the "Waters of the Minnetonka," with its wood wind accompanimental figure and its swinging climax and the insidiously delicate "Oh, Joseph."

One sees all one's friends and some of one's enemies at the recording laboratories and the exchange of experience between the classicist and "coonshouter," the string quartette and the clarinet jazz band is illuminating for everybody.

Not long ago, Rosa Ponselle, Mischa Elman and I were all recording at the Victor, though in different laboratories. We had lunch together and regardless of the fact that the temperature was above 90, the great dramatic soprano demonstrated a dance step for us in the best Broadway style. Then we sat for our pictures, she in her bungalow apron, Elman minus collar and coat and I in plus four knickerbockers.

It interested me that the singer should have been familiar with the current fox trot step, for with the almost weekly changes in the dance I had begun to believe that only orchestra leaders and college boys could possibly keep pace. We have even to anticipate the change and that has become our chief problem as the public is well aware. Dancers and musicians, as a rule, are harder to bring together than the various labor unions working on a big building. Ballroom dancers persistently refuse to conform to accepted or classical styles, or to any styles which they do not determine for themselves in the ballrooms of the hour. Any study of the long list of our fox trots will reveal peculiarities in tempo, rhythm and general style not to be accounted for on the basis of "individual variation," or the time-honored principle that "nature makes no two faces alike"; the simple truth of the matter is, that a dance, almost, is no sooner in the hands of the public than the style changes.

During the past half-dozen years there have been several powerfully marked variations in the ordinary, or "two-step" fox trot. The original "glide two-step" fox trot of the "Japanese Sandman" period soon was succeeded by the "radio roll" or the "scandal walk" (the two passed into one another) by the "blues," which was officially earlier but in point of fact later in the experience of many dancers than the "collegiate," which set up an entirely new style of dancing and called for an entirely new type of music. The "tango fox trot" prevailed in a few cities, the "military fox trot," and entirely local dances with fanciful, and in some cases meaningless, names, in others.

All of these changes of style or local and individual caprices in taste, have to be ministered to by a dance organization as large as ours, or we soon perish. Few new dances, except those for stage use, are ever brought forward by teachers; they are developed, in public, by persons of no particular skill, and with little or no knowledge of the dance as an art. It is avowed, and on excellent authority, that the "collegiate" sprang from the use of rubber-soled summer footwear and slow, sticky dance floors at public resorts, where the skate-like slides and pivots of the old-style dancer were impossible. With footwear of this sort it was possible to do little else than stamp up and down. From this developed a polka-like dance with crude hops and jumps, calling for agility, but with no great degree of sophisticated grace.

Small items like this determine the whole power of survival of an orchestra. When a method crystallizes or a dance is standardized, it is done. For the younger generation everywhere who invented it, without half knowing most of the time what they were about, are now through with it.

One phenomenon I noted when I was playing dance music at the Palais Royal on Broadway. A fox trot was played in a rhythm exactly that of the Habanera or Tango, but much swifter in time. The result was that the easy "chasse" skips peculiar to this type of dance became impossible to the dancers who thereby changed their rhythm from that of the tango to the easier two-step with the result that six hundred fox-trotters—not all of whom could be charged with profound musical knowledge—automatically were dancing in cross rhythm.

# 2. Big Band Swing Music
## Race and Power in the Music Business

The music most canonized as jazz during the 1920s—the small, hot combos led by Louis Armstrong, the ragtime-influenced compositions of Jelly Roll Morton—was largely the province of African American listeners and white jazz connoisseurs and did not find a mass audience. This situation changed radically in the 1930s, when popular music and what is now heard as "real jazz" began to be closely intertwined. The period from the mid-1930s through the early 1940s is commonly referred to as "The Swing Era" or "The Big Band Era," named after the large ensembles that proliferated at that time and the type of jazz they played ("Swing"). The two entries included here examine the racial politics of the Swing Era, demonstrating that contemporary writers were aware of how music that had initially been made largely by and for African Americans had been popularized mainly by white bandleaders.[1]

Marvin Freedman's article appeared in *Down Beat,* one of the first publications in the United States to cater to jazz connoisseurs. Freedman discusses the distinction between "sweet" bands (e.g., Guy Lombardo, Sammy Kaye) and those that play a "hotter" type of "swinging" jazz (Count Basie, Duke Ellington, Benny Goodman, Artie Shaw). His valuation of black musicians over white ones may seem to counter common stereotypes about white superiority, yet some stereotypes are still at

---

1. Both articles are discussed in Scott DeVeaux's excellent examination of the transformation of swing into bebop, *The Birth of Bebop: A Social and Musical History* (Berkeley: University of California Press, 1997).

work in his article: Freedman identifies black musicians with the body and natural spontaneity, while he identifies whites with the mind, calculation, and "femininity" (after all, as he writes, "even college girls" like white swing bands, such as Jimmy Dorsey's). His history of the relationship between race and the ability to play jazz is overly simple at best: Few would now agree that white musicians dominated jazz during the years 1927–31, though several of the greatest white jazz musicians produced fine music during that period. Clearly, Freedman recognizes that the relationship between race and musical style is important in jazz, but he never distinguishes whether these differences are social or biological, thus leading to a type of stereotyping that modern cultural theorists might describe as "essentialist" (the notion that "black music" consists of a fixed repertoire of stylistic elements that is transmitted genetically), although he does state that a musician does not have to be black to sound black. The article is valuable in that it shows how public awareness of the racial politics of popular music is not necessarily of recent provenance. Freedman may have been one of the first white writers to recognize so explicitly how white musicians learn from and admire black musicians.

## BLACK MUSIC'S ON TOP; WHITE JAZZ STAGNANT
### *Marvin Freedman*

Any good scientist will tell you there's no difference between the blood of a Negro and the blood of a white man. But you can still tell the color of a jazz musician by listening to the music he plays. There may be a lot of greys in between, but it's a long way from black to white.

The history of American music has been the story of two great conflicts. One of them, the fight between commercial dance music and jazz is all over. Some Guerilla warfare is going on, but the sweet corn has taken the Siegfried, Maginot, and Mannerheim lines. The other great fight, between white and black, is still in progress. Now, a good fight is worth any cause. So long as it's strictly man to man, and nixy on the brass knucks. There's conflict *inside* music. In classical music you call it counterpoint. In American music you call it swing. The soloist swinging against the rhythm section is battling it so as not to get sucked into an "on beat" Busse solo. The rhythm section is shoving the soloist to prevent him from pulling them into a Joe Daniels "military" rhythm. A sweet band can't play music, because everyone in the sweet band is docilely going in the same direction with everyone else. You can't build musical structure by merely swelling your volume. There's got to be a conflict, swing, counterpoint. That's what's good about a jam session, an old fashioned "carving" session. Everyone fight everyone to give out or to give up—then you produce your best music. The fight between black and white is good because it keeps both sides on their toes.

### Bix and Tesch Whites

Now, don't get the idea that white or black is just a difference in the color of the musician. It's a difference in the music itself. White jazz is colder, cleaner, more conscious; black music

*Source:* Marvin Freedman, "Black Music's on Top; White Jazz Stagnant," *Down Beat,* April 1, 1940, pp. 7, 20. Used with permission of Down Beat.

is richer, looser, more relaxed. Beiderbecke and Teschemacher were probably the whitest; Armstrong, Bechet, Hawkins probably the blackest. I can't tell you the difference. You either know it or you don't.

Right now, it's black on top, and white isn't climbing. Sure, there are a lot of white men playing jazz, but are they playing white or black? And when they play white is it good white?

Count Basie's band is the strongest influence in jazz. When Shaw's band beat out Goodman's, it did so by playing Basie music—weakened and commercialized Basie, but still the same black Kansas City style. Glenn Miller's band would probably fall off the stand if it heard itself swing a note, but it's getting by as a swing band, and it's black music again—Count Basie diluted some more. Charlie Barnet's band is as black a band as you'll ever hear, and that band is one of the idols of the growing white musicians. Ask Barnet if he doesn't think white men can swing only by imitating blacks.

## Crosby "Canadian Capers"

There's no white vitality anywhere in jazz. Glen Gray stayed white, and stopped playing jazz. Crosby sounds like Canadian Capers except when it imitates black New Orleans style. Dorsey wears Lord Fauntleroy pants, and even college girls like his style. Goodman imitates Basie, or imitates the Goodman of five years ago, or doesn't swing. James wishes he was Louis Armstrong or Joe Smith. Is the great Teagarden as good as he used to be? Why does a fine old timer like Fud Livingston need a Stanley? Have the last 10 years done Krupa any good?

The white Chicagoans, Pee-Wee Russell, Freeman, Kaminsky, Joe Sullivan, Condon, are walking in the footprints they made 10 years ago. At their best they're almost as good as they were then. Spanier plays as well or better than ever, but the only thing white about his music is the color of the face behind the horn.

Meanwhile, men like Basie, Hawkins, Hines, Hampton are still going forward and upward. Not all the time, but every now and then a great colored musician comes out with something new that knocks you over. Louis Armstrong isn't trying any more, but every time you listen to him you'll come away with at least one new idea. Lionel Hampton is twice as good as he was five years ago. Chu Berry, Teddy Bunn, Frankie Newton, Al Morgan, Benny Carter, Cozy Cole—they're all growing. Even old timers like Jelly Roll Morton and Sidney Bechet come out and put some of the finest jazz of all time on wax.

## Harry James Plays Black Music

When young white musicians want to encourage themselves, they listen to black music. When a white arranger wants ideas he listens to Basie or Lunceford or Redman. In the last year or so you hear white musicians say that they've got to play like colored musicians, or their music doesn't swing. Even a great musician like Harry James forsakes the white cause, and carries out the ideas of colored musicians.

It wasn't always black music. A dozen years ago, white jazz was on top. The hottest music came from white men in Chicago. Teshemacher was probably the hottest musician alive. Bud Freeman was starting out, and full of energy, as were Krupa, Condon, Sullivan. Young musicians were getting their kicks from white music. From about 1927 until as late as 1931–32 (when Bix and Tesch died), colored musicians imitated the white style. And you can prove that by listening to Fletcher Henderson records of those times. White music was so far in front that bands like Red Nichols', playing pure white style, were tremendously popular. The public liked white jazz so much that even men like Whiteman let their men play some good jazz.

## Goodman Took Up the Fight

Unfortunately for the white cause, they have no reserves. When Bix and Tesch died that took all of the strength out of white music. The white Chicagoans remained good (or great), but none of them had the necessary genius to lead a whole musical style. As white music got worse, the public and musicians discarded it. Goodman's band in about 1935 took up the fight again, and squeezed out some good white jazz. It wasn't enough, however, and I've told you the rest.

Maybe it doesn't matter. Music is music, black or white. But maybe it does. If Bix and Tesch had lived and if white music had developed (or if it develops anyway), it might have gotten (or it might get) better than Bix or Teschemacher, Louis, or any of them have done. Maybe white jazz could even conquer commercial dance music and Tin Pan Alley.

> Irving Kolodin's article touches on issues similar to those discussed by Freedman, framing them with an in-depth description of the network of live performances (frequently played in hotel ballrooms), radio broadcasts, and recordings that sustained the big bands at the apex of their success. By sticking to the different treatment received by black and white musicians, rather than trying to theorize why they sound different, Kolodin avoids some of the problems with stereotypes that haunt Freedman. The tone of the article was undoubtedly influenced by its inclusion in *Harper's*, a general-interest magazine, rather than one directed toward jazz fans, such as *Down Beat*. The article thus has more of the quality of a "human-interest" story in contrast to Freedman's essay, which conveys the passion of a fan participating in an ongoing debate.

## THE DANCE BAND BUSINESS: A STUDY IN BLACK AND WHITE

### *Irving Kolodin*

Those with a finger on the pulse of this capricious industry have an amazing instinct for estimating the moment when a band is truly "hot," in a sense unrelated to the kind of music it plays. It is at such a moment, when sales of records suddenly swing upward, and a fan club is started in Baton Rouge, and another leader tries to buy off the hitherto obscure arranger who has given the band its distinctive personality, and radio agents file requests for the band to audition, and even Winchell[2] recommends its performance, that a shrewd booker realizes that the time is at hand to tour the band on as long a series of one-nighters as the men can endure. In two months of the early summer of 1937 the Goodman band played a sequence of dates that carried it from New York to California and never found the band in the same town for two days. The Goodman share was nearly $90,000 in two months during what could hardly be called a boom period. How quickly (and mysteriously) a band can find itself in such a category is illustrated by the career of Glenn Miller. As recently as New Year's Day of 1939 Miller was playing an engagement (at union scale, or about $1,050 a week for the entire organization) at the Paradise Restaurant in New York, humbled to

---

2. Walter Winchell, famous theater and music critic based in New York City.

*Source:* Irving Kolodin, "The Dance Band Business: A Study in Black and White," *Harper's Magazine* (1941), pp. 78–82. Copyright © 1941 by *Harper's Magazine*. All Rights Reserved. Reproduced from the June issue by special permission.

second billing below the clownish group known as Freddie "Schnickelfritz" Fisher and his orchestra. For purposes of economy Miller pared his band to thirteen dispensing with a guitar player—in this profession almost a confession of bankruptcy. In the few months that followed Miller played one-night engagements for as little as $400.

During the dismal stand at the Paradise, however, Miller had made a disk of his signature music which he called "Moonlight Serenade." It embodied a curious blending of reed instruments, in which two clarinets played the melody in unison with the saxophones, but an octave higher. And from this record, and the amazing vacillations of popular enthusiasms, Miller's rise may be traced. An engagement at Dailey's Meadowbrook during the late spring of the same year tested out Miller's new style, and through radio sustaining time,[3] impressed it on a wide public. When his manager told him, during the summer of 1939, that the band would never sell for less than $700 for a one-nighter thenceforth, Miller told him he was a dreamer with a perverted sense of humor.

But less than a year later Miller's band played two successive dates to a total of 13,000 people. On one night, in St. Louis, they drew 5,400; and on the following night, in Kansas City, Missouri, they broke every record (including the inaccurate ones) for attendance at such a public, unsponsored dance by attracting 7,800 people to the Kansas City Convention Hall. Miller received $4,680 for his night's work. "It's an inspiring sight," he recalls, "to look down from the balcony on the heads of 7,000 people swaying on a dance floor—especially when you are getting $600 for every thousand of them." Concurrently, Miller held a contract for three fifteen-minute broadcasts a week for Chesterfield, which brought him a quarter of a million dollars in the first year and has recently been renewed for a second; and he was negotiating a contract for a moving picture (now in production) with $100,000 as the band's fee for eight weeks' work. It is not likely that Miller will ever use his Social Security card.

Now perhaps you can see why a band leader who has won his way to a second and a third engagement in a prominent New York hotel is rarely overjoyed with his situation. He is spending the hours from seven to two each night to earn a sum which will not cover his expenses; he is also aware that someone else might come along to take the money out of a territory he is eager to play before his popularity wanes. It might be someone as little known to the general public as Glenn Miller was at the Paradise when Goodman was blowing his clarinet in the Empire Room of the Waldorf. In this business the public does not merely want to be entertained—it wants to be entertained by a succession of new personalities, with a different instrument prominent in this year's "sensational" band than in the one they were ecstatic about the year before.

That it is possible to write a survey of this kind with no more than historic reference to the names of Paul Whiteman, Vincent Lopez, Fred Waring, Ted Lewis, Rudy Vallee, and other celebrities of the so-called Jazz Age is evidence that they have, substantially, been passed by. However, by less than the exalted standards of their highest popularity, they are not faring so badly. Waring, for example, very likely earns nearly as much now as he ever did, playing a series of brief, almost daily broadcasts for a cigarette company. Lopez still makes theater and dance-hall appearances and derives as well a moderate income from one of the lesser weekly radio shows. Vallee's radio career is momentarily in suspension, but his recent radio activities have had practically nothing to do with music anyhow. Lewis is still a person of consequence in the hinterlands, cavorting as ever with clarinet and silk hat, moaning "Is Everybody Happy?" and employing good musicians with traditional shrewdness. However, the infrequency of his appearances in New York is not altogether involuntary;

---

3. "Sustaining time": Late-night radio broadcasts paid for by the hotel from which the performance originated rather than by the radio network.

what he has to offer now he is showman enough to realize is not for sophisticates. As for Whiteman, who has made the most eager effort to adapt himself to the new mode in music, he was last heard from in Florida (after a lapse from public prominence due to illness), organizing a new band, principally for radio work.

It is rather more curious that another group of names has been even less conspicuous in this inquiry, for it embraces musicians who are in no sense moribund, and very much a part of the contemporary jazz picture. It is a list which begins with the name of Duke Ellington, and continues with those of "Count" Basie, Jimmy [Jimmie] Lunceford, Louis Armstrong, Fletcher Henderson, Ella Fitzgerald, Cab Calloway, Teddy Wilson, Andy Kirk, John Kirby, Coleman Hawkins, Erskine Hawkins, Lionel Hampton, Roy Eldridge, and sundry others. They are names with a familiar echo even to a public unfamiliar with this subject; but they are almost never to be encountered in a prominent hotel, and never on a commercial radio program.

They are of course all Negro musicians—and rigorously excluded, as if by Congressional decree, from these two principal sources of prestige and financial reward. Thus, though each enjoys a serious repute among students of jazz music, and substantial income from records and theater engagements and dance-hall appearances, they can never hope to equal the fabulous earnings of Goodman, Shaw, or Glenn Miller. Nor can the working musicians in their bands hope to attain the degree of public prominence which Gene Krupa enjoyed when he received $500 a week from Benny Goodman.

A few Northern hotels have made an exception occasionally for a particular band— Duke Ellington has played in the Panther Room of the Hotel Sherman in Chicago several times, and the Ritz-Carlton in Boston has been hospitable to both Ellington and Basie. More recently, the Pump Room of the Ambassador East in Chicago has opened its doors to Teddy Wilson, John Kirby, and "Fats" Waller, of the glib piano and raucous voice, but this is a minor room in the hotel, with little social réclame.

The single effort of a New York hotel to take advantage of the undeniable popularity of Negro swing bands was so surrounded by compromises that it collapsed quickly under the burden of its own un-certainty. It was the roof-top Cocoanut Grove of the Park Central Hotel, which placed its premises at the disposal of the late "Chick" Webb and Ella Fitzgerald when the latter was still the "A-tisket A-tasket" girl two years ago. Instead of letting the band perform as it was accustomed to, the management encouraged a kind of exhibitionism which had a disastrous effect on the playing of the musicians. There was so much "Jim Crow" in the air, together with the kind of antics which the white public believes to be inseparable from the colored man's expression of his immortal soul, that the musicians were humiliated, the knowing public repelled, and the engagement a failure.

Considering the stratagems which a hotel manager will employ to attract business to his establishment, this avoidance of such established attractions as Ellington, Basie, Armstrong, Lunceford, and Calloway can only be regarded as pathological. There is a legend that the transient trade of the large "commercial" hotels in New York includes many persons from the South, and that they would be offended to find themselves in a dining room where the musicians were colored. But the Goodman Trio and Quartet (with its Negro virtuosi Wilson, Hampton, and Christian) were ecstatically applauded when they appeared in the Empire Room of the Waldorf-Astoria though they were identified, somewhat disingenuously, as "special entertainers."

It is simply an exaggerated prejudice which no hotel manager has the enterprise to challenge or the courage to disregard. When one is driven to such a decision by such straits as influenced Weitman to experiment with bands at the Paramount it is probable that a vogue of Negro orchestras in hotels will ensue.

However the outlook is not too hopeful, Even a colored guest star on a dance band's radio commercial may bring angry mutterings from the South and one which regularly employs such musicians may write off, in advance, any hope of sales appeal in Georgia, Louisiana, and Mississippi.

If the swing fever is not what it was in 1938-39, there is still a substantial public for the orchestras which play music with precision and drive, life and flexibility—the qualities which were all but unknown in the dance music of commerce in the middle twenties and early thirties. The trend-followers and sensation-seekers who made of swing (and themselves) a public nuisance three years ago have gone on to some new enthusiasm. The youngsters who grew up with swing are sufficiently sure of their liking not to require the exhibitionistic simulation of it which made their older brothers and sisters subjects for the psychologists. Moreover, an increasingly large number of adults through the country have found swing and swing musicians an absorbing phase of general musical interest and will continue to be diverted by it regardless of its fate as a social phenomenon. Benny Goodman, Artie Shaw, Jack Teagarden, the Dorseys, Duke Ellington, and the rest continue to be important people in their lives.

# 3. Solo Pop Singers and "Der Bingle"

Bing Crosby (1903–77), the most successful solo singer of the pre–rock 'n' roll era, skillfully combined many of the distinctive qualities of the preceding generation of popular singers: the energy and rhythmic vivaciousness of Al Jolson, the use of new amplification technology to project the sensitivity of crooners like Rudy Vallee, and the spontaneity and swing of Louis Armstrong. Crosby succeeded in all the media available to him at that time—records, radio, movies—to become the first international, multmedia superstar. While he had first achieved prominence with Paul Whiteman's band in the late 1920s, Crosby was best known as a solo performer during the 1930s and 1940s, recording with studio orchestras (or occasionally smaller ensembles that had more in common with jazz groups), singing and acting in movies, and hosting his own network radio show. The only other star who could possibly rival him in the 1930s was Fred Astaire, who had an extraordinarily successful career as a dancer, actor, and singer. During World War II, a number of factors led to solo singers gradually supplanting the supremacy of big bands: the recording ban of 1943, the expense of operating a large band, the decrease in demand for dancing, and the increasing demand for sentimentality as the war progressed. The newfound dominance of solo singers also contributed to the increasing separation between popular music and jazz, as solo singers relied less on swinging rhythm, improvisation, and blues tonality.

In this excerpt from his autobiography, Bing describes how Jack Kapp encouraged him to experiment with stylistic eclecticism. This development
is significant because Crosby's eclecticism introduced pop audiences to
"hillbilly" and "race" material, albeit in cover versions, and anticipated
the eclecticism of pop music during the 1946–55 period—an important
factor that paved the way for the emergence of rock 'n' roll. The tone of
Crosby's autobiography is an extension of his homespun, folksy, and
self-deprecating public persona.

## *from* CALL ME LUCKY
### *Bing Crosby (as told to Pete Martin)*

One of the activities my family was able to help me with when they rallied around was
handling the financial affairs connected with my recordings. When I started to make
records with the Brunswick Record Corporation, Jack Kapp was the recording manager. To
my sorrow, Jack is no longer among the living, but when a disk outfit called Decca was
born, Jack went over to Decca from Brunswick and wound up as its president. It was Jack
who formulated my recording plans. He even selected the numbers I sang. He was wise
enough to have me work with a variety of bands and sing duets with different artists, so as
to give the listeners a change of pace. This policy helped keep me alive as a recording artist
long after the average performer is washed up.

Jack's progressive plans for me were due to the fact that he had a much higher opinion
of me than I had of myself. He was always striving to make me the top figure in recording.
He selected things for me a cut above ordinary popular songs, although of course I sang
those, too. In fact, Jack saw to it that I achieved a musical variety very few other recording
artists—with my limitations—were able to. I sang hillbillies and blues, ballads and Victor
Herbert, traditional songs and patriotic songs, light opera, and even an opera aria or two.

Jack wouldn't let me get typed. He kept me spread out. In addition to his desire to
make money for Decca, he took a personal interest in me. This resulted in my getting the
cream of the recording dates and opportunities.

I also worked with a lot of different arrangers. An arranger is the guiding spirit in making a successful record. He is the one who makes the vocal sound good, or he can kill a good
vocal or a good song if he's not skillful or not interested in the singer. Jack always had a lot
of those fellows available. Whenever a good arranger or a good band was free and without
previous contractual obligations, he grabbed them for a few dates with me.

If there was a chance to get the Boswell Sisters, or the Andrews Sisters, or the Mills
Brothers or the Dorsey Brothers or Woody Herman or Duke Ellington or Louis Armstrong
or Louis Jordan, Jack would give me an opportunity to work with them. That kind of backing contributes a lot toward the success of a record. This is particularly true of Louis
Armstrong. On any record we made together, I was really supporting Louis instead of vice
versa.

*Source:* Bing Crosby (as told to Pete Martin), *Call Me Lucky* (New York: Da Capo Press, [1953] 1993),
pp. 139–140.

# 4. Hillbilly and Race Music

In addition to the category of popular music, during the 1920s the music industry developed categories for music that catered to African Americans and rural, white Americans, dubbed "race" and "hillbilly," respectively. This article on the beginnings of these two latter categories appeared in *Collier's* in 1938. The faint tone of condescension found here would continue for many years in mainstream writing about these musics.[1] Astonishment mixed with condescension as writers conveyed their surprise at the success of musicians originating outside the ambit of New York's professional music circuit. Not discussed in this article is the phenomenon of the "Latin Tinge" creeping into mainstream popular music during this time via novelty numbers, such as Don Azpiazu's 1930 hit, "El Manisero (The Peanut Vendor)."[2] The author does, however, mention in passing other ethnic sources of variety for the mainstream, such as "Calypso people in the West Indies, [and] the Cajuns of Louisiana."

## THAR'S GOLD IN THEM HILLBILLIES
### Kyle Crichton

The young man with the Adam's apple seemed out of place in a New York elevator. Very definitely he was not a New Yorker and in addition he was not welcome in the crowded car because he carried under his arm a case that looked like a rough box for a horse.

"Will y'all pahdon me?" he said plaintively. "Ah'm havin' some trouble with this here git-tar."

He carried the trouble with him when he got off at the eleventh floor and was presently in a room before a microphone having an audition for phonograph records. He said, with some hesitation, that he would do imitations of Jimmie Rodgers and started in a thin wailing voice to do Blue Yodel, No.1, which has for its theme: "T for Texas, T for Tennessee and T for Thelma." It seemed that Thelma had made a bum out of somebody and was to receive a bullet from a .44 through her middle—"just for to see her jump and fall."

This was the rare thing of a New York audition for hillbilly songs and race records. The general practice is to take a recording outfit into the territory where such songs grow and

---

1. A discussion of an assortment of bemused articles about "hillbilly" music may be found in David Brackett, *Interpreting Popular Music* (Berkeley: University of California Press, [1995] 200), 101–05.

2. For more on the Latin tinge in American popular music, see John Storm Roberts, *The Latin Tinge: The Impact of Latin American Music on the United States*, 2nd ed. (New York: Oxford University Press, [1979] 1999).

*Source:* Kyle Crichton, "Thar's Gold in Them Hillbillies," *Collier's* (April 30, 1938), pp. 26–27.

out of this endeavor have come such classics as The Wreck of Old 97, Floyd Collins in the Cave, Little Old Log Cabin in the Lane, The Old Hen Cackles and The Rooster's Goin' ta Crow, Crazy Blues, Jimmie Rodgers and his Blue Yodels (Nos. 1 to 12), That Thing Called Love, Just Because, Deep Elam Blues, The Prisoner's Song, Comin' Round the Mountain, Hand Me Down My Walkin' Cane, Casey Jones, Twenty-one Years, and hundreds of others.

South of a point that might roughly be regarded as St. Albans, West Virginia, the grapevine system of news distribution still beats anything known to modern science. A hint from New York that David Kapp of Decca or Eli Oberstein of Victor is headed South will find the tidings flying over mountains and the result will be that when the city slickers arrive they will be unable to get into their hotels for the presence of mouth organ virtuosos, yodelers, blues singers and specialty bands equipped with instruments made up of tissue paper on combs, washboards, assorted saws and rutabaga gourds.

If there needs to be another picture at this point, the camera can leap agilely to such distant parts of South African and Australia where the native bushmen are busily humming a little number written by Jimmie Davis of Shreveport, Louisiana, and entitled Nobody's Darling but Mine. In short, no matter what the citizens of the United States think about their native songs, the world ranks the hillbilly ballads among the folk-tune wonders of the universe.

It started back in 1921 when Ralph S. Peer was with Okeh records. Sophie Tucker had agreed to do You Can't Keep a Good Man Down but it was found at the last moment that another contract prevented her from working for Okeh. In this crisis Perry Bradford, who was a colored song plugger for W. C. Handy (St. Louis Blues, Memphis Blues, etc.), informed Mr. Peer that he could furnish a girl who was as good as Sophie. She turned out to be Mamie Smith, a colored girl who was working as [sic] cleaning woman in a theatre. She made the Good Man song, and for the other side of the record did That Thing Called Love. Mamie had a loud raucous voice and there was great difficulty with recordings in that day of poor equipment, but the Okeh people knew they had something when the record sold 75,000 copies the first month. Mamie was forthwith yanked back into the studio and this time she brought with her a horrendous five-piece band known as Mamie Smith's Jazz Hounds. They made Crazy Blues and It's Right Here for You.

## A Market Nobody Thought Of

Bert Williams, the colored comedian, had been making records for Columbia for many years but the companies never imagined that the Negroes themselves might be a market for Negro records. In fact, the companies carefully hid the fact that colored singers were being used. About this time, dealers in New York began to report a curious trend in the business. It seemed that Negro Pullman porters on trains going South invariably left New York with as many as twenty-five records apiece under their arms. Since the records cost one dollar each, the business was big stuff and Mr. Peer went South to investigate. He found (a) that the Negroes were buying records of their own people in great quantities and (b) that the Negroes of Richmond, Virginia, invariably referred to themselves as The Race.

"We had records by all foreign groups," says Mr. Peer. "German records, Swedish records, Polish records, but we were afraid to advertise Negro records. So I listed them in the catalogue as 'race' records and they are still known as that."

About this time the vogue of Mamie Smith at Okeh was swamped by the arrival of the great Bessie Smith on Columbia records. Bessie Smith has now become almost a legendary figure and her records have lately been reissued in a new form and are considered classics in blues singing by the experts. Her most famous was Gold Coast Blues, which originally sold into the millions. It may be remarked that at the present day a sale of 100,000 records is held to be sensational in any field.

With Bessie Smith being so successful, Okeh was under the necessity of digging up a new sensation, and Mr. Peer took a portable recording outfit to Atlanta and began looking around. For some reason Atlanta is the worst town in the South for Negro talent (then and now), and Mr. Peer was soon stumped. At the suggestion of a local dealer who guaranteed to sell enough records to cover the cost, he did a few recordings by Fiddler John Carson, a white mountaineer who arrived for the recordings in overalls. Old John had been a bally-hoo man with a circus, had a repertory of hillbilly songs that never ended, and he could sing a bit with his fiddling. He made Little Old Log Cabin in the Lane, and The Old Hen Cackles and The Rooster's Goin' ta Crow.

"It was so bad that we didn't even put a serial number on the records, thinking that when the local dealer got his supply, that would be the end of it," says Mr. Peer. "We sent him 1,000 records, which he received on a Thursday. That night he called New York on the phone and ordered 5,000 more sent by express and 10,000 by freight. When the national sale got to 500,000, we were so ashamed we had Fiddler John come up to New York and do a re-recording of the numbers."

The matter of the name arose again in this connection. It was obviously impossible to list them under the designation of each section (mountaineer, "Georgia Cracker," etc.) and Mr. Peer, who had come from Kansas City and was well acquainted with the Ozarks, named them hillbilly records. The result is that the word has come to have a general application, and mountaineers of all sections are now known as hillbillies.

The greatest success of all time was made by The Prisoner's Song, which was introduced almost as an afterthought by Vernon Dalhart, who had done The Wreck of Old 97 and was desperate for something for the other side of the record. It eventually sold 2,500,000 records for the Victor company. It cost the company seven cents to make the record (all expenses included) and the wholesale price they received was thirty-seven cents a record.

## The Singing Brakeman

The greatest of all romances in the hillbilly business centers about Jimmie Rodgers, the little railroad brakeman who fought desperately against poverty and the ravages of tuberculosis until Mr. Peer discovered him in Bristol, Tennessee, and started him on a career that was fabulous even in the phonograph industry. It is estimated that the Blue Yodel records sold over 5,000,000 copies. Jimmie Rodgers is now dead and his records do not have the fame with collectors that has come to those of Bessie Smith, but he has left a mark on all hillbilly music.

When David Kapp goes out to Dallas now for Decca to record hillbilly and race records, he will do as many as 325 selections in fifteen days. The big stars now are Jimmie Davis, clerk of the Criminal Court in Shreveport, Louisiana, and Gene Autry, the singing cowboy of the movies. Another favorite group is the Carter Family of Maces Springs, Virginia, who sing and play and make marvelous didos with such instruments as the guitar and autoharp, which is really a zither with keys.

The best colored singer since Bessie Smith is said to be Georgia White, and it is in this field that some of the most remarkable records are made. There are colored numbers so strictly African and special that nobody but a Negro could understand them or appreciate them. When Sleepy John Estes does his own Negro compositions, they seem to be in another language. The melodies are strange, the words are like something out of a voodoo chant and the manner of delivery is such that they make no sense whatever to the untrained white mind. The recordings by Petie [sic] Wheatstraw come in the same class, and when Kokomo Arnold does the "sebastapool" on his guitar, effects are made that seem unearthly.

Unless the artist is also the writer of his own material and hence shares in the royalty for composers, the rewards of recording are not great, being on an average of $25 a "side." The payment is outright and there is no bookkeeping.

Among the novelty records are those made by the Calypso people in the West Indies, the Cajuns of Louisiana and Corny Allen Greer and his band.

The loyalty of the hillbilly audience to its heroes can be seen in the titles of the songs. When Jimmie Davis wrote Nobody's Darling But Mine, he immediately made a sequel entitled An Answer to Nobody's Darling. That was followed by A Woman's Answer to Nobody's Darling. Bob and Joe Shelton, who also come from Shreveport, wrote Just Because in collaboration with Leon Chappalear. When it became a success, they followed *that* with Just Because III. It is quite possible that the thing could go on forever.

Students are convinced that Bessie Smith and particularly the players who accompanied Bessie Smith on her records have had a great part in stimulating that disease known as swing music, which has now gripped the nation. Bessie had such men doing her accompaniments as Louis Armstrong, Fletcher Henderson, Joe Smith, Fred Longshaw, Charlie Green and the late James P. Johnson, one of the most spectacular of the hot pianists. Musicians are the keenest people in the world at admiring new talent and just as Benny Goodman will sit goggle-eyed now listening to the "hotteties" of Count Basie, the colored demon of Kansas City, so did the orchestra leaders of ten years ago go insane over the berserk playing of Bessie Smith's boys. From that interest came the change in orchestra music that is now so pronounced in the work of Goodman, Tommy Dorsey, Glen Gray, Jimmy Dorsey and others.

The traditional folk songs of the Southern mountaineers and the spirituals have not been included in this discussion because they occupy a special position in the art of song. In the strictest sense the mountaineer ballads are old English folk songs, some of them even traceable to old Gregorian chants; and as such they are not strictly American products. New York was recently visited by the Rev. John William Dawson, pastor of the Dry Fork Primitive Baptist Church of Morehead, Kentucky, who sang Lord, Spare Me for Another Year and The Wayfaring Stranger. The words seemed to have grown out of local legends of the mountains but the tunes stemmed back to the earliest days of American history when the first settlers crossed from the old country. Most strictly in the American tradition are the songs of Aunt Molly Jackson of Harlan County, Kentucky, who has told the story of the labor struggles of that section. Her songs are richly evocative and thrilling, carrying the troubadour quality of old.

## Fans Are Delighted

But it's when Sleepy John Estes on his guitar and Hammie Nix on his mouth organ get wound up that the newfound fans start yammering with delight. There are isolated groups in all sections of the world prepared to fight to the death to prove that Maxine Sullivan, from the Onyx Club, is a greater artist than Lily Pons. Miss Sullivan became the storm center of radio controversy as the first person to swing Loch Lomond and other old ballads. There are strange individuals who wouldn't give a Georgia White and Rhubarb Red (guitar) record for anything made by Caruso.

The cult of the hillbillies may be a passing fancy but it is significant that Ambrose, the swankiest orchestra conductor in London, has made an arrangement of Nobody's Darling But Mine. When the St. Louis Blues is made into a Metropolitan Opera, the truth will finally be evident. In the meanwhile, the nasal-voiced boys and girls of the hinterlands who have most curious things to say about love and My Gal Sal. There seems to be an awful lot of double-crossing done by the ladies in the "mountings," and they invariably pay for it. This makes art.

# 5. *Blues People* and the Classic Blues

As indicated in the preceding article, from the 1920s through the 1940s, the music industry classified most of the music made by and directed toward African Americans as "race music." Notwithstanding this practice of musical segregation, several notable African American bands were marketed in the "popular" category and heard over network radio shows; they included swing bands led by Duke Ellington, Count Basie, Jimmie Lunceford, and some of the close harmony groups, such as the Mills Brothers and the Ink Spots. The "race music" category, on the other hand, included blues, gospel tunes, piano boogie-woogies, small jazz groups, and the funkier swing bands unknown to the white public. During the 1920s, the category of race music also included types of music that would later not be closely associated with African Americans, such as music for jug bands and string bands.[1]

The name of the category itself, "race music," probably carried pejorative connotations to the executives who coined it; yet, for African Americans during this period, it also carried positive meanings: In the Harlem Renaissance of the 1920s up through the 1940s, to be a "race man" was to be active in the fight for equal rights and the recognition of black achievement and ability; this designation was obviously not limited to the "Negroes of Richmond, Virginia'" as implied by the previous article.

The previous article from *Collier's* also mentioned how the late 1920s witnessed the growing importance of newly composed gospel music in addition to secular music. Thomas Dorsey, a pianist and songwriter who had provided material and worked as an accompanist for Ma Rainey, began to write sacred material and to work with female singers, such as Mahalia Jackson and Willie Mae Ford Smith. Dorsey, known as the "Father of Gospel Music," was a major force in the development of modern gospel music and its rise to prominence in a network of African American Baptist churches across northern and Midwestern cities. As gospel developed into an important component of the "race" records category, gospel quartets like the Golden Gate Quartet and the Five Blind Boys made successful recordings throughout the 1930s and 1940s. This

---

1. For an excellent assortment of "race" and "hillbilly" recordings from the late 1920s, see the now-classic *Anthology of American Folk Music,* compiled by Harry Smith. For a discussion of the diversity of traditions issued on race records, see Paul Oliver, *Songsters and Saints: Vocal Traditions on Race Records* (Cambridge, England: Cambridge University Press, 1984). The usefulness of the term "race music" for understanding post-1940 forms of African American popular music is explored by Guthrie P. Ramsey, Jr., in *Race Music: Black Cultures from Bebop to Hip-Hop* (Berkeley: University of California Press, 2003).

style of gospel performance would play a major role in the development of "doo-wop" a capella singing, which would, in turn, play a major role in rhythm and blues, beginning in the late 1940s, and later in early rock 'n' roll. While sacred and secular music had been intertwined previously, the vitality of gospel music provided a major resource (and training ground) to which African American popular musicians continually returned.

Amiri Baraka, widely known as a poet, playwright, and associate of the Beat writers, wrote what was arguably the first social history of African American music in the early 1960s (when he was known as Leroi Jones). His *Blues People* has been much debated, its theses argued and disputed, but Jones's strong views of his subject continue to encourage readers to focus on the political aspects of this history.[2] Baraka's account is valuable both for its perspectives on the relationship between changing social conditions and the development of the classic blues and for his discussion of the historical linkages among classic blues, minstrelsy, and vaudeville. Many have argued that Baraka's views of the "whitening" of African American genres is overly simplistic and that his ideas about the connections between racial identity and musical style betray traces of essentialism.[3] He may also be faulted now for his use of the "reflection" theory between culture and art that posits a straightforward and direct relationship between social change and musical change, and others have challenged his scholarly assertions. Nonetheless, the passion and moral authority with which Jones asserts his analysis and the imaginative way in which he illuminates the aural manifestations of social forces all continue to make knowledge of this text invaluable for the student of American popular music.

## *from* BLUES PEOPLE: THE NEGRO EXPERIENCE IN WHITE AMERICA AND THE MUSIC THAT DEVELOPED FROM IT
### *Leroi Jones*

What has been called "classic blues" was the result of more diverse sociological and musical influences than any other kind of American Negro music called blues. Musically, classic blues showed the Negro singer's appropriation of a great many elements of popular American music, notably the music associated with popular theater or vaudeville. The

---

2. The most famous rejoinder came from Ralph Ellison; see his "Blues People," in *Shadow and Act* (New York: Vintage Books, [1964] 1972), 247–58.

3. Baraka modified this notion himself with the development of the idea of black music as a "changing same." See Amiri Baraka, "The Changing Same (R&B and New Black Music)," *Black Music* (New York: William Morrow, 1967), 180–211.

*Source:* Leroi Jones, from *Blues People: The Negro Experience in White America and the Music that Developed from It* (New York: William Morrow and Company, 1963), pp. 81–94. Copyright © 1963 by Leroi Jones. Reprinted by permission of HarperCollins Publishers, Inc.

instrumental music that accompanied classic blues also reflected this development, as it did the Negro musician's maturing awareness of a more instrumental style, possibly as a foil to be used with his naturally vocal style. Classic blues appeared in America at about the same time as ragtime, the most instrumental or nonvocal music to issue from Negro inspiration. Ragtime is also a music that is closely associated with the popular theater of the late nineteenth and early twentieth centuries. Although ragtime must be considered as a separate kind of music, borrowing more European elements than any other music commonly associated with Negroes, it contributed greatly to the development of Negro music from an almost purely vocal tradition to one that could begin to include the melodic and harmonic complexities of instrumental music.

Socially, classic blues and the instrumental styles that went with it represented the Negro's entrance into the world of professional entertainment and the assumption of the psychological imperatives that must accompany such a phenomenon. Blues was a music that arose from the needs of a group, although it was assumed that each man had his *own* blues and that he would sing them. As such, the music was private and personal, although the wandering country blues singers of earlier times had from time to time casual audiences who would sometimes respond with gifts of food, clothes, or even money. But again it was assumed that *anybody* could sing the blues. If someone had lived in this world into manhood, it was taken for granted that he had been given the content of his verses, and as I pointed out earlier, musical training was not a part of African tradition—music like any art was the result of natural inclination.[4] Given the deeply personal quality of blues-singing there could be no particular method for *learning* blues. As a verse form, it was the lyrics which were most important, and they issued from life. But classic blues took on a certain degree of professionalism. It was no longer strictly the group singing to ease their labors or the casual expression of personal deliberations on the world. It became a music that could be used to entertain others *formally*. The artisan, the professional blues singer, appeared; blues-singing no longer had to be merely a passionately felt avocation, it could now become a way of making a living. An external and sophisticated idea of performance had come to the blues, moving it past the casualness of the "folk" to the conditioned emotional gesture of the "public."

This professionalism came from the Negro theater: the black minstrel shows, traveling road shows, medicine shows, vaudeville shows, carnivals, and tiny circuses all included blues singers and small or large bands. The Negro theater, in form, was modeled on the earlier white minstrel shows and traveling shows which played around America, especially in rural areas where there was no other formal entertainment. The Negro theater did not, of course, come into being until after the Civil War, but the minstrel show is traceable back to the beginning of the nineteenth century. White performers using blackface to do "imitations of Negro life" appeared in America around 1800, usually in solo performances. By the 1840's, however, blackface was the rage of the country, and there were minstrel shows from America traveling all over the world. It was at least thirty more years before there were groups of traveling entertainers who did not have to use burnt cork or greasepaint.

It is essential to realize that minstrelsy was an extremely important sociological phenomenon in America. The idea of white men imitating, or caricaturing, what they consider certain generic characteristics of the black man's life in America to entertain other white men is important if only because of the Negro's reaction to it. (And it is the Negro's *reaction to* America, first white and then black and white America, that I consider to have made him such a unique member of this society.)

---

4. This is an example of one of Baraka's assertions that would be hotly questioned by contemporary scholars.

The reasons for the existence of minstrelsy are important also because in considering them we find out even more about the way in which the white man's concept of the Negro changed and why it changed. This gradual change, no matter how it was manifested, makes a graph of the movement of the Negro through American society, and provides an historical context for the rest of my speculations.

I suppose the "childlike" qualities of the African must have always been amusing to the American. I mentioned before how the black man's penchant for the supernatural was held up for ridicule by his white captors, as were other characteristics of African culture. Also, I am certain that most white Americans never thought of the plight of the black man as tragic. Even the Christian Church justified slavery until well into the nineteenth century. The "darky" at his most human excursion into the mainstream of American society was a comic figure. The idea that somehow the slavery of the black man in America was a tragic situation did not occur to white Americans until the growth of the Abolition movement. But it is interesting that minstrelsy grew as the Abolition movement grew. I would say that as the "wild savage" took on more and more of what New England Humanists and church workers considered a human aspect, there was also more in his way of life that Americans found amusing. (And who has not laughed at the cork-faced "Negro" lawmakers in D. W. Griffiths' *Birth of a Nation*? It is a ridiculous situation, ignorant savages pretending they know as much as Southern senators.) As the image of the Negro in America was given more basic human qualities, e.g., the ability to feel pain, perhaps the only consistent way of justifying what had been done to him—now that he had reached what can be called a post-bestial stage—was to demonstrate the ridiculousness of his inability to act as a "normal" human being. American Negroes were much funnier than Africans. (And I hope that Negro "low" comedy persists even long after all the gangsters on television are named Smith and Brown.)

The white minstrel shows were, at their best, merely parodies of Negro life, though I do not think that the idea of "the parody" was always present. It was sufficiently amusing for a white man with a painted face to attempt to reproduce some easily identifiable characteristic of "the darky." There was room for artistic imprecision in a minstrel show because it wasn't so much the performance that was side-splitting as the very idea of the show itself: "Watch these Niggers." Among the typical "Negro" material performed by the white minstrels are these two songs which perhaps indicate the nature of the parody white minstrelsy proposed to make of Negro life:

### The Traveling Coon
*Once there was a traveling coon*
*Who was born in Tennessee.*
*He made his living stealing chickens*
*. . . And everything else he could see.*
*Well, he traveled and he was known for miles around,*
*And he didn't get enough, he didn't get enough,*
*Till the police shot him down.*

### The Voodoo Man
*I've been hoodooed, hoodooed*
*Hoodooed by a negro voodoo;*
*I've been hoodooed, hoodooed,*
*Hoodooed by a big black coon.*

*A coon for me had a great infatuation;*
*Wanted for to marry me but had no situation.*
*When I refused, that coon he got wild.*
*Says he, "I'm bound for to hoodoo this child."*

*He went out and got a rabbit's foot and burned it with a frog*
*Right by the road where I had to pass along.*
*Ever since that time my head's been wrong.*

The black minstrel shows were also what might be called parodies, or exaggerations, of certain aspects of Negro life in America. But in one sense the colored minstrel was poking fun at himself, and in another and probably more profound sense he was poking fun at the white man. The minstrel show was appropriated from the white man—the first Negro minstrels wore the "traditional" blackface over their own—but only the general form of the black minstrel show really resembled the white. It goes without saying that the black minstrels were "more authentic," and the black shows, although they did originate from white burlesques of Negro mores, were given a vitality and solid humor that the earlier shows never had.

The minstrel shows introduced new dance steps to what could then be considered a mass audience. The cakewalk was one of the most famous dance steps to come out of minstrelsy; it has been described as "a take-off on the high manners of the white folks in the 'big house.'" (If the cakewalk is a Negro dance caricaturing certain white customs, what is that dance when, say, a white theater company attempts to satirize it as a Negro dance? I find the idea of white minstrels in blackface satirizing a dance satirizing themselves a remarkable kind of irony—which, I suppose, is the whole point of minstrel shows.)

Early Negro minstrel companies like the Georgia Minstrels, Pringle Minstrels, McCabe and Young Minstrels, provided the first real employment for Negro entertainers. Blues singers, musicians, dancers, comedians, all found fairly steady work with these large touring shows. For the first time Negro music was heard on a wider scale throughout the country, and began to exert a tremendous influence on the mainstream of the American entertainment world; a great many of the shows even made extensive tours of England and the Continent, introducing the older forms of blues as well as classic blues and early jazz to the entire world.

Classic blues is called "classic" because it was the music that seemed to contain all the diverse and conflicting elements of Negro music, plus the smoother emotional appeal of the "performance." It was the first Negro music that appeared in a formal context as entertainment, though it still contained the harsh, uncompromising reality of the earlier blues forms.[5] It was, in effect, the perfect balance between the two worlds, and as such, it represented a clearly definable step by the Negro back into the mainstream of American society. Primitive blues had been almost a conscious expression of the Negro's *individuality* and equally important, his *separateness*. The first years after the Civil War saw the Negro as far away from the whole of American society as it was ever possible for him to be. Such a separation was never possible again. To the idea of the meta-society is opposed the concept of integration, two concepts that must always be present in any discussion of Negro life in America.

The emergence of classic blues indicated that many changes had taken place in the Negro. His sense of place, or status, within the superstructure of American society had changed radically since the days of the field holler. Perhaps what is so apparent in classic

---

*From Newman Ivey White, ed., *The Frank C. Brown Collection of North Carolina Folklore* (Durham, N.C.: Duke University Press, 1962), 88–89.

5. By "earlier blues forms," I am assuming Jones is referring to what blues scholars would term the "country blues" or the "downhome blues." These blues genres are discussed later in Part 1.

blues is the sense for the first time that the Negro felt he was a *part* of that superstructure at all. The lyrics of classic blues become concerned with situations and ideas that are recognizable as having issued from one area of a much larger human concern. Classic blues is less obscure to white America for these reasons, less involuted, and certainly less *precise*. Classic blues attempts a universality that earlier blues forms could not even envision. But with the attainment of such broad human meaning, the meanings which existed in blues *only for Negroes* grew less pointed. The professionalism of classic blues moved it to a certain extent out of the lives of Negroes. It became the stylized response, even though a great many of the social and emotional preoccupations of primitive blues remained. Now large groups of Negroes could sit quietly in a show and listen to a performer re-create certain serious areas of their lives. The following blues was written by Porter Grainger and sung by Bessie Smith:

### Put It Right Here or Keep It Out There
*I've had a man for fifteen years, give him his room and board;*
*Once he was like a Cadillac, now he's like an old, worn-out Ford;*
*He never brought me a lousy dime and put it in my hand;*
*So there'll be some changes from now on, according to my plan*

*He's got to get it, bring it, and put it right here,*
*Or else he's goin' to keep it out there;*
*If he must steal it, beg it, or borrow it somewhere,*
*Long as he gets it, I don't care.*

*I'm tired of buyin' porkchops to grease his fat lips,*
*And he has to find another place for to park his old hips;*
*He must get it, and bring it, and put it right here.*
*Or else he's goin' to keep it out there.*

*The bee gets the honey and brings it to the comb,*
*Else he's kicked out of his home sweet home.*
*To show you that they brings it, watch the dog and the cat;*
*Everything even brings it, from a mule to a gnat.*

*The rooster gets the worm and brings it to the hen;*
*That oughta be a tip to all you no-good men.*
*The groundhog even brings it and puts it in his hole,*
*So my man is got to bring it—dog gone his soul.*

The "separate society" was moving to make some parallels with the larger world. An idea of theater had come to the blues, and this movement toward performance turned some of the emotional climate of the Negro's life into artifact and entertainment. But there was still enough intimacy between the real world and the artifact to make that artifact beautiful and unbelievably moving.

Classic blues formalized blues even more than primitive blues had formalized earlier forms of Negro secular music. Just as the wandering primitive blues singers had spread a certain style of blues-singing, the performers of classic blues served as models and helped standardize certain styles. Singers like Gertrude "Ma" Rainey were responsible for creating the classic blues style. She was one of the most imitated and influential classic blues singers, and perhaps the one who can be called the *link* between the earlier, less polished blues styles and the smoother theatrical style of most of the later urban blues singers. Ma Rainey's singing can be placed squarely between the harsher, more spontaneous country styles and the somewhat calculated emotionalism of the performers. Madame Rainey, as she was sometimes known, toured the South for years with a company called the Rabbit Foot Minstrels and became widely known in Negro communities everywhere in America. It was she who taught Bessie Smith, perhaps the most famous of all the classic blues singers. Both these women, along with such performers as Clara Smith, Trixie Smith, Ida Cox, Sarah Martin, Chippie Hill, Sippie Wallace, brought a professionalism and theatrical polish to blues that it had never had before. They worked the innumerable little gin towns with minstrel shows.

By the turn of the century there were hundreds of tiny colored troupes, and some larger ones like The Rabbit Foot, Silas Green's, Mahara's. There were medicine shows, vaudevilles, and circuses when minstrel shows finally died. By the early twenties there were also certain theater circuits that offered tours for blues singers, jazz bands, and other Negro entertainers. One of the most famous, or most infamous, was the old T.O.B.A. (Theatre Owners' Booking Agency), or as the performers called it, "Tough On Black Artists" (or "Asses"). Tours arranged by these agencies usually went through the larger Southern and Midwestern cities.

While the country singers accompanied themselves usually on guitar or banjo, the classic blues singers usually had a band backing them up. They worked well with the jazz and blues bands, something the earlier singers would not have been able to do. Classic blues was much more an instrumental style; though the classic singers did not lose touch with the vocal tradition, they did augment the earlier forms in order to utilize the more intricate styles of the jazz bands to good effect.

The great classic blues singers were women. Ma Rainey, Bessie Smith, and the others all came into blues-singing as professionals, and all at comparatively early ages. (Ma Rainey started at fourteen, Bessie Smith before she was twenty.) Howard W. Odum and Guy B. Johnson note from a list of predominantly classic blues titles, taken from the record catalogues of three "race" companies. "The majority of these formal blues are sung from the point of view of woman . . . upwards of seventy-five per cent of the songs are written from the woman's point of view. Among the blues singers who have gained a more or less national recognition there is scarcely a man's name to be found."* However, the great country blues singers, with exceptions like Ida May Mack or Bessie Tucker, were almost always men. But the country blues singers were not recorded until much later, during the great swell of blues and "race" recordings when the companies were willing to try almost any black singer or musician because they were still ecstatic about their newly discovered market. The first recordings of blues were classic blues; it was the classic singers who first brought blues into general notice in the United States.

There were several reasons why women became the best classic blues singers. Most of the best-known country singers were wanderers, migratory farm workers, or men who went from place to place seeking employment. In those times, unless she traveled with her family it was almost impossible for a woman to move about like a man. It was also unnecessary since women could almost always obtain domestic employment. Until the emergence of the Negro theater, Negro women either sang in the church (they were always more consistent in their churchgoing) or sang their own personal sadnesses over brown wood tubs. In the slave fields, men and women worked side by side—the work songs and hollers served both. (Given such social circumstance, one must assume that it was only the physiological inequality of the black woman, e.g., not infrequent pregnancies, that provided some measure of superiority for the male, or at least some reticence for the female.)

*I'm a big fat mama, got the meat shakin' on my bones*
*I'm a big fat mama, got the meat shakin' on my bones*
*And every time I shake, some skinny gal loses her home.*

---

*Negro Workaday Songs* (Chapel Hill, University of North Carolina Press, 1926), p. 38.

Only in the post-bellum society did the Christian Church come to mean social place-
ment, as it did for white women, as much as spiritual salvation. (Social demeanor as a basic
indication of spiritual worth is not everybody's idea. Sexual intercourse, for instance, is not
thought filthy by a great many gods.) It was possible to be quite promiscuous, if it came to
that, and still be a person capable of "being moved by the spirit." But in post-bellum Negro
society, Christianity did begin to assume the spirituality of the social register; the Church
became an institution through which, quite sophisticatedly, secular distinction was be-
stowed. The black woman had to belong to the Church, even if she was one of the chief
vestals of the most mysterious cult of Shango, or be thought "a bad woman." This was a
legacy of white American Protestantism. But the incredibly beautiful Jesus of Negro spirituals is so much a man of flesh and blood, whether he is sung of by the church women or
those women who left the Church to sing the "devil songs."

> *Dark was de night an' cold was de groun'*
> *On which de Lawd had laid;*
> *Drops of sweat run down,*
> *In agony he prayed.*
>
> *Would thou despise my bleedin' lam'*
> *An' choose de way to hell,*
> *Still steppin' down to de tomb,*
> *An' yet prepared no mo'?*
>
> *I love Jesus,*
> *I love Jesus,*
> *I love Jesus,*
> *O yes, I do,*
> *Yes, Lawdy.\**

Minstrelsy and vaudeville not only provided employment for a great many women
blues singers but helped to develop the concept of the professional Negro female entertainer. Also, the reverence in which most of white society was held by Negroes gave to those
Negro entertainers an enormous amount of prestige. Their success was also boosted at the
beginning of this century by the emergence of many white women as entertainers and in
the twenties, by the great swell of distaff protest regarding women's suffage. All these factors came together to make the entertainment field a glamourous one for Negro women,
providing an independence and importance not available in other areas open to them—the
church, domestic work, or prostitution.

The emergence of classic blues and the popularization of jazz occurred around the
same time. Both are the results of social and psychological changes within the Negro group
as it moved toward the mainstream of American society, a movement that tended to have
very significant results. The Negro's idea of America as the place where he lived and would
spend his life was broadened; there was a realization by Negroes (in varying degrees, depending upon their particular socio-economic status) of a more human hypothesis on
which to base their lives. Negro culture was affected: jazz is easily the most cosmopolitan of
any Negro music, able to utilize almost any foreign influence within its broader spectrum.
And blues benefited: it was richer, more universal, and itself became a strong influence on
the culture it had depended upon for its growth.

---

\*From *Negro Workaday Songs*, p. 196.

*Ragtime, dixieland, jazz,* are all American terms. When they are mentioned anywhere in the world, they relate to America and an American experience. But the term *blues* relates directly to the Negro, and his *personal* involvement in America. And even though ragtime, dixieland, and jazz are all dependent upon blues for their existence in any degree of authenticity, the terms themselves relate to a broader reference than blues. *Blues* means a Negro experience, it is the one music the Negro made that could not be transferred into a more general significance than the one the Negro gave it initially. Classic blues differs a great deal from older blues forms in the content of its lyrics, its musical accompaniment, and in the fact that it was a music that moved into its most beautiful form as a *public entertainment,* but it is still a form of blues, and it is still a music that relates directly to the Negro experience. Bessie Smith was not an American, though the experience she relates could hardly have existed outside America; she was a Negro. Her music still remained outside the mainstream of American thought, but it was much closer than any Negro music before it.

# 6. The Empress of the Blues

Amiri Baraka concludes his discussion of the classic blues with a reference to Bessie Smith (1894–1937), the "Empress of the Blues," the most popular and influential of the classic blues singers and one of the most popular recording artists of the 1920s. Gaining her experience from traveling vaudeville shows, Smith developed a powerful voice that could project in large spaces without amplification. Unlike the country and Delta blues singers, many of her songs were tailormade for her by professional songwriters. Thus, while she incorporates conventional blues phrasing and harmonic patterns in her singing, she also incorporates formal devices from contemporary popular song as well (this is true of "St. Louis Blues," the most famous song associated with her). The persona projected by Smith—strong, sassy, sensual—has become almost an archetype in representations of classic blues.[1] Her influence on subsequent female blues, jazz, and rock singers was strong and was felt by everyone, from Billie Holiday to Dinah Washington to Janis Joplin.

---

1. For more on issues of sexuality and place in the classic blues, see Hazel V. Carby, "'It Jus' Be's Dat Way Sometime': The Sexual Politics of Women's Blues," *Radical America* 20, no. 4 (1986): 9–24; reprinted in Robert Walser, ed., *Keeping Time: Readings in Jazz History* (New York: Oxford University Press, 1999), 351–65; see also Daphne Duval Harrison, *Black Pearls: Blues Queens of the 1920s* (New Brunswick, N.J.: Rutgers University Press, 1988); and Angela Y. Davis, *Blues Legacies and Black Feminism: Getrude "Ma" Rainey, Bessie Smith, and Billie Holiday* (New York: Vintage Books, 1999).

In the following discussion from Nat Shapiro and Nat Hentoff's classic oral history of jazz, *Hear Me Talkin' to Ya*, we hear from Frank Walker (a record company executive who was a central figure in the development of both "race" and "hillbilly" categories), Clarence Williams (a pianist and songwriter who worked with Bessie Smith), Danny Barker and Buster Bailey (musicians who accompanied her), Mezz Mezzrow (a jazz musician of the period), and Alberta Hunter (a songwriter and blues singer in her own right).

## *from* HEAR ME TALKIN' TO YA: THE STORY OF JAZZ AS TOLD BY THE MEN WHO MADE IT
### Nat Shapiro and Nat Hentoff

## Frank Walker

I don't think there could have been more than fifty people up North who had heard about Bessie Smith when I sent Clarence Williams down South to get her. Clarence did a lot of work for me then. He was very important in coaching and teaching and working on our artists. He could somehow manage to get the best out of them, and to this day hasn't received the credit he really deserves.

Clarence really wasn't much of a pianist though, he'll tell you that himself. When he was back home in New Orleans he played piano in one of those honky-tonks and could only play by ear—maybe knowing a half a dozen songs. Then some inebriate might come in and ask for a song he didn't know, and Clarence would say, "Come back tomorrow night." The next day he'd go down to the five-and-ten-cent store, to the sheet music counter, and pull out the song for the piano player to demonstrate. He would hear it once and know it. If that customer came back, Clarence would play the song and maybe pick up a dime tip. It was like some of our hillbilly artists say about songs, "I can write them down, but I can't note them."

Anyway, I told Clarence about the Smith girl and said, "This is what you've got to do. Go down there and find her and bring her back up here."

He found her, and I'm telling you that the girl he brought back looked like anything *but* a singer. She looked about seventeen—tall and fat and scared to death—just awful! But all of this you forgot when you heard her sing, because when Bessie sang the blues, she meant it. Blues were her life. She was blues from the time she got up in the morning until she went to bed at night. Oh, she had a sense of humor all right, and she could laugh too. But it didn't last long.

Her first record was *Down Hearted Blues* and it was a tremendous hit. And there was one line in that blues that did it. It was the first time it was used and it made that record a hit. It was "Got the world in a jug, got the stopper in my hand."

I don't know that there was anyone closer to Bessie than I was. She came to me for advice; I took care of her money and bookings (at one time she was probably the highest-paid

*Source:* Nat Shapiro and Nat Hentoff, *Hear Me Talkin' to Ya: The Story of Jazz as Told by the Men Who Made It* (New York: Dover Publications [1955] 1966), 239–41, 243, 244–45, 245–48.

Negro performer in vaudeville—next to Bert Williams, that is)[2]. She knew that we looked at her and treated her as a human being and not a piece of property.

It was all a matter of feeling with her. It was inside. Not that there was any repression. It all came out in her singing. Almost all of the blues she sang told sort of a story, and they were written especially for her. I don't want to give you the idea that Bessie Smith was incapable of writing her own blues, not at all. She probably could have. She would get an idea, then we would discuss it. But once she started to sing, nobody told her what to do. Nobody interfered. That was one of the reasons she liked Fletcher Henderson so much. He was quiet and never butted in. He did what Bessie told him to.

I suppose that lots of people remember and think of Bessie as a rough-and-tumble sort of person. Still, that wasn't the only side of her. They didn't know about things like her buying a rooming house for her friends to live in, and hundreds of other little things which cost her barrels of money. Yes, Bessie had a heart as big as all outdoors, but she gave it all away.

Later on, when the blues began to spread out and became established, new people were coming along and Bessie began to lose heart. You might say she didn't have a hitching post to tie her horse to. She began to lose interest in life. She had no heart left and was singing differently.

There was bitterness in her, and, you know, the blues aren't bitter.

## Danny Barker

Bessie Smith was a fabulous deal to watch. She was a pretty large woman and she could sing the blues. She had a church deal mixed up in it. She dominated a stage. You didn't turn your head when she went on. You just watched Bessie. You didn't read any newspapers in a night club when she went on. She just upset you. When you say Bessie—that was it. She was unconscious of her surroundings. She never paid anybody any mind. When you went to see Bessie and she came out, that was it. If you had any church background, like people who came from the South as I did, you would recognize a similarity between what she was doing and what those preachers and evangelists from there did, and how they moved people. The South had fabulous preachers and evangelists. Some would stand on corners and move the crowds from there. Bessie did the same thing on stage. She, in a sense, was like people like Billy Graham are today. Bessie was in a class with those people. She could bring about mass hypnotism. When she was performing, you could hear a pin drop.

## Buster Bailey

Bessie Smith was a kind of roughish sort of woman. She was good-hearted and big-hearted, and she liked to juice, and she liked to sing her blues slow. She didn't want no fast stuff. She had a style of phrasing, what they used to call swing—she had a certain way she used to sing. I hear a lot of singers now trying to sing something like that. Like this record that came out a few years ago—*Why Don't You Do Right?*—they're trying to imitate her.

We didn't have any rehearsals for Bessie's records. She'd just go with us to the studio around Columbus Circle. None of us rehearsed the things we recorded with her. We'd just go to the studio; Fletcher would get the key. This, by the way, applied not only to Bessie but to almost all the blues singers. The singers might have something written out to remind them what the verse was but there was no music written on it. On a lot of the records by Bessie you'll see lyrics by Bessie Smith and music by George Brooks. That was Fletcher.

---

2. Bert Williams was the most famous black minstrel performer of the period.

We recorded by the horn. You know the way they used to record in those days. We'd monkey around until we had a good balance and we'd make two or three but we never made more than two masters on a tune. We'd make only two sides in a session and at that time we got more money for that than we do now.

For Bessie, singing was just a living. She didn't consider it anything special. She was certainly recognized among blues singers—a shouter, they called her. They all respected her because she had a powerful pair of lungs. There were no microphones in those days. She could fill up Carnegie Hall, Madison Square Garden, or a cabaret. She could fill it up from her muscle and she could last all night. There was none of this whispering jive.

## Mezz Mezzrow

Bessie was a real woman, all woman, all the femaleness the world ever saw in one sweet package. She was tall and brown-skinned, with great big dimples creasing her creeks, dripping good looks—just this side of voluptuous, buxom shapely as a hourglass, with a high-voltage magnet for a personality.

You ever hear what happened to that fine, full-of-life female woman? You know how she died? Well, she went on for years, being robbed by stinchy managers who would murder their own mothers for a deuce of blips, having to parade around in gaudy gowns full of dime-store junk and throwaway her great art while the lushes and morons made cracks about her size and shape. She drank a lot, and there must have been plenty of nights when she got the blues she couldn't lose, but she went on singing, pouring out the richness and the beauty in her that never dried up. Then one day in 1937 she was in an automobile crash down in Mississippi, the Murder State, and her arm was almost tore out of its socket. They brought her to the hospital but it seemed like there wasn't any room for her just then—the people around there didn't care for the color of her skin. The car turned around and drove away, with Bessie's blood dripping on the floor mat. She was finally admitted to another hospital where the officials must have been color-blind, but by that time she had lost so much blood that they couldn't operate on her, and a little later she died. *See that lonesome road, Lawd, it got to end*, she used to sing. That was how the lonesome road ended up for the greatest folk singer this country ever heard—with Jim Crow directing the traffic.

## Buster Bailey

Alberta Hunter was another singer of the type I mean. She didn't need a mike. Bricktop was also in that gang. She was a good singer and she could dance. You had to sing and dance in those days. Bricktop was the one who later had a club of her own in Paris and now has one in Rome. Ma Rainey was good—you can't leave her out. But they all considered Bessie the best, like they put Louis on top. Bessie was the Louis Armstrong of the blues singers. She had more original ideas for blues and things than the others did.

## Alberta Hunter

The blues? Why the blues are a part of me. To me, the blues are—well, almost religious. They're like a chant. The blues are like spirituals, almost sacred. When we sing blues, we're singin' out our hearts, we're singin' out our feelings. Maybe we're hurt and just can't answer back, then we sing or maybe even hum the blues. Yes, to us, the blues are sacred. When I sing:

> "I walk the floor, wring my hands and cry.
> "Yes, I walk the floor, wring my hands and cry. . . ."

what I'm doing is letting my soul out.

Blues are a part of me, and when I knew nothing about music, or even about such a thing as music being written down, I was singing blues and picking them out on the piano with one finger. I was less than eleven years old when I started writing *Down Hearted Blues,* just before I ran away from home. Later on, I recorded it for Paramount Records and it was a tremendous hit. That was before Frank Walker sent for Bessie Smith. Bessie made it after it had been recorded on almost all the labels and even on piano rolls. We thought that it was exhausted, but it was Bessie's first record and it sold 780,000 copies!

No, they don't have blues singers now like they had then, except maybe Dinah Washington. There was Sara Martin, Ida Cox, Chippie Hill, Victoria Spivey, Trixie Smith, and Clara Smith and Mamie Smith, who made it possible for all of us with her recording of *Crazy Blues,* the first blues record.

But Bessie Smith was the greatest of them all. There never was one like her and there'll never be one like her again. Even though she was raucous and loud, she had a sort of a tear—no, not a tear, but there was a misery in what she did. It was as though there was something she had to get out, something she just had to bring to the fore. Nobody, least of all today, could ever match Bessie Smith.

# 7. At the Crossroads with Robert Johnson, as Told by Johnny Shines

Of the many musical forms associated with African Americans, the country blues, along with work songs and the religious ring shout, has most often been linked with West African musical practices, such as those used by the *jali* singers of the Gambia region.[1] While both *jalis* and blues singers are (frequently) troubador-like solo singers who accompany themselves on string instruments while telling stories, crucial differences exist as well: A

---

1. For the connection between country blues and the music of the *jalis,* see Paul Oliver, *Savannah Syncopators: African Retentions in the Blues* (New York: Stein and Day, 1970); and Samuel Charters, *The Roots of the Blues: An African Search* (New York: Da Capo Press, 1981). For more in-depth accounts of the *jali* tradition, see Sidia Jatta, "Born Musicians: Traditional Music from the Gambia," in Geoffrey Haydon and Dennis Marks, eds., *Repercussions: A Celebration of African-American Music* (London: Century Publishing, 1985), 14–29; and Eric Charry, *Mande Music: Traditional and Modern Music of the Maninka and Mandinka of Western Africa* (Chicago: University of Chicago Press, 2000).

*jali* sings the history of his or her people, while a blues singer describes personal experiences and the blues musician uses Western musical techniques, such as harmonic progressions and instruments based on equal temperament. Nonetheless, some view the expressive note bending and the use of multi- or polyrhythm in the blues as musical connections to *jalis,* in particular, and to West African musicmaking, in general.

In contrast to the classic blues, the country blues singers tended to be men from the rural South. The earliest recordings date from the 1920s, not too long after the first classic blues, but no country blues singer ever enjoyed the widespread success of a Bessie Smith or Ma Rainey. Of the country blues artists who recorded in the 1920s, the best known, most influential, and perhaps the most successful was Blind Lemon Jefferson (1897–1930), who sang in a high-pitched wailing style, accompanied himself on the guitar with a mixture of single-note runs and chords, and featured an extremely flexible rhythmic sense in recordings, such as "Matchbox Blues," "Black Snake Moan," and "See That My Grave Is Kept Clean."

The Delta blues were a specific variety of country blues that developed in the Mississippi Delta and featured a more driving, extroverted style of blues than that recorded by singers such as Blind Lemon Jefferson, who hailed from Texas. Other innovations, such as bottleneck or "slide" guitar and blues harmonica, also first became widespread in the Delta region. Of these Delta blues musicians, none had more impact or influence than did Robert Johnson (1911–38). Johnson, who left behind a mere 29 recordings, wrote some of the most well-known blues songs, including "I Believe I'll Dust My Broom," "Sweet Home Chicago," "Cross Road Blues," and "Come On in My Kitchen." The release of his collected recordings by Columbia in the early 1960s was one of the most important events in spurring the blues revival of that decade. Although Johnson played unamplified guitar, his style influenced numerous electric blues artists who were instrumental in the later development of Chicago blues, such as Muddy Waters and Elmore James. The drive and intensity of his guitar playing and singing were also undoubtedly responsible for the continuing popularity and influence of his recordings on subsequent generations of blues aficionados.

The following account of Robert Johnson's musical style and personality comes from an interview with Johnny Shines, who was a powerful blues performer in his own right. Shines gives a firsthand account of the social context in which he and Johnson operated and of many aspects of the Johnson myth; primary among them is how he owed his skill to a pact with the devil and how his irresistible attraction for women played a role in his untimely demise. Shines also attests to Johnson's musical prowess and skill as a performer. The magazine in which this interview appeared, *Living Blues,* is also part of the legacy of the blues revival, since it was one of a number of publications to cater to folklorists, historians, and record collectors.

# INTERVIEW WITH JOHNNY SHINES
## *Pete Welding*

Back in Hughes (Ark.) a guy named M&O, a piano player—I never did know his name [Jerry Hooks—Ed.]—him and I were playing together. Him and Robert Parnell. Piano Slim and Roosevelt Caramac, all were piano players around through there. Roosevelt Caramac was considered one of the better piano players, and Piano Slim was considered better than him because he played jazz—jazz, pop, ballads and so on, things like that. Well, we blues players called those guys "scat" players. "Oh, he ain't playing nothing but scat music." After all, we had to get back at them with something.

I worked with M&O for a while, playing blues. He was a very good blues player; he was considered one of the good piano players around there. I began to learn how to play slide too. Then, M&O he kept on after me about this boy Robert, Robert Johnson. He kept telling me about Robert Johnson. Robert Johnson, how good he was. He wanted us to meet. Because a lot of guys then, they got a thrill out of a guy getting his head bumped, you know. He wanted me to meet this boy Robert Johnson, so finally we went to Helena (Ark.) to find him. He was supposed to have been living there.

This was about 1934 or '35 that M&O took me over there to look for Robert. It was in the summertime, Helena was a pretty nice-sized town then; had its own bus service, I remember. Wasn't a city, more of a town. The joints, the places that we would play at, naturally they were in the colored section of town, which was pretty big because there were quite a lot of colored people living there then. Lots of music around too. There was Peck (Curtis), Dudlow (Taylor), fellow called Fat Man—he played a trombone or something like that, some air instrument—and I heard talk of Sonny Boy, Rice Miller, but I didn't know him then; and quite a few others. The town was loaded with musicians.

And lots of places to play there too. Juke joints, I'd guess you'd call them. The guys running them had the protection of the police—not state protection but the local police—so they kept the places open through those means. Now, a juke joint is a place where people go to play cards, gamble, drink and so on. So far as serving drinks like you would in a bar or tavern, no, it wasn't like that. Beer was served in cups; whiskey you had to drink out of the bottle. You didn't have no glasses to drink the whiskey out of, so you drank it from the bottle or you used your beer cup, and they were tin cans usually. See, they couldn't use mugs in there because the people would commit mayhem, tear people's head up with those mugs. Rough places they were. When you were playing in a place like that, you just sit there on the floor in a cane-bottomed chair, just rear back and cut loose. There were no microphones or P.A. setups there; you just sing out loud as you can.

The way you'd get those kind of jobs, if the guy owned it heard of you he'd come around and get you, tell you what he paid, and you take it or leave it. Some places was paying a dollar and a half a night but then you got many tips by playing requests, and like that. Sometimes people just throw you money anyway, just come and chuck it in your guitar. People attempt to pour whiskey in your guitar. Beer in your guitar, anything! They'd get to drinking, see, and you'd have to watch out for people like that. Most of those places were pretty rough but I didn't have too much trouble, being a good-sized fellow.

When we got to Helena, Robert was playing there, playing somewhere near every night. I thought he was about the greatest guitar player I'd ever heard. The things he was

*Source:* Pete Welding, "Interview with Johnny Shines," *Living Blues* 22 (July–August 1975): 23–24, 25–29.

doing was things that I'd never heard nobody else do. And I wanted to learn it, especially a lot of his slide stuff. He got me a job with another guy right across from where he was playing at. M&O got a job playing someplace else and later on he and I got a chance to work at this same place where I was. I got him in there.

We played there for a while and we begin to swap back and forth—Robert would come over on his break and I'd go over to where he was on my break. In the day time him and I would meet up and we would just play and, as I say, where ever you stopped with a guitar or two, why, it was a party. Truthfully, I mostly hung around where he was because Robert wasn't particular about anybody being with him. He wasn't too favorable to nobody. As I understand, he was more favorable to me than he was to most people. That was his personality; that was just his make. You had to be able to deal with him if you wanted to know him, and he was kind of long-armed. What I mean by that, he'd kind of keep you away from him. He tried at all times to keep people away from him. He wasn't interested in individuals other than . . . well, him and I had ways kind of alike, in some ways. He liked to be around older people, and I did too.

Now, Robert Jr. Lockwood's mother was Robert Johnson's old lady and she lived there in Helena. Robert Jr. and I are about the same age, I'd say. Robert Johnson was a couple of years older than me but when you try to tell people that, they won't believe it, They believe he was younger than me, but he was not. Now, Robert Jr. Lockwood's mother was his old lady even though he was very young. He was much younger than she was but she was his old lady and he wasn't but two or three years older than Robert Jr. and myself.

And for showmanship, he had a built-in showmanship radar! He could just stop anywhere and draw a crowd of people, doing anything. Now he wasn't a clown or anything like that. Here's an example. We was staying in West Memphis at a place called John Hunt's and this place burnt down and burnt our guitars up. I didn't know that he knew anything about harmonica at all but he come up with this old harmonica. We were out on Highway 61 and he started blowing this harmonica and slapping his hands—patting his hands, blowing and singing—and in a few minutes the whole highway was almost blocked off with cars, people pitching us nickels, dimes, quarters. He'd sing, I would sing. And when we got to Steels, Mo., we bought ourselves little guitars. We had money to buy guitars with! And truthfully speaking, we didn't have no money when we started out.

With the harmonica he played most of the same songs he played with the guitar, though he did play some songs that I never heard him play before but later on I did hear him play them on the guitar. He was just a guy would could pull something out of the sky.

People might consider him wild because he didn't think nothing of just taking off from where ever he was, just pack up and go. He had that about traveling. If Robert wasn't drinking he wasn't really wild, but once he got a few drinks in him it didn't make him and [sic] difference what he did. He wasn't able to take care of himself when he started drinking. As a matter of fact he wasn't man enough to take care of himself when he wasn't drinking. He couldn't punch hisself out of a wet paper sack. He just wasn't able to maneuver and take care of himself, for some reason. I've seen many people with the same build that he had that were much more capable of taking care of themselves than he was. He wasn't a scrapper or a fighter, but he tried, and he'd get the hell beat out of YOU if you didn't watch out. 'Cause he'd jump on a gang of guys just as quick as he would one and if you went to defend him, why, naturally you'd get it!

Robert didn't just perform his own songs. He did anything that he heard over the radio, ANYTHING that he heard. When I say "anything," I mean ANYTHING—popular songs, ballads, blues, anything. It didn't make him no difference what it was. If he liked it, he did it. He'd be sitting there listening to the radio—and you wouldn't even know he was paying any attention to it—and later that evening, maybe, he'd walk out on the streets and play the same songs that were played over the radio. Four or five songs he'd liked out of the whole session over the radio, and he'd play them all that evening and he'd continue to play them.

Funny thing. I never saw him just sit down and fool around with his guitar the way I did. I was steady working with mine. He'd sit down and play his guitar and whatsoever came to his mind to play, that's what he played. I never seen him sit down and try to work out a piece like I would. It seemed that he had already done that in the past and yet from what I know other people to tell me, he hadn't been playing no heck of a long time either.

When I knew him he had a Kalamazoo guitar—either that or a Kay. It was an F-hole guitar. I don't know why he chose that over a round-hole guitar but I do know it had a beautiful sound. Robert sang pretty loud and most of the time he sang in a high-pitched voice, and, naturally, his voice was carrying. We didn't have too much trouble in having ourselves heard in those places we played in. The people that was dancing, they'd just pick up the beat and if they got out of earshot, I guess the rhythm just stayed with them and they kept right on dancing. Because the whole house had the same motion, it wasn't hard for them to stay in rhythm. People would ask you to play things and that's where you made your money from, because people would ask for different requests.

See, recordings were a great thing then. At that time they didn't have nothing but these big discs on the vendors. I could take 15 cents and go to a vendor and learn any song on there, music and lyrics. And lots of things would come over the radio, and I could catch it, but not as good as Robert could. You didn't hardly hear no blues on the radio. If you heard blues on the radio it was what you might call a city blues; it wasn't none of the country blues. You got THAT stuff on the vendors and through records that you'd buy. Then, too, you picked them up from different guys along the way. Now, I don't know when the vendors started but when I was playing in those places in the '30s they were already there. In those places, the juke joints, there'd be quite a few blues on the vendors and at that time you also had Duke Ellington, Cab Calloway, Fatha Hines, Teddy Wilson, a variety of guys, piano players and things like that who had those numbers on there. Quite a bit of jazz on those vendors.

# 8. From Race Music to Rhythm and Blues
## T-Bone Walker

The migration of a large number of African Americans to northern and western cities also led to new contexts for the performance of blues and sacred music. Singers, such as Muddy Waters, who moved from Mississippi to Chicago in the 1940s, were increasingly accompanied by small ensembles that included electrically amplified guitars, harmonica, bass, and drums. The widespread popularity of big band swing during the years 1935–45 also encouraged blues musicians to add saxophones and brass instruments to their bands and to incorporate techniques of jazz arranging. Finally, some jazz musicians, many of whom had played in big bands, began to play in smaller groups and to simplify some of the harmonic and rhythmic devices of jazz in order to adapt to less favorable economic conditions for big bands and to provide danceable music. All these elements began to coalesce in the mid- to late 1940s in a new genre known as "rhythm and blues": a blues-based music that used jazz elements but was designed to meet the dancing and partying needs of an urban, African American audience. While this sound had been anticipated during the 1930s by some of the small groups led by jazz pianist and bandleader William "Count" Basie and by the boogie-woogie piano craze, the sides waxed in the early 1940s by Louis Jordan and Nat "King" Cole (both jazz musicians) demonstrated that blues performed in an urbane style could find the same kind of widespread success as the classic blues.

In 1949, *Billboard* magazine began to use the term "rhythm and blues" for all black secular popular music, conflating genres now recognized as urban blues, Chicago blues, doo-wop, small-band jazz, and rhythm and blues. The name, now shortened to "R&B," still persists as the name for the industry category and consumer genre associated with black popular music.

---

T-Bone Walker (1910–75) was one of the first blues guitar players to exploit the possibilities of the electric guitar opened up by the great jazz guitarist Charlie Christian. Walker's fusion of downhome blues with jazzy, single-note lines backed by a horn section, set the stage for the development of "urban blues" musicians, such as B. B. King and Otis Rush. The following article, written shortly after Walker's death, discusses his early influences and the development of his guitar style and includes the recollections of a number of his contemporaries. The emphasis on Walker's guitar technique springs from the publication of this article in *Guitar Player,* one of a number of magazines directed toward a specialized audience of music practitioners that began in the late 1960s and early 1970s.

## T-BONE WALKER: FATHER OF THE BLUES
### *Kevin Sheridan and Peter Sheridan*

"It's awful late, isn't it?" Blues singer Jimmy Witherspoon pauses and lets the disappointment in his statement sink in.

"It's a shame all those trade magazines didn't even write nothing about this man before he died," declares Spoon [who later recorded with Walker on *Evenin' Blues* (Prestige, 7300)]. "Most black artists are victims of this shit. I'm not being paranoid either. It's pitiful, man, it's a damn shame. A lot of these artists could have helped people like T-Bone—exposed them to a lot of youngsters by putting them on the bill with themselves. A lot of pop English groups, a lot of pop American groups—at least they could give each other exposure and let people hear you."

---

*Source:* Kevin Sheridan and Peter Sheridan, "T-Bone Walker: Father of the Blues," *Guitar Player* (March 1977): 22, 48–56.

In 1939 a young Witherspoon went to a club, Little Harlem, in East Los Angeles where T-Bone was playing. "I always wanted to sing," he recalls. "I told him I wanted to sing, and he called me up. I was just an amateur, and he let me sing. All I can say is that he's the Charlie Parker of guitars when it comes to blues. And in jazz guitarists, he's right with Charlie Christian. No one else can touch T-Bone in the blues on guitar."

The respect evident in Witherspoon's tone is almost consistent to a man when it comes to the subject of T-Bone Walker "He brought the blues guitar back in style," blues guitarist Lowell Fulson states with the resolve to set the record straight. "Blues guitar players wasn't much back in those days; if you couldn't blow a horn, why, you was just out. And T-Bone came out with "Bobby Sox Blues" in '46, then guitar players were able to work a little more, get a decent price. I always give him credit, because he's the first man brought the blues guitar—matter of fact, brought the *guitar* back in style, playing lead.

"Back in those times," Fulson goes on, "the average guitar player, if he was pretty positive into music, he wanted to be a Charlie Christian. When T-Bone brought the blues guitar out, you ought to have seen the guys going back and studying and playing and really trying to get their licks in, because the man was the only one being talked about."

Oklahoma-born Lowell Fulson met T-Bone in 1944 while in the Navy. At that time Lowell was playing guitar but not regularly; "just a little playing off the base on liberty." T-Bone was in San Diego at the Silver Slipper, and as Lowell puts it, "I never seen nobody like him at that time. Since, either."

Lowell didn't see Walker again until 1949, four years after his discharge. Bone was well on his way to legend while Lowell was just beginning to break into touring, having cut "Everyday I Have The Blues." Fulson recounts, "As I improved, agents began getting a package together called the Battle Of The Blues. It seemed at the time, me and T-Bone was pretty good drawing cards for promoters. I'll never forget—they used to call us The Big Three: me, T-Bone, and Big Joe Turner. We'd each play a separate set. I was the newest in the game, so I'd open the show. Well, Joe Turner, he didn't play an instrument, so he'd come on in the middle (instead of having both guitars together). Then T-Bone played on the end. On the last set we'd all get together and have a jam session. I really enjoyed working with those men.

"Bone used to tell me, 'Swing the blues a little more, Fulson. You can play it, swing it a little more. Put a little life into it, a little pep; rock into it. Tap your foot off of what you're doing.' It was wonderful advice; then I began to get into better houses, playing."

Lowell leans back in his chair and smiles. "He used to knock me out, because he was the only guy I'd seen play the guitar behind his head and do the splits with it. He'd tear the house up!"

T-Bone was indeed a master showman—the best according to his present peers and disciples. He did the splits without missing a beat, played leads behind his head (more than a decade before Jimi Hendrix brought the trick to rock audiences). He repeatedly excited crowds, whose women reacted by throwing purses, clothing, and even their husbands' paychecks onto the stage.

In 1942, at the age of sixteen, Riley B. King first heard T-Bone on a 78 in a jukebox. "I lived in the country, and I went to town that particular day, to this little cafe, and heard this record playing, I went to the jukebox and saw the name 'T-Bone Walker.' And I've never forgotten it; it seems like yesterday."

By that time, T-Bone's distinctive sound was well in hand, and he was playing the rocking blues with a swing touch as he would continue to do for the next three decades. "I don't think it was any particular amp," states B.B., in reference to Walker's one-of-a-kind tone; "T-Bone would play any guitar, any amp, and he would get the same sound. It was the man. I have no idea how he got his sound, but I remember Bone later telling me that he used to play banjo. I guess that was one of the things that started him playing single strings. But he was the first guy I ever heard play blues using a 9th chord."

Bone even held his guitar "different than anybody else," adds King; always slanted out, away from his body, with his chording hand curling around the neck." I think it's kind of like Wes Montgomery playing with his thumb," explains B.B. "It was comfortable for him. The only people I saw playing guitar like T-Bone played his, I saw a few guys playing steel guitar, had it around their neck. They played with the left hand free, with the bar. But to actually note it, to fret with the left hand, I haven't seen anybody else do that."

Lowell Fulson elaborates, "He was the only guitar player I've ever seen hold his guitar flat and watch his whole hand. I don't know how that man could hold his wrist over like that, playing the guitar, and not miss a note. He laid it flat like you were going to play piano or keyboards. That's the one thing other guys couldn't do. Oh, they tried to put the guitar behind their heads and do the splits—some of the younger players came up and could do that pretty good—but they never could hold the guitar out like that, so they finally let that alone.

"All his lead playing he did like that." Lowell continues, "and when he got ready to riff, he'd drop it down so he could swing his box, you understand. But when he really got down to playing, he'd turn it up, push it out from him, and go to work on it."

"His touch was so clear," B.B. states with envy. "I don't think he did much up-and-down strokes; I think he mostly picked down. Whenever he hit the strings he hit them with authority. It was almost a measured touch. You don't find too many people who have that kind of control, especially in the blues; you find it more in jazz."

Inevitably, when anyone sits down to reminisce about T-Bone Walker—guitarists, bluesmen, whomever—the conversation turns to his classic "Stormy Monday."

"To me, 'Stormy Monday' tells such a good story," stresses B.B. King, "especially for the working man. It's a very unique song."

"It's true everyday life," declares Fulson, "about the average guy. It's smooth. It goes between a ballad and a blues. It's a type of tune that will fit in any kind of club. I rate it along with 'St. Louis Blues'—you can sing it anywhere, if you can sing."

Jimmy Witherspoon is even more emphatic about his love for the tune: "It's just like a national anthem; it tells the truth. It tells the strife of working people getting paid on Friday, Saturday they go out and have a ball."

"Everybody tried to do it," adds Pee Wee Crayton, putting things into perspective, "can't anybody do it like him."

Bone's importance, concludes Spoon, lies in the fact that "he's one of the few people who put dignity into the blues. That the right word, dignity."

# 9. Jumpin' the Blues with Louis Jordan

Louis Jordan's (1908–75) role in the transition of race music to rhythm and blues is second to none. His group, the Tympany Five (which usually consisted of seven members), established the concept of the swinging small band with rhythm section (piano, bass, drums, and occasionally guitar) and a horn section consisting of two saxophones and one or two trumpets. Jordan's use of simplified swing rhythm (which became known as "shuffle rhythm"), blues harmonic patterns, and witty, vaudeville-influenced lyrics led to his achieving unprecedented popularity for an African American artist during the years 1942–49. While reviews from the period and statements from musicians who were his contemporaries stress his musicianship and his professionalism, Jordan departed from other jazz-oriented players of the day in his emphasis on pleasing audiences and his unabashed embrace of commercialism.

The following article from *Down Beat* comes from a period when Jordan was beginning to broaden his audience. The anonymous reviewer notes how Jordan is merging aspects of jazz, blues, and pop with novelty and "jump numbers." Although the writer criticizes Jordan for monotony, he acknowledges that Jordan's emphasis on entertainment results in a crowd-pleasing show. He also looks somewhat askance at those stage mannerisms that Jordan retained from his days as a vaudeville-minstrel entertainer. *Down Beat*, as mentioned earlier, was one of the first magazines to cater to jazz fans. As such, the criticisms of Jordan allude to ongoing debates among jazz critics about the relationship between jazz and commercialism.[1]

## BANDS DUG BY THE BEAT: LOUIS JORDAN
### *Down Beat*

Dynamic is the word for Jordan's compact jazz machine. One of the strongest contributing factors to Jordan's phenomenal success has been his unrelenting insistence on a continuous performance. The band came on the Savoy bandstand at ten and played one number on top of the other until two ayem [sic] with only a twenty-minute intermission. This group really works hard and manages to keep the same tension intact all through their appearance. Another very important factor contributing to the shining of Jordan's star has been those innumerable juke box sides. Playing this dance job, they took advantage of the nickel grabbers and played their recorded repertoire, most of which features the leader vocally. Louis gave with his usual gestures and rolling of the eyes but did not bother to don any stage garb to depict *Deacon Jones*. In fact, he kept the pure novelty numbers at a minimum and featured blues to a great extent with a very fine reception from the Savoy throng. Consequently there was a good deal of jazz played with Louis himself playing fine alto and some quite acceptable tenor plus a little clarinet.

---

1. These debates over value in the jazz press have received a fair amount of scholarly attention; for two studies, see Bernard Gendron, "Moldy Figs and Modernists," *Between Montmartre and the Mudd Club: Popular Music and the Avant-Garde* (Chicago: University of Chicago Press, 2002), 121–42; and Scott DeVeaux, "Constructing the Jazz Tradition: Jazz Historiography," *Black American Literature Forum* 25, no. 3 (Fall 1991): 525–60.

*Source:* "Bands Dug by the Beat: Louis Jordan," *Down Beat*, September 1, 1944, p. 4. Used with permission by *Down Beat*.

The group is closely knit and jumps like mad when really wound up. Louis' vocal on every number tended to slow up the winding however. When Eddie Roane, a fine trumpet, got a break he made the most of it and played some amazing things. His wah-wah muting accompaniment to the blues vocals showed a variety of ideas for that type of playing. His open horn is clean and full-toned. Both Louis and Eddie worked over a full and driving beat furnished by the rhythm trio, which in itself is stellar. The original Jordan pianist, Arnold Thomas, played relaxed and his fillins are well worth listening to. Al Morgan, considered one of the finest bass men still slapping the bass, fitted into the rhythm trio perfectly. Wilmore (Slick) Jones, the late Fats Waller's favorite drummer, also helped keep the rhythm going at [a] terrific pace.

Louis Jordan has versatility and one feature is some good jazz playing. One criticism, however, is the fact that every number played in jump tempo with Louis' singing is likely to become monotonous. His renditions of *G. I. Jive, Straighten Up and Fly Right*, and *Is You Is Or Is You Ain't My Baby* all sound alike. Although the band is versatile in presenting novelties, blues, jump numbers and pops, it still retains a sameness in the style of playing various types.

> In the next entry, Jordan describes his background in minstrel shows and large swing bands and his role in the development of "jump blues," a genre using a small band, blues-based forms, and shuffle rhythms. Throughout his recollections, Jordan shows a concern for the makeup of his audience, and although he recognized that he needed to please white audiences to achieve commercial success, he also believed that much of the vitality of his music came from his continued connection with black listeners. This belief is apparent in Jordan's telling account of an engagement he shared with the Mills Brothers, a band with much less connection to blues and jazz.

## *from* HONKERS AND SHOUTERS: THE GOLDEN YEARS OF RHYTHM AND BLUES
### *Arnold Shaw*

"It was a saxophone in a store window. I could see myself in the polished brass—that started me off. I ran errands all over Brinkley [Arkansas] until my feet were sore, and I saved until I could make a down payment on that shiny instrument. My father taught me music. I was still a teen-ager when I played my first gig. It was vacation time, and I blew with Rudy Williams—he was known as 'Tuna Boy' Williams. It was at The Green Gables in Hot Springs. That was about 150 miles west of Brinkley where I was born. Little Rock is in between, and about 100 miles from my hometown. I went to Arkansas Baptist College there and majored in music.[2]

---

2. While Jordan wanted to attend college, he was never able to for financial reasons despite many statements to the contrary. See John Chilton, *Let the Good Times Roll: The Story of Louis Jordan and His Music* (Ann Arbor: University of Michigan Press, 1997), 17.

*Source:* Pages 65–68, 70–71 from *Honkers and Shouters: The Golden Years of Rhythm & Blues* by Arnold Shaw. Reprinted with permission of Scribner, an imprint of Simon & Schuster Adult Publishing Group. Copyright © by Ghita M. Shaw.

"My first professional job was with The Rabbit Foot Minstrels. Ma Rainey was once the star, and Bessie Smith got her start with them. I played clarinet and danced all through the South. Around 1932, I went North, settled in Philadelphia and got connected with Charlie Gaines's band. I had eyes, you know, on the Big Apple—New York City. But it took several years before I could get a union card in Local 802.

"I worked with several bands. Joe Marshall was one. He was a drummer with Fletcher Henderson. We played the Elks Rendezvous in Harlem for a while. Around 1936 I joined Chick Webb at The Savoy. Played alto, sang, and announced numbers. Chick was a little man, hunchback, but a great drummer. He had big ears for talent—like Ella Fitzgerald, whom he adopted so she could sing with the band. But he was no showman and some people thought I was the leader because I introduced numbers.

"I loved playing jazz with a big band. Loved singing the blues. But I really wanted to be an entertainer—that's me—on my own. I wanted to play for the people, for millions, not just a few hep cats.

"When Chick died in 1938, I cut out and formed my own band. Nine pieces, and we had a regular gig at the Elks Rendezvous. Four-sixty-four Lenox Avenue was the address. Also played club dates 'off nights.' Those were nights when a band was off. I played up and down Swing Street, Fifty-second Street. After a while, I cut the nine pieces down to six. Later I added a guitar and made it seven. Once I got known as Louis Jordan and His Tympany Five, I kept the name. But I always had seven or eight men.

"After that Fifty-second Street bit, I started playing proms, like at Yale and Amherst. That's when friends began saying, 'Why don't you get out of New York, Louis? It's taking too long for you to get started.' So they came and asked me if I would play with the Mills Brothers in Chicago. The Capitol Lounge was for white folks. It was across the alley from the Chicago Theater. Not many Negroes came because they felt they weren't welcome. They wanted me to play intermission for the Mills Brothers. I started not to go—that was a big mistake.

"At first I was doing ten minutes; then they raised me to fifteen; then I got to half an hour. The Mills Brothers went over big. 'Cause the people who came to hear them and Maurice Rocco—he was the third act—they had *their* following and he had *his*. And after a while, I had *my* following. The Capitol Lounge couldn't hold two hundred people. But they would have a hundred twenty sittin' down and maybe a hundred eighty standin' at the bar. After that booking, I was gone!

"The Fox Head in Cedar Rapids was a great turning point in my career. It was there I found 'If It's Love You Want, Baby, That's Me' and a gang of blues—'Ration Blues,' 'Inflation Blues,' and others. Now, it was just a beer joint. It ran from a street to an alley. Beer was fifteen cents. The owner was a ham radio operator. He insisted that I stay at his house. He was a wonderful man.

"After my records started to sell, we drew mixed audiences to clubs like The Tick Tock in Boston, Billy Berg's Swing Club in Los Angeles, The Garrick in Chicago and The Top Hat in Toronto. The first time I played the Adams Theatre in Newark, I played with a fellow who sings like Perry Como. He was in Vic Damone's bag. And the second time I played there, I appeared with a society band like Meyer Davis. I was the Negro part, and they played the white part. That's how we did it in the early forties, so that we drew everybody. I was trying to do what they told me: straddle the fence.

"I made just as much money off white people as I did off colored. I could play a white joint this week and a colored next. The Oriental Theatre in Chicago was a white theater for the hep crowd. The State Theatre in Hartford was the same. It drew the college crowd. Same with the Riverside Theatre in Milwaukee. Any time I played a white theater, my black following was there. The Paradise Theatre in Detroit was on the borderline. The Negroes lived on that side of Woodward, and the whites on this side. Oh yeah, the Royal in Baltimore was a colored theater. But white people came to see me. The Beachcomber in Omaha was basically a Negro place. When I played there, I had white audiences. Many nights we had more white than colored, because my records were geared to the white as well as colored, and they came to hear me do my records.

"For Negroes, there were three basic theaters: Howard in Washington, Regal in Chicago, and Apollo in Harlem. In the big years, we played the Paramount on Broadway— a four-week engagement every year—and the Apollo twice a year. We appeared at the Regal in Chicago every Easter week and the Apollo every Christmas week.

"Not all of my hits was written by Negroes. 'Knock Me a Kiss' was by a white man, Mike Jackson, though Andy Razaf wrote some special words. Two white guys came up with 'Choo Choo Ch' Boogie.' I believe that Vaughn Horton and Denver Darling were really country-western writers. The song was played to me in the studio. We were recording with Milt Gabler, who handled all my Decca sessions. He brought the words and asked what I could do with them. At that time I had Wild Bill Davis playing piano. All of my things are based on the blues, twelve-bar blues. So I asked Bill to play some blues in B-flat. I was using the shuffle boogie then. He started shuffling off in B-flat, a twelve-bar phrase—and that's how we got the record together.

"'Blue Light Boogie' was by a colored woman, Jessie Mae Robinson. She was the best-oriented colored songwriter. She didn't write white songs. 'Don't Worry 'bout That Mule' was written by colored. 'Beans and Cornbread' was by a colored boy, Freddie Clark. 'The Chicks I Pick Are Slender, Tender, and Tall,' 'What's the Use of Getting Sober?,' 'Somebody Done Changed the Lock on My Door,' 'That'll just about Knock You Out,' started from a white man in Grand Forks, North Dakota. The boss of the place had a husky voice. [Imitating] He'd say it all the time. That's where we wrote the song from.

"'Saturday Night Fish Fry' was the work of a colored girl. 'Let the Good Times Roll' was by Sam Theard, a black comedian. 'Mama Blues' was by a black writer, and so was 'Small Town Boy.' That was written by Dallas Bartley, my bass man, who comes from a small town. But 'Five Guys Named Moe' was by a white guy. It was done with a Negro feel. [Sings lyrics and some of the instrumental licks] 'Beware, Brother, Beware' and 'Buzz Me' were both written by white guys. 'Early in the Mornin' ' was by a mixed group—Leo Hickman, a white man; Dallas Bartley, my bassman; and me.

"I had five tunes that sold a million records, and 'Is You Is, or Is You Ain't (Ma' Baby)?' was by a white man. I was playing at Lakota's Lounge on Wisconsin Avenue in Milwaukee. He was a little humpback fellow about the size of Chick Webb. He'd come in every night and talk to this girl. They'd have dinner and stay for lunch. He just loved me and he'd hang around so long as I was there. She'd be talkin' to someone else and he'd say to her, 'Is you is or is you ain't ma baby?' And he was strictly Caucasian—no black blood in him at all. Soon I started sayin' it. And he said, 'Let's write a song.' You can't say because of color or race that a person would not say a thing or would not do a thing.

"'Caldonia' was by a black writer, meaning me. Fleecie Moore's name is on it, but she didn't have anything to do with it. That was my wife at the time, and we put it in her name. She didn't know nothin' about no music at all. Her name is on this song and that song, and she's still getting money.

# 10. On the Bandstand with Johnny Otis and Wynonie Harris

Although not well known to many rock 'n' roll fans, Johnny Otis (b. 1921) was a major force in rhythm and blues from the late 1940s throughout the 1950s. He worked as a bandleader, record producer, disc jockey, and entrepreneur. Otis's collaborators included Willie Mae "Big Mama" Thornton (Otis played drums and produced her recording of "Hound Dog"), Little Esther, and Etta James, among others. After numerous rhythm and blues hits throughout the 1950s, in 1958 he led a recording of "Willie and the Hand Jive," which used a rhythm common throughout the African diaspora (sometimes rendered as "shave and a haircut, six bits") and became a crossover hit when revived by Eric Clapton in 1974.[1] Otis's involvement in rhythm and blues for over 50 years is remarkable for another reason; although biologically white, Otis identified with African Americans from an early age, becoming culturally, if not racially, black. His life serves as an important reminder of the instability of racial categories. As dedicated to social causes as he is to music, Otis continues to be a sterling advocate of African American popular music and political interests. Otis is also a master storyteller, and his autobiography, *Upside Your Head!* deserves to be read in its entirety.

## *from* UPSIDE YOUR HEAD! RHYTHM AND BLUES ON CENTRAL AVENUE
### *Johnny Otis*

From my vantage point on the drummer's stool in the Club Alabam, I could see the music that was to be named rhythm and blues taking shape. First in Harlan Leonard's Kansas City Rockets and later, with my own big swing band, the blues and jazz elements were

---

1. In addition to the uses of this rhythm in African American music, which are described in the following excerpt, this rhythm, in slightly varied form, also forms the basic clave rhythm of the Cuban *son*, which, in turn, provides provides the rhythmic underpinning for much salsa. For a concise exploration of this connection, see Peter Manuel, *Caribbean Currents: Caribbean Music from Rumba to Reggae* (Philadelphia: Temple University Press, 1995).

*Source:* Johnny Otis, from *Upside Your Head! Rhythm and Blues on Central Avenue* (Hanover, N.H.; Wesleyan University Press and University Press of New England, 1993), 46–47, 50. Copyright © 1993 by Johnny Otis. Reprinted by permission of the University Press of New England.

coming together. Neither Harlan's band nor mine could have been described as rhythm and blues, but the acts we were backing at the Alabam in the early and mid-forties were certainly the forerunners of the R&B style. Wynonie Harris, Jo Jo Adams, Marion Abernathy, T-Bone Walker, Little Miss Cornshucks, and Mabel Scott were the kind of artists who headlined the shows. Each of them and the many other blues-oriented performers who starred at the Alabam in those years, had a down-to-earth, uninhibited approach that set them apart from the more formal and formatted jazz and swing performers of the preceding era.

These new show stoppers grew out of the Lionel Hampton, Louis Jordan, Ray Nance, Jimmy Rushing, Illinois Jacquet tradition. The high-spirited exuberance of the African American church tradition and of the little honky-tonk clubs around America was being felt on the stages of the larger, more prestigious Black entertainment rooms. They were demonstrating that artistry, energy, and fun could coexist in Black music without sacrificing artistic integrity. Louis Armstrong had always performed in this way, and now, more and more, the deadpan stiff concept was giving way to a freer, bluesier, more entertaining form. Even in the more conservative world of bebop music, the great Dizzy Gillespie began to use dancing, good humor, and earthiness as a kind of act of love, and his burgeoning popularity among both the music experts and the general public proved him commercially and artistically correct.

During the thirties and forties and perhaps as far back as the 1920s, there evolved an interesting breed of musicians. They inhabited that musical never-never land that exists somewhere between southern blues and so-called jazz. Usually working for peanuts, in small undistinguished clubs, they made up for whatever technical shortcomings they may have had with enthusiasm and showmanship. They probably regarded themselves as "jazz" players and singers but could be tagged more accurately barrel-house or jump music stylists. A typical jazz musician wouldn't have lasted five minutes in those clubs. The customers weren't interested in musical subtlety or even virtuosity—they wanted spirited entertainment and fun. The bigger the beat, the stronger the boogie woogie flavor, and the bawdier the lyrics, the better.

Of course, bawdy by those standards would hardly raise an eyebrow today. An example of a very daring lyric for that time was the blues Count Otis Matthews sang when we played in those West Oakland greasy spoon dives. It went, "Oohwee, baby, I ain't gonna' do it no more, 'Cause every time I do it, it makes my wee wee sore!" The audience would squeal with delight.

One night in 1941, at the Peavine Club—a tacky Black joint in Reno, Nevada—Count Otis sang his risqué little verse, and a burly, white plainclothes cop materialized out of the shadows and snarled, "Sing one more dirty, filthy song and I'm taking all you niggers down!" After that, our most daring number was "Mama Bought a Chicken."

A rhythm and blues "shouter" who had a large influence on early rock 'n' roll singing, Wynonie Harris (1915–69) developed his style in midwestern swing bands and in the emerging Los Angeles rhythm and blues scene, where he worked with Johnny Otis. After scoring R&B hits with Lucky Millinder's band, Harris recorded under his own name, frequently working with jazz-influenced combos. His recordings for King Records, under the guidance of Henry Glover, were eclectic, including both the prototypical rocker, "Good Rockin' Tonight" and country western-derived material.

In this self-penned article, which appeared in the African American monthly, *Tan*, Harris describes how he consciously exploits the sexual connotations of R&B and manipulates stereotypes about the sexuality of blues performers. Along the way, he makes numerous insightful observations about the relationship between gospel and R&B, his eclectic use of materials, and the source of his appeal.

## WOMEN WON'T LET ME ALONE
### *Wynonie "Mr. Blues" Harris*

I've made dozens of records and most of them have sold over the 250,000 mark. Among them were *Young and Wild*, for which Walter Winchell once gave me an orchid. This was highly unusual, for Broadway columnists like Winchell don't dig the Negro blues. I stole *Good Rocking Tonight* from my man, Roy Brown, and also his *Miss Fanny Brown*, and made bigger hits out of them and more money off them than he ever did.

My version of *Good Rocking* started the present vogue of "rocking" blues tunes. When I say I stole the tunes, I mean that I waited until Roy had made his sides and then out-sang him with my own interpretation. *Papa Tree Top* and *Lollypop* were a couple of other big sellers for me.

I reached into the hillbilly feedbag and got hold of Hank Snow's *Don't Roll Them Bloodshot Eyes At Me*. It was a scorcher. So was *Good Morning, Judge*, another hillbilly.

There was once an impression that the blues had driven me stone crazy. I agree. I'm crazy like a fox for I've got enough to retire on tomorrow when I get tired of having fun. I'm not like a lot of fellows who are now on their heels and haven't even got started because they let the women go to their heads and threw their money away to help prove it. I draw a definite line. I play to create impressions. The women who really know me also know part of my secret. We can laugh about it together for they know how women can get stirred up by a man who seems cruel, ornery, vulgar and arrogant.

But no woman will ever completely dig me for such a woman hasn't yet been born. I'm cool about it because I know what I'm doing and the chicks who try to be as slick as I don't know I know what's going on. To them I say, I'm glad to see you with it because I saw you go and get it. Those who can't dig that most assuredly can't dig me.

Oh, yes. There was once a lot of publicity around about me going into the ministry. They said that I was quitting the blues singing business and getting myself lined up for a pulpit job. Well, I don't mix the Lord and the Devil. They are the two I'm most afraid of. As long as I'm with the Devil, I'm going to shake him down for everything, every dime I can get. But when I quit him, It'll be time enough for me to thumb my nose at him and tell him to go plumb straight back to hell!

*Source:* Wynonie "Mr. Blues" Harris, "Women Won't Let Me Alone," *Tan* (October 1954), p. 77.

# 11. The Producers Answer Back

## The Emergence of the "Indie" Record Company

The article reproduced in chapter 4, "Thar's Gold in Them Hillbillies," discussed the position of the "race" and "hillbilly" categories in relation to mainstream "popular" music during the 1920s and 1930s. What that article did not really discuss or analyze was how the structure of the music industry in the United States discriminated against popular musicians outside the "mainstream." Radio was dominated by national network shows (somewhat analogous to network television), which played a broad range of programs: music variety, dramas, comedies, news, concerts, and so forth. The music featured on these shows tended to consist of songs written by professionals employed in Tin Pan Alley. These songwriters also were responsible for the vast majority of Broadway (and, after 1930, Hollywood) musicals. The main organization responsible for securing royalties for songwriters was a publishing-rights organization known as the American Society of Composers and Publishers (ASCAP). ASCAP had stringent rules about whom they would accept as a composer, and most composers of hillbilly and race music did not fit their guidelines. These songwriters were thus excluded both from receiving exposure via radio broadcasts and from collecting revenue from their songs (which might accrue from either jukebox play, sales of recordings, public performance, or radio broadcasts).[1]

This situation began to change on several fronts in the late 1930s. A publishing-rights organization, Broadcast Music Incorporated (BMI), formed with somewhat looser guidelines than ASCAP about what constituted an acceptable composition and about what type of people might qualify as acceptable composers. Small, local radio stations proliferated that began to play "hillbilly" music (stations devoted to "race" music developed a bit later). "Barn Dance" shows, such as the Grand Ole Opry, and the WLS *National Barn Dance*, both of which had been broadcasting since 1925, reached larger audiences, and the Grand Ole Opry even procured a half-hour Saturday night slot on the NBC radio network. Recording bans during 1942 and 1943 increased interest by the radio networks in alternative sources for recordings, a development that also facilitated crossovers and cover tunes of both hillbilly and race music. And, immediately following the war, the number of independent record companies

---

1. See John Ryan, *The Production of Culture in the Music Industry: The ASCAP-BMI Controversy* (New York: Rowman and Littlefield, 1985); Russell Sanjek and David Sanjek, *Pennies from Heaven: The American Popular Music Business in the Twentieth Century* (New York: Da Capo Press, 1996); and Philip T. Ennis, *The Seventh Stream: The Emergence of Rocknroll in American Popular Music* (Hanover: University Press of New England, 1992).

catering to these types of music grew at an unprecedented rate. All these developments set the stage for a massive shift in the role played by hillbilly and race music in popular music.

---

The following article demonstrates the music industry's awareness of the growing role of independent record companies. During the late 1940s, four major companies dominated record sales: RCA Victor, Columbia, Decca, and Capitol. Nevertheless, the percentage of sales controlled by the "majors" slipped between 1948 and 1955, presaging a major decentralization of record sales by the late 1950s.[2] This article was published in *Billboard*, the leading music industry weekly, whose editorial policy took for granted the centrality and superiority of music originating in Tin Pan Alley. While somewhat condescending, the author nonetheless recognizes the entrepreneurial skill and the organizational advantages (which include flexibility, underpaying recording artists, and smaller expenses for "disc jockey promotion")[3] held by small companies in "nonmainstream" categories, such as polka, Polish, Latin, rhythm and blues, and country and western.

## INDIES' SURPRISE SURVIVAL: SMALL LABELS' INGENUITY AND SKILL PAY OFF
### *Bill Simon*

It's almost a year ago that James C. Petrillo signed with the record companies to end his historic recording ban. At that time most prognosticators foresaw the early demise of the indie companies as the majors threatened to grab their proven artists and methods in all categories. It was reasoned then that distribution and exploitation power, plus slicker recording facilities would spell the end to the indie era. Now it appears that a number of indie label producers have by creative ability, ingenuity and sharp business acumen, carved special niches in the market and actually outsold the majors in several fields. Many indie-produced disks have racked sensational sales figures despite the fact that the artists and tunes were unknown, distribution spotty and exploitation funds virtually nonexistent.

---

2. For an in-depth analysis of record companies during this period, see Richard A. Peterson and David G. Berger, "Cycles in Symbol Production: The Case of Popular Music," *American Sociological Review* 40 (1975); reprinted in Simon Frith and Andrew Goodwin, eds., *On Record: Rock, Pop, and the Written Word* (New York: Pantheon, 1990), 140–59.

3. This practice, acknowledged openly at this point, later became the focus of a backlash against early rock 'n' roll when certain disc jockeys were prosecuted for accepting such "promotional fees," which were subsequently labeled "payola." See Part 2 for articles documenting this late 1950s "scandal."

*Source:* Bill Simon, "Indies' Surprise Survival: Small Labels' Ingenuity and Skill Pay Off," *The Billboard*, December 3, 1949, pp. 3, 13, 18. © 1949 VNU Business Media, Inc. Reprinted with permission.

It has become more and more obvious that the gimmick makes the hit, and these indies have been able to come up with the gimmicks. The hit then makes its own distribution. The indie topper, who usually acts as artists-repertoire chief, recording director, business manager and promotion man has got out in the field to dig up new talent with that different, provocative sound. And he's kept his door open to all sorts of new writers and performers. Since overhead is low, and he's not expected to pay the kind of fees a major pays a name artist, he can afford to take chances. And he often has the boldness and the imagination to do so.

Some of the small diskeries have taken advantage of the majors' weakness in certain departments such as rhythm-blues, folk, Latin-American and Polish, and by clever concentration have nabbed the leadership in the various markets. They have consistently attracted the salable new talent and tunes. They have learned their field thoroly [sic], and maintain a close contact with the buying public. They have set up their distribution where it counts.

With low talent and recording costs and with the low, or non-existent royalty rates that are paid out for original material, the indie can usually get off his recording nut with a sale of 5,000 records. A major usually has to go three times that figure to break even. Where the majors pay $275,000 or even more annually for disk jockey promotion, some of the indies will go no higher than $150 a month, usually divided between a couple of key jocks. Some send out vinylites but they know exactly which spinners can use them, and few are wasted.

## Rhythm and Blues

In the rhythm-and-blues field, such indies as Atlantic, King, Alladin, Miracle, Supreme, and Savoy have come up sensational sellers. Most of their sides have displayed an acute awareness of their market's ephemeral predictions. Savoy's Herman Lubinsky and Teddy Reig have led the way on many occasions, and the label's original waxing of *The Hucklebuck* is reported to have hit around 500,000. Atlantic's Herb Abramson, who once came up with an *Open the Door, Richard* for National, and also waxed that label's big sides with The Ravens and Billy Eckstine, has come up with a new star, Ruth Brown, on his own label. Her first record, *So Long*, has been out three months and sold 65,000. The label's big click was Stick McGhee's *Drinkin' Wine Spo-Dee-O-Dee*, released in March and, according to publisher's statement, hitting 170,000 at the end of the last quarter. It's now up to about 200,000 and is enjoying a late spurt. Joe Morris's small combo disking of *Beans and Corn Bread* has done 70,000 to date. The diskery anticipates a total sale of 950,000 disks this year.

Sensation, another rhythm-blues outfit, has had several platters hit between 70,000 and 100,000 sales this year. A Crystalette sleeper, *Ain't She Sweet?*, by Mr. Goon Bones, has sold close to 500,000. The Tempo etching of *Margie*, by the original Mr. Bones, hit 376,000 between the first of the year and the end of the last quarter. This platter, which retails at $1.05, was the first of the gimmicked "Bones" novelties to hit.

## Hillbillies Score

King, 4-Star, Imperial and several more are racking up startling figures in Country-Western territories. The original disking of *Why Don't You Haul Off and Love Me?*, cut for King by Wayne Raney, has hit 250,000 and versions are now available on all major labels. None of these, however, has approached Raney's mark. Another King disk, *Blues Stay 'Way From Me?*, by the Delmore Brothers, is close to 125,000 in six weeks, and the other companies have just begun to cover the tune. King, masterminded by Sid Nathan, virtually dominated the folk field during some months of this year.

> One of the unsung heroes of early R&B and rock 'n' roll, and one of a handful of African Americans with some clout in the recording industry at this time, Henry Glover was a songwriter, arranger, producer, and A&R (artists and repertoire) director at King records, an independent label located in Cincinnati specializing in rhythm and blues and country music. Glover was the musical brains behind King who helped label owner Syd Nathan realize his goal of having country artists record rhythm and blues songs and rhythm and blues artists record country songs (see Wynonie Harris, chapter 10)—usually they would have one artist from each category record the same song. Glover's arrangements and skills as a producer enabled these ideas to work musically.[4] Here Glover recounts King Records' crossover strategy.

## *from* HONKERS AND SHOUTERS: THE GOLDEN YEARS OF RHYTHM AND BLUES
### *Arnold Shaw*

"Sam Phillips has received great recognition because he did the novel thing of recording R&B with white country boys. He deserves credit, considering that Elvis Presley, Jerry Lee Lewis, Roy Orbison, Carl Perkins, and Johnny Cash all emerged from the Sun label. But the fact is that King Records was covering R&B with country singers almost from the beginning of my work with Syd Nathan. We had a duo called The York Brothers who recorded many of the day's R&B hits back in '47–'48. They sounded something like the Everly Brothers, whom they probably influenced. We were more successful in doing the reverse—covering C&W hits with R&B singers. In '49, as you already know, Bull Moose Jackson's hit "Why Don't You Haul Off and Love Me" was a cover of a Wayne Raney country hit. And Wynonie Harris's "Bloodshot Eyes"—on R&B charts in '51—was originally a Hank Penny country record. I'll confess that we didn't think we were doing anything remarkable. It's just that we had both types of artists, and when a song happened in one field, Syd Nathan wanted it moved into the other.

---

4. For more on the literature on rhythm and blues with an emphasis on the role of producers, A&R men, and record company owners, see David Sanjek, "One Size Does Not Fit All: The Precarious Position of the African American Entrepreneur in Post–WWII American Popular Music," *American Music* 15, no. 4 (Winter 1997): 535–62. For a longer interview with Glover, see John Rumble, "The Roots of Rock & Roll: Henry Glover of King Records," *Journal of Country Music* 14, no. 2 (1992): 30–42.

"You see it was a matter of Cincinnati's population. You couldn't sell Wynonie Harris to country folk, and black folk weren't buying Hank Penny. But black folk might buy Wynonie Harris doing a country tune. And since Syd published most of the tunes we recorded, he was also augmenting his publishing income and building important copyrights. He was a smart businessman and didn't miss a trick."

Cofounder of rhythm and blues independent Atlantic, Ahmet Ertegun was one of the most important behind-the-scenes personages in the development of the "uptown" R&B that began to crossover to white audiences. His career intersects with many of the leading names of not only 1950s and but of 1970s rock as well. Near the end of this entry, Ertegun claims that part of Atlantic's success was due to the loyalty of the artists engendered through generous contracts and the creation of a sense of "family." It is interesting to compare Ertegun's recollections with Ruth Brown's account (in chapter 16) of how she and other Atlantic artists from that period were treated.

"When I was studying for my doctorate at Georgetown University in Washington, D.C., I hung around a record store not far from the Howard Theatre. That's where I got my doctorate in black music, at the Howard Theatre. What I learned at Max Silverman's Quality Music Shop was that black people didn't buy jazz. They bought country blues singers like Washboard Sam; they bought city blues men like Charles Brown; and they bought rhythm-and-bluesmen like The Ravens. My Atlantic partner, Herb Abramson, had been making these records on National. When we cut Brownie McGhee's brother, Stick McGhee, doing an old blues, our direction was set. 'Drinkin' Wine, Spo-Dee-O-Dee' was our first R&B hit in 1949.

"Black people were clamoring for blues records, blues with a sock dance beat. Around 1949, that was their main means of entertainment. Harlem folks couldn't go downtown to the Broadway theaters and movie houses. Downtown clubs had their ropes up when they came to the door. They weren't even welcome on Fifty-second Street where all the big performers were black. Black people had to find entertainment in their homes—and the record was it.

"Even radio was white oriented. You couldn't find a black performer on network radio. And when it came to disk jockeys on the big wattage stations, they wouldn't play a black record. We had a real tough time getting our records played—even Ruth Brown, who didn't sound particularly black. All the jocks had to see was the Atlantic label and the name of the artist and we were dead. We'd say, 'Just listen and give your listeners a chance to listen.' But they had a set of stock excuses: 'Too loud'; 'Too rough'; 'Doesn't fit our format.' They'd never say, 'We don't play black artists.' But then they'd turn around and play a record of the very same song that was a copy of our record, only it was by a white artist.

"The breakthrough didn't come, as you might expect, in the North. No, it was 'prejudiced' white Southerners who began programming R&B. They began playing Fats Domino, Ivory Joe Hunter, Roy Milton, Ruth Brown, Amos Milburn because young white teen-agers heard them on those top-of-the-dial stations and began requesting them. What the hell was Elvis listening to when he was growing up?

"From the beginning, our records were really accessible to white listeners. Our artists weren't down-home bluesmen. They didn't come from red-clay country. And our backup groups were either studio musicians or jazzmen. Working with these sophisticated cats, we did try to get an authentic blues feeling. And how could you beat a polished performance of down-to-earth blues material? It has mass appeal, white as well as black.

"We worked at getting a strong and clean rhythm sound. This was partly a matter of engineering. We were among the first independents to mike instruments in the rhythm section separately—a separate mike for drums, bass, and guitar. But to get that clean rhythmic punch, we found it necessary to use written arrangements. This was a major departure in R&B recording. Experienced black arrangers like Jesse Stone, Howard Biggs, Budd Johnson, Bert Keyes, and Teacho Willshire, later white arrangers like Ray Ellis and Stan Applebaum, helped develop a blues arranging style. Some writers have described the Atlantic Sound as R&B with strings or arranged R&B, and there's some merit in that.

"In later years, the Atlantic Sound acquired what Jelly Roll Morton spoke of as 'the Spanish tinge.' Leiber and Stoller introduced a shuffling Latin beat in some of The Drifters' records. Bert Berns also had a big feeling for Spanish music. W. C. Handy used the habanera rhythm in his 'St. Louis Blues.' In the late fifties the samba beat, guaracha, baion, and other Afro-Cuban rhythms added color and excitement to the basic drive of R&B.

"Atlantic grew and survived when most other independents disappeared because it had great flexibility and responded to change. A record company needs engineers, creative producers, and smart promoters. But more than anything else, it needs artists. We established a reputation early for paying established artists top royalty—and did pay. This trade secret attracted many performers to our doors. And after we signed them, we worked to make them feel at home and to search out the best material we could find for recording. We're probably too big now to cultivate the family feeling that was ours for years, but we still like to think of ourselves as a big, happy, soulful family."

# 12. Country Music as Folk Music, Country Music as Novelty

Several articles have already touched upon the position of country (or "hillbilly") music within the post-1920 music industry. Country music, in its modern, commercial, mechanically reproducible form, began in the 1920s as a conglomeration of separate genres: ballads derived from British Isles traditional music, string band music, fiddle tunes, hymns, and blues. As the inclusion of "blues" in the preceding list indicates, musical elements that would later be associated exclusively with African Americans formed a powerful part of the mix. The early music industry name for this category of music, "hillbilly," was a pejorative term used by rural, white southerners in the spirit of affectionate self-deprecation; however, its use by music executives in New York City arose from a misunderstanding and conveyed a supercilious attitude toward the music.[1]

New genres of country music developed in the 1930s in response to changing performance contexts and increasing contact with other popular idioms. One new genre, Western Swing, arose from a conjunction of fiddle-led, string band dance music and big band swing. Breaking with country music tradition by using drums, Western Swing also featured amplified guitars, horns, and piano, alongside bass and fiddle. From the rough barrooms of the rural South came another new genre, "honky-tonk" music, named after the venues in which it was featured. Honky-tonk also featured amplifed guitars and produced stars in the late 1930s and early 1940s, such as Ernest Tubb, Cliff Bruner, and Ted Daffan.

In the early 1940s, both Western Swing and honky-tonk produced "crossover" hits: songs that appeared on the popular music charts and were heard on national network radio broadcasts. Songs like "New San Antonio Rose" by Bob Wills, "Born to Lose" by Ted Daffan, and "Walking the Floor Over You" by Ernest Tubb found large audiences that cut across the demographic spectrum, a development aided by pop artists, such as Bing Crosby, who recorded their own "cover" versions of the songs. Country music, in turn, was influenced by mainstream popular music in terms of songwriting conventions, instrumentation, and rhythm (as in the "swing" of Western Swing).

Beginning in 1939, the popularity of country music began to be tracked in the music industry publication, *Billboard*, in a chart initially titled "hillbilly." The number of songs represented in this chart increased throughout the 1940s as the name vacillated, changing to "American folk" in 1945, before finally settling down to "country and western" in 1949. This name reflected what were perceived at the time as two different types of music: "Country" included honky-tonk music and music descended from fiddle tunes, ballads, waltzes, and novelty tunes, while "western" referred to Western Swing and cowboy songs.

---

The unsigned article that begins this chapter marks an increase of interest in country music in music industry publications. The author correctly points out the link between country music of the 1940s and the traditional music of Euro-Americans (particularly in the rural South) prior to the advent of recording. The tone is faintly apologetic as if anticipating a skeptical readership, which, since the article was appearing in *Billboard*, was not unreasonable. The explanation that the spread of country music's popularity reflects demographic shifts has some validity but implies that the music could appeal only to southerners (or their friends),

---

1. For a more thorough description of the history of this term, see Bill Malone, *Country Music U.S.A.*, rev. and enlarged ed. (Austin: University of Texas Press, 1985); and Archie Green, "Hillbilly Music: Source and Symbol," *Journal of American Folklore* 78 (July–September 1965): 204–28.

an explanation that turned out to be overly pessimistic. The article also refers to a phenomenon that was only beginning: the writing of country tunes by Tin Pan Alley tunesmiths.

## AMERICAN FOLK TUNES: COWBOY AND HILLBILLY TUNES AND TUNESTERS
### *Billboard*

### People's Music

Folk music, tho highly sectional, has always been the music of the people as a whole. Plaintive or catchy, the melodies are easily remembered and easily sung. Written from the heart, the words more often than not are imperfect grammatically, but they express the feeling of the people more clearly than would even perfect poetry. To be sure, many folk tunes have been written by commercial writers and some corrupted by the South American influence, but the majority are written by people who find music as the outlet for their thoughts and emotions. They stress the ordinary sorrows and joys of people which are experienced by everyone, be he rich or poor. Love, hate, loyalty, infidelity, all have their place in folk music. Early American folk music told the tales of heroes, good and bad. Sung by people as they pioneered the country, the songs were a means of spreading news. The story of many a famous battle has been told in a folk song. Today's folk music has changed but little from the early songs. While they are no longer need [sic] to carry news the basic components have remained the same.

Another major factor in the increasing popularity of folk music was the migration of country dweller to the city during the war. The country dweller demanded the music with which he was familiar at night clubs, theaters, dance halls and amusement parks. He organized square dances, jamborees and hayrides, and as a result of this activity, the city dweller, once too sophisticated for the simple music, found himself enjoying it as he attended the square dances in the company of his country friends.

A third factor was the cognizance of the trend by show business. Ever on the alert for the changing moods of its audiences, show business eagerly complied with the request for folk music. Folk artists were imported from country fairs to theaters and night clubs. Entertainers in the popular and concert fields included folk music on their programs. Radio increased its folk shows. Motion pictures included folk artists and folk music in pictures other than Westerns. Thus more and more people became acquainted with folk music and the interest in it spread from coast to coast.

That this rise in popularity of folk tunes will continue is certain, for today efforts are being made to catalog, categorize and compile folk music for the first time in its history. Whether or not folk music will ever entirely supplant the so-called popular music is not certain. At any rate, folk music is here to stay.

In the late 1940s, the profile of country music among the general public continued to increase. However, the most successful recordings of country tunes in the "popular" category during this period were not by

*Source:* "American Folk Tunes: Cowboy and Hillbilly Tunes and Tunesters," *Billboard*, August 17, 1946, p. 120. © 1946 VNU Business Media, Inc. Reprinted with permission.

country artists, but were "cover tunes" of country songs by pop artists, or pseudo-country songs written by Tin Pan Alley songwriters.[2] In 1950, the phenomenon of country music's crossover success reached an apex: "The Tennesse Waltz," recorded and composed by country artist Pee Wee King in 1948, was released in a cover version by pop singer Patti Page in 1950 and became one of the best-selling recordings up to that time, spawning an additional six cover versions by pop artists that made the best-seller charts during 1951.[3]

By 1949, the presence of tunes originating in the country field had grown to the point where mass circulation magazines, such as *Newsweek,* felt the need to give their readers some background on the phenomenon. The title of the following article, "Corn of Plenty," tells readers all they need to know about the cultural status of the music under discussion (and shows how impressions of country music had changed little since the 1938 *Collier's* article reprinted in chapter 4). The article refers to the increasing prominence of country tunes on the popular Hit Parade, and discusses the prominence of Eddy Arnold in particular. Because of the prevalence of cover versions, Arnold's songs were heard by the popular music audience in recordings by pop singers, despite the fact that his own versions sold over a million copies. The overall impression conveyed by this article is the sense of a vacuum in mainstream popular music that the music industry ("in its chronic fluttery state") is filling with country music and other sorts of "simpler songs."

## CORN OF PLENTY

### *Newsweek*

"The corn is as high as an elephant's eye—and so are the profits." A hard-bitten Tin Pan Alley character shook his head in amazement, for he was talking about hillbilly songs—the current wonder of the music world.

Always a steady factor in record and sheet sales, hillbilly music is now such a vogue that it is "just about pushing popular tunes, jazz, swing, bebop, and everything else right out of the picture," noted *Down Beat* magazine. While the rest of the music business remained in its chronic fluttery state, the hillbilly output remained fairly constant. But the demand for it has multiplied fivefold since the war. This week the industry was still moving in concentric circles and nothing was dependable—except hillbilly music.

---

2. This phenomenon is noted in the following entry and was the focus of an article in the *New York Times Magazine*: "Tin Pan Alley's Git-tar Blues," *New York Times Magazine,* July 15, 1951, 8, 36, 37.

3. For a more in-depth account of "Tennessee Waltz" and its significance for both the country and popular music fields, see James M. Manheim, "B-side Sentimentalizer: 'Tennessee Waltz' in the History of Popular Music," *Musical Quarterly* 76, no. 3 (Fall 1992): 37–56.

## Out of the Hills

Ten years ago, if a hillbilly record sold 10,000 copies, it was a hit; today a 50,000 sale is mediocre. Once a specialty product marketed in the Deep South, it now has a nationwide sales field. The South is still lapping it up (some radio stations play hillbilly music eighteen hours a day), but Pennsylvania and New York are right behind. City slickers are square-dancing from Ciro's in Hollywood to the Pierre in New York, and the cowpoke "Riders in the Sky" is the most popular song in the nation.

With the war, hillbilly music quickly came out of the hills. Most of the large training camps were in the South, and GI's who might have never been exposed to this relatively unfamiliar music heard it constantly. They liked it—and brought the songs home with them. Postwar shifts in population helped spread it; and disk jockeys followed through and aired "country" music to a widening audience. It all tied in with the current trend toward simpler songs—and nothing is simpler than country music.

## Rich Soil

From the plains, prairies, and hills the songs are now coming—ballads (love stories), narratives, sacred songs, and dance tunes. Titles range from "My Daddy Is Only a Picture" to "Life Gits Tee-jus, Don't It?" Songs celebrating news events pop up overnight. For example, only three days after little Kathy Fiscus of San Marino, Calif., died in an abandoned well, the record companies were swamped with songs about her. And no Tin Pan Alley tunesmith can turn out songs faster than country-song writers—men like Fred Rose, Bob Miller, and Carson Robison.

But country music has spilled over into the more conventional popular field, and many numbers are being recorded in both straight and country styles. Jo Stafford's raucous hayseed version of "Timtayshun" undoubtedly started something, and it would seem that all a singer needs is a hoedown fiddle, a steel guitar, a mandolin, and new inflection in his voice—and he's set for the bonanza. Dinah Shore did just that and changed the schmaltzy European waltz "Forever and Ever" into a backwoods ditty.

Back in 1930 country singers started going highly commercial when Gene Autry pioneered the way. Following him came a long procession of names, led today by Hank Williams, George Morgan, Red Foley, Roy Acuff, Jimmy Wakely—and the kingpin of them all—Eddy Arnold.

## Barefoot Boys

In New Orleans last February, Eddy Arnold guest-starred on the Spike Jones show. Laying aside his guitar, he did a skit in which he was murdered by a storekeeper. As Arnold sagged dying to the floor, Jones bawled to the other actor: "You jut killed RCA Victor's biggest asset!"

He wasn't far wrong, for Eddy Arnold ranks with Perry Como and Vaughn Monroe among RCA's top popular names. Just another country boy five years ago, today he is the pace setter in the whole country-music field.

Arnold was born on his father's farm near Henderson, Tenn., 30 years ago. As a child, he picked cotton and husked corn on land that barely gave his family enough to eat. "I figured," he recalls, "there must be a better way of makin' a livin'."

When he was 10, his cousin gave him an old Sears, Roebuck guitar, and Arnold started fooling around with it. Soon he was good enough to play with local outfits. At 15 he took four lessons at 75 cents apiece from an iteinerant musicians—the only music lessons he ever had.

## Pay Dirt

By the time he was 18, he signed up with Pee Wee King and His Golden West Cowboys, and from there he struck out on his own. On a six-day-a-week stint over Station WSM at Nashville, the 6-foot, drawling baritone sang, played the guitar, and called himself "The Tennessee Plowboy"—a sobriquet he still uses. There RCA heard him and signed him up in 1944.

In 1946 along came "That's How Much I Love You," and the ball started rolling. It picked up momentum with "I'll Hold You in My Heart" and last year's "Bouquet of Roses," which sold a million and a half records and is still going strong. Ever since Arnold made the big time, no record of his has sold less than 400,000 copies. His current number, "One Kiss Too Many," hit the 250,000 mark last week—with only six weeks' sales.

Arnold is tied up with RCA Victor until 1956. He also has a radio show on Mutual and a two-picture deal with Columbia. He is now star-gazing in Hollywood while making "Hoedown," but somehow, "I'm real downright homesick for my wife an' kids an' my mom back home."

Today the barefoot boy has an annual gross income of $250,000, a great cure for homesickness.

# 13. Country Music Approaches the Mainstream

In contrast to the bemused accounts in the late 1940s in publications, such as *Billboard* and *Newsweek,* country music had so succeeded by 1953 that it earned a feature story in a business magazine. The period 1949 to 1953 witnessed numerous cover versions of country songs (especially those written and recorded by Hank Williams) that succeeded on the pop charts, as well as some crossover hits by country stars, such as Red Foley and Tennessee Ernie Ford. While this article shares with the earlier entries a somewhat condescending tone (note especially the description of the audience), it nevertheless enthusiastically discusses the spread of country music to Europe and Asia. Another important focus is the history provided of that enduring institution, the Grand Ole Opry, and its development in tandem with the rest of the Nashville-based country music industry (which is, after all, what one may expect to find in a business magazine). The article concludes with a brief interview with Hank Williams (1923–53), arguably the most significant songwriter and performer during this period in country music and one of the most influential musicians in country music history. An unwritten requirement of any piece on Williams is that it must include a reference to Tee-Tot, an African American guitarist and street musician who was an early mentor of Williams.

## COUNTRY MUSIC GOES TO TOWN

### Rufus Jarman

What brought this homely music out of the back-roads and into great popularity nationally—and now internationally—was radio in general and in particular station WSM, owned by the National Life & Accident Insurance Company. Through country music, Nashville is now a phonograph-recording center comparable to New York and Hollywood. WSM has become the "big time" to country musicians, as the old Palace once was to vaudeville. The

*Source:* Rufus Jarman, "Country Music Goes to Town," *Nation's Business*, February 1953.

*Wall Street Journal* has estimated that country music in Nashville now amounts to a $25,000,000-a-year industry.

What baffles conservative Nashvillians are the crowds that swarm into town each week to see the program, which lasts four and one-half hours. All of it is broadcast over WSM's powerful, clear-channel station, and 30 minutes of it has been broadcast for a dozen years over the NBC network, sponsored by Prince Albert Tobacco. Red Foley is the master of ceremonies. In addition to the music of bands and quartets, there are two immensely popular comedians, Red Brasfield of Hohenwald, Tenn., and Cousin Minnie Pearl, a product of Centerville, Tenn.

Only the network portion of the show is rehearsed and that only once, for timing. About 125 stars and their "side men" take part in this whole jamboree, which is marked by great informality. Performers, some in outlandish costumes, stroll about the stage, join in with their instruments with units of the show other than their own, and occasionally toss one another playfully into a tub of iced drinks that is kept on the stage at all times.

The audience ranges from a few people who think the term "Opry" means they should come formal to those who take off their shoes and nurse their babies during the show. Many of them come in trucks.

In Nashville hotels, they often bed down eight to a room, and bring along their food. They clean their hotel rooms, never having heard of maid service. Many of them never heard of tipping either. Bellboys and elevator operators, when the management isn't looking, may make up for this over-sight by charging ten cents per elevator ride.

Besides their radio programs and records, the Opry stars constantly manifest themselves to their followers through personal appearances, arranged by the WSM Artist Service Bureau, under Jim Denny. Every night one or more troupes of Opry stars are appearing in some city about the land. They have crammed Carnegie Hall in New York and played before sellout audiences in white ties and tails in Constitution Hall in Washington. More often they appear on Sundays in picnic groves in Pennsylvania, Illinois or Ohio. Not long ago, one troupe played to 65,000 persons in four days in Texas.

To fill this schedule, the Opry stars live a hard life. They usually leave Nashville in their cars on Sundays, and drive hard from one engagement to another, heading back to Nashville in time for Saturday. Often they don't sleep in a bed for nights on end, but take turns driving.

They keep their car radios tuned to hillbilly broadcasts at all times, and when they hear some local rustic singer who sounds promising, they tip off Jack Stapp, the Opry's program director.

The touring stars have simple living tastes. One observer who has travelled with them reports that some stars, making hundreds of thousands of dollars a year will eat the same meal three times a day—fried potatoes, fried eggs and fried pork chops. For, in spite of their fancy clothes, big cars and abundant money, the Opry stars remain simple people who "were raised hard and live hard," as one of them has said. Some of them do not know a note of music, but their great appeal as entertainers is in the rawness of their emotions and their sincerity in conveying them.

Hank Williams was discussing that shortly before his death in January. Williams was a lank, erratic countryman who learned to play a guitar from an old Negro named Teetot in his home village of Georgiana, Ala.

"You ask what makes our kind of music successful," Williams was saying. "I'll tell you. It can be explained in just one word: sincerity. When a hillbilly sings a crazy song, he feels crazy. When he sings, 'I Laid My Mother Away,' he sees her a-laying right there in the coffin.

"He sings more sincere than most entertainers because the hillbilly was raised rougher than most entertainers. You got to know a lot about hard work. You got to have smelt a lot of mule manure before you can sing like a hillbilly. The people who has been raised something like the way the hillbilly has knows what he is singing about and appreciates it.

"For what he is singing is the hopes and prayers and dreams and experiences of what some call the 'common people.' I call them the 'best people,' because they are the ones that the world is made up most of. They're really the ones who make things tick, wherever they are in this country or in any country.

"They're the ones who understand what we're singing about, and that's why our kind of music is sweeping the world. There ain't nothing strange about our popularity these days. It's just that there are more people who are like us than there are the educated, cultured kind.

"There ain't nothing at all queer about them Europeans liking our kind of singing. It's liable to teach them more about what everyday Americans are really like than any thing else."

# 14. Hank Williams on Songwriting

Despite the evidence presented in the passage that ends the previous article, Williams was remarkably recalcitrant about granting interviews. He did, however, publish a book in 1951 (in collaboration with songwriter Jimmy Rule) about songwriting. Although much of the book describes how to approach the business and technical aspects of songwriting (and, from all accounts, owes more to Rule than to Williams), it does feature a passage that is interesting for how it reflects on the moral stance projected by the lyrics. If Williams was indeed responsible for this paragraph, it greatly simplifies the moral ambiguity found in his songs, which enact a struggle between sin (exemplified in such songs as the ode to partying, "Honky Tonkin'") and redemption (exemplified in the hymnlike "I Saw the Light" and songs recorded by his alter ego "Luke the Drifter").[1]

---

1. For a further exploration of this struggle enacted by Williams's different personae, see David Brackett, *Interpreting Popular Music*, pp. 75–107. Within the vast biographical literature on Hank Williams, Chet Flippo's controversial, *Your Cheatin' Heart: A Biography of Hank Williams* (Garden City, N.Y.: Doubleday, 1981), most thoroughly examines the dualities in Williams's music and psyche. Barbara Ching discusses the continuing struggles of country music with its low cultural status in *Wrong's What I Do Best: Hard Country Music and Contemporary Culture* (New York: Oxford University Press, 2001); and Richard Peterson offers an account of the long historical *durée* of authenticity in country music in *Creating Country Music: Fabricating Authenticity* (Chicago: University of Chicago Press, 1997).

*from* **HOW TO WRITE FOLK AND WESTERN MUSIC TO SELL**
*Hank Williams (with Jimmy Rule)*

Now a few words in regard to the words to your song. It has already been stated that you should keep your song simple and appealing. The next advice would be to keep your song in good taste. Don't write any song which might offend a certain class of people. You should avoid especially the offending of any religious groups or any races. It goes without saying that you must observe all standards of decency. Avoid writing songs that have or could have double meanings or could be interpreted in any indecent manner. While certain songs bordering on the indecent have enjoyed some degree of popularity, they usually are banned from the air and the good name of the writer is hurt.

# 15. Rhythm and Blues in the Early 1950s

## B. B. King

The music industry category rhythm and blues included within it a great diversity of distinct musical genres. The three musicians examined more closely in this and subsequent chapters—B. B. King, Ruth Brown, and Ray Charles—represent three important strands of R&B during the early 1950s: the transformation of the country blues into urban blues; the development of a more carefully arranged form of R&B; and the increasing use of vocal techniques derived from solo gospel singing.

Riley "B. B." ("Blues Boy") King (b. 1925) already appeared as an interviewee in the article about T-Bone Walker in chapter 8. One of the most popular rhythm and blues performers of the 1950s and early 1960s, B. B. King was responsible for spreading and popularizing many of Walker's innovations: the jazzy, single-note improvisations on guitar, the gospel-influenced vocal style, and the large band arrangements featuring horns.[1] A widely imitated guitarist, King became known to many fans of rock music through his influence on rock guitarists, such as Eric Clapton, and

---

1. A fascinating account of King during this period can be found in Charles Keil, *Urban Blues* (Chicago: University of Chicago Press, 1966).

*Source:* Hank Williams (with Jimmy Rule), from *How to Write Folk and Western Music to Sell* (Nashville: Harpeth Publishing Co., 1951), p. 21.

through the tributes paid to him by Clapton and other white artists. Despite the acclaim generated by such attention and by successful albums like *Live at the Regal* (1964), King had to wait until 1970 for his greatest mainstream success with "The Thrill Is Gone." In this interview, recorded in 1978, King talks about how he learned to entertain audiences, some unsuspected relationships between sacred and secular music, and what the blues mean to him. King comments on the shifting nature of music industry classifications and how in many ways they seem determined more by sociological factors than musical ones.

## *from* HONKERS AND SHOUTERS:
## THE GOLDEN YEARS OF RHYTHM AND BLUES
### *Arnold Shaw*

"I left Indianola in 1946, hitchhiking to Memphis. I had been singing with a gospel quartet called the St. John Gospel Singers. There were a lot of groups around, and material would pass from group to group so that we did some new gospel songs. We picked most of our material from what we heard on records, radio, jukeboxes. Poor people were beginning to afford a radio and they got to know the name groups and their songs. CBS and a few of the networks were presenting groups like The Trumpeteers and the Golden Gate Quartet. Then, out of Nashville, we could hear the Fairfield Four. The Soul Stirrers came into our area, and that was when I first met Sam Cooke—around 1948, I guess.

"The distinctions that I hear writers make between blues and rhythm and blues I regard as artificial. Most of the people that we hear playing the blues came from the same area, even though they may be living in other areas. We hear of the Chicago blues because many of the Mississippi crowd lives in Chicago. When I was on the radio in Memphis, we used to get *Billboard, Cash Box,* and they classed things that Louis Jordan was doing as rhythm and blues. Or they would call it 'race.' And that's how you could distinguish what he and others like him did from so-called pop. But today, for instance, James Brown is considered rhythm and blues. Aretha Franklin is considered soul or rhythm and blues—and I am considered blues. [Chuckling] In Memphis, I was considered rhythm and blues. I personally think that it's all rhythm and blues because it's blues and it has rhythm. I guess that you could break it down if you wanted to. I remember that Dinah Washington was considered R&B or 'race.' But Dinah sang anything that anybody else sang. She just sang it her own way. She was doing all of the popular tunes of the late forties and early fifties. So were Ella Fitzgerald, Nat Cole, and Louis Armstrong—these were the top black recording artists. Louis Jordan, too, and The Ink Spots. But they were classed differently. Ella was more pop than most of the black female singers, but she still covered most of the bluesy tunes. But Dinah stayed with them, and Louis Jordan stayed with them, and they came up with some very big records. I remember Dinah covering 'Three Coins in a Fountain.' Mercury Records was using her to sell records to black record buyers. But when she did these pop tunes in her way, they were classed as rhythm and blues.

*Source:* Pages 220–25 from *Honkers and Shouters: The Golden Years of Rhythm & Blues* by Arnold Shaw. Reprinted with permission of Scribner, an imprint of Simon & Schuster Adult Publishing Group. Copyright © by Ghita M. Shaw.

"It's true that after the big band era, blues singers started being accompanied by horns and rhythm groups instead of just guitar and harp. But the reason that this happened was because, before that, blues singers just could not afford to be backed by bands. They wanted it. In the delta, there was a band called the Red Caps that had all kinds of instruments. They were playing like Jimmie Lunceford. They were stationed right there in Greenville, Mississippi. They were among the lucky few that could afford band instrumentation. Incidentally, the Red Caps I'm talking about were not the Red Caps of Steve Gibson that had 'Wedding Bells Are Breaking Up That Old Gang of Mine.' But they played the socials around Greenville, and they had a very varied repertoire. They played bluesy things and jazz. What I'm trying to say is that if we had the money or even a music store where we could borrow instruments—why we had to go twenty-five miles to the nearest music store. We did not have one in Indianola, Greenwood or Greenville was the nearest place. And when you went to one of these stores, you had to pay cash. They didn't know you, and you didn't have any credit. At that time, a horn was costing like $100. Gosh, in those days, it would take me five months to make $100. Out of the twenty-two fifty a week I was making, after you bought groceries and other necessities, you could save only seven to eight dollars. So you bought whatever instrument you could afford— and that was the guitar. As for a piano, you could forget about that. Or an organ. But my aunt had one that you had to paddle with your feet. It's so funny to see people now playing notes on an organ with their feet. Well, then you had to use your feet to get air flowing through the organ pipes. I don't know how she got that organ. My aunt was one of those people who said that a person had to have something for themselves. And she did. She had a phonograph, or as we called them, a Victrola. When I was a good boy—and I stayed a good boy around her—she would let me play the Victrola. And that's how I got into those old blues records like Lemon Jefferson. I had a chance to fool with the organ, and that's how I learned to play a few chords.

"My first hit record was Lowell Fulson's tune, 'Three O'Clock Blues.' I always did like his work. In fact, I idolized Lowell. But I probably like his singing better than his playing. It's nice of him to say that I do 'Every Day I Have the Blues' better than he does, but he had a hit on it. Several of us had hits on that Memphis Slim tune. But Lowell was the one who influenced me to do the tune. He and Joe Williams. You know, a lot of people don't know that Williams cut 'Every Day I Have the Blues' before he made it with Basie. He first made it with King Kolak's band. That was the one, along with Lowell's record, that made me think that I could get a hit on it. And luckily I did. But then, when Joe Williams got with Basie, he did it again, and that was the master one. But Lowell is a great artist. He is one of the sleeping giants in the blues.

"When I first started performing, it was me alone. Then I got a trio on the radio: Johnny Ace on piano, Earl Forest on drums. It was hard to keep a bass player. Later on is when I got Billy Duncan on tenor sax. That's when I made 'Three O'Clock Blues.' We recorded our first hit in the YMCA in Memphis. One of my biggest hits, 'Darling, I Love You,' was recorded at Tuff Green's home, the same fellow that made the first record with me.

"By 1955 I was pretty well known, and we were booked for like five to seven hundred dollars a day. That was our guarantee. Then it went up to a thousand and, if we were lucky, twelve hundred. But then I had my own bus and a very big group. We ran it up to about thirteen pieces, and we kept that until I went broke. [Chuckling] Then I dropped down to five: organ, drums, tenor, trumpet, and alto. Kept that for a while, and when things started to pick up, we added more men. I like the big band sound. I guess one of the reasons is my being brought up in the church. I can always hear the choir singing behind me, and that's what I hear when the horns are playing behind me. The little tricky things they do, like rhythms within rhythms—this is what puts spice on. Blues is usually slow, melancholy, and if you have some little figures going on with the horns, it makes it more interesting.

"The blues is the blues. They don't change. But sounds do change. And I've just had to make some changes in my band after working with some men for many years. For some time, I've been asking them to listen to the sounds behind James Brown, behind Aretha, behind Wilson Pickett. Audiences feel the difference. But it was like I wasn't saying anything. Each year, I give my men four weeks off, two with pay and two without. This was to give them a chance to make a change if they wanted to. And this year, I felt that I had to. It wasn't easy, especially since some of the men are Memphis friends from way back. I understand their feelings. But you either change with the times or you find yourself looking at empty seats. . . ."

# 16. "The House That Ruth Brown Built"

Ruth Brown (b. 1928), along with Dinah Washington, was the biggest female R&B star of the 1950s. Like other R&B and soul stars, Brown's formative musical experiences occurred in the church, and her early musical influences also included field hollers and blues. By the time she began to sing professionally, she had also been exposed to a great variety of music via records and radio and had acquired a background in jazz and mainstream popular music. In 1948, she signed with manager Blanche Calloway, who helped arrange a contract with Atlantic records. Shortly after signing with Atlantic, Brown was hobbled by a serious auto accident. Nevertheless, she began recording as soon as she possibly could, and her first session resulted in a major R&B hit, "So Long." Subsequent sessions were marked by eclecticism and uncertainty about how to repeat the success. The search for a follow-up was finally rewarded when Brown, in tandem with arranger Jesse Stone and producers Ahmet Ertegun and Herb Abramson, began to develop a style that fused elements of blues, jazz, and pop. As Brown further refined this fusion into a trademark form of smooth "uptown" rhythm and blues, her continuing success led to Atlantic being known as "The House That Ruth Brown Built."[1]

---

1. This phrase is a play on the description of Yankee Stadium as "The House That Ruth Built."

In her autobiography, *Miss Rhythm*, Ruth Brown describes her contributions to Atlantic, the origins of her biggest hits, and the development of her business relationship with Atlantic. Brown devotes a lot of space to detailing how companies, such as Atlantic, exploited her and other rhythm and blues artists of the time. One of the factors that gave the companies almost unlimited leverage in withholding royalties was the onerous practice of charging "session fees" to the leader of the date. She also describes the difficulties of touring in the Jim Crow South, a hardship compounded by being the only female in the entourage as well as the star of the show. Brown's autobiography offers an insightful view of the relationship between rhythm and blues artists in the fifties and the owners of independent companies like Atlantic.

## *from* Miss Rhythm: The Autobiography of Ruth Brown, Rhythm and Blues Legend
### *Ruth Brown (with Andrew Yule)*

On April 6, [1949], still on crutches and wearing a leg brace, I hobbled into the Apex Studio at the tail end of a John "Texas Johnny" Brown session, with Amos Milburn sitting hunched over the piano. I sang "Rain Is a Bringdown," a tune I'd doodled in the hospital just to give Ahmet and Herb an idea of how my voice came over on disc. Then Herb began to talk material, mentioning "So Long," the bluesy ballad we all knew from Little Miss Cornshuck's version. We talked a little bit about the tempo and treatment, and Herb said he'd have an arrangement worked out by the time we were set to record at WOR the following month. We recorded the song with Eddie Condon's orchestra on May 25, and after listening to the playback Ahmet and Herb decided the track was strong enough for my first A-side. "It's Raining" formed the B-side.

Within a few weeks of its release "So Long" was selling well, climbing to number six on Billboard's R-and-B chart. It was only the company's second hit after Sticks McGhee's "Drinkin' Wine, Spo-dee-o-dee," and everybody at Atlantic was thrilled to see the company's name back on the charts. Me too, believe it! This time they were determined it would be no one-hit wonder.

After four of my follow-up releases to "So Long" went nowhere however, it was time for a reappraisal. The problem on Atlantic's side was they couldn't figure out what to do with me. I was recorded with the Delta Rhythm Boys, singing spirituals, even flirting with Yiddish songs in English. *"Too* darn versatile," I heard Herb mutter more than once. The problem I posed, in turn, was my resistance to singing anything but my first love, ballads. I wanted to tell stories in songs, to explore emotions, to the lush sounds of velvety string accompaniments I'd always conjured up when dreaming of recording. A solution had to be found; meanwhile I was working regularly, and for decent money, although I was hampered by the legacy of that car crash.

The house writer that broke the dry spell after "So Long" was Rudolph "Rudy" Toombs. The song Rudy composed especially for me, "Teardrops from My Eyes," took me to the top

---

of the R-and-B chart in October 1950. And there it stayed for eleven solid weeks, with a total chart run of twenty-six weeks. One-hit wonder? Not me, baby! The disc also became a tiny piece of history, being Atlantic's first record made available on seven-inch 45-rpm vinyl as well as the standard ten-inch 78-rpm shellac.

Rudy was my good friend, a man who was simply bursting with life, as effervescent as any of his songs. The things he did for me were different rhythmically from what I was into, but I finally had to give in to the fact that Ahmet, Herb and their team were a step ahead of the accepted sound of the day. Taking a deep breath, I went along with it. Although I had no right of veto in my contract, that did not stop me from fighting if I wasn't happy with what came up. On most issues we reached common ground, with Ahmet and Herb resigned to my singing the occasional ballad, if only for a B-side. Although Herb was the man in charge of my sessions, many of the decisions regarding material were made by Ahmet and arranger Jesse Stone, whose remarkable body of compositions ranged from "Smack Dab in the Middle" all the way to "Shake, Rattle and Roll." He was the man behind so many of the great things that came out of Atlantic, together, of course, with the engineering wizard, Tom Dowd. Tommy had impeccable intuition and was a fixture in the control booth with Ahmet and Herb.

A couple of times during early morning sessions, with sunshine streaming through the windows, I remember protesting it was the wrong time of day to capture a blue mood. "Ruth, just sing like you've got tears in your eyes," Herb would direct me. Another time it would be, "Give me that million-dollar squeal." There were occasions when my throat felt sore, or what I used to call "rusty." "I *like* your sound when it's like that," Herb would enthuse. "It has an earthy quality, a sexiness." "*Down*, boy!" I'd kid him.

Soon I felt like the Queen of the One-Nighters, with dates stretching through the Litchman Theater chain from New York to Washington, Baltimore, Richmond, and near home again at the Booker T in Norfolk. One-night dance dates followed into the Carolinas and all the way down to Georgia, Alabama and Tennessee, bringing me face to face with all those racial problems, rubbing my nose in them. We did close on seventy one-nighters on the trot, spending most days riding the tour bus. When we hit Atlanta we set up camp and made excursions to neighboring towns like Columbus and Augusta, and in Atlanta itself there were lots of clubs to work.

On stage I took to wearing multicolored petticoats and accordion-pleated skirts, featuring all the colors of the rainbow, and from the brighter end of the spectrum: peacock blue, surprise pink, sunshine yellow, orange and lavender. Apart from fellow performers, you had the audiences to compete with, who came along dressed to the nines. Our dates were once-in-a-lifetime-style affairs, a big night out, with posters up months before we arrived. In the South it was even trickier; you had to watch in case a member of the audience was wearing the same dress as you and took offense.

Some people to this day call Atlantic "The House that Ruth Brown Built," and even if this is an exaggeration, few would deny that I contributed a solid portion of the foundation as well as quite a few of the actual bricks. No doubt the cement was the matchless team at the company, Ahmet, Herb, Jesse and Tommy, together with the incredible mix of outstanding musical talent they employed and nurtured.

Rudy Toombs was responsible for the next smash I enjoyed. His original title was "5-10-15" Minutes (Of Your Love)" until Herb coolly informed him that "minutes" was no longer enough now that we were in the era of Billy Ward and the Dominoes' *Sixty-Minute Man*. Presto, it became "5-10-15 Hours (Of Your Love)." The song followed "Daddy, Daddy" into the R-and-B chart in '52 and lodged at number one for seven weeks. Ruth Brown? Hotter than a pistol!

Caught up in the euphoria of having a contract to sign at all, I had taken no advice beyond a quick word with Blanche before signing with Atlantic. Ahmet had a great pitch that settled any questions: "Only Bing Crosby gets five percent at Decca." Ruth Brown on the same percentage as Der Bingle? Sure sounded good to me, although I knew I was starting at the bottom as far as advances were concerned—I'm sure Bing had long since worked his way past sixty-nine dollars a side. I also understood that I was responsible for certain production costs, but how big a deal could they be if I sold enough records?

Strangely enough, despite my continuing chart success, I had to ask every time I needed cash. Any real money I made came from touring, and I was always out there promoting the records. Back then any record by a black artist needed every ounce of help it could get. The expression "R-and-B chart" was another way in the late forties and early fifties to list "race and black" as well as "rhythm and blues" records. And the reason so few discs by black artists crossed over to Billboard's mainstream chart was simple: it was compiled from white-owned radio station playlists featuring music by white artists, with our list confined to stations catering to blacks. As Jerry Wexler, Herb's successor at Atlantic, put it when asked if it was difficult to get R-and-B records played on general-audience stations in the early fifties, "*Difficult* would have been easy. It was *impossible.*"

It very gradually became less so, of course, as R-and-B artists broke through the barriers by the sheer strength and quality of their music. But it took time, and throughout my biggest hit-making period I was forced to stand by as white singers like Georgia Gibbs and Patti Page duplicated my records note for note and were able to plug them on top television shows like *The Ed Sullivan Show,* to which I had no access.

Chuck Willis wrote "Oh, What a Dream" especially for me, and it was my favorite song, but it was Patti Page, with an identical arrangement, who got to sing it on national television. Even topical stuff like my "Mambo Baby" had a Georgia Gibbs duplicate rushed out. My labelmate and good friend LaVern Baker, who joined Atlantic in '53, suffered the same fate on her original of "Tweedle Dee"—another note-for-note copy by Her Nibs Miss Gibbs. There was no pretense, either, that they were anything but duplicates. Mercury actually called up Tommy Dowd on the day they were cutting "Tweedle Dee" and said, "Look, we've got the same arrangement, musicians and tempo, we might as well have the same sound engineer too."

It was tough enough coming up with hit sounds, therefore doubly galling to see them stolen from under our noses. Few seemed to stop and question the morality of this, least of all the publishers, to whom it was a case of the more the merrier. LaVern for one did, protesting to her congressman over her treatment at Mercury's hands, but then as now, there was no copyright protection on arrangements.

I was denied sales abroad as well, although I knew nothing of this at the time. "Abroad," as far as the feedback from Atlantic's accounting department was concerned, could have been the moon. Having made number three on Billboard's R-and-B chart in the States, and actually crossing over to their pop charts as well, reaching number twenty-five, my version of "Lucky Lips" was ignored in Britain.

It was because of Willis[2] that I couldn't relate to "Mama, He Treats Your Daughter Mean" when it was first presented to me at Atlantic. Maybe it reminded me of a past relationship I wanted to forget, maybe I felt that singing it would put a jinx on us. I had to be coaxed into it by Herb, who upped the tempo from the slow ballad it had been. The tune had been

---

2. The "Willis" in question is Willis "Gator Tail" Jackson, tenor saxophonist on many Atlantic recordings from the period including Brown's, and the person Brown describes as "the love of her life."

written by two friends of mine, Herb Lance and Johnny Wallace (brother to a young fighter named Coley, who played the champion in *The Joe Louis Story*). There was a lot of joking around the night we recorded it, for everyone present knew I was less than keen. And Willis was absent, off doing a session of his own. "Does *your man* treat you mean, Ruthie?" drummer Connie Kay inquired, mock-anxiety written all over his teasin' face."Anybody here seen Gator?" trumpeter Taft Jordan chimed in. I tell you, spitfires can be a target themselves sometimes.

During the first playback Herb and the others all looked at me expectantly. Although I still didn't like it, there was something so comical about their concern that I had to smile and relax into the second take. This time we hit it just right. I can't put my finger on what was so special about that record, for the rhythm pattern was similar to a lot of stuff that was out there, but boy, did it take a trick. I was never so wrong about any piece of material in my life.

# 17. Ray Charles, or, When Saturday Night Mixed It Up with Sunday Morning

Ray Charles (1930–2004) is almost bewilderingly talented: a pianist, singer, songwriter, arranger, saxophonist, and bandleader, he is also an extraordinarily eclectic musician, skilled in jazz, gospel, blues, country, pop, and classical musics. After initial experiences playing jazz and country music in Florida, Charles moved to Seattle in 1948 and began playing clubs and recording in a sophisticated rhythm and blues style indebted to Nat "King" Cole and Charles Brown. Charles' real breakthrough came in 1953–55 when he developed an earthy adaptation of gospel music that fused the melodies, singing style, and harmonic and rhythmic patterns of gospel with secular lyrics and rhythm and blues instrumentation.

Prior to Charles, the first rhythm and blues singer to attract attention for his indebtedness to gospel technique was Clyde McPhatter, who had been the lead singer on many hit recordings made in the early- to mid-1950s with Billy Ward and the Dominoes and with the Drifters. These recordings featured McPhatter's impassioned melismas and call-and-response alternations between him and the other singers in the band to a greater extent than had been evident in previous R&B recordings. What distinguished McPhatter from singers in earlier gospel-derived male groups, such as the Ink Spots and the Mills Brothers, was the way in which he adopted the dynamic solo style of female singers, such as Mahalia Jackson and Clara Ward, to songs with gospel-derived harmonic progressions in which the change of a single word ("Have Mercy Baby" to

"Have Mercy Lord") could transform the song back into a gospel number. Also important during the late 1950s was McPhatter's successor in the Dominoes, Jackie Wilson, a dynamic performer who employed gospel-derived vocal techniques in a pop-oriented idiom.

It was Charles, however, who brought many of McPhatter's innovations to fruition in a series of recordings beginning in 1954. Thinly veiled adaptations of gospel songs, such as "I've Got a Woman" (1954), "This Little Girl of Mine" (1955), "Drowning in My Own Tears" (1956), and "Hallelujah, I Love Her So" (1956), became major rhythm and blues hits while raising charges of blasphemy in the African American community. On these recordings, Charles sings in a raspy, exuberant tone full of whoops, cries, bent notes, melismas, and shouts, engaging in call-and-response patterns with either the horns (a combination of saxophones, trumpets, and trombones) or a female backup trio named the Raelettes, and accompanying himself with gospel-style piano. The apotheosis of this approach comes in Charles's 1959 recording "What'd I Say," which not only imported musical elements from gospel music, but produced a condensed simulation of an African American Holiness religious service. Charles succeeded with yet another innovative fusion in 1962 with his *Modern Sounds in Country and Western Music*. Although it caught his fans and the music industry off guard, he was merely bringing sounds together that he had been hearing and performing since his childhood.

---

Ray Charles's autobiography, *Brother Ray*, conveys his charming and irascible personality and details the rise of a poor, blind, African American country boy in the Deep South to become one of the world's most successful entertainers. The path to this success was paved by his voracious appetite for diverse styles and his ability to synthesize them. The passages reproduced here focus on the years during which he developed his proto-soul sound and address the controversy aroused by his adaptation of preexisting gospel material. Throughout these passages, Charles displays a keen sensitivity about the relationship his style and the makeup of his audience, enabling him to explain quite clearly the difference between the music he was making in the mid-1950s and early rock 'n' roll.

## *from* BROTHER RAY: RAY CHARLES' OWN STORY
### *Ray Charles and David Ritz*

These are the years—'53, '54, '55—when I became myself. I opened up floodgates, let myself do things I hadn't done before, created sounds which, people told me afterward, had never been created before. If I was inventing something new, I wasn't aware of it. In my mind, I

*Source:* Ray Charles and David Ritz, from *Brother Ray: Ray Charles' Own Story* (New York: Dial Press, 1978), pp. 148–51, 173–75, 176–78, 190–92, 222–23. Reprinted by permission of the Aaron M. Priest Literary Agency.

was just bringing out more of me. I started taking gospel lines and turning them into regular songs.

Now, I'd been singing spirituals since I was three, and I'd been hearing the blues for just as long. These were my two main musical currents. So what could be more natural than to combine them? It didn't take any thinking, didn't take any calculating. All the sounds were there, right at the top of my head.

Many of those first tunes were adaptations of spirituals I had sung in quartets back in school. "You Better Leave That Woman Alone" was originally something called "You Better Leave That Liar Alone." "Lonely Avenue" was based on a spiritual that Jess Whitaker used to sing with the Pilgrim Travelers. "Talkin' 'Bout You" was another song which I had been singing my whole life in another form.

None of the spirituals had copyrights. How could they? Black folk had been singing 'em through the hollow logs as far back as anyone could remember. And often my new tunes would be based on three or four gospel numbers—not just one.

But the basic line, the basic structure, the basic chord changes were throwbacks to the earliest part of my life on earth. Nothing was more familiar to me, nothing more natural.

Imitating Nat Cole had required a certain calculation on my part. I had to gird myself; I had to fix my voice into position. I loved doing it, but it certainly wasn't effortless. This new combination of blues and gospel was. It required nothing of me but being true to my very first music.

Now with my band I could rebuild my own little musical world that I first heard in Greensville. In fact, this was the heaviest writing period of my life. When Ahmet Ertegun or Jerry Wexler at Atlantic sent me songs they thought I should record, I often didn't like them. That inspired me to begin writing more tunes of my own.

Atlantic let me record anything I wanted to. They never said, "No, do our songs, not yours." They trusted me and left me alone.

The same thing had been true with Jack Lauderdale when I was recording for Swingtime. And it would be no different years later when I would start making records for ABC.

I've never had what they call a producer to oversee me. I've always produced myself. And during my Atlantic days, I always came into the studio with the tunes already picked and the arrangements already written. There was nothing left for a producer to do.

You might ask: How could a young kid like me—at twenty-two or twenty-three or twenty-four—have that kind of power? I still wasn't much of a name. And I certainly didn't have any right to go round demanding or dictating a goddamn thing. Well, these record people saw that I was developing and that I needed space to find myself. Even though I was young and tender, they let me make my own mistakes, let me produce my own small triumphs.

Only one time at Atlantic—and that was a very minor incident—did one of the cats suggest that I listen to Fats Domino and maybe do something on the style of "Blueberry Hill." I told the guy that I was *for* Fats, but that I wasn't Fats. I was Brother Ray. That quieted him down.

So I was lucky. Lucky to have my own band at this point in my career. Lucky to be able to construct my musical building to my exact specifications. And lucky in another way:

While I was stomping around New Orleans, I had met a trumpeter named Renolds Richard who by this time was in my band. One day he brought me some words to a song. I dressed them up a little and put them to music. The tune was called "I Got a Woman," and it was another one of those spirituals which I refashioned in my own way.

"I Got a Woman" was my first real smash, much bigger than "Baby, Let Me Hold Your Hand." This spiritual-and-blues combination of mine was starting to hit.

But even though this record, made toward the end of 1954, was very big, that didn't mean I was making very big money. It was like that story I told before about Joe Morris. He had a hit, but he still had to hustle like crazy. Well, now *I was* Joe Morris. The success of my record meant I'd get to work more often. But the black promoters—the men I dealt with—still paid very little. And as for royalties, well, they took a long, long time to start coming in, and when they did I used the money for things like new tires for the car.

At the time this was happening, not everyone approved. I got letters accusing me of bastardizing God's work. A big-time preacher in New York scolded me before his congregation. Many folks saw my music as sacrilegious. They said I was taking church songs and making people dance to 'em in bars and nightclubs.

Must tell you that none of those reactions bothered me. I'd always thought that the blues and spirituals were close—close musically, close emotionally—and I was happy to hook' em up. I was determined to go all out and just be natural. Everything else would spring from that. I really didn't give a shit about that kind of criticism.

After "I Got a Woman," my three big records were "A Fool for You," "Drown in My Own Tears" and "Hallelujah, I Love Her So." These were the songs which caught on, the tunes which kept me working.

"Hallelujah" was probably the most important. I did it in late 1955, at the same session as "Drown," and, as far as I was concerned, it was just another number I'd written. I didn't ascribe any great importance to it, and actually the lyrics were a little more lighthearted than the ones I usually wrote.

When I was writing songs, I concentrated on problems or feelings everyone could understand. I wouldn't call the tunes biographical; I just made' em up. But I always tried to stick to common themes—love heartaches, money heartaches, pleasures of the flesh and pleasures of the soul.

"Hallelujah" clicked. It sold big among blacks, and I guess it was my first record to enjoy some popularity among whites.

If these early hits sold two hundred thousand copies, I was pleased. That was almost all in one market—the black market—and two hundred thousand were a lot of records in those days. Oh, sure, there'd be whites who bought my sides—even *sneak* and buy 'em if they had to—but up until "Hallelujah," the overwhelming majority of those listening to me were black.

When I stopped imitating Nat Cole and slid into my own voice, I saw that my successes were exclusively at black clubs and black dances. My music had roots which I'd dug up from my own childhood, musical roots buried in the darkest soil. Naturally it was music blacks could immediately take to heart.

Little by little, though, beginning around 1956, I saw that my music had appeal beyond my own people. I saw it breaking through to other markets, and now and then there'd be a date in a city auditorium where whites would come along with blacks. It probably took me longer to digest this gradual change than it would have taken someone else. I couldn't see the increasing number of white faces.

It meant more work and more money. But it wasn't going to change my music, and it wasn't going to change me. The more people there were who liked my stuff, the happier I was. But at this point in my life that only convinced me to stick to my guns and follow my program. Most of the material the band was playing was our own. Ninety-five percent of everything we did in those years was written by me. There were the original songs—maybe fifteen or twenty that we played. And there were also Latin numbers and hard-driving jazz tunes which I arranged. I remember writing a chart of Dizzy's "Manteca," and we also did a bolero thing on "In a Little Spanish Town" and "Frenesi."

I might write arrangements on ballads like "Funny Valentine" or "If I Had You." I loved old standards and always had them in the book. From the first days the band was together, we played a mixture of the different music I found myself drawn to.

The cats in the band could play the blues. That came first. Show me a guy who can't play the blues and I'm through with him before he can get started. If you can't get nasty and grovel down in the gutter, something's missing.

It's not that the blues are complicated. They're not; they're basic. There are hundreds of versions of the same blues—the same changes, the same patterns—just as there are hundreds of versions of the same spirituals. The music is simple. But the feeling—the low-down gut-bucket feeling—has to be there or it's all for nothing.

My cats could also play serious jazz. Donald Wilkerson, for example, could kick the ass of almost any tenor player in the country. For my money, he's one of the best saxophonists of the century. Fathead[1] was right there next to him, playing with a lyricism and a sweetness which Donald lacked. Fathead didn't have Donald's speed and maybe not as much fire, but he could make his sax sing the song like no one else.

In this period, I loved to watch Donald attack Fathead on the stand. Course that was good for David, and it brought out the best in both cats. When someone tries to stomp on you, naturally you're going to respond. And together—blowing out in front of the band—they'd be burning up the place.

Most of my original compositions—the ones with my own words and my own music—found their way to the recording studio, but I'd guess there must have been three times that number of songs—maybe as many as a hundred—which I arranged and never recorded.

I like to think I'm a half-ass composer. I ain't no Duke Ellington, but I *can* write. There isn't that much to making a song—jazz or otherwise. There are lyrics, and then there are notes, melody lines which you set up.

As I told you before, I could write on demand—especially when we were about to go into the studio. And I suspect that if you asked me tonight to write you a song, and if I wasn't too sleepy, I'd have it done by morning.

I noticed some interesting developments in popular music. White singers were picking up on black songs on a much more widespread basis. They had always done it, but now it was happening much more frequently. Georgia Gibbs and Pat Boone and Carl Perkins and Elvis were doing tunes which originally had been rhythm-and-blues hits.

It didn't bother me. It was just one of those American things. I've said before that I believe in mixed musical marriages, and there's no way to copyright a feeling or a rhythm or a style of singing. Besides, it meant that White America was getting hipper.

Something else happened in this time slot: rock 'n' roll. I have a hard time defining schools of music, and I've never been one to even try. I've been arguing against labels my whole life—I hate it when they're slapped on me—but finally they become so popular that even I have to use them.

I never considered myself part of rock 'n' roll. I didn't believe that I was among the forerunners of the music, and I've never given myself a lick of credit for either inventing it or having anything to do with its birth.

When I think of the true rock 'n' roll, cats like Chuck Berry and Little Richard and Bo Diddley come to mind. I think they're the main men. And there's a towering difference between their music and mine. My stuff was more adult. It was more difficult for teenagers to relate to; so much of my music was sad or down.

A tune like Little Richard's "Tutti Frutti" was fun. Less serious. And the kids could identify with it a lot easier than my "A Fool for You" or "Drown in My Own Tears."

I don't want to put down the others, and I don't want to butter myself up. Richard and Chuck and Bo sold millions of records, and they helped the whole industry. They did some

---

1. "Fathead" was David Newman, Charles's long-time tenor sax player.

spirited music and it broke through some thick barriers. Those guys sold a hell of a lot more records than I did back then. They sold to whites by the truckloads. Fats Domino had huge hits in the white market—"Blueberry Hill" and "Ain't It a Shame"—and I wasn't even in the same league.

Rock 'n' roll was also music that the teenagers were able to play themselves. Little Richard's or Jerry Lee Lewis's piano style—taking your thumb and scraping all the way up the keyboard—had a flare and a sound that the kids loved. And which they could duplicate. I sang some happy songs, and I played tunes with tempos that moved. But if you compare, let's say, my "Don't You Know, Baby?" to Little Richard's "Long Tall Sally," you'll hear the difference; my music is more serious, filled with more despair than anything you'd associate with rock 'n' roll.

Since I couldn't see people dancing, the dance crazes passed me by. I didn't try to write any jitterbugs or twists. I wrote rhythms which moved me and figured they'd also make other folk move.

I've heard the Beatles say that they listened to me when they were coming up. I believe them, but I also think that my influence on them wasn't nearly as great as these other artists. I was really in a different world, and if any description of me comes close, it's the tag "rhythm and blues." I've fooled around in the same way that blacks have been doing for years—playing the blues to different rhythms.

The style requires pure heart singing. Later on they'd call it soul music. But the names don't matter. It's the same mixture of gospel and blues with maybe a sweet melody thrown in for good measure. It's the sort of music where you can't fake the feeling.

Earlier I was telling you how I never test songs on the public before I record them. I've always been my own private testing service. But there was one exception to this rule, even though I didn't mean for it to happen the way it did. I'm talking about the accidental birth of "What I Say."

We happened to be playing one of my last dances—somewhere in the Midwest—and I had another twelve minutes to kill before the set closed. A typical gig of that kind lasted four hours, including a thirty-minute intermission. We played from 9:00 till 11:30, took a half-hour break, and then did the final hour.

It was nearly 1:00 A.M., I remember, and we had played our whole book. There was nothing left that I could think of, so I finally said to the band and the Raeletts, "Listen, I'm going to fool around and y'all just follow me."

So I began noodling. Just a little riff which floated up into my head. It felt good and I kept on going. One thing led to another, and suddenly I found myself singing and wanting the girls to repeat after me. So I told 'em, "Now'"

Then I could feel the whole room bouncing and shaking and carrying on something fierce. So I kept the thing going, tightening it up a little here, adding a dash of Latin rhythm there. When I got through, folk came up and asked where they could buy the record. "Ain't no record," I said, "just something I made up to kill a little time."

The next night I started fooling with it again, adding a few more lyrics and refining the riffs for the band. I did that for several straight evenings until the song froze into place. And each time I sang it, the reaction was wild.

I called Jerry Wexler from the road and told him that I was coming to New York with something new to record. "I've been playing it," I said, "and it's pretty nice." That was further than I usually went with Jerry. I don't believe in giving myself advance notices, but I figured this song merited it.

We made the record in 1959, and it became my biggest hit to date. Like "Hallelujah," it sold to whites and blacks alike, although not everyone dug it. It was banned by several radio stations. They said it was suggestive. Well, I agreed. I'm not one to interpret my own songs, but if you can't figure out "What I Say," then something's wrong. Either that, or you're not accustomed to the sweet sounds of love.

Later on, I saw that many of the stations which had banned the tune started playing it when it was covered by white artists. That seemed strange to me, as though white sex was cleaner than black sex. But once they began playing the white version, they lifted the ban and also played the original.

These bans didn't bother me none, mainly 'cause I could see, feel, and smell royalties rolling in. At this point, it was bread I really needed.

The biggest of the concept albums involved country-and-western music. And it came about because I had been planning it for years. If I had remained on Atlantic, I would have done the country thing a year or two earlier. I knew, however, that ABC thought of me as a rhythm-and-blues singer, and I didn't want to shock the label too badly or too quickly. So I waited till the beginning of 1962. That seemed like a reasonable time.

My contract was up for its three-year renewal and, to my way of thinking, I had done well for ABC. They hadn't hassled me before, and I had no reason to believe they would bother me now. Still, my country music idea might have hit them as half-cocked and completely crazy.

What better time to test their faith in me? If they were really behind me, they'd let me do what I wanted. And if they weren't with me all the way, I'd get to learn that right now.

I called Sid Feller and asked him to gather up the great country hits of all time. He sounded a little bewildered, but he was nice enough to do what I asked. Later on, the ABC executives mildly protested—but all in good taste.

They told me how this might injure my career. They told me how all my fans had been loyal to me. They explained how I might irritate some people, how I might lose my following. And even though I listened and understood what they were saying, I ignored them and made the record anyway. We had no contract problems.

I didn't plan on making a killing on the country stuff; I had no commercial scheme in mind. I just wanted to try my hand at hillbilly music. After all, the Grand Ole Opry had been performing inside my head since I was a kid in the country.

To show you how naive I was about the sales potential of this material, I put "I Can't Stop Loving You" as the fifth song on the B side. I called the album *Modern Sounds in Country and Western Music.*

I had no special plans for the arrangements. In fact, I set some of the songs against strings with a choir, the way I was doing much of my material then. Other tunes were done with a big band—my big band—which had just been formed.

I was only interested in two things: being true to myself and being true to the music. I wasn't trying to be the first black country singer. I only wanted to take country songs and sing them my way, not the country way. I wasn't aware of any bold act on my part or any big breakthrough.

It was just blind luck that the tunes—"I Can't Stop Loving You," "Born to Lose," and later, "Take These Chains," "You Are My Sunshine," "Busted," and "You Don't Know Me"—hit with such impact. These country hits wound up giving me a bigger white audience than black, and today when I play concerts, there are still usually more whites than blacks.

At the same time, "I Can't Stop Loving You" was a big song among blacks. It didn't get the initial air play that it might have, but that's 'cause it wasn't the kind of song black jocks normally programmed. And also I was led to believe by some of these cats that they just didn't like ABC. They told me that they played my songs only because it was me. Finally, "I Can't Stop Loving You" made the black stations simply cause they had no choice; the record was too important to be ignored.

# 18. Jerry Wexler

## A Life in R&B

A colorful character who had a hand in recording numerous R&B and soul greats, Jerry Wexler (b. 1917), along with Ahmet Ertegun, ran Atlantic records in from the mid-1950s through the 1960s. These excerpts from his autobiography look both backward—to "race" records of the 1940s—and forward—to the transformation of rhythm and blues into rock 'n' roll. He describes the situation at Atlantic records when he joined as codirector with Ahmet Ertegun and presents his analysis of the social and historical context in the early 1950s in which R&B recordings began to appeal to white teenagers. Always engaging and opinionated, Wexler offers his views on cross-cultural collaboration, the "White Negro" syndrome,[1] and on the relationship between commercialism and notions of expressive sincerity (or "authenticity"). Not surprisingly, both he and Ertegun take a rather different view of Atlantic's relationship with its artists than the artists themselves do.

## *from* RHYTHM AND THE BLUES: A LIFE IN AMERICAN MUSIC
### *Jerry Wexler and David Ritz*

The early catalogue [at Atlantic] was eclectic. There were Eddie Safranski's Poll Cats; Stan Kenton band members like Art Pepper, Shelly Manne, Pete Rugolo, and Bob Cooper. There were guitarist Tiny Grimes; Swing Era jazzmen like Rex Stewart; vocal groups like the Delta Rhythm Boys, the Clovers, and the Cardinals; pianists Erroll Gamer and Mal Waldron; boppers Howard McGhee, James Moody, and Dizzy Gillespie; scat singers Jackie and Roy; Sarah Vaughan; blues legends Leadbelly and Sonny Terry; Mary Lou Williams; clarinetist Bamey Bigard; cafe society singers Mabel Mercer and Bobby Short; Billie Holiday–based Sylvia Syms; boogie-woogie virtuoso Meade Lux Lewis. In short, there was everything.

At the same time, nothing was selling big except for that single Stick McGhee hit—"Drinkin' Wine Spo-Dee-O-Dee"—and some Ruth Brown and Joe Turner. In spite of a noble attempt to represent a broad spectrum of jazz and jazz-tinged music, it was rhythm and blues and rhythm and blues alone that paid the rent—a situation that wouldn't change for a long time to come.

---

1. The "White Negro" syndrome refers to a famous article by Normal Mailer, "The White Negro: Superficial Reflections on the Hipster," *Dissent* 4 (Summer 1957): 276–93. Wexler discusses Mailer's article in this excerpt.

*Source:* Jerry Wexler and David Ritz, from *Rhythm and the Blues: A Life in American Music* (New York: Alfred A. Knopf, 1993), pp. 78–79, 85–87, 90–92. Copyright © 1993 by Jerry Wexler and David Ritz. Used by permission of Alfred A. Knopf, a division of Random House, Inc.

So when I came along, the agenda was already set. Ahmet ran it down to me in no un-certain terms. "Here's the sort of record we need to make," he explained. "There's a black man living in the outskirts of Opelousas, Louisiana. He works hard for his money; he has to be tight with a dollar. One morning he hears a song on the radio. It's urgent, bluesy, authentic, irresistible. He becomes obsessed. He can't live without this record, He drops everything, jumps in his pickup, and drives twenty-five miles to the first record store he finds. If we can make that kind music, we can make it in the business."

It's interesting that Ahmet's decree makes no mention of cross-over—the notion of selling black music to whites. That idea wasn't yet in the air. When I started working at Atlantic, I certainly had no such notions. I knew that the postwar rhythm-and-blues phe-nomenon had been spearheaded by independent labels. The war had caused a scarcity in shellac, and the majors were recording only their big-selling white acts and very few blacks. Thus black buyers' demand for black records was great. That's the slot the indies filled in the forties. And to a large extent, in the early fifties that was still the deal.

*It happened before,* I wrote in an essay for *Cashbox* in 1954. "It happened in the twenties when Perry Bradford and Spencer Williams were as hot as Irving Berlin; it happened when Bessie Smith and Ethel Waters sold their records into millions of white parlors. Now it's happening again. The blues will get stronger before the blues get weaker. Regardless of its impact on the pop field, the blues will surely go on."

I was talking about the present state of rhythm and blues and the beginnings of rock 'n' roll. In significant numbers, white people were listening to, buying, and playing black music. Atlantic's black-and-red label carried the slogan "Leads the Field in Rhythm and Blues," but it was clear that our market, once exclusively black, was expanding.[2]

The first hint came when my friend Howie Richmond called to say that something new was happening in the South and Southwest. They were calling it "cat music," the pre-rock-'n'-roll handle for rhythm and blues selling to whites. Immediately I glommed on to the name, and we started a "Cat" subsidiary label. That had two advantages: first, I hoped the name would pick up on the trend; and secondly, another label allowed us to use other distributors in major markets. (We usually made exclusive agreements with a single dis-tributor in each city, when in fact there were any number of excellent distributors.) We had black artists on Cat—Little Sylvia Vanderpool (later of Mickey and Sylvia), Mike Cordon and the El Tempos, and the Chords, whose record of "Sh-Boom" would be copied (and buried) by the Crewcuts, a white group.

A picture was beginning to emerge: Kids, especially kids down South, were taking newly invented transistor radios to the beach. White Southerners, I believe, in spite of the traditional aura of racial bigotry, have always enjoyed the most passionate rapport with black music, itself a Southern phenomenon. And in the fifties, white Southern teenagers started the charge towards ballsy rhythm and blues. As the Eisenhower decade became more conformist, the music became more rebellious, more blatantly sexual, climaxing in the remarkable persona of Elvis Presley, a Memphis boy raised on the pure sounds of the black South.

In the wake of postwar prosperity, teenagers were becoming a market of their own. Their buying power was real, their emotional needs immediate, their libidinous drive no longer reflected by the dead-and-gone fox-trots of their parents. Suddenly there was another force at work—old but new, primal yet complex, a music informed by the black

2. This assertion is borne out by a spate of articles that appeared in music industry publications around this time; see Bob Rolontz and Joel Friedman, "Teen-Agers Demand Music with a Beat, Spur Rhythm-Blues: Field Reaps $15,000,000; Radio, Juke Boxes Answer Big Demands," *Billboard,* April 24, 1954, 1, 18, 24, 50; and other articles reprinted or cited later.

genius for expressing pent-up frustration, joy, rage, or ecstasy in a poetic context marked by hip humor and irresistible rhythm.

Ahmet had already anticipated this evolution, the best example being his seminal work with Joe Turner. Big Joe was the blues-shouting bartender from Kansas City whom I'd heard back in my student days. A mountain of a man, his voice was among the most powerful in the history of the form. History had placed him in a niche with Pete Johnson, his boogie-woogie-piano-playing partner, and Count Basie, whose band he'd joined when Ahmet caught him at the Apollo in the early fifties.

"Joe took Jimmy Rushing's place," says Ahmet, "but unlike Jimmy, Joe didn't fit. Musically, he and Basie were fighting each other, and it was depressing. The crowd didn't like it, Joe didn't like it, and afterwards I found him in a bar where he told me Columbia had dropped him from the label. Joe really had the blues. I think you're the greatest blues singer in the world,' I told him. 'All you need is fresh material. Sign with Atlantic and we'll make hits.'"

Ahmet's "Chains of Love" hit the charts in 1951, followed by "Sweet Sixteen," "Honey Hush," and "TV Mama." It was "Shake, Rattle and Roll," though, that opened the floodgates for Joe. The song was written by Jesse Stone, a brilliant black arranger with roots back to Jelly Roll Morton. Jesse's musical mind had as much to do as anyone's with the transformation of traditional blues to pop blues—or rhythm and blues, or cat music, or rock 'n' roll, or whatever the hell you want to call it. Jesse was a master, and an integral part of the sound we were developing. He had the unique gift of maintaining a hang-loose boogie-shuffle feel in the context of a formal chart. Jesse was a record producer's dream come true. I always felt he viewed me with a slightly jaundiced eye, as though I might sign the checks but was in on a pass, not knowing shit about the music. Jessie seemed to know everything.

He'd written hits for Jimmy Dorsey. He'd written "Idaho," whose sophisticated chord structure became a favorite vehicle for the beboppers. In "Shake, Rattle and Roll," under the pseudonym of Charles Calhoun, he also wrote, "you wear those dresses, the sun comes shining through, I can't believe my eyes, all that mess belongs to you"—one of my favorite images of erotic poetry. In Bill Haley's white cover, whose sales outstripped Turner's version, the sex was stripped off," the lyrics bleached clean. No matter; Joe's reading remains a gem.

Highly imitated as innovators, Jesse Stone and Howard Biggs (another fabulous arranger) were absolutely essential to the good rockin' feel of our early-fifties hits. Howard is gone, but Jesse is still with us. In his eighties, he is living in Florida, alert and in full possession of all his faculties.

*Those first* couple of years at Atlantic had me flying high. With the aid of Miriam Abramson, who shared my zeal for the nitty-gritty of daily detail, the business side was clean-cut and straight-ahead. Ahmet was cooking in the studio, and I was at his side soaking up the make-it-up-as-you-go-along recipes.

Luckily, my arrival came at that fortunate point in American music when the lines between black and white were starting to fade. Things were getting blurry in a hurry, and Atlantic both benefited from and contributed to that breakdown. Hip disc jockeys—white guys who talked black—were starting to play black music to an audience that was increasingly white. Cats like Zenas "Daddy" Sears in Atlanta, George "Hound Dog" Lorenz in Buffalo, Hunter Hancock in Los Angeles, Bob "Wolfman Jack" Smith in Shreveport and Del Rio, Ken "Jack the Cat" Elliott and Clarence "Poppa Stoppa" Hamman in New Orleans, Gene Nobles and John Richbourg and Hoss Allen in Nashville, not to mention a man destined for national prominence, Alan "Moondog" Freed in Cleveland—these were all white guys who broadcasted black, speaking with the timing and rhyming of the ghetto. Both in the existential sense of Norman Mailer's term ("The source of Hip is the Negro," he wrote, "for he has been living on the margin between totalitarianism and democracy for two centuries") and in the sense of pure entertainment, these were White Negroes. Their significance cannot be overemphasized. These sons-of-bitches not only pointed to the future of American popular music but were also the makers and the breakers of our records.

The black style represented a diverting departure from the mid-fifties blahs. You could segregate schoolrooms and buses, but not the airwaves. Radio could not resist the music's universality—its intrinsic charm, its empathy for human foibles, its direct application to the teen-age condition.

The hip of my generation, who were teenagers in the thirties, had always been drawn to black culture. In fact, I had always known White Negroes, not pretenders or voyeurs but guys who had opted to leave the white world, married black women, and made Harlem or Watts their habitat. These guys *converted*. Clarinetist Mezz Mezzrow—of the famous joints—was the most colorful example; Teddy Reig, the three-hundred-pound soul man who managed Count Basie and Chuck Berry and produced Charlie Parker, was another. Symphony Syd, jazz voice of the night in New York City; Johnny Otis, pioneering rhythm-and-blues band leader, creator of "Willie and the Hand Jive," discoverer of Esther Phillips and Etta James in Los Angeles; Monte Kay, bebop impresario, manager of the Modern Jazz Quartet, whose kinky coif might have been the first Jewfro in hair-fashion history—these were all friends.

I dug cross-cultural collaborations and craved commercial success, which is maybe why Ahmet and I got on so well. We could have developed a label along the lines of Blue Note, Prestige, Vanguard, or Folkways, fastidious documentarians of core American music. Bobby Weinstock, Alfred Lion, Moe Ash, Orrin Keepnews, Manny Solomon, and the other keepers of the flame were doing God's work. Ahmet and I, however, didn't feature ourselves as divinely elected. We weren't looking for canonization; we lusted for hits. Hits were the cash flow, the lifeblood, the heavenly ichor—the wherewithal of survival. While we couldn't divorce ourselves from our tastes and inclinations, neither could we deny our interest in income. Nor could we stand still; we believed to our souls that the way of the independent label was either growth or death. Every month, it seemed, another indie would hit the dust. Our competitors in commercial black music—Lew Chudd at Imperial, Sam and Hymie Weiss at Old Town, Syd Nathan at King, Art Rupe at Specialty, Don Robey at Duke/Peacock, Jules and Saul Bihari at Modern, Bess Berman at Apollo, Herman Lubinsky at Savoy, Phil and Leonard Chess—weren't exactly pushovers. If we slipped, these sweethearts would be right behind us picking up the pieces. This was a pushy, get-to-the-distributor, get-to-the-deejay, get-the-goddamn-song-on-the-air business.

Consequently, the term "commercial" was not a pejorative for me—wasn't then, isn't now. If "commercial" meant a song with a strong hook, an inviting refrain, melodic variety, and a rhythm pattern with a walloping bass line—well, give me commercial and lots of it. The merry jingle of cash registers was music to my ears. As a kid, I might have been cavalier about money. But this was a different deal. I had a family to support; people were working for me. Fear of bankruptcy was always around the corner—deep-depression, nothing-to-eat, nowhere-to-sleep fear. Given my high level of chain-smoking anxiety, I still wonder that I didn't develop ulcers early on.

Yet the tonic wasn't money; it was music. Substantial financial rewards wouldn't come until well into the sixties. In the precarious fifties, my fascination with the glories of the music seemed to push me beyond my own limitations. If now and then Ahmet or I might begin to worry during a session, unnecessarily afraid that LaVern or Ray was getting too hoarse or the drummer was dragging, the natural abilities of our artists would eventually pull things together. We also had the benefit of Dowd's engineering talents, arrangers like Jesse, and a large pool of New York City session musicians, many of whom—drummers Connie Kay and Panama Francis, tenor men Budd Johnson and Sam Taylor, pianists Hank Jones and Dick Hyman—were jazz musicians of the first order.

# 19. The Growing Threat of Rhythm and Blues

While the early 1950s witnessed numerous crossovers and cover versions of country songs, such developments occurred more slowly in rhythm and blues. As described by Jerry Wexler and Ruth Brown, however, by 1954 people in the music industry were aware of the broadening appeal of R&B. The expanding audience for R&B began to be reflected in a growing number of pop cover versions of R&B hits, as well as in the occasional crossover, such as "Crying in the Chapel" in July 1953 by the Orioles or "Gee" by the Crows in March 1954, both "doo-wop"-style vocal numbers. Diverse factors played a role in heightening public awareness of black popular music: the spread of R&B to juke boxes and record stores in white neighborhoods, the integrated audiences at rhythm and blues shows emceed by Alan Freed, new technology (the introduction of the inexpensive and durable "45," affordable tape recorders, transistor radios), and a growing number of radio shows devoted to R&B.

In early 1955, a series of articles appeared in *Variety* (one of the three most important music industry publications, along with *Billboard* and *Cashbox*) describing the effect of the increasing popularity of rhythm and blues on popular music. These articles generally lamented the incursion of R&B, citing the difficulties created for old-fashioned pop tunes and in the music publishing business. As one article observed, "R&B is strictly a sound phenom"—i.e., it is the particular sound of a recorded performance of a R&B record that listeners find attractive, rather than the more abstract sense of melody and harmony provided by sheet music that may retain its appeal through numerous competing recordings or performances (as in the pop tunes of the Tin Pan Alley era).[1]

As the weeks went by, the sense of panic in *Variety*'s pages increased. The following article provides evidence of this tone in its assertions of the displacement of pop vocalists by rhythm and blues artists. *Variety*'s own popularity charts contradict this, however, as cover versions were far more popular than the original versions of these tunes. For example, Georgia Gibbs's version of "Tweedle-Dee" (discussed in the following article) ranked number nine, while LaVern Baker's (R&B) version was not listed at all during the week this article was published. At any rate, regardless of whether its assertions were well grounded, *Variety* clearly found the presence of *any* R&B recordings or covers on the pop charts profoundly *upsetting*.

---

1. "Music Biz Now R&B Punchy: Even Hillbillies Are Doing It," *Variety*, February 9, 1955, 51, 54.

# TOP NAMES NOW SINGING THE BLUES AS NEWCOMERS ROLL ON R&B TIDE

## *Variety*

Like the major disk companies, the established pop vocalists are finding the current rhythm & blues phase of the music biz to be tough sledding. At the present time, the only veteran names in the topselling brackets are Perry Como and Georgia Gibbs. Both are rolling with the cycle and have turned r&b tunes, such as "Ko Ko Mo" and "Tweedle Dee," into top hits.

The major diskers are not finding it easy to crack the r&b formula. For one thing, most of the artists & repertoire chiefs frankly can't recognize a potential r&b hit when they hear one. As a result, they are all waiting for the tunes to break through on the indie labels and then they decide to cover.

However, unlike a straight pop tune on which a major could usually take the play away from an indie, this does not necessarily hold true of r&b tunes. The kids not only are going for the tunes and the beat, but they seem to be going for the original interpretations as well. Several covers of r&b tunes by pop names have not been able to gain ground because they lacked that authentic low-down quality accented on the indie labels.

The major labels are not only being knocked over by the r&b cycle, but by the general demand for offbeat stuff. Femme vocal groups, which used to be a drug on the market only a few month ago, are now hitting big. Such combos as the McGuire Sisters, Fontane Sisters, and DeJohn Sisters are one, two, three disk attractions currently.

The Crew-Cuts is another combo mopping up in the current tune trend, as is Bill Haley & His Comets. The Penguins, on the indie Dootone label, have also been clicking with their original r&b interpretation of "Earth Angel," although the Crew-Cuts are outpacing them in sales.

Like the influx of hillbilly names into the pop market about four years ago, the r&b cycle is turning up its share of new combos and singers. These include The Charms, The Five Keys, Lavern Baker, Fats Domino, Gene & Eunice, the Moonglows, and a flock of other such combos.

Topsyturvy nature of the current disk biz is spotlighted by the dominance of the small labels among the top 10 or 15 disks. Companies like Dot, Cadence, Coral, Epic and Mercury are riding roughshod over the Big Four of Victor, Columbia, Decca and Capitol.

That there's no completely uniform pattern to the music biz is revealed by the presence of an oldie ballad like "Melody of Love" among the topsellers. Also a legitimate tune like "That's All I Want From You" continues to hold up despite the demand for the "Ko Ko Mos" and "Tweedle-Dees."

*Variety*'s anxiety reached its shrillest pitch in the following editorial, which appeared the same week as the preceding article. "Abel" (the pseudonym used by the author of this piece) seems particularly upset about companies who are irresponsibly pursuing the "filthy fast buck" by foisting R&B on an unsuspecting public. This idea, which verges on a conspiracy theory, implies the unlikely historical scenario whereby the music business, prior to its defilement by popular music sporting "leer-ics," was engaged in a philanthropic, rather than a capitalistic, activity. Abel blames payola even though independent companies spent less money on "promotion" (the official term for payola) than the majors.[2]

The following week's edition of *Variety* printed letters from several prominent people in the entertainment industry who supported the editorial, along with one anonymous writer who argued in favor of the independent record companies.[3] That the writers who favored the editorial were allied with the superstructure supporting old-style pop music— ASCAP, a major record company, and a Broadway theater—should not be too surprising. None of these people stood to profit from the expansion of rhythm and blues into the pop market. Though never overt, the issue of race informs the editorial and the responses to it: The concern about the inroads made by R&B is unimaginable without the widely held associations between race and certain categories of popular music and the way in which the structure of popular music at that time mirrored the segregation of U.S. society (as the editorial reminded its readers, "this sort of lyric was off in a corner by itself. It was the music underworld—not the main stream").[4]

Of greater interest, though, and a bit more perplexing, is that Abel doesn't provide examples of offending songs. Which particular "leer-ic" does he have in mind? Two somewhat salacious songs had experienced a minor degree of crossover success in the preceding year: Joe Turner's "Shake, Rattle, and Roll" and the Midnighters' "Work with Me Annie" both of which were huge R&B hits (another suggestive song, "Sixty-Minute Man" had followed a similar pattern three years earlier). However, as Jerry Wexler noted in his autobiography, another version of "Shake, Rattle, and Roll," a cover by Bill Haley which toned down the lyrics of the Joe Turner version, had been much more successful on the pop charts.[5] On the other hand, nothing in the lyrics of songs of other recent crossovers from this period, such as "Earth Angel" and "Tweedle-Dee," explains why they might cause offense. The plentiful cover songs on the charts at the time of the editorial also offer no explanation for this fear of

---

2. For more on panics surrounding early rock 'n' roll concerts, see "'Rock & Roll' to Get Ofay Theatre Showcasing; Freed Set for Par, B'kln," *Variety,* February 1955, 47; "Cleve. Cats Are Clipped by Cops' Crackdown on Jock's Jive Jamboree," *Variety* February 9, 1955: 58; "Jocks Junk Payola Platters," *Variety* February 16, 1955, 39.

3. "Trade Execs Generally Support Stand vs. Indigo R&B Lyrics," *Variety,* March 2, 1955, 51.

4. I discuss the moment in greater detail in "Music," in *Key Terms in Popular Music and Culture,* ed. Bruce Horner and Thomas Swiss (Malden, Mass.: Blackwells, 1999). For an in-depth account, see Trent Hill, "the Enemy Within: Censorship in Rock Music in the 1950s," *South Atlantic Quarterly,* 90, no. 4 (Fall 1991), 675–708. Charles Hamm also discusses this editorial and the series of articles in *Variety* (in *Yesterdays: Popular Song in America* (New York: W. W. Norton, 1979), 401–2).

5. The original recording of "Shake, Rattle, and Roll," by Joe Turner reached 22 in the pop juke box charts and spent a total of two weeks in the Top 30 during August 1954. "Work with Me Annie" performed similarly in the pop charts in June 1954. After Etta James had an R&B hit with a reply song, "The Wallflower (Roll with Me Henry)," Georgia Gibbs had a huge hit with a watered-down version, entitled "Dance with Me Henry," in April 1955.

an invasion of "euphemisms which are attempting a total breakdown of all reticences about sex." One can only speculate that this panic is being driven by fears about aspects of the music style, the threat to the established structure of the music industry, and the breakdown of extant social barriers that would accompany an unprecedented integration of African American performers into white society. Despite the fact that these reactions seem out of proportion to what was actually going on in the popular music of the time, they proved remarkably prescient. By 1956, African American artists playing what would by then be termed "rock 'n' roll" were thoroughly integrated into the mainstream pop charts.

## A WARNING TO THE MUSIC BUSINESS
### *Variety*

Music "leer-ics" are touching new lows and if the fast-buck songsmiths and music makers are incapable of social responsibility and self-restraint then regulation—policing, if you will—have to come from more responsible sources. Meaning the phonograph record manufacturers and their network daddies. These companies have a longterm stake rather than a quick turn-around role. It won't wash for them to echo the cheap cynicism of the songsmiths who justify their "leer-ic" garbage by declaring "that's what the kids want" or "that's the only thing that sells today."

What are we talking about? We're talking about "rock and roll," about "hug," and "squeeze," and kindred euphemisms which are attempting a total breakdown of reticences about sex. In the past such material was common enough but restricted to special places and out-and-out barrelhouses. Today "leer-ics" are offered as standard popular music for general consumption, including consumption by teenagers. Our teenagers are already setting something of a record in delinquency without this raw musical idiom to smell up the environment still more.

The time is now for some serious soul-searching by the popular music industry. This is a call to the conscience of that business. Don't invite the Governmental and religious lightning that is sure to strike. Forget the filthy fast buck. Nor is it just the little music "independents" who are heedless of responsibility.

The major diskeries, with the apparently same disregard as to where the blue notes may fall, are as guilty. Guiltier, perhaps, considering the greater obligation—their maturer backgrounds—their time-honored relations with the record-buying public.

The most casual look at the current crop of "lyrics" must tell even the most naive that dirty postcards have been translated into songs. Compared to some of the language that loosely passes for song "lyrics" today, the "pool-table papa" and "jellyroll" terminology of yesteryear is polite palaver. Only difference is that this sort of lyric then was off in a corner by itself. It was the music underworld—not the main stream.

For the music men—publishers and dlskeries—to say that "that's what the kids want" and "that's the only thing that sells nowadays," is akin to condoning publication of back-fence language. Earthy dialog may belong in "art novels" but mass media have tremendous obligation. If they forget, they'll hear from authority. Seemingly that is not the case in the music business.

Before it's too late for the welfare of the industry—forgetting for the moment the welfare of young Americans—VARIETY urges a strong self-examination of the record business by its most responsible chief executive officers. A strong suspicion lingers with VARIETY that these business men are too concerned with the profit statements to take stock of what's causing some of their items to sell. Or maybe they just don't care. A suspicion has been expressed that even the network-affiliated and Hollywood-affiliated record companies brush things off with "that's the music business." This is illogical because it is morally wrong and in the longrun it's wrong financially.

Today's "angles" and sharp practices in the music business are an intra-trade problem. Much of it, time-dishonored. The promulgation and propagation of a pop song, ever since there was a Tin Pan Alley, was synonymous with shrewdness, astuteness and deviousness that often bordered on racketeering in its subornation of talent, subsidy, cajolery and out-and-out bribery.

In its trade functions no trade paper, VARIETY included, wants to be accused of "blowing the whistle." But the music business is flirting with the shrill commands of an outer influence if it doesn't wake up and police itself. This is not the first time VARIETY has spotlighted the pyramiding evils of the music business as it operates today. One of the roots is the payola. If some freak "beat" captures the kids' imagination, the boys are in there quick, wooing, romancing, cajoling the a&r men.

Here is where the responsible chief officers of the major diskeries should come in. They can continue to either blind themselves, as apparently seems to be the case, or they can compel their moral obligations to stand in the way of a little quick profit. This has an accumulative force, because their own radio outlets can limit the exploitation of this spurious stuff. Not only the commodities of their own affiliation, but others.

Some may argue that this is a proposal of "censorship." Not at all. It is a plea to ownership to assume the responsibilities of ownership and eliminate practices which will otherwise invite censorship. In short, chums, do it yourself or have it done for you. You're not going to get or have it done for you.

*Abel.*

# 20. Langston Hughes Responds

The following article addresses the issue of "cover" songs from a quite different perspective from that found in the trade publications of the time. Written by Langston Hughes, the renowned African American poet and essayist, and published in the *Chicago Defender* (an African American newspaper), it considers not whether cover versions of R&B are perverting mainstream popular music, but rather how such a practice perpetuates the syndrome that Steve Chapple and Reebee Garofalo termed "Black Roots/White Fruits."[1] A lawsuit by Lavern Baker several months earlier had touched on this issue. Baker contended that Georgia Gibbs's cover version of "Tweedle-Dee" had duplicated the arrangement used on her (Baker's) recording.[2] This suit raises questions about what constitutes a "composition": The Copyright Act of 1909 defines it according to what can be notated, thereby reproducing the standards of originality developed for classical music, which favored the production model used by Tin Pan Alley songwriters. However, these standards did not protect R&B and country musicians who depended on a unique "sound" and the nuances of performance more than on a unique melody and harmonic progression.

## HIGHWAY ROBBERY ACROSS THE COLOR LINE IN RHYTHM AND BLUES
### Langston Hughes

Young people nowadays seem to think that all the white popular singers who copied the singing styles of Billie Holiday, Sara Vaughan, Dinah Washington, Ethel Waters, Billie Daniels, King Cole, La Vern Baker, and Mahalia Jackson are doing something new. Not true at all! White singers have been copying Negro singing styles for over 100 years.

Almost as fast as the Negro originates something new in the world of music, the whites take it and go, sometimes even claiming it as their own creation.

A white band in Chicago in the early 1920s claimed to be the creators of jazz since they beat King Oliver and Louis Armstrong in the North by a few months.

In New York a bit later Paul Whiteman took unto himself the title of "The King of Jazz," and gave the first jazz concert in Aeolian Hall. George Gershwin wrote the first jazz concerto, also the first blues opera—and made himself not only famous, but rich. Some of the poor guys who originated jazz and are still living, are on relief.

It is the same with dancing. Back in 1830 the first of the white minstrels, Dan Rice, copied the jig of a Negro stable boy in Louisville, called it Jump Jim Crow, and made himself famous.

When the Charleston first came to fame in Harlem in the 1920s some whites quickly and jerkily learned it, and claimed—unsuccessfully for once—to have originated it. A bit later Gilda Gray had claimed the shimmy.

And I would not be surprised to read any day now where some white singer originated the blues. Some have just that much nerve.

That hundreds of white performers are today copying note for note and slur for slur the rhythms and blues styles of Negro performers is a compliment to Negro artists—artistically, if not commercially.

"Imitation is the sincerest form of flattery," so the saying goes. What the Negro artists are saying is, "It's nice to have white performers imitate us—but cut us in on the jobs and the dough, too."

---

1. Steve Chapple and Reebee Garofalo, *Rock 'n' Roll Is Here to Pay: The History and Politics of the Music Industry* (Chicago: Nelson-Hall, 1977).

2. See "Lavern Baker Claims 15G Royalty Loss on Lifting of Song Arrangements," *Variety*, March 2, 1955, 51.

*Source:* Langston Hughes, "Highway Robbery Across the Color Line in Rhythm and Blues," *Chicago Defender* (July 2, 1955), p. 9.

But it just happens that the white performers can carry their copies of Negro material into the best night clubs, the biggest theaters, and onto the movie screens of Hollywood where poor Negroes hardly ever get a look in—not to speak of the fields of radio and television where colored performers with regular jobs are few and very, very far between.

In other words, in commercial entertainment, "the white man is still in the lead." He makes the money, we make the basic music. What to do about it? Who knows? From coast to coast, and uptown to down, Broadway to Central Ave., Vine St. to W. 125th St. where stands the Hotel Theresa, the colored performer is yowling to high heaven, "They got me and gone!"

# 21. From Rhythm and Blues to Rock 'n' Roll
## The Songs of Chuck Berry

In chapter 17, Ray Charles described several factors that defined the difference between him, a rhythm and blues artist, and rock 'n' rollers, such as Chuck Berry and Little Richard; these factors included the intended audience for his recordings (more adult for R&B, more teenage for rock 'n' roll), and the level of emotional gravity (rock 'n' roll projected more unadulterated "fun," while rhythm and blues was more serious). During 1955, Chuck Berry, Little Richard, Bo Diddley, and Fats Domino all developed a new form of rhythm and blues that lent itself to being marketed to an interracial teenage audience.[1] Of these three, Chuck Berry (b. 1926) in many ways represented the prototypical rock 'n' roller because of his abilities as a singer, songwriter, and guitarist (the quality that separated him from Little Richard and Fats Domino, both pianists). More than the other two, Berry was also the master of creating miniature stories depicting experiences that were widespread enough (cars, dating, frustrating high school experiences) to transcend many social boundaries. This does not mean that Berry was motivated solely by a desire to cross over. Musically, he remained rooted in blues and the guitar styles of Muddy Waters, T-Bone Walker, and Charlie Christian, although he experimented early on with incorporating influences from country and pop music, developing a fusion that would prove important to his success. He

---

1. Some may argue that of the three, Fats Domino's success resulted the least from a change of style, since he had been recording songs similar in sound since the late forties. In this case, changes in the audience and the popular music mainstream may be more responsible for his sudden success in the pop market.

also occasionally wrote lyrics that expressed subtle social commentary ("Too Much Monkey Business") and even racial pride ("Brown Eyed Handsome Man").

In his autobiography, first published in 1987 and one of the few such efforts not to involve a ghost writer, Chuck Berry displays the same love of language found in his lyrics.[2] In addition to discussing significant events in his career, he provides insights into the writing of some of his most famous songs and illuminates the tension that inevitably exists between calculation and inspiration in creative endeavors. Beyond his songs and his recordings of them, Berry's legacy lives on in the numerous rock 'n' roll artists who owe a large part of their style to him, including the Beach Boys, the Beatles, and the Rolling Stones, to name only the most famous. Learning his trademark guitar licks and boogie-style accompaniment has become a rite of passage for every would-be rock guitarist, and his songs still feature prominently in many country and rock 'n' roll bar bands.[3]

## *from* CHUCK BERRY: THE AUTOBIOGRAPHY
### *Chuck Berry*

With the recorder, I started hanging around more with Ira Harris. I picked up a lot of new swing riffs and ideas from Ira's playing, which was similar to the style of Charlie Christian's. Ira showed me many licks and riffs on the guitar that came to be the foundation of the style that is said to be Chuck Berry's. Carl Hogan, the guitarist in Louis Jordan's Tympany Five, was another idol of mine. I buckled down and started taking seriously the task of learning to play the guitar. I studied a book of guitar chords by Nick Mannaloft and practiced daily. The chord book led to my getting a textbook explaining the basics of theory and harmony and the fundamental functions of notes, staff, and scale. It's amazing how much you can learn if your intentions are truly earnest.

On June 13, 1952, Tommy Stevens phoned me to ask if I could sing with his three-piece combo at Huff's Garden. It was to be our first time to play together since the All Men's Review yet we had seen each other at many intervals. My heart leaped as I answered, "When?" We squared away the address, agreed on the finances, and I showed up shouting that Saturday and every Saturday thereafter on through to December, earning six dollars a night. It was my first paid nightclub appearance.

The combo, a small group, consisted of Tommy on lead guitars, Pee Wee (can't remember his last name) was on alto sax, and I was on guitar singing the blues. Muddy Waters,

---

2. The release of the book coincided with the release of a semi-autobiographical movie, *Hail! Hail! Rock 'n' Roll.*

3. For more on Berry's guitar style, see Steve Waksman, *Instruments of Desire: The Electric Guitar and the Shaping of Musical Experience* (Cambridge, Mass.: Harvard University Press, 1999), 148–66; R. Vito, "The Chuck Berry Style: A Modern Rocker Pays Tribute to the Master," *Guitar Player* (June 1984), 72–75.

Elmore James, and Joe Turner with his "Chains of Love" were the favorites of all the black disk jockeys' turntables while Nat Cole sang love songs and Harry Belafonte was popular also on the tropical scene. These were the types of songs that made up our selections, along with the backbone of our program, which was always the blues.

My work was divided into day and night with music. While Tommy Stevens didn't have the stage personality of some musicians I had encountered, he did have a congenial personality. He had no objection or reservations whatsoever about my presenting ideas and tactics that often went beyond his own showmanship, in fact he encouraged me. For example, I would suddenly break out with a hillbilly selection that had no business in the repertoire of a soul-music-loving audience and the simple audacity of playing such a foreign number was enough to trigger the program into becoming sensational entertainment.

We were making a little name for ourselves, enough to keep the club packed every Saturday night until that Thanksgiving, when the owner added on Friday nights. After the first two weeks of two nights straight we were drawing a full house. The owner agreed to our salaries being raised to eight dollars per man for each night. As Christmas approached, a rumor was out that a good band was at Huff's Garden and Tommy was telling us that we were being sought by larger nightclubs for jobs.

On December 30, a piano player named Johnnie Johnson phoned me, asking me to join his Sir John's Trio for a gig on the eve of the year of 1953. The nightclub he mentioned was four times as big as Huff's Garden, six times as plush, and ten times as popular. It had been renovated from a supermarket and named the Cosmopolitan Club, which is still located on the corner of 17th and Bond Street in East St. Louis, Illinois. It was on New Year's Eve of 1953 that my career took its first firm step. If I could have stored the drinks that were offered me that night, I think I could have set up everyone in the house twice. The owner of the Cosmo Club, Joe Lewis, asked Johnnie to have me come back the following week to start singing steady.

Johnnie Johnson was the leader and the pianist, Ebby Hardy was the drummer, and I replaced somebody to play guitar and sing. On holidays, Joe Lewis hired a bass to fill out the music more completely. By the Easter holidays we kept a steady packed house on weekends with a well-rounded repertoire programmed to the varied clientele.

The music played most around St. Louis was country-western, which was usually called hillbilly music, and swing. Curiosity provoked me to lay a lot of the country stuff on our predominantly black audience and some of the club goers started whispering, "Who is that black hillbilly at the Cosmo?" After they laughed at me a few times, they began requesting the hillbilly stuff and enjoyed trying to dance to it. If you ever want to see something that is far out, watch a crowd of colored folk, half high, wholeheartedly doing the hoedown barefooted.

Johnnie Johnson was reserved and jolly just like Tommy Stevens, and we didn't have any clash on stage when I would express myself and perform in excess of his own performance. In the beginning, when I would get applause for a gesture, I would look back at Johnnie and see him smiling in approval of what I'd spontaneously added to the song or the show. We made a name for ourselves there at the Cosmopolitan Club.

Toddy [Berry's wife] would get the biggest kick out of our rehearsals around the house, hearing me sing the country stuff. She cared less for country music, being a blues lover, and saw only the fictitious impressions I would insert in a tune to impress the audience with my hilarious hilly and basic billy delivery of the song. It could have been because of my country-western songs that the white spectators showed up in greater numbers as we continued playing at the Cosmo Club, bringing the fairly crowded showplace to a full house. Sometimes nearly forty percent of the clients were Caucasian, causing the event to be worthy of publicity across the river in St. Louis.

The state of Illinois in the beginning of the 1950s was a bit more liberal than Missouri in regards to relations between blacks and whites. A traveler might notice a considerable difference in the community just across the Mississippi in East St. Louis. For one thing, if a black and white couple were stopped by a squad car there they did not have to go to a police station and get a mandatory shot for venereal disease, as was the custom across the river in St. Louis. Nightclub people were known to flock across the river to the east side, where they could escape the bounds of Missouri's early-closing blue laws and continue their enjoyment.

Over half of the songs I was singing at the Cosmo Club were directly from the recordings of Nat "King" Cole and Muddy Waters. They are the major chords in the staff of music I have composed. Listening to my idol Nat Cole prompted me to sing sentimental songs with distinct diction. The songs of Muddy Waters impelled me to deliver the down-home blues in the language they came from, Negro dialect. When I played hillbilly songs, I stressed my diction so that it was harder and whiter. All in all it was my intention to hold both the black and the white clientele by voicing the different kinds of songs in their customary tongues.

Way back then, to me, a gig was played for the purpose of entertaining the patrons. So many times I have sat listening to a group knocking themselves out playing three-week-long songs that have the audience taking pit stops. I can never see why any group would not terminate a song that has boredom showing from the audience. But then some groups don't seem to consider that pleasing the patrons is their main objective. The varied audience at the Cosmo Club gave me an early start at judging the state or the people to be entertained.

[Following a successful audition for Chess records in Chicago] I traveled down from U.S. Highway 66, [and] I contacted Johnnie Johnson and Ebby Hardy and began arranging rehearsals. Johnnie, Ebby, and I had been playing other people's music ever since we started at the Cosmo, but for this tape I did not want to cover other artist's tunes. Leonard Chess had explained that it would be better for me if I had original songs. I was very glad to hear this because I had created many extra verses for other people's songs and I was eager to do an entire creation of my own. The four that I wrote may have been influenced melodically by other songs, but, believe me, the lyrics were solely my own. Before the week had ended, I brought fresh recorded tapes to the ears of the Chess brothers in Chicago.

Chess was in the heart of the Southside of Chicago amid a cultural district I knew all too well. Leonard told me he had formerly had a bar in the neighborhood as well, which accounted for his easy relations with black people. When I carried the new tape up I immediately found out from a poster on the office wall that Muddy, Little Walter, Howlin' Wolf, and Bo Diddley were recording there. In fact Bo Diddley dropped by the studio that day.

Leonard listened to my tape and when he heard one hillbilly selection I'd included called "Ida May," played back on the one-mike, one-track home recorder, it struck him most as being commercial. He couldn't believe that a country tune (he called it a "hillbilly song") could be written and sung by a black guy. He said he wanted us to record that particular song, and he scheduled a recording session for May 21, 1955, promising me a contract at that time.

[After arriving in NYC on a trip to promote "Maybellene"] I phoned Jack Hook, Alan Freed, and Gene Goodman, who were New York business affiliates of Leonard Chess. Leonard had asked me to phone them to introduce me to his New York contacts and them to the guy who wrote "Maybellene."

Jack had a distributing shop in Manhattan where our number-one, and only one, record was being shipped out to dealers. He persuaded us to come immediately over to his storefront business on 8th Street, where I observed boxes and boxes of disks bearing the label of MAYBELLENE, CHESS, CHICAGO. They were triple stacked ceiling high covering one

entire wall. We were stepping over opened boxes scattered about on the floor of the combination office-warehouse.

Between steps on the way to his desk in the back corner, I thought well of the amount
of product carrying my identity on each item. Still it never entered my mind how much
wealth such quantities should bring in sales. I didn't have any idea that Alan Freed was
being compensated for giving special attention to "Maybellene" on his radio program by a
gift from Leonard registering him part of the writer's credit to the song. In fact I didn't know
then that a person also got compensation for writing as well as recording a song. My first
royalty statement made me aware that some person named Russ Fratto and the Alan Freed
I had phoned were also part composers of the song. When I later mentioned to Leonard
Chess the strange names added to the writer's royalties, he claimed that the song would get
more attention with big names involved. With me being unknown, this made sense to me,
especially since he failed to mention that there was a split in the royalties as well.

I have been asked many times, "Where did you get the idea to write that song, Chuck?" Off
hand, I wouldn't know, but I always refer to the story within the song, which usually recalls
my inspiration. Or sometimes the melodic lines bring me in sync with the time and place
where the tune got its origin. The embarrassing thing is that sometimes when I have been
asked about a song's origin I have made up a reason that is dramatic enough to get by the
question. But the origins have varied under different circumstances or with different interviewers. In the pages that follow I'll recall whatever I can about a few of my songs' *true* origins. They appear in the order, according to my records and memory, that I recorded them.

Writing a song can be a peculiar task. So much time can pass during the intervals I
would be putting a song together that each time I'd get back to it, the tune or story it was
following would likely take an entirely different route.

The kind of music I liked then, thereafter, right now and forever, is the kind I heard
when I was a teenager. So the guitar styles of Carl Hogan, T-Bone Walker, Charlie Christian,
and Elmore James, not to leave out many of my peers who I've heard on the road, must be
the total of what is called Chuck Berry's style. So far as the Chuck Berry guitar intro that
identifies many of my songs, it is only back to the future of what came in the past. As you
know, and I believe it must be true, "there is nothing new under the sun." So don't blame
me for being first, just let it last.

To quote the lyrics the genius Ray Charles sang, "Sometimes I get sideways and stay up
all night with a tune. . . . I like what I am doing and sho' hope it don't end too soon." The
nature and back-bone of my beat is boogie and the muscle of my music is melodies that are
simple. Call it what you may: jive, jazz, jump, swing, soul, rhythm, rock, or even punk, it's
still boogie so far as I'm connected with it. When I can't connect to it, I have no right to dispute its title. When it's boogie, but with an alien title, the connection is still boogie and my
kind of music.

So here are the stories of how and why a few of my earlier compositions came about. The
entire catalogue of all my songs will be in a *Chuck Berry Songbook* that will follow this one
with much data of when, where, and who were involved in the recordings plus information
on every concert I ever played.

"Maybellene" was my effort to sing country-western, which I had always liked. The
Cosmo club goers didn't know any of the words to those songs, which gave me a chance to
improvise and add comical lines to the lyrics. "Mountain Dew," "Jambalaya," and "Ida
Red" were the favorites of the Cosmo audience, mainly because of the honky-tonk gestures
I inserted while singing the songs.

"Maybellene" was written from the inspiration that grew out of the country song "Ida
Red." I'd heard it sung long before when I was a teenager and thought it was rhythmic and

amusing to hear. I'd sung it in the yard gatherings and parties around home when I was first learning to strum the guitar in my high-school days. Later in life, at the Cosmo Club, I added my bit to the song and still I enjoyed a good response so I coined it a good one to sing.

Later when I learned, upon entering a recording contract, that original songs written by a person were copyrighted and had various rewards for the composer, I welcomed the legal arrangement of the music business. I enjoyed creating songs of my own and was pleased to learn I could have some return from the effort. When I wrote "Maybellene" I had originally titled it "Ida May," but when I took the song to Chess Records I was advised to change its title. That was simple because the rhythmic swing of the three syllables fit with many other names. The music progression itself is close to the feeling that I received when hearing the song "Ida Red," but the story in "Maybellene" is completely different.

The body of the story of "Maybellene" was composed from memories of high school and trying to get girls to ride in my 1934 V-8 Ford. I even put seat-covers in it to accommodate the girls that the football players would take riding in it while I was in class.

"Roll Over Beethoven" was written based on the feelings I had when my sister would monopolize the piano at home during our youthful school years. In fact most of the words were aimed at [my sister] Lucy instead of the Maestro Ludwig Van Beethoven. Thelma [my other sister] also took piano lessons in classical music but Lucy was the culprit that delayed rock 'n' roll music twenty years. Telling Mother in an attempt to get support for my kind of music did no good, but writing a letter and mailing it to a local DJ might have, as stated in the opening of the song.

What sounds like, "Way lay in the . . ." is really "Early in the morning, I'm giving you a warning." Out of my sometimes unbelievably imaginative mind, the rest of the self-explanatory lyrics came forth.

"Too Much Monkey Business" was meant to describe most of the kinds of hassles a person encounters in everyday life. When I got into writing on this theory, I realized I needed over a hundred verses to portray the major areas that bug people the most. I was even making up words then like "botheration" to emphasize the nuisances that bothered people. I tried to use (or make up) words that wouldn't be hard to decipher by anyone from the fifth grade on. I hadn't received any kickback about using "motorvating" in "Maybellene," so why not compete with Noah Webster again? Anyway, the first verse was directed toward a family supporter paying bills, while the filling station attendant, the seduced, the student, and the veteran all declare their problems in the lyrics.

"Brown Eyed Handsome Man" came to mind when I was touring California for the first time. After leaving St. Louis with six inches of snow lying under sub-freezing temperatures, I found green grass under clear blue skies with eighty-degree breezes loitering along the evening sunset.

What I didn't see, at least in the areas I was booked in, was too many blue eyes. The auditoriums were predominantly filled with Hispanics and "us." But then I did see unbelievable harmony among the mix, which got the idea of the song started. I saw, during the length of the tour, quite a few situations concerning the life of the Mexican people. For example, a Caucasian officer was picking up a fairly handsome male loiterer near the auditorium when some woman came up shouting for the policeman to let him go. He promptly did so, laughingly saluting the feminine rescuer. The verse in the song is situated a bit differently but was derived from that incident. The verse about Venus De Milo (believe it or not) came from thoughts out of a book I had come upon entitled *Venus in Furs* and the last verse from a fictional condition always appreciated in a baseball game.

"School Days" was born from the memories of my own experience in high school. The lyrics depict the way it was in my time. I had no idea what was going on in the classes during the time I composed it, much less what's happening today. The phrases came to me spontaneously, and rhyming took up most of the time that was spent on the song. I remember leaving it twice to go get coffee and while out having some major lines come to me that would enhance the story in the song, causing me to rush back to my room to get them down. Recording the song with breaks in the rhythm was intended to emphasize the jumps and changes I found in classes in high school compared to the one room and one teacher I had in elementary school. That's 90 percent of the song; I suppose the remainder could have been talent.

# 22. Little Richard

## Boldly Going Where No Man Had Gone Before

Compared to Chuck Berry, Little Richard (b. 1932) came from a far more rural and humble background, and his early experiences in a backwoods Pentecostal church played a stronger role in his musical style than Berry's. Little Richard's extroverted and energetic singing, piano playing, and songwriting made him one of the biggest stars of the rock 'n' roll era. His vocal style, in particular, had an impact on many subsequent musicians, including James Brown, Otis Redding, Paul McCartney, and John Fogerty (of Creedence Clearwater Revival). After making several unsuccessful recordings in the early 1950s, he recorded "Tutti Frutti" in September 1955, which rose high on both the R&B and pop charts. "Tutti Frutti" set the tone for the hits that followed between 1956 and 1958: over a fast boogie-shuffle rhythm with many stop-time breaks, Richard would sing playful double entendres near the top of his range in a searing timbre interspersed with trademark falsetto whoops. His piano playing derives from boogie-woogie style, emphasizes the upbeat, and features a great many glissandi. In performance, Richard would frequently leave the piano to dance exuberantly, occasionally on top of the piano itself.

    In addition to his uninhibited presence as a singer, pianist, and dancer, Richard's visual appearance added to the sense of his outrageousness: With his large pompadour, liberal use of makeup, and gaudy clothing, he raised the spectre of cross-dressing and ambiguous sexuality at a time when such issues were strictly taboo. In pondering the improbability of Richard's mass acceptance at the time, one possible explanation suggests itself: His outrageous performance style camouflaged (and perhaps deflected and deflated) whatever threat he posed to heterosexual norms. After several more hits and appearances in three films (*Don't Knock the*

*Rock* and *The Girl Can' t Help It,* both in 1956, and *Mister Rock 'n' Roll,* in 1957), Richard decided abruptly to quit his career for the ministry because of a vision he had during a flight back to the States from Australia.

The following excerpts come from an "oral history" of Little Richard, rather than an autobiography. Thus, in addition to Richard's voice, we hear from Bumps Blackwell, a famous A&R man for Specialty records (an independent record company specializing in African American sacred and secular music). An academically trained composer, Blackwell, along with Henry Glover and Jesse Stone, was one of the few African American A&R men at the time. His astute comments derive from the important role that he played in Little Richard's early recordings: In addition to producing, he cowrote many of Richard's best-known songs. Richard presents his own views on how his music mapped racial relations, on the interesting origins of "Lucille," and on Alan Freed.

## *from* THE LIFE AND TIMES OF LITTLE RICHARD: THE QUASAR OF ROCK
### *Charles White*

You'd hear people singing all the time. The women would be outside in the back doing the washing, rubbing away on the rub-boards, and somebody else sweeping the yard, and somebody else would start singing "We-e-e-ll . . . Nobody knows the trouble I've seen. . . ." And gradually other people would pick it up, until the whole of the street would be singing. Or "Sometimes I feel like a motherless child, a long way from home. . . ." Everybody singing. I used to go up and down the street, some streets were paved, but our street was dirt, just singing at the top of my voice. There'd be guitar players playing on the street—old Slim, Willie Amos, and my cousin, Buddy Penniman. I remember Bamalama, this feller with one eye, who'd play the wash-board with a thimble. He had a bell like the school-teacher's, and he'd sing, "A-bamalam, you shall be free, and in the mornin' you shall be free." See, there was so much poverty, so much prejudice in those days. I imagine people had to sing to feel their connection with God. To sing their trials away, sing their problems away, to make their burdens easier and the load lighter. That's the beginning. That's where it started.

    We used to have a group called the Penniman Singers—all of us, the whole family. We used to go around and sing in all the churches, and we used to sing in contests with other family groups, like the Brown Singers, in what they called the Battle of the Gospels. We used to have some good nights. I remember one time. I could always sing *loud* and I kept changing the key upward. Marquette said it ruined his voice trying to sing tenor behind me! The sisters didn't like me screaming and singing and threw their hats and purses at us, shouting "Hush, hush, boys—hush!" They called me War Hawk because of my hollerin' and screamin' and they stopped me singing in church.

From a boy, I wanted to be a preacher. I wanted to be like Brother Joe May, the singing evangelist, who they called the Thunderbolt of the West. My daddy's father, Walter Penniman, was a preacher, and so was my mother's brother, Reverend Louis Stuart, who's now pastor of a Baptist church in Philadelphia. And I have a cousin, Amos Penniman, who's a minister in the Pentecostal Church. I have always been basically a religious person—in fact most of the black people where I'm from was. I went to the New Hope Baptist Church, on Third Avenue, where my mother was a member. My daddy's people were members of Foundation Templar AME Church, a Methodist church on Madison Street, and my mother's father was with the Holiness Temple Baptist Church, downtown in Macon. So I was kind of mixed up in it right from the start. Of all the churches, I used to like going to the Pentecostal Church, because of the music

Clint Brantley set up a tour around Georgia and Tennessee—Nashville, Knoxville, Milledgeville, Sparta, Fitzgerald, and Tallahassee, places like that. We used to draw the crowds all the time. The places were always packed. I was popular around those states before Chuck and Lee Diamond joined the band. I got two sax players and named the band the Upsetters. It made me outstanding in Macon at that time, to have this fantastic band in a little town like this. The other bands couldn't compete. So when it said "Little Richard and the Upsetters" everybody wanted to come. We had a station wagon with the name written on it, and I thought it was fantastic.

We were each making fifteen dollars a night, and there was a lot you could do with fifteen dollars. We would play three, four nights a week—that's fifty dollars. And sometimes we would play at a place on the outskirts of Macon at a midnight dance. That would pay ten dollars and all the fried chicken you could eat. We were playing some of Roy Brown's tunes, a lot of Fats Domino tunes, some B. B. King tunes, and I believe a couple of Little Walter's and a few things by Billy Wright. I really looked up to Billy Wright. That's where I got the hairstyle from and everything. "Keep Your Hand on Your Heart," that was one of them. We'd play all around Georgia, Tennessee, and Kentucky, cos we had a big name around those places. We would draw packed houses every place and we'd get a guarantee and a percentage of the take over the guarantee. We were making a darned good living. One song which would really tear the house down was "Tutti Frutti." The lyrics were kind of vulgar, "Tutti Frutti good booty—if it don't fit don't force it. . . ." It would crack the crowd up. We were playing without a bass and Chuck would have to bang real hard on his bass drum in order to get a bass-fiddle effect.

BUMPS BLACKWELL: When I got to New Orleans, Cosimo Matassa, the studio owner, called and said, "Hey, man, this boy's down here waiting for you." When I walked in, there's this cat in this loud shirt, with hair waved up six inches above his head. He was talking wild, thinking up stuff just to be different, you know? I could tell he was a mega-personality. So we got to the studio, on Rampart and Dumaine. I had the Studio Band in— Lee Allen on tenor sax, Alvin "Red" Tyler on baritone sax, Earl Palmer on drums, Edgar Blanchard and Justin Adams on guitar, Huey "Piano" Smith and James Booker on piano, Frank Fields, bass, all of them the best in New Orleans. They were Fats Domino's session men.

Let me tell you about the recording methods we used in those days. Recording technicians of today, surrounded by huge banks of computer-controlled sound technology, would find the engineering techniques available in the 1950s as primitive as the *Kitty Hawk* is to the space shuttle. When I started there was no tape. It was disk to disk. There was no such thing as overdubbing. Those things we did at Cosimo's were on tape, but they were all done straight ahead. The tracks you heard were the tracks as they were recorded from beginning to end. We would take sixty or seventy takes. We were recording two tracks. Maybe we might go to surgery and intercut a track or cut a track at the end or something, but we didn't know what overdubbing was. The studio was just a back room in a furniture store, like an ordinary motel room. For the whole orchestra. There'd be a grand piano just as you came in the door. I'd have the grand's lid up with a mike in the keys and Alvin Tyler and Lee Allen would be blowing into that. Earl Palmer's drums were out of the door, where I had one mike, as well. The bassman would be way over the other side of the studio. You see, the bass would cut and bleed in, so I could get the bass.

The recording equipment was a little old quarter-inch single-channel Ampex Model 300 in the next room. I would go in there and listen with earphones. If it didn't sound right I'd just keep moving the mikes around. I would have to set up all those things. But, you see, once I had got my sound, my room sound, well then I would just start running my numbers straight down. It might take me forty-five minutes, an hour, to get that balance within the room, but once those guys hit a groove you could go on all night. When we got it, we got it. I would like to see some of these great producers today produce on monaural or binaural equipment with the same atmosphere. Cos the problem is, if you're going to get a room sound with the timbre of the instruments, you can't put them together as a band and just start playing. All of a sudden one horn's going to stick out. So I had to place the mikes very carefully and put the drummer outside the door.

Well, the first session was to run six hours, and we planned to cut eight sides. Richard ran through the songs on his audition tape. "He's My Star" was very disappointing. I did not even record it. But "Wonderin' " we got in two takes. Then we got "I'm Just a Lonely Guy," which was written by a local girl called Dorothy La Bostrie who was always pestering me to record her stuff. Then "The Most I Can Offer," and then "Baby." So far so good. But it wasn't really what I was looking for. I had heard that Richard's stage act was really wild, but in the studio that day he was very inhibited. Possibly his ego was pushing him to show his spiritual feeling or something, but it certainly wasn't coming together like I had expected and hoped.

The problem was that what he looked like, and what he sounded like didn't come together. If you look like Tarzan and sound like Mickey Mouse it just doesn't work out. So I'm thinking, Oh, Jesus . . . You know what it's like when you don't know what to do? It's "Let's take a break. Let's go to lunch." I had to think. I didn't know what to do. I couldn't go back to Rupe[1] with the material I had because there was nothing there that I could put out. Nothing that I could ask anyone to put a promotion on. Nothing to merchandise. And I was paying out serious money.

So here we go over to the Dew Drop Inn, and, of course, Richard's like any other ham. We walk into the place and, you know, the girls are there and the boys are there and he's got an audience. There's a piano, and that's his crutch. He's on stage reckoning to show Lee Allen his piano style. So WOW! He gets to going. He hits that piano, dididididididididi . . . and starts to sing "Awop-bop-a-Loo-Mop a-good Goddam—Tutti Frutti, good booty. . . ." I said, "WOW! That's what I want from you, Richard. That's a hit!" I knew that the lyrics were too lewd and suggestive to record. It would never have got played on the air. So I got hold of Dorothy La Bostrie, who had come over to see how the recording of her song was going. I brought her to the Dew Drop.

Dorothy was a little colored girl so thin she looked like six o'clock. She just had to close one eye and she looked like a needle. Dorothy had songs stacked this high and was always asking me to record them. She'd been singing these songs to me, but the trouble was they all sounded like Dinah Washington's "Blowtop Blues." They were all composed to the same

1. Art Rupe, owner of Specialty Records.

melody. But looking through her words, I could see that she was a prolific writer. She just didn't understand melody. So I said to her, "Look. You come and write some lyrics to this, cos I can't use the lyrics Richard's got." He had some terrible words in there. Well, Richard was embarrassed to sing the song and she was not certain that she wanted to hear it. Time was running out, and I *knew* it could be a hit. I talked, using every argument I could think of. I asked him if he had a grudge against making money. I told her that she was over twenty-one, had a houseful of kids and no husband and needed the money. And finally, I convinced them. Richard turned to face the wall and sang the song two or three times and Dorothy listened.

Break time was over, and we went back to the studio to finish the session, leaving Dorothy to write the words. I think the first thing we did was "Directly from My Heart to You." Now that, and "I'm Just a Lonely Guy," could have made it. Those two I could have gotten by with—just by the skin of my teeth. Fifteen minutes before the session was to end, the chick comes in and puts these little trite lyrics in front of me. I put them in front of Richard. Richard says he ain't got no voice left. I said, "Richard, you've *got* to sing it."

There had been no chance to write an arrangement, so I had to take the chance on Richard playing the piano himself. That wild piano was essential to the success of the song. It was impossible for the other piano players to learn it in the short time we had. I put a microphone between Richard and the piano and another inside the piano, and we started to record it. It took three takes, and in fifteen minutes we had it. "Tutti Frutti."

BUMPS BLACKWELL: The white radio stations wouldn't play Richard's version of "Tutti Frutti" and made Boone's cover number one. So we decided to up the tempo on the follow-up and get the lyrics going so fast that Boone wouldn't be able to get his mouth together to do it! The follow-up was "Long Tall Sally." It was written by a girl named Enortis Johnson and the story of how she came to us seems unbelievable today.

I got a call from a big disk jockey called Honey Chile. She *had* to see me. Very urgent. I went, because we relied on the jocks to push the records, and the last thing you said to them was no. I went along to this awful downtown hotel, and there was Honey Chile with this young girl, about sixteen, seventeen, with plaits, who reminded you of one of these little sisters at a Baptist meeting, all white starched collars and everything. She looked like someone who's just been scrubbed—so out of place in this joint filled with pimps and unsavory characters just waiting to scoop her up when she's left alone, you know?

So Honey Chile said to me, "Bumps, you got to do something about this girl. She's walked all the way from Appaloosa, Mississippi, to sell this song to Richard, cos her auntie's sick and she needs money to put her in the hospital." I said okay, let's hear the song, and this little clean-cut kid, all bows and things, says, "Well, I don't have a melody yet. I thought maybe you or Richard could do that." So I said okay, what *have* you got, and she pulls out this piece of paper. It looked like toilet paper with a few words written on it:

*Saw Uncle John with Long Tall Sally*
*They saw Aunt Mary comin,*
*So they ducked back in the alley*

And she said, "Aunt Mary is sick. And I'm going to tell her about Uncle John. Cos he was out there with Long Tall Sally, and I saw 'em. They saw Aunt Mary comin' and they ducked back in the alley.

I said, "They did, huh? And this is a song? You walked all the way from Appaloosa, Mississippi, with this piece of paper?" (I'd give my right arm if I could find it now. I kept it for years. It was a classic. Just a few words on a used doily!)

Honey Chile said, "Bumps, you gotta do something for this child." So I went back to the studio. I told Richard. He didn't want to do it. I said, "Richard, Honey Chile will get mad at us. . . ." I kept hearing "Duck back in the alley, duck back in the alley." We kept adding words and music to it, to put it right. Richard started to sing it—and all of a sudden there was "Have some fun tonight." That was the hook. Richard loved it cos the hottest thing then was the shuffle.

Richard was reciting that thing. He got on the piano and got the music going and it just started growing and growing. We kept trying, trying it, and I pulled the musicians in and we pulled stuff from everybody. That's where Richard's "Ooooooh" first came in. That's what he taught to Paul McCartney. Well, we kept rerecording because I wanted it faster. I drilled Richard with "Duck back in the alley" faster and faster until it burned, it was so fast. When it was finished I turned to Richard and said, "Let's see Pat Boone get his mouth together to do *this* song."* That's how it was done, and if you look at the copyright you'll see it's Johnson, Penniman, and Blackwell.

LITTLE RICHARD: We were breaking through the racial barrier. The white kids had to hide my records cos they daren't let their parents know they had them in the house. We decided that my image should be crazy and way-out so that the adults would think I was harmless. I'd appear in one show dressed as the Queen of England and in the next as the pope.

They were exciting times. The fans would go really wild. Nearly every place we went, the people got unruly. They'd want to get to me and tear my clothes off. It would be standing-room-only crowds and 90 percent of the audience would be white. I've always thought that Rock 'n' Roll brought the races together. Although I was black, the fans didn't care. I used to feel good about that. Especially being from the South, where you see the barriers, having all these people who we thought hated us, showing all this *love.*

A lot of songs I sang to crowds first to watch their reaction, that's how I knew they'd hit, but we recorded them over and over again. "Lucille" was after a female impersonator in my hometown. We used to call him Queen Sonya. I just took the rhythm of an old song of mine called "Directly from My Heart to You" slowed down and I used to do that riff and go "Sonya!" and I made it into "Lucille." My cousin used to live in a place called Barn Hop Bottom in Macon, right by the railway line, and when the trains came past they'd shake the houses—*chocka-chocka-chocka*—and that's how I got the rhythm for "Directly from My Heart" and "Lucille." I was playing it way before I met Bumps. I was playing "Lucille" and "Slippin' and Slidin'" in my room in Macon way before I started recording for Specialty. I'd make up the music while I was making the words fit.

"Good Golly Miss Molly" I first heard a D.J. using that name. His name was Jimmy Pennick, but you know it was Jackie Brenston that gave me the musical inspiration. Jackie Brenston was a sax player with Ike Turner's Kings of Rhythm when he did "Rocket 88" and "Juiced," and Ike Turner's band backed him, but they didn't take any credits because of their contracts. I always liked that record, and I used to use the riff in my act, so when we were looking for a lead-in to "Good Golly Miss Molly" I did that and it fitted."

---

*Boone did cover "Long Tall Sally." An anemic version in which he reverses the Midas touch and turns gold into dross, managing to sound as though he is not quite sure what he is singing about. It sold a million.

# 23. Elvis Presley, Sam Phillips, and Rockabilly

As the most successful artist of the mid-1950s rock 'n' roll explosion, Elvis Presley (1935–77) had a profound impact on popular music. His sense of style, musical and personal, was both the focal point of the media reaction to early rock 'n' roll and the inspiration for some of the most important rock musicians to follow. The narrative of his meteoric rise and subsequent decline amid mysterious and tawdry circumstances fueled many myths both during his life and after his death at 42.[1]

The earliest musical experiences of Presley, who was raised in poverty in the Deep South, came in the Pentecostal services of the First Assembly of God Church.[2] Other formative influences included popular tunes of the day, country music, blues, and rhythm and blues. Although he had little experience as a performer, in 1954, at age 19, he came to the attention of Sam Phillips, owner of a Memphis recording company, Sun Records. Philips teamed Presley, who sang and played guitar, with local country and western musicians, Scotty Moore (guitar) and Bill Black (bass). During their first recording session in June 1954, the trio recorded a single with "That's All Right, Mama" (originally recorded in 1946 by blues singer Arthur "Big Boy" Crudup) on one side and "Blue Moon of Kentucky" (originally recorded in 1946 by bluegrass pioneer Bill Monroe) on the other. The group's style blended elements of country and rhythm and blues without being identifiable as either; the distinctive sound included Moore's rhythmically oriented lead guitar playing, Black's slapped bass, and Presley's forceful, if crude, rhythm guitar, with the recording swathed in a distinctive electronic echo effect. Presley's voice, however, attracted the most attention: Swooping almost two octaves at times, changing timbre from a croon to a growl instantaneously, he seemed not so much to be synthesizing preexisting styles as to be juxtaposing them, sometimes within the course of a single phrase.[3] While the trio's initial record provoked enthusiastic responses immediately upon being broadcast on

---

1. The mythologizing after his death has been prolific enough to spawn at least two books that are devoted to understanding it, as well as numerous articles; see Gilbert
Rodman, *Elvis After Elvis: The Posthumous Career of a Living Legend* (New York: Routledge, 1996); and Greil Marcus, *Dead Elvis: A Chronicle of a Cultural Obsession* (New York: Doubleday, 1991).

2. C. Wolfe: "Presley and the Gospel Tradition," in *The Elvis Reader: Texts and Sources on the King of Rock 'n' Roll*, ed. K. Quain (New York: St. Martin's Press, 1992), 13–27.

3. These aspects of Presley's style are described in Richard Middleton, "All Shook Up," in *The Elvis Reader*, 3–12.

Memphis radio, it confused audiences, who wondered if the singer was white or black. And although white musicians' music had incorporated African American instrumental and vocal approaches since the earliest "hillbilly" recordings of the 1920s, no previous white singer had so successfully forged an individual style clearly rooted in a contemporaneous African American idiom.

Presley, Moore, and Black released four more singles on Sun during 1954–55; each one featured a blues or rhythm and blues song backed with a country-style number. Presley's uninhibited, sexually charged performances throughout the Southeast provoked frenzied responses and influenced other musicians: By the end of 1955, performers, such as Carl Perkins and Johnny Cash, had emerged with a style (coined "rockabilly") that resembled Presley's.

Presley's growing popularity attracted the attention of promoter "Colonel" Tom Parker, who negotiated the sale of Presley's contract to RCA records for the then unheard-of sum of $35,000. Presley's first recording for RCA, "Heartbreak Hotel" (released in March 1956), achieved the unprecedented feat of reaching the Top 5 on the pop, rhythm and blues, and country charts simultaneously. This recording and the songs that followed in 1956 all combined aspects of his spare Sun recordings with increasingly heavy instrumentation—including piano, drums, and background singers—that moved the sound closer to that of mainstream pop. Both sides of his third RCA single "Hound Dog"/"Don't Be Cruel" hit number one on all three charts. "Hound Dog" radically transformed Willie Mae "Big Mama" Thornton's 1952 R&B hit, while "Don't Be Cruel" was a more pop-oriented recording written specifically for Presley by Otis Blackwell. Presley's vocal style already showed signs of mannerism, trading the unpredictable exchanges of different voices of the early recordings for a single affect throughout each song.

Although Elvis Presley did participate in some interviews throughout his career, the questions and his answers in these interviews tended toward the perfunctory (e.g., in response to questions about rock 'n' roll, Elvis responded "It's hard to explain rock 'n' roll. It's not what you call folk music. It's a beat that gets you. You feel it.").[4] In contrast, Presley's first producer, Sam Phillips, has reflected at length on those early recording sessions and the conditions that gave rise to rockabilly. Prior to recording Presley's first five singles and Elvis's rockabilly successors at Sun, such as Carl Perkins, Jerry Lee Lewis, Johnny Cash, and Roy Orbison, Phillips recorded local blues and R&B musicians like B. B. King, Ike Turner, and Howlin' Wolf, including a session that resulted in the important proto-rock 'n' roll recording, Jackie Brenston's "Rocket 88" (with a band led by Turner) in 1951. Phillips is also a natural-born storyteller, as revealed by many of the anecdotes in this interview.

---

4. This quote comes from Mick Farren and Pearce Marchbank: *Elvis in His Own Words* (London: Omnibus Press, 1977), 27.

# SAM PHILLIPS INTERVIEW
## Elizabeth Kaye

*There are many stories about how Elvis came to Sun in 1954. I'd like to hear your version of it.*

He was working for Crown Electric. I'd seen the truck go back and forth outside, and I thought, "They sure are doing a hell of a lot of business around here." But I never saw it stop anywhere. So Elvis had . . . he had cased the joint a long time before he stopped the truck and got out. And there's no telling how many days and nights behind that wheel he was figuring out some way to come in and make a record without saying, "Mr. Phillips, would you audition me?" So his mother's birthday gave him the opportunity to come in and make a little personal record. [Elvis claimed he was making the record for his mother, but her birthday was, in fact, months away, so perhaps he had other motives.]

*The first song he recorded was "My Happiness." What do you think when you heard it?*

There wasn't anything that striking about Elvis, except his sideburns were down to here [*gestures*], which I kind of thought, well, you know, "That's pretty cool, man. Ain't nobody else got them that damn long." We talked in the studio. And I played the record back for him in the control room on the little crystal turntable and walked up front and told Marion [Philips's assistant, Marion Keisker] to write down Elvis' name and a number and how we can get ahold of him.

*You called him back to cut a ballad called "Without You." That song was never released. What went wrong?*

We got some pretty good cuts on the thing, but I wanted to check him out other ways before I made a final decision as to which route we were going to attempt to go with him.

And I decided I wanted to look at things with a little tempo, because you can really hang yourself out on ballads or when you go up against Perry Como or Eddie Fisher or even Patti Page, all of those people. I wasn't looking for anything that greatly polished.

*After that, you put Elvis with a band, Scotty Moore on guitar and Bill Black on bass. Why did you choose them?*

The two of them, they'd been around the studio, Lord, I don't know how many damned times, you know? Scotty had been playing with different bands, and although he hadn't ever done a session for me, I knew he had the patience and he wasn't afraid to try anything, and that's so important when you're doing laboratory experiments.

Scotty was also the type of person who could take instruction real good. And I kidded him a lot. I said, "If you don't quit trying to copy Chet Atkins, I'll throw you out of this damn place." And Bill, he was just Bill Black, and the best slap bass player in the city.

*What were you trying to achieve with Elvis?*

Now you've got to keep in mind Elvis Presley probably innately was the most introverted person that came into that studio. Because he didn't play with bands. He didn't go to this little club and pick and grin. All he did was set with his guitar on the side of his bed at home. I don't think he even played on the front porch.

So I had to try to establish a direction for him. And I had to look into the market, and if the market was full of one type of thing, why try to go in there? There's only so many pieces in a pie. That's how I figured it. I knew from the beginning that I was going to have to do something different and that it might be harder to get it going. But if I got it going, I might have something.

*Source:* Elizabeth Kaye, "Sam Phillips Interview," from *Rolling Stone*, February 13, 1986, pp. 54–58, 86–88.

*How did you come to cut "That's All Right"?*

That night we had gone through a number of things, and I was getting ready to fold it up. But I didn't want to discourage the damn people, you understand? I knew how enthusiastic Elvis was to try to do something naturally. I knew also that Scotty Moore was staying there till he dropped dead, you know? I don't remember exactly what I said, but it was light hearted. I think I told him, "There ain't a damn song you can do that sounds worth a damn," or something like that. He knew it was tongue in cheek. But it was getting to be a critical time, because we had been in the studio a lot. Well, I went back into the booth. I left the mikes open, and I think Elvis felt like, really, "What the hell have I got to lose? I'm really gonna blow his head off, man." And they cut down on "That's All Right," and hell, man, they was just as instinctive as they could be.

*It's said that you heard him singing it, and you said, "What are you doing?" and he said, "I don't know," and you said, "Do it again." Is that true?*

I don't remember exactly verbatim. But it was something along the lines that I've been quoted.

*Scotty Moore says that when he heard the playback he thought he'd be run out of town. How did you feel when you heard it?*

First of all, Scotty wasn't shocked at any damned thing I attempted to do. Scotty isn't shockable. And for me, that damned thing came through so loud and clear it was just like a big flash of lightning and the thunder that follows. I knew it was what I was looking for for Elvis. When anybody tells you they know they've got a hit, they don't know what the hell they're talking about. But I knew I had it on "That's All Right." I just knew I had found a groove. In my opinion. And that's all I had to go on, honey. I mean I let people hear it. But I didn't ask them their damn opinions.

*Then what happened?*

I let Scotty, Bill and Elvis know I was pretty damn pleased. Then I made an acetate dub of it and took it up to [Memphis disc jockey] Dewey Phillips and played him the tape. And Daddy-O Dewey wanted to hear it again. "Goddamn, man," he says, "I got to have it." Red, hot and blue. You'd have to know Dewey.

And two nights later he played that thing, and the phones started ringing. Honey, I'll tell you, all hell broke loose. People were calling that station, and it really actually surprised me, because I knew nobody knew Elvis. Elvis just didn't have friends, didn't have a bunch of guys he ran with or anything, you know? Anyway, it was just fantastic. To my knowledge, there weren't any adverse calls.

*Why did you decide to back "That's All Right" with "Blue Moon of Kentucky"?*

This was before anybody thought of young people being interested in bluegrass. But we did this thing, and it just had an intrigue. And that's the one where I thought maybe there was a good possibility of getting run out of town, 'cause hey, man, you didn't mess with bluegrass. Bluegrass is kind of sacred, you know.

*Once the record was released, there was an incredible furor. How did it affect you?*

Rock & roll probably put more money in the collection boxes of the churches across America than anything the preacher could have said. I certainly know that to be a fact. Not only them. Disc jockeys broke the hell out of my records. Broke 'em on the air. Slam them over the damn microphone. Now if I *hadn't* affected people like that, I might have been in trouble.

*Do you remember the session for "Good Rockin' Tonight"?*

Oh, God, we all loved that song, man. I took Bill, and I said, "I don't want none of this damned slapping. I want you to pull them damned strings, boy."

*Your contract with Elvis had him completely locked up, so the only way Colonel Parker could have become involved was as a concert booker. Why did you decide to sell his contract just a year and a half after he started with you?*

I had looked at everything for how I could take a little extra money and get myself out of a real bind. I mean, I wasn't broke, but man, it was hand-to-mouth. I made an offer to Tom Parker, but the whole thing was that I made an offer I didn't think they'd even consider—$35,000, plus I owed Elvis $4000 or $5000.

*So you thought the offer was so high no one would take it?*

I didn't necessarily want them *not* to take it.

*Did you realize how much Elvis was worth?*

Hell, no. I didn't have any idea the man was going to be the biggest thing that ever happened to the industry.

*Were you ever sorry you let him go?*

No. That was the best judgment call I could make at the time, and I still think it is. And Sun went on and did many, many things. I hoped the one thing that wouldn't happen to me was that I would be a one-artist or a one-hit label.

*Did you give Elvis any advice when he left Sun?*

The one real ammunition I gave him was "Don't let them tell you what to do. Don't lose your individuality."

*Then how did you feel when he started making the type of movies he made?*

They were just things that you could make for nothing and make millions off of, and Elvis didn't have anything to do with it. That was Colonel Tom Parker and the moguls at the different studios. I think it was almost sinister, I really do.

*Did you ever think of becoming a manager?*

I'm insane. But I'm not that insane.

*Once Elvis was gone, were you banking Sun's future on Carl Perkins?*

Absolutely. And there was another one of those instincts. I was giving up some kind of a cat, man, but, sure enough, I sold him, and that's what financed "Blue Suede Shoes."

*Steve Sholes of RCA called you at the time "Blue Suede Shoes" was climbing the charts. RCA couldn't get anything going with Elvis, and Sholes asked you, "Did we buy the wrong guy?" What did you tell him?*

I told him, "You haven't bought the wrong person." And I gave him the reasons. Number one, Elvis certainly had the talent. And unlike Carl, he was single and had no children and was a helluva-looking man. He said, "Well, would you be mad at us if we put out 'Blue Suede Shoes'?" Man, that staggered me. I said, "Steve, you all are big enough to kill me, you know." But they didn't put it out as a single. They released it as an EP.

*Did it outsell Perkins' version?*

Hell, no. Well, I guess over the years when it was put in nineteen packages. But the only reason Carl is not recognized for "Blue Suede Shoes" is that Elvis became so mammothly big.

*When did you realize how big Elvis would be?*

Not when I heard "Heartbreak Hotel." That was the worst record. I knew it when I heard "Don't Be Cruel." I was driving back from the first vacation I'd had in my life, and it came on the radio, and I said, "Wait a minute. Jesus, he's off and gone, man." I'd like to run off the road.

*Were you jealous?*

Hell, no, 'cause when I heard "Heartbreak Hotel," I said, "Damned sons of bitches are going to mess this man up." Then, boy, I heard "Don't Be Cruel," and I was the happiest man in the world.

*What was the difference in what you were trying to achieve first with Elvis, then with Perkins?*

With Elvis I kind of wanted to lean more toward the blues. I wanted to get Carl more into modifying country music.

*What was your favorite Perkins song?*

This is the craziest thing, but one of the cutest songs I ever heard was his "Movie Magg." And "Boppin' the Blues."

*Do you remember when you first heard Jerry Lee?*

It was the day after I first heard "Don't Be Cruel." Jerry had come to Memphis with his cousin, staying at his house. He was a pretty determined person, and he made up his mind he was going to see Sam Phillips. Jack Clement [Sun's producer] was at the studio, and Jerry didn't even want to audition for him. But they cut this little audition tape. And when I went to the studio, Jack says, "Man, I got a cat I want you to hear." Well, I had been looking for somebody that could do tricks on the piano as a lead instrument. Lo and behold, man, I hear this guy and his total spontaneity.

*Then, when you met Jerry Lee and he played for you, you're supposed to have told him, "You are a rich man."*

I probably did. Not in the connotation of money, but of talent.

*You've said that Jerry Lee was the most talented person you ever worked with but that you don't think he could have been bigger than Elvis. Why is that?*

That gets into the thing of the total effect of the person. There is no question that the most talented person I ever worked with is Jerry Lee Lewis. Black or white. But Elvis had a certain type of total charisma that was just almost untouchable by any other human that I know of or have ever seen.

But this is a tough comparison for me to make. It looks like I'm drawing lines between two of the most talented people in the world, and I don't like to do that. But I would say that if they were both at their peak, and Elvis was booked for a show but Jerry Lee showed up, no one would be disappointed. Is there a better answer you can think of than that?

*What do you remember about recording "Great Balls of Fire"?*

That was the toughest record I ever recorded in my life. Otis Blackwell had done the demo.[5] When I heard it, I said, "What in the hell are they doing sending me a record like this? It ought to be out." He'd written the damn thing on a napkin in a bar he owed a lot of money to. And we worked our ass off because those breaks . . . with Jerry having to do his piano, it had to be exactly synced with his voice.

*You didn't do any overdubbing on it?*

Hell, no. We didn't have nothing to overdub with.

*When Elvis died, you said that he died of a broken heart. Can you amplify that?*

When you really don't have something to look forward to with a good, sweet, beautiful attitude, you're in trouble. I don't care who you are. You're also in trouble if you're in

---

5. Blackwell also wrote many songs for Presley, including "Don't Be Cruel," "All Shook Up," and "Jailhouse Rock."

bondage in any way. I'm talking about emotional entrapment. That's deep stuff. And it's serious stuff. And no matter what happens to you in this world, if you don't make it your business to be happy, then you may have gained the whole world and lost your spirit and maybe even your damned soul.

*But wasn't Elvis entrapped by circumstance?*
Absolutely.

*What could he have done differently?*
Been hardheaded like me and said, "I will break your damned neck, I don't care—you can't scare me. Monetary factors can't scare me. Starvation can't scare me. Threats can't scare me." I mean you have to have that attitude.

Elvis also knew that success wasn't enough. It's like Mac Davis said, man, and I think this is one of the greatest quotes, Bible included: "Stop and smell the roses." Now that's where we can all find ourselves if we don't stop and smell the roses.

And the sad thing about it is dying before you actually physically die. I mean, you know, bless his heart.

# 24. Rock 'n' Roll Meets the Popular Press

Beginning in 1956—after the first wave of national hits by Fats Domino, Chuck Berry, Little Richard, and Elvis Presley—articles on rock 'n' roll began appearing in mainstream newspapers, such as the *New York Times,* and in magazines like *Time, Newsweek,* and *Life.* These articles recall and amplify some of the topics presented in the series of *Variety* articles included earlier: The tone, by and large, is condescending, making frequent references to the connections among rock 'n' roll and sex, violence, and juvenile delinquency. In particular, descriptions abound of audiences and performers trespassing societal norms, and this aberrant behavior (one article describes "snake-dancing around town and smashing windows")[1] is typically linked to the influence of the beat or rhythm of the music. The four excerpts that follow are representative of the invective directed toward early rock 'n' roll, although they constitute but a small portion of it.

---

1. This phrase comes from "Yeh-Heh-Heh-Hes, Baby," *Time,* June 18, 1956, 54. Part of this article is reprinted here, but not this particular passage.

# Rock-and-Roll Called Communicable Disease
## *New York Times*

Conn. March 27 (UP)—A noted psychiatrist described "rock-and-roll" music today as a "communicable disease" and another sign of adolescent rebellion."

Dr. Francis J. Braceland, psychiatrist in chief of the Institute of Living, called rock-and-roll a "cannibalistic and tribalistic" form of music. He was commenting on the disturbances that led to eleven arrests during the week-end at a local theatre.

It is insecurity and "rebellion," Dr. Braceland said, that impels teenagers to affect "ducktail" haircuts, wear zoot-suits and carry on boisterously at rock-and-roll affairs.

# Yeh-Heh-Heh-Hes, Baby
## *Time*

When [the names of the stars] appear on theater and dance-hall marquees announcing a stage show or "record hop," the stampede is on. The theater is jammed with adolescents from the 9 a.m. curtain to closing and it rings and shrieks like the jungle bird house at the zoo. If one of the current heroes is announced—groups such as Bill Haley and His Comets or The Platters or a soloist such as Elvis Presley—the shrieks become deafening.[2] The tumult completely drowns the sound of the spastically gyrating performers despite fully powered amplification. Only the obsessive beat pounds through, stimulating the crowd to such rhythmical movements as clapping in tempo and jumping and dancing in the aisles. Sometimes the place vibrates with the beat of music and stamping feet, and not infrequently kids have been moved to charging the stage, rushing ushers and theater guards.

## Suggestive as Swing

There is no denying that rock 'n' roll evokes a physical response from even its most reluctant listeners, for that giant pulse matches the rhythmical operations of the human body, and the performers are all too willing to specify it. Said an Oakland, Calif. policeman, after watching Elvis Presley last week: "If he did that in the street we'd arrest him." On the other hand, the fans' dances are far from intimate—the wiggling 12- and 13-year-olds (and up) barely touch hands and appear oblivious of one another. Psychologists feel that rock 'n' roll's deepest appeal is to the teeners' need to belong; the results bear passing resemblance to Hitler mass meetings.

---

2. Elvis Presley, in fact, became a focus of the media's reaction to rock 'n' roll's "lewdness" and "degeneracy." For examples of early responses to Elvis's TV performances, see "Teeners' Hero," *Time*, May 14, 1956, 53–54; and Jack Gould, "TV: New Phenomenon—Elvis Presley Rises to Fame as Vocalist Who Is Virtuoso of Hootchy-Kootchy," *New York Times*, June 6, 1956, p. 67.

*Source:* "Rock-and-Roll Called Communicable Disease," *New York Times*, March 28, 1956, p. 33.
*Source:* "Yeh-Heh-Heh-Hes, Baby," *Time*, June 18, 1956, p. 54.

# Rock 'n' Roll's Pulse Taken

## *New York Times*

Oct. 26—(UP)—Herbert von Karajan, conductor of the touring Berlin Philharmonic Orchestra has offered an explanation for Rock 'n' Roll. "Strange things happen in the blood stream when a musical resonance coincides with the beat of the human pulse."

# Why They Rock 'n' Roll—and Should They?

## Gertrude Samuels

In show business circles there has been bitter controversy about the worth and effects of rock 'n' roll.

Frank Sinatra, a veteran showman, was quoted in a Paris magazine recently as follows: "Rock 'n' roll smells phony and false. It is sung, played and written for the most part by cretinous goons and by means of its almost imbecilic reiteration and sly, lewd, in plain fact, dirty lyrics, it manages to be the martial music of every sideburned delinquent on the face of the earth."

# 25. The *Chicago Defender* Defends Rock 'n' Roll

The landmark U.S. Supreme Court decision of 1954, *Brown v. Board of Education*, which in effect mandated integration of public schools, sent shockwaves through U.S. society. The struggles around civil rights for African Americans that intensified after this decision received considerable media attention from the mid-1950s through the 1960s. The following article attests to the interconnection between early rock 'n' roll and the increasing public pressure to end racial segregation, an interconnection that was especially important to those who were most concerned with resisting integration. While Asa Carter (head of the North Alabama White Citizens Council) makes claims that may seem extreme in the context of previous media reactions (e.g., rock 'n' roll pulls "the white man

*Source:* "Rock 'n' Roll's Pulse Taken," *New York Times,* October 27, 1956, p. 58.

*Source:* Gertrude Samuels, "Why They Rock 'n' Roll—And Should They?," *New York Times Sunday Magazine,* January 12, 1958, pp. 19–20.

down to the level of the Negro"), these statements bring out what was implicit in the earlier "Warning to the Music Business" published in *Variety*. In lighthearted fashion, Rob Roy (the author of this article) makes overt the linkages between the threats of both rock 'n' roll and integration to U.S. social conventions of the era. The publication of this article in the African American newspaper, the *Chicago Defender*, indicates some of the issues related to rock 'n' roll that concerned the black community at the time.

Roy's experiences in Alabama were hardly unique, nor were they the most extreme instance of harassment: Three days after this article was published, an attack on Nat "King" Cole during a concert in Birmingham by the White Citizens Council illustrates to what lengths such groups could go. This attack led to the cancellation of the remainder of Cole's southern tour. Cole was certainly not a rock 'n' roller by any stretch of the imagination, representing the persistence of older-style pop music into the late 1950s (and into the 1960s), but he was also assuredly African American, obviously a factor that was more important to the White Citizens Council than the type of music he was playing.[1]

## Bias Against "Rock 'n' Roll" Latest Bombshell in Dixie

### *Rob Roy*

In a small town in Alabama not so many moons ago, and after several "moonshines" (at a rear bar) this corner [i.e., the author] attempted to play a number on [a] juke box that was situated near a front bar. The bartender yelled, "No, no, no" so no music was played. That will not happen again.

One of the reasons is factual—this corner will hardly be in a position to reach a juke box in that little town again. Then there is the other reason: Should council leader Asa Carter of Birmingham have his way there will be no Rock 'N' Roll numbers on the juke box and of course no reason for this corner to wish to spend his dime. Even in Birmingham a dime is a dime.

Councilman Asa Carter says "Rock 'N' Roll" music is nothing but a plot by [the] NAACP to lower American youth's morals. He indicates he'll ask blacklisting of juke box operators who carry "Rock 'N' Roll" records on their vendors. Only thing wrong here is Mr. Carter, if successful, wouldn't be hurting the NAACP or the customers who wish to play the music but the juke box operators and the tavern owners.

Fancy if you can, a group of youngsters, patronizing a dancehall tavern and having to waltz each number that isn't a fox trot. "What, no jitterbugging,"? they'd say on the way out of the place. In that case who would be hurt? Of course Mr. Carter would hardly be hurt. One must feel that he does not operate a tavern. Nor is it likely that his accomplishments

---

1. For a report on this incident, see "Alabamans Attack 'King' Cole on Stage," *New York Times*, April 11, 1956, 1, 27.

*Source:* Rob Roy, "Bias Against 'Rock 'n' Roll' Latest Bombshell in Dixie," *Chicago Defender*, April 7, 1956, p. 14.

include the jitterbug or rugcutting dance. To do either one must be alert of limb, fast, think what is the next move just naturally, and a few more sensible things. If Asa's feet match his expressed mind and actions they are too sluggish and out of line for even a dancer. Just an old story? "Free schools yet dumb people."

Carter, executive secretary of the powerful pro-segregation group, declared that citizen's councils through the state were circulating petitions demanding that "rock and roll" music be banned from jukeboxes.

He said in an interview that what he called "this generate music" was being encouraged by the NAACP and other pro-integration groups, adding:

"The NAACP uses this type of music as a means of pulling the white man down to the level of the Negro."

He declared that "rock and roll" as well as other forms of jazz, was undermining the morals of American youth with its "degenerate, anamalistic [sic] beats and rhythms." He added:

"This savage and primitive type of music which comes straight from Africa brings out the base things in man."

"Rock and Roll" music, he said, got its start in Negro night clubs and Negro radio broadcasts and its influence was spread by the NAACP.

"Instead of opposing it in an attempt to raise the morals of the Negro," he said, "the NAACP encouraged it slowly for the purpose of undermining the morals of white people."

He estimated that 300,000 signatures would be collected by the petitions and added:

"If jukebox operators hope to stay in business they better get rid of these smutty records with their dirty lyrics."

# 26. The Music Industry Fight Against Rock 'n' Roll

## Dick Clark's Teen-Pop Empire and the Payola Scandal

The 1950s ended on a bum note for rock 'n' roll: Chuck Berry was on the verge of being convicted for having transported a minor across state lines; Elvis was in the army; Little Richard had left popular music for the ministry; Jerry Lee Lewis had effectively been blacklisted for having married his 13-year-old cousin; and Buddy Holly, Richie Valens, and the Big Bopper (all of whom had scored major hits during 1957–58) had died in a plane crash. As early as 1956, defenders of pop music's old guard, represented by ASCAP officials and songwriters-performers associated with ASCAP, mounted an attack on rock 'n' roll by linking it to the rise of BMI and by accusing BMI of manipulating public taste owing to its undue influence in the broadcast media. Several rounds of public hearings resulted.[1] The repeatedly asserted link between BMI and radio stations was specious: All broadcasters at that time had licenses from both BMI and ASCAP that required them to pay a fee for using music affiliated with those organizations, and even radio stations that owned stock in BMI did not receive dividends. No, the battle's focus truly lay in a conjunction of aesthetics and politics.[2] The old guard were defending their business interests, as well as their taste in music. The analyses of BMI's power, while inaccurate, could have been applied quite fairly to the position of ASCAP before BMI-affiliated music began making inroads in the pop music mainstream during the late 1940s.[3]

The payola hearings (which grew out of congressional hearings into crooked practices on television quiz shows) represented yet another official intervention into the business and media practices associated with early rock 'n' roll. In media accounts of payola, one is struck by how politicians were so quick to believe that the popularity of rock 'n' roll was due to either a conspiracy with BMI or payola; in other words, they thought that the music was so horrible that there had to be some form of external coercion involved for people to want to listen to it.

A new form of rock 'n' roll emerged that was designed to please both politicians and teenagers. The main variety of this new rock 'n' roll, "teen pop," was promoted by a nationally syndicated television show, *American Bandstand*, hosted by Dick Clark, a figure at once youthful and nonthreatening. Teen pop adopted older techniques of pop music production to late-1950s' popular music, incorporating aspects of rock 'n' roll while reinstating the separate roles of songwriter, instrumentalist, and singer that had been collapsed by artists like Chuck Berry and Little Richard. *American Bandstand* largely featured the stars of teen pop, known as "teen idols": good-looking young people from the Philadelphia area (where *American Bandstand* originated) singing music that was produced with a vague resemblance to rock 'n' roll.

Equally striking as the official, public response to rock 'n' roll was the disparate fates of Alan Freed and Dick Clark: The Jewish Freed rose to success by playing black popular music to white kids and by promoting concerts at which both performers and audiences were integrated. The

---

1. For a summary and analysis of these hearings, see Trent Hill, "The Enemy Within: Censorship in Rock Music in the 1950s," *South Atlantic Quarterly* 90, No. 4 (Fall 1991), 675–708. The hearings lasted from 1956 into 1958. For accounts in the press, see "Rock 'n' Roll Laid to B. M. I. Control: Billy Rose Tells House Unit That 'Electronic Curtain' Furthers 'Monstrosities," *New York Times*, September 19, 1956, 75; Val Adams, "Networks Held Biased on Music: Senate Unit Hears Charges That They Promote Products of Their Own Affiliates," *New York Times*, March 12, 1958, 63; Val Adams, "Hanson Decries Hillbilly Music: Tells Senate Unit Hearing Tunes Heard on Air Are 'Madison Ave.' Version," *New York Times*, March 14, 1958, 51.

2. See Reebee Garofalo, *Rockin' Out: Popular Music in the USA* (Boston: Allyn and Bacon, 1997), p. 172; and Russell Sanjek, "The War on Rock," *Downbeat Music '72 Yearbook* (Chicago: Maher, 1972).

3. See Richard A. Peterson and David G. Berger, "Cycles in Symbol Production: The Case of Popular Music," in *On Record: Rock, Pop, and the Written Word* (New York: Pantheon Books, 1990), 140–59.

clean-cut, All-American Clark's signature show, *American Bandstand*, featured a virtually all-white audience and was cautious about integration on the air.[4] Freed's career was effectively ended by the scandal; Clark's career, as of this writing, was still going strong, and he hosted *American Bandstand* until 1989.[5]

---

The following article from *Life* describes the payola hearings of late 1959–early 1960 and focuses on the host of *American Bandstand*, Dick Clark. This article reproduces many of the criticisms and stereotypes found in early media reports on rock 'n' roll, even suggesting in the opening paragraph that a teenager murdered his mother because she refused to let him watch *American Bandstand*. More evenhanded than some other mainstream reports of the time, the article gives space to the views of fans of the show in order to explain why they like it. And while the familiar condescending tone is present, most of the comments critical to rock 'n' roll are ascribed to the members of the Senate committee. Along the way, a history and explanation of payola is presented and contrasted with the specifics of Clark's business operation so as to anticipate his ultimate exoneration.

## Music Biz Goes Round and Round: It Comes Out Clarkola
### *Peter Bunzel*

Back in September 1958 a roly-poly Tulsa boy named Billy Jay Killion came home from high school and wanted to watch Dick Clark's television program, *American Bandstand*. His mother, who didn't particularly care for rock 'n' roll music, was all set to watch a different program, so she told Billy "No." He seethed the whole night long. Then in the morning Billy took out a rifle and shot his mother dead.

Millions of American teen-agers feel just as strongly about Dick Clark, though no others have vented their feelings so violently. Last week their loyalty was put to the supreme test, for Clark was up before Congress to answer for mayhem of another kind. For six months the Harris Committee had been investigating payola in music and broadcasting, and had developed a greedy image of the whole industry. A long succession of disk jockeys admitted taking payments from music companies. But the one man the committee had always been gunning for was Dick Clark, the biggest disk jockey of all and a symbol, in giant screen, of the whole questionable business.

"I have never," Clark told the committee, "agreed to play a record in return for payment in cash or any other consideration." This statement seemed more and more astonishing to the committee as Clark went on to admit that in the last three years he had parlayed

---

4. That this was recognized by African American viewers is substantiated by the article from the African American newspaper, the *New York Age*, reprinted in this chapter.

5. For a thorough history of *American Bandstand*, see John A. Jackson, *American Bandstand: Dick Clark and the Making of a Rock 'n' Roll Empire* (New York: Oxford University Press, 1997).

*Source:* Peter Bunzel, "Music Biz Goes Round and Round: It Comes Out Clarkola," *Life*, May 16, 1960, pp. 118–122. © 1960 TIME, Inc., reprinted by permission.

his position into a whopping personal fortune of $576,590. "Plugola," "royola" and "Clarkola," the committeemen variously called it.

But their skepticism did not alter Clark's mien as he sat on the stand giving off the same air of proper respectability he does on TV. He wore a blue suit, button-down shirt and black loafers. Every strand of his hair was neatly lacquered into place. His voice had the bland, dulcet tone of the TV announcer that he is.

## A Most Important Commercial

His tone was appropriate, for 30-year-old Richard Wagstaff Clark was delivering the most important commercial of his life. He is out to sell his highly select adult audience the same moralistic image of himself that he has convincingly sold to the nation's teen-agers. It was an image he had peddled not only on the air but in a book of adolescent etiquette called *Your Happiest Years*. In this work he made a strong pitch for neatness and good manners, pausing briefly for little homilies: "Don't make the mistake of thinking those TV cameras are branches of the United States mint. Contrary to popular opinion, dollar bills don't come out of them like bread from a bakery oven."

Clark himself made the mistake he warned his public against, but it turned out fine for him. After all, he was in a unique spot to profit by his error. Most disk jockeys perform on radio. Clark is on TV. Most others are only on local stations. He is on a national network and he reaches some 16 million people with his stock in trade, rock 'n' roll. This form of music is alien to most adults, for whom it has all the soothing charm of a chorus of pneumatic drills. "But we love it," said a teen-age girl from Charleston, W. Va., who attended the Clark hearings. "When I hear a Beethoven symphony, I don't feel anything. When I hear our kind of music, I feel something way down deep, like oatmeal."

## Payola as a Compliment

The same adults who disparage rock 'n' roll unwittingly helped get it going. When long-playing records came in, grown-ups stopped buying single records. Manufacturers of singles had to aim their products at teen-age taste and rock 'n' roll became the staple. The singles are easy and cheap to make and 600 record companies are expelling a constant flow. But the big problem is selling them.

First the records get a test run in such "break-out" cities as Cleveland, Boston or Detroit to see which can be sold—or which the public can be conned into buying. A sure way to boost the songs has been to put money on the line to disk jockeys. Many deejays were proud to be bribed, for, in their curious little fraternity, payments became a status symbol. "Payola comes to the top disk jockeys, not the others," said one. "If you are in show business, don't you want to be at the top? Isn't this the greatest compliment?"

A large number of fraternity brothers felt the same way, for the Federal Trade Commission estimates that 250 disk jockeys accepted the compliment. Generally the recipients deny that there is any connection between paying and playing. But remarked Congressman John Moss of the committee, "Some kind of telepathic communication seems to take place. By intellectual osmosis between the disk jockey and the record manufacturer, money is passed and records get played."

Actually the committee should not be so surprised at payola. It is old stuff in the music business. In Victorian England, before he teamed up with William Gilbert, a young composer named Arthur Sullivan dashed off a song called *Thou'rt Passing Hence*. He got it performed in public by giving a share of the royalties to Sir Charles Santley, a leading baritone of the time. Sir Charles was still collecting his payoff when the tune was played at Sullivan's funeral.

In the U.S., in the 1890s, the music publishers paid to have their songs played in beer gardens. Later, top stars like Al Jolson and Eddie Cantor were offered enormously tempting payola deals—and in the '30s maestros of big-name bands got a cut of the royalties for playing new tunes on network radio.

Until the payola scandals broke, disk jockeys had no pangs of conscience about benefiting from a practice with such a tradition. Payola was simply the way they did business and they imagined that everyone else did it that way too. "This seems to be the American way of life," said Boston's Stan Richards, "which is a wonderful way of life. It is primarily built on romance: 'I'll do for you. What will you do for me?'"

What Dick Clark did for music people was to give them a pre-sold market and what they gave him in return was a windfall. He did not rely on conventional cash payola but worked out a far more complex and profitable system. It hinged on his numerous corporate holdings which included financial interests in three record companies, six music publishing houses, a record pressing plant, a record distributing firm and a company which manages singers. The music, the records and the singers involved with these companies gained a special place in Clark's programs, which the committee said gave them systematic preference.

A statistical breakdown showed how his system worked. In a period of 27 months Clark gave far less air time to a top star like Elvis Presley than to a newcomer named Duane Eddy, one of the several singers whom he has helped make into a star. Clark had no stake in Presley. But firms in which he held stock both managed and recorded Eddy. During the same 27 months Clark played only one record by Bing Crosby (the almost mandatory *White Christmas*) and none at all by Frank Sinatra. "You sought to exploit your position as a network personality," said Moss. "By almost any reasonable test records you had an interest in were played more than the ones you didn't." Replied Clark, "I did not consciously favor such records. Maybe I did so without realizing it."

## "You Laid It On"

Nor did Clark neglect revenues from copyright ownership. He owned 160 songs, and of these 143 came to him as outright gifts, much as Gilbert's *Thou'rt Passing Hence* came to Santley. "Once you acquired an interest," said Moss, "then you really laid it on."

A shining example was a record called *16 Candles*. Before getting the copyright, Clark spun it only four times in 10 weeks, and it got nowhere. Once he owned it, Clark played it 27 times in less than three months and it went up like a rocket. Each time the record was purchased Clark shared in the profits to the merry tune of $12,000. This pattern was duplicated with a song called *Butterfly*—and for his trouble the publisher gave him $7,000.

Many of his deals afforded Clark a special tax break. In May 1957 he invested $125 in the Jamie Record Company, which was then $450 in the red. Once he was a stockholder, Clark found Jamie records very attractive. By plugging them on his show he helped make many of them hits. When he sold out last December for $15,000, Clark had a cool profit of $11,900, and he could declare it all as capital gains. Clark granted the accuracy of these figures but explained, "I followed the ground rules that existed." He was familiar with the rules from another angle. Although he denied *he* had taken payola he admitted, paradoxically, that one of his record companies had passed out payola to get its wares plugged.

Coming back again and again to rock 'n' roll, the committee members strongly implied that Clark had deliberately foisted it on teen-agers. "I don't know of any time in our history when we had comparably bad, uniformly bad music," said Moss. Clark replied, "Popular music has always become popular because of young people. You can't force the public to like anything they don't want. If they don't want it, it won't become a hit."

Clark's soft sell made him an effective, if slippery, witness. At the end Chairman Oren Harris remarked, "You're not the inventor of the system or even its architect. You're a product of it." Then showing as much perspicacity as any 15-year-old, the congressman added, "Obviously you're a fine young man."

This encomium was sweet music to teen-agers who came to the hearing to see their hero in his hour of travail. Seated in the front row were two sisters from West Orange, N.J., whose parents had brought them to Washington to view the sights. To them the loveliest sight of all was Dick Clark.

"I don't care if he took payola," said Karen Katz, 13. "He gets to us as kids. The reason *16 Candles* took off is because we liked it. They say he didn't play enough Bing Crosby. Look, his show isn't for grandmothers. And Frank Sinatra, who needs him?"

The final verdict on Clark rests in part with teen-agers like Karen, but even more with his many sponsors. If they decide that his value as a pitchman has been hurt, then they will drop him like a cracked record. Already the danger signals are up. "We aren't happy about this thing," said the account executive for Hollywood Candy Bars, "and neither are any of the other ad agencies. We want to keep our noses clean."

The American Broadcasting Company is playing it cautious, waiting to see which way the wind will blow. Its stake in Clark is huge, for the network carries both of his shows, and each year they bring $6 million in advertising revenue. At least one disk jockey, a Miami man, says that ABC has already lined him up as Clark's replacement, just in case—and he is waiting for word to catch the next plane north.

But the sponsors had better think twice before dropping Clark. The teen-agers feel an almost fanatical bond with him. An investigator for the committee named James Kelly ran into this fanaticism right in his own family. Kelly's wife has a 15-year-old sister and they used to be great pals. But ever since Kelly started prying into Dick Clark's affairs, the girl has cut him absolutely dead.

> The concluding article for this chapter, published in the *New York Age*, an African American newspaper, explores an aspect of *American Bandstand*'s "all-American" appeal ignored by the previous article.

## MR. CLARK AND COLORED PAYOLA
### *New York Age*

With all of the publicity focusing on disc jockey payola, we are concerned about another matter which has never seemed to bother many people. This is the question of Negro participation on the various TV bandstand programs.

If there's one shining star in the constellation of Alan Freed's career, it has been his determined, quiet, but effective war on racial bigotry in the music business. Largely as a result of his efforts, several Negro singing groups are top successes today because of his encouragement and fairness.

At the same time, his "Big Party" has always had Negro kids right in there putting down a tough "slop" with the best of them.

Have you even seen Negro kids on Dick Clark's program? Perhaps, a few times, but the unspoken rule operates—Negro kids simply have been quietly barred from the "American Bandstand."

Somebody should raise the question as to whether there was ever any payola to keep Negro kids off of Dick Clark's American Bandstand TV program.

---

*Source:* "Mr. Clark and Colored Payola," *New York Age*, December 5, 1959, p. 6.

## 27. Brill Building, the Girl Groups, and Phil Spector

The payola hearings, one of the most publicized aspects of popular music as the 1950s ended and the 1960s began, highlighted some of the dominant trends in the mainstream: The early wave of rock 'n' roll, represented by Alan Freed and promoted by independent recording companies, lay dormant while teen idols coexisted with continuations of previous popular styles embodied in soundtrack themes and new versions of standards.[1] Until recently, histories of popular music describing this period tended to trace an arc of declining quality, as authentic, virile rock 'n' roll was supplanted by mass-produced schlock.

A closer inspection of popular music circa 1960, however, leads one to resist such tidy characterizations. It is true that music industry centers, such as the Brill Building in New York City, did revive some of the production practices of Tin Pan Alley, but not all their efforts can be dismissed as "schlock-rock." A breed of young songwriters combined the youthful energy of rock 'n' roll with the sophisticated harmonic and melodic techniques of earlier popular music to create new forms of soulful, dance-oriented popular music. These songwriters—who included among their ranks newcomers, such as the teams of Carole King and Gerry Goffin, Barry Mann and Cynthia Weil, Ellie Greenwich and Jeff Barry, and Burt Bacharach and Hal David, along with seasoned pros like Jerry Leiber and Mike Stoller—created new syntheses working with young singers, many of whom were African American and female. Thus, the period 1961–63 witnessed the emergence and success of numerous "girl groups," marking the first time that female subjectivity had been so widely represented, perhaps because many of the people just noted who

---

1. Reebee Garofalo and Steve Chapple use the term "schlock-rock" to refer to the music developed around teen idols (*Rock and Roll Is Here to Pay* [Chicago: Nelson-Hall, 1977]). By the mid-sixties, recordings of pre-rock 'n' roll pop music led to the creation of a new category, "easy listening," alternately referred to as "middle-of-the-road" or even as "good music." Despite the lack of attention paid in this book and almost every history of popular music to this type of music after the 1950s, it continued to be extremely popular; soundtracks and original cast recordings of musicals remained among the best-selling albums up through the late 1960s.

were involved with the songwriting and production of the girl groups were women (also a new development). Production teams in New York and Philadelphia also participated in the creation and promotion of dance crazes: songs based in R&B and rock 'n' roll that named and described a particular dance (e.g., the "jerk," the "limbo," the "mashed potatoes"). The most successful of these songs was "The Twist," which became a Number One hit for Chubby Checker *twice*, in 1960 and 1961.

In what is probably not a paradox, the most widely celebrated figure connected with the "girl-group" genre was a man, producer-songwriter Phil Spector (b. 1940). Spector developed a trademark sonic quality on his recordings, known as the "Wall of Sound," that featured a dense, reverberant texture filled with instruments that were often difficult to separate aurally from one another. This sound has often been inaccurately compared to the textural approach of European Romantic art-music composers, such as Richard Wagner; what Spector shared with Wagner was a grandiosity of vision and a tendency toward self-aggrandizement. The following essay by Tom Wolfe, notable as an example of "new journalism" (i.e., journalism that attempts to convey a sense of the inner state of the writer and/or the essay's subject, forgoing attempts at objective representation and linear narrative exposition) portrays Spector at the height of his fame in late 1964.

# THE FIRST TYCOON OF TEEN
## *Tom Wolfe*

Spector is sitting in a little cream room in his office suite at 440 East 62nd Street with his back to a window that is practically on top of the East Side Drive [East River Drive]. Twenty-three years old—he has a complex of corporations known as Phil Spector Productions. One of them is Mother Bertha Productions, named after his mother, Bertha. She works for his office in Los Angeles, but only because she wants to. The main organization is Philles Records. Spector has produced 21 "single" Philles records since October, 1962—and sold more than 13 million copies. All rock and roll. His most recent big hit, "Walking in the Rain," by the Ronettes, went as high as No. 20 on the *Cashbox* chart and has sold more than 250,000 copies. His latest record, "You've Lost That Lovin' Feelin'," by the Righteous Brothers, rose from the 70's to No. 37 with a "bullet" beside it—meaning "going up fast." He has produced seven albums. The first teen-age tycoon! He is leaning back in the chair. He has on his suede jerkin, his Italian pants, a pair of pointy British boots with Cuban heels. His hair hangs down to his shoulders in back.

Danny Davis, his promotion man, is talking on the phone in the inner office. A fellow sits across from Spector with his legs crossed and a huge chocolate brown Borsalino hat over his bent knee, like he was just trying it on. He says,

"Phil, why do you do—"

---

"I'm moving the whole thing to California," says Phil Spector. "I can't stand flying anymore."

"—why do you do these things?"

Spector—without his beard, Spector has a small chin, a small head, his face looks at first like all those little kids with bad hair and reedy voices from the Bronx, where he was born. But—an *ordinary* Phil Spector? Phil Spector has the only pure American voice. He was brought up not in the Bronx, but California. It meanders, quietly, shaking, through his doldrum fury, out to somewhere beyond cynical, beyond cool, beyond teen-age world-weary. It is thin, broken and soft. He is only twenty-three years old, for godsake, the first millionaire businessman to rise up out of the teen-age netherworld, king of the rock and roll record producers.

Spector jumps out of the chair.

"Wait a minute," he says. "Just a minute. They're making deals in here."

Spector walks into the inner office, gingerly, like a cowboy, because of the way the English boots lift him up off the floor. He is slight, five feet seven, 130 pounds. His hair shakes faintly behind. It is a big room, like a living room, all beige except for nine gold-plated rock and roll records on the wall, some of Phil Spector's "goldies," one million sales each. "He's a Rebel," by the Crystals, "Zip-a-dee-doo-dah," by Bob B. Soxx and the Blue Jeans, "Be My Baby," by the Ronettes, "Da Do Ron Ron," "Then He Kissed Me," "Uptown," "He's Sure the Boy I Love," all by the Crystals, "Wait Til My Baby Gets Home," by Darlene Love. And beige walls, beige telephones all over the place, a beige upright piano, beige paintings, beige tables, with Danny Davis crowding over a beige desk, talking on the telephone.

"Sure, Sal," says Danny, "I'll ask Phil. Maybe we can work something out on that."

Spector starts motioning thumbs down.

"Just a minute, Sal." Danny puts his hand over the mouthpiece and says,

"We *need* this guy, Phil. He's the biggest distributor out there. He wants the one thousand guarantee."

Phil's hands go up like he is lifting a slaughtered lamb up on top of an ice box.

"I don't care. I'm not interested in the money, I've got millions of dollars of money, I don't care who needs this animal. I'm interested in selling records, O.K.? Why should I give him a guarantee? He orders the records, I guarantee I'll buy a thousand back from him if he can't sell them; he sells them, then after the record dies, he buys up 500 cut rate from somebody, sends them back and cries for his money. Why should we have to be eating his singles later?"

Danny takes his hand away and says into the mouthpiece:

"Look, Sal, there's one thing I forgot. Phil says this record he can't give the guarantee. But you don't have anything to worry about. . . . I know what I said, but Phil says . . . look, Sal, don't worry, 'Walking in the Rain,' this is a tremendous record, tremendous, a very big record. . . . What? . . . I'm not reading off a paper, Sal. . . . Wait a minute, Sal—"

"Who needs these animals?" Phil Spector tells Danny.

"Look, Sal," Danny says, "this man never made a bad record in his life. You tell me one. Nothing but hits."

"Tell him to go to hell" says Spector.

"Sal—"

"Who needs these animals!" says Spector, so loud this time that Danny cups his hand around the receiver and puts his mouth down close.

"Nothing, Sal," says Danny, "that was somebody came in."

"Joan," says Phil, and a girl, Joan Berg, comes in out of another room. "Will you turn the lights off?" he says.

She turns the lights off, and now in the middle of the day the offices of Philles Records and Mother Bertha Productions are all dark except for the light from Danny Davis' lamp. Danny crowds into the pool of light, hunched over the phone, talking to Sal.

Phil puts his fingers between his eyes and wraps his eyebrows around them.

"Phil, it's dark in here," says the fellow with the large hat. "Why do you do these things?"

"I'm paying a doctor $600 a week to find out," says Phil without looking up.

He sits there in the dark, his fingers buried between his eyes. Just over his head one can make out a painting. The painting is kind of came-with-the-frame surrealist. It show a single musical note, a half note, suspended over what looks like the desert outside Las Vegas. Danny has to sit there huddled in his own pool of light talking to this animal on the telephone.

"This is a primitive country," says Phil Spector. "I was at Shepheard's, the discotheque, and these guys start saying these things. It's unbelievable. These people are animals."

"What kind of things, Phil?"

"I don't know. They look at, you know, my hair—my wife and I are dancing, and, I mean, it's unbelievable, I feel somebody yanking on my hair in the back. I turn around, here's this guy, a grown man, and he is saying these unbelievable things to me. So I tell him, like this, 'I'm going to tell you this one time, that's all—don't ever try that again.' And the guy—it's unbelievable—he shoves me with the heel of his hand and I go sprawling back into a table—"

—Spector pauses—

"—I mean, I've studied karate for years. I could literally *kill* a guy like that. You know? Size means nothing. A couple of these—" he cocks his elbow in the gloom and brings up the flat of his forearm—"but what am I going to do, start a fight every time I go out? Why should I even have to listen to anything from these animals? I find this country very condemning. I don't have this kind of trouble in Europe. The people of America are just not born with culture."

Not born with culture! If only David Susskind and William B. Williams could hear that. Susskind invited Phil Spector to the *Open End* television program one evening "to talk about the record business." Suddenly Susskind and "William B.," station WNEW's old-nostalgia disc jockey, were condemning Spector as some kind of sharpie poisoning American culture, rotting the minds of Youth and so forth. That was how it all hit Spector. It was as if he were some kind of short-armed fatty in the Brill Building, the music center on Broadway, with a spread-collar shirt and a bald olive skull with strands of black hair pulled up over it from above one ear. There was something very ironic about that. Spector is one record producer who wouldn't go near Broadway. His setup is practically out in the East River, up by the Rockefeller Institute. The Rockefeller Institute, for godsake. Susskind and Williams kept throwing Spector's songs at him—"He's a Rebel," "Da Do Ron Ron," "Be My Baby," "Fine Fine Boy," "Breakin' Up"—as if he were astutely conning millions of the cretins out there with this stuff. Spector didn't know exactly what to tell them. He *likes* the music he produces. He writes it himself. He is something new, the first teen-age millionaire, the first boy to become a millionaire within America's teen-age netherworld. It was never a simple question of him taking a look at the rock and roll universe from the outside and exploiting it. He stayed within it himself. He *liked* the music.

Spector, while still in his teens, seemed to comprehend the prole vitality of rock and roll that has made it the kind of darling holy beast of intellectuals in the United States, England and France. Intellectuals, generally, no longer take jazz seriously. Monk, Mingus, Ferguson—it has all been left to little executive trainees with their first apartment and a mahogany African mask from the free-port shop in Haiti—let me *tell* you!—and a hi-fi. But rock and roll! Poor old arteriosclerotic lawyers with pocky layers of fat over their ribs are out there right now twisting with obscene clumsiness to rock and roll. Their wives wear stretch pants to the seafood shoppe. A style of life! There have been teen-agers who have made a million dollars before, but invariably they are entertainers, they are steered by older people, such as good Colonel Tom Parker steers Elvis Presley. But Phil Spector is the bona-fide Genius of Teen. Every baroque period has a flowering genius who rises up as the most glorious expression of its style of life—in latter-day Rome, the Emperor Commodus; in Renaissance Italy, Benvenuto Cellini; in late Augustan England, the Earl of Chesterfield; in the sal volatile Victorian age, Dante Gabriel Rossetti; in late fancy neo-Greek Federal America, Thomas Jefferson; and in Teen America Phil Spector is the bona-fide Genius of Teen. In point of fact, he had turned twenty-one when he made his first clear million. But it was as a teenager working within the teen-age milieu, starting at the age of seventeen, that Phil Spector developed into a great American business man, the greatest of the independent rock and roll record producers. Spector's mother, Bertha took him from the Bronx to California when he was nine. California! Teen Heaven! By the time he was sixteen he was playing guitar with some jazz group. Then he got interested in rock and roll, which he does not call rock and roll but "pop blues." That is because—well, that is a complicated subject. Anyway, Phil Spector likes this music. He genuinely likes it. He is not a short-armed fatty hustling nutball fads.

"I get a little angry when people say it's bad music," Spector tells the man with the brown hat. "This music has a spontaneity that doesn't exist in any other kind of music, and it's what is here now. It's unfair to classify it as rock and roll and condemn it. It has limited chord changes, and people are always saying the words are banal and doesn't anybody write lyrics like Cole Porter anymore, but we don't have any presidents like Lincoln anymore either. You know? Actually, its more like the blues. It's pop blues. I feel it's very American. It's very *today*. It's what people respond to today. It's not just the kids. I hear cab drivers, everybody, listening to it."

And Susskind sits there on his show reading one of Spector's songs out loud, no music, just reading the words, from the Top Sixty or whatever it is, "Fine Fine Boy," to show how banal rock and roll is. The song just keeps repeating "He's a fine fine boy." So Spector starts drumming on the big coffee table there with the flat of his hands in time to Susskind's voice and says, "What you're missing is the beat." Blam blam.

Everybody is getting a little sore with Susskind reading these simple lyrics and Spector blamming away on the coffee table. Finally, Spector says the hell with it and, being more . . . hip . . . than Susskind or William B. Williams, starts cutting them up. He starts asking Williams how many times he plays Verdi on his show—Monteverdi?—D. Scarlatti?—A. Scarlatti?—that's good music, why don't you play that, you keep saying you play only good music, I don't hear you playing that. Williams doesn't know what to say. Spector tells Susskind he didn't come on the show to listen to somebody tell him he was corrupting the Youth of America—he could be home making money. Susskind—well uh, all right, Phil everybody is testy.

Making money. Yes! At the age of seventeen, Spector wrote a rock and roll song called "To Know Him Is To Love Him." He took the title off his father's tombstone. That was what his mother had had engraved on his father's tombstone out in Beth David cemetery in Elmont L.I. He doesn't say much about his father, just that he was "average lower middle class." Spector wrote the song, sang it and played the guitar in the recording with a group called the Teddy Bears. He made $20,000 on that record, but somebody ran off with $17,000 of it, and, well, no use going into that. Then he was going to UCLA, but he couldn't afford it and became a court reporter, one of the people who sit at the shorthand machine, taking down testimony. He decided to come to New York and get a job as an interpreter at the UN. His mother had taught him French. But he got to New York and the night before the interview, he fell in with some musicians and never got there. The hell with stenography. He wrote another hit that year, "Spanish Harlem." *There is a rose in Spanish Ha-a-a-a-ar-a-lem.* And then—only nineteen—he became head of A & R, artists and repertoire, for Atlantic Records. By 1961 he was a free-lance producer, producing records for the companies, working with Connie Francis, Elvis Presley, Ray Peterson, the Paris Sisters. All this time, Spector would write a song and run all phases of making records: get the artists, direct the recording sessions, everything. Spector could work with these hairy goslin kids who make these records because he was a kid himself, in one sense. God knows what the music business biggies thought of Phil Spector—he already wore his hair like Salvador Dali did at that age or like an old mezzotint of Mozart at the Academy or something. And he was somehow *one of them,* the natives, the kids who sang and responded to this . . . music. Phil Spector could get in one of those studios with the heron microphones, a representative of the adult world that makes money from records, and it became all one thing—the kids comprehended him.

Spector had an ideal, Archie Bleyer. Bleyer was a band leader who founded a record company, Cadence Records. Spector formed a partnership with two other people in 1961, then bought them out and went on his own as Philles Records in October of 1962. His first big hit was "He's a Rebel," by the Crystals. Spector had a system. The big record companies put out records like buckshot, 10, maybe 15 rock and roll records a month, and if one of them catches on, they can make money. Spector's system is to put them out one at a time and pour everything into each one. Spector does the whole thing. He writes the words and the music, scouts and signs up the talent. He takes them out to a recording studio in Los Angeles and runs the recording session himself. He puts them through hours and days of recording to get the two or three minutes he wants. Two or three minutes out of the whole struggle. He handles the control dial like an electronic maestro, tuning various instruments or sounds up, down, out, every which way, using things like two pianos, a harpsichord and three guitars on one record; then re-recording the whole thing with esoteric dubbing and over-dubbing effects—reinforcing instruments or voices—coming out with what is known throughout the industry as "the Spector sound."

The only thing he doesn't keep control of is the actual manufacture, the pressing, of the records and the distribution. The only people around to give him any trouble all this time are the distributors—cigar-chewing fatties . . . and—well, to be honest, there is a lot that gives Phil Spector trouble, and not so much any kind of or any group of people as much as his . . . status. A teen-age Tycoon! It is too wacked out. He is betwixt and between. He identifies with the teen-age netherworld, he defends it, but he is already too mature for it. As a millionaire, a business genius, living in a penthouse 22 stories up over the East River, with his wife, Annette, who is twenty, a student at Hunter College, and with a four-room suite downstairs on the ground floor as his office, and a limousine, and a chauffeur, and a bodyguard, and a staff, Danny and Joan Berg and everybody, and a doorman who directs people to Mr. Spector's office—well, that makes Phil Spector *one of them,* the universe of arteriosclerotic, hypocritical, cigar-chewing, hopeless, larded adults, infarcted vultures, one meets in the music business. And so here in the dark is a twenty-three year-old man with a Shelley visage, a suede shirt, a kind of page-boy bob and winkle-picker boots, the symbol of the one, sitting in the dark in this great beige office, the symbol of the other, in the middle of the day, in the dark, tamping his frontal lobes with his fingers in the gloom.

One of the beige phones rings and Danny answers. Then he presses the "hold" button and tells Phil Spector, "It's the Rolling Stones, they just got in."

Spector comes alive with that. He gets up on his ginger toes and goes to the telephone. He is lively and he spins on the balls of his feet a little as he stands by the phone.

"Hello Andrew," he says. He is talking with Andrew Oldham, the manager of the Rolling Stones. And then he puts on a cockney accent. "Are you all in?" he says.

The Rolling Stones; all right. The Rolling Stones, English group, and Andrew Oldham, are like him. They grew up in the teen-age netherworld and made it, and they all want to have it all too, kids' style of life and the adult's . . . money . . . and not cop out on one side or the other, larded and arteriosclerotic. God! Phil Spector's British trip! That was where suddenly he had it all.

Phil Spector is here! The British have the ability to look at all sorts of rebel baddies and alienated thin young fellows and say coo and absorb them like a great soggy lukewarm, mother's poultice. The Beatles, Beatlemania rock and roll, suddenly it is all absorbed into the center of things as if it could have been there all along if it only asked. Phil Spector arrives at London Airport and, Santa Barranza, there are photographers all over the place, for him, Phil Spector, and the next morning he is all over the center fold of the *London Daily Mirror*, the biggest newspaper in the Western World, five million circulation: "The 23-year-old American rock and roll magnate." He is in the magazines as the "U.S. Recording Tycoon." Invitations go out to come to the receptions to meet "America's outstanding hit maker, Phil Spector." And then he lands back at Idlewild and waiting are, yes, the same bunch of cheese-breath cabbies, and he takes a cab on back to 440 E. 62nd St. and goes into his beige world, the phones are ringing and it is all the same, the same—

"Cigar-smoking sharpies," says Phil Spector. He is in a livelier mood after the talk with Andrew Oldham. "They're a bunch of cigar-smoking sharpies in record distribution. They've all been in the business for years and they resent you if you're young. That's one reason so many kids go broke in this business. They're always starting new record companies, or they used to, the business is very soft right now, they start a company and pour all their money into a record, and it can be successful and they're still broke, because these characters don't even pay you until you've had three or four hit records in a row. They order the records and sell them and don't pay you. They don't pay you because they know they don't have to. You start yelling for the money and they tell you, 'Whattya mean, I have all these records coming back from the retailers and what about my right to return records, and blah-blah.' What are you going to do? Sue twenty guys in twenty different courts in United States?

"They look at everything as a product. They don't care about the work and sweat you put into a record. They respect me now because I keep turning out hits, and after that they become sort of honest . . . in their own decayed way."

Status! What is his status? He produces "rock and roll," and, therefore, he is not a serious person, and he won't join the Young Presidents or whatever the hell kind of organization jaycee geniuses would join for their own good.

"Phil," says the man in the hat, "why don't you hire a press agent, a P. R. man—"

Phil is tamping his frontal lobes in the gloom. Danny Davis is hunched up in the little pool of light on his desk. Danny is doing his level best for Phil.

"Jack? Danny Davis . . . Yeah . . . No, I'm with Phil Spector now . . . Right! It's the best move I ever made. You know Phil . . . I'm in the best shape of my career . . . Jack, I just want to tell you we've got—"

"A press agent?" Phil says to the man in the hat. "In the first place, I couldn't stand to hear what he'd say about me."

"—Got two tremendous records going, Jack, 'Walking in the Rain,' the Ronettes, and—"

"In the second place," Phil says, "there's no way my image can be bought."

"—And 'You've Lost That Lovin' Feelin'' by The Righteous Brothers," says Danny. ". . . Right, Jack . . . I appreciate that, Jack . . ."

"The only thing I could do—you know what I'd like to do? I'd like to do a recording session in the office of *Life* or *Esquire* or *Time*, and then they could see it. That's the only chance I've got. Because I'm dealing in rock and roll, I'm, like I'm not a bona-fide human being—"

". . . Absolutely! . . . If there's anything we can do for you on this end, Jack, let us know. O.K.? Great, Jack . . ."

". . . and I even have trouble with people who should never say *any*thing. I go over to Gristede's to get a quart of milk or something and the woman at the cash register has to start in. So I tell her, 'There's a war in Viet Nam, they fired Khrushchev, the Republican party is falling to pieces, the Ku Klux Klan is running around loose, and you're worrying about my hair. . . .'"

America's first teen-age tycoon, a business genius, a musical genius—and it is as if he were still on the corner of Hoffman Street in the Bronx when the big kids come by in a hideous fraternity, the way these people act. What is he now? Who is he in this weird country? Danny talks in the phone in the little pool of light, Joan is typing up whatever it is, Phil is tamping his frontal lobes.

Another airplane! It levels off, and the man in the seat by the window, next to Phil Spector, lights a cigarette, pure as virgin snow. Phil Spector sits there with his kind of pageboy bob pressed down in back and a checked shirt and tight black pants. The man with the cigarette keeps working himself up to something. Finally, he says, "If you don't mind me asking— have I seen you on television or something? What's your name, I mean, if you don't mind me asking?" Phil Spector presses back into the seat but his head won't disappear. Then he says, "I'm Goddard Lieberson."

"Gottfried Lieberman?"

Marvelous! Reassuring! Nobody ever heard of Goddard Lieberson, either. Who the hell is Goddard Lieberson! He is the president of Columbia Records, all those nice straight cookie jar "tunes" William B. Williams would go for, very big—and who the hell knows who he is?

"I'm the president of Columbia records."

The man sucks on his cigarette a moment. A skinny ash, all limp, hangs out.

"Well—you must be kind of young."

Phil Spector lies back. Then he says,

"I was only kidding. I'm Chubby Checker. That's who I really am."

"Chubby Checker?"

Who the hell is Chubby Checker? Yes! Who the hell has *any*body ever heard of? It's like the last time when he said he was Paul Desmond. Who the hell is Paul Desmond? Or Peter Sellers's cousin. Or Monsieur Fouquet, of the de Gaulle underground. Or . . . who the hell is *any*body? Phil Spector tamps his frontal lobes and closes his eyes and holds his breath. As long as he holds his breath, it will not rain, there will be no raindrops, no schizoid water wobbling, sideways, straight back, it will be an even, even, even, even, even, even, even world.

# 28. From Surf to *Smile*

Concurrent with the dance crazes and girl-group phenomenon, the American imagination increasingly shifted westward to the land of fruit and nuts, as California rapidly became the most populous and economically important of the 50 states. Out of the sun-drenched expanses of the rapidly growing suburbs in Southern California came surf music, with its litany of beaches, blondes, and Bonneville sport coupes. Initially, an instrumental genre led by guitarist Dick Dale (a real, live surfer) and by guitar-dominated instrumental bands, such as the Ventures, surf came to be associated most strongly with the Beach Boys, a band that developed a distinctive, contrapuntal, falsetto-led vocal style.

The group was a family affair, consisting of three Wilson brothers (Brian, Carl, and Dennis), cousin Mike Love, and pal Al Jardine. The eldest brother, Brian (b. 1942), was the musical mastermind of the group, concocting a potent brew of multipart harmony singing (derived from 1950s' vocal groups, such as the jazz-influenced Four Freshmen and the Hi-Los), Chuck Berry riffs, trebly guitar timbres (a holdover from surf instrumental groups), and lyrics extolling the ennui of beach-loving, middle-class, white teens. The early hits of 1962–63 all hewed close to these themes in one way or another, although the emotional range and the harmonic palette expanded in ballads like "Surfer Girl" and "In My Room." Their first major national hit, "Surfin' U.S.A.," owed so much to Chuck Berry's "Sweet Little Sixteen" that Berry was eventually awarded songwriting credit for it.

The following excerpts from Brian Wilson's autobiography describe a period after Wilson suffered a nervous breakdown in 1964 and subsequently stopped touring, a move that enabled him to devote more energy to songwriting and production. While his songs had continuously increased in musical complexity beginning with the Beach Boys' first recordings in 1962, the Beatles' *Rubber Soul*, released in December 1965, inspired Wilson to try and surpass his earlier efforts. The result? *Pet Sounds*, one of the first "concept" albums, and one of the first to feature overt studio experimentation (including elaborate overdubbing and mixing, unusual instruments, and songs with multiple tempi). Although *Pet Sounds* did not equal the success of earlier Beach Boys' albums (managing nevertheless to reach the Top 10), it, and the commercially successful single that followed, "Good Vibrations," subsequently established critical high-water marks for the band. Here, Wilson describes the creation of these recordings.[1]

## *from* WOULDN'T IT BE NICE: MY OWN STORY
### *Brian Wilson (with Todd Gold)*

In December, the Beatles' latest LP, *Rubber Soul*, hit Number One in Britain and the U.S. I heard individual cuts but didn't listen to the entire LP until someone from my expanding circle of friends, most of whom I'd inherited from Loren [Loren Schwartz, a close friend of Wilson during this period], brought it over to my house in early 1966 and insisted I listen and give my opinion, as if I were some kind of oracle.

Under a cloud of pot smoke, it was a ceremonial event. A bunch of us sat around the dining room table, gazing out the window at the expanse of city lights shimmering below, smoking joints as the album played. No one ventured an opinion until I expressed mine. That was easy. I was knocked out. Every song from "Michelle" to "Norwegian Wood" to "In My Life," and "The Word" was great.

"I'm flipped by it," I exclaimed. "I can't believe it."

"John and Paul, those guys are geniuses," Loren said.

"That album is just blowing my mind," I continued, excited by its amazing consistency. "They put only great stuff on the album. That's what I want to do."

"What?" he asked.

"I want to make a whole album a gas!" I said.

Around January 1966 I had all these pieces of music, feels,[2] and they needed lyrics. I remembered that five months earlier Loren had brought a friend of his to Western, where I was in the midst of laying tracks on the *Summer Days* album. Tony Asher was a bright young copy-and-jingle writer for Carson/Roberts, an advertising agency. During a break, I'd played them one of my feels and asked for an opinion. Then Tony played a little melody he had written.

Among our first songs was "You're So Good to Me," one of Tony's favorites. He thought it was a good pop song, light and hummable. I agreed but explained that those qualities were what I wanted to get away from.

"I want to show that the Beach Boys know *music*," I said. "I don't want to do the easy stuff"

"I understand," he said.

Our next song was done with the record company breathing so hard down my neck for a new single that I began every day by unplugging the phone. One of the prettiest, most personal songs I've ever written, "Caroline, No" concerned growing up and the loss of innocence. I'd reminisced to Tony about my high school crush on Carol Mountain and sighed,

---

1. For a portrait of Wilson during the period following "Good Vibrations" while he worked on *Smile*, the imploding follow-up to *Pet Sounds*, see Jules Siegel, "A Teen-age Hymn to God," in William McKeen, ed., *Rock and Roll Is Here to Stay: An Anthology* (New York: W. W. Norton, 2000), 387–99. Written in 1967.

2. "Feels" was a term that Wilson used to refer to unfinished fragments of music.

*Source:* Brian Wilson (with Todd Gold), *Wouldn't It Be Nice: My Own Story* (New York: HarperCollins Publishers, 1991), pp. 129–30, 131, 134–35, 138–41, 145, 147–48.

"If I saw her today, I'd probably think, God, she's lost something, because growing up does that to people."

But the song was most influenced by the changes Marilyn [Wilson's wife] and I had gone through since meeting at Pandora's Box. We were young, Marilyn nearing twenty and me closing in on twenty-four, yet I thought we'd lost the innocence of our youth in the heavy seriousness of our lives. The lightness that had once been ours was fading. Subconsciously, I might've sensed that the power allowing me to do special things naturally might not last too much longer.

All that made me sad.

The first time I played the melody of "Caroline, No" he told me the song had single potential. He took a tape home, embellished on my concept, and completed the words. The Beach Boys were on the road when it came time to record "Caroline, No," though between the pressure Capitol was putting on me to get a single ready, the song's intensely personal nature, and the creative space I was in at the time, I didn't think about waiting for them to get back to town. Instead, I did it myself.

It took seventeen takes before the song sounded the way I wanted, perfect. At the end of the seventeenth take, tears were streaming down my eyes, and I knew I'd nailed it. But it still wasn't finished."

I played "Caroline, No" for my dad. Though our contact was minimal, for some reason I continued to solicit his opinion. He praised the song but suggested that I change the key from C to D. The engineer put a wrap around the recording head, a technique which sped up the playback, and the two of us listened again. My dad was right, and I took his advice.

As work progressed, I began to consider making the album a solo project. I kept the thought private, but it reflected my growing intuition that the guys, when they began hearing the music, wouldn't like or understand it. The songs were a telling self-portrait of my troubled psyche: "I Just Wasn't Made for These Times" was a lament about being too advanced and having to leave people behind; "Let's Go Away for a While," a Burt Bacharach tribute, was explained by the title. The track originally included lyrics but worked better as an instrumental and became one of the most satisfying of my songs.

I pulled myself out of bed, went to the piano to save myself, and resumed work with Tony. It was mid-February. I played him the song I'd written titled "Good, Good, Good Vibrations." I had the chorus but no lyrics for the verses. He loved the song but was a little weirded out when I explained why I'd written the song and what I wanted it to convey.

"My mom told me dogs discriminate between people," I said. "They like some because the people give off good vibrations. They bite others because they give off bad vibrations. I have a feeling this is a very spiritual song, and I want it to give off good vibrations."

He tried his hand at writing lyrics, and things were going so well that I put "Good, Good, Good Vibrations" on the preliminary list of songs I told Capitol would be on the album. Two weeks later, though, I changed my mind and took the song off. The time wasn't right. I couldn't produce it yet.

With plenty of other good songs needing work, Tony and I turned our attention to "God Only Knows," the song about which I felt the strongest and proudest. The melody was inspired by a John Sebastian record I'd been listening to, and the idea summarized everything I was trying to express in a single song. But it began with an argument. I hated the opening line, "I may not always love you." I didn't think it was the right way to begin a love song. It was too negative.

"Brian, that's real life," Tony argued. "People who are in love may not always stay in love with each other. But consider the next line."

Then Tony sang: "'But as long as the stars are above you, you'll never need to doubt me . . .'"

"'The love we're writing about will last until the stars burn out,'" he sang.'" "'And that won't ever happen.'"

That made me feel better. Then we had another argument over the word God. No one had ever recorded it before in a popular song. I was concerned that with God in the song we wouldn't get any radio airplay. Tony understood, but he was adamant about not compromising the artistic integrity. I eventually agreed too. First, because God was a spiritual word, and second, because we'd be breaking ground. Both were good reasons to leave it unchanged.

People who were at the "God Only Knows" sessions still tell me that they were the most magical, beautiful musical experiences they've ever heard. I gathered twenty-three musicians in one studio, an extraordinary number for a pop record. Everyone played simultaneously, the different sounds bleeding into one other, producing a rich, heavenly blanket of music.

It wasn't like making records is today, with seventy-eight tracks and every instrument recorded individually and mixed later. Then, everyone had to play live. It either worked or it didn't. The ability to make the type of snap decisions a production of that size required was what separated Spector from the pack. I excelled there too, but I still did twenty takes before the tracks sounded the way I heard them in my head.

"Goddamnit, that was beautiful," Dennis said afterward. "How'd you write that?"

"I prayed," I answered. "I prayed to God."

"Well, I pray to God it sells," Mike interjected.

Indeed, not everyone appreciated what they heard. I played bits and pieces of songs to Mike and Carl over long-distance telephone, but by the time of the "God Only Knows" sessions they still hadn't heard any completed songs and didn't know whether they liked what they'd heard. Al complained that he spent three months singing the chorus to "Wouldn't It Be Nice" before he ever knew the verses. Then I decided not to use the guys playing instruments on the album, the first LP on which none of the Beach Boys does anything more than sing.

By March 1966, the time at which they began listening to the songs Tony and I had done, which was around the "God Only Knows" sessions, they were prepared not to like the music. And they didn't. First, they were put off by the fact that I didn't need them. The tracks and vocals were all well developed without them. I think their egos were bruised. But the guys also weren't prepared for how different the music was from the songs we'd done in the past.

Especially Mike, whose biggest concern was, Will it sell? He hated everything. He criticized it as "ego music." He complained that the songs were too avant-garde and didn't sound like the old stuff. He refused to sing on "Hang On to Your Ego" until the lyrics were reworked to "I Know There's an Answer." After one stormy vocal session, he let his disgust surface and snapped at me, "Who's gonna hear this shit? The ears of a dog?"

Ironically, Mike's barb inspired the album's title, *Pet Sounds*. It was quite clear that none of them, except Dennis, who was always my biggest supporter in the studio, and Bruce Johnston, who loved everything, understood the album's significance to me. I'd poured my soul into these songs. The pain, the joy, the conflicts, the sadness, the love. They were everything to me, my flesh and blood. They only knew the songs weren't about sun, fun, and bikini-clad buns.

But that's always been the core difference between me and the Beach Boys. To the guys, the group was a great gig, a terrific job. The pay was good, the fringe benefits even better. They just wanted me to crank out the songs like a machine. Stick in a nickel, pull the handle, take five dollars. Money never entered my mind when I wrote a song. Writing songs was what I did.

*Pet Sounds* represented the maturing of my talent, the single-minded pursuit of a personal vision. I wasn't just entertaining people, I was speaking directly to them, directly from my heart.

The clash of egos wasn't helped any when it was decided to release "Caroline, No" in early March, not as the first Beach Boys single off *Pet Sounds* but as a Brian Wilson solo. Despite protests from the group, Capitol supported the idea as a means of broadening our marketability. Lennon and McCartney were as widely known by themselves as the Beatles. Likewise, Mick Jagger and the Rolling Stones. Yet the Beach Boys were as bland personalitywise as the sand on the beach.

Having given up on my dream of making *Pet Sounds* a Brian Wilson album, I liked the idea of releasing "Caroline, No" as a solo record, but I still made it clear to the guys that they didn't have to worry about me leaving the Beach Boys for a career of my own. That wasn't my goal. I'd worked too hard mother-henning the band to where it was. Besides, they were my family.

Unfortunately, "Caroline, No" got no higher than twenty-three, causing the record company to jump on Mike's side and ask, "What the hell is going on with the music?"

They immediately rushed out "Sloop John B," which was more in line with the Beach Boys' formula, and by May 1966 it was at number three. That was more like it.

At the peak of a creative streak that had begun during the *Summer Days* album and found itself in the making of *Pet Sounds,* I talked about going further, breaking old boundaries and setting new standards, and I knew the song I began working on immediately after *Pet Sounds* was the one that was going to catapult me to that place.

"Good Vibrations" was going to be the summation of my musical vision, a harmonic convergence of imagination and talent, production values and craft, songwriting and spirituality. I'd written it five months earlier and imagined the grand, Spectorlike production while on the LSD trip I'd described so enthusiastically for Al [Jardine, member of the Beach Boys]. Instinctively, I knew it was the right song at the right time.

Written in three separate parts, "Good Vibrations" required seventeen sessions and six weeks—not six months as has always been reported—spread over three months, to record, costing a sum somewhere between $50,000 and $75,000, then an unheard amount for one song. I threw everything I could think of into the stew: fuzz bass, clarinet, cello, harp, and a theremin, a strange, electronic instrument. Chuck Britz, who worked the board on all seventeen sessions, always said the first session was the best. Glen Campbell, one of the nearly twenty musicians used that day, agreed, exclaiming, "Whew, Brian! What were you smokin' when you wrote that?"

In August, I finished the final edit, mixed the tracks down to mono, and knew, during the playback, that it was right. Throughout, I repeatedly thought, Oh my God, this is a real mindblower. I played it for Mike, Carl, Dennis, Al, and Bruce the following day, and when the song finished they looked at me with bewilderment. They'd never heard anything like it, and they honestly didn't know whether or not it was any good. It was just different.

Finally, Bruce spoke up: "We're gonna have either the biggest hit in the world," he said. "Or the Beach Boys' career is over."

# 29. Urban Folk Revival

The whole notion of "urban folk" summons a number of paradoxes: If we take "folk music" to mean music that survives in an oral, rather than a written, tradition, preserved in face-to-face encounters between people who recognize one another as belonging to the same community, then the idea of "urban folk," in which the music exists among widely dispersed city dwellers and is shared through mass-mediated technology, seems at least somewhat contradictory. If we try to retain some sense of American folk music as connected to the rural folk in a premodern era, the term "urban folk" similarly involves a suspension of disbelief.

The idea of urban folk music first gathered momentum in the 1930s. Many of the early performers were either black or white southerners who had been brought (or encouraged to come) to New York City by folklorists-musicologists who were associated with the leftist Popular Front political movement, such as John and Alan Lomax and Charles Seeger.[1] While early urban folk performers did include African American blues singers like "Leadbelly" (Huddie Ledbetter) and Josh White among their ranks, the dominant musical style derived, in large part, from the ballad tradition of white, rural Southerners and thus shared qualities with the "hillbilly" music of the period. Many of the differences between "hillbilly" and "folk" were, in fact, more sociological than musicological: Rather than the utilitarian, overtly commercial aims of 1920s and 1930s hillbilly music, urban folk used the associations of rural, traditional music to evoke a sense of timeless purity.

Of all the performers who are associated with the urban folk movement, Woody Guthrie (1912–67) became the most recognized. Born and raised in Oklahoma, Guthrie wrote original songs (using melodies with strong connections to traditional tunes) that chronicled the tribulations of dust-bowl refugees—"Okies" like those memorialized in John Steinbeck's *Grapes of Wrath*—and the hardships endured by the common "folk." Guthrie's lyrics were pro-labor and pro-working class, but sufficiently populist so that people from various political perspectives could adopt a song like "This Land Is Your Land," especially when the most explicitly left-wing verses were excised. For example, the

---

1. For more on the popular front and the urban folk revival, see Michael Denning, *The Cultural Front: The Laboring of American Culture in the Twentieth Century* (New York: Verso, 1997); Robert Cantwell, *When We Were Good: The Folk Revival* (Cambridge, Mass.: Harvard University Press, 1996); Benjamin Filene, *Romancing the Folk: Public Memory and American Roots Music* (Chapel Hill: The University of North Carolina Press, 2000); Bryan Carman, *A Race of Singers: Whitman's Working-Class Hero from Guthrie to Springsteen* (Chapel Hill: University of North Carolina Press, 2000).

often-deleted fourth verse of "This Land Is Your Land" protests the negative effects of land ownership: "Was a high wall there that tried to stop
me/A sign was painted said: Private Property."[2] Guthrie also developed a
ramblin', gamblin' persona in many witty talking blues that had much in
common with personae developed later by Beat writers, such as Jack
Kerouac, and that influenced many male singers of the 1960s.

   In 1941, Guthrie joined the Almanac Singers, a group that included
among its members, Pete Seeger (b. 1919), son of the noted musicologist
Charles Seeger. The Almanac Singers continued to stress political and
social issues, such as the importance of civil rights and labor unions.
Seeger then formed the Weavers, a group that continued to be associated with the liberal themes of the Almanac Singers, while their richly
harmonized (and thickly orchestrated) versions of songs, such as Leadbelly's "Goodnight Irene" (Number One for 13 weeks in 1950!) and
Guthrie's "So Long It's Been Good to Know You" (Number Four in 1951)
were sufficiently successful to enter the popular music mainstream. Although the Weavers' hits eschewed strong political messages, their left-
wing views brought them to the attention of Joseph McCarthy and the
House Un-American Activities Committee, the proceedings of which led
to the group's demise in 1953.

   Despite their blacklisting, the Weavers and other folk musicians like
Burl Ives planted seeds for the popularity of urban folk music that led
some of their fans to an awareness of Guthrie, Leadbelly, Josh White, and
others. Although the McCarthy hearings effectively suppressed urban
folk music, artists like Harry Belafonte—who found success with several
Caribbean-flavored recordings in 1956–57—and the Kingston Trio—
whose "Tom Dooley" went to Number One in 1958—maintained the
mass-mediated presence of folk music, and the music gained popularity
among college-age audiences. Urban folk music also maintained its
paradoxical stature as the anticommercial form of popular music and was
heard by many as the antidote to mainstream pop music and early rock
'n' roll.

The article that follows describes the links between many of the artists
associated with the urban folk music of the 1930s and 1940s and their
successors in the late 1950s and early 1960s. The article notes how, from
the late 1950s onward, urban folk reasserted its political connotations
(which for many it had never lost) and how distinctions were already
being made between overtly commercial folk groups (the Kingston Trio)
and artists who were viewed (rightly or wrongly) as making few, if any,
concessions to mass taste. The civil rights movement provided the
strongest public cause for this new confluence of folk music (dubbed by
historians the urban folk music *revival*) and politics, and, as the article
notes, the fight for civil rights provided the strongest motivation for the

---

2. The sixth verse of this song, also usually omitted, describes the devastating effects of poverty in the
United States.

"nonconformity" exhibited by folk music fans. It is significant that, despite the prominence of several African American performers within the movement and its strong commitment to civil rights, the vast majority of the performers and audience members were white, college educated, and middle class, thereby forming another link with the 1930s urban folk scene.

## SONGS OF THE SILENT GENERATION
### *Gene Bluestein*

*Mademoiselle,* the magazine which specializes in telling smart young women what the bright young men of Madison Avenue think they ought to know, got around to explaining (in its December 1960 issue) what the "folksong fad" is all about. Notwithstanding a brief nod in the direction of anthropology and social psychology (folksinging provides students with a sense of "togetherness," it helps them channelize their feelings toward a "brutal and threatening" world), what *Mademoiselle* wants to emphasize is the fact that this generation of college students are "hungry for a small, safe taste of an unslick, underground world" and folksong, like pizza and popcorn, takes the edge off their appetites.

*Mademoiselle*'s description of the college "folkniks" as a "student middle class" which has adapted "the trappings and tastes of a Bohemian minority group" is based on the assumption that the students draw their main inspiration from the bearded "beatniks" who inhabit the countless coffee houses which have sprung up around the country. But as Kenneth Rexroth has been pointing out from the beginning, the "beatnik" is the creature of Time, Inc; it is a popular view of the artist as irresponsible, incomprehensible, and "maladjusted." And, as in the case of the new young poets, the analogy is false.

Neither does the college folksong addict flip over the antics of commercial folksong groups which have become standard property in the stables of such bigtime operators as RCA Victor, Decca, and Columbia. (The Kingston Trio was so out of place at the first Newport Folk Festival that it did not appear at the second one.) The repertoires of these groups do consist mainly of traditional songs but they are adapted, dislocated, expurgated or, when the occasion is right, turned into popular songs. Often the appeal of the big time night club singers comes less from their vocal or instrumental skill than from the patter *in between* the songs; the routines are second-rate imitations of the humor developed by the "sick" comics.

But the interest of large numbers of college students in folksong goes far beyond the limits of wisecracks accompanied by banjo and guitar. Even *Mademoiselle* noticed this, for its reporter can't quite understand what attracts these middle class kids to a music which evokes "the ideas and emotions of the downtrodden and the heartbroken, of garage mechanics and mill workers and miners and backwoods farmers"—a lineup of materials which reflects neither the world of the beats nor of the slick trios.

Here is where a little historical perspective would help. As Harold Taylor has pointed out recently, this generation of college students has begun to react against being treated like adolescents. If they have not been ideological, Mr. Taylor points out, they have been willing to associate themselves with non-conformist movements, despite warnings by parents and

*Source:* Gene Bluestein, "Songs of the Silent Generation," *New Republic,* 144, no. 11 (March 13, 1961), pp. 21–22. Reprinted by permission of The New Republic, © 1961, The New Republic, LLC.

teachers that such activities will endanger their personal as well as their job security. The moral leadership for this so-called "silent generation," Mr. Taylor notes, was "established by the Negro students in the South who quietly and courageously began to assert their rights with the sit-in strikes at lunch counters." And as TV coverage of events in the South has revealed, the passive resistance movement of young people and adults is a singing movement as well.

Martin Luther King's meetings with Negro college students almost always conclude with a song—a popular one has its roots in the spiritual: "We shall overcome—Oh Lord, Deep in my heart, I do believe, we shall overcome some day." A Huntley-Brinkley special on the sit-ins showed students singing a West Indian work song which they had sung in jail—"Daylight's comin' and I wanna go home." The same program featured snatches of a song which told how the "cops went wild over me, and they locked me up and threw away the key." The words were up to date, but it was unmistakably the IWW protest song called the "Popular Wobbly." Earlier, the bus-boycotters in Mongomery, Alabama, had sung, "Walk Along Together."

That spirituals, work songs, and other protest songs should figure prominently in the expression of the students in the South is not surprising. What is significant is that the main stream of the song traditions that interest college students in general derive from similar materials. Almost fifty years ago, John Lomax told a meeting of academic folklorists that the significance of American folksong was to be seen not in transplanted ballads, but in songs of the miners, lumbermen, Great Lakes sailors, railroad men, cowboys, and Negroes. (A special category singled out "songs of the down and out classes—the outcast girls, the dope fiend, the convict, the jail bird and the tramp.") It was a shocking revision of the academic approach to American folksong, for in 1913, as today, the professional folklorist tends to be concerned mainly with ballads, and especially the relationship between American and British ballads. But as Lomax continued to collect in the field the vitality of non-ballad traditions impressed upon him. With the help of his son Alan, John Lomax explored the prisons of the South, uncovering such singers as Huddie Ledbetter (Lead Belly), Vera Hall, Dock Reed; they were impressed by the songs of the dust bowl songmaker, Woodie Guthrie, but especially by "the singers who have moved us beyond all others that we have heard . . . the Negroes, who in our opinion have made the most important and original contributions to American folksong . . ."

Long before folksongs became commercially profitable, singers like Guthrie, Lead Belly, and Pete Seeger were spreading the Lomax gospel on picket lines, at union meetings, and through the recordings made by quixotic Moses Asch, whose supreme devotion to traditional material kept his record companies producing even when he had neither a large audience nor a source of capital. Through the thirties and forties Guthrie kept a constant streams of songs flowing like an underground river—about the dust bowl, hoboes, folk heroes (including the Oklahoma Robin Hood, Pretty Boy Floyd), the Grand Coulee Dam, New York City, mining disasters, as well as a Whitmanesque catalogue about America called "This Land Is Your Land." Lead Belly popularized such songs as "Good Night Irene," "The Midnight Special," The Rock Island Line," and dozens of blues including "Bourgeois Blues," based on his attempt to find housing in Jim Crow Washington, D.C. Seeger, whose sensitivity to vocal and instrumental traditions is unrivalled, has been, since the early forties, a Johnny Appleseed encouraging his audience to pick up a banjo and make music.

Lead Belly died in 1949, just before the Weavers put "Good Night Irene" at the top of the hit parade, paving the way for a mass folksong audience. But like other serious arts in America, folksongs resist the mass production and standardization of tin-pan alley. (Lee Hays, who sings bass with the Weavers, commented that the success of "Good Night Irene" made tin-pan alley believe America was ready for a waltz revival!) Guthrie has become seriously ill and is unable to appreciate fully the response to his songs and his artistry which has developed among enthusiasts in America and in England. Pete Seeger is today the most sought after performer on college campuses, more often through the insistence of student groups than the promotion by official university concert bureaus. With obvious respect for his materials and the people who produced them, Seeger continues in the tradition of the Lomaxes, Guthrie and Leadbelly.

This is still a young movement, composed of students who are filled with the stubborn idealism that permeates the songs of Negro slaves, miners, hoboes, and blues singers. If the Kennedy administration is serious in its proposal to recruit them into a corps which will work to push the new frontiers, they will respond en masse and bring their guitars with them.

> The second, brief article describes a new phase of the urban folk music revival that gathered momentum in 1963: the protest song movement, which sought to express the folk revival's political concerns with newly composed songs that addressed topical matters.[3] Here, Pete Seeger was again a pioneer: He had written songs with topical themes dating back to the 1940s—"I Had a Hammer," cowritten by Seeger and Weavers' band mate Lee Hays in 1949, was a hit for Peter, Paul, and Mary in 1962— and several of his songs, such as "Where Have All the Flowers Gone?" and "Turn, Turn, Turn," figured prominently in the new wave of politically inspired material. This article also describes the participation of one Bob Dylan, the singer who became identified more than any other with the protest movement.

## FOLK MUSIC: THEY HEAR AMERICA SINGING
### *Time*

Pete Seeger, Theodore Bikel and Bob Dylan are three of the most sought-after folk singers in the business. But last week they were doing the seeking. At a voter registration rally two miles out of Greenwood, Miss., all three stood on a flatbed truck parked on a dusty field beside Highway 82 and sang the gospel-like *We Shall Overcome*. The audience, 200 Negro dirt farmers, lustily joined in:

> *We shall overcome—some day*
> *Oh, deep in my heart.*
> *I do believe.*
> *We shall overcome—some day*

---

3. This article does not mention one of the most important musicians of the folk music revival, Joan Baez, who had begun including protest songs in her concerts by 1963. Baez was the focus of a somewhat earlier article in *Time* on folk music, which, however, paid as much attention to personal eccentricities (including her lack of makeup and "loose" approach to sexual relationships) as it did to her political concerns. See "Folk Singing: Sibyl with Guitar," *Time*, November 23, 1962, 54–60.

All over the U.S., folk singers are doing what folk singers are classically supposed to do—singing about current crises. Not since the Civil War era have they done so in such numbers or with such intensity. Instead of keening over the poor old cowpoke who died in the streets of Laredo or chronicling the life cycle of the blue-tailed fly (the sort of thing that fired the great postwar revival of folk song), they are singing with hot-eyed fervor about police dogs and racial murder. Sometimes they use serviceable old tunes, but just as often they are writing new ones about fresh heroes and villains, from Martin Luther King to Bull Connor. In Chicago, integrationist songs are sung not only at the North Side's grubby Fickle Pickle but also in the Camellia House of The Drake. In a cocktail lounge in Ogunquit, ME., a college girl shouts out: "Sing something about integration." Seeger has done so before a crowd of 45,000 at the Boston Arts Festival; and the Peter, Paul and Mary recording of Bob Dylan's *Blowin' in the Wind* is, according to Warner Bros. Records, the fastest selling single the company has ever cut. *Blowin'* is young Dylan at his lyrically honest best. It sounds as country-airy as *Turkey in the Straw*, but it has a cutting edge.

# 30. Bringing It All Back Home

## Dylan at Newport

Early in 1961, Bob Dylan (b. 1941) left Minneapolis, arrived in New York City's Greenwich Village, and quickly made his way to the forefront of the folk music scene there. Early signs of outward encouragement came in September 1961 with a glowing review from the *New York Times* critic Robert Shelton[1] and with a contract from Columbia Records (the largest record company at the time) that resulted in his first album, the eponymous *Bob Dylan*, recorded in November 1961 and released in March 1962. In keeping with the practice of the folk revival at the time, the album relied heavily on preexisting material, containing only two originals, both heavily indebted to Dylan's idol Woody Guthrie. The other songs on the album reveal what set Dylan apart from the rest of the folk performers: an eclectic mixture of material, which included renditions of hard-driving country blues that were first recorded by Blind Lemon Jefferson and Bukka White.

In fact, Dylan's performance style at this time owed a lot to the high-energy performances of the musicians he had emulated in high school: Little Richard, Jerry Lee Lewis, and Hank Williams. This performance style, which he combined in concert with Chaplinesque physical humor and a moodiness derived from the image of James Dean, makes it easy in

---

1. "Bob Dylan: A Distinctive Folk-Song Stylist," *New York Times*, September 29, 1961.

retrospect to see what made Dylan appear much hipper than the other "pure" folkies who tended to project a kind of somber earnestness. Furthermore, in another atypical move for a "folky," Dylan never denied the influence of overtly commercial musicians, and he moved quickly toward writing the majority of the songs he performed. Many of Dylan's protest songs, which addressed topical concerns of the day, stood out from other songs of their ilk in their use of allusion rather than straightforward description, a quality evident in his most famous song in the protest genre, "Blowin' in the Wind."

As described in the preceding article, Peter, Paul, and Mary's recording of "Blowin' in the Wind" provided a commercial breakthrough for Dylan, albeit as a songwriter, rather than as a performer. The trio followed with another hit recording of Dylan's "Don't Think Twice, It's Alright," and Dylan himself performed at one of the keystones of the civil rights movement in August 1963—the March on Washington in front of 200,000 people—an event that featured Dr. Martin Luther King's famous "I Have a Dream" speech. These events sealed an image of Dylan with the public as the conscience of his generation.[2]

With the arrival of the Beatles and other British groups, along with the emergence of Motown in 1964, folk music had already slipped from its 1963 peak of popularity even as it retained its core audience. However, the album Dylan recorded early in 1965, *Bringing It All Back Home*, along with the single released from it, "Subterranean Homesick Blues," constituted a serious threat to the aesthetic and political beliefs of the folk movement. Many of Dylan's new songs featured a driving rock 'n' roll beat, and the lyrics became increasingly surrealistic, drawing from the Beat poets, Walt Whitman, and the French symbolist Artur Rimbaud. While the songs did not directly address any recognizable political causes, their sarcastic and bizarrely imaginative humor contained a critique of society, albeit a fairly abstract one. Rather than specific causes, the targets were now the moral fabric and cultural assumptions of Western society itself, including sexual repression; materialism; received notions of "normality"; and the taken-for-granted beliefs in "reality," "truth," and "rationality."

In June 1965, Dylan followed *Bringing It All Back Home* with "Like a Rolling Stone," which featured the organ and electric guitar-led backing that would be most associated with him during this period. "Rolling Stone" ran over six-minutes long, an unheard-of length for a single, and became his biggest hit, reaching number two on the pop charts. "Rolling Stone" had been preceded onto the charts by an electrified version of Dylan's "Mr. Tambourine Man," recorded by the Los Angeles-based rock

---

2. For a vivid portrait of this period, see David Hajdu's account of the relationships among Dylan; Joan Baez; Baez's sister, Mimi (a folksinger in her own right); and Richard Fariña, husband of Mimi and author of *Been Down So Long It Looks Like Up to Me* (Hajdu, *Positively Fourth Street: The Lives and Times of Joan Baez, Bob Dylan, Mimi Baez Fariña, and Richard Fariña* [New York: Farrar, Straus and Giroux, 2001]). And, for an almost hagiographical depiction of Dylan and Baez circa 1964, see Fariña's article, "Baez and Dylan: A Generation Singing Out," *Mademoiselle*, 59, no. 4 (August 1964).

band, the Byrds. While Dylan's recording of "Tambourine Man" had appeared on *Bringing It All Back Home* with a muted electric guitar added to Dylan's voice, acoustic guitar, and harmonica, the Byrds added a rhythm used in recent hits, such as the Beach Boys' "Don't Worry Baby," and overlaid it with leader Roger McGuinn's electric 12-string guitar, and the distinctive harmony singing of David Crosby. The music industry and mass media recognized the combined impact of these recordings with the swiftly coined label, "folk-rock." Numerous cover versions of Dylan songs with electric backing, as well as countless imitations, swiftly appeared, all with "deep" and "relevant" lyrics—the most commercially successful of these imitations was "Eve of Destruction," recorded by Barry McGuire and written by P. F. Sloan (August 1965).[3]

As the folk-rock craze was gathering momentum, Dylan appeared in late July at the Newport Folk Festival, accompanied by members of the Butterfield Blues Band. A storm of controversy followed: The folk movement could no longer ignore Dylan's "defection," nor could certain contradictions in folk music's opposition to commerce be ignored. Dylan's hit single and his use of a rock 'n' roll band seemed to embody the very commercial forces to which the folk revival had seen itself in revolt.

The following two articles appeared in *Sing Out*, a major publication devoted to folk music, and they chart the reaction to Dylan's Newport appearance and a subsequent appearance in August at Forest Hills, New York. To folk purists, Dylan's move toward amplification and rock 'n' roll smacked of a "sellout"; to supporters of his new style, Dylan's music was becoming more personalized and conveyed a truer picture of the contemporary world. However, as the descriptions of the other performers at Newport indicate, even the split between "pure" folk and pop music revealed unsuspected complexity: All was not well with the urban folk music world's equation of simple, acoustic music with left-wing politics.

# Newport Folk Festival, 1965
## *Irwin Silber*

The Festival's most controversial scene was played out on the dramatically-lit giant stage halfway through the final night's concert when Bob Dylan emerged from his cult-imposed aura of mystery to demonstrate the new "folk rock," and [*sic*] expression that has already begun to find its way into the "Top Forty" charts by which musical success is measured. To many, it seemed that it was not very good "rock," while other disappointed legions did not think it was very good Dylan. Most of these erupted into silence at the conclusion of

---

3. For a contemporary overview of some of these recordings, see Robert Shelton, "On Records: The Folk-Rock Rage," *New York Times*, January 30, 1966, 17–18.

Dylan's songs, while a few booed their once-and-former idol. Others cheered and demanded encores, finding in the "new" Dylan an expression of themselves, just as teen aged social activists of 1963 had found themselves summed up in the angry young poet's vision.

Shocked and somewhat disoriented by the mixed reaction of the crowd, a tearful Dylan returned to the stage unelectrified and strained to communicate his sense of unexpected displacement through the words and music of a song he made fearfully appropriate, "It's All Over Now, Baby Blue."

But if the audience thought that the Dylan scene represented a premature climax to the evening, more was yet to come. A double finale (presumably a Newport tradition by now) saw hordes of singers, musicians, self-appointed participants and temporary freaks take over the stage in a tasteless exhibition of frenzied incest that seemed to have been taken from a Hollywood set. One singer called it a "nightmare of pop art," which was one of the more apt and gentle of the comments heard in the audience. The stage invasion took place during the singing of Mrs. Fannie Lou Hamer, one of that incredible band of Mississippi heroines who are in the process of reshaping America for us all. It seemed as though everyone wanted to make sure they were in on the big "civil rights act," and a moment that might have become the highpoint of the entire weekend was suddenly turned into a scene of opportunistic chaos—duplicated once again after the inevitable Peter, Paul and Mary finale and reducing the meaning of Newport to the sense of a carnival gone mad.

At the height of the frenzy, it was easy to forget the music and the conviction that had come before. There were many who thought they sensed a feeling of revulsion even among some of the Newport directors who were themselves participating in the debacle. And when the end finally came, the crowd filed out to the sound of a mournful and lonesome harmonica playing "Rock of Ages." It was the most optimistic note of the evening.

Here is the second of the accounts of the 1965 Newport Folk Festival.

## Newport Folk Festival, 1965

### *Paul Nelson*

For all its emphasis on tradition and its quiet highpoints (Roscoe Holcomb and Jean Ritchie singing "Wandering Boy" was my favorite among many), Newport is still a place for the Big Moment, the Great Wham, that minuscule second of High Drama that freezes the blood and sparks the brain into the kind of excitement that stays forever in one's memory. Nothing approaching such a moment happened at Newport in 1964 (it was a dull circus), but Bob Dylan provided it on Sunday night this year: the most dramatic scene I've ever witnessed in folk music.

Here are two accounts of it, the first sketched quickly in my notebook at the time:

"Dylan doing his new R&R, R&B, R&? stuff knocked me out. . . . I think his new stuff is as exciting as anything I've heard lately in any field. The Newport crowd actually booed the electric guitar numbers he did, and there followed the most dramatic thing I've seen: Dylan walking off the stage, the audience booing and yelling 'Get rid of that electric guitar,' Peter Yarrow trying to talk the audience into clapping and trying to talk Dylan into coming back,

Yarrow announcing that Dylan was coming back, George Wein asking Yarrow in disbelief '*Is* he coming back?' Dylan coming back with tears in his eyes and singing 'It's All Over Now, Baby Blue,' a song that I took to be his farewell to Newport, an incredible sadness over Dylan and the audience finally clapping now because the electric guitar was gone, etc." (Dylan did only his first three numbers with electric guitar and band.)

The second account is from a long report on Newport by Jim Rooney of Cambridge, Massachusetts:

"Nothing else in the festival caused such controversy. His (Dylan's) was the only appearance that was genuinely disturbing. It was disturbing to the Old Guard, I think, for several reasons. Bob is no longer a neo-Woody Guthrie, with whom they could identify. He has thrown away his dungarees and shaggy jacket. He has stopped singing talking blues and songs about 'causes'—peace or civil rights. The highway he travels now is unfamiliar to those who bummed around in the thirties during the Depression. He travels by plane. He wears high-heel shoes and high-style clothes from Europe. The mountains and valleys he knows are those of the mind—a mind extremely aware of the violence of the inner and outer world. 'The people' so loved by Pete Seeger are 'the mob' so hated by Dylan. In the face of violence, he has chosen to preserve himself alone. No one else. And he defies everyone else to have the courage to be as alone, as unconnected . . . as he. He screams through organ and drums and electric guitar, 'How does it feel to be on your own?' And there is no mistaking the hostility, the defiance, the contempt for all those thousands sitting before him who aren't on their own. Who can't make it. And they seemed to understand that night for the first time what Dylan has been trying to say for over a year—that he is not theirs or anyone else's—and they didn't like what they heard and booed. They wanted to throw him out. He had fooled them before when they thought he was theirs. . . . Pete (Seeger) had begun the night with the sound of a newborn baby crying, and asked that everyone sing to that baby and tell it what kind of a world it would be growing up into. But Pete already knew what he wanted others to sing. They were going to sing that it was a world of pollution, bombs, hunger, and injustice, but that PEOPLE would OVERCOME. . . . (But) can there be no songs as violent as the age? Must a folk song be of mountains, valleys, and love between my brother and my sister all over this land? Do we allow for despair only in the blues? . . . (That's all) very comfortable and safe. But is that what we should be saying to that baby? Maybe, maybe not. But we should ask the question. And the only one in the entire festival who questioned our position was Bob Dylan. Maybe he didn't put it in the best way. Maybe he was rude. But he shook us. And that is why we have poets and artists."

Indeed, that's why we have poets and artists. Newport 1965, interestingly enough, split apart forever the two biggest names in folk music: Pete Seeger, who saw in Sunday night a chance to project his vision of the world and sought to have all others convey his impression (thereby restricting their performances), and Bob Dylan, like some fierce young Spanish outlaw in dress leather jacket, a man who could no longer accept the older singer's vague humanistic generalities, a man who, like Nathaniel West, had his own angry vision to project in such driving electric songs as "Like a Rolling Stone" and "Maggie's Farm."

And, like it or not, the audience had to choose. Whether, on the one hand, to take the word of a dignified and great humanitarian whose personal sincerity is beyond question but whose public career more and more seems to be sliding like that other old radical Max Eastman's toward a *Reader's Digest* Norman Rockwell version of how things are (Pete's idea of singing peace songs to a newborn baby makes even the most middlebrow *Digest* ideas seem as far-out as anything William Burroughs ever did!); or whether to accept as truth the Donleavy-Westian-Brechtian world of Bob Dylan, where things aren't often pretty, where there isn't often hope, where man isn't always noble, but where, most importantly, there exists a reality that coincides with that of this planet. Was it to be marshmallows and cotton candy or meat and potatoes? Rose colored glasses or a magnifying glass? A nice guy who has subjugated and weakened his art through his constant insistence on a world that never was and never can be, or an angry, passionate poet who demands his art to be all, who demands not to be owned, not to be restricted or predicted, but only, like Picasso, to be left alone from petty criticisms to do his business, wherever that may take him?

Make no mistake, the audience had to make a clear-cut choice and they made it: Pete Seeger. They chose to boo Dylan off the stage for something as superficially silly as an electric guitar or something as stagnatingly sickening as their idea of owning an artist. They chose the safety of wishful thinking rather than the painful, always difficult stab of art. They might have believed they were choosing humanity over a reckless me-for-me attitude, but they weren't. They were choosing suffocation over invention and adventure, backwards over forwards, a dead hand instead of a live one. They were afraid, as was Pete Seeger (who was profoundly disturbed by Dylan's performance), to make a leap, to admit, to consider, to think. Instead, they took refuge in the Seeger vision as translated by the other less-pure-at-heart singers on the program, indeed, by all other than Seeger: the ghastly second half of Sunday night's program, where practically all forms of Social Significance ran completely out of control in a sickening display of egomania and a desperate grasping for publicity and fame [see Irwin Silber's account earlier in this chapter]. The second half of Sunday night (from all reports) was more ugly and hysterical than anything in a Dylan song; and, remember, the impetus for it was not Dylan at all, but Pete Seeger. (Ironically, although the audience chose the Seeger vision, it was a hollow victory for Pete, who felt he'd failed badly.)

It was a sad parting of the ways for many, myself included. I choose Dylan, I choose art. I will stand behind Dylan and his "new" songs, and I'll bet my critical reputation (such as it may be) that I'm right.

# 31. "Chaos Is a Friend of Mine"

With his move from self-accompanied topical songs to surrealistic lyrics accompanied by a rock band, Dylan's music became the focal point for a number of issues that still figure prominently in critical and fan discourse. Foremost among them is the issue of personal sincerity, or "authenticity," meaning, in this case, that the persona projected in performance is identical with the lived experience of the performer and that the performer is motivated by a desire to express his or her own feelings, not by a desire for financial gain. This idea of authenticity, as we have seen, figured prominently in the urban folk revival, which had adopted this idea from traditional music, where it was assumed that the participants were motivated by a desire to perpetuate a sense of community, rather than by commercial purposes. Some of this attitude transferred into the value system of the counterculture, which was sometimes described as a "community" (as in "Woodstock Nation"). Loyal fans of Dylan brought these ideas with them as he changed styles. Dylan (along with critics and fans) also merged this discourse of authenticity with another idea about authenticity—the notion, derived from Euro-modernism, that "artistic expression" is opposed to commercial interests as well (see, for example, Paul Nelson's article reprinted in chapter 30).[1]

Often arguments about authenticity in Dylan's songs were transferred to the ground of aesthetics (a transference that followed from the modernist view of the separation of art from commerce). Whereas arguments had previously raged over the quality of Dylan's voice, now these arguments were joined to discussions of whether or not his lyrics were poetry. University classes attempted to parse the meanings of his songs, and interviewers naively asked him to expound on his philosophy. These forms of attention signaled a new attitude toward popular music, as critical stances previously reserved for high art (or perhaps for urban folk music) were now shifted to certain types of popular music. This new critical attitude toward popular music is perhaps the most significant legacy of folk and folk-rock, in general, and of Dylan's musical career, in particular: Despite his relatively brief stay in the national media limelight, Dylan (together with the Beatles) demonstrated that the forms of rock 'n' roll did not forswear the possibility of "serious" content and that these forms were open to numerous permutations. Almost overnight, as it were, college audiences now found the most hip and intellectual forms of popular music to be acceptable listening material for dorm room pot-smoking sessions.[2]

What this newfound seriousness toward Dylan's lyrics seemed to miss at first is that whatever "profundity" the lyrics possessed was due as much to their delivery (i.e., the fact that they were sung by Dylan) and surrounding musical context as to their relative complexity compared to other folk and popular music—which isn't to say that Dylan didn't do more than any other individual to expand the subject matter of popular music and change notions of what song lyrics could be.[3] As for Dylan's singing, the fact that it wasn't conventionally "pretty" in the vein of many

1. The transference of the idea of community from the urban folk revival to rock music is explored by Simon Frith in "'The Magic That Can Set You Free': the Ideology of Folk and the Myth of the Rock Community." In *Popular Music 1: Folk or Popular? Distinctions, Influences, Continuities,* ed. David Horn and Richard Middleton, (Cambridge, England: Cambridge University Press, 1981), 159–68; for a discussion of Dylan as modernist artist, see Greil Marcus, *Invisible Republic: Bob Dylan's Basement Tapes* (New York: Henry Holt, 1997), 1–41.

2. See Nick Bromell, *Tomorrow Never Knows: Rock and Psychedelics in the 1960s* (Chicago: University of Chicago Press, 2000).

3. An illuminating contemporary discussion of this phenomenon is Robert Christgau's, "Rock Lyrics Are Poetry (Maybe)," in Jonathan Eisen, ed., *The Age of Rock: Sounds of the American Cultural Revolution* (New York: Random House, 1969), 230–43. First published in *Cheetah* in December 1967.

other folk singers owed much to his early interest in rock 'n' roll and country blues. When his voice is heard with this background in mind, the "shift" to rock 'n' roll does not come as a surprise.

One amusing result of the sudden increase in public interest in Dylan, much of it by media that had previously avoided popular music or had condescended to it, was a vast increase in the number of interviews given by Dylan. These media performances throughout 1965–66 grew increasingly surreal as Dylan took a creative approach to the interview situation. Because his lyrics were more "serious" and "poetic" than those found in previous pop songs, he was barraged with questions about what the songs meant, which he steadfastly refused to answer. One of the most famous interviews from that period, conducted by Nat Hentoff (a famous jazz critic, social commentator, and a writer who was not likely to ask naive questions), provides a particularly amusing exchange on the subject of "message songs." When asked why he thought message songs were vulgar, Dylan replied, "You've got to respect other people's right to also have a message themselves. Myself, what I'm going to do is rent Town Hall and put about 30 Western Union boys on the bill. I mean, then there'll *really* be some messages. People will be able to come and hear more messages than they've ever heard before in their life."[4]

The following interview, from 1965, occurred after Dylan's Forest Hills, New York, concert in August and was conducted by Nora Ephron and Susan Edmiston. Ephron, who began her career in journalism, is now well known for her work in films as a screenwriter, director, and producer (*When Harry Met Sally, Sleepless in Seattle, You've Got Mail,* and many others). This interview provides glimpses of Dylan's surreal humor, as Ephron and Edmiston found him in an unusually agreeable mood. Particular points of interest are Dylan's comments on folk music, the value of contemporary R&B, and his critique of the institutions of high art.

## BOB DYLAN INTERVIEW
### *Nora Ephron and Susan Edmiston*

*This interview took place in late summer of 1965 in the office of Dylan's manager Albert Grossman. Dylan had just been booed in the historic Forest Hills concert where he abandoned folk purity to the use of electric accompaniment. He was wearing a red-and-navy op-art shirt, a navy blazer and pointy high-heeled boots. His face so sharp and harsh when translated through the media, was then*

---

4. Nat Hentoff, "The Playboy Interview: Bob Dylan—A Candid Conversation with the Iconoclastic Idol of the Folk-Rock Set," *Playboy* (March 1966); reprinted in *Bob Dylan: The Early Years: A Retrospective,* ed. Craig McGregor (New York: Da Capo Press, [1972] 1990), 132–33.

*Source:* Nora Ephron and Susan Edmiston, "Bob Dylan Interview," in Craig McGregor, ed., *Bob Dylan: The Early Years: A Retrospective*, 82–90. New York: William Morrow, 1972.

*infinitely soft and delicate. His hair was not bushy or electric or Afro; it was fine-spun soft froth like the foam of a wave. He looked like an underfed angel with a nose from the land of the Chosen People.*

*Some American folk singers—Carolyn Hester, for example—say that what you're now doing, the new sound, "folk rock," is liberating them.*
Did Carolyn say that? You tell her she can come around and see me any time now that she's liberated.

*Does labeling, using the term "folk rock," tend to obscure what's happening?*
Yes.

*It's like "pop gospel." What does the term mean to you?*
Yeah, classical gospel could be the next trend. There's country rock, rockabilly. What does it mean to me? Folk rock. I've never even said that word. It has a hard gutter sound. Circussy atmosphere. It's nose thumbing. Sound like you're looking down on what is . . . fantastic, great music.

*The definition most often given of folk rock is the combination of the electric sound of rock and roll with the meaningful lyrics of folk music. Does that sum up what you're doing?*
Yes. It's very complicated to play with electricity. You play with other people. You're dealing with other people. Most people don't like to work with other people, it's more difficult. It takes a lot. Most people who don't like rock and roll can't relate to other people.

*You mention the Apollo Theatre in Harlem on one of your album covers. Do you go there often?*
Oh, I couldn't go up there. I used to go up there a lot about four years ago. I even wanted to play in one of the amateur nights, but I got scared. Bad things can happen to you. I saw what the audience did to a couple of guys they didn't like. And I would have had a couple of things against me right away when I stepped out on the stage.

*Who is Mr. Jones in "Ballad of a Thin Man"?*
He's a real person. You know him, but not by that name.

*Like Mr. Charlie?*
No. He's more than Mr. Charlie. He's actually a person. Like I saw him come into the room one night and he looked like a camel. He proceeded to put his eyes in his pocket. I asked this guy who he was and he said, "That's Mr. Jones." Then I asked this cat, "Doesn't he do anything but put his eyes in his pocket?" And he told me, "He puts his nose on the ground." It's all there, it's a true story.

*Where did you get that shirt?*
California. Do you like it? You should see my others. You can't get clothes like that here. There are a lot of things out there we haven't got here.

*Isn't California on the way here?*
It's uptight here compared to there. Hollywood I mean. It's not really breathable here. It's like there's air out there. The Sunset Strip can't be compared to anything here, like 42nd Street. The people there look different, they look more like . . . you want to kiss them out there.

*Do you spend a lot of time out there?*
I don't have much time to spend anywhere: The same thing in England. In England everybody looks very hip East Side. They wear things . . . they don't wear things that bore you. They've got other hang-ups in other directions.

*Do you consider yourself primarily a poet?*
No. We have our ideas about poets. The word doesn't mean any more than the word "house." There are people who write *po*ems and people who write po*ems*. Other people write *poems*. Everybody who writes poems do you call them a poet? There's a certain kind of rhythm in some kind of way that's visible. You don't necessarily have to write to be a poet. Some people work in gas stations and they're poets. I don't call myself a poet because I don't like the word. I'm a trapeze artist.

*What I meant was, do you think your words stand without the music?*
They would stand but I don't read them. I'd rather sing them. I write things that aren't songs—I have a book coming out.

*What is it?*
It's a book of words.

*Is it like the back of your albums? It seemed to me that the album copy you write is a lot like the writing of William Burroughs. Some of the accidental sentences—*
Cut-ups.

*Yes, and some of the imagery and anecdotes. I wondered if you had read anything by him.*
I haven't read *Naked Lunch* but I read some of his shorter things in little magazines, foreign magazines. I read one in Rome. I know him. I don't really know him—I just met him once. I think he's a great man.

*Burroughs keeps an album, a collection of photographs that illustrate his writing. Do you have anything similar to that?*
I do that too. I have photographs of "Gates of Eden" and "It's All Over Now, Baby Blue." I saw them after I wrote the songs. People send me a lot of things and a lot of the things are pictures, so other people must have that idea too. I gotta admit, maybe I wouldn't have chosen them, but I can see what it is about the pictures.

*I heard you used to play the piano for Buddy Holly.*
No. I used to play the rock and roll piano, but I don't want to say who it was for because the cat will try to get hold of me. I don't want to see the cat. He'll try to reclaim the friendship. I did it a long time ago, when I was seventeen years old. I used to play a country piano too.

*This was before you became interested in folk music?*
Yes. I became interested in folk music because I had to make it somehow. Obviously I'm not a hard-working cat. I played the guitar, that was all I did. I thought it was great music. Certainly I haven't turned my back on it or anything like that. There is—and I'm sure nobody realizes this, all the authorities who write about what it is and what it should be, when they say keep things simple, they should be easily understood—folk music is the only music where it isn't simple. It's never been simple. It's weird, man, full of legend, myth, Bible and ghosts. I've never written anything hard to understand, not in my head anyway, and nothing as far out as some of the old songs. They were out of sight.

*Like what songs?*
"Little Brown Dog." "I bought a little brown dog, its face is all gray. Now I'm going to Turkey flying on my bottle." And "Nottemun Town," that's like a herd of ghosts passing through on the way to Tangiers. "Lord Edward," "Barbara Allen," they're full of myth.

*And contradictions?*
Yeah, contradictions.

*And chaos?*
Chaos, watermelon, clocks, everything.

*You wrote on the back on one album, "I accept chaos but does chaos accept me."*
Chaos is a friend of mine. It's like I accept him, does he accept me.

*Do you see the world as chaos?*
Truth is chaos. Maybe beauty is chaos.

*Poets like Eliot and Yeats—*
I haven't read Yeats.

*They saw the world as chaos, accepted it as chaos and attempted to bring order from it. Are you trying to do that?*
No. It exists and that's all there is to it. It's been here longer than I have. What can I do about it? I don't know what the songs I write are. That's all I do is write songs, right? Write. I collect things too.

*Monkey wrenches?*
Where did you read about that? Has that been in print? I told this guy out on the coast that I collected monkey wrenches, all sizes and shapes of monkey wrenches, and he didn't believe me. I don't think you believe me either. And I collect the pictures too. Have you talked to Sonny and Cher?

*No.*
They're a drag. A cat gets kicked out of a restaurant and he went home and wrote a song about it.[5]

*They say your fan mail has radically increased since you switched sounds.*
Yeah. I don't have time to read all of it, but I want you to put that I answer half of it. I don't really. A girl does that for me.

*Does she save any for you—any particularly interesting letters?*
She knows my head. Not the ones that just ask for pictures, there's a file for them. Not the ones that say, I want to make it with you, they go in another file. She saves two kinds. The violently put-down—

*The ones that call you a sellout?*
Yeah. Sellout, fink, Fascist, Red, everything in the book. I really dig those. And ones from old friends.

*Like, "You don't remember me but I was in the fourth grade with you"?*
No. I never had any friends then. These are letters from people who knew me in New York five, six years ago. My first fans. Not the people who call themselves my first fans. They came in three years ago, two years ago. They aren't really my first fans.

*How do you feel about being booed at your concert at Forest Hills?*
I thought it was great, I really did. If I said anything else I'd be a liar.

*And at the Newport Folk Festival?*
That was different. They twisted the sound. They didn't like what I was going to play and they twisted the sound on me before I began.

---

5. Dylan is referring here to lyrics of the song "Laugh at Me," which were credited to Sonny of Sonny and Cher. The song was popular at the time of this interview.

*I heard you were wearing a sellout jacket.*
What kind of jacket is a sellout jacket?

*Black leather.*
I've had black leather jackets since I was five years old. I've been wearing black leather all my life.

*I wonder if we could talk about electronic music and what made you decide to use it.*
I was doing fine, you know, singing and playing my guitar. It was a sure thing, don't you understand, it was a sure thing. I was getting very bored with that. I couldn't go out and play like that. I was thinking of quitting. Out front it was a sure thing. I knew what the audience was gonna do, how they would react. It was very automatic. Your mind just drifts unless you can find some way to get in there and remain totally there. It's so much of a fight remaining totally there all by yourself. It takes too much. I'm not ready to cut that much out of my life. You can't have nobody around. You can't be bothered with anybody else's world. And I like people. What I'm doing now—it's a whole other thing. We're not playing rock music. It's not a hard sound. These people call it folk rock—if they want to call it that, something that simple, it's good for selling records. As far as it being what it is, I don't know what it is. I can't call it folk rock. It's a whole way of doing things. It has been picked up on, I've heard songs on the radio that have picked it up. I'm not talking about words. It's a certain feeling, and it's been on every single record I've ever made. That has not changed. I know it hasn't changed. As far as what I was totally, before, maybe I was pushing it a little then. I'm not pushing things now. I know it. I know very well how to do it. The problem of how I want to play something—I know it in front. I know what I'm going to say, what I'm going to do. I don't have to work it out. The band I work with—they wouldn't be playing with me if they didn't play like I want them to. I have this song, "Queen Jane Approximately"—

*Who is Queen Jane?*
Queen Jane is a man.

*Was there something that made you decide to change sounds? Your trip to England?*
I like the sound. I like what I'm doing now. I would have done it before. It wasn't practical to do it before. I spent most of my time writing. I wouldn't have had the time. I had to get where I was going all alone. I don't know what I'm going to do next. I probably will record with strings some time, but it doesn't necessarily change. It's just a different color. And I know that it's real. No matter what anybody says. They can boo till the end of time. I know that the music is real, more real than the boos.

*How do you work?*
Most of the time I work at night. I don't really like to think of it as work. I don't know how important it is. It's not important to the average cat who works eight hours a day. What does he care? The world can get along very well without it. I'm hip to that.

*Sure, but the world can get along without any number of things.*
I'll give you a comparison. Rudy Vallee. Now that was a lie, that was a downright lie. Rudy Vallee being popular. What kind of people could have dug him? You know, your grandmothers and mothers. But what kind of people were they? He was so sexless. If you want to find out about those times and you listen to his music you're not going to find out anything about the times. His music was a pipedream. All escapes. There are no more escapes. If you want to find out anything that's happening now, you have to listen to the music. I don't mean the words, although "Eve of Destruction" will tell you something about it. The words are not really gonna tell it, not really. You gotta listen to

the Stapes Singers, Smokey and the Miracles, Martha and the Vandellas. That's scary to a lot of people. It's sex that's involved. It's not hidden. It's real. You can overdo it. It's not only sex, it's a whole beautiful feeling.

*But Negro rhythm and blues has been around underground for at least twelve years. What brought it out now?*

The English did that. They brought it out. They hipped everybody. You read an interview asking who the Beatles' favorite singer was and they say Chuck Berry. You never used to hear Chuck Berry records on the radio, hard blues. The English did that. England is great and beautiful, though in other ways kinda messy. Though not outside London.

*In what way messy?*

There's a snobbishness. What you see people doing to other people. It's not only class. It's not that simple. It's a kind of Queen kind of thing. Some people are royalty and some are not. Here, man, somebody don't like you he tells you. There it's very tight, tight kinds of expressions, their whole tone of speaking changes. It's an everyday kind of thing. But the kids are a whole other thing. Great. They're just more free. I hope you don't think I take this too seriously—I just have a headache.

*I think you started out to say that music was more in tune with what's happening than other art forms.*

Great paintings shouldn't be in museums. Have you ever been in a museum? Museums are cemeteries. Paintings should be on the walls of restaurants, in dime stores, in gas stations, in men's rooms. Great paintings should be where people hang out. The only thing where it's happening is on the radio and records, that's where people hang out. You can't see great paintings. You pay half a million and hang one in your house and one guest sees it. That's not art. That's a shame, a crime. Music is the only thing that's in tune with what's happening. It's not in book form, it's not on the stage. All this art they've been talking about is nonexistent. It just remains on the shelf. It doesn't make anyone happier. Just think how many people would really feel great if they could see a Picasso in their daily diner. It's not the bomb that has to go, man, it's the museums.

# 32. From R&B to Soul

The mid-1950s represented a time of relative rapprochement between rhythm and blues and mainstream pop that found its greatest expression in early rock 'n' roll. Despite the overlapping of the two categories, however, rhythm and blues did maintain a distinct style, as well as its own audience and set of connotations. As Ray Charles noted in the excerpt from his autobiography in chapter 17, before the release of "What'd I Say" in 1959, his music had not been programmed on Top 40 radio, nor had it found much support among the portion of the rock 'n' roll audience constituted by white teenagers. The same is true of numerous other R&B stars, including Dinah Washington and James Brown, who enjoyed a succession of hits on the R&B charts but rarely, if ever, crossed over.[1] These singers' styles were heavily indebted to gospel music, and the singers continued to embrace themes in their lyrics that were not obviously directed toward teenagers. The use of gospel vocal technique in secular music, as pioneered by Charles and Clyde McPhatter, was increasingly adopted by R&B singers as the 1950s waned, and was one of the main musical factors involved in the gradual acquisition of a new name for R&B: soul music. In addition to its association with a cluster of musical practices, the ascendancy of the term "soul music" is inextricably linked to the growth of the civil rights movement.

Along with Ray Charles and James Brown (who began recording in 1956), two other artists form an important link between the gospel-influenced R&B of the 1950s and soul music of the 1960s: Sam Cooke (1935–64) and Jackie Wilson (1934–84). Although both artists experienced crossover success in the late 1950s and early 1960s, Cooke's career formed an early template for the extensive mainstream success of the African American singers who were to follow. Cooke used the smooth and sophisticated vocal technique that he developed in the popular gospel group, the Soul Stirrers, to record a major crossover hit in 1957, "You Send Me," as well as numerous other hits. Cooke's approach to ballads, which conveyed an understated spirituality and sensuality, was a major influence on soul singers of the 1960s and 1970s, such as Otis Redding and Al Green, while his involvement in the management of his own career also established an important precedent for subsequent black stars.

It was a number of newcomers, however, who signaled the stirrings of a recognizable soul genre when they began in the early 1960s to record songs that merged spiritual fervor with secular topics. Among the many emerging talents were Solomon Burke ("Cry to Me," 1962), Wilson Pickett ("I Found a Love," with the Falcons, 1962), Otis Redding ("These Arms of Mine," 1962), and Etta James (who, after an early hit as a teenager with "The Wallflower," racked up a string of hits in the early 1960s). In addition to the melismas, bent notes, and wide range of timbres employed by these singers, their hit recordings from this period (almost all of which were in a slow tempo) prominently featured triplet subdivisions that were often articulated in arpeggiations played by piano or guitar; they also frequently featured interjected "sermons" that usually took the form of romantic advice addressed to the audience. Many of these artists recorded for either Atlantic or Stax, which had a distribution deal with Atlantic for a time.

While it may seem as if no genre could make stronger claims about cultural purity than soul music, Solomon Burke describes the unique blend—"multicultural" before the phrase existed—that contributed to

---

1. Dinah Washington did enjoy several pop hits beginning in the late fifties until her death in 1963 after she started recording with increasingly lush arrangements.

the Atlantic sound:

> Ahmet would come in to a session and ask you if you wanted a pastrami sandwich. He'd order it from the Jewish deli, then start yakking in French on another phone. Some wheezy cat from Bogalusa's on tenor sax, working at a carton of takeout Cantonese. A pleasant Jewish man name of Wexler is cussing out a late drummer with some mighty greasy Lenox Avenue jive. Me, the black preacher, the apprentice mortician from Philadelphia, standing at the mike. Singing country and western. Now what would I call those years at Atlantic? Broadway fricassee.[2]

The excerpt from James Baldwin's novel, *The Fire Next Time*, vividly depicts the central importance of the church and gospel music in the upbringing of African Americans of his generation. This wellspring of ecstatic spiritual power received more and more direct expression in African American popular music during the 1960s.

## *from* THE FIRE NEXT TIME
### *James Baldwin*

There is no music like that music, no drama like the drama of the saints rejoicing, the sinners moaning, the tambourines racing, and all those voices coming together and crying holy unto the Lord. I have never seen anything to equal the fire and excitement that sometimes, without warning, fill a church, causing the church, as Leadbelly and so many others have testified, to "rock." Nothing that has happened to me since equals the power and the glory that I sometimes felt when . . . the church and I were one. Their pain and their joy were mine, and mine were theirs . . . and their cries of "Amen!" "Hallelujah!" and "Yes, Lord!" "Praise His name!" "Preach it brother!" sustained and whipped on my solos until we all became equal, wringing wet singing and dancing in anguish and rejoicing, at the foot of the altar.

There was a zest and a joy and a capacity for facing and surviving disaster that are very moving and very rare. Perhaps we were, all of us—pimps whores, racketeers, church members, and children—bound together by the nature of our oppression. If so, within these limits we sometimes achieved with each other a freedom that was close to love. I remember, anyway, church suppers and outings, and, later, after I left the church, rent and waistline parties where rage and sorrow sat in the darkness and did not stir, and we ate and drank and talked and laughed and danced and forgot all about "the man."

This is the freedom that one hears in some gospel songs, for example, and in jazz. In all jazz, and especially in the blues, there is something tart and ironic, authoritative and double edged. White Americans do not understand the depths out of which such an ironic tenacity comes but they suspect that the force is sensual. To be sensual, I think, is to respect and rejoice in the force of life, of life itself, and to be present in all that one does, from the effort of living to the breaking of bread.

> Because of his position of importance at Atlantic, Jerry Wexler held a good vantage point for recounting central events in the R&B world during the early- to mid-1960s. In this excerpt from his autobiography, he describes his work with Wilson Pickett and Stax records and the memorable occasion of the recording of "In the Midnight Hour."

---

2. Gerri Hirshey, *Nowhere to Run: The Story of Soul Music* (New York: Penguin Books, [1984] 1985), 80.

*Source:* James Baldwin, *The Fire Next Time* (excerpt). (New York: Dial Press, 1963).

# from RHYTHM AND THE BLUES: A LIFE IN AMERICAN MUSIC

## Jerry Wexler and David Ritz

*Pickett* was a pistol. I called him the Black Panther even before the phrase was political. He had matinee-idol looks, flaming eyes, lustrous ebony skin, a sleek, muscular torso. His temperament was fire, his flash-and-fury singing style a study in controlled aggression, his blood-curdling scream always musical, always in tune. In the mid-sixties Wicked Wilson Pickett mainlined American music with a hefty dose of undiluted soul. Three decades later, his steel-belted hits like "Funky Broadway," "Mustang Sally," "In the Midnight Hour," and "Midnight Mover" have lost none of their tread.

Pickett told me he wanted to be on Atlantic when we met in my Broadway office in 1964. This was only a year after the fight over "If You Need Me"—Wilson Pickett versus Solomon Burke—and I asked if that hadn't pissed him off.[3]

"Fuck that," he said. "I need the bread."

I sent Wilson into the studio with Bert Berns . . . but all I got back was a single, a seven-thousand-dollar production bill (outrageous for those days), and no hits. Pickett was obstreperous, and Bert abrasive; the chemistry couldn't work. So I took it upon myself to find the songs; but what I liked, Wilson didn't, and vice versa. For a year we did the dance of the fireflies. We couldn't get it together. I knew what a powerhouse singer he was, and it was killing me.

Finally I got an idea—not for a song but for a trip: me and Pickett to Memphis, whose freshness just might give us the edge. And instead of trying to provide material, I urged him—with local genius Steve Cropper—to create his own. I put the two of them in a hotel room with a bottle of Jack Daniel's and the simple exhortation—"Write!"—which they did. When we got in that beat-up old movie theater on East McLemore, the place was rocking, the speakers nearly blown by the power of Wayne Jackson's punctuated horns. One of the songs was "In the Midnight Hour." I loved the lyric and the gospel fervor; Cropper inspired Pickett's truest passion. Originally from Prattville, Alabama, the Wicked One was back home, raising hell.

I was taken with everything but the rhythm pattern. Jim Stewart was at the board setting knobs, and I was working the talkback, directing the vocal, when I suddenly realized I was on the wrong side of the glass.

"Jerry amazed us," Cropper told Jann Wenner for a piece in *Rolling Stone*. "He ran out of the booth and started dancing."

"The bass thing was Wexler's idea," Duck Dunn said. "We were going another way when Jerry started doing the jerk dance."

I was shaking my booty to a groove made popular by the Larks' "The Jerk," a mid-sixties hit. The idea was to push the second beat while holding back the fourth—something easier demonstrated than explained. The boys caught it, put it in the pocket, and sent Pickett flying up the charts. "Midnight Hour" was a stone smash, Wilson's vocal a cyclone of conviction. The song became a bar-band anthem; the MG's incorporated the little rhythm variation into their playing from then on.

---

3. The previous year, Wexler and Atlantic records had released a cover of Pickett's "If You Need Me," recorded by Solomon Burke, that surpassed the sales of Pickett's recording.

*Source:* From *Rhythm and the Blues: A Life in American Music* by Jerry Wexler and David Ritz, pp. 175–76. Copyright © 1993 by Jerry Wexler and David Ritz. Used by permission of Alfred A. Knopf, a division of Random House, Inc.

# 33. No Town Like Motown

As the term "soul music" began to enter mainstream usage, black popular music increasingly cut its ties with 1950s rhythm and blues to establish a distinctive 1960s soul genre. At the same time, differences began to emerge between a down-home, "southern" soul style—identified with the Stax and Atlantic recording companies and with studios based in Memphis and Muscle Shoals, Alabama–and a "northern," "smooth," or "uptown" soul style—identified primarily with Motown Records based in Detroit.

The story of Motown is so remarkable as to become the stuff of myth. Aspiring songwriter Berry Gordy (b. 1929 and the writer of Jackie Wilson's biggest hit, "Lonely Teardrops") began the company on a family loan of $700 in 1959. Gordy's keen ear for catchy tunes and infectious rhythms, along with his deft judgment of personnel and his business sense, combined to establish Motown as both the most successful independent record company and the most successful black-owned business in the United States by the mid-1960s.

Initially, Motown's musical style blended in with other developments in R&B and pop with its successful recordings by girl groups (e.g., the Marvellettes, "Please Mr. Postman," 1961) and soulful ballads (e.g., the Miracles, "You Really Got a Hold on Me," 1963). Gradually a distinctive style began to coalesce; "Heat Wave" (1963) by Martha and the Vandellas provides a template: Written and produced by the songwriting team of Holland-Dozier-Holland (the most successful of such teams at the company), the recording features Martha Reeves's gospel-influenced vocal over an irresistibly danceable groove and an instantly memorable melody. Between 1964 and 1972, Motown produced an extraordinary number of hits; its roster of artists included many of the leading names of 1960s soul: (in addition to those already noted) the Supremes, the Four Tops, the Temptations, Marvin Gaye, Mary Wells, Junior Walker and the All Stars, Smokey Robinson (songwriter and leader of the Miracles), Stevie Wonder, the Isley Brothers, and Gladys Knight and the Pips. The sound, while frequently stereotyped as being only "sweet" and "pop," actually ranged from the pop stylings of the Supremes ("Where Did Our Love Go?" "Baby Love," "Come See About Me"—all from 1964–65) to the downright fonkiness of Junior Walker and the All Stars ("Shotgun," 1965).[1]

---

1. For more on the stylistic range of Motown, see Jon Fitzgerald, "Motown Crossover Hits 1963–1966 and the Creative Process," *Popular Music*, 14, no. 1 (January 1995): 1–12; for a less-than-flattering account of the company, see Nelson George, *Where Did Our Love Go? The Rise and Fall of the Motown Sound* (New York: St. Martin's Press, 1985).

The following portrait of life at Motown consists of excerpts from Berry Gordy's autobiography. Here Gordy discusses many aspects of Motown that made the company unique: the importance of Motown's house band and its approach to recording, the development of a "finishing school" to ensure a consistent public style and image for Motown artists, and strategies for dealing with race. These excerpts include Gordy's profiles of many of the most important artists to record for the company, including the discovery of the Jackson Five. Gordy, begins by discussing Motown's house band, the Funk Brothers, who, while responsible for the distinctive instrumental sound of the 1960s' recordings, received no credit on the liner notes.[2]

## *from* TO BE LOVED: THE MUSIC, THE MAGIC, THE MEMORIES OF MOTOWN
### *Berry Gordy*

Probably the two musicians who were the key for me in this loosely organized group were Benny Benjamin on drums and James Jamerson on bass. The other two members that made up the core of the Funk Brothers were Earl Van Dyke (on piano) and Robert White (on guitar). Others included from time to time Joe Hunter (piano), Eddie Willis (guitar), Johnny Griffith (piano), Joe Messina and David Hamilton (guitar), drummers Uriel Jones and Richard "Pistol" Allen, and percussionists Eddie "Bongo" Brown, Jack Ashford, and Jack Brokensha. Our saxophonist/flute player extraordinaire was Thomas "Beans" Bowles—nicknamed "Beans" for being tall and thin like a stringbean. I had first spotted him at the Flame Show Bar, playing in Maurice King's band, and used him on the "Come To Me" session. Maurice King also joined Motown, where he wore many hats.

Whenever a new player came into the group the sound would change slightly, based on his style.

Artists sang background on each other's sessions, or played the tambourine or clapped their hands; any employee who could carry a tune or keep a beat was used.

Each person—whether directly in the creative process or behind the scenes—somehow affected the mix.

The love we felt for each other when we were playing is the most undisputed truth about our music. I sometimes referred to our sound as a combination of rats, roaches, soul, guts and love.

On my sessions we'd work from handwritten chord sheets. The "feel" was usually the first thing I'd go for. After locking in the drumbeat, I'd hum a line for each musician to start. Once we got going, we'd usually ad lib all over the place until we got the groove I wanted. Many of these guys came from a Jazz background. I understood their instincts to turn things

---

2. A recent documentary, *Standing in the Shadows of Motown* (2002) seeks to redress this neglect of the Funk Brothers. George's *Where Did Our Love Go* also gives the musicians their due.

*Source:* Berry Gordy, *To Be Loved: The Music, the Magic, the Memories of Motown* (New York: Warner Books, Inc., 1994), pp. 129–30, 230–34, 253–55, 290–91, 313–16.

around to their liking, but I also knew what I wanted, to hear—commercially. So when they went too far, I'd stop them and stress, "We gotta get back to the funk—stay in that groove." Then I'd make it as plain as possible: I would extend my arms a certain distance apart, saying, "I want to stay between here and there. Do whatever you want but stay in this range, in the pocket." But between "here and there" they did all kinds of stuff—always pushing me to the limit and beyond. Especially Jamerson.

James Jamerson was a genius on the bass. He was an incredible improviser in the studio and someone I always wanted on my sessions. He'd get a simple chord sheet and build his own bass line so intricately it was hard to duplicate. Even he had trouble. That was great for the record, but when he stayed in Detroit and other musicians went out on the road to play the song live, they'd go crazy trying to play his lines. Some of the stuff he did on the bass, people are still trying to figure out today.

Another musician I had to have on all my sessions was Benny Benjamin. He was so good on the drums and had a feel no one could match. He had a distinctive knack for executing various rhythms all at the same time. He had a pulse, a steadiness that kept the tempo better than a metronome. Benny was my man.

Long before there were electronic synthesizers, I was looking for new ways to create different sound effects, We would try anything to get a unique percussion sound: two blocks of wood slapped together, striking little mallets on glass ashtrays, shaking jars of dried peas—anything. I might see a producer dragging in big bike chains or getting a whole group of people stomping on the floor.

Never having forgotten that big orchestral sound from the Jackie Wilson "Lonely Teardrops" session, I tried to recreate it in our own studio, often bringing in string players from the Detroit Symphony. At first they had no idea what to make of me or how their music would fit into ours. But in time they became an integral part of the Motown family and our sound.

Another regular aspect of our early productions was the background voices of the Andantes—Judith Barrow, Louvain Demps, Jacqueline Hicks—another backup group.

Since many producers, myself included, lacked a lot of formal music education, when it came time to merge all these different elements, we sometimes looked for help from some of our arrangers. In the process, the talents of such people as Johnny Allen, Willie Shorter, Paul Riser and Hank Cosby would also leave a distinctive mark on our music.

Mixing was so important to me that it seemed I spent half my life at the mixing board. To get just the right sound, just the right blend, I would mix and mix and then remix. Smokey and I had a running joke over what a mix maniac I was.

Often the differences between the various mixes were subtle; but those subtleties, I felt, could make or break a record.

Whether I was cutting a record, mixing it or listening to someone else's, I was open to just about anything.

I may not have always known what I was looking for exactly, but when I found it I knew it. While open to a broad range of influences—Gospel, Pop, Rhythm & Blues, Jazz, Doo-Wop, Country—I always emphasized simple, clear communication.

When I look back at these years from 1965 to 1968 it seems we could do no wrong. The stream of hits was endless. The whole world was fast becoming aware of our overall success—our artists, our songs, our sound. I was being called the star maker, the magic man.

During that time, at Hitsville, a battle for another kind of supremacy continued. For our first five years the strongest thread in our musical tapestry had been sewn by Smokey with his clever, poetic lines pushing the Miracles, Mary Wells and the Tempts to the top. Now the texture was being dominated by the Holland-Dozier-Holland hooky, simple—yet deep, driving, melodic overtures. But the competition to stay on top was no small matter for HDH. When they gave Marvin another hit with "How Sweet It Is (To Be Loved By You)" Smokey answered with "My Girl" on the Temptations, their first #1 record. HDH then hit again on Martha and the Vandellas with "Nowhere To Run." Smokey came back with one of the sexiest records of his career, "Ooo Baby Baby," on the Miracles.

There was no stopping HDH, whose #1 "I Hear A Symphony" on the Supremes became one of my favorites of that era. HDH seemed to hit as easily on newer artists like the Isley Brothers' "This Old Heart Of Mine (Is Weak For You)," Shorty Long's "Function At The Junction" and the Elgins's "Heaven Must Have Sent You."

HDH benefited from my policy that, if two records under consideration were equally strong, the release would be given to the producer who had the last hit. In addition to the monster hits on the Supremes, in the next couple years they would give the Four Tops five smashes: "I Can't Help Myself (Sugar Pie, Honey Bunch)," "It's The Same Old Song," "Reach Out I'll Be There," "Standing In The Shadows Of Love" and "Bernadette." I loved them all but for me "Bernadette" would epitomize the Holland-Dozier-Holland genius for capturing a listener's ear and not letting it go. It also helped fuel my belief that Levi Stubbs of the Four Tops could interpret and deliver the meaning of a song better than anybody. He made Bernadette live. I wanted to meet her myself.

What was equally remarkable was that though Smokey was on the road most of the time he continued to compete, often writing or producing with fellow Miracles Ronnie White, Pete Moore and Bobby Rogers, as well as longtime friend, Marv Tarplin, the group's guitar player. These different collaborators produced hits on the Miracles like "Going To A Go-Go," "The Tracks Of My Tears," "I Second that Emotion" and "More Love," and on other artists like the Marvelettes with "Don't Mess With Bill" and Marvin Gaye with "I'll Be Doggone" and "Ain't that Peculiar."

"Tracks Of My Tears" brought out something about Marv Tarplin and Smokey working together that always touched a dramatic chord with me. It became my favorite song of theirs. I began calling it a masterpiece.

Smokey was now more confident than ever. It looked like he couldn't lose. Then, after he had kept almost a complete hold on the Tempts for about three years, he did "Get Ready" in early 1966. It went to #1 on the R&B charts but couldn't get past #29 Pop. A crack in Smokey's armor. That was all Norman Whitfield needed.

At the Friday meeting Norman sat confidently as we listened to his new production on the Tempts—"Ain't Too Proud To Beg." The reactions were mixed, from "I hate it" to "It's a big hit."

I was the last one to give my opinion. "I love the feel—it's street," I said. "But it doesn't have enough meat. I gotta hear more story."

The next week Norman was back with an improved "Ain't Too Proud To Beg." It got more votes, but was again rejected. Norman looked crushed when the group went along with my "Not quite there."

But the following week he was back—and taking no prisoners. David Ruffin's voice came jumping off that record begging like I'd never heard before—

*I know you wonna leave me,*
*but I refuse to let you go.*
*If I have to beg, plead for your sympathy,*
*I don't mind 'cause you mean that much to me.*
*Ain't too proud to beg. . . .*

Just as HDH had a lock on the Supremes and Tops, so began Norman's on the Temptations. He had snatched them right out of Smokey's pocket.

Norman had such passion. He was relentless. When a song wasn't a hit on one artist he'd produce it over and over again on other artists. After "Ain't Too Proud To Beg," he continued with hits like "Beauty Is Only Skin Deep," (I Know) I'm Losing You," "You're My Everything" and "I Wish It Would Rain." Each song was different, but there was always something undeniably Whitfield about Norman's productions. He was versatile, unique and getting stronger and cockier with every hit.

I told him he had fire deep in his soul and a little would come out each time he produced a record.

Though I was finding less and less time to get into the studio, early in '65 I, too, jumped into the mix, co-producing a record with engineer Lawrence Horn. It was a tune called "Shotgun," written by Jr. Walker for himself and his group the All Stars.

Junior was incredible. His saxophone sound was like nobody else's. The down-home feeling he and his band got when he sang and played his horn made it easy to produce him. All we had to do was get a good sound balance in the studio and just wait. He could put together some of the damnedest lyrics you'd ever heard—and come out with a smash:

> *Shotgun, shoot 'em fore he run now*
> *Do the jerk baby, do the jerk now*
> *Put on your high heel shoes*
> *We're goin' down here now and listen to 'em play the Blues*
> *We're gonna dig potatoes*
> *We're gonna pick tomatoes. . . .*

He broke every rule in the book, but I still loved it.

New people were coming all the time and from everywhere. When I think of the two young songwriters who came to us from New York around this time one word comes to mind— TALENTED! Nickolas Ashford and Valerie Simpson had joined our growing writing staff at Jobete after an earlier hit they'd written for Ray Charles, "Let's Go Get Stoned." When I first saw them they both seemed warm and quiet. While that held true, I later found out Valerie was a pint-sized ball of dynamite, especially when working in the studio.

One day Harvey Fuqua, in his quest for material for a duo he had put together— Marvin Gaye and Tammi Terrell—listened to a demo of their songs. Liking what he heard, he and Johnny Bristol produced "Ain't No Mountain High Enough" and "Your Precious Love." Both songs became big hits.

Sooner or later just about every songwriter, and some performers, want to produce their own records. But talent in one area doesn't always mean you have it in another. With Nick and Val it did. The success of their songs earned them a chance to produce some of their own material.

Their production of Nick's lyrics with Valerie's melodies and arrangements added a new sophisticated element to our overall sound. When their production on Marvin and Tammi was brought into the Friday morning meeting there was no debate. "Ain't Nothing Like the Real Thing" was voted a smash and it was. When their next record on the same duo, "You're All I Need To Get By" was played it sounded so great to me I didn't bother to take a vote. No one complained. It is still one of my all-time favorites.

When selling records to the mainstream market I had learned long before that you had to deal with people's prejudices.

I had not forgotten the hurt I felt when my brother's record, "Everyone Was There," had died when the public realized that this white-sounding record was performed by a black artist.

That was why we released some of our early albums without showing the artists' faces on them. The Marvelettes' album *Please Mr. Postman* had a picture of a mailbox on it; *Bye Bye Baby* by Mary Wells, a love letter. We put a cartoon of an ape on the cover of *The Miracles' Doing Mickey's Monkey;* and an Isley Brothers album had two white lovers at the beach on its cover.

This practice became less necessary as our music's popularity started overcoming the prejudices.

But there were so many other color barriers to overcome. I remember one day sitting in Barney's [Barney Ales, head of the sales department at Motown] office in a meeting when I noticed I was the only black person in the room. My own company!

After the meeting I talked to Barney and Phil [Jones, a member of the promotion staff]. "How come there's nothing but white folks in the Sales Department?"

"You just now noticed?" Barney asked.

I smiled. "I guess I never saw black and white, I only saw record sales."

Of course, I knew the Sales Department was all white. Barney had built it with experienced people he knew in the business. They were a powerful team. With their know-how they not only dealt successfully with the distributors with one-stops and a new sector of the market known as rackjobbers—the guys who sold records in large quantities to supermarkets and drugstores.

"You always told me you wanted a general market company, and that's what we got here," Barney said. "We want to sell our records across the board and when I put my team together, there were no black salesmen I knew out there that had ever done that or that could do it the way we needed it done."

"Have you tried to find any?"

"Well, no."

"Well I think you should. If black promotion men can get white stations to play a record, why can't black get white distributors to buy them as well?"

I could see Barney was surprised because he had never known me to challenge him on the basis of race. I felt a little strange myself.

"Getting radio play is one thing, but selling records is another. The distributors are going to give you a lot more resistance than any DJ," he said. "It would be really tough—especially in the South."

"That may be. But I think we're so strong now we can change things. It's time."

"He's right,' Phil jumped in. "I think we can." It was rare for any of Barney's people to side with me—in front of him.

But Barney was all for it. "Let's get on it," he told Phil,

"But we can't hire just any black guy," Phil said. "He's got to be real special, strong."

They were lucky. They found Miller London. He was shortish and thinnish, with a pleasant face and a great smile that he used a lot. My first impression was that he might be too fragile. I was wrong.

Soon he was joined by other black sales and promotion men—Chuck Young, Eddie Gilreath, Ralph Thompson and Skip Miller.

Phil enjoyed telling about one of the first incidents when he sent Miller London on a trip to the South.

As soon as Miller arrived for his first appointment at one of our major Southern distributors, Phil got a hysterical call.

"Phil," the distributor screamed, "you sent a nigger down here to sell white Pop accounts? Are you fuckin' nuts?"

"How much money do you make a year off Motown?" Phil responded.

"Oh, I don't know. Quite a bit I guess."

"Well, if you want to keep making that 'quite a bit,' you better get used to looking in that nigger's face."

Miller had been waiting in an outer office. As soon as the distributor got off the phone he rushed out smiling: "Miller, nice to see you, come on in, my friend."

Miller was in. But it took about a year of insults, threats and narrow escapes before he could breathe easily.

> In the next excerpt, Berry recalls his first encounter with the Jackson Five and the young star of the group, Michael Jackson.

When I look at it today I can still remember the intensity we all felt standing there that July morning [in 1968] watching those five young boys from Gary, Indiana, perform. Nine-year-old Michael, eleven-year-old Marion, fourteen-year-old Jermaine, and fifteen- and seventeen-year-old Tito and Jackie meant business. All of them moved, sang and played instruments like winners.

They tore into the Temptations' "Ain't Too Proud to Beg" all moving together like little David Ruffins, with a style all their own. When they sang "I Wish It Would Rain" and "Tobacco Road," they made the songs sound like they were written just for them. They wound up with Michael doing James Brown's "I Got The Feelin'." His dazzling footwork would have certainly made the Godfather proud.

This little kid had an incredible knowingness about him that really made me take notice. He sang his songs with such feeling, inspiration and pain—as if he had experienced everything he was singing about. In between songs he kept his eyes on me the whole time, as if he was studying me.

All the right clues were there—their professionalism, their discipline, their talent. And something else that Michael had, an unknown quality that I didn't completely understand but I knew was special. Somehow even at that first meeting he let me know of his hunger to learn, and how willing he was to work as hard as necessary to be great, to go to the top. He let me know he believed I was the person who could get him there.

# 34. The Godfather of Soul and the Beginnings of Funk

James Brown (b. either 1928 or 1933) stands out as one of the most influential and successful musicians in the history of R&B. While his innovations as a singer, performer, composer, arranger, and bandleader virtually defined the genre of funk and contributed mightily to the development of hip-hop, his achievements cannot be measured only in terms of his musical contributions: During the height of his popularity, he became a cultural icon in the African American community, exploring the limits of economic self-determination for a black performer and demonstrating how crossover success could be achieved without forswearing the black vernacular.

Born into extreme poverty in the rural South (in Barnwell, South Carolina, near Augusta, Georgia), Brown began his career as a professional musician with the gospel-based Flames in the early 1950s. By 1956, the group had recorded the R&B hit, "Please, Please, Please" and changed their name to "James Brown and the Famous Flames." This early recording established what was to become a stylistic trademark: insistent repetition of a single phrase (in this case consisting of the song's title) resulting in a kind of ecstatic trance. This trademark and Brown's characteristic raspy vocal timbre and impassioned melismas display his debt to the African American gospel tradition. His stage shows, dancing, and inspired call-and-response interactions with the audience also convey the fervor of a sanctified preacher.

The subsequent highpoints of his career are numerous: the surprising smash success of his 1962 recording, *Live at the Apollo;* his development of funk during the years 1964–65 with three successive hits, "Out of Sight," "Papa's Got a Brand New Bag," and "I Got You (I Feel Good)"; his continued crossover success with a string of recordings—including "Cold Sweat," "Say It Loud (I'm Black and I'm Proud)," "Superbad," "Hot Pants"—that further defined the funk genre during the years 1967–72. In recordings, such as "Cold Sweat," verse-chorus structures were replaced by sections of irregular length, defined by densely overlapping ostinati played by all the instruments. Brown's lyrics grew increasingly impressionistic, celebrating black vernacular speech (often creating slang in the process) and emphasizing racial pride.[1]

In a book organized by decades, where does one place a musician who was active and influential in three of them (the 1950s, 1960s, and 1970s) and continues to perform and record up to the present day? While funk will be discussed at greater length in Part 4, I placed Brown in this chapter because it was during the 1960s that he developed the innovations that were felt and continue to be felt across a broad musical spectrum.

The following excerpts come from Brown's autobiography, *The Godfather of Soul,* and detail his early experiences and eclectic influences, his indebtedness to gospel music and charismatic preaching styles, the importance of audience-performer interaction (also learned in church), his firsthand experience of the ring shout, and the somewhat surprising link between minstrel shows (and professional wrestling!) and the later development of his stage act. He also charts the development of soul and

---

1. For an essay exploring how Brown's funk expressed an African American aesthetic in its conjunction of music and lyrics, see David Brackett, "James Brown's 'Superbad' and the Double-Voiced Utterance," *Interpreting Popular Music* (Berkeley: University of California Press, [1995] 2000), 108–56.

funk, the circumstances of the famous *Live at the Apollo* album, and his business philosophy and profiles several of the well-known musicians who worked for him.

## *from* THE GODFATHER OF SOUL
### *James Brown (with Bruce Tucker)*

I liked gospel and pop songs best of all. I got all the Hit Parade books and learned all the pop tunes—Bing Crosby's "Buttermilk Sky," Sinatra's "Saturday Night Is the Loneliest Night of the Week," "String of Pearls." I also admired Count Basie's "One O'Clock Jump," but I couldn't play piano good enough to do it.

I heard a lot or church music, too, because I went to all the different churches with a crippled man named Charlie Brown who lived in one of the shacks in Helmuth Alley. He had to walk with two sticks or with somebody on each side holding his arms. On Sundays when we weren't shining shoes, Junior and I walked Mr. Charlie to one or another of the churches because they'd take up collections for people like him.

At the churches there was a lot of singing and handclapping and usually an organ and tambourines, and then the preacher would really get down. I liked that even more than the music. I had been to a revival service and had seen a preacher who really had a lot of fire. He was just screaming and yelling and stomping his foot and then he dropped to his knees. The people got into it with him, answering him and shouting and clapping time. After that, when I went to church with Mr. Charlie, I watched the preachers real close. Then I'd go home and imitate them because *I* wanted to preach. I thought that was the answer to it.

Audience participation in church is something the darker race of people has going because of a lot of trials and tribulations, because of things that we understand about human nature. It's something I can't explain, but I can bring it out of people. I'm not the only person who has the ability, but I *work* at it, and I'm sure a lot of my stage show came out of the church.

One thing I never saw in the churches was drums until I went to Bishop Grace's House of Prayer. Those folks were sanctified—they *had* the beat. See, you got sanctified and you got holy. Sanctified people got more fire; holy people are more secluded—sort of like Democrats versus Republicans. I'm holy myself, but I have a lot of sanctified in me.

Bishop Grace was a big man, the richest and most powerful of that kind of preacher in the country, bigger than Father Divine or any of 'em. He had houses of prayer in more than thirty cities in the East and South, and he had these "Grace Societies" that just took in the money. Every year when he came back to Augusta there was a monstrous parade down Gwinnett Street for him, with decorated floats and cars and brass bands. Everybody in the Terry[2] turned out for it, and other people came from as far away as Philadelphia to march in it. You could join in it with your car or, if you had a musical instrument, you could fall in with one of the bands.

---

2. The name for the African American neighborhood where Brown lived.

*Source:* James Brown with Bruce Tucker, from *The Godfather of Soul*, pp. 17–19, 23–24, 106–07, 120, 134–36, 138–39, 157–58, 178–79, 218–19, 221–22, 224, 227, 242–43. Reprinted with permission of Scribner, an imprint of Simon and Schuster Adult Publishing Group. Copyright © 1986 by James Brown and Bruce Tucker.

He was called "Daddy" Grace, and he was like a god on earth. He wore a cape and sat on a throne on the biggest float, with people fanning him while he threw candy and things to the children. He had long curly hair, and real long fingernails, and suits made out of money.

His House of Prayer on Wrightsboro Road in Augusta resembled a warehouse. A sign over the door said: "Great joy! Come to the House of Prayer and forget your troubles." And everybody *did* come at one time or another, even people who didn't believe in him, because he put on such a show. Inside there were plank benches, a dirt floor covered with sawdust, and crepe paper streamers on the ceiling. At one end there was a stage where Daddy Grace sat on a red throne.

He'd get to preaching and the people would get in a ring and they'd go round and round and go right behind one another, just shouting. Sometimes they'd fall out right there in the sawdust, shaking and jerking and having convulsions. The posts in the place were padded so the people wouldn't hurt themselves. There was a big old tin tub sitting there, too, and every time they went by the tub, they threw something in it. See who could give the most. Later on he had various big vases out there, like urns, one for five-dollar bills, one for tens and twenties, and one for hundreds. It seemed like the poorest people sacrificed the most for him.

Daddy Grace had to be a prophet, but seeing him I knew I was an outsider because I couldn't believe in him. I believed in God so that made me an outsider right away.

The Lenox [Theater in Augusta] was where I first saw films of Louis Jordan performing. Louis Jordan and His Tympany Five. They played a kind of jumping R&B and jazz at the same time, and they were something else. They did a lot of comedy, but they could play a blues if they had to, or anything in between. The films were shorts of Louis doing whatever his latest song was, and they showed them before the regular picture. He played alto sax *real* good and sang *pretty* good. Louis Jordan was the man in those days, though a lot of people have forgotten it. His stuff was popular with blacks *and* whites, and he usually had several hits at one time, a lot of 'em that sold a million. "Choo Choo Ch'Boogie," "Early in the Morning," "Saturday Night Fish Fry," and "Ain't Nobody Here but Us Chickens" were all his. When I first saw him I think he had out "G. I. Jive" and "Is You Is, or Is You Ain't (Ma' Baby)?" but the one that knocked me out was "Caldonia, What Makes Your Big Head So Hard?" especially the way he'd go up real high; Cal-don-*ya*! I learned the words as quick as I could, picked it out on the piano, and started playing it and singing it whenever I got the chance.

"Caldonia" was a song you could really put on a show with, and I guess that Louis Jordan short is what first started me thinking along those lines. That and the preachers. The circus and the minstrel shows that came through town played a part, too.

Johnny J. Jones was my favorite circus. Junior and I used to crawl through a hole in the fence in the back of the fairgrounds to see him. Since he stayed for a whole week, they called it a fair, but it was really a circus. A circus is supposed to do all its stuff in one night and then move on to the next town, the way I did with my show years later.

We had to pay to get into the minstrel shows, but only because we couldn't figure out a way to sneak in. Silas Green from New Or-leans was the best. He presented a complete varied program with singers, dancers, musicians, and comics. That's what I tried to do fifteen years later when I put together the James Brown Revue.

It's strange: Even though I'd seen just about everything there was to see in the house on Twiggs Street,[3] I thought the short dresses on Silas Green's girls were unbelievable. To me, those brown skinned models were the prettiest things in the world. I saw some top talent in

---

3. The "house on Twiggs Street" refers to the whorehouse where Brown spent many of his formative years.

those shows, too, like Willie Mae Thornton, who first did "Hound Dog." I saw a lot of great comedians, too. In those days the comics still worked in blackface, but like everybody else I just thought it was funny.

Ever since the Uptown we'd worked on our closing routine with "Please." I'd fall to my knees and out would come the coat to go around my shoulders. At first, we used anybody's coat that was laying around. Might belong to one of the Flames or one of the fellas in the band. It worked fine until people started hiding their coats; cleaning bills were mounting up, and didn't nobody want their coat to be the one. So they started bringing me a towel, like for a boxer. That was effective, too. Then one night in Chattanooga on a bill with B. B. King and Bobby "Blue" Bland they brought me the towel, and after a little bit I threw it into the audience. They loved it, so we did it that way for a good while.

Later on in that tour, when we were in Atlanta, we sat around the hotel one day watching wrestling on television. Gorgeous George was on, and when he got through killing whoever he was killing, he started walking around the ring taking his bows. A handler followed him and threw a robe over his shoulders. Gorgeous shook it off, went to another side of the ring, and took another bow. The fella threw the robe him again, and George shook it off and took another bow. Watching it, I said, "We got to get a robe." So we went out and got some store-bought robes. Later on we got capes that I signed and had tailor-made, but the whole thing really started coming together while watching Gorgeous George.

Willie John or somebody might have said we were using more tricks to get over, but they didn't understand that everything was developing at once—the stage show, the band, the dancing, the music. There were a lot of different aspects to what we were doing. I wanted people to appreciate them so I decided to record the band on an instrumental and kind of popularize the mashed potatoes at the same time. Most entertainers today never really understand that show business means just that, show business.

You can hear the thing starting to change on the records I put out during the beginning of 1960. I was changing before that, but that's when you can *hear* it. "I'll Go Crazy" came out in January; "Think" and "You've Got the Power" were released in May. "I'll Go Crazy" is a blues, but it's a different kind of blues, up-tempo, a kind of jazz blues. "Think" is a combination of gospel and jazz—a rhythm hold is what we used to call it. Soul really started right there, or at least my kind did. See when people talk about soul music they talk only about gospel and R & B coming together. That's accurate about a lot of soul, but if you're going to talk about mine, you have to remember the jazz in it. That's what made my music so different and allowed it to change and grow after soul was finished.

Once Mr. [Syd] Nathan [owner of King Records] saw I was going to go ahead with the live recording [from a performance at the Apollo in 1962], he started cooperating. Mr. Neely took care of getting the equipment from A-1 Sound in New York, the only ones who had portable stuff—Magnacorders, I think. Matter of fact, Mr. Nathan started cooperating *too* much. He sent word that he wanted us to use cue cards to direct the audience participation. I said, "Now if y'all are going to pay for it, then I'll do it the way y'all want to, but if I'm going to pay for it, then please leave it alone. All I want y'all to do is tape the stuff."[4] That was the end of it.

We had opened on the nineteenth and were building up to recording on the twenty-fourth, a Wednesday, which meant amateur night. I wanted that wild amateur-night crowd because I knew they'd do plenty of hollering. The plan was to record all four shows that day

---

4. Brown was paying for the recording because of Nathan's initial objections.

so we'd have enough tape to work with. I think Mr. Neely and Chuck Seitz, the engineers, had six or eight mikes, two crowd monitors in front, one above the crowd, and then the mikes on me, the band, and the Flames.

The other acts on the bill were Olatunji, the Sensations, Curley Mays, and Pigmeat Markham. Yvonne Fair had a solo spot, and so did Baby Lloyd. On the twenty-fourth I was going around backstage telling the Flames and the band not to get nervous, and I guess I was probably the most nervous of all. I wasn't worried about performing; I was worried about the recording coming off good. I had a lot riding on it, not just my own money but my reputation because here I was having to prove myself to Mr. Nathan and them all over again, just like when I had to demo "Try Me." I was standing in the wings thinking about all this when Fats stepped up to the microphone and did his intro:

"So now, ladies and gentlemen, it is startime. Are you ready for startime?" *Yeah!* "Thank you and thank you very kindly. It is indeed a great pleasure to present to you at this particular time, nationally and internationally known as the *Hardest* Working Man in Show Business, the man that sings, 'I'll Go Crazy'" . . . *a fanfare from the band: Taaaaa!* "'You've Got the Power'" . . . *Taaaaa!* "'Think'" . . . *Taaaaa!* "'If You Want Me'" . . . *Taaaaa!* "'I Don't Mind'" . . . *Taaaaa!* "'Bewildered'" . . . *Taaaaa!* "million-dollar seller 'Lost Someone'" . . . *Taaaaa!* "the very latest release, 'Night Train'" . . . *Taaaaa!* "Let's everybody 'Shout and Shimmy'" . . . *Taaaaa!* "Mr. Dynamite, the amazing Mr. 'Please Please' himself, the star of the show . . . James Brown and the Famous Flames."

Then the band went into the chaser—the little up-tempo vamp we used between songs—and I hit the stage. As soon as I was into "I'll Go Crazy" I knew it was one of those good times. That's a hard feeling to describe—being on stage, performing, and knowing that you've really got it that night. It feels like God is blessing you, and you give more and more. The audience was with me, screaming and hollering on all the songs, and I thought, "Man, this is really going to do it."

It's a funny thing, though. When I'm up on stage I'm very aware of everything that's going on around me—what the band and the backup singers are doing, how the audience is reacting, how the sound system's working, all that. When you work small clubs you watch the door, check out how rough the crowd looks, listen for little pitch changes in your one little amplifier that tell you it's about to blow out. You can't just be thinking about the song or how pretty you look up there. You learn to be aware.

As the show went along I started noticing little things and filing them away in my mind. Every now and then the band made a mistake or the Flames were a half tone off. Sometimes I hollered where I usually didn't in the song, and some of the audience down front was too enthusiastic. A little old lady down front kept yelling, "Sing it motherf——r, sing it!" She looked like she must have been seventy-five years old. I could hear her the whole time and knew the overhead crowd mike was right above her. Mr. Neely had strung it on a wire between the two side balconies. Most times none of those things would've mattered, but we were recording and I was thinking, "Oh, Lord, this take's ruined."

During a quiet stretch of "Lost Someone" the woman let out a loud scream, and the audience laughed right in the middle of this serious song. I thought "Well, there goes that song, too." Then I thought I had better try to fix it some kind of way so I started preaching: "You know we all make mistakes sometimes, and the only way we can correct our mistakes is we got to try one more time. So I got to sing this song to you one more time." I stretched out the song, hoping we could get something we could use; then I went into "Please."

Mr. Neely brought the tape into a back room between the first two shows and played it for us on a little tape recorder. As soon as we heard the little old lady, we all busted out laughing. He didn't understand. All he could hear was her high piercing voice, but he didn't really understand what she was saying even though it was clear as a bell. Finally, somebody told him. *Then* he understood.

"Oh no," he said. "I can't' have that. I have to get it out of there and make sure she's not here for the other shows, too. This is terrible."

He was getting all worked up, while all the cats were listening to it over and over, laughing, having a great time, and getting other cats to listen to it. After a while, watching everybody carry on, Mr. Neely settled himself down and said, "Hey, maybe we've got something here."

He found the lady down front and told her he'd buy her candy and popcorn and give her $10 if she'd stay for the other three shows—he didn't tell her why. He moved the overhead mike so it wouldn't pick her up so strong. We were using two-track, which meant practically mixing as we went along. She stayed for the next three shows and hollered the same thing every time I did a spin or something she liked. It was like it was on cue. I think the shows got even better as the day went along. By the end of the last one we had four reels of tape. Mr. Neely was so excited he brought the master up to the dressing rooms and passed around the headphones for us to listen. None of us had ever heard ourselves live like that. It sounded fantastic. We knew we really had something.

By this time we had completely forgotten about the finale, where all the acts change clothes and come out on stage together to close the show. Everybody else had changed and was waiting backstage, but we were listening to the tape over and over. Never did do that finale.

A lot of people don't understand about the hollering I do. A man once came up to me in a hotel lobby and said, "So you're James Brown. You make a million dollars, and all you do is scream and holler."

"Yes," I said, very quiet, "but I scream and holler on key."

I was branching out in a lot of directions. At the end of 1962 I formed my own song publishing company, Jim Jam Music, and got King to give me my own label, Try Me. I had already been producing on Federal and King and Dade and wanted to bring it all together on Try Me. I wasn't content to be only a performer and be used by other people; I wanted to be a complete show business person: artist, businessman, entrepreneur. It was important to be because people of my origin hadn't been allowed to get into the *business* end of show business before, just the *show* part.

By this time Mr. Neely had finished editing the *Live at the Apollo* tape. He had a good mix of the performance and the audience, and he had fixed all the cussing so it wasn't right up front. He figured it would become an underground thing for people who knew what the lady was screaming; he was right too. He worked on the tape a long time and did a fantastic job of mixing it.

When Mr. Nathan finally heard the tape he hated it. "This is not coming out," he said. "We have a certain standard, and we're going to stick with it." What he didn't like now was the way we went from one tune to another without stopping. He just couldn't understand that. I guess he was expecting exact copies of our earlier records, but with people politely applauding in between. He had all kinds of theories about how records should be. He wanted the hook right up front because he knew that disc jockeys auditioned hundreds of records every week by putting the needle down and playing only the first fifteen or twenty seconds. If that didn't grab them, they went on to the next record. The same thing happened in record stores, where they usually let you hear fifteen or twenty seconds on a player on the counter. A lot of my things were more like stage numbers, and he couldn't understand that. After more conversation, he finally agreed to put the album out. I think Mr. Neely was the one who finally sold him on it.

After all the editing and all the arguing it was January 1963 before *Live at the Apollo* was finally released. Then discussion began about what singles to release off it. Byrd thought "Think" should be spun off it, especially since the live version was so different from the version we'd put out before. Some people thought "Try Me" was going to do it again, some people had faith in "Lost Someone."

The idea of a smash *album* was far from anybody's mind. Those were the days when most popular albums had only one hit on them plus filler. Mr. Nathan was waiting to see which tune the radio stations were going to play from the album, and then he would shoot it out as a single. I said, "What do you mean? We're not going to take any singles off it. Sell it the way it is."

"James," he said, "all the money I've made in this business I made off singles. That's how it's done. As soon as we get the reports from the radio stations, we're going to start releasing singles."

"Nosir, Mr. Nathan," I said. 'No singles."

"You've been paid. You have no say in it anymore, James."

I didn't give him no more argument. I still had faith in the album. While he was waiting to see what would break off the album, King put out the "Prisoner of Love" single in April; it crossed over into the pop market and made it to the top twenty. It was very different from the raw stuff on the *Live* album, which was starting to build momentum.

When Mr. Nathan checked the radio stations to see what was being played off the album, he got a surprise; They told him that there *wasn't* a tune the stations were playing. They were playing the whole album. It was unheard of for a station to play a whole album uninterrupted, but a lot of stations with black programming were doing it. You could tune in at a certain time each night to some of them and they would be playing it. Mr. Nathan couldn't believe it, but it convinced him to let the album keep going on its own.

Meantime, it was a standoff between King Records and Mercury.[5] I started to think there was something funny about it; Mercury seemed more interested in putting Mr. Nathan out of business than in recording me on vocals. The doors at King were all but closed; they had beat him, he had nothing to fight with. I felt bad about it, so I went to Arthur Smith's studio in Charlotte, North Carolina, cut "Papa's Got a Brand New Bag," and sent the tape to Mr. Nathan. It was done underground—I had to sneak the tape to him.

The song started out as a vamp we did during the stage show. There was a little instrumental riff and I hollered: "Papa's got a bag of his own!" I decided to expand it into a song and cut it pretty quick to help Mr. Nathan, so when we went into the studio I was holding a lyric sheet in my hand while I recorded it. We were still going for that live-in-the-studio sound, so we cranked up and did the first take.

It's hard to describe what it was I was going for; the song has gospel feel, but it's put together out of jazz licks. And it has a different sound—a snappy, fast-hitting thing from the bass and the guitars. You can hear Jimmy Nolen, my guitar player at the time, starting to play scratch guitar, where you squeeze the strings tight and quick against the frets so the sound is hard and fast without any sustain. He was what we called a chanker; instead of playing the whole chord and using all the strings, he hit his chords on just three strings. And Maceo played a fantastic sax solo on the break. We had been doing the vamp on the show for a while, so most of it was fine, but the lyrics were so new I think I might have gotten some of them mixed-up on the take. We stopped to listen to the playback to see what we needed to do on the next take. While we were listening, I looked around the studio. Everybody—the band, the studio people, *me*—was dancing. Nobody was standing still.

Pop said, "If I'm paying for this, I don't want to cut any more. This is it."

---

5. Brown had tried to get out of his contract with King and had released a single on Mercury. This single, "Out of Sight," was an important precursor to "Papa's Got a Brand New Bag" (see *The Godfather of Soul*, 148–49, and Brown's uptempo performance of the song in the famous *T.A.M.I. Show* from late in 1964).

And that *was* it. That's the way it went out. I had an acetate made and took it to Frankie Crocker, a deejay in New York. He thought it was terrible, but he put it on the air and the phones lit up. Then he admitted I was right about it.

"Papa's Bag" was years ahead of its time. In 1965 soul was just really getting popular. Aretha and Otis and Wilson Pickett were out there and getting big. I was still called a soul singer—I still call myself that—but musically I had already gone off in a different direction. I had discovered that my strength was not in the horns, it was in the rhythm. I was hearing everything, even the guitars, like they were drums. I had found out how to make it happen. On playbacks, when I saw the speakers jumping, vibrating a certain way, I knew that was it: deliverance. I could tell from looking at the speakers that the rhythm was right. What I'd started on "Out of Sight" I took all the way on "Papa's Bag." Later on they said it was the beginning of funk. I just thought of it as where my music was going. The title told it all: I had a new bag.

My music was changing as fast as the country. The things I'd started doing in "Papa's Bag" and "Cold Sweat," and other tunes around that time, I was taking even further now. In the middle of 1967 Nat Jones left the band and was replaced by Alfred "Pee Wee" Ellis as musical director. He was really in sync with what I was trying to do. He played alto, tenor, and some keyboards. Maceo, after a hitch in the army, came back in April that year. I still had St. Clair Pinkney and L. D. Williams on saxes. Joe Dupars and Waymond Reed played trumpets; Jimmy Nolen and Alphonso Kellum gave me that distinctive scratch guitar sound; and John "Jabo" Starks and Clyde Stubblefield were two of the funkiest drummers you could find. They did it to *death.*

I started off 1968 by buying my first radio station. I got into the radio business because of all the things going on in the country. I believed in human rights—not civil rights, *human* rights of *all* people everywhere—and I loved my country. But I would speak out for my people, too. That was part of loving my country. I thought we needed pride and economic power and, most important of all, education. So I bought WGYW which I changed to WJBE, in Knoxville, Tennessee.

I know people might not believe it but I didn't go into it to make money. First, I thought black communities need stations that really served them and represented them. The station I bought in Knoxville had been a black-oriented station, but it had gone off the air. When I put it back on I kept a format of soul and gospel and jazz—the whole spectrum of black music. We had talk shows, too, and editorials and programs directed at the kids to get them to stay in school. We directed a lot of it at their parents, too, encouraging them to give their kids the support they needed.

Second, I wanted my station to be a media training ground so black people could do more than just be jocks. I wanted them to learn advertising, programming, and management at all levels. Third, as owner I wanted to be a symbol of the black entrepreneur. All three of these reasons were, to me, part of education. That was real black power.

Eventually I bought two more radio stations, WEBB in Baltimore and WRDW in Augusta. At that time there were around five hundred black-oriented radio stations in the country, but only five of them were owned by black people—three of those were mine. I did the same thing with my other two stations that I did in Knoxville. We used to joke that WEBB really stood for "We Enjoy Being Black." WRDW was really special because that was in my hometown.

We did many political things on the stations, editorials that irritated a lot of people. Sometimes I would cut an editorial and just say what I was really thinking. I wasn't a radio professional, so some of 'em were a little too raw for the FCC and they got on us every now and then. With the war in Vietnam and the unrest at home, you couldn't avoid politics during that time.

Brown re-formed his band in 1970. New members included bassist "Bootsy" Collins, and his brother, guitarist "Catfish" Collins. Bootsy later went on to fame with Parliament-Funkadelic and with his own Rubber Band.

Bootsy and the others turned out to be the nucleus of a very good band. They were studio musicians so when I hummed out solos and things they knew how to give me what I wanted. I think Bootsy learned a lot from me. When I met him he was playing a lot of bass— the ifs, the ands and the buts. I got him to see the importance of the *one* in funk—the down-beat at the beginning of every bar. I got him to key in on the dynamic parts of the one in-stead of playing all around it. Then he could do all his other stuff in the right places—*after* the one.

I think the first thing of my own I recorded with the new band was "Hot Pants (She Got to Use What She Got to Get What She Wants)," and it was one of my biggest records.[6] It came out in July 1971 and went to number 1 on the soul charts and number 15 on the pop charts. At the same time I recorded another live album at the Apollo, *Revolution of the Mind*, a two-record set that came out in December. In August I followed up "Hot Pants" with "Make It Funky," which went to number 1 on the soul chart, and with "I'm a Greedy Man," which went to number 7. Those songs did well on the pop charts, too. Most of my music right on through the mid-seventies did, but a funny thing was happening to music on the radio then. It was starting to get segregated again, not just by black and white but by *kinds:* country, pop, hard rock, soft rock, every kind you could name. Radio formats became very rigid. Be-cause of that and because of my political thing, about 80 percent of the popular stations in the country would not play James Brown records. But my sales were so strong to Afro-Americans and some hip whites that they couldn't keep me off the pop charts. Matter of fact, in all of the seventies I tied with Elvis for the most charted pop hits—thirty-eight. The bad thing about it is that I was making some of my strongest music during that period, and I think most whites have been deprived of it.

Because of my stuff, Polydor was really starting to hit the charts for the first time. My first album for them, *Hot Pants*, came out soon after I signed. *Revolution of the Mind* came out in December. At the beginning of 1972 I released "Talkin' Loud and Sayin' Nothing" and "King Heroin," which was a rap song like "Get Up, Get Into It, Get Involved" and "America Is My Home." But, really the very first rap in my career was a thing I did back in 1963 called "Choo-Choo (Locomotion)." We were in the studio at King one night recording it and it just wasn't happening. It was about two or three in the morning, and Mr. Neely said, "Why don't you just play conductor and call off the names of the towns and talk about them?" So that's what I did.

In August 1972 I opened the Festival of Hope at Roosevelt Raceway on Long Island. It was the first rock festival held to help an *established* charity, the Crippled Children's Society. It was a big show: us, Chuck Berry, Ike and Tina Turner, Billy Preston, Sly and the Family Stone, Stephen Stills, Jefferson Airplane, Commander Cody, and so on. The festival didn't bring in as much money as everybody hoped, but it was worth it if it brought in anything. I had visited an Easter Seal summer day camp in Albertson, New York, and my heart went out to those kids.

---

6. The "new band" referred to here is the one Brown formed after the Collins brothers departed and included Fred Wesley as arranger and trombonist.

Right before the festival I put out "Get on the Good Foot." Afrika Bambaataa says it's the song that people first started break dancing to. I feel solidarity with the breakers and rappers and the whole hip hop thing—as long as it's clean. Their stuff is an extension of things I was doing for a long time: rapping over a funky beat about pride and respect and education and drugs and all kinds of issues. I did what I said in the songs: I got up, got into it, and got involved. I was determined to have a say, and I thought anybody with a big following had a responsibility to speak out like I'd done with "America Is My Home" and with "Black and Proud."

By the middle of 1975 disco had broken big. Disco is a simplification of a lot of what I was doing, of what they *thought* I was doing. Disco is a very small part of funk. It's the end of the song, the repetitious part, like a vamp. The difference is that in funk, you dig into a groove, you don't stay on the surface. Disco stayed on the surface. See, I taught 'em everything *they* know, but not everything *I* know.

Disco was easy for artists to get into because they really didn't have to do anything. It was all electronic sequencers and beats-per-minute—it was done with machines. They just cheated on the music world. They thought they could dress up in a Superfly outfit, play one note, and that would make them a star. But that was not the answer. It destroyed the musical basis many people worked so hard to build up in the sixties. The record companies loved disco because it was a producer's music. You don't really need artists to make disco. They didn't have to worry about an artist not cooperating; machines can't talk back and, unlike artists, they don't have to be paid. What disco became was a lawyer's recording; the attorneys were making records.

Disco hurt me in a lot of ways. I was trying to make good hard funk records that Polydor was trying to soften up, while people were buying records that had no substance. The disco people copied off me and tried to throw me away and go with young people. You can't do that. You have to come back to the source. Disco hurt live music in general. The black concert business was already hurting. Whites wouldn't come even if the black artist had big record sales. Black America was in a serious recession; there was just no money in the black community. Later on, that situation hurt records sales, too. For everybody.

# 35. "The Blues Changes from Day to Day"

During 1965–66, the Southern Soul sound gained prominence in tandem with Motown. Southern Soul recordings tended to eschew some of the complexities of Motown arrangements, emphasizing (like Brown) the gospel roots of the music and presenting a looser, more spontaneous-seeming sound. Among these artists, Otis Redding (1941–67), from Macon, Georgia, achieved a special sort of notoriety with the white counterculture by being the only soul artist to appear at the Monterey Pop Festival in 1967. While Redding had been one of the most consistently successful artists associated with Stax and a staple on the R&B radio for years, his exposure to the white audience had been fairly limited up to that time. His greatest commercial triumph, with "(Sittin' on) The Dock of the Bay" (Number One pop and R&B early in 1968), followed his death in a plane crash in December 1967. The following interview from 1967 reflects the newfound interest in Redding among the pop and rock audiences and touches on Redding's views about the musical relationships between black and white performers, as well as the differences between Motown and Stax. The initials "J. D." stand for Jim Delehant, the editor of *Hit Parader* who conducted the interview in the summer of 1967.

## OTIS REDDING INTERVIEW

### *Jim Delehant*

**J.D:**  *What do you dislike about England?*

**Otis:**  Nothing. I loved England from head to toe. I love the weather, the people. I was there in the summer and it was nice. The people are so groovy; they treated me like I was somebody. They took me wherever I wanted to go. I loved Paris too.

**J.D:**  *Did you find any language problems with your audiences in Paris?*

**Otis:**  No, they sang along with almost all the songs. But England is a beautiful country. If I were to leave the U.S, I'd live in England. But I'd never leave the U.S. I own a 400-acre farm in Macon, Georgia. I raise cattle and hogs. I own horses too. I love horses as much as singing. I'd like to hunt on horseback.

**J.D:**  *Tell us about the album you recorded with Carla Thomas.*

**Otis:**  Carla and I worked on this album for three days. We do things like "It Takes Two" that Marvin Gaye and Kim Weston did. And we do "Tramp" by Lowell Fulsom. I wrote an original called "Oo Wee Baby." We do "Tell It Like It Is." There's a lot of great stuff on it.

**J.D:**  *Your voices are so different. Did you have any problems working together?*

**Otis:**  My voice right today is hoarse from working on the album. We didn't have any problems working at all. I went in first and sang my part, and then she came in and overdubbed her part. We used Booker T. & MG's too. Booker played both the piano and the organ. We cut eleven songs in three days.

**J.D:**  *How did you write "Respect"?*

**Otis:**  That's one of my favorite songs because it has a better groove than any of my records. It says something too: "What you want, baby you got it. What you need baby, you got it. All I'm asking for is a little respect when I come home." The song lyrics are great. The band track is beautiful. It took me a whole day to write it and about twenty minutes to arrange it. We cut it once and that was it. Everybody wants respect, you know.

**J.D:**  *Why did you choose to do "Satisfaction"?*

**Otis:**  That came from Steve Cropper and Booker. We were all in the studio one day to record an album and they suggested I do "Satisfaction." They asked me if I had heard the new Rolling Stones song but I hadn't heard it. They played the record for me and everybody liked it except me. If you notice, I use a lot of words different from the Stones' version—that's because I made it up.

---

*Source:* Jim Delehant, "Otis Redding Interview," *Hit Parader* (September 1967).

**J.D:**   *Were you in the music business before you joined Stax?*

**Otis:**   No, I used to be a well driller. I made a $1.25 an hour drilling wells in Macon, Georgia. One day I drove a friend of mine, Johnny Jenkins, up to do a recording session. They had thirty minutes left in the studio and I asked if I could do a song, "These Arms of Mine." They did it and it sold about 800,000 copies. I've been going ever since. I wrote that song in 1960 when I wasn't even thinking about the music business. I recorded it in November, 1962. I tried the song out with a small recording company but it didn't do anything. I knew it was saying something though. I dug the words.

**J.D:**   *What was the first music you heard that impressed you deeply?*

**Otis:**   My mother and father and I used to go to parties when I was a kid. We used to go out to a place called Sawyer's Lake in Macon. There was a calypso song out then called "Run, Joe." My mother and daddy used to play that for me all the time. I just dug the groove. Ever since then I've been playing music. As I was growing up, I did a lot of talent shows. I won fifteen Sunday nights straight in a series of talent shows in Macon. I showed up the sixteenth night and they wouldn't let me go on anymore. Whatever success I had was through the help of the good Lord.

**J.D:**   *What do you think of people like Muddy Waters and Jimmy Reed?*

**Otis:**   I dig them because they give me a lot of ideas. I listen to them a lot.

**J.D:**   *Do you like harmonica?*

**Otis:**   Yes, I love harmonica. I haven't done one on record, yet, but I might try. I play it a little. It's easy. I play piano too—the chords. I write songs with my guitar.

**J.D:**   *How many pieces do you have in your band?*

**Otis:**   I used to have ten, but now I have eight. I cut it down because it was getting away from my sound. I have two trumpets, two tenors, guitar, bass, drums and organ.

**J.D:**   *What do you think of Sam and Dave and the Righteous Brothers?*

**Otis:**   I'll tell you. When I first heard the Righteous Brothers, I thought they were colored. I think they sing better than Sam and Dave. But Sam and Dave are much better showmen. Sam and Dave have been together for ten or twelve years. I think Sam and Dave are my favorites.

**J.D:**   *Why do you think white blues performers are so much more successful than the originals?*

**Otis:**   Because the white population is much larger than the colored. I like what these rock and roll kids are doing. Sometimes they take things from us, but I take things from them too. The things that are beautiful, and they do a lot of beautiful things.

**J.D:**   *What do you think of Eric Burdon?*

**Otis:**   Now, Eric is one of the best friends I have. He's a great guy. I like the way he works. I like the way he sings, too. He's a good blues performer. I've seen him work in a club in England. This boy came on stage with a blues song and he tore the house up. They called me up on stage after he finished and I wouldn't go up. I knew I couldn't do anything to top it. Eric can really sing blues.

**J.D:**   *Any blues by the Stones you like?*

**Otis:**   No. I like their uptempo songs. They really groove on "Satisfaction." It's too much. I like their original things better. They can't do anybody else's songs.

**J.D:**   *You're a producer and manager now, aren't you?*

**Otis:**   I have an artist that just came out on Atlantic Records named Arthur Conley. He does one of my songs, "Sweet Soul Music." It's uptempo and he does it beautifully. I manage him and record him. My band is on the record too.

**J.D:**  *What's the difference between rock and roll and rhythm and blues?*
**Otis:**  Everybody thinks that all the songs by colored people are rhythm and blues but that's not true. Johnny Taylor, Muddy Waters and B. B. King are blues musicians. James Brown is not a blues singer. He has a rock and roll beat and he can sing slow pop songs. My own songs "Respect" and "Mr. Pitiful," aren't blues songs. I'm speaking in terms of the beat and structure of the music. A blues is a song that goes twelve bars all the way through. Most of my songs are soul songs. When I go in to record a song, I only have the title and maybe a first verse. The rest I make up as we're recording. We'll cut it three of four times and I'll sing it different every time. You know, once I cut a song, I can't pantomime it on a TV show. I've goofed TV shows every time. I missed the lyrics. I'd be going my own way but then I'd catch up.

**J.D:**  *What's the difference between the Stax sound and the Motown sound?*
**Otis:**  Motown does a lot of overdubbing. It's mechanically done. At Stax the rule is what-ever you feel, play it. We cut everything together—horns, rhythm, and vocals. We'll do it three or four times, go back and listen to the results and pick the best one. If some-body doesn't like a line in the song, we'll go back and cut the whole song over. Until last year, we didn't even have a four-track tape recorder. You can't overdub on a one-track machine. Like yesterday, we cut six songs in five hours for my album with Carla. They were perfect songs, and they'll all be in the album.

**J.D:**  *Do you think R&B has changed a great deal?*
**Otis:**  Yes, I'd like to say something to the R&B singers who were around ten years ago. They've got to get out of the old bag. Listen to the beat of today and use it on records. Don't say we're gonna go back ten years and use this old swing shuffle. That's not it. I know what the kids want today, and I aim all my stuff at them. I'd like to see all those singers make it again. I'd like to take Fats Domino, Little Richard, Big Joe Turner, Clyde McPhatter and bring them into the bag of today. They'd have hits all over again. The blues changes from day to day. It all depends on what the kids will be dancing to, what they're moving to. I watch people when I sing. If they're stompin' their foot, or snappin' their fingers, then I know I got something. But if they don't move, then you don't have anything. Five years from now, I know the kids are going to be tired of my singing. If I can keep a good mind with the help of the good Lord, I'm gonna keep producing records. You can't have anything else on your mind but the music business. When I go into the studio, I'm strictly for business. I can go in there any time of the day and cut six songs if I want to. I don't like any fooling around in the studio.

**J.D:**  *Do you like country and western music?*
**Otis:**  Oh yeah. Before I started singing, maybe ten years ago, I loved anything that Hank Williams sang. Eddy Arnold does some groovy things, too. Everybody's got their own bag and if they're doing something good, I can hear it.

**J.D:**  *From your experience, what's the best advice you could give to someone who wants to get in the business?*
**Otis:**  If you want to be a singer, you've got to concentrate on it 24 hours a day. You can't be a well driller, too. You've got to concentrate on the business of entertaining and writ-ing songs. Always think different from the next person. Don't ever do a song as you heard somebody else do it. Concentrate and practice every single day. It took me four years to get into show business in a big way. Also I think it's very important to write your own songs.

# 36. Aretha Franklin Meets the Mainstream

In 1967–68, Aretha Franklin's version of Otis Redding's "Respect" and James Brown's "Say It Loud (I'm Black and I'm Proud)" signaled soul music's entry into a new phase of political engagement. The emergence of Aretha Franklin (b. 1942), one of the first solo female stars in the genre, had a huge impact: Her tremendous range, mastery of all aspects of gospel singing technique, and driving gospel piano playing, applied to consistently excellent material (some of which she wrote or cowrote), resulted in a series of brilliant recordings in 1967–70, during which time she sold more records than any other African American artist. Her recordings from the late 1960s include, in addition to "Respect," such anthems as "I Never Loved a Man (the Way I Love You)," "Natural Woman (You Make Me Feel Like a)," "Chain of Fools," and "Think." While her other recordings did not have quite the broad political resonance of "Respect," these hits did convey a sense of pride and strength not previously expressed by black female singers.

Thanks, in large part, to the success of Aretha Franklin, the profile of soul had risen by 1968 to the point where a mass-circulation weekly, such as *Time,* could do a feature on it. The tone of the following article may strike contemporary readers as a rather unhip way of approaching soul music, but this awkward match of tone and topic is indicative of the newness of such subjects in mainstream forums. Franklin herself disliked this article, since a section of it dwelled on her marital problems and other aspects of her personal life in ways that she did not feel were accurate.[1] Those sections have been omitted from the version reprinted here. What remains is an account of the broad importance of soul in the late 1960s to American music and society, with a focus on Franklin's career. Franklin's background

---

1. Tales of Franklin's difficult marriage to Ted White during this period surface in many accounts of her, particularly those that recount the circumstances of her first and only recording date at Muscle Shoals, Alabama (mistakenly referred to as Memphis in the *Time* article), the date responsible for "I Never Loved a Man (the Way I Love You)," and her first session for Atlantic. This tale has become one of the most often-told of the whole late 1960s' soul music era, summing up either racial tension, marital tension, or poor judgment in the consumption of alcohol, depending on who is telling the story. See the accounts in Jerry Wexler and David Ritz, *Rhythm and the Blues: A Life in American Music* (New York: Alfred A. Knopf, 1993), 208–11; and Peter Guralnick, *Sweet Soul Music: Rhythm and Blues and the Southern Dream of Freedom* (New York: Harper and Row, 1986), 339–42. Franklin's own story does not paint a picture of marital harmony; for her account, as well as her response to the *Time* article reprinted here, see Aretha Franklin (and David Ritz), *Aretha: From These Roots* (New York: Villard, 1999), 109–10, 123–24.

in gospel music is outlined, from her father's career as a famous preacher to her own early experiences as a teenage gospel singer. This piece underscores the importance of her switch from Columbia to Atlantic records and the simultaneous move from an "easy listening" pop-jazz style to one based more on her gospel roots.

The relationship of soul music and "soul" in general to the black church and to changing notions of black racial self-consciousness is another focus of the article, which came at a moment when racial politics were assuming a higher and more militant profile and as public awareness was increasing about the Black Power movement and groups like the Black Panthers. These larger political currents form (at least part of) the context that enabled recordings like "Respect" and "Think" to resonate so strongly with African American audiences.

## LADY SOUL: SINGING IT LIKE IT IS

### *Time*

Has it got soul? Man, that's the question of the hour. If it has soul, then it's tough, beautiful, out of sight. It passes the test of with-itness. It has the authenticity of collard greens boiling on the stove, the sassy style of the boogaloo in a hip discotheque, the solidarity signified by "Soul Brother" scrawled on a ghetto storefront.

But what *is* soul? "It's like electricity—we don't really know what it is," says Singer Ray Charles. "But it's a force that can light a room." The force radiates from a sense of selfhood, a sense of knowing where you've been and what it means. Soul is a way of life—but it is always the hard way. Its essence is ingrained in those who suffer and endure to laugh about it later. Soul is happening everywhere, in esthetics and anthropology, history and dietetics, haberdashery and politics—although Hubert Humphrey's recent declaration to college students that he was a "soul brother" was all wrong. Soul is letting *others* say you're a soul brother. Soul is not needing others to say it.

Where soul is really at today is pop music. It emanates from the rumble of gospel chords and the plaintive cry of the blues. It is compounded of raw emotion, pulsing rhythm and spare, earthy lyrics—all suffused with the sensual, somewhat melancholy vibrations of the Negro idiom. Always the Negro idiom. LeRoi Jones, the militant Negro playwright, says: "Soul music is music coming out of the black spirit." For decades, it only reverberated around the edges of white pop music, injecting its native accent here and there; now it has penetrated to the core, and its tone and beat are triumphant.

### No Moon in June

Soul music is sincerity, a homely distillation of everybody's daily portion of pain and joy. "It pulls the cover off," explains Jim Stewart, a former banker and country fiddler who heads Memphis' soul-oriented Stax Records. "It's not the moon in June. It's life. Sometimes it's violence and sex. That's the way it is in this world. Sometimes there's animal in it; but let's face it, we've got a lot of animal in us." The difference between Tin Pan Alley and Soul is not hard to define. A conventional tunesmith might write: "You're still near, my darling, though we're

*Source:* "Lady Soul: Singing It Like Is," *Time*, June 28, 1968, pp. 62–66. © 1968 Time, Inc., reprinted by permission.

apart/I'll hold you always in my heart." The soul singer might put it: "Baby, since you split the scene the rent's come due/Without you or your money it's hard, yeah, hard to be true."

In all its power, lyricism and ecstatic anguish, soul is a chunky, 5-ft. 5-in. girl of 26 named Aretha Franklin singing from the stage of a packed Philharmonic Hall in Manhattan. She leans her head back, forehead gleaming with perspiration, features twisted by her intensity, and her voice—plangent and supple—pierces the hall:

> *Oh baby, what you done to me. . . .*
> *You make me feel, you make me feel, you make me feel like a natural*
> *woman.*

"Tell it like it is," her listeners exhort, on their feet, clapping and cheering. She goes into a "holiness shout"—a writhing dance derived from gospel services, all the while singing over the tumult. This is why her admirers call her Lady Soul.

## Bearing Witness

Aretha's vocal technique is simple enough: a direct, natural style of delivery that ranges over a full four octaves, and the breath control to spin out long phrases that curl sinuously around the beat and dangle tantalizingly from blue notes. But what really accounts for her impact goes beyond technique: it is her fierce, gritty conviction. She flexes her rich, cutting voice like a whip; she lashes her listeners—in her words—"to the bone, for deepness." "Aretha's music makes you sweaty, gives you a chill, makes you want to stomp your feet," says Bobby Taylor, leader of a soul group called Bobby and the Vancouvers. More simply, a 19-year-old Chicago fan named Lorraine Williams explains: "If Aretha says it, then it's important."

She does not seem to be performing so much as bearing witness to a reality so simple and compelling that she could not possibly fake it. In her selection of songs, whether written by others or by herself, she unfailingly opts for those that frame her own view of life. "If a song's about something I've experienced or that could've happened to me, it's good," she says. "But if it's alien to me, I couldn't lend anything to it. Because that's what soul is about—just living and having to get along."

For Aretha, as for soul singers generally, "just living and having to get along" mostly involves love—seeking it, celebrating its fulfillment, and especially bemoaning its loss. Aretha pleads in *Since You've Been Gone:*

> *I'm cryin'! Take me back, consider me please;*
> *If you walk in that door I can get up off my knees.*

And in the earthy candor of the soul sound, love is inescapably, bluntly physical. In *Respect*, she wails:

> *I'm out to give you all of my money,*
> *And all I'm askin' in return, Honey,*
> *Is to give me my propers when you get home . . .*
> *Yeah, baby, whip it to me when you get home.* *

---

*"Sock it to me," one of Aretha's variations on "whip it," is another in the long list of sexual terms from blues or jazz that have passed into respectable everyday language. Having come to prominence through such recordings as Aretha's and Mitch Ryder's, "Sock it to me" is now used in a neutral sense as a catch-phrase on TV's *Rowan and Martin's Laugh-In* and is a common sight on bumper stickers and even political placards. *Jazz* (originally a copulative verb) and *"rock 'n' roll"* (from a blues lyric, "My baby rocks me with a steady roll") are other examples.

"That's what most of the soul songs are all about," says Negro Comedian Godfrey Cambridge. Take Aretha's *Dr. Feelgood:*

*Don't send me no doctor fillin' me up with all of those pills;*
*Got me a man named Dr. Feelgood and, oh yeah,*
*That man takes care of all of my pains and my ills.*

"A woman works all day cooking and cleaning house for white folks, then comes home and has to cook and clean for her man. Sex is the only thing she's got to look forward to, to set her up to face the next day."

Aretha's father, the Rev. C. L. Franklin was—and is—pastor of Detroit's 4,500-member New Bethel Baptist Church, where the preaching is so fiery that two white-uniformed nurses stand by to aid overwrought parishioners. Franklin commands up to $4,000 per appearance as a barnstorming evangelist, has recorded 70 steadily selling LPs of his sermons. He may not be a member of the Baptist Ministers Conference, but his Cadillac, diamond stickpins and $60 alligator shoes testify to an eminently successful pastorate. Just how successful is not altogether clear, although when he was convicted last year for failing to file federal tax returns, the Government had shown that his income between 1959 and 1962 was more than $76,000. Franklin paid a $25,000 fine. Now 51, he is a strapping, stentorious charmer who has never let his spiritual calling inhibit his fun-loving ways.

Through her father, Aretha became immersed in gospel music at home as well as in church. Such stars as Mahalia Jackson, Clara Ward and James Cleveland often came by the house for jam sessions, whooping and clapping, singing and playing all through the night while Aretha watched intently from a corner. Once, at a funeral for an aunt of Aretha's, Clara Ward was singing the gospel tune *Peace in the Valley;* in her fervor, she tore off her hat and flung it on the ground. "That," says Aretha, "was when I wanted to become a singer." Aretha had the spirit, all right; after her first solo in church at the age of twelve, excited parishioners crowded around her father, saying, "Oh, that child can sure enough sing."

## Cutting Loose

Two years later, she was a featured performer with her father's gospel caravan, an evangelist show that crisscrossed the country by car (except for Franklin, who preferred to travel by plane). Though it ripened her vocal and professional skills, the experience of touring was in other ways a harsh initiation for Aretha. Says Cecil dryly: "Driving eight or ten hours trying to make a gig, and being hungry and passing restaurants all along the road, and having to go off the highway into some little city to find a place to eat because you're black—that had its effect." And the post-performance parties among older troupers in hotel rooms, where the liquor and sex were both plentiful—they had their effect too.

At 18, inspired by the example of former Gospel Singer Sam Cooke, Aretha decided to try the pop field. She started by auditioning for a New York manager named Jo King. "Aretha did everything wrong," recalls Mrs. King, "but it came out right. She had something—a concept of her own about music that needed no gimmickry. She was a completely honest musician." Groomed by Mrs. King, signed to a Columbia Records contract, Aretha began playing a sometimes seamy circuit of jazz and rhythm & blues clubs—with disheartening results. "I was afraid," she says. "I sang to the floor a lot." In the recording studio, she cut side after side with stereotyped pop arrangements—which sold indifferently. Deep down, she knew what was wrong with her repertory of standards, jazz tunes and novelties: "It wasn't really me."

Then 18 months ago she switched to Atlantic Records, which for two decades has specialized in bedrock rhythm & blues. Savvy Producer Jerry Wexler backed her with a funky Memphis rhythm section (which she ably joined on piano), and cut her loose to swing into the soul groove. Her first disk, *I Never Loved a Man,* sold a million copies. "It had looked for the longest time like I would never have a gold record," she says. "I wanted one so bad."

It was only the beginning. Aretha embarked on a remarkable year. She collected four more gold single records, sold a total of 1,200,000 albums, won two Grammy awards for record performances, and was cited by *Billboard* magazine as the top female vocalist of 1967. She toured Europe and was hailed in England as the new Bessie Smith—the first (1894–1937) of the great blues belters. Ray Charles called her "one of the greatest I've heard any time." Janis Joplin, 25, probably the most powerful singer to emerge from the white rock movement, ranked her as "the best chick singer since Billie Holiday." Her troubles were over.

## Badge of Identity

By all the commercial yardsticks used in the trade, soul has arrived—and it has arrived in the the hit parade as well as the "race market," in the suburbs as well as the ghettos, in the Midwestern campuses as well as Harlem's Apollo Theater.

By yardsticks used outside the trade, soul's arrival is even more significant. Since its tortuous evolution is so intertwined with Negro history and so expressive of Negro culture, Negroes naturally tend to value it as a sort of badge of black identity. "The abiding moods expressed in our most vital popular art form are not simply a matter of entertainment," says Negro Novelist Ralph Ellison. "They also tell us who and where we are."

Militant young Negroes put a more defiant slant on it. Explains Charles Keil, a white ethnomusicologist and the author of *Urban Blues:* "For a Negro to say 'B. B. King is my main man' is to say 'I take pride in who I am.' With this self-acceptance, a measure of unity is gained, and a demand is made upon white America: 'Accept us on our own terms.'"

Yet when soul solidarity is founded on a fellowship of suffering, it may involve not a demand for white acceptance but an outright exclusion of whites, as Godfrey Cambridge makes clear. "Soul is getting kicked in the ass until you don't know what it's for," he says. "It's being broke and down and out, and people telling you you're no good. It's the language of the subculture; but you can't learn it, because no one can give you black lessons."

Used in this way, the soul concept becomes a mystique, a glorification of Negritude in all its manifestations. The soul brother makes a point of emphasizing Negro inflections such as "yo" for "your," of abandoning slang words and phrases as soon as they reach universal currency, of eating foods such as chitlins, pig's feet and black-eyed peas, in mastering a lose, cocky way of walking down the street—in doing all the things that are closed off or alien to Whitey.

## Blue-Eyed Soul

Does this mean that white musicians by definition don't have soul? A very few Negroes will concede that such white singers as Frank Sinatra and Peggy Lee have it, and Aretha also nominates Frenchman Charles Aznavour. A few more will accept such blues-oriented whites as the Righteous Brothers, Paul Butterfield, and England's Stevie Winwood—largely because their sound is almost indistinguishable from Negro performers'. But for the most part, Negroes leave it up to whites to defend the idea of "blue-eyed soul," whether by the criterion of talent, experience or temperament. Janis Joplin argues it this way: "There's no patent on it. It's just feeling things. A housewife in Nebraska has soul, but she represses it, makes it conform to a lot of rules like marriage, or sugar-coats it."

If the earnest racial jockeying can be suspended, the question of who has soul actually becomes intriguing, if rather fanciful fun. The very elusiveness of the soul concept invites a freewheeling, parlor-game approach. Not long ago, in an eleven-page feature on the soul mystique, *Esquire* half seriously argued that there are only two kinds of people in the world: the haves and the have-nots—soulwise. Others have taken up the sport, which prompts the engaging notion that important personalities of history and legend can be classed in these terms.

As for those to whom soul is anything but a parlor game, one thing is certain: the closer a Negro gets to a "white" sound nowadays, the less soulful he is considered to be, and the more he is regarded as having betrayed his heritage. Dionne Warwick singing *Alfie?* Impure! Diana Ross and the Supremes recording an album of Rodgers and Hart songs? Unacceptable! Yet many "deviations" may be solid professionalism, a matter of adapting to changing audiences. As Lou Rawls says, "Show business is so vast—why should I limit myself to any one aspect if I have the capabilities to do more?"

On the other hand, some soul singers are so deeply imbued with the enduring streams of blues and gospel, so consumed by those primal currents of racial experience and emotion, that they could never be anything but soulful. Aretha Franklin is one of them. No matter what she sings, Aretha will never go white, and that certainty is as gratifying to her white fans as to her Negro ones.

## Going Home

The depth of Aretha's fidelity to her own heritage can be heard on an occasional Sunday night when she is in Detroit. Just as she did a dozen years ago, she goes to her father's services to sing a solo. She was there one recent evening, standing somewhat apart at first, a little dressy in mink-trimmed pink, preoccupied and somber. A drenching rain was falling outside, but 1,000 parishioners had shown up: Aretha was back.

She decided to sing the gospel song *Precious Lord.* The words, as the congregation knew them, were straightforward and simple:

*Precious Lord, take my hand.*
*Lead me on, let me stand.*
*I get tired,*
*I get weak and worn.*
*Hear my cry,*
*Hear my call.*
*Hold my hand,*
*Lest I fall.*
*Take my hand,*
*Precious Lord,*
*Lead me on.*

As the first mellow chords rippled from the organ and piano, Aretha stepped out of the robed choir that was massed on tiers behind the altar. Moving in front of a lectern, she closed her eyes and sang: "Precious Lord, take my hand. . . ." The congregation nodded or swayed gently in their seats. "Sing it!" they cried, clapping hands. "Amen, amen!" Her melodic lines curved out in steadily rising arcs as she let her spirit dictate variations on the lyrics, finally straining upward in pure soul:

*Please! Please! Please! Hear my call,*
*'Cause I'm gonna need you to hold on to my hand,*
*And I'm gonna need my friends right now 'cause I might fall . . .*

"All right!" answered the congregation. She was with them now. Her voice spiraled down to a breathy whisper, then broke into intense, halting phrases as she almost talked to the end:

*You know what's happening . . . and it's bad times right now;*
*Just lead us, just lead us, lead us on—*
*We've got to get home.*

Afterward, spent and exalted, Lady Soul said something that nobody in the church that night needed to be told: "My heart is still there in gospel music. It never left."

# 37. The Beatles, the "British Invasion," and Cultural Respectability

The Beatles' music emerged with such distinctiveness from the other popular music of the time that the bands' popularity became a media sensation, first in the United Kingdom during 1963, then in the United States in 1964. In the United States, the novelty of a *British* pop group contributed to their singularity and set them apart. The energy and enthusiasm conveyed by their recordings and performances, the variety of repertoire, the musicality and skill of the singing and playing, all conveyed with an irreverence toward establishment figures—these qualities created an effect of overwhelming charisma, especially for the white, middle-class teenagers who made up the bulk of their early audience.

The Beatles consisted of four members: rhythm guitarist John Lennon (1940–80) and bass guitarist Paul McCartney (b. 1942) wrote most of the songs and sang most of the lead vocals, while lead guitarist George Harrison (1943–2001) occasionally contributed songs and sang, with drummer Ringo Starr (Richard Starkey, b. 1940) rounding out the group. In combining the functions of songwriting, singing, and playing, the band recalled some of the pioneers of rock 'n' roll, particularly Chuck Berry, with the important innovation that they were a *band* whose recordings reproduced almost uncannily their sense of camaraderie (in this, they were preceded to some extent by the girl groups and the Beach Boys). The producer of all but one of their albums, George Martin, was also an unusually sympathetic partner; he ensured that the recordings possessed remarkable clarity, gave them a classically trained ear to help with arrangements, and had a knack for recognizing and capturing peak performances.[1] Martin also contributed much to the originality of the Beatles' use of orchestral instruments when they began to use them in 1965. Despite the importance of his contribution, skeptics of the Beatles who assign all credit for their success to Martin are surely overstating their case.

In light of the Beatles' impressive originality, it is easy to lose sight of where they came from. Somewhat in the manner of earlier international, multimedia superstars, such as Bing Crosby and Elvis Presley, at least some of that originality resulted from the synthesis of preexisting strains of popular music that had been kept more or less separate. From their start in "skiffle" (a form of folk music performed in a highly rhythmic manner borrowed from "trad" jazz, a British adaptation of New Orleans-style jazz), the Beatles' early performing repertory in numerous nightclub and dance performances consisted of liberal doses of 1950s' rhythm and blues (especially Chuck Berry and Little Richard), rockabilly (especially Elvis, Carl Perkins, and the Everly Brothers), Brill Building-produced pop music (especially the songs and arrangements of the girl groups), and the songs and performing style associated with Motown. The Beatles also occasionally included "standards" from pre–rock 'n' roll pop music, especially those that had been recently rerecorded by other artists, and influences from British music hall, a style dating back to the 19th-century, also occasionally appeared in their compositions. The Beatles' first two albums, *Please Please Me* and *With the Beatles,* released in the United Kingdom in 1963, mixed cover tunes of their nightclub repertory with original compositions.

---

The significance of the Beatles extends far beyond their popularity or their ability to create something fresh from a synthesis of previous styles: The Beatles, along with Bob Dylan, did more than any other pop musicians to shift the perception of popular music in the mainstream media.[2] The early article presented here—originally printed unsigned but later attributed to the London *Times* music critic William Mann—shows how critics were taking the Beatles seriously even during the first year of their popularity. Mann, with his musicological terminology, even compares the Beatles' musical processes to those used by Austrian composer, Gustav Mahler (1860–1911). While some of their most dedicated fans may dispute the appropriateness of this terminology for the Beatles' music, the fact that a music critic for the London *Times* would deign to analyze the music in this way (and approvingly at that) was significant and a harbinger of things to come.

---

1. Close listening to the Beatles' *Anthology* (three double-CD albums filled with rare recordings and alternate takes) sets provokes few quibbles about whether the best take of a given song was included on the official release.

2. Bernard Gendron termed this phenomenon "cultural accreditation." This chapter on the Beatles is much indebted to the chapters in Gendron's book dealing with the band; see *From Montmartre to the Mudd Club: Popular Music and the Avant-Garde* (Chicago: University of Chicago Press, 2002), chaps. 8–9.

# What Songs the Beatles Sang . . .

## *William Mann*

The outstanding English composers of 1963 must seem to have been John Lennon and Paul McCartney, the talented young musicians from Liverpool whose songs have been sweeping the country since last Christmas, whether performed by their own group, The Beatles, or by the numerous other teams of English troubadours that they also supply with songs.

I am not concerned here with the social phenomenon of Beatlemania, which finds expression in handbags, balloons and other articles bearing the likenesses of the loved ones, or in the hysterical screaming of young girls whenever the Beatle Quartet performs in public, but with the musical phenomenon. For several decades, in fact since the decline of the music-hall, England has taken her popular songs from the United States, either directly or by mimicry. But the songs of Lennon and McCartney are distinctly indigenous in character, the most imaginative and inventive examples of a style that has been developing on Merseyside during the past few years. And there is a nice, rather flattering irony in the news that The Beatles have now become prime favourites in America too.[3]

The strength of character in pop songs seems, and quite understandably, to be determined usually by the number of composers involved; when three or four people are required to make the original tunesmith's work publicly presentable, it is unlikely to retain much individuality or to wear very well. The virtue of The Beatles' repertory is that, apparently, they do it themselves; three of the four are composers, they are versatile instrumentalists, and when they do borrow a song from another repertory, their treatment is idiosyncratic—as when Paul McCartney sings 'Till there was you' from *The Music Man,* a cool, easy, tasteful version of this ballad, quite without artificial sentimentality.

Their noisy items are the ones that arouse teenagers' excitement. Glutinous crooning is generally out of fashion these days, and even a song about "Misery" sounds fundamentally quite cheerful; the slow, sad song about "This boy," which figures prominently in Beatle programmes, is expressively unusual for its lugubrious music, but harmonically it is one of their most intriguing, with its chains of pandiatonic clusters, and the sentiment is acceptable because voiced cleanly and crisply. But harmonic interest is typical of their quicker songs too, and one gets the impression that they think simultaneously of harmony and melody, so firmly are the major tonic sevenths and ninths built into their tunes, and the flat—submediant key—switches, so natural is the Aeolian cadence at the end of "Not a second time" (the chord progression which ends Mahler's *Song of the Earth*).

Those submediant switches from C major into A-flat major, and to a lesser extent mediant ones (e.g. the octave ascent in the famous "I want to hold your hand") are a trademark of Lennon-McCartney songs—they do not figure much in other pop repertories, or in The Beatles' arrangements of borrowed material—and show signs of becoming a mannerism. The other trademark of their compositions is a firm and purposeful bass line with a musical life of its own; how Lennon and McCartney divide their creative responsibilities I have yet to discover, but it is perhaps significant that Paul is the bass guitarist of the group. It may also be significant that George Harrison's song "Don't bother me" is harmonically a good deal more primitive, though it is nicely enough presented.

I suppose it is the sheer loudness of the music that appeals to Beatles admirers (there is something to be heard even through the squeals), and many parents must have cursed the

---

3. This statement was a bit premature when this article was published; no Beatles' recordings entered *Billboard*'s Hot 100 until January 11, 1964.

*Source:* From Our Music Critic [William Mann], "What Songs the Beatles Sang . . . ," *The Times*, December 27, 1963, p. 4. © The Times, December 27, 1963. Used by permission.

electric guitar's amplification this Christmas—how fresh and euphonious the ordinary guitars sound in The Beatles' version of "Till there was you"—but parents who are still managing to survive the decibels and, after copious repetition over several months, still deriving some musical pleasure from the overhearing, do so because there is a good deal of variety—oh, so welcome in pop music—about what they sing.

The autocratic but not by any means ungrammatical attitude to tonality (closer to, say, Peter Maxwell Davies's carols in *O Magnum Mysterium* than to Gershwin or Loewe or even Lionel Bart); the exhilarating and often quasi-instrumental vocal duetting, sometimes in scat or in falsetto, behind the melodic line; the melismas with altered vowels ("I saw her yesterday-ee-ay") which have not quite become mannered, and the discreet, sometimes subtle, varieties of instrumentation—a suspicion of piano or organ, a few bars of mouth-organ obbligato, an excursion on the claves or maracas; the translation of African blues or American Western idioms (in "Baby, it's you," the Magyar 8/8 meter too) into tough, sensitive Merseyside.

These are some of the qualities that make one wonder with interest what The Beatles, and particularly Lennon and McCartney, will do next, and if America will spoil them or hold on to them, and if their next record will wear as well as the others. They have brought a distinctive and exhilarating flavour into a genre of music that was in danger of ceasing to be music at all.

> The following article by Theodore Strongin (music critic for the *New York Times*), published two months after Mann's piece, demonstrates how the intellectual apparatus of high culture could be marshaled against pop music. Strongin's article perpetuates a tradition that goes back to dismissive academic descriptions of jazz and swing.[4]

## MUSICOLOGICALLY . . .
### *Theodore Strongin*

"You can tell right away it's the Beatles and not anyone else," is the opinion of a 15-year-old specialist on the subject who saw the Beatles on the Ed Sullivan show last night. The age of 15 or 16 or 14 or 13 is essential in a Beatles expert.

Taking the above axiom as gospel, this listener made an attempt to find out just what is musically unique about the British visitors.

The Beatles are directly in the mainstream of Western tradition: that much may be immediately ascertained. Their harmony is unmistakably diatonic. A learned British colleague, writing on his home ground, has described it as pandiatonic, but I disagree.

The Beatles have a tendency to build phrases around unresolved, leading tones. This precipitates the ear into a false modal frame that temporarily turns the fifth of the scale into a tonic, momentarily suggesting the Mixylydian [*sic*] mode. But everything always ends as plain diatonic all the same.

---

4. For numerous examples of such descriptions, see Walser, *Keeping Time: Readings in Jazz History* (New York and Oxford: Oxford University Press, 1999).

*Source:* Theodore Strongin, "Musicologically . . ." *New York Times*, February 10, 1964, p. 53. Copyright © 1964 by the New York Times Co. Reprinted with permission.

Meanwhile, the result is the addition of a very, very slight touch of British countryside nostalgia with a trace of Vaughan Williams to the familiar elements of the rock and roll prototype. "It's just that English rock and roll is more sophisticated," explained the 15-year-old authority.

As to instrumentation, three of the four Beatles (George Harrison, Paul McCartney, and John Lennon) play different sizes of electronically amplified plucked-stringed instruments. Ringo Starr ("He's just like a little puppy, he's so cute," said our specialist) plays the drums. The Beatles vocal quality can be described as hoarsely incoherent, with the minimal enunciation necessary to communicate schematic texts.

Two theories were offered in at least one household to explain the Beatles' popularity. The specialist said "We haven't had an idol in a few years. The Beatles are different, and we have to get rid of our excess energy somehow."

The other theory is that the longer parents object with such high dudgeon, the longer children will squeal so hysterically.

# 38. *A Hard Day's Night*

The Beatles' third British album, *A Hard Day's Night* (1964), was also the title of their first movie, and their first consisting entirely of original compositions. The movie, however, rather than the album, won them a whole legion of new converts among high-middlebrow cultural authorities and audiences. Andrew Sarris's review is indicative of the pleasantly surprised reception that greeted *A Hard Day's Night* among the intelligentsia, and he was not alone in applauding the film for its incorporation of sophisticated cinematic style derived, at least partly, from the French *nouvelle vague* (or "New Wave").[1]

## BRAVO BEATLES!
### *Andrew Sarris*

*A Hard Day's Night* is a particularly pleasant surprise in a year so full of unexpectedly unpleasant surprises. I have no idea who is the most responsible—director Richard Lester or screenwriter Alun Owen or the Messrs John Lennon, Paul McCartney, George Harrison,

---

1. For another, even more surprised-sounding review, see Bosley Crowther, "The Four Beatles in 'A Hard Day's Night,'" *New York Times*, August 12, 1964, 41.

*Source:* Andrew Sarris, "Bravo Beatles!" *Village Voice*, August 27, 1964, p. 13.

and Ringo Starr, better known collectively as The Beatles. Perhaps it was all a happy accident, and the lightning of inspiration will never strike again in the same spot. The fact remains that *A Hard Day's Night* has turned out to be the *Citizen Kane* of jukebox musicals, the brilliant crystallisation of such diverse cultural particles as the pop movie, rock 'n' roll, *cinéma vérité*, the *nouvelle vague*, free cinema, the affectedly hand-held camera, frenzied cutting, the cult of the sexless sub-adolescent, the semi-documentary, and studied spontaneity. So help me, I resisted The Beatles as long as I could. As a cab driver acquaintance observed, "So what's new about The Beatles? Didn't you ever hear of Ish Kabibble?" Alas, I had. I kept looking for openings to put down The Beatles. Some of their sly crows' humour at the expense of a Colonel Blimp character in a train compartment is a bit too deliberate. "I fought the war for people like you," sez he. "Bet you're sorry you won," sez they. Old Osborne ooze, sez I. But just previously, the fruitiest looking of the four predators had looked up enticingly at the bug-eyed Blimp and whimpered "Give us a kiss." Depravity of such honest frankness is worth a hundred pseudo-literary exercises like Becket.

Stylistically, *A Hard Day's Night* is everything Tony Richardson's version of *Tom Jones* tried to be and wasn't. Thematically, it is everything Peter Brook's version of *Lord of the Flies* tried to be and wasn't. Fielding's satiric gusto is coupled here with Golding's primordial evil, and the strain hardly shows. I could have done with a bit less of a false sabre-toothed, rattling wreck of an old man tagged with sickeningly repetitive irony as a "clean" old man. The pop movie mannerisms of the inane running joke about one of the boys' managers being sensitively shorter than the other might have been dispensed with at no great loss.

The foregoing are trifling reservations, however, about a movie that works on every level for every kind of audience. The open-field helicopter-shot sequence of The Beatles on a spree is one of the most exhilarating expressions of high spirits I have seen on the screen.[2] The razor-slashing wit of the dialogue must be heard to be believed and appreciated. One as horribly addicted to alliteration as this otherwise sensible scribe can hardly resist a line like "Ringo's drums loom large in his legend."

I must say I enjoyed even the music enormously, possibly because I have not yet been traumatised by transistors into open rebellion against the "Top 40" and such. (I just heard "Hello, Dolly" for the first time the other day, and the lyrics had been changed to "Hello, Lyndon.") Nevertheless I think there is a tendency to underrate rock 'n' roll because the lyrics look so silly in cold print. I would make two points here. First, it is unfair to compare R&R with Gershwin, Rodgers, Porter, Kern, et al., as if all pre-R&R music from Tin Pan Alley was an uninterrupted flow of melodiousness. This is the familiar fallacy of nostalgia. I remember too much brassy noise from the big-band era to be stricken by the incursions of R&R. I like the songs The Beatles sing despite the banality of the lyrics, but the words in R&R only mask the poundingly ritualistic meaning of the beat. It is in the beat that the passion and togetherness is most movingly expressed, and it is the beat that the kids in the audience pick up with their shrieks as they drown out the words they have already heard a thousand times. To watch The Beatles in action with their constituents is to watch the kind of direct theater that went out with Aristophanes, or perhaps even the Australian bushman. There is an empathy there that a million Lincoln Center Repertory companies cannot duplicate. Toward the end of *A Hard Day's Night* I began to understand the mystique of

---

2. This scene, accompanied by "Can't Buy Me Love" on the soundtrack, was one of the clearest antecedents of post-MTV music video and of contemporary rock film scoring; see Jeff Smith, *The Sounds of Commerce: Marketing Popular Film Music* (New York: Columbia University Press, 1998), 159–60.

The Beatles. Lester's crane shot facing the audience from behind The Beatles established the emotional unity of the performers and their audience. It is a beautifully Bazinian deep-focus shot of hysteria to a slow beat punctuated by the kind of zoom shots I have always deplored in theory but must now admire in practice. Let's face it. My critical theories and preconceptions are all shook up, and I am profoundly grateful to The Beatles for such a pleasurable softening of hardening aesthetic arteries.

As to what the Beatles "mean," I hesitate to speculate. The trouble with sociological analysis is that it is unconcerned with aesthetic values. *A Hard Day's Night* could have been a complete stinker of a movie and still be reasonably "meaningful." I like The Beatles in this moment in film history not merely because they mean something but rather because they express effectively a great many aspects of modernity that have converged inspiredly in their personalities. When I speak affectionately of their depravity, I am not commenting on their private lives, about which I know less than nothing. The wedding ring on Ringo's finger startles a great many people as a subtle Pirandellian switch from a character like Dopey of the Seven Dwarfs to a performer who chooses to project an ambiguous identity. It hardly matters.

What interests me about The Beatles is not what they are but what they choose to express. Their Ish Kabibble hairdos,[3] for example, serve two functions. They become unique as a group and interchangeable as individuals. Except for Ringo, the favourite of the fans, the other three Beatles tend to get lost in the shuffle. And yet each is a distinctly personable individual behind their collective façade of androgynous selflessness—a façade appropriate, incidentally, to the undifferentiated sexuality of their sub-adolescent fans. The Beatles are not merely objects, however. A frequent refrain of their middle-aged admirers is that The Beatles don't take themselves too seriously. They take themselves seriously enough, all right; it is their middle-aged admirers and detractors they don't take too seriously. The Beatles are a sly bunch of anti-Establishment anarchists, but they are too slick to tip their hand to the authorities. People who have watched them handle their fans and the press tell me that they make Sinatra and his clan look like a bunch of rubes at a county fair. Of course, they have been shrewdly promoted, and a great deal of the hysteria surrounding them has been rigged with classic fakery and exaggeration. They may not be worth a paragraph in six months, but right now their entertaining message seems to be that everyone is "people." Beatles and squealing sub-adolescents as much as Negroes and women and so-called senior citizens, and that however much alike "people" may look in a group or a mass or a stereotype, there is in each soul a unique and irreducible individuality.

---

3. Ish Kabibble was a trumpeter and novelty singer with Kay Kyser's swing band during the 1930s and 1940s. Kabibble wore a distinctive "pudding basin"-style haircut.

# 39. England Swings, and the Beatles Evolve on *Revolver* and *Sgt. Pepper*

The album *A Hard Day's Night,* along with the two that followed— *Beatles for Sale* (1964) and *Help!* (1965, also the title of their second movie)—featured a steady expansion of musical and technological resources. The Beatles had begun to use four-track recording on *A Hard Day's Night,* which increased the possibilities of overdubbing (i.e., layering vocal and instrumental parts in succession, rather than recording everything at once). The expansion of instrumentation was modest on these albums but nonetheless significant as more songs featured acoustic guitars, additional percussion instruments, and piano and organ, as well as unusual instrumental effects, such as the guitar feedback that opens "I Feel Fine" (1964, from *Beatles for Sale*). One song from *Help!,* "Yesterday," was the first Beatles' song to feature orchestral instruments. Compared to the thick texture found in most pop recordings employing orchestral instruments, the chamber ensemble texture of the string quartet on "Yesterday" produced a novel and relatively transparent sound.

The modest sense of evolution found in the Beatles' early albums, regardless of its novelty for a rock 'n' roll group, did little to prepare the public for what was to happen next. On *Rubber Soul,* released late in 1965, the combination of subtle instrumentation with introspection of lyric content and an "artsy" cover photo was novel within the pop music context of the time.[1] The U.S. version of the album enhanced the effect of seriousness by deleting several of the songs with clearer ties to rock 'n' roll and by adding some quieter acoustic tracks that had been left off the U.S. release of *Help.*[2] Many listeners shared Brian Wilson's reaction to *Rubber Soul* (described earlier in the excerpt from Wilson's autobiography; see chapter 28). On the eve of the explosion of media attention to the counterculture and psychedelia, *Rubber Soul* and its successor *Revolver* (1966), along with the concurrent albums of Bob Dylan, convinced many that rock could be the music of adults, even those with intellectual inclinations. While Dylan had primarily brought notions of artistic sincerity with him from the folk music movement, where such

---

1. One recent article described the cover of *Rubber Soul* as "the first suggestion of psychedelia . . . with its hallucinatory photo of the band and distorted Art Nouveau-derived lettering"). See Steve Jones and Martin Sorger, "Covering Music: A Brief History and Analysis of Album Cover Design," *Journal of Popular Music Studies,* 11–12 (1999–2000): 68–102.

2. British albums typically contained 14 songs, rather than 12 in the United States, resulting in different versions of albums released on both sides of the Atlantic.

notions were connected to creating a sense of community between performer and audience, the Beatles achieved their sense of authenticity through their allusions to high art. Sarris's review, in chapter 38, described how *A Hard Day's Night* helped accomplish this cultural accreditation, but many of the songs released in 1965–66 achieved a sense of artiness musically via formal complexity, textural variety, and lyrical introspection.

With Richard Goldstein's review of *Revolver*, we enter the realm of a new form of criticism that arises from a sensibility and milieu similar to that of the music it describes. While earlier critics, such as Robert Shelton, Nat Hentoff, and Ralph J. Gleason, had written sympathetically about popular music, their critical sensibilities were honed in the 1940s and 1950s on jazz and folk music. Goldstein was among the first of a new breed of critic who had come of age with "rock music" (now distinct from the earlier "rock 'n' roll") and who were trying to articulate an alternative aesthetic that might correspond with the new music. Goldstein asserts his belief in the validity of aesthetic contemplation for rock when he writes "we will view this album in retrospect as a key work in the development of rock 'n' roll into an artistic pursuit." That Goldstein (and other early rock critics) devoted a lot of space to the Beatles was not fortuitous: he wrote in a later piece (on *Sgt. Pepper*) that "Without [the Beatles] there could be no such discipline as 'rock criticism.' The new music is their thing."[3]

## POP EYE: ON "REVOLVER"
### *Richard Goldstein*

SWINGING LONDON, August 17—As though displaying unswerving loyalty to its idols, British youth has flipped completely over the new Beatles album "Revolver." The single chosen from these songs—"Yellow Submarine b/w Eleanor Rigby"—came on the charts one week ago at number four. Today it is number one. The entire album is in the top twenty. Large record stores and tiny street stalls feature mass displays of the art-nouveau-ish album jacket. The sound of "Revolver" blares from window after window. John harmonizes with Paul in greengrocers and boutiques. George plays his sitar from cars stalled in traffic. Ringo ricochets from the dome of St. Paul's. The Beatles are harder to avoid than even the Americans.

But there is more than mere adulation behind the sudden conquest of Britain by this particular LP. "Revolver" is a revolutionary record, as important to the expansion of pop territory as was "Rubber Soul." It was apparent last year that the 12 songs in "Rubber Soul"

---

3. Richard Goldstein, "Pop Eye: I Blew My Cool Through the New York Times," *Village Voice*, July 20, 1967: 14, 25–26.

*Source:* Richard Goldstein, "Pop Eye: On 'Revolver,'" *Village Voice*, August 25, 1966, pp. 23, 25. Reprinted with permission by the author.

represented an important advance. "Revolver" is the great leap forward. Hear it once and you know it's important. Hear it twice, it makes sense. Third time around, it's fun. Fourth time, it's subtle. On the fifth hearing, "Revolver" becomes profound.

If "Rubber Soul" opened up areas of baroque progression and Oriental instrumentation to pop commercialization, "Revolver" does the same for electronic music. Much of the sound in this new LP is atonal, and a good deal of the vocal is dissonant. Instead of drowning poor voices in echo-chamber acoustics, "Revolver" presents the mechanics of pop music openly, as an integral part of musical composition. Instead of sugar and sex, what we get from the control knobs here is a bent and pulverized sound. John Cage move over, the Beatles are now reaching a super-receptive audience with electronic sound.

## Resemble Mantra

The key number on the album is that last track, "Tomorrow Never Knows." No one can say what actually inspired the song, but its place in the pantheon of psychedelic music is assured. The lyrics resemble a mantra in form and message:

> *Turn off your mind*
> *Relax and float downstream*
> *This is not dying*
> *This is not dying*
>
> *Lay down all thought*
> *Surrender to the void*
> *It is shining*
> *It is shining*
>
> *That you may see*
> *the meaning of within*
> *It is being*
> *It is being*
>
> *Love is all*
> *and love is everyone*
> *It is knowing*
> *It is knowing . . .*

While not unprecedented, the combination of acid-Buddhist imagery and rock beat had never before been attempted with such complexity. At first, the orchestration sounds like Custer's last stand. Foghorn-like organ chords and the sound of bird-like screeching overshadows the vocal. But the overall effect of this hodge-podge is a very effective suspension of musical reality. John's vocal sounds distant and God-like. What he is saying transcends almost everything in what was once called pop music. The boundaries will now have to be re-negotiated.

"Revolver" also represents a fulfillment of the raga-Beatle sound. A George Harrison composition, "Love You To," is a functioning raga, with a natural beat and an engaging vocal advising: "Make love all day long/Make love singing songs."

"Eleanor Rigby" is an orchestrated ballad about the agony of loneliness. Its characters, Eleanor herself and Father McKenzie, represent sterility. Eleanor "died in the church and was buried along with her name." The good father writes "words to the sermon that no one will hear. No one comes near." As a commentary on the state of modern religion, this song will hardly be appreciated by those who see John Lennon as an anti-Christ.[4] But "Eleanor Rigby" is really about the unloved and un-cared for. When Eleanor makes up, the narrator asks: "Who is it for?" While the father darns his socks, the question is: "What does he care?"

## More Next Door

"Yellow Submarine" is as whimsical and child-like as its flip side is metaphysical. Its subject is an undersea utopia where "our friends are all aboard/many more of them live next door," and where "we live a life of ease/Every one of us has all he needs."

"For No One" is one of the most poignant songs on the record. Its structure approaches madrigal form—with an effective horn-solo counterpoint. Its lyrics are in an evocative Aznavour bag.

"Taxman" is the album's example of political cheek, in which George enumerates Britain's current economic woes. At one point, the group joins in to identify the villains. "Taxman—Mr. Wilson . . . Taxman—Mr. Heath." They lay it right on the non-partisan line.

There is some mediocre material on this album. But the mystique forming around "Revolver" is based on more than one or two choice tracks—it encompasses the record as a whole.

It is a bit difficult to gauge the importance of "Revolver" from this city, where it has become gospel and where other beat groups are turning out cover copies like Guttenberg Bibles. But is seems now that we will view this album in retrospect as a key work in the development of rock 'n' roll into an artistic pursuit.

If nothing else, "Revolver" must reduce the number of cynics where the future of pop music is concerned—even on the violent side of the Atlantic.

> The Beatles' critical acceptance reached new heights with the release of their next album, *Sgt. Pepper's Lonely Hearts Club Band* (1967). The album was a loosely organized "concept" album, simulating a concert given by the Beatles' alter egos—the namesake of the album. The album made extensive use of the recording studio, incorporating numerous sound effects, tape collages, orchestral instruments, and sound processing. The brief article that follows appeared in *Newsweek* and documents how *Sgt. Pepper* won over even those middlebrow publications that had maintained a condescending stance toward popular music until that point, although the author cannot completely relinquish the patronizing tone of yore adopted by such publications. While the album won new admirers for the Beatles' music, and most rock fans and critics were dazzled, not all agreed. One of the disenchanted, Richard Goldstein, published a review of the album and a defense of the review; in both cases, he argued that innovations in instrumentation and recording techniques were leading formal innovations in songwriting, rather than the other way around, much to the detriment of the Beatles' music.[5] The release of

---

4. This is probably a reference to Lennon's remarks, published in March 1966, that the Beatles were "more popular than Jesus," a comment that when repeated in the United States caused a furor on the eve of their 1966 tour.

5. Richard Goldstein, "We Still Need the Beatles, but . . . ," *New York Times*, June 18, 1967, sec. II, p. 24; and idem., "Pop Eye: I Blew My Cool Through the New York Times," *Village Voice*, July 20, 1967: 14, 25–26.

Sgt. Pepper coincided with the Beatles' withdrawal from "live" performance, a coincidence that suggested to Goldstein that performance has
the potential to rein in excesses that result from the pursuit of dazzling
effects in the recording studio.

## IT'S GETTING BETTER . . .
### *Jack Kroll*

The problem of choosing Britain's new Poet Laureate is easy. The obvious choice is the
Beatles. They would be the first laureates to be really popular since Tennyson—their extraordinary new LP, "Sgt. Pepper's Lonely Hearts Club Band," has been out for two weeks
and has already sold 1.5 million copies in the U.S. alone. And the Beatles' recent LP's "Rubber Soul," "Revolver," and now "Sgt. Pepper" are really volumes of aural poetry in the
McLuhan age.[6]

Indeed, "Sgt. Pepper" is such an organic work (it took four months to make) that it is
like a pop "Façade," the suite of poems by Edith Sitwell musicalized by William Walton.
Like "Façade," "Sgt. Pepper" is a rollicking, probing language-and-sound vaudeville,
which grafts skin from all three brows—high, middle, and low—into a pulsating collage
about mid-century manners and madness.

The vaudeville starts immediately on the first track, in which the Beatles, adding several horn players, create the "persona" of the album—Sgt. Pepper's band, oompahing
madly away with the elephant-footed rhythm, evoking the good old days when music
spoke straight to the people with tongues of brass, while dubbed in crowds cheer and
applaud as the Beatles make raucous fun of their own colossal popularity.

After this euphoric, ironic, nostalgic fanfare, the Beatles leave Sgt. Pepper polishing his
coronet in the wings and go on with the show, creating little lyrics, dramas, and satires on
homely virtues, homely disasters, homely people and all the ambiguities of home. "She's
leaving home," sing John and Paul, as a harp flutters, a string group makes genteel aspidis-
tra sounds and a lugubrious cello wraps the soggy English weather around the listener's
ears. The song is a flabby family fiasco in miniature, spiking the horrors of the British hearth
like a stripped down Osborne play. "Me used to be an angry young man," sings Paul in
"Getting Better," and adds "it's getting better all the time," as the group sarcastically repeats
"get-ting bet-ter, get-ting bet-ter" in those Liverpudlian accents.

### Vision

Getting better? Well, there's John's vision of a vinyl Arcadia, with it's Sitwellian images:
"Cellophane flowers of yellow and green . . . Plasticine porters with looking-glass ties"
which turns Wordsworth's idealized Lucy into a mod goddess, "Lucy in the sky with diamonds." And then there's Paul announcing "I'm painting my room in the colorful
way/And when my mind is wandering/There I will go/And it really doesn't matter if I'm

---

6. This reference to Marshall McLuhan echoes remarks made by Richard Goldstein in an article
reprinted in chapter 48; see "Pop Eye: Evaluating Media," *Village Voice*, July 14, 1966, 6–7.

*Source:* Jack Kroll, "It's Getting Better . . . ," *Newsweek*, June 26, 1967, p. 70. © 1967 Newsweek, Inc. All
rights reserved. Reprinted by permission.

wrong I'm right/Where I belong I'm right." But even this manifestation of psychedelic individualism is undercut as George's sitar boings one note relentlessly like a giant mocking frog.

"Within You Without You" is George Harrison's beautiful new cuddle-up with Mother India. Backed by three cellos, eight violins, three tambouras, a dilruba, a tabla, and a table-harp, George plays the sitar as he chants Vedantic verities such as "The time will come when you see we're all one, and life flows on within you and without you." These Himalayan homilies are given powerful effect by the wailing, undulating cascade of sound which turns the curved, infinite universe of Indian music into a perfect tonal setting for the new pantheism of the young. But even here, the Beatles, like Chaplin, deflate their own seriousness as the song ends—to be followed by a crowd laughing.

Some critics have already berated the Beatles for the supersophisticated electronic technology on this record. But it is useless to lament the simple old days of the Mersey sound. The Beatles have lost their innocence, certainly, but loss of innocence is, increasingly, their theme and the theme of a more "serious" new art from the stories of Donald Barthelme to the plays of Harold Pinter.

The new Beatles are justified by the marvelous last number alone: "A Day in the Life," which was foolishly banned by the BBC because of its refrain "I'd love to turn you on." But this line means many things, coming as it does after a series of beautifully sorrowful stanzas in which John confronts the world's incessant bad news sighing "Oh boy" with a perfect blend of innocence and spiritual exhaustion. Evoking the catatonic metropolitan crown (like Eliot's living dead flowing across London Bridge), John's wish to "turn you on" is a desire to start the bogged-down juices of life itself. This point is underscored by an overwhelming musical effect, using a 41-piece orchestra—a growling, bone-grinding crescendo that drones up like a giant crippled turbine struggling to spin new power into a foundered civilization. This number is the Beatles' "Waste Land," a superb achievement of their brilliant and startlingly effective popular art.

# 40. Art School and the British Blues Revival

The Beatles hailed from Liverpool, a seaport on England's northwest coast. Liverpool had long had access to the latest releases from the United States, and, consequently, other bands (in addition to the Beatles) developed a blend of rockabilly, pop, and R&B for playing in local dance halls and nightclubs, resulting in a style dubbed "Merseybeat" by the British music press. In the wake of the Beatles, other Merseybeat artists, such as Gerry and the Pacemakers, Billy J. Kramer and the Dakotas, and Peter and Gordon (not from Liverpool but with a song written by Lennon and McCartney) had hits in the United States, thus inspiring the media to coin the term "British Invasion" to describe the phenomenon. It had been rare for any British artists to penetrate the American pop market until that time, and this sudden success set off a fad for all things British.

Concurrent with the pop-oriented Merseybeat artists, a more blues-oriented music scene was thriving down in London, fueled by record enthusiasts and collectors, along with refugees from British art schools. The role of art schools cannot be underestimated in the development of a distinctive form of British rock 'n' roll: With no real equivalent in the United States, art schools in Britain filled a gap somewhere between university (which during the 1950s and 1960s was still a fairly exclusive affair) and technical or trade schools. Better-than-average students with some vague artistic inclination were often sent to art school, where they would presumably learn a trade, such as graphic design. These schools became hotbeds for aspiring pop musicians, some of whom even absorbed some fashionable theories about art along the way.[1] The Rolling Stones' lead guitarist, Keith Richards (b. 1942), memorably described his experience: "I mean in England, if you're lucky, you can get into art school. It's somewhere they put you if they can't put you anywhere else. If you can't saw wood straight or file metal. It's where they put me to learn graphic design because I happened to be good at drawing apples or something. Fifteen . . . I was there for three years and meanwhile I learned how to play guitar. Lotta guitar players in art school. A lot of terrible artists too. It's funny."[2]

Several groups from the London blues and British art school scenes achieved commercial success during this period, most notably the Kinks, the Who, the Yardbirds, and the Rolling Stones. The Kinks scored three hits in a row in the United States in late 1964–early 1965 with "You Really Got Me," "All Day and All of the Night," and "Tired of Waiting." The first two of these songs were proto-heavy metal, constructed around primal riffs played on a highly distorted electric guitar. Subsequent Kinks' recordings saw them developing a style based on British music hall influences and ironic, detached personae ("Well-Respected Man," "Sunny Afternoon"), presenting an interesting antithesis to the "authentic" ethos so prevalent during the era. Many have viewed this self-consciousness and the nonblues sound of their later music as peculiarly representative of a British-identified pop, with main songwriter Ray Davies (b. 1944) seen as particularly responsible for this sensibility.

The Yardbirds, on the other hand, came out of the same London blues scene as the Rolling Stones and recorded numerous covers of American blues recordings, especially songs associated with the Chicago blues. Their American hits included both bluesy songs, such as "I'm a

---

1. For an extensive study of the impact of British art school on the development of British rock, see Simon Frith and Howard Horne, *Art into Pop* (London: Methuen, 1987).

2. Robert Greenfield, "Keith Richard: Got to Keep it Growing," in *The Rolling Stone Interviews, Vol. 2* (New York: Straight Arrow, 1973, 218; first published in *Rolling Stone* in August 1971).

Man," and the more pop-oriented "For Your Love." The Yardbirds are also notable for having featured a succession of guitarists who eventually became famous on their own or as leaders of other groups: Eric Clapton (b. 1945), Jeff Beck (b. 1944), and Jimmy Page (b. 1944).

The Who have a main songwriter, Pete Townshend (b. 1945), who did time in art school. The band was associated with the Mods, a London subculture of the mid-1960s that worshipped American R&B and had a particular fondness for motor scooters, smart clothes, and amphetamines. The Who's music included blues influences at times, along with generous dollops of ironic self-consciousness. Master manipulators of mass cultural symbols, the band began wearing clothing redolent of "old England" years before *Sgt. Pepper*. They were also practitioners of performance art—their stage act featured a kind of highly theatricalized violence, which for a time included the destruction of their equipment. Pete Townshend became one of the more articulate spokespeople for understanding 1960s rock through the prism of modernist theories about art. The Who's music presented two somewhat opposed tendencies: an emphasis on performance and the enduring values of early rock 'n' roll and the blues, and an exploration of extended forms associated with art music, which reached its apogee in the "rock opera," *Tommy*.[3]

The Rolling Stones were the most famous band to emerge from the early 1960s London blues scene, and they had roots in art school as well. The Stones were quickly pegged in the press as a scruffy foil to the Beatles' bohemian charm. The following article is one of the earliest in the British music press to seize upon the rebellious image of the Stones, an image that seemed to flaunt its artificiality. The music press did little to hide its complicity in the production of this image: An article appearing a month later, in March 1964, featured a headline screaming, "Would You Let Your Sister Go with a Rolling Stone?"; the headline, however, had little to do with the content of the article, which was little more than a profile of "life on the road" with the band.[4] The article reprinted here appeared in *Melody Maker*, one of the two leading British popular music magazines, along with the *New Musical Express*. At a time when no real equivalents existed in the United States, these magazines mixed informative profiles with tabloid-style sensationalism. The author, Ray Coleman, who later went on to write respectable biographies of pop musicians, seems to be writing with tongue firmly placed in cheek.

3. For Pete Townshend's witty appraisal of the Who's career from 1965 to 1971, see Peter Townshend, Review of "The Who: *Meaty, Beaty, Big, and Bouncy,*" *Rolling Stone,* December 7, 1971.

4. Ray Coleman, "Would You Let Your Sister Go with a Rolling Stone?" *Melody Maker,* March 14, 1964, 8. Note that this article was written by the same author as, and appeared in the same magazine a mere month later than, the article reprinted in this anthology.

# REBELS WITH A BEAT

## *Ray Coleman*

"Wasn't that the Rolling Stones you just left?" asked the taxi driver as I left a restaurant in London's Mayfair.

"Yes. What do you think of them?"

"A bunch of right 'erberts!" he replied with the cutting pertinence so typical of the London cabbie. "'Ere, aren't they the boys they say are trying to knock the Beatles off the top?"

While cab drivers are often noted for their lack of tact, some have rare perception. Had I been an agent or a record chief, I would probably have signed that taxi driver immediately as my trends adviser.

The Rolling Stones might have had other ideas, like punching him on the nose. Because they deeply resent any suggestion that they are attempting to overtake the Beatles.

Yet if the Beatles are to be knocked from their perch in the future, by a British group, the popular notion is that the Rolling Stones could easily be their successors.

Why? Their image is perfect . . . five disheveled rebels who have already made a firm imprint on the hit parade, who have gained a huge following among young people, who never wear stage uniforms, and who JUST DON'T CARE.

There are even rumblings inside show business of a swing against the Beatles in favor of the Rolling Stones. Many observers endorse the view of an alert writer to Melody Maker's Mailbag.

She asserted that young pop fans instinctively turn against an idol whom their parents endorse, like the Beatles. Fans actually enjoy hearing their elders spurning their worship of their heroes. That way, there is an outlet for their emotional involvement.

## Horrors

That taxi driver we met earlier was aged 42. He loathed the Rolling Stones. Like certain others he considers them downright scruffy, hairy horrors who need a severe talking-to from Lord Montgomery.

I have no psychiatric or sociological qualifications, but I think I can confirm that the Rolling Stones are 100 percent human beings, acutely aware of what is going on.

They have no leader, but Mick Jagger, 19-year-old ex-economics student (lead singer, harmonica) and Keith Richard (19, ex-art student, guitarist) do most of the talking.

The others are Brian Jones, aged 20 (harmonica, guitar), whom the rest describe as an ex-layabout; Bill Wyman (22, bass guitarist, former electronics man); and 22-year-old drummer Charlie Watts, a man of few words who claims to have been a brilliant advertising executive before turning to music.

They all come from Southern England, and have a close association with Richmond, where they played a seven-month residency when started under their present title 18 months ago.

"Yes!" replied Jagger when I asked if they were jealous of the Beatles' success. "No!" said the others. With that formality over, we switched to talk of images and money, untidiness and fans.

Jagger spoke: "Yeah, we know about the image. I think most groups need one. You see, you can get so far without an image in people's minds, but as soon as you make a not-so-hot record, you feel it.

*Source:* Ray Coleman, "Rebels with a Beat," *Melody Maker,* February 8, 1964, p. 11. © Ray Coleman/Melody Maker/IPC Syndication. Used by permission.

"If you've got an image, you sell the records on the image, if you see what I mean, and you can always rely on a following whatever you do.

## Strange

"But we didn't all sit down and say 'right, let's be untidy and let's not have uniforms and let's grow our hair long like the Beatles' or anything like that'."

Wyman said: "The image was a thing that just happened. We always carried on like this. People thought, when we started, that we were so strange to look at. Now we're lumbered with the image."

The difference [between the Stones and the Beatles] is that Keith and Mick do not write their own material, but work on orders for songs from other groups and solo artists.

Visually, the Rolling Stones are not the prettiest quintet in the land. Although they deny it, the truth is that they are angry young rebels who scorn conformity.

## Groan

"We're not deliberately untidy," says Keith. "We think a lot of this 'rebel' thing has been brought up by people thinking too much about it. People like you come up to us and say 'are you rebels?' The answer's no."

To which one could reply that they are either rebels or blatant exhibitionists.

Said Charlie Watts: "We like it this way—we like to please ourselves what we do. We don't like this 'big star' bit. We get treated by the fans as just ordinary blokes, and that's good. There's none of this 'fab gear' and all that."

I asked how much they earned today and how much they earned when they started. At once, their publicist and co-manager, 20-year-old Andrew Oldham, joined the conversation.

"It's about 20 times more than we got when we started," Mick Jagger stated.

"About £1,500 a week for personal appearances, that's between them, and excluding record royalties," said Andrew, who now sports a Rolling Stone-type hair style.

And what about that hair style? There was a groan of horror at the mere suggestion that it had been described as Beatle-ish.

"Look," said Keith, "These hair styles had been quite common down in London long before the Beatles and the rest of the country caught on. At art school and years ago, ours had always been the same."

"Look at Jimmy Savile," urged Jagger. "He had his like it is long before others started that style. It's the same with us."

"And Adam Faith," added Bill Wyman. "He had hair like the Beatles years ago, didn't he?"

"I dunno," Richard said to Wyman. "I reckon your style came direct from the Three Stooges."

They talked about extravagancies now they had money, and disclosed that they had few. "Nobody's gone really mad with money," said Keith, "except that Charlie's bought a blue suede coat."

"I spend a lot of money on records," said Wyman. "Six new LPs a week." "You can't," declared Keith. "There aren't six good LPs issued a week." "Well, I do, and that's where the money goes," said Bill.

"Charlie likes jazz," said Jagger. "He's the only one in the group who does, really." Wyman said he preferred R&B from Chuck Berry, Jerry Lee Lewis, "and Fats Waller." "I go for singers like Ben E. King" said Jagger. "So do I," said Keith. "And Muddy Waters."

## Mates

Do the Stones call themselves an R&B group? "We claim to be R&B as much as anyone," Richard said. "We were playing R&B material long before this beat craze got going.

"You know, the beat craze that's going on at the moment will last longer than a lot of people think. Kids realize that having four or five stars, like a group, is better than having one star, and groups are improving tremendously all the time.

"The Searchers' 'Needle and Pins' is the best record they ever made."

Was there any prejudice from promoters because of their dress habits? "Sometimes," said Keith. "They used to have this attitude of 'that scruffy lot from London who don't turn up on time and are nasty to look at."

"But once we appear, we always get re-booked."

"They just think we're layabouts," added Wyman.

"Well, they can lump it," announced Keith.

"They call us the ugliest pop group in the country," admitted Wyman. "We could name a few uglier people in the business," said Jagger, whose face creases into a mammoth smile at the slightest provocation. "Yes, quite a few more. . . ."

"Do you know," said Wyman, "some places we go, they bill us as London's answer to the Beatles. They don't like it when we say we don't do 'Twist and shout.'"

"Yes," said Jagger. "And whatever you do, don't write that article saying we're knocking the Beatles. They're good mates of ours. We like 'em and they've done so much good for the whole scene see?"

"The cancer business doesn't scare me," said Wyman, lighting up. They all smoke about 20 a day and drink moderately. "We not boozers," said Richard, "but we enjoy a drink and fags like anybody else."

"No, it doesn't scare me at all," affirmed Wyman. "Let's face it, if you have got to go, you have got to go."

"I'll probably die of electric shock," said Keith, the guitarist. He lit up. They all trailed out of the restaurant.

People eating lunch looked up, aghast at such a sight. Unkempt the Rolling Stones may be, but their music has vitality and they are mentally sharp.

AND COMMERCIAL.

# 41. The Stones Versus the Beatles

The preceding chapter described some of the ways in which the Rolling Stones, especially lead singer Mick Jagger (b. 1942), projected an ironic detachment, arrogance, and aggressive sexuality that made them seem as if they were the opposite of the cuter, more polite public image of the Beatles. The rawer, blues-based sound of the Stones also seems at odds with the polished, more conventionally melodic, pop of the Beatles. This apparent difference masked many similarities: Both bands were influenced by the rock 'n' roll of the 1950s (the Stones more by Chicago blues, the Beatles more by rockabilly), and by the soul music of the early 1960s (the Stones more by "down-home" singers, such as Solomon Burke, and the Beatles more by Motown). As the Stones began writing their own material, the Beatles' influence became clearer. Although they tended to retain a less polished sound, the Stones followed the Beatles closely in the use of strings ("As Tears Go By," late 1965, after "Yesterday"), the sitar ("Paint It Black," 1966, after "Norwegian Wood"), and psychedelia (*Their Satanic Majesties Request,* late 1967, after *Sgt. Pepper*). Following *Satanic Majesties,* the Stones began developing their own brand of hard rock; "Jumpin' Jack Flash" (1968) stands as both the inaugural and archetypal song in this style, with its hypnotic syncopated riff based on a fragment of the blues scale.

The following article by Ellen Willis dates from 1969 and explicitly compares what were then the two latest releases of the Stones and Beatles, *Beggar's Banquet* and *The Beatles* (aka, "The White Album"). Willis captures well the Stones' appeal and uniqueness within the pop context. She also refers to debates about the Stones' imitations of the Beatles that were rampant at that point and discusses the connection between rock and politics, another hot topic among critics, fans, and musicians. Both bands had produced songs that had brought political involvement into the foreground—the Stones with "Street Fighting Man," the Beatles with "Revolution"—during 1968, the year when the relationship between the counterculture and politics began to become more pressing and contentious. The sources of this shift were numerous: the growth of the antiwar movement, riots at the Democratic convention in Chicago, and the assassinations of Dr. Martin Luther King, Jr., and Robert Kennedy all played a role.

A curious aspect of this article, in retrospect, is Willis's failure to mention the Stones' misogyny, something she was to comment upon later. Willis was one of the first female rock critics, and the lack of consciousness on this subject was symptomatic of the lack of feminism within the counterculture at this time. The paradox becomes more palpable in that Willis subsequently became better known as a writer about cultural politics and feminism than as a rock critic.[1]

---

1. Curiously, this issue had been debated in a series of articles on the Stones in the Marxist journal, *The New Left Review.* See Alan Beckett/Richard Merton, "Stones/Comment," in Jonathan Eisen, ed., *The Age of Rock: Sounds of the American Cultural Revolution* (New York: Random House, 1969), 109–17; and Michael Parsons, "Rolling Stones," in Eisen, ed., *The Age of Rock,* 118–20. These articles originally appeared in the *New Left Review* in 1968, issues 47 and 48. For more of Willis's writings, see *Beginning to See the Light: Sex, Hope, and Rock-and-Roll* (Hanover, N.H.: Wesleyan University Press and University Press of New England, 1992).

# Records: Rock, Etc.— the Big Ones
## *Ellen Willis*

It's my theory that rock and roll happens between fans and stars, rather then between listeners and musicians—that you have to be a screaming teen-ager, at least in your heart, to know what's going on. Yet I must admit I was never much of a screaming teen-ager myself. I loved rock and roll, but I felt no emotional identification with the performers. Elvis Presley was my favorite singer, and I bought all his records; just the same, he was a stupid, slicked-up hillbilly, a bit too fat and soft to be really good-looking, and I was a middle-class adolescent snob. Jerry Lee Lewis? More revolting than Elvis. Buddy Holly? I didn't even know what he looked like. Fats Domino? He was *comic*—and black. When I went to rock shows, I screamed, all right, but only so I wouldn't be conspicuous. Actually, I grooved much more easily with records than with concerts, which forced me to recognize the social chasm separating me from the performers (and, for that matter, from much of the audience). The social-distance factor became more acute as I got older; that was one reason I defected to folk music. By the time the Beatles came on the scene, I wasn't paying much attention to rock. Naturally, I was *aware* of them, but I didn't have the slightest inkling of their importance. Their kookiness had the same effect on kids that Elvis's dirtiness had had; as far as I was concerned, the two phenomena were identical, and neither had much to do with me. I didn't realize that Elvis was to the Beatles as a Campbell Soup can is to an Andy Warhol replica. (Of course, the Beatles probably didn't realize it, either.) At first, I reacted to the Stones with equal incomprehension. Mick Jagger had his gimmick: he was a hood. The j.-d. [juvenile delinquent] image was a familiar one, though Mick played the role with more than the usual élan. He was so aggressively illiterate, his sexual come-on was so exaggerated and tasteless that it never occurred to me he might be smart. (I didn't know then that he'd gone to the London School of Economics.) But his songs, which had all the energetic virtues of rock and roll, also displayed the honesty and clear-headedness I expected only from blues. I loved both rock and blues, but in each case my response was incomplete: rock was too superficial, blues too alien. The Stones' music was the perfect blend. And, I came to realize, so was Mick's personality; he was an outcast, but he was also thoroughly indigenous to mass society. Because he was so unequivocally native, he touched a part of me that the black bluesmen and alienated folk singer could never reach. And because I couldn't condescend to him—his "vulgarity" represented a set of social and aesthetic attitudes as sophisticated as mine, if not more so—he shook me in a way Elvis had not. I became a true Stones fan— i.e., an inward screamer—and I've been one ever since.

As a fan, I feel ambivalent about "Beggars Banquet." It's a good album—the Stones have never put out a bad one—but something of an anti-climax. This is the first Stones L.P. in a year, and there have been no major performances since 1966. When stars have as little contact with their public as this, everyone's fantasies get so baroque that the eventual reality rarely satisfies. (Bob Dylan has got away with this sort of thing twice; if he tries it again, he'll be pressing his luck.) Besides, "Beggar's Banquet" had an unusually long gestation— the rumors of its imminent appearance began back in August. Through the fall, I followed the Stones' hassle with (British) Decca over that men's-room-with-graffiti-album cover. I took it for granted they'd win. The cover was really pretty innocent, and, anyway, what mere record company could thwart the Rolling Stones? But they lost. For the first time, I had to think of the Stones as losers. So even before I heard the record the reality—that black and white jacket designed to look like an engraved invitation—was a letdown from the fantasy.

*Source:* Ellen Willis, "Records: Rock, Etc.—the Big Ones," *The New Yorker,* 44, no. 50, February 1, 1969, pp. 55–63. Reprinted by permission of the Charlotte Sheedy Agency.

There's another reason, also having to do with contact, that "Beggar's Banquet" doesn't quite make it: I have the feeling that Jagger is responding more to the Beatles than to the world, and that the album gets to us only after bouncing off John Lennon. In a very general way, the Stones' sensibility has always been—at least in part—a revision of and a reaction to the Beatles. But the symbiosis—or, rather, the competition—has become more pronounced and specific since "Sergeant Pepper" forced them to respond with "Their Satanic Majesties Request." I'm not putting down "Satanic Majesties" as a mere imitation, or parody, or comment. There was nothing mere about that album. The Stones showed they could do the studio thing; they did it with just the right amount of extravagance and wit, and with beautiful songs. Anyway, they could scarcely have ignored an event of "Sergeant Pepper's" magnitude. But "Satanic Majesties" was a special record for a special time. In practice it was good, in principle very dangerous. While "Satanic Majesties" was still in the works, the Beatles released "All You Need Is Love," and the Stones countered with "We Love You," a better-conceived and more powerful song. Now the best track on "Beggar's Banquet" is "Street Fighting Man," which is infinitely more intelligent than "Revolution." I sense an unworthy effort to expose John as callow (Callowness is part of his charm anyway.) It may be that anything the Beatles do, the Stones can do better, but it never pays to work on someone else's terms. In this case, there is a special risk. What has made the Stones the Stones, more than anything else, is a passionate, thrusting ego. The Beatles' identity is collective, but the Stones are Mick Jagger. The Beatles' magic inheres in their glittering surface, the Stones' in Jagger's genius for visceral communication. Yet in this album, as in "Satanic Majesties," Mick is—the only word for it is "leashed." "Parachute Woman" and "Stray Cat Blues" do show traces of the old self-assertion, but in both of them bad production has made the lyrics nearly impossible to catch. In the other songs that have an "I" at all, it is weak, even passive—"Take me to the station,/And put me on a train./I've got no expectations/To pass through here again," or "But what can a poor boy do/'Cept to sing for a rock-and-roll band?/Guess in sleepy London town there's just no place for a street fighting man"—or else, as in "Sympathy for the Devil," it belongs to a stock character. Most of the songs are impersonal artifacts. The "Factory Girl" is just described, not loved or sneered at. "Salt of the Earth" is positively alienating, in the Brechtian sense. What can it mean for Mick Jagger to toast the workers? Is he being sarcastic? Is the song just a musical exercise? Or is he making a sincere, if rather simple-minded, political statement? Like the Beatles, the Stones play with forms: "Prodigal Son," flawless folk blues (another political statement?); "Dear Doctor," a rather overdone parody of country music; "Jig-Saw Puzzle," proof that Jagger (or Richard) can write lyrics exactly like Dylan's. My response to these songs is purely cerebral. "Street Fighting Man" is my favorite, because it really gets down to the ambiguous relation of rock and roll to rebellion. It does with politics what early rock did with sex. (Are they deliberately using the tradition, or unconsciously re-creating it?) The lyrics of the old songs had to be bland enough to be played on the radio, but the beat and arrangements that emphasized a phrase out of context here, a double-entendre there got the message across. Taken together, the words of "Street Fighting Man" are innocuous. But somehow the only line that comes though loud and clear is "Summer's here, and the time is right for fighting in the streets." Then, there's the heavy beat and all that chaotic noise in the background. So Mick leaves no doubt where his instincts are. (And he didn't fool the censors, either; the single of "Street Fighting Man" was virtually boycotted by AM stations, though "Revolution" was played constantly.) But what can a poor boy do—if he wants to make some bread—'cept to sing for a rock and roll band? There it is. Rock is a socially acceptable, lucrative substitute for anarchy; being a rock and roll star is a way of beating the system, of being free in the midst of unfreedom. And I know Jagger understands the ironies involved and has no illusions about himself. (Which isn't to say he's cynical—I suspect that his famous cynicism has always been more metaphor than fact.) Still, there was a time when he applied equal energy to having no illusions about other people. It's the direct link between subject and object that I miss.

Apparently, the Stones, too, are worried that all is not right; I hear they're planning an American tour in the spring. Whether that decision stems from a desire for artistic renewal or from nervousness about declining sales doesn't matter. It's wonderful news. The Stones were never meant to be studio recluses. They need to get out and face the people.

The Beatles have also found it necessary to define themselves politically. But unlike the Stones, they have little insight into their situation. Instead, they have taken refuge in self-righteousness, facile optimism, and status mongering (revolution isn't hip, you'll scare away the chicks). Not that I believe the Beatles have any obligation to be political activists, or even political sophisticates. There are many ways to serve mankind, and one is to give pleasure. Who among the Beatles' detractors has so enriched the lives of millions of kids? No, all I ask of the Beatles is a little taste. When Bob Dylan renounced politics, he also renounced preaching. "Revolution," in contrast, reminds me of the man who refuses a pan-handler and then can't resist lecturing him on the error of his ways. It takes a lot of chutz-pah for a millionaire to assure the rest of us, "You know it's gonna be alright." And Lennon's "Change your head" line is just an up-to-date version of "Let them eat cake"; anyone in a position to follow such advice doesn't need it.

We may as well face it. Deep within John Lennon, there's a fusty old Tory struggling to get out. Yet I think "Revolution" protests too much. It had been obvious for a while—ever since all the Beatles grew beards and/or mustaches and George announced "We're tired of that kiddie image"—that they're suffering growing pains from the who-am-I-and-where-am-I-going-and-how-do-my-money-and-my-fame-fit-in variety. When they were four silly kids jumping around on a stage, making tons of money was a rebellious act—they were thumbing their noses at the Protestant ethic. But once Leonard Bernstein had certified them as bona-fide artists they began in the eyes of society to *deserve* all that money. They could no longer accept it as part of the lark. It's no accident that the Maharishi was not only a believer in transcendental meditation but a believer in the virtue of material things. And would John have needed to write "Revolution" if on some level he hadn't felt a little defensive? He can see that all those student revolutionaries are sufficiently well-off to do more or less what he's done, if on a less spectacular scale—that is, to find a personal solution within the system—yet, they've chosen a far less comfortable route. I notice that in the album version of "Revolution" he has put the ambivalence right into the song: "Don't you know that you can count me out—in?" And he admitted to a *Rolling Stone* reporter that if he were black, he might not be so "meek and mild." Good.

Everybody has to grow up, but few people have done it as late and publicly as Lennon. Though Dylan also went through a protracted adolescence in front of a mass audience, he at least battled the media for every scrap of his private life. John takes us through all the changes—LSD, religion, politics, broken marriage, love affair.[2] In the context of this

---

2. Lennon discussed these topics at great length in a famous interview published in *Rolling Stone* following the Beatles' breakup. See Jann Wenner, *Lennon Remembers: The Rolling Stone Interviews* (New York: Popular Library, 1971). This interview is also important in that Lennon goes to great lengths to debunk what he already saw as the dominant myth of the sixties as a period dominated by an ethos of "peace and love." For another contemporary debunking (albeit an allegorical one), see the "fictional review" by J. R. Young reprinted in chapter 49.

openness, the nude pictures of him and Yoko are very touching. I'm sure he didn't analyze what he was doing—isn't everyone undressing these days?—But he certainly gets my most-inspired-whim-of-the-year-award. What makes the pictures beautiful is that the bodies *aren't* beautiful; by choosing to reveal them, John is telling his fans that celebrities aren't gods, that people shouldn't be ashamed of their bodies just because they're imperfect, that even a Beatle can love a woman who isn't a pinup. When I think of both of them looking so vulnerable, I don't resent "Revolution" so much. How can I expect someone to be right all the time?

About the new album. To get it over with, here's what I *don't* like:

1. Calling the album "The Beatles" and packaging it in a white cover. Everyone's going back to the basics, and it's getting boring. The right cover should have been John and Yoko, clothed.
2. The slowed-down version of "Revolution." Aside from the lyrics, the song was fine: good, heavy hard rock. You could even dance to it. Why do it at half the speed? So that we can hear the words better?
3. "Revolution 9." Though I know nothing about electronic music, it sounds to me like the worst kind of pretentious nonsense. Friends who are more knowledgeable than I am concur.
4. The album is just a bit too in-groupy. It parodies Bob Dylan, Tiny Tim, the Beach Boys, fifties gospel, rock, blues, and music-hall songs; a whole song is devoted to discussing the Beatles' previous work; and one of the songs on the record alludes to another. But it's all done so well that this is a minor criticism.

Otherwise, this album is very satisfying. The Beatles have always blended sentimentality with irreverence. Lately, the sentimentality has become fantasy and the irreverence a whimsical disregard of linguistic conventions. Whether or not it has anything to do with their politics, "The Beatles," even more than "Magical Mystery Tour," belongs to a private world. And what doesn't work in life works fine is art. By "private" I don't mean exclusive; the Beatles world is one anybody can get into. "The Beatles" is a terrific children's album—much better than Donovan's "For the Little Ones"—yet there is nothing prohibitively childish about it. The songs are funny (especially "Piggies" and "Why Don't We Do It in the Road?"), moving ("I'm So Tired" and "Julia"), clever ("Rocky Raccoon"), singable ("Ob-la-di, Ob-la-da" and "Back in the U.S.S.R."). For sheer fun with language, none of the lyrics quite come up to "I Am the Walrus," but the general level is high. A special treat is Ringo Starr's first song, "Don't Pass Me By." It's beautiful, especially the verse that goes, "I'm sorry that I doubted you, / I was so unfair. / You were in a car crash, / And you lost your hair." Ringo, you keep us all sane. The Beatles might still be with the giggling guru if you hadn't turned up your nose at the curry. "Don't Pass Me By" makes up for all George Harrison's Indian songs, plus "The Fool on the Hill." The screaming teenager in me wants to know how your Beatle museum is coming along, and sends her love to Maureen and the kids—and to you.

# 42. If You're Goin' to San Francisco . . .

Psychedelic rock provided rock critics with more evidence (in addition to the work of Dylan and the Beatles) for their belief that rock music had become a form of "art." Taking its cue from a hodgepodge of elements derived from early 20th-century modernism, psychedelic rock was particularly enamored of notions of the unconscious derived from Freud. Symbolist poetry of Rimbaud and Baudelaire, filtered through Beat writers, such as Jack Keroauc and Allen Ginsburg; "stream of consciousness" writing as practiced by James Joyce and Virginia Woolf; existentialist philosophy as espoused by Jean-Paul Sartre and Albert Camus; visual imagery drawn from surrealism and expressionism; and Eastern philosophy: all were cultural threads that the counterculture and psychedelic music drew upon. The first flowering of psychedelic rock occurred in San Francisco, also one of the geographic centers for the Beat movement, and where liberal politics and the lack of a "blue-blood" social hierarchy conjoined to encourage artistic experimentation.

The lyric style of psychedelic rock, while drawing on the literary influences just noted, was filtered most directly through Dylan's work of 1965–66. In musical terms, psychedelic rock drew from many sources, most notably from the emphasis on improvisation found in blues, jazz, and South Asian classical music, particularly that of the North Indian, or Hindustani, tradition. The earliest songs recognized as psychedelic, such as the Byrds' "Eight Miles High" or the Beatles "Tomorrow Never Knows" (both recorded early in 1966), combined surrealistic lyrics with drones and modal improvisation influenced by Indian classical music. "Tomorrow Never Knows" used *musique concrète* (recorded sounds manipulated with a tape recorder), a technique borrowed from avant-garde art music, to create an "otherworldly" effect, a technique soon adapted by many other bands.[1] Dissonance and atonality were other musical elements derived from avant-garde jazz and classical music that came to connote the "psychedelic" within the rock music context.

Psychedelic rock, as it developed in the San Francisco Bay Area, London, Los Angeles, and elsewhere, was connected to local hippy subcultures through large outdoor concerts and other, more experimental,

---

1. The Mothers of Invention were probably the pioneers in the use of *musique concrete* in popular music, since their *Freak Out!* was released prior to *Revolver* (the Beatles' album containing "Tomorrow Never Knows"). Despite this, it is safe to say that the Beatles did the most to expose the public (and other pop musicians) to this practice. See Richard Goldstein's review of *Revolver*, reprinted in chapter 39.

performance practices. These performances incorporated multimedia approaches from the avant-garde and included light shows, projections,
and film. In San Francisco, many of these events were connected to mass
"dosings" of LSD, in which much of the audience ingested the hallucino-
gen. Author Ken Kesey (*One Flew Over the Cuckoo's Nest*) and his gang
of cohorts, the Merry Pranksters, were important organizers of many of
these events, dubbed the "Acid Tests."[2] The "Human Be-In," a public concert held in San Francisco's Golden Gate Park in January 1967, brought
these happenings into public awareness. The three-day-long Monterey
Pop Festival (held in June 1967),[3] demonstrated some of the commercial
potential of such gatherings and impressed even the "straight" press
with how peaceful the participants were.

The San Francisco psychedelic rock scene was one of the first popular music movements ever to receive attention by the mass media before
many people had heard the music or before much of it had even been
recorded. The first group to record, the Jefferson Airplane, was also the
first to achieve commercial success; after an initial album, *The Jefferson
Airplane Takes Off* (1966) failed to attract many buyers, the second,
*Surrealistic Pillow* (1967) sold several million copies and, much to the
surprise of the group and its followers, generated two Top 10 singles,
"Somebody to Love" and "White Rabbit."

The Airplane, with their backgrounds in folk music and blues; their
modal harmonies and dissonant, contrapuntal textures; and their charismatic female vocalist, Grace Slick, were only the most public face of the
San Francisco scene. The colorful names of other San Francisco bands
caught the fancy of the national media: the Grateful Dead, the Quicksilver Messenger Service, Moby Grape, Country Joe and the Fish, Big
Brother and the Holding Company. Of these, the Grateful Dead enjoyed
the most sustained success and influence, surviving as primarily a con-
certizing unit until leader Jerry Garcia's death in 1995.

The first two entries on psychedelic rock consist of an article and an interview conducted by Ralph J. Gleason. Gleason was the jazz and pop
music critic for the *San Francisco Chronicle* from the 1940s through the
1960s and one of the first established critics to write about rock music
with the seriousness previously accorded jazz. Gleason became an advocate of the San Francisco bands and cofounded *Rolling Stone* with Jann
Wenner in 1967. The first of Gleason's essays portrays the Grateful Dead
circa 1967 and reflects on the development of their style and the San
Francisco psychedelic scene in general.

2. This scene was memorably recorded by Tom Wolfe in his *Electric Kool-Aid Acid Test*.
3. And commemorated in a documentary by D. A. Pennebaker, *Monterey Pop.*

# DEAD LIKE LIVE THUNDER
## Ralph J. Gleason

San Francisco has become the Liverpool of America in recent months, a giant pool of talent for the new music world of rock.

The number of recording company executives casing the scene at the Fillmore and the Avalon is equaled only by the number of anthropologists and sociologists studying the Haight-Ashbury hippy culture.

Nowhere else in the country has a whole community of rock music developed to the degree it has here.

At dances at the Fillmore and the Avalon and the other, more occasional affairs, thousands upon thousands of people support several dozen rock 'n' roll bands that play all over the area for dancing each week. Nothing like it has occurred since the heyday of Glenn Miller, Benny Goodman, and Tommy Dorsey. It is a new dancing age.

The local band with the greatest underground reputation (now that the Jefferson Airplane has gone national via two LP's and several single records) is a group of young minstrels with the vivid name, The Grateful Dead.


## A Celebration

Their lead guitar player, a former folk musician from Palo Alto named Jerry Garcia and their organist, harmonica player and blues singer Pig Pen (Ron McKernan) have been pictured in national magazines and TV documentaries. Richard Goldstein in the *Village Voice* has referred to the band as the most exciting group in the Bay Area and comments, "Together, the Grateful Dead sound like live thunder."

Tomorrow The Grateful Dead celebrate the release of their first album on the Warner Brothers label. It's called simply "The Grateful Dead" and the group is throwing a record promotion party for press and radio at Fugazi Hall.

The Dead's album release comes on the first day as their first single release, two sides from the album—"Golden Road" and "Cream Puff War."

The Dead, as their fans call them, got their exotic name when guitarist Garcia, a learned and highly articulate man, was browsing through a dictionary. "It just popped out at me. The phrase—'The Grateful Dead.' We were looking for a name at the time and I knew that was it."

The Grateful Dead later discovered the name was from an Egyptian prayer: "We grateful dead praise you, Osiris. . . . "

Garcia, who is a self-taught guitarist ("my first instrument was an electrical guitar; then I went into folk music and played a flat-top guitar, a regular guitar. But Chuck Berry was my influence!") is at a loss to describe the band's music, despite his expressiveness.

The Grateful Dead draws from at least five idioms, Garcia said, including Negro blues, country and western, popular music, even classical. (Phil Lesh, the bass player, is a composer who has spent several years working with serial and electronic music.)

"He doesn't play bass like anybody else; he doesn't listen to other bass players, he listens to his head," Garcia said.

Pig Pen, the blues vocalist, "has a style that is the sum of several styles," Garcia pointed out, including that of country blues singers such as Lightnin' Hopkins, as well as the more modern, urban blues men.

"When we give him a song to sing, it doesn't sound like someone else, it comes out Pig Pen's way." Pig Pen's father, by the way, is Phil McKernan, who for years had the rhythm and blues show on KRE, the predecessor of KPAT in Berkeley.

Bill Sommers [usually known as Bill Kreutzmann], the drummer, is a former jazz and rhythm and blues drummer. "He worked at the same music store I did in Palo Alto. I was teaching guitar and he was teaching drums," Garcia said. He is especially good at laying rhythms under a solo line played by the guitars. Bob Weir, the rhythm guitarist, "doesn't play that much straight rhythm," Garcia said, "he thinks of all these lovely, pretty things to do."

The Dead (they were originally known as the Warlocks) have been playing together for over two years now. They spend at least five or six hours a day rehearsing or playing or "just fooling around," Garcia continued.

"We're working with dynamics now. We've spent two years with loud, and we've spent six months with deafening! I think we're moving out of our loud stage. We've learned after these past two years, that what's really important is that the music be groovy, and if it's groovy enough and it's well played enough, it doesn't have to be too loud."

## Dance Band

The Dead's material comes from all the strains in American music. "We'll take an idea and develop it; we're interested in form. We still feel that our function is as a dance band and that's what we like to do; we like to play for dancers. We're trying to do new things of course, but not arrange our material to death. I'd say we've stolen freely from everywhere, and we have no qualms about mixing our idioms. You might hear some traditional style classical counterpoint cropping up in the middle of some rowdy thing, you know!"

The eclectic electric music has won the Dead its Warner Brothers contract, offers of work in films, a dedicated group of fans who follow them faithfully and the prospect of national tours, engagements in New York and elsewhere. But Garcia, who is universally loved by the rock musicians and fans, is characteristically calm about it all. "I'm just a student guitar player," he concluded, "I'm trying to get better and learn how to play. We're all novices."

> The following interview with Grace Slick (b. 1939) was excerpted from Gleason's *The Jefferson Airplane and the San Francisco Sound.* Although the book contains interviews with all six members of the Jefferson Airplane, the interview with Slick was selected because of her unique position within rock music at the time. The lead singer on both of the band's national hits, the composer of the controversial "White Rabbit," and a former model, Slick received more attention from the mass media than the rest of the group. As the first nationally famous female *rock* (as opposed to pop, folk, or soul) singer, Slick expanded the range of possibilities for female musicians.
>
> This excerpt begins with one of the themes that Gleason returned to repeatedly in the interviews in his book, all of which were conducted during 1967–68: the notion that the bands and audience in the San Francisco scene are a "community," and that U.S. society is on the verge of a new order in which psychedelic rock music is leading the way.

# GRACE SLICK, VOCALS, COMPOSER
## Ralph J. Gleason

**RJG:** *Do you see all this music as a sort of a crest of a whole revolution?*

**Grace:** Probably. Part of it. I think the music's probably at the top. It hasn't been in the past as close to being the . . . as closely integrated with a revolutionary movement. Usually, music was only part of life . . . just period . . . not part of a movement, because of communication. Music goes over the radio, music is what people listen to on all this fantastic amount of communications system that we have and probably the wonder of it's easier to get your ideas across pleasantly, same thing as being anti-war, music is a pleasant way of getting your ideas across, rather than a speech which is dull unless you're a fantastic orator. There are too few of those for any amount of people listening plus even if they are good, nobody cares! Look at Stevenson, very interesting guy, you know. People didn't care, didn't understand him.

**RJG:** *Did you ever think of music in the beginning as offering that opportunity?*

**Grace:** Oh sure. One of the first songs I wrote, a song called "Father Bruce."

**RJG:** *Was that the first song you wrote?*

**Grace:** Well, it was one of the first. I wrote, well they said, "Now we're gonna have a group," my husband, brother-in-law and these other people, "Now we need some songs, so write some songs." So I wrote about 13 of them, all at once, within a period of a month or so.[4]

**RJG:** *Now a song like "White Rabbit," which in a way is a kind of complicated idea, did that come to you easily or was that the end process of a long thing?*

**Grace:** No, that was a fairly quick thing. Spanish music, which I feel, for some reason, well, I can tell you the reason, it even overrides the rock thing, actually, except the story that the kids are getting into, but it's still all electric so it is categorized in that our stuff is all electric, but Spanish music is actually very universal, and I feel that for some reason or other, it's spade music and it's Eastern music, European, both North and South, and I can hear all the stuff that's gone on with all these different people, within that one music and that's the only music that is that way. Everybody else's music, it's either the Delta, or the Scottish Highlands, or it's this or that.

**RJG:** *Have you thought about why that is?*

**Grace:** Why Spanish? Yeah. Islam. It's proximity to all those places. Religious conquering of various sorts. So I like Spanish music about better than any other kind of music I can think of. And then of course, "Alice in Wonderland," it's obvious why that is used.

**RJG:** *Your voice doesn't sound like anyone else's. I hear no overtones of other people's singing in your voice, which is a very curious thing.*

**Grace:** Probably because I can't sing. It's just whatever comes out. . . .

**RJG:** *Yes, but that control. . . .*

**Grace:** There isn't any control. I keep telling Spencer [Dryden, drummer for the Jefferson Airplane]. He has talked to me about whatever it is I'm doing, and it really isn't a matter so much of singing as it is of pronunciation of words. When you pronounce words

---

4. Slick is referring to her first group, The Great Society, which included her first husband, Jerry Slick, and her brother-in-law, Darby Slick (writer of "Somebody to Love").

*Source:* Ralph J. Gleason, "Grace Slick, Vocals, Composer," from *The Jefferson Airplane and the San Francisco Sound* (New York: Ballantine Books, 1969), pp. 155–56, 159–60, 164–65, 165–66, 174.

a certain way, you can get a certain tone out of your voice, and the only thing I'm really doing is talking and I hope that I hit the right notes while I'm talking. Do you know what I mean? So that's why people say, "What do you do for a living?" And I sort of stumble around, you know, "Well, I, uh, I'm involved with music, I'm an entertainer." I don't really consider myself a singer though, it's more a lyrical way of talking or a funny way of talking.

You asked me who influences? It's electric guitars! Not singers so much as the instruments! That's probably it, as a matter of fact. Your asking me makes me figure out what it is. But it's more than those funny sounds. That's interesting, see, 'cause it seems very logical too, 'cause I didn't sing before there were electrical instruments. I started right out electric. Most everybody was doing the folk thing or something, so any influence I have is all electric. Except for chords, but that has nothing to do with the voice. Sounds that I hear that I'll try and duplicate has been the stuff that I hear coming out of the amplifiers.

**RJG:** *Did you get all the fashion magazines running at you? Interviewing?*
**Grace:** No, not really. They've called before and they say, "Do you want to do this or that or the other thing," and usually I don't because for one thing, I'm not interested in propagating anybody's idea of the American girl. They'll say, "We're gonna put you in these Bermuda shorts and you'll be standing next to Janis [Joplin], or somebody, like that whose gonna have this little plaid beanies on and we're gonna have your hair done," and I don't want to tell anybody how to look, so when they call for interviews mostly I just say I think people ought to wear what they feel like or a costume of one sort or another or just walk around nude. I don't, I really don't care, you know? Most of the time I wear black, that's an occupational thing, though. To keep up with five men, you can't really wear chiffon unless you have millions of dollars because it'd get ripped and slobbered on so fast. . . .

# 43. The Kozmic Blues of Janis Joplin

Although she first gained prominence as the lead singer with the San Francisco psychedelic band Big Brother and the Holding Company, Janis Joplin's (1943–70) fame soon superseded her band's. She departed Big Brother in 1968, following a successful year that included a critically acclaimed performance at the Monterey Pop Festival, a major recording contract with Columbia records, and a pop hit with the single "Piece of My Heart." The career of this dynamic, blues-influenced singer was riddled with contradictions: Joplin was labeled the first "hippy poster girl," yet claimed by progressive writers as a proto-feminist for her assertive performing style, extroverted public persona, and status as a band-leader.

Often described as the "the best white blues singer of all time," she clearly modeled her style after blues and R&B singers in contrast to the more "folk"-influenced vocal approach favored by other popular white female singers of the era (with the obvious exception of Grace Slick, with whom she was often compared). These influences also con-trasted with the effort by some of the San Francisco bands to distance themselves from African American sources.[1] The perception of her per-formances as completely uninhibited was reinforced by her hard-living, hard-drinking image, which she emphasized on stage and in interviews. Another contradiction surfaces in the contrast between this "one-of-the-boys" image and the image of Joplin as a "victim," an image pro-moted by the tales of suffering outlined in many of her songs and by re-ports of her personal life.[2] Regardless of these aspects of her persona, her brief recording career, which included four albums released be-tween 1967 and 1971, displays increasing vocal refinement from the all-out, larynx-shattering performance of "Ball and Chain" on *Cheap Thrills* with Big Brother and the Holding Company (1968; also captured in the film *Monterey Pop*, 1967), to the carefully nuanced buildup in her most commercially successful recording, "Me and Bobby McGee," recorded shortly before her death in 1970 and released posthumously in 1971 on *Pearl*.

The article that follows charts the broadening awareness of Joplin and her reception in New York early in 1968 shortly before her split with Big Brother and the Holding Company. This portrayal of Joplin by Nat Hentoff is based on an interview in which Joplin discusses her influences, the connection between "soul" and race, and her approach to performing. Hentoff's role in the criticism of rock music resembles that of Ralph J. Gleason's in that Hentoff was well known initially as a jazz critic in the 1950s, and the "oral history" of Bessie Smith in chapter 6 is excerpted from a volume coedited by him. Hentoff's relationship with jazz musicians was less adversarial than that of many white critics, sharing

---

1. For examples of this "anxiety of (African American) influence, see the following: the exchange between Gleason and Nick Gravenites in *Rolling Stone* over white bluesman Mike Bloomfield's "cultural authenticity"—Gleason, "Perspectives: Stop This Shuck, Mike Bloomfield," *RS*, May 11, 1968, p. 10; and Gravenites, "Gravenites: Stop This Shuck, Ralph Gleason, *RS*, May 25, 1968, p. 17; Ed Ward's review of *The Worst of the Jefferson Airplane (Rolling Stone*, February 4, 1971); and many of Gleason's comments and questions in *The Jefferson Airplane and the San Francisco Sound*. In the piece reprinted here, Joplin betrays her own anxieties about seeming to be *too* influenced by black singers.

2. These aspects of Joplin's persona are brilliantly addressed by Ellen Willis in "Janis Joplin," *Begin-ning to See the Light: Sex, Hope, and Rock-and-Roll* (Hanover, N.H.: Wesleyan University Press and University Press of New England, 1992), 61–67. First published in 1976.

close personal relationships with musicians otherwise known for their irascible personalities, such as Charles Mingus. Hentoff moved into writing about other forms of popular music somewhat earlier than Gleason, however, writing a well-known profile of Bob Dylan in 1964 and conducting one of the most-celebrated interviews of Dylan late in 1965.[3] Clearly, Hentoff had a gift for earning the trust of musicians who were wary of journalists. His empathy for Joplin is clearly apparent in the profile that follows.

# WE LOOK AT OUR PARENTS AND . . .
## *Nat Hentoff*

The only girl in the group (Big Brother and the Holding Company), Janis Joplin has exploded the increasingly mandarin categories of rock music by being so intensely, so jovially herself. Her singing with that unit is a celebration—her voice and body hurled with larruping power that leaves her limp and this member of her audience feeling that he has been in contact with an overwhelming life force. Part of that force is an open sensuality, with no tinge of coyness or come-on. It's not that she is beautiful by ordinary standards (a phrase that makes her wince). Rather, she brings *all* of herself into a performance. "The sex thing they keep trying to lay on me," Miss Joplin says, "is always in the receiver's head, which is where it should be. If I turn on anyone that way—great! Because that's what it's all about."

The triumphs of Janis Joplin began last June when she lifted a huge audience at the Monterey International Pop Festival to a standing ovation. The glory of her abandon has continued to draw open-mouthed attention as she and the group travel more and more widely from their San Francisco base, most recently having touched here at Generation, a new rock cellar room in Greenwich Village. The hosannas from the most flinty of the rock critics sound like hyperbole until you see her—"the best rock singer since Ray Charles"; "the best popular stylist since Billie Holiday, and certainly the most impressive woman on the rock scene"; "the major female voice of her generation."

The best single description of Janis Joplin I've seen appeared in Cashbox, not usually a source of memorable metaphor: "She's a kind of a mixture of Leadbelly, a steam engine, Calamity Jane, Bessie Smith, an oil derrick, and rot gut bourbon funneled into the 20th century somewhere between El Paso and San Francisco." Not entirely complete: her drink of preference is Southern Comfort, not bourbon, and that choice also indicates the gentleness at the core of her corybantic devotions.

Having seen her at Fillmore East on Second Avenue a few weeks ago, I wanted to know more. More than the biological facts—born in Port Arthur, Texas; a dropout from four colleges; a singer of country music in Texas and blues in San Francisco; a drifter until she found a molten center of gravity in Big Brother and the Holding Company two years ago.

We met in the darkly uninviting bar of the Chelsea Hotel, where she stays when she is in New York. Her long hair is brown, her eyes blue-gray, her figure trim, and her hands are

---

3. *Mademoiselle* (1964); and "The Playboy Interview: Bob Dylan," *Playboy* (March 1966).

*Source:* Nat Hentoff, "We Look at Our Parents and . . . ," *New York Times*, April 21, 1968, sec. 2, pp. 17, 19.

always moving. When she's not wielding a microphone, her voice is soft but not guarded; and her face, as on stage, is a kaleidoscope of swiftly changing emotions. I asked her, because I was concerned, how long her voice can hold out since she spends it without stint in performance. "I was worried about that for a while," she grinned, "and so for a couple of weeks, I consciously held back—like maybe a third of what I could do. And it was *nothing*! I'm not doing that anymore. Maybe I won't last as long as other singers, but I think you can destroy your now by worrying about tomorrow. If I hold back, I'm no good *now*, and I think I'd rather be good sometimes than holding back all the time. I'm 25 and, like others of my generation and younger, we look back at our parents and see how they gave up and compromised and wound up with very little. So the kids want a lot of something now rather than a little of hardly anything spread over 70 years."

She frowned, "But that's what *I* think. I'm still not used to being asked about my opinions, I'm still not used to all this attention. Nobody gave a damn about me before the Monterey Festival. Look, I'm not a spokesman for my generation. I don't even use acid. I drink." She laughed. "The reason I drink," she had had enough of the generation talk, "is that it loosens me up while the guys are tuning their instruments. I close my eyes and feel things. If I were a musician, it might be a lot harder to get all that feeling out, but I'm really fortunate because my gig is just feeling things." She laughed, again. "I'm really lucky. It doesn't always happen the way I want. It's not always a supreme emotional experience, but when everything is together—the band, me, the audience, it's boss! It's just like magic. I don't think I could ever feel that way about a man. It seems to be the kind of feeling a woman would like to have about a man. I hope I do someday."

New York had gotten in the way of that boss feeling for a while. "At first," she shook her head in exasperation, "this city seemed to have made us all crazy; it was dividing the unity of the band." Miss Joplin hadn't received quite the drink she'd ordered and I waved to the waiter. Slowly, grumblingly, he acceded to the request. "The first three weeks here," she went on, "we all got superaggressive, separate, sour. Something like that waiter there. San Francisco's different. I don't mean it's perfect, but the rock bands there didn't start because they wanted to make it. They dug getting stoned and playing for people dancing. Here they want to MAKE it. What we've had to do is learn to control success, put it in perspective and not lose the essence of what we're doing—the music. Well, we played a gig in Philadelphia recently, and the minute we walked offstage after the first set, it all fell back into place. We all looked at each other, like 'Remember me?' We all remembered what it was all about. We're learning how to handle New York."

San Francisco had been a saving place for her. "In Texas, I was a beatnik, a weirdo, and since I wasn't making it the way I am now, my parents thought I was a goner. Now my mother writes and asks what kinds of clothes a 1968 blues singer wears. That's kind of groovy, since we've been on opposite sides since I was 14. Texas is O.K. if you want to settle down and do your own thing quietly, but it's not for outrageous people, and I was always outrageous. I got treated very badly in Texas." She smiled grimly. "They don't treat beatniks too good in Texas."

Janis Joplin didn't get into music until she was 17, when hard, basic blues changed her from being a painter. "It was Leadbelly first. I knew what it was all about from the very front. I was right into the blues." She moved into a bluegrass band in Austin, dug Bob Dylan and Woody Guthrie, but the blues were always her base. She went to San Francisco to stay in 1962, and sang in folk clubs and bars until she joined the Holding Company.

I told her that she was the first white blues singer (female) I'd heard since Teddy Grace who sang the blues out of black influences but had developed her own sound and phrasing. She'd never heard of Teddy Grace, also a Southern girl, but she beamed. "God, I'm glad you think that. I keep trying to tell people that whites have soul too. There's no patent on soul. It's just feeling things. I sure loved Otis Redding, and Bessie Smith before him, but I don't think I copy anybody much. I've got country in my music too, but what changed things was singing with an electric band. All that power behind you—that pulsating power. I had to react to what was behind me, and my style got different. You can't sing a Bessie Smith vocal with a rock band, so I had to make up my own way of doing it."

Do you categorize yourself at all? I asked. Would you call yourself a jazz singer? "No, I don't feel quite free enough with my phrasing to say I'm a jazz singer. I sing with a more demanding beat, a steady rather than a lilting beat. I don't riff over the band; I try to punctuate the rhythm with my voice. That's why Otis Redding is so great. You can't get away from him; he pounds on you; you can't help but *feel* him. He was a man! Still is! Categories? I regard myself as a blues singer but then I regard myself as a rock singer. Actually, I don't feel there's any separation now. I'm a chick singer, that's what I am."

We had another drink. "You know how that whole myth of black soul came up? That only they have soul?" She wasn't asking, she was telling. "Because white people don't allow themselves to feel things. Housewives in Nebraska have pain and joy; they've got soul if they'd give in to it. It's hard. And it isn't all a ball when you do. Me, I never seemed to be able to control my feelings, to keep them down. When I was young, my mother would try to get me to be like everybody else. 'Think before you speak.' 'Learn how to behave yourself.' And I never would. But before getting into this band, it tore my life apart. When you feel that much, you have superhorrible downs. I was always victim to myself. I'd do wrong things, run away, freak out, go crazy. Now, though, I've made feeling work for me, through music, instead of destroying me. It's superfortunate. Man, if it hadn't been for the music, I probably would have done myself in."

She looked tired, not so much from present feeling as from an all-night record session the night before. Being made for Columbia, the album, due this spring, will be the first to fully reflect—she hopes—what Big Brother and the Holding Company are all about. (A previous, poorly recorded set, made much earlier, was issued despite the group's vehement protests.) "Making this record hasn't been easy," she said. "We're not the best technicians around. We're not the kind of dispassionate professionals who can go into a studio and produce something quick and polished. We're passionate; that's all we are. And what we're trying to get on record is what we're good at—insisting, getting people out of their chairs."

"What also makes it hard for John Simon, who's producing the album, is that we're kinda sloppy at the same time as we're happy. Last night he was trying to get something done and said 'Come on, who's the head of this band?' There was a pause because, well, no one is. We vote on things. We're democratic. But I think we're getting what we want into the recording." She sighed. "We've got complete control over this one, and if it's no good, it's our fault."

Janis leaned back, smiled again. "Like I said, it's hard to be free, but when it works, it's sure worth it."

# 44. Santana's Psychedelic Salsa

Guitarist Carlos Santana (b. 1947) and his band arrived on the San Francisco scene in the late 1960s, recording their first album in 1969 and making a splash at the Woodstock festival during the summer of that year. Santana's significance—in addition to his fiery guitar work and infectious songs—lies in his overt introduction of Latin rhythms to the improvisatory, jamming style of psychedelic rock. Santana's career made a remarkable resurgence in 1999 with the release of *Supernatural,* which featured collaborations between the guitarist and numerous younger musicians, sold umpteen million copies, and won ten Grammy awards.

Greg Tate's essay on Santana is one of the few in the collection that was neither written within a few years of the events described nor told in the words of one of the principals involved. I chose it nevertheless because Tate captures something important about Carlos Santana (guitarist and bandleader) as well as Santana (the band): the way his and their music spoke to an audience that merged fans of funk, psychedelic rock, and jazz-fusion, a quality that Santana shared with several other artists, including Sly and the Family Stone, War, and Miles Davis (all of whom are discussed in Part 4). This "fictional review," written in response to Santana's 1983 release *Havana Moon,* depicts a group of African American baby boomers gathering for a high school reunion. Tate disturbs easy assumptions about linkages between musical taste and race, while conveying the passion of a true fan (albeit in a fanciful way) and commenting on Santana's stylistic shifts since his late-1960s–early-1970s heyday.

## CALL ME ABRAXAS: SANTANA
### Greg Tate

Tetragrammaton and Homeboy fell into high school reunion scooping for old band members and eventually lucked up on Bayray, Romeo, and Kidd Funkadelic. After an exchange of yo muhfuhs the conversation quickly turned to good sex and old girlfriends before Kidd canned the booty tales to give it up to his once-upon-a-true love.

"You all know who I was really digging on more than any dame back then was Carlos Santana."

*Source:* Greg Tate, "Call Me Abraxas: Santana," from *Flyboy in the Buttermilk: Essays on Contemporary America* (New York: Simon & Schuster, 1992), pp. 90–93. Used by permission of Greg Tate.

Bayray: "Yep, *yep*, that's right, that's right—Santana used to be your *heart*, boy. Cold-blooded even."

Homeboy: "I swear. Couldn't *nobody* go over this wild muhfuh's crib without getting blasted right out of the joint by some *Abraxas* and doohickey."

Tetragrammaton, head mystic in the circle, mused: "Ah yes, Abraxas: signifying as Hesse learned from the gnostics that God and the devil may be one and the same, signifying as well Santana's coaxial synthesis of jazz, rock, and more ancient Abyssinian systems of polyrhythmic possession."

Picking up on this thread, Kidd ejaculated: "Oh yeah, buddy, oh yeah. Like you check how they threw that *Bitches Brew* on the top of that *Electric Ladyland* on top of that *Santamaria santeria* thang. Man, that music filled the serious *void*, you hear me?"

Romeo: "That Strauss ripoff they segued between 'Black Magic Woman' and 'Gypsy Queen' was baad, jim—twothousandandonespaceodyssey *down*."

Kidd reflected: "1 used to know all them solos man."

"Yep, yep, that's right, that's right—you even be onstage gritting and squinting and clenching like Carlos too man."

"Remember when you wanted us to name the band Funkatana, Kidd? Like, what was you, in love with the bitch, or what was you gonna do, marry the muhfuh, take half his name and doohickey or what?"

"Yep, yep, like that Miles line 'bout Al Green where Miles say if Al had one tit I would a married the motherfucker, ha-ha-ha!"

"Aw man, ya'll know it wasn't just me 'cause you used to be hearing Santana-style jams all over the place, like with War, Mandrill, Maurice and Verdine and them, Maxayn, Osibisa. Shee, Rolling Stones even."

"So what happened man, howcum they ain't into no more progressive Latin-jazz, like some *Caravanserai.* Why they coming out this lame AOR type groove nowadays?"

"Bayray, you remember when Carlos got all holy and big-headed behind discovering God and Mahavishnu and fired all them cats from the original band and then they put Journey together and so now Journey's making all that cash so Santana can't cut a record without jumping on board that Journey train, so they apartheid-orientedrock *down!*"[1]

"Hey, Kidd, you know your boy Carlos got a new solo jam out and doohickey."

"Yep, yep, that's right, that's right, *Havana Moon* or some shit like that."

"Do it righteously jam Homeboy? Because that last one he did was a depressant to me."

"Well, I can't say it *jam*-jams, Kidd. I mean it don't get off like the whipping dick or nothing like that. I mean it's spozed to be a boogie-type jam but it sound to me like it could use a square kick in the ass. I like the feeling on it though, reminds me of Santana when they first hit, with that Latin blues feeling. Carlos got them white boogie boys outta Texas on it, the Fabulous Thunderbirds, but they be undercranking sound like to me. But in a way it's good 'cause look like Carlos going back to his roots for that feeling—'cause they do some Chuck Berry, some Bo Diddley, even some of that Mexican mariachi shit. He ain't really into nothing new guitarwise but the, *huh*, album cover is real *purty*, ha-ha-ha."

"Check it: Even when that boy's music ain't shit his album covers always been the bomb—trulypsychedelic *down!*"

Kidd picked up on his vibe: "Santana used to have that mystique thang happening like Miles and Jimi."

---

1. This is a reference to "AOR" or album-oriented rock, a radio format derived from late 1960s "underground" radio and notorious for its refusal to program recordings by black artists. See Part 5 for further discussion of radio programming in the early 1980s.

Always the slow one, Bayray turned to Tetragrammaton and said: "So that's what *Abraxas* meant, huh? I always wondered 'bout that like I always wondered 'bout some Tetragrammaton like what kind of name is that for a. . . .

"Brother, I take my name from the Hebraic quadralineal which is the name of Jehovah deconstructed into the consonants JHWH, also known as Jahweh, or here in the Black Atlantic world as JAH, a triangular reconstruction which etymologically envisions Rastafari repatriation and the demise of the triangular slave trade now grown global as the Trilateral Commission. Further revelations on these matters are contained in my MS Tetragrammatonic Bicameralism: A Breakdown of Tabloid Wildstyle and the Afro-Gonzo Aesthetic as It Relates to Other Subversive Vernaculars—such as neohoodooism, Ikonoklast Panzerism, P-Funkism, rappism, dubbism, and magic realism. All being systems wherein blood beating in Babylon become Babel-on brother, or deeper still, chant down Babylon to the beat, blood."

Lost in reverie, Kidd spoke: "Every couple years a band comes along that can't be labeled this or that, a band that plugs into all styles and systems. First it was the Beatles, then Sly and Jimi, then Santana, P-Funk, Stevie Wonder, Weather Report, and Miles; now it's the Police and Talking Heads you know."

"Tell me something Kidd, you still playing and doohickey?"

"I'm still waiting, man."

"For?"

"New Talking Heads."

"What they calling this one, *(not just) Knee Deep parts three and four?*"

"No brother," said Tetragrammaton. "*Speaking in Tongues.*"

"How you know, chump?"

"Because dread eyes read the trades, muhfuh."

# 45. Jimi Hendrix and the Electronic Guitar

Like Janis Joplin, Jimi Hendrix (1942–70) first achieved prominence through a form of highly amplified blues merged with psychedelic rock. Hendrix's path to that point, however, followed a very different trajectory from Joplin's: an African American raised in Seattle, Hendrix toured as a sideman for R&B artists, such as Wilson Pickett and Little Richard, before he moved to London, where he launched his solo career. While clearly steeped in the blues, Hendrix made the most significant contribution of any guitarist of his generation toward conceiving of the electric guitar as an electronic instrument, rather than merely an amplified guitar. Distortion no longer occurred as a by-product of turning up an amplifier:

Hendrix made sustain and feedback an integral part of his technique, and he pioneered the use of electronic devices, such as fuzztones and wah-wah pedals (he may not have been the first to use these, but he was the first to incorporate them fully as more than gimmicks).

Again, like Joplin, Hendrix first came to the attention of American audiences during the 1967 Monterey Pop festival. Early commentaries (including those about this festival) all center on his highly theatrical stage performance, which involved playing the guitar behind his head and with his teeth, licking it (all techniques used by earlier blues and R&B musicians, such as T-Bone Walker), lighting it on fire, and finally destroying it (in a gesture perhaps adapted from the Who's Peter Townshend). The highly sexualized performance of a black man in front of a white band and (mostly) white audience also attracted attention and evoked some uncomfortable contradictions within the counterculture, which (as I discussed earlier) was almost entirely white despite a professed ethos of inclusion.[1]

Hendrix's compositions drew on blues and R&B, but also on psychedelic innovations in sound and recording, as well as on Dylan's approach to lyrics; as such, he was an innovator and synthesizer with few previous peers among rock musicians.[2] Hendrix freely acknowledged his indebtedness to Dylan, both in interviews and by recording Dylan's "Like a Rolling Stone" (at Monterey Pop) and "All Along the Watchtower" (which Dylan later said he preferred to his own version). His performance of the "Star Spangled Banner" was a highlight of the Woodstock festival; Hendrix used his guitar wizardry to simulate exploding bombs and sky-diving aircraft, turning the U.S. national anthem into an antiwar protest song. Some of his comments to interviewers and his abandonment of the Jimi Hendrix Experience (which was two-thirds white) toward the end of his career revealed that Hendrix was wrestling with the relationship of his music to his identity as an African American.[3] He died in September 1970 in his sleep from an accidental overdose of barbituates.

The critical response to Jimi Hendrix during his life featured much debate about whether the highly theatrical performances early in his career were a "gimmick" or not. Also common in the press were comparisons to Eric Clapton and Cream, who achieved prominence at roughly the same time

    1. For a fuller discussion of these issues, see Steve Waksman, *Instruments of Desire:* The Electric Guitar and the Shaping of Musical Experience (Cambridge, Mass.: Harvard University Press, 1999), 167–206.

    2. See Greg Tate's comments in chapter 44 and in his interview with George Clinton (*Flyboy in the Buttermilk: Essays on Contemporary America* (New York: Fireside/Simon and Schuster, 1992), 39–40, 92–93).

    3. Again, see Waksman, *Instruments of Desire,* for a discussion of Hendrix in the context of the black arts movement; and Samuel A. Floyd, *The Power of Black Music: Interpreting Its History from Africa to the United States* (New York: Oxford University Press, 1995), for a discussion that includes Hendrix within a broader, theoretically informed conception of "black music."

with the same trio format and who also featured long, blues-based improvisations. While all writers conceded the quality of Hendrix's guitar playing, many criticized his singing and his ability as a lyricist. The English music press viewed him as part of the London scene (as indeed he was for several years), and this article from the British music magazine, *Melody Maker*, provides a good example of that perspective. The article also shows Hendrix in transition from the flashy theatrics of his trio and reveals his awareness of earlier criticisms. Like so many articles from this period (and after), this article raises the opposition of art versus mass culture. Because the author accepts the terms of this opposition, "showmanship" of the kind associated with Hendrix must result from an artistic compromise—appealing to teenyboppers—rather than from continuity with previous African American approaches to performance.

## SECOND DIMENSION: JIMI HENDRIX IN ACTION
### *Bob Dawbarn*

Jimi Hendrix—like Eric Clapton, the Nice, the Pink Floyd and many others—is faced with one major problem.

He is trying to produce music with claims to permanent value, yet the outlets for that music are the mass media which, as yet, seem unable to distinguish between a Jimi Hendrix or a Donald Peers.

This means that a Hendrix must continually compromise in order to conform to the patterns demanded by his means of communication.

To stay in business he must make singles, he finds he is forced into acts of showmanship to get his music across, he must make use of publicity machines geared to the needs of teenyboppers.

Before his Albert Hall concert last Tuesday he told me: "I just hope the concert turns out all right. We haven't played in a long time and we concentrate on the music now.

"As long as people come to listen rather than to see us, then everything will be all right. It's when they come to expect to see you doing certain things on stage that you can get hung up."

Jimi dislikes miming on TV. "If you play live, nobody can stop you or dictate what you play beyond setting a time limit."

A good example was his recent appearance on the Lulu show when he surprised everybody in the studio by suddenly shifting from "Hey Joe" into "Sunshine Of Your Love" as a tribute to Cream.

"It was the same old thing," explained Jimi, "with people telling us what to do. They wanted to make us play 'Hey Joe.' I was uptight about it, so I caught Noel's and Mitch's attention and we went into the other thing.

"I dream about having our own show where we would have all contemporary artists as guest stars. Everybody seems to be busy showing what polished performers they are and that means nothing these days—it's how you feel about what you are doing that matters.

*Source:* Bob Dawbarn, "Second Dimension: Jimi Hendrix in Action," *Melody Maker*, March 1, 1969, pp. 14–15.

"I just cross off people who are just in it for the own ego scene instead of trying to show off another style of music.

Jimi admits that he feels a little restricted by the Trio format.

"It restricts everybody—Noel and Mitch, too," he said. "Now and then I'd like to break away and do a bit of classic blues. Mitch wants to get into a jazz thing and Noel has this thing with Fat mattress and wants to go on an English rock thing—how about Anglo Rock. A patriotic blues-rock music."

As a performer, Hendrix seems to be going through a period of change at the moment leaning towards extended performances.

Personally, I find his playing has great impact when disciplined by a four minute track. The longer things on the "Electric Ladyland" album don't always come off, his ideas seem to get diffused. But this is no doubt a time of transition.

Nobody is better at conveying an atmosphere in a few phrases—there was the menace of "Purple Haze," the raw, immensely masculine "Hey Joe," the blues influence of "Foxy Lady." And listen to the way guitar and voice complement each other on something like "51st Anniversary." Or the way he shows blues can be utterly contemporary on "Voodoo Chile."

"You have to make people identify with the music," explains Jimi. "You make a record in the hope that the public may want to buy it, so you have to make it presentable in some way. They have to have an identification mark.

"The trouble is that a single has to be under six minutes—it used to be under three, which was a real hang-up. It's like you used to be able to give them just one page of a book, now you can give them two or three pages—but never the whole book.

'The music is what matters. If an audience are really digging you on a show, then naturally you get excited and it helps. But a bad audience really doesn't bother me that much because then it is a practice session, a chance to get things together.

"I always enjoy playing, whether it's before ten people or 10,000. And I don't even care if they boo, as long as it isn't out of key.

"I don't try to move an audience—it's up to them what they get from the music. If they have paid to see us then we are going to do our thing.

"If we add a bit of the trampoline side of entertainment then that is a fringe benefit but we are there to play music. If we stand up there all night and play our best and they don't dig it, then they just don't dig us and that's all there is to it."

Jimi is rather underrated as a songwriter—the imagery of the lyric of "The Wind Cries Mary," for example, could not have been written by anyone else.

"I've not written too many heavy things recently," he told me. "Most of what I have done will come out on the next LP in the late summer. I don't try to make a thing about my songs when I put them on record. I try to make them honest and there doesn't seem to much point in talking about them.

The people who listen to them are the ones who will know whether they are successful or not."

One of the things Jimi seems to be cutting out of his personal appearances is playing guitar with his teeth.

"The idea of doing that came to me in a town in Tennessee," he recalled. "Down there you have to play with your teeth or else you get shot. There's a trail of broken teeth all over the stage.

"It was another way of letting out things and you have to know what you are doing or you might hurt yourself. The trouble was audiences took it as something they must see or they don't enjoy the show. So I don't do it much any more. We don't do too much of anything any more, except play music."

Jimi says it is usually the lyrics that attract him to a song.

"Maybe a lyric has only five words and the music takes care of the rest," he said. "I don't mean my lyrics to be clever. What I want is for people to listen to the music and words together, as one thing. Sometimes you get wrapped up in the words and forget the music—in that case I don't think the song can be completely successful.

"Generally, I don't do other people's songs unless they really say something to me."

Jimi laughed when I said I thought I could detect church music influences in some of his things.

"Spiritual music, maybe," he said. "But if you say you are playing electric church music people go 'gasp, gasp' or 'exclaim, exclaim.'"

"The word church is too identified with religion and music is my religion. Jesus shouldn't have died so early and then he could have got twice as much across.

"They killed him and then twisted so many of the best things he said. Human hands started messing it all up and now so much of religion is hogswash.

"So much of it is negative—Thou Shalt Not. Look at sex. It's been screwed around so much I'm surprised babies are still being born.

"Don't get me wrong. I'm not trying to stop people going to church. But as long as I'm not hurting anybody else I don't see why they should tell me how to live and what to do."

# 46. Rock Meets the Avant-Garde

## Frank Zappa

Frank Zappa's (1940–93) persona presents an imposing conundrum: immensely talented and witty to his fans, unbearably obnoxious to his detractors. After an involvement in a diverse range of musical activities and genres, Zappa formed the Mothers of Invention, signed a recording contract with Verve Records (known primarily as a jazz label), and recorded *Freak Out!* (released in August 1966), one of the first, if not the first, album to be organized around a concept, rather than simply presenting an assemblage of songs (the other contender for this distinction is the Beach Boys' *Pet Sounds,* released in May 1966). *Freak Out!* was also one of the first rock albums to feature classical avant-garde approaches to composition, electronics, and sound—in fact, even describing the album as "rock" demonstrates the breadth of that generic label. Other artists, primarily the Beatles, received more attention for their incorporation of such techniques, primarily because their music was heard by a larger audience, but none pursued the use of such experimentation within a rock context as zealously as Zappa.

Zappa's use of parody also stands out in the context of the time: He seemed simultaneously to belong to the counterculture and to mock it. Although it is doubtful that a figure like Zappa could have emerged at any other time and found an audience even as large as the one he had (meaning that he owed something to the social context of the time, and, hence, to the counterculture), the parodic aspects of his music and his separation from the counterculture became more obvious with the release of successive albums. His incorporation of an avant-garde classical performance approach also became more aggressive over time, as did his guitar pyrotechnics. While not really part of the (mostly British) progressive- or art-rock genre per se, Zappa's concern with integrating art music approaches to rock overlaps to some extent with that of such progressive rock bands as King Crimson and Yes.

This 1968 article captures Frank Zappa's role in his band, The Mothers of Invention, as analogous to that of a conductor of a classical music ensemble and comments upon and provides examples of Zappa's ironic verbal style. The description of Zappa as a modernist is apt, particularly with regard to his disdain of the audience; his attitude seems to personify the modernist credo—"if it's popular, it must be bad." Nevertheless, the tone of general approval in the article reveals the increasing acceptance of such high-art notions within the public discourse of rock music. At this moment, the rock audience, writ large, was understood to have room for highly intellectualized parodies of itself.

## ZAPPA AND THE MOTHERS: UGLY CAN BE BEAUTIFUL
### Sally Kempton

It is 1 A.M. on a Friday night and the Mothers of Invention are recording part of the soundtrack for their forthcoming movie. Ian is playing the harpsichord and Bunk is playing the flute. They huddle together in a cluster of microphones, Bunk leaning over Ian's shoulder to read the music propped up on the harpsichord stand. Bunk wears a goatee and a matching moustache, and his long thick hair is gray (in the studio light it looks like a powered [sic] wig). Resembling a figure in an old etching, he bends closer to Ian, his flute poised, and Ian straightens his back and places his fingers on the harpsichord keys. Poised like musicians at a nineteenth-century musicale, they wait for a signal to begin. One feels they are waiting to play a Mozart sonata.

Inside the control booth Frank Zappa, wearing a T-shirt bearing the legend "Herzl Camp, Garner, Wisconsin," is fiddling with knobs on the control board. "You're going to have to do the parody notes more staccato, Ian," he says through the intercom.

"You want a little bebop vibrato on that too?" calls Ian.

"Yeah, a little bebop a go go," says Frank. Dick Cunk, the engineer, flips the "record" switch.

*Source:* Sally Kempton, "Zappa and the Mothers: Ugly Can Be Beautiful," *Village Voice,* January 11, 1968, pp. 1, 10.

"OK, for fame and stardom," says Frank. "You ready?"

Ian and Bunk begin to play a series of dissonant, rhythmic, oddly beautiful chords. The people in the control booth listen intently.

"This is going to be a nice soundtrack," someone says.

Frank Zappa is bent over a music sheet, writing out the next piece. "Yeah," he says. "This is one the folks can enjoy listening to at home."

Frank Zappa is an ironist. He is also a serious composer, a social satirist, a promoter, a recording genius, but his most striking characteristic is his irony. Irony permeates his music, which is riddled with parodies of Charles Ives and Guy Lombardo, of Bartók and the Penguins and Bo Diddly and Ravel and Archie Shepp and Stravinsky and a whole army of obscure fifties rhythm and blues singers. It permeates his lyrics, which are filled with outlandish sexual metaphors and evocations of the culture of the American high school and the American hippie.

Irony is the basis of his public image. In pursuit of absurdity he has had himself photographed sitting naked on the toilet. His latest album is titled *We're Only in It for the Money*. And he has appeared on television speaking in well-rounded periods about music and society and The Scene, all the while emanating a kind of inspired freakishness. Zappa's is the sort or irony which arises from an immense self-consciousness, a distrust of one's own seriousness. It is the most modernist of defense mechanisms, and Zappa is an almost prototypically modernist figure; there are moments when he seems to be living out a parody of the contemporary sensibility.

And now he and his group are teenage idols, or anti-idols, and Zappa's irony, which, because it is so often expressed through contemporary clichés, is the most accessible part of his musical idiom, turns on audiences and makes the Mothers, in addition to everything else, a splendid comedy act. Until recently Zappa's voice, the paradigm California voice, could be heard on the radio doing "greasy teen-age commercials" for Hagstrom Guitars. During the Mothers' live appearances he sits on a stool, his expression deadpan above his bandillero moustache, and occasionally he will lean over and spit on the floor under the bandstand, saying to the audience: "Pigs!"

"Actually, we don't turn on audiences," he said the other day. "Not in the sense that other groups do, anyway. I think of that sort of thing as the strobes going and everybody dancing and love-rock-at-the-Fillmore bullshit—if anybody felt like that about us it'd be for the wrong reasons. Last week we were playing in Philadelphia and we got seven requests, so we played them all at once. It was fantastic. Sherwood was playing the sax part to one song: the whole thing, even the rests. It was really great. But nobody knew what we were playing. They couldn't even tell the songs apart. Half the time, when we're really doing something, the audience doesn't know what it is. Sometimes the guys in the band don't know."

But the Mothers' first album sold a quarter of a million copies and the second has done almost as well. And when they played a long stretch at the Garrick last summer they were beset by loyal groupies. Perhaps the groupies sensed the presence of a governing intelligence, perhaps they simply dug perversity. In any case, the Mothers have an audience.

Frank Zappa is twenty-seven years old. He was born in Baltimore and began playing drums in a rock-and-roll band in Sacramento when he was fifteen.

"It's almost impossible to convey what the r and b scene was like in Sacramento," he says. "There were gangs there, and every gang was loyal to a particular band. They weren't called groups, they were called bands. They were mostly Negro and Mexican, and they tried to get the baddest sound they could. It was very important not to sound like jazz. And there was a real oral tradition of music. Everybody played the same songs, with the same arrangements, and they tried to play as close as possible to the original record. But the thing was that half the time the guys in the band had never heard the record—somebody's older brother would own the record, and the kid would memorize it and teach it to everybody else. At one point all the bands in Sacramento were playing the same arrangement of 'Okey Dokey Stomp' by Clarence Gatemouth Brown. The amazing thing was that it sounded almost note for note like the record."

Zappa was lying in bed, eating breakfast and playing with his three-month-old baby. He lives with his wife, Gail, and the baby, in a long basement apartment in the West Village. The apartment has a garden and its walls are papered with posters and music sheets and clippings from magazines; there is a full-length poster of Frank in the hall and a rocking chair in the living room with a crocheted cover that says "Why, what pigs?"

Frank was in bed because he had been up all night before, recording. "The reason I can stand New York is because I spend all my time here or at the studio," he said.

"Mostly at the studio," said his wife, smiling.

"Let's see, my life," he said. "Well, when I was sixteen my father moved us to a little town out in the country. That was terrible, I hated it. I was used to Sacramento, you see. I was the strangest thing that ever hit that high school. They were so anxious to get rid of me they even gave me a couple of awards when I graduated. After that my father wanted me to go to college. I said no, I was interested in music, I didn't want to go to college. So I hung out at home for awhile, but there was nobody to talk to, everybody else being at college, so I finally decided I should go too. That was very ugly. I stayed for a year. In the meantime I had shacked up with this girl and married her. We stayed married for five years during which time I held a number of jobs" (he listed the jobs). "Then in 1963 we were living in Cucamonga and there was a recording studio there which I bought for $1000, also assuming the former owner's debts. He had hundreds of tapes, among them such big hits as" (he named three or four obscure songs) "and I took the tapes and the equipment and began fooling around. About that time I got divorced and moved into the studio. I spent all my time experimenting; a lot of stuff the Mothers do was worked out there."

A year later the studio was torn down to make room for a widened road, but by that time he had gotten the Mothers together. "We were playing at local beer joints for like six dollars a night. I finally decided this would not do, so I began calling up all the clubs in the area. This was in 1965, and to get work you had to sound like the Beatles or the Rolling Stones. You also had to have long hair and due to an unfortunate circumstance all my hair had been cut off. I used to tell club managers that we sounded exactly like the Rolling Stones. Anyway we finally got a booking in a club in Pomona, and were something of a hit. It was more because of our act than because of our music. People used to go away and tell their friends that here was this group that insulted the audience.

"Then M-G-M sent someone around to sign us to a contract. Their guy came into the club during a set of 'Brain Police' and he said, 'Aha, a protest rhythm and blues group,' so they paid us accordingly. The fee we got for signing was incredibly small, particularly considering the number of guys in the group."

Nowadays, of course, Zappa runs something of an empire. He has an advertising agency ("mostly to push our own products, at least so far"), and a movie coming out which someone else shot but for which they are going to do the soundtrack. The movie is a surrealistic documentary called "Uncle Meat"; it is shot in a style Zappa refers to as "hand-held Pennebaker bullshit," and it will be edited to fit the music.

"Then we're going to do a monster movie in Japan—Japan is where they do the best monster work. And we're starting our own record company. We'll record our own stuff and also some obsure new groups."

It was time for him to go to the studio. The Mothers have rented Apostolic Studios on Tenth Street for the entire month of January. "One hundred and eighty hours—not as much time as the Beatles use, of course, we can't afford that"—and that is where Zappa spends most of his time. He puts on a brown leather greatcoat, pulls a red knitted cap over his ears, and sets out, talking about his music as he walks.

"Stockhausen isn't really an influence," he says. "That is, I have some of his records but I don't play them much. Cage is a big influence. We've done a thing with voices, with talking that is very like one of his pieces, except that of course in our piece the guys are talking about working in an airplane factory, or their cars.

"It was very tough getting the group together in the beginning. A lot of guys didn't want to submit to our packaging. They didn't like making themselves ugly, but they especially didn't like playing ugly. It's hard getting a musician to play ugly, it contradicts all his training. It's hard to make them understand that all that ugliness taken together can come out sounding quite beautiful."

The studio, when he arrived, was nearly deserted, except for Mother Don Preston, who sat at the organ wearing earphones and playing a piece audible only to himself. "Can you run a playback on the violins?" he asked when Frank came in.

"Sure," said Frank. "We recorded this thing last night. I found some violins in a closet and I gave them to three of the guys. None of them had ever played a violin before. They were making all these weird sounds on them, and then in the middle I got them to add some farts. It's a concerto for farts and violins."

But instead of playing back the violin thing, Dick put on a tape of "Lumpy Gravy," one of the Mothers' new records, an instrumental piece, framed at the beginning and end with cocktail music, and interspersed with quiet, hollow, surreal voices talking behind a continuous hum of resonating piano strings. The music has overtones of Bartòk and Ives, but by some stylistic alchemy it ends by sounding like nothing but Zappa. It is an impressive record. Three or four people had drifted into the control room while it was playing, and after it was over someone said, "I love that piece."

"Yeah, but will the kids go for it," said Frank.

"It's good to have it out," said Don, "so people will know what you can do."

"No, no," Frank said. "It's good to have it out so I can take it home and listen to it."

# 47. Pop/Bubblegum/Monkees

Although the emergence of rock criticism during 1966–67 led to an unprecedented amount of writing about popular music, this writing focused on only a portion of the popular music circulating at the time. Omitted from rock criticism was "pop": music that continued the tradition of teen idols, of schlock-rock, of "middle-of-the-road," "easy listening" pop, resembling nothing so much as the popular music that antedated rock 'n' roll. While rock music and the counterculture were attracting ever-increasing amounts of media attention, it is important to remember that Frank Sinatra ("Strangers in the Night"), Nancy Sinatra ("These Boots Are Made for Walkin'"), Frank and Nancy Sinatra ("Somethin' Stupid"), and

Sgt. Barry Sadler ("The Ballad of the Green Berets") all had Number One pop hits during the years (1966–67) in which rock criticism emerged.

Among acts catering to young consumers, the Monkees were by far the most successful. A made-for-TV group, the Monkees were modeled on the Beatles, and their television series, which began broadcasting in 1966, adapted aspects of the humor and cinematic style of the Beatles' early movies. The Monkees' music represented (at least initially) an attempt by some of the best professional songwriters (many of them holdovers from the Brill Building) to write in the style of the "new rock."[1]

Robert Christgau is probably best known to readers as the primary pop music critic and editor for the *Village Voice,* a position he has held since the early 1970s. Christgau was one of the few "new rock" critics to grapple with the phenomenon of the Monkees or, for that matter, with unabashedly commercial music in general. Christgau is concerned, in these essays and others written around the same time, that rock be a "popular art." When he states, as he does here, that "good rock is largely a matter of production and publicity," or when he compares the Monkees' latest single release favorably to the Beatles' because of its superior commercial performance, he is implicitly confronting the growing critical orthodoxy that artistry in rock music must be opposed to commercialism.[2]

## *from* ANY OLD WAY YOU CHOOSE IT: ROCK AND OTHER POP MUSIC, 1967–1973
### *Robert Christgau*

*June, 1967.* The Monkees are four young men who star in an adolescent TV comedy of the same name and make records that rise to the top of the charts like jellyfish. They were chosen (from a hirsute field of 437) not for musical ability but for exuberance and irreverence,

---

1. For an attempt to view the Monkees as a representation of the counterculture, rather than its antithesis, see Aniko Bodroghkozy, *Groove Tube: Sixties Television and the Youth Rebellion* (Durham, N.C: Duke University Press, 2001), 66–75. For a contemporary mainstream account, see "Romp! Romp!," *Newsweek,* October 24, 1966, 102.

2. A particularly good example of Christgau's ecumenical approach may be found in his "Rock Lyrics Are Poetry (Maybe)," in *The Age of Rock: Sounds of the American Cultural Revolution,* ed. Jonathan Eisen (New York: Random House, 1969), 230–43 (first published in *Cheetah* in December 1967), in which he discusses the work of Dylan and other "heavy rock" artists alongside the more overtly commercial work of Simon and Garfunkel and the Mamas and the Papas.

*Source:* Robert Christgau, *Any Old Way You Choose It: Rock and Other Pop Music, 1967–1973* (New York: Cooper Square Press, 2000), pp. 38–39, 47–48. Originally published in June 1967 and December 1967 in *Esquire.* Reprinted by permission of Robert Christgau.

qualities salient in the chaps who were in those very successful Richard Lester movies. You remember.

You'd better, because the Monkees, conceived as a haircut on *A Hard Day's Night* and *Help!,* find themselves sole inheritors of the great Beatle tradition. The originals have abdicated, withdrawing from teeny idolatry into their music, which is popular but personal and exotic. Young fans, confused, miss those nice floppy Englishmen they fell for three years ago, and the Monkees provide a wholesome American substitute (with an English-man added for remembrance). They're not too handsome, not too pretentious, and every week they do silly things for thirty minutes, not counting commercials. At the moment the kids seem to love them.

For similar reasons, serious rock fans hate them. They know the Monkees are together by happenstance, that they are not too irreverent, too precocious, too sexual—too anything. They know they are lousy singers and can hardly play their instruments. They note that Micky Dolenz was once "Circus Boy" and forget that Mike Nesmith has had a respectably bumpy folk-rock career. And they conclude that the music stinks.

It doesn't. It's not great, but it is good, better than much of what makes top ten—an important test if rock is truly a popular art. The group's second album, *More of the Mon-kees,* is hard to criticize objectively. Do I hear that dishonest edge in a funny, raucous song like "Your Auntie Grizelda" because it's there or because I expect it to be? Who can tell? With a couple of horrible exceptions, the songs sound OK, testimony to the truth that good rock is largely a matter of production and publicity. "Mary, Mary," which Nesmith wrote and produced, is very successful. He is their clearest talent and a bit of a real rebel. One would hope that he and not Dolenz will dominate the group. Something may come of this yet.

But whatever it is, it won't be the Beatles.

*December, 1967.* It is time for a progress report on the Monkees, who took a big gamble by re-leasing an album and a single at about the same time as the big fellas from England. The album, *Headquarters,* has not done as well as *Sgt. Pepper,* but "Pleasant Valley Sunday" b/w "Words" is two-sided top ten, whereas "All You Need Is Love" is one-sided.

My original analysis of the group pitted Mike Nesmith (struggling singer, hence good) against Micky Dolenz (ex-child actor, hence bad). As it turns out, the real baddie seems to be the other ex-child actor, Davy Jones, a repulsive showbiz type, cute as a push button. The rest? Peter Tork is an anxiety-prone phony, Dolenz a likable oaf with a strong voice, and Nesmith still the most talented of the four, which may not be saying much. His "You Just May Be the One" and "Sunny Girlfriend" are by far the best songs on *Headquarters* and would sound good anywhere.

The Monkees began, if you'll remember, as poor vocalists and no musicians at all, but now, as a note on the album proclaims, they are Doing It Themselves. This means they are venturing live performances. I saw them at Forest Hills, and they stank. That crisp studio sound was weak and ragged on stage, and their Act (they tell the press that the kids won't go for "four dots" anymore) was unbelievably corny. The kids screamed, of course, but the stadium was far from full, and the one lonely rush at the stage quickly stymied by a bored and overstaffed security force. Good signs.

# 48. The Aesthetics of Rock

An important part of a history in documents about popular music is the way in which writing about popular music changed over time. Prior to the 1960s, one period in particular stands out for the amount of print expended on popular music: The late 1930s and early 1940s witnessed the birth of several publications devoted to jazz, precisely at the moment when debates about "authenticity" and "commercialism" in jazz were becoming more common. The aesthetic and historical issues in the mid-1960s were similar in many respects. As I mentioned earlier, music criticism devoted to rock blossomed parallel to a shift in the seriousness of the audience for popular (especially "rock") music. Several new publications appeared in response to these changes in reception. *Crawdaddy!* led the way early in 1966 and was quickly followed by *Rolling Stone* in 1967 and *Creem* in 1968. In addition to these, several older, more established publications published articles by critics that discussed popular music in a tone previously reserved for classical music and jazz (some of these articles appeared earlier in Part 3). The *Village Voice* earned the distinction of being the first established publication to hire a member of the counterculture, Richard Goldstein, as their rock critic in 1966. Other publications followed suit: *Cheetah* hired Robert Christgau in 1967; the toney *New Yorker* broke down in 1968 and hired Ellen Willis, one of the first female rock critics. Meanwhile other notables of rock criticism, such as Greil Marcus, Jon Landau, and Dave Marsh, were getting their start at one or the other of the above-named countercultural publications.[1]

Compared to the previous generation of critics and to mainstream publications, such as *Time* and *Newsweek*, these countercultural writers brought with them a new sensibility. What follows are articles that explicitly address the notion of rock aesthetics—in other words, what is it that makes rock music good or beautiful? And how does the specificity of late sixties' rock demand a different approach to answering these questions compared to other types of music?

---

1. For a more in-depth account of the development of rock criticism, see Gendron, *From Montmartre to the Mudd Club: Popular Music and the Avant-Garde* (Chicago: University of Chicago Press, 2002) (Gendron discusses the debates about jazz aesthetics in the early 1940s as well); Steve Jones and Kevin Featherly, "Re-Viewing Rock Writing: Narratives of Popular Music Criticism," in Steve Jones, ed., *Pop Music and the Press* (Philadelphia: Temple University Press, 2002), 19–40; and other essays in *Pop Music and the Press*. Richard Meltzer, another critic who began with *Crawdaddy,* authored a book with the title of this section, *The Aesthetics of Rock* (New York: Something Else Press, 1970).

The first entry in this chapter consists of the introductory editorial to the first issue of *Crawdaddy!*, by that magazine's founder, Paul Williams, then a 17-year-old freshman at Swarthmore College. Here, Williams explains the rationale for a new type of publication devoted to the criticism of rock.

## GET OFF OF MY CLOUD

### *Paul Williams*

You are looking at the first issue of a magazine of rock 'n' roll criticism. *Crawdaddy!* will feature neither pin-ups nor news briefs; the specialty of this magazine is intelligent writing about pop music. *Billboard*, *Cash Box*, etc., serve very well as trade news magazines; but their idea of a review is: "a hard-driving rhythm number that should spiral rapidly up the charts just as (previous hit by the same group) slides." And the teen magazines are devoted to rock 'n' roll, but their idea of discussion is a string of superlatives below a fold-out photograph. *Crawdaddy!* believes that someone in the United States might be interested in what others have to say about the music they like.

This is not a service magazine. We fully expect and intend to be of great use to the trade: by pushing new 45s that might have otherwise been overlooked, by aiding radio stations in deciding on their playlists, by giving manufacturers some indication of response to a record other than sales, by providing buyers with critiques of new LPs so that they'll have some idea what they're getting before they buy, and, most important, by offering rock 'n' roll artists some sort of critical response to their work. But we are not a service magazine.

The aim of this magazine is readability. We are trying to appeal to people interested in rock 'n' roll, both professionally and casually. If we could predict the exact amount of sales of each record we heard, it would not interest us to do so. If we could somehow pat every single pop artist on the back in a manner calculated to please him and his fans, we would not bother. What we want to do is write reviews and articles that you will not want to put down, and produce a magazine that you will read thoroughly every week. And we think we can do it.

The second entry in this chapter is an early article by Richard Goldstein that takes Marshall McLuhan's ideas about the effects of electronic media on communications as its point of departure. One of the first attempts to articulate why rock music demanded a new way of listening and a new context for evaluation, this article aligns rock with McLuhan's "cool media," which, according to McLuhan, counteract the serial, unitary logic of hot media (such as print) with an "intuitive mosaic of instantaneous communication" (McLuhan uses television as an example of the latter).[2] Goldstein's innovative move here is to apply McLuhan's often-quoted statement, "the medium is the message" to rock music in the service of

---

2. See Marshall McLuhan, *Understanding Media: The Extensions of Man* (New York: Signet Books, 1964).

*Source:* Paul Williams, "Get Off of My Cloud [editorial]," *Crawdaddy!* February 7, 1966. Reprinted in Paul Williams, ed., *The Crawdaddy! Book: Writings (and Images) from The Magazine of Rock* (Milwaukee: Hal Leonard Co., 2002), 10–11.

developing a type of criticism specific to it. Part of the urgency of this project for Goldstein stems from a reaction to the modernist tendency to dismiss pop because of its inescapable association with commerce.

# POP EYE: EVALUATING MEDIA
## *Richard Goldstein*

The most disturbing thing about Marshall McLuhan's "Understanding Media" to most
readers of this column will be its insistence that those who attempt to impose standards
upon the "cool" electronic media based on their aesthetic experiences with the printed
word are cultural illiterates. They are as far from understanding radio, television, cinema,
or mixed media discotheques as non-literate cultures are from comprehending the scope of
literature.

Many of those absorbed in criticizing these new media "are typically book-orientated
individuals who have no competence in the grammars of newspaper or radio or film but
who look askew and askance at all non-book media," according to McLuhan. Such critics
would be hard pressed to understand why "Death of a Salesman" could be an "evening of
exalted theatre" (to quote Jack Gould of the Times) and still be mediocre television, while a
series like "I Spy," with no literary aspirations, can use the spontaneous and informal qualities of television to maximum advantage.

What McLuhan's oft-quoted and oft-vilified statement—"the medium is the message"—means to criticism is that no longer can aestheticians separate form from content.
McLuhan differentiates between "hot" media, which provide a maximum amount of information to one specific sense, and "cool" media, which provide low definition images and
invite the audience to fill in the gaps.

To tell a professor of literature that Marvel Comics are artistic extensions of the comic
book form is probably futile because few professors choose to consider the possibility that
the cartoon—which McLuhan calls a "cool" pictorial form—can be artistic. To speak of the
New Journalism is useless because, many critics will maintain, reporting facts in a mosaic
rather than a sequential fashion cannot possibly be artistic.

To tell the connoisseur that a happening is a "cool" or participational approach to theatre is an impudence. To discuss seriously recent exhibits such as the USCO show, which
combined throbbing light, oscilloscopic patterns, flashing color sparks, and electronic
music to create an intimate "psychedelic" art-experience is self-defeating. Such approaches
will be considered irrelevant to the real stuff of art by those whose academic backgrounds
have enabled them to "appreciate" only the hot techniques in painting, music, and especially the printed word.

McLuhan refers to the "ancient book" and places our literary standards in opposition
to the newer pop arts. "Genteel art," he claims, "is a kind of repeat of the specialized acrobatic feats of an industrialized world. Popular art is the clown reminding us of all the life
and faculty that we have omitted from our daily routines. . . . The highbrow, from Joyce to
Picasso, has long been devoted to American popular art because he finds in it an authentic
imaginative reaction to official action."

Pop aestheticism has found its maximum support among the young intellectuals because its emergence as a meaningful experience can best be appreciated by those who have
been nursed on the 24-inch flickering box. For the great majority of our youth, pop culture

*Source:* Richard Goldstein, "Pop Eye: Evaluating Media," *Village Voice*, July 14, 1966, pp. 6–7. Reprinted
with permission by the author.

becomes a pervasive reality long before the age of artistic discrimination. McLuhan tells us that "every American home has a Berlin Wall" between it's youthful and adult occupants.

The dichotomy between classic and pop, between hot and cool, between high and low art forms, is especially apparent in the area of popular music. Adult intellectuals may never be able to comprehend why Bob Dylan is worshipped by legions of pubescent "teeny-boppers" and, at the same time, considered a major American poet by many serious students. These parochial critics face a practically insurmountable obstacle in their unwillingness to accept the fact that a poet can work in a medium such as rock 'n' roll—that this is an age of electronic troubadours.

They reply that rock 'n' roll cannot possibly be artistic because it is self-limiting in form, because it is not musically complex, because it has traditionally been commercial and therefore anti-artistic. When we mention that rock 'n' roll is musical television, that it is the language of the streets and increasingly of the campus, that it comes closest to being a universal means of communication, we are met with impatient snickering from those who inhabit the other side of the wall.

Just as reprehensible as the widespread ignorance of the classics among the young is the widespread ignorance of the current among adults. Yet, many of those churning out words and music to feed the sensibilities of our youth are becoming particular about the product they produce. A sure sign of this new sense of potential is the trend toward censorship of pop music by radio officials. Pop, we are told, is warping the tastes of our young. We are confronted with songs about pre-marital sex, the drug experience, war and peace, poverty, and lack of communication, and many, many shades of love. The basic Italian sound which came out of Philadelphia in the late 50's—the sound of Fabian, Frankie Avalon, and Connie Francis, among others—has nearly disappeared from popular view. In its place we have more variation in pop-sounds than ever before.

From the Negro ghettos of the North comes soul, with its gospel flavor. And from the South comes the Chuck Berry heritage of "hard" rhythm-and-blues. Far removed from the basic soul approach is the Motown sound, from Negro Detroit. It features a smooth, driving beat, reliance upon heavy orchestration, and a syrupy vocal quality. The lyrics are repetitive and rarely present any poetic ideas; the beauty is in the "sound."

The surf-sound from California presents us with loud, direct harmonies and subject matter that is materialistic and happy. By way of contrast, the California folk sound—exemplified by the Mamas and the Papas and new groups from the San Francisco Bay Area—is spiritual and often "psychedelic."

Psychedelic music—the most controversial sound—emphasizes melodic ambiguity, a free association approach to lyrics, and many electronic and atonal touches. It encompasses performers like the new Bob Dylan, Simon and Garfunkel, Bob Lind, and groups such as the Lovin' Spoonful, the Byrds the Yardbirds, and the Fugs.[3]

Jazz-rock, a new hybrid, has enabled groups like the Ramsey Lewis Trio, the Blues Project, and the Alan Price Set to experiment with sound-stretching. Folk-rock is, by now, an almost meaningless generalization since it labels the diverse work of the protest writers, the balladeers, and almost anyone who accompanies himself on a guitar. But any number of folk purists have made the electronic discovery that the big beat can be ethnic. Joan Baez has just recorded a rock album; three years ago, she parodied rock regularly in her concerts.

---

3. This is an early description of "psychedelic" music and differs considerably from later appraisals. Some of the other descriptions also diverge considerably from estimations that were current at the time and that were to become prominent shortly thereafter (e.g., Motown and Southern Soul).

The English Renaissance did much more than add a broad "a" to pop music; it brought to the fore a number of angry young troubadours who sing, almost obsessively, of the struggles between the poor and the rich, young and old, boss and worker. The Rolling Stones, the Animals, and the Kinks specialize in scathing put-downs. They sing Clifford Odets with an echo chamber.

And, of course, there are the Beatles. Their ascendancy covers almost every style mentioned above. They initiated Baroque-rock—making the classical style an integral part of their sound rather than the flourishing touch it has always been to rock 'n' roll. They are widely credited with awakening an interest in Eastern music and instrumentation which goes under the lamentable name of Raga-Rock. In their latest releases, the Beatles too seem to be drifting in the direction of electronic feedback and atonal rock and roll.

There are hacks working in pop music, but there is mediocrity on both sides of the wall. Rock 'n' roll may not be the most flexible form, but it is the one most with us today and the form most of our youth chooses to participate in. True artists are always aware of the limitations in their form. But they must receive an intense satisfaction in the realization that they are reaching a wider, more receptive, and more diversified audience through rock 'n' roll than ever before. And they are making money at it.

Their craft—rock 'n' roll—needs a critic. McLuhan complains that our educational apparatus educates principally with regard to the printed word. We learn to tell Dostoevsky from Spillane, but we know nothing about the flicks. We learn to tell Rembrandt from Keane, but we know nothing about advertising. We learn to deal with classical music and legitimate theater but we know nothing about the sights and sounds which bombard us perpetually in the name of pop.

And pop is not mere entertainment; it is anything but passive and conventional. Television, radio, advertising and cinema have radically changed the perceptions of every man on any street. The question now is how to deal with pop—how do we screen the fallout from Madison Avenue? How do we evaluate our responses to the electronic waves racing through our living room? How do we tell what is noise and what is good, even artistic, rock 'n' roll?

A pop critic needs his eyes, his ears, a typewriter, and an impressive German vocabulary. But most important, he needs his youth. Understanding media is hardly enough; we must learn to evaluate as well. And, in rock 'n' roll at least, the child may be father to the man.

> Ellen Willis's article, written two years after Goldstein's, analyzes the effects of the new seriousness of rock, particularly the emphasis on instrumental virtuosity. Willis relates musical developments to changes in dissemination and material culture, discussing how radio and recording formats also articulated the rock-pop divide: albums (rock) versus 45s (pop), FM-Free-form broadcasting (rock) versus AM-Top 40 (pop). She explicitly refers to an important shift that figured implicitly in the previous article: the way in which more people were beginning to consider the formal, aesthetic analysis of pop music to be as valid, if not more so, than the sociological analysis that previously dominated serious discussion. Willis's article marks a new stage in the development of a rock aesthetic, however, in that she argues *against* embracing standards of aesthetic merit derived from "high" culture. She extends Goldstein's argument for a criticism uniquely adapted for contemporary popular music, but now the increased technical complexity of rock during the interval since

Goldstein's article spurs Willis on to greater specificity about what such criticism may look like. Her article may be interpreted, then, as arguing for a resistance to the incorporation of modernist priorities into rock and rock criticism.[4]

## MUSICAL EVENTS—RECORDS: ROCK, ETC.

### *Ellen Willis*

The sociology of rock and post-rock has been based on three concepts: the star, the sound, and the scene. That sociology, like most, is firmly rooted in economics. Since the simplicity that gave rock its mass appeal also made it relatively easy to create, performers and the businessmen behind them faced a problem familiar to the makers of cigarettes and cars: How do you outsell a horde of competitors whose products are as good as yours? The solution was equally familiar: attractive packaging. The crucial elements in the package were charisma and sound—the artist's trademark, the gimmick that unified his work and set it apart (Little Richard's scream, the Everly Brothers' close harmonies, the Beatles' falsetto). If a performer or group did not have a unique sound, it helped to identify with a collective sound—usually that of a subculture (rockabilly, the Mersey sound) or of a creative producer (Phil Spector, Berry Gordy). I do not mean to conjure up the spectre of hucksters sitting around the Brill Building cold-bloodedly inventing salable gimmicks. Sometimes it worked that way. But mostly the process was unconscious: performers whose personal style was naturally gimmicky, or whose managers understood intuitively how to get attention, survived and bred imitators. Actually, before rock and roll became self-conscious, commercial and aesthetic considerations were almost indistinguishable; the geniuses of that period, from Chuck Berry to the early Beatles and Stones, owed their greatness to the same qualities that made them best-sellers. (Presley was an exception, and he ended up in Hollywood singing ballads.)

The Beatles were transitional figures. For one thing, their charisma was much more interesting than that of any previous rock-and-roll stars. Their image—that androgynous, childlike insouciance, the way they revelled in their fame and wealth without ever taking it or themselves seriously—sold records, which is what Brian Epstein had in mind when he made them wear mop tops and Edwardian suits. But it was also a comment on success, an embodiment of ingenuous youth in the affluent society—and "comments" and "embodiments" are, after all, aesthetic categories. Similarly, the Beatles' sound—a deliberate attempt *not* to sound black, contrary to custom—was at once a commercial novelty and an artistic self-assertion. These developments fascinated Pop artists and others for whom the aesthetic significance of commercial phenomena was a major preoccupation—enter the first self-conscious rock fans. The Beatles were also responsible for the bohemianization of rock. The concept of the rock "scene"—a term borrowed from jazz and implying an élite In group as much as a place—originated in Mod London and spread to San Francisco. Rock became identified less with particular superstars or sounds than with a whole lifestyle; "psychedelic" music was not so much a sound as a spirit. In 1965, the average person, asked to

---

4. For another attempt to establish a rock aesthetic by a prominent critic of the time, see Jon Landau, "Rock and Art," *Rolling Stone*, July 20, 1968, 18–19.

*Source:* Ellen Willis, "Musical Events—Records: Rock, Etc.," *The New Yorker*, July 6, 1968, pp. 56–58. Reprinted by permission of the Charlotte Sheedy Literary Agency.

associate to the phrase "rock and roll," would probably have said "Beatles;" by 1967 the answer would more likely have been "hippies," "drugs," or "long hair." When American bohemians took up rock, they brought along their very un-Beatlish distinctions between art and Mammon, and for the first time people talked about "serious," as opposed to merely commercial, rock. Yet if such talk was possible, it was only because the Beatles (with a lot of help from Bob Dylan) had paced a miraculous escalation in the quality of pop songs. Since "Sgt. Pepper," few people deny that "serious" pop is serious art. And though there is still some overlap, the split between the AM-radio-singles-teenie market and the FM-L.P.-student-hippie-intellectual audience is a fact of life.

With this evolution has come a shift in the way the music is perceived. There is, for example, an unprecedented demand for technical virtuosity. Good musicianship was once as irrelevant to rock as it was rare; the whole point of electric guitars and dubbing and echo chambers was that kids with no special talent could make nice noises. But now the music has enough scope to attract excellent instrumentalists, as well as an audience interested in traditional criteria of quality. Not that this audience's taste necessarily lives up to its pretensions; often flash is mistaken for skill. Still, a few years ago it would have been impossible for an Eric Clapton or a Mike Bloomfield to make it in pop music on the strength of fine guitar playing. The new audience also favors complex music and lyrics—a trend that threatened to get totally out of hand until Dylan's "John Wesley Harding" provided some timely propaganda for simplicity. What all this adds up to is an increasing tendency to judge pop music intrinsically, the way poetry or jazz is judged. Social context is still important, as it is for most art. But although social and economic factors were once an integral part of the rock aesthetic—indeed, defined that aesthetic—they are now subordinate to the "music itself."

On balance, in spite of all the good music that would never have happened otherwise, I think this tendency is regrettable. What it means is that rock has been co-opted by high culture, forced to adopt its standards—chief of which is the integrity of the art object. It means the end of rock as a radical experiment in creating mass culture on its own terms, ignoring elite definitions of what is or is not intrinsic to aesthetic experience. The reason the Beatles, the Stones, and Dylan are the unchallenged—and probably unchallengeable—giants of pop is that through and beyond their work their personalities have a continuing impact on the public consciousness that, if it is not aesthetic, is something just as good. (This is especially true of Dylan, an indifferent musician who never bothered to become a studio expert.) The new standards are bound to inhibit further exploration in this area. In addition, lack of a compelling image puts the new performer at an almost insuperable disadvantage in trying to make an impression on a public whose imagination is deeply involved with established artists. At best, new performers are taking longer to be recognized, and fewer and fewer will attain that special relationship to the public psyche that is so often uncomprehendingly dismissed as "mere celebrity." I'm thinking, for example, of the Sweet Inspirations, a Gospel-oriented quartet whose first album came out a while ago. They're great, and by all rights should take over the position of preeminent girl group last held by the Supremes and before that by the Shirelles. But though they have a hit single ("Sweet Inspiration"), I doubt that they will make that pinnacle. So what? Well, part of the fun of listening to the Supremes was that they were the *Supremes*.

A related problem is the loss of the mass audience. Whether the upgrading of the music is in itself responsible for that loss is questionable. The Beatles held the loyalty of their original teenage fans long after they had stopped making simple, happy dance music; when the kids finally turned off, it was less because the Beatles were esoteric than because they were old hat. More recently, the Doors and Jefferson Airplane have done very well outside the coterie. Jimi Hendrix, on the other hand, has not, though he has all the accoutrements of the superstar—a distinctive personality (he's the only expatriate black hippie around), a distinctive sound (achieved by choke-neck playing on the electric guitar), and a spectacular live act (he plucks his guitar with his teeth, sets fire to it, and breaks it up). What *is* certain is that the new music has thoroughly confused the record industry; no one can figure out how to promote it. Since the beginning of this year, the sheer quantity of serious pop, as well as its immense variety, has defied sloganeering. Most of the new musicians are not interested in gimmickry or image-making; they just want to make music. It's no longer possible to attract notice with a fancy album cover and a way-out name. And the scenes are dying. The Small Faces are the only interesting British group to break since Cream. The best first albums of this year's San Francisco crop come from two of the original underground groups, the Loading Zone and Quicksilver Messenger Service; except for a little-known group called Serpent Power, and Blue Cheer, which has a certain crude energy going for it (what I mean is, it's loud), the "second generation" San Francisco groups are a disaster. Early this year, MGM Records, out of naïveté or desperation, tried to invent a new scene, and a few other companies went along. It was called the Boston Sound (though there was no special sound involved) and was promoted as anti-drug and anti-exotic—rather negative premises on which to build a scene. The groups themselves were a dreary lot, ranging from the competently frenetic Beacon Street Union to the sublimely ridiculous Earth Opera. (By the time the E. O. album was released, the vibrations were pretty bad, so the group was billed as a *Cambridge* product. It didn't help.) Moral: scenes may be made, but they have to be born first.

For the sake of completeness, I ought to note that there are two areas of pop music in which sociology still dominates. First, *negative* charisma is very potent. A group that is thought of as a teenybopper band won't be accepted by most serious rock fans no matter how good it is. Ask someone in the audience at the Fillmore East what he thinks of the Hollies or the Young Rascals. Second, there is a minor cult of sensitive adolescent folkies like Tim Buckley and Steve Noonan, for no reason I can discern except that they are probably just like the kids who idolize them. In the case of Richie Havens, the attraction must be that he is black and friendly—an irresistible combination these days.

# 49. Festivals

## The Good, the Bad, and the Ugly

While stadium concerts featuring several bands had been occurring since at least 1964, the Monterey Pop Festival in the summer of 1967 inaugurated a new era in which a "rock festival" spanned several days and somehow managed to connote antimaterialism within what were still basically capitalist enterprises. The decade ended with two major festivals. Woodstock, held in August 1969, was widely viewed as a successful event by the national media, and attendance became a kind of retroactive litmus test for hipness (if not hippieness). The idea of the "Woodstock Nation" gained widespread currency among hippies and media observers and became a metonym for the "new age" of peace and love that many hoped the change in lifestyles would bring.

Less than four months later, however, the Altamont "festival" (actually a one-day event) brought such fantasies to a crashing halt. Organized at the behest of the Rolling Stones as the finale of their tour late in 1969, the concert took place near the San Francisco Bay Area and featured local bands, such as the Grateful Dead, the Jefferson Airplane, and Santana. The Hell's Angels were hired as security and were at least partially responsible for the feelings of paranoia that many audience members remember as characterizing the event.[1]

Some of the most thoughtful accounts of Woodstock discuss the contradictions between the peace-and-love ethos projected by the event and the effort required by entrepreneurs to produce that effect. At the same time, few writers could resist an optimistic interpretation of Woodstock, still believing in the "reality of a new culture of opposition" that was basically antimaterialist.[2] J. R. Young's "fictional" review of the album, *Woodstock*, released almost a year after the festival, brings out some of the self-delusion involved in the counterculture at the level of interpersonal relationships; in other words, even if the counterculture managed to resist the lures of materialism, status and prestige were still important, even when acquired nonmaterialistically. Many of Young's other fictional reviews address issues of conformity and the persistence of prehippie values within the counterculture.[3]

---

1. It is interesting to compare the films from all three of these events: *Monterey Pop* and *Woodstock* both seem in sympathy with the hippy milieu. *Woodstock*, in particular, coordinated as it was with the release of a triple-album (perhaps the first of its kind), ran over three hours in length, meaning that consumption of both the album and movie required feats of endurance similar to those needed to survive the original event. *Gimme Shelter*, on the other hand, is a different story altogether: Begun as a documentary of the Rolling Stones "triumphal" 1969 American tour as the "undisputed" greatest rock 'n' roll band in the world (now that the Beatles were no longer touring), the harrowing footage of Altamont turns the movie into a tragedy. Both the cinematic accounts of Woodstock and Altamont emphasized certain elements of those events that downplayed the range of audience reactions.

2. See Andrew Kopkind, "Woodstock Nation," in Jonathan Eisen, ed., *The Age of Rock 2: Sights and Sounds of the American Cultural Revolution* (New York: Random House, 1970), 312–18. Originally published in *Hard Times* in 1969.

3. See, for example, J. R. Young, review of The Grateful Dead, *Live Dead* (Warner Brothers 1830), *Rolling Stone,* February 7, 1970; and J. R. Young, review of Crosby, Stills, Nash, Young, Taylor, and Reeves, *Déjà Vu* (Atlantic SD 7200), *Rolling Stone,* April 30, 1970.

# REVIEW OF VARIOUS ARTISTS, *WOODSTOCK*

## *J. R. Young*

Bill hadn't been to Woodstock that August weekend the summer before, although Plattsburgh, his home, was less than 300 miles due north on the Northway. He'd gone drinking at Filion's Friday night, and when he awakened terribly hungover the next afternoon, as did most of his 18-year-old buddies, it was too late to make the trip down to Bethel. You couldn't have convinced anyone in the months that ensued, however, that not only was Bill not *at* the Music and Art Show in the alfalfa fields, but that he hadn't also played some integral part in the whole proceeding—a dope runner for the Airplane, perhaps ("Hey, Bill, you got a bomber?" Grace, resplendent in white, tits high and firm, asked him standing behind the giant platform as the Who finished up their set with the sun edging orange up the mountain from its resting place), or a candy bar for Jerry Garcia. Bill believed, too, and if pressed he had a whole Abbie Hoffman Rap about the "actuality" of being there not actually being the important thing, but only a minor side trip.

"I *live* in Woodstock nation," Bill told people when the topic came up, "If you can dig it. I mean how many were actually there. You don't know. We'll never know. But it doesn't make any difference. The Woodstock actuality has become a media trip. That's where it's at. More cameras, writers, and that kind of shit than at Kennedy's funeral. Like the people on the outside probably know more than those who were actually there. What it's come down to is Woodstock Nation, and Woodstock Nation, man, is in your head if you want it to be."

Probably. But Bill still knew a whole lot about the Music Show itself, and took great pains to seek out said information. He had clippings, articles, ads, the illustrious *Life* Magazine Special Edition, *Rolling Stone's Woodstock*, the *Village Voice* issue, and now in late spring had seen the movie three times at four bucks a throw, and also had the album committed to memory. His head, in fact, was a living monument to the whole Woodstock thing, even down to the little things. Somehow Bill had found someone who had some of the infamous "brown acid." He paid ten bucks for the tab so that he could find out "what was going down." True to form, he took it the second time he saw *Woodstock*.

"Man, that brown acid at Woodstock was a real bummer," he told assorted freaks at assorted gatherings. "A real bummer. Knocked me out for hours. Paranoia personified."

As time passed, Bill became more assertive in such situations. No one now bothered to question him directly as to whether he had been there, but merely what was it like. Bill went along with them because he felt he really knew what it was like.

"Cocker was crazy, man, beautiful. And Alvin Lee, wow."

"Were there really a lot of naked people," a far out chick asked handing him a joint, "like cunt and cock and everything?"

"Well," Bill would smile, "you saw the movie didn't you?"

"Yeh."

"What else do you want to know?"

"Far out."

Woodstock was now the new American Dream, a pipe dream, how it had been those three glorious days of sun and rain, mud and music, and the 500,000 patriots whose ranks were growing day by day, patriots of Woodstock "flying their freak flags high," Groupies, the Dope, and good ol' Rock & Roll, and the national anthem, understood for the first time by Hendrix and his buzz saw guitar. It was all coming home to rest now, and Bill, like many,

*Source:* Record review of *Woodstock* (Cotillion SD 3-500), by J. R. Young from *Rolling Stone*, July 9, 1970.

was proud to stand up and be counted for his own People, for Life, Liberty, and the Pursuit of Happiness, for his Country. Woodstock Nation was a reality.

So it was, until one night at a party in West Chazy when the conversation once more found its way to Woodstock as it always did whenever Bill happened to show. Bill dropped facts and recollections amidst the circle of listeners who sat rapt about him like Leary dropped acid. They all shook their heads at the good dope being passed and at the general incredulity of the whole Woodstock affair. But they believed. That is, all but one believed, and this one hairy ragamuffin of hipdom lay back against a sofa, hitting on his own kief, and coolly taking in Bill's polished exposition. He listened for a long time. At some point, indiscernible to the rest of the gathering, he apparently had heard enough.

"Hey, man," he said, leaning his well-coiffed head into the circle. "Did you ever understand what happened down front just before the Band went on?"

Bill looked up and smiled.

"No, I wasn't there when that happened. I must have been somewhere else. What happened?"

"I don't know. I was sitting about 50 yards out." The kid leaned back out again.

Bill eyed him for a moment, and then continued on from the point where he had disengaged. He had his stuff down.

Seconds later however, the kid again poked his head inside the circle.

"What happened, man, when that weird rumor. . . ."

"About Dylan showing up?" Bill cut him off in stride.

"No, man, that was a media hype. No, the rumor just before Creedence Clearwater went on about the latrines?"

Bill looked at the kid again, and didn't answer for the longest time. And then it was only a reticent shrug.

"Well, where, man, did you take a dump after that? Where'd you spend most of your time?"

Everyone turned and looked at Bill, but Bill had nothing to say, no one to look at, nowhere to go.

"I mean," the kid went on, driving his point home, "when I arrived, the can situation, and that strange tale, well, it was weird. Right? You do remember that, don't you?"

"Sure, but. . . ."

"Did you fork out any bread to get in?"

"No," Bill answered, looking down at the flickering candle, "but. . . ."

"Did you get back to Leon's down the. . . ."

"Groovy Way?"

"Wrong direction, man, wrong direction."

There was a silence, a certain moment of embarrassment because now everyone knew. Bill didn't look up.

"You're right, though," the kid finally said, "the movie was pretty far out. But it wasn't like being there. Nothing was like being there." A second silence followed, and then the kid turned to the far out chick. "Hey, you got anything to drink or eat, man? This is your place, isn't it?"

"Yeh," someone echoed, and in seconds the crowd was on its feet, eager to be up and away. Everyone but Bill. He was still on the floor staring into the flame. The rest of the gang trooped to the kitchen.

"Look, man, it was clear he hadn't been there if you'd been there."

"And you'd been there," the girl said.

"Yeh. Anybody who had would have known immediately he was shucking us. It was obvious, if you knew."

"Sure, maybe, but dig where it's at. Two wrongs don't necessarily make a right, as my grandmother used to tell me, if there were even two wrongs. You know what I mean?"

"But, look. He'd been sold a bill of goods, man, a product that had little to do with anything but money, and that's what he was selling. What, I'm supposed to feel bad for coming down on him for fucking around with us? He's an asshole, it's that simple. I mean, like he really believes it, and that's weird."

"Apparently you believe it too. Perhaps more so than Bill. But then you *were* there. You are Woodstock Nation, and if it's come down to this, then that's sad. That's why there will never really be a Woodstock Nation. You won't let anybody live on your land. You were there. Bill wasn't. Bang, bang. Sad. It's too bad you didn't remember what Dylan said."

"What?"

"'Those dreams are only in your head.'" She turned and walked away. At the door she paused and looked back at the kid, and smiled. "'I'll let you be in my dreams, if I can be in yours.'"

> The following account of Altamont by George Csicsery explores the cultural ramifications of the event. Many hip commentators of the time viewed Altamont as the symbolic and literal "end of the sixties" and a "loss of innocence," an interpretation that grew stronger in retrospect. In the following article, Csicsery discusses how Altamont revealed that the counterculture's emphasis on peace and love had not excised fear and violence but, rather, had displaced it so that it was perceived as existing only in the rest of society. The question forced to the surface here is how separate a subculture can really be.

## ALTAMONT, CALIFORNIA, DECEMBER 6, 1969
### *George Paul Csicsery*

In the beginning there was rock 'n' roll. The Beatles came and made it good with love and the bluebird of Paradise. But even while the children lifted their faces to the sun, Mick Jagger coiled himself around the tree of flesh, offering a sweet bite of chaos. Saturday, the children swallowed that bite, after chewing and tasting their alliance with evil for nearly a decade.

Until Saturday, evil was value-free, something to dig for its own sake. A lot of people who thought they were children of chaos dropped out of their sugar-coated camp trips Saturday to see the core of their religion at work.

Altamont, like the massacre of Song My, exploded the myth of innocence for a section of America. As the country grows more sophisticated, it learns to confront its own guilt.

The media projected WOODSTOCK. A great people event put on by the younger generation to celebrate its freedom. Traffic jams creating technological time-space motion transcending normal blurb time events. Birth, death, dope, violence, groovy teenyboppers dancing—an instant consumer package of life. Look at all the hippies, America. They're grooving while the rest of you schmucks have to watch it on TV, because you're too uptight.

*Source:* George Paul Csicsery, "Altamont, California, December 6, 1969," in Jonathan Eisen, ed., *The Age of Rock 2: Sights and Sounds of the American Cultural Revolution* (New York: Random House, 1970), pp. 145–48. Used by permission of the author.

The media needs hippies now more than ever, to show there is still someone in America who can dig on a scene.

But this time it didn't work. The helicopters could not feel that something more than a happening with three hundred thousand people was going on below. Altamont was America. Years of spreading dope, hair, music, and politics came together and reflected nothing less than the whole trip.

Those who expected the illusion of their own inherent goodness to last forever are still freaked. Others who pay less attention to the rhetoric of a cultural revolution say they had a good time. Putting it all together reads like America's pulse NOW. After all we not only make beautiful music, love, and beadwork; we pay our pigs to exterminate Black Panthers, we fry Vietnamese in their own homes, and we elect Spiro Agnew to govern our lives.

Altamont was a lesson in micro-society with no holds barred. Bringing a lot of people together used to be cool. Human Be-Ins, Woodstock, even a Hell's Angel funeral, were creative communal events because their center was everywhere. People would play together, performing, participating, sharing, and going home with a feeling that somehow the communal idea would replace the grim isolation wrought on us by a jealous competitive mother culture.

But at Altamont we were the mother culture. The locust generation come to consume crumbs from the hands of an entertainment industry we helped create. Our one-day micro-society was bound to the death-throes of capitalist greed. The freeway culture delivered the crowd, separate, self-contained in Methedrine isolation, to an event where they could not function as private individuals. The crowd came from a country where everything is done for you. Welfare state—relax, work, and pay your taxes. We'll take care of the war in Vietnam and the war at home.

Yeah, but nobody made sure the machine would function at Altamont. Three hundred thousand people sucked on a dry nipple because it was free. Everyone tried to get to the same place all by himself, and since everyone made it there was no pie. The pie was watching yourself at the spectacle, watching the spectacle watching you at the spectacle doing your own thing watching.

America at Altamont could only muster one common response. Everybody grooved on fear. One communal terror of fascist repression. The rest was all separate, people helping, people walking, people eating, people standing in line to shit. The revolutionaries were there too. Everybody related to people freaking out as well as the mother culture relates to Yippies. Here they were running through the crowd naked, stoned, trampling on our thinning privacy.

They expressed our own lack of control, our desire for space, for the freedom to live out our own body lives. But the crowd reacted with blind hatred, paranoia pressing them forward to get a better look at their own private crush on his satanic majesty.

But it wasn't all a freakout. Back up the slopes of Altamont Speedway, as in the secluded suburbs and woods of America, people kept to the illusions of better dope and more space. The loners, couples, and communes saw nothing, heard nothing and cared less about the crowded valley of fear. Most of them say they had a good time, but few escaped the heavy vibes from below.

Around the stage, at the epi-center, the Angels lost control. Their violence united the crowd in fear. Even people who had no fear of the Angels grew tense from a repressed feeling of panic that swirled around the stage. Mostly it was a fear of being trampled that was intensified by fights and people who did freak out. Since the Angels were the only group there who were together enough to organize their violence they became a clear focus of crowd hatred. Thousands of times we've blamed pigs for less while holding the myth of right-wing Anarchist sacred. Marlon Brando, freewheelin' agent of chaos, another of Saturday's toppled camp heroes.

The Angels protected Mick, their diabolic prince, well. He escaped without serious injury. Later on KSAN they too defended their actions on the grounds that their private property was violated. "... ain't nobody going to kick an Angel's bike and get away with it ..." The official cover-up came Ronald Reagan style from the Stones' Manager Sam Cutler. When asked about the Angels' violence he answered "... regrettable, but if you're asking for a condemnation of the Angels ..."

It was over. No explanation was needed, only a feeble plea for someone in America to clean it up. The stirrings of a young but growing movement to salvage our environment. The job of cleaning up Altamont, or America, is still up for grabs. America wallows in the hope that someone, somewhere, can set it straight. Clearly nobody is in control. Not the Angels, not the people. Not Richard Nixon or his pigs. Nobody. America is up for grabs, as it sinks slowly into Methedrine suffocation with an occasional fascist kick to make her groan with satisfaction.

# 50. Where Did the Sixties Go?

Histories of popular music often describe the late 1960s–early 1970s as a time of "splintering," when the supposedly monolithic counterculture audience divided itself among an ever-growing assemblage of genres. According to this view, middle-class, college-educated listeners gravitated toward singer-songwriters, art rock, and what remained of improvisation-oriented blues and psychedelic rock, while younger, middle- and working-class listeners favored the emerging heavy-metal and hard rock. At the same time, Top 40 music for early teens grew increasingly disconnected from all the above, ending the brief convergence of the most experimental rock and soul with mainstream pop. Such generalizations are true up to a point, but they obscure divisions that already existed, as well as commonalities that persisted. Earlier large-scale divisions among and within white pop, black pop, and country continued, but in new forms, while fissures appeared in the critical firmament. New bands, such as Led Zeppelin, for example, appealed to many readers of *Rolling Stone,* but elicited the approbation of critics on *Rolling Stone's* staff.[1]

The music industry did seem to recover from its bewildered response to the anarchic eclecticism that had surfaced between 1965 and 1969. Top 40 radio more and more featured bubblegum groups and one-off novelties, while some of the most challenging funk, soul, and rock faded from mass circulation. This is not to say to that all one could hear on Top 40 were the Archies, the Partridge Family, and the 1910 Fruitgum Company; hits by Aretha Franklin, James Brown, Sly and the Family Stone, Santana, the Rolling Stones, Janis Joplin, and many others were still played heavily for several years into the 1970s. Nevertheless, "soul" radio, FM progressive, and AM Top 40 all diverged during this period. "Easy listening" pop, the holdover from pre–rock 'n' roll popular music, continued to fade, although chestnuts, such as "Theme from Love Story" by Andy Williams (from 1971), surfaced occasionally.

---

1. See the exchange in *Rolling Stone* (part of which is reprinted in chapter 56) of reviews and letters about Led Zeppelin's first two albums in *The Rolling Stone Record Review* (New York: Pocket Books, 1971). Originally published in *Rolling Stone* on March 15, 1969, and December 13, 1969.

While many saw the end of the 1960s as representing the end of the counterculture, quite a few of the musical predilections of the late 1960s continued. Bands like the Beatles (and the solo efforts of former Beatles once the band split up); the Band; the Grateful Dead; Led Zeppelin; the Allman Brothers; Crosby, Stills, Nash, and Young; and many others shared an emphasis on technical virtuosity and either formal complexity or improvisational ability (or both), while featuring lyrics that displayed psychedelic influences and expressed utopian sentiments. Although all these bands might—only a short time later—be categorized according to different genres, this was not necessarily apparent to listeners at the beginning of the 1970s.

The continuities between the late 1960s and early 1970s illustrate the difficulties with periodization schemes organized by decades. When one thinks of that cultural-historical moment known as the 1960s in terms of how the subculture of white, Western youths, usually referred to as "hippies," intersected with larger political and economic patterns, a strong case can be made for the persistence of "the 1960s" until 1972 or 1973. In this scheme, the end of the 1960s is marked by (take your pick) the failed U.S. presidential campaign of George McGovern, the oil crisis of 1973, the Watergate scandal of 1973–74, or the reconsolidation of the recording industry. The musical analogy of these various crises and scandals was the near-banishment of hard funk and deep soul to black radio and of countercultural rock to "progressive" FM by the mid-1970s.

The continuing and almost subliminal emphasis on technique derived from "high art" music within many evolving genres of rock music forms a large part of the context for the excerpt by Lester Bangs included here. Bangs advances an aesthetic similar to that described by Ellen Willis in chapter 48, one that opposes the virtues of rock 'n' roll to those of "artiness." For Bangs, the artless simplicity of Iggy and the Stooges represents an antidote to the pretentiousness of the "heavy" rock bands, with the Stooges' music synthesizing desirable qualities taken from both free jazz and the garage bands of the mid-1960s, both of which Bangs applauds for their acceptance and creative use of noise. A particularly influential aspect of this account is how the Velvet Underground emerges as an important link between the proto-punk of the 1960s and the Stooges. Both free jazz and the Velvet Underground (and hence the Stooges) reveal affinities for the New York avant-garde aesthetic of the 1960s, sharing the avant-garde's enthusiasm for confronting and shocking the audience.[2]

To support his argument, Bangs presents a synopsis of rock music from the mid-1960s to 1970 when this article was written. Bangs adds crucially to previous accounts of a rock aesthetic by enlarging the frame

---

2. Bangs expands further on the relevance of the Velvet Underground for revitalizing 1970s rock in "Dead Lie the Velvet Underground," *Creem* (May 1971): 44–49, 64–67.

of reference to include jazz and by recognizing the connection between the influence of ex-folkies and the attitudes of purism and of disdain for simple rock 'n' roll that wielded a large influence over late 1960s' rock.[3] Bangs became one of the most important theoreticians of punk rock, and this article serves as an early statement of the values that found fruition in the musical developments of the mid- to late 1970s. The major forum for the dissemination of Bangs's views was *Creem* magazine, a publication whose aesthetic tone was set primarily by Bangs and his colleague, Dave Marsh, beginning in 1970. *Creem* draped its proto-punk philosophy in proletarian garb, appearing as a populist alternative to *Rolling Stone*, which largely valued the continuation of a 1960s, countercultural aesthetic. In *Creem's* scheme of things, the main culprits in the decline of rock were Elton John, James Taylor, Led Zeppelin, and Chicago—i.e., bloated, "professional" entertainers.[4]

## OF POP AND PIES AND FUN
### Lester Bangs

The first thing to remember about Stooge music is that it is monotonous and simplistic on purpose, and that within the seemingly circumscribed confines of this fuzz-feedback territory the Stooges work deftly with musical ideas that may not be highly sophisticated (God forbid) but are certainly advanced. The stunningly simple two-chord guitar line mechanically reiterated all through "1969" on their first album, for instance, is nothing by itself, but within the context of the song it takes on a muted but very compelling power as an ominous, and yes, in the words of Ed Ward which were more perceptive (and more of an accolade) than he ever suspected, "mindless" rhythmic pulsation repeating itself into infinity and providing effective hypnotic counterpoint to the sullen plaint of Iggy's words (and incidentally, Ig writes some of the best throwaway lines in rock, meaning some of the best *lines* in rock, which is basically a music meant to be tossed over the shoulder and off the wall: "Now I'm gonna be twenty-two/I say my-my and-a boo-hoo"—that's classic—he couldn't've picked a better line to complete the rhyme if he'd labored into 1970 and threw the *I Ching* into the bargain—thank God somebody making rock 'n' roll records still has the good sense, understood by our zoot-jive forefathers but few bloated current bands, to know when to just throw down a line and let it lie).

---

3. See Andrew Chester's near-contemporaneous attempt to articulate a rock aesthetic in "For a Rock Aesthetic." Chester's account, while written for a more academic readership, nevertheless shares much with Willis and Bangs in his recognition that value in rock music is not synonymous with value in classical music and was itself part of an ongoing debate in *New Left Review*. See Andrew Chester, "Second Thoughts on a Rock Aesthetic: The Band," *New Left Review* 62 (1970): 75–82.

4. For more on how the writings of *Creem* and of Bangs, in particular, prefigure the values that would dominate punk, see Bernard Gendron, "Punk before Punk," in *Between Montmartre and the Mudd Club* (Chicago: University of Chicago Press, 2002), 227–47.

Now *there's* a song just packed with ideas for you, simplistic and "stupid" though it may seem and well be. A trained monkey could probably learn to play that two-chord line underneath, but no monkeys and very few indeed of their cousins half a dozen rungs up on the evolutionary ladder, the "heavy" white rock bands, could think of utilizing it in the vivid way it is here, with a simplicity so basic it's almost pristine. Seemingly the most obvious thing in the world, I would call it a stroke of genius at least equal to Question Mark and the Mysterians' endless one-finger one-key organ drone behind the choruses of "96 Tears," which is one of the greatest rock and roll songs of all time and the real beginning of my story, for it was indeed a complex chronology, the peculiar machinations of rock 'n' roll history from about 1965 on, which ultimately made the Stooges imperative.

## Part Two: Brief History Lesson

I used to hate groups like Question Mark and the Mysterians. They seemed to represent everything simpleminded and dead-endish about rock in a time when groups like the Who and the Yardbirds were writing whole new chapters of musical prophecy almost monthly; certainly we've never known music more advanced at the time of its inception than the likes of "I'm a Man," "Anyway Anyhow Anywhere," "My Generation" and "Shapes of Things." The Yardbirds I especially idolized. Eventually, though, I wised up to the fact that the Yardbirds for all their greatness would finally fizzle out in an eclectic morass of confused experiments and bad judgments, and hardest of all to learn was that the only spawn possible to them were lumbering sloths like Led Zeppelin, because the musicians in the Yardbirds were just too *good,* too accomplished and cocky to do anything but fuck up in the aftermath of an experiment that none of them seemed to understand anyway. And similarly, the Who, erupting with some of the most trail-blazing music ever waxed, got "good" and arty with subtle eccentric songs and fine philosophy, a steadily dilating rep, and all this accomplishment sailing them steadily further from the great experiment they'd begun.

So all these beautiful ideas and raw materials were just lying around waiting for *anybody* to pick them up and elaborate them further into vast baroque structures that would retain the primordial rock and roll drive whilst shattering all the accumulated straitjackets of key and time signature which vanguard jazz musicians had begun to dispose of almost a decade before. By now jazz was in the second stage of its finest experimental flowering, in that beautiful night of headlong adventure before the stale trailoff workaday era which has now set in. The Albert Ayler who is now spooning out quasi-cosmic concept albums cluttered with inept rock ripoffs and sloppy playing was then exploding with works like *Spiritual Unity's* free-flying Ozark-tinged "Ghosts," and Archie Shepp had not yet passed from *Fire Music* into increasingly virulent Crow-Jim nihilism. Jazz was way out front, clearing a path into a new era of truly free music, where the only limits were the musician's own consciousness and imagination, a music that cut across all boundaries yet still made perfect sense and swung like no music had ever swung before.

Clearly, rock had a lot of catching up to do. We could all see the possibilities for controlling the distortions of Who/Yardbirds feedback and fuzz for a new free music that would combine the rambling adventurousness of the new free jazz with the steady, compelling heartbeat of rock, but the strange part was that nobody with these ideas seemed to play guitar or any of the necessary instruments, while all the budding guitarists weaned on Lonnie Mack and Dick Dale and Duane Eddy and now presumably ready to set out for the unknown were too busy picking up on the sudden proliferation of borrowed, more accessible forms that came with the sixties renaissance. Christ, why go fuck with screaming noise when there were Mike Bloomfield's and George Harrison's newest ideas and all that folk rock to woodshed with?

About this time it also began to look like a decided majority of the rising bands were composed of ex-folkies, as opposed to previous waves whose roots had lain in fifties rock and R&B but never crossed paths with the college mobs of coffee house banjo-pickers, who almost unanimously, from Kingston Trio frat sweaters to hip Baez/Lightnin' Hopkins "purists," looked down their noses at that ugly juvenile noise called rock 'n' roll which they all presumed to have grown out of into more esthetically rewarding tastes (or, in other words, a buncha fuckin' effete snobs).

Well, I never grew out of liking noise, from Little Richard to Cecil Taylor to John Cage to the Stooges, so I always liked rock and grabbed hungrily at the Yardbirds/Who development, expecting great things. Meanwhile, all these folkies who grew out of the jolly Kennedy era camaraderie of "This Land Is Your Land" singalongs into grass and increasing alienation were deciding that the rock 'n' roll stuff warn't so bad: it, not they, was getting better (I'm sure I'm simplifying this a bit, but not much, I fear, not much). So they got electric guitars and started mixing all the musics stored in their well-educated little beans up together, and before we knew it we had Art-rock.

Some of the groups that came out of this watershed were among rock's best ever: the Byrds, the early Airplane, etc. But the total effect, I think, was to set the experiment begun by those second-string English bands back by at least two years. You kept listening for something really creative and free to emerge from all the syntheses, but in the end it mostly just seemed competent and predictable. Raga-rock and other such phases with marginal potential came and went, and the Byrds did a few far-out but seldom followed-up things like "Eight Miles High," while the Stones kept on being great following the trends like the old standbys they had already become. The Airplane hinted at a truly radical (in the musical sense) evolution in *After Bathing at Baxter's,* but the most advanced statement they could seem to manage was the Sandy Bull-like standardized electric guitar raga of "Spare Chaynge." Clearly something was wrong. Rock soaked up influences like some big sponge and went meandering on, but no one in the day's pantheon would really risk it out on the outer-edge tightrope of true noise. 1967 brought *Sgt. Pepper* and psychedelia: the former, after our initial acid-vibes infatuation with it, threatening to herald an era of rock-as-movie-soundtrack, and the latter suggesting the possibility of real (if most likely unconscious) breakthrough in all the fuzztone and groping space jams. Even local bands were beginning to experiment with feedback but neither they nor the names they followed knew what to do with it.

Meanwhile, rumblings were beginning to be heard almost simultaneously on both coasts: Ken Kesey embarked the Acid Tests with the Grateful Dead in Frisco, and Andy Warhol left New York to tour the nation with his Exploding Plastic Inevitable shock show (a violent, sadomasochistic barrage on the senses and the sensibilities of which Alice Cooper is the comparatively innocuous comic book reflection) and the Velvet Underground. Both groups on both coasts claimed to be utilizing the possibilities of feedback and distortion, and both claimed to be the avatars of the psychedelic multimedia trend. Who got the jump on who between Kesey and Warhol is insignificant, but it seems likely that the Velvet Underground were definitely eclipsing the Dead from the start when it came to a new experimental music. The Velvets, for all the seeming crudity of their music, were interested in the possibilities of noise right from the start, and had John Cale's extensive conservatory training to help shape their experiments, while the Dead seemed more like a group of ex-folkies just dabbling in distortion (as their albums eventually bore out).

By the time the Velvets recorded "Sister Ray," they seemed to have carried the Yardbirds/Who project to its ultimate extension, and turned in their third album to more "conventionally" lyrical material. Also, their two largely experimental albums had earned them little more than derision (if not outright animosity) among critics and the listening audience at large. Their music, which might at first hearing seem merely primitive, unmusicianly and chaotic, had at its best sharply drawn subtleties and outer sonances cutting across a stiff, simplistic beat that was sometimes ("Heroin") even lost, and many of the basic guitar lines were simple in the extreme when compared with the much more refined (but also more *defined,* prevented by its very form and purposes from ever leaping free) work of groups like the Byrds and Airplane. I was finally beginning to grasp something.

Sixties avant-garde jazz is in large part a very complex music. The most basic, classic rock, on the other hand, is almost idiotically simple, monotonous melodies over two or three chords and a four-four beat. What was suddenly becoming apparent was that there was no reason why you couldn't play truly free music to a basic backbeat, gaining the best of both worlds. Many jazz drummers, like Milford Graves and Sunny Murray, were distending the beat into a whirling flurry that was almost arrhythmic, or even throwing it out altogether. So if you could do that, why couldn't you find some way of fitting some of the new jazz ideas in with a Question Mark and the Mysterians type format?

It was also becoming evident that the nascent generation of ex-folkie rock stars, like the British beat and R&B groups which preceded them in '64, were never going to get off their rich idolized asses to even take a fling at any kind of free music. They simply knew too much about established musical forms which the last three decades of this century should make moribund, and were too smug about it to do anything else. So the only hope for a free rock 'n' roll renaissance which would be true to the original form, rescue us from all this ill-conceived dilettantish pap so far removed from the soil of jive, and leave some hope for truly adventurous small-guitar-group experiments in the future, would be if all those ignorant teenage dudes out there learning guitar in hick towns and forming bands to play "96 Tears" and "Wooly Bully" at sock hops, evolving exposed to all the eclectic trips but relatively fresh and free too (at least they hadn't grown up feeling snobbish about being among the intellectual elite who could appreciate some arcane folksong), if only they could somehow, some of them somewhere, escape the folk/*Sgt. Pepper* virus, pick up on nothing but roots and noise and the possibilities inherent in approaching the guitar fresh in the age of multiple amp distorting switches, maybe even get exposed to a little of the free jazz which itself seemed rapidly to be fading into its own kind of anachronism, then, just *maybe,* given all those ifs, we might have some hope.

Well, maybe the gods were with us this time around, because sure enough it happened. On a small scale, of course—the majority of people listening to and playing rock were still mired in blues and abortive "classical" hybrids and new shitkicker rock and every other conceivable manner of uninventively "artistic" jerkoff. But there were some bands coming up. Captain Beefheart burst upon us with the monolithic *Trout Mask Replica,* making history and distilling the best of both idioms into new styles undreamed of, but somehow we still wanted something else, something closer to the mechanical, mindless heart of noise and the relentless piston rhythms which seemed to represent the essence of both American life and American rock 'n' roll.

Bands were sprouting and decaying like ragweed everywhere. The MC5 came on with a pre-records hype that promised the moon, and failed to get off the launching pad. Black Pearl appeared with a promising first album—no real experiments, but a distinct Yardbirds echo in the metallic clanging cacophony of precisely distorted guitars. Their second LP fizzled out in bad soul music.

## Part Three: The Outline of Cure

And, finally, the Stooges. The Stooges were the first young American group to acknowledge the influence of the Velvet Underground—and it shows heavily in their second album. The early Velvets had the good sense to realize that whatever your capabilities, music with a simple base was the best. Thus, "Sister Ray" evolved from a most basic funk riff seventeen minutes into stark sound structures of incredible complexity. The Stooges started out not being able to do anything else *but* play rock-bottom simple—they formed the concept of the band before half of them knew how to play, which figures—probably just another bunch of disgruntled cats with ideas watching all the bullshit going down. Except that the Stooges decided to do something about it. None of them have been playing their instruments for more than two or three years, but that's *good*—now they won't have to unlearn any of the stuff which ruins so many other promising young musicians: flash blues, folk-pickin', Wes Montgomery-style jazz, etc. Fuck that, said Asheton and Alexander, we can't play it anyway, so why bother trying to learn? Especially since even most of those styles' virtuosos are so fucking boring you wonder how anyone with half a brain can listen to them.

Cecil Taylor, in A. B. Spellman's moving book *Four Lives in the Bebop Business,* once told a story about an experience he had in the mid-fifties, when almost every club owner, jazz writer and listener in New York was turned off to his music because it was still so new and so advanced that they could not begin to grasp it yet. Well, one night he was playing in one of these clubs when in walked this dude off the street with a double bass and asked if he could sit in. Why not, said Taylor, even though the cat seemed very freaked out. So they jammed, and it soon became apparent to Taylor that the man had never had any formal training on bass, knew almost nothing about it beyond the basic rudiments, and probably couldn't play one *known* song or chord progression. Nothing. The guy had just picked up the bass, decided he was going to play it, and a very short time later walked cold into a New York jazz club and bluffed his way onto the bandstand. He didn't even know how to hold the instrument, so he just explored as a child would, pursuing songs or evocative sounds through the tangles of his ignorance. And after a while, Taylor said, he began to hear something coming out, something deeply felt and almost but never quite controlled, veering between a brand-new type of song which cannot be taught because it comes from an unschooled innocence which cuts across known systems, and chaos, which playing the player and spilling garble, sometimes begins to write its own songs. Something was beginning to take shape which, though erratic, was unique in all this world: Quite abruptly, though, the man disappeared, most likely to freak himself into oblivion, because Taylor never saw or heard of him again. But he added that if the cat had kept on playing, he would have been one of the first great free bassists.

The Stooges' music is like that. It comes out of an illiterate chaos gradually taking shape as a uniquely personal style, emerges from a tradition of American music that runs from the wooly rags of backwoods string bands up to the magic promise eternally made and occasionally fulfilled by rock; that a band can start out bone-primitive, untutored and uncertain, and evolve into a powerful and eloquent ensemble. It's happened again and again; the Beatles, Kinks, Velvets, etc. But the Stooges are probably the first name group to actually form before they even knew how to play. This is possibly the ultimate rock 'n' roll story, because rock is mainly about beginnings, about youth and uncertainty and growing through and out of them. And asserting yourself way before you know what the fuck you're doing. Which answers the question raised earlier of what the early Stooges' adolescent mopings had to do with rock 'n' roll. Rock is basically an adolescent music, reflecting the rhythms, concerns and aspirations of a very specialized age group. It *can't* grow up—when it does, it turns into something else which may be just as valid but is still very different from the original. Personally I believe that real rock 'n' roll may be on the way out, just like adolescence as a relatively innocent transitional period is on the way out. What we will have instead is a small island of new free music surrounded by some good reworkings of past idioms and a vast sargasso sea of absolute garbage. And the Stooges' songs may have some of the last great rock 'n' roll lyrics, because everybody else seems either too sophisticated at the outset or hopelessly poisoned by the effects of big ideas on little minds. A little knowledge is still a dangerous thing.

# 51. The Sound of Autobiography

## Singer-Songwriters, James Taylor

From the ashes of the folk revival rose the very antithesis of Bangs's "cure"—the singer-songwriter genre. While Bob Dylan's early work up through *Blonde on Blonde* forms the obvious prototype for this genre, one can look back further and find an even earlier model in Woody Guthrie, who wrote his own songs, accompanied himself on guitar, and presented a romantic image of poetic individualism, albeit without the strong autobiographical currents that run through Dylan's work. While Dylan acknowledged Guthrie as his major influence, we should not forget the blues and country musicians (especially a figure such as Hank Williams who wrote songs with strong autobiographical connotations) who also embodied many of the qualities just ascribed to Guthrie.

Among the many musicians influenced by Dylan, two, in particular, were important for setting the stage for the singer-songwriter movement: Joan Baez (b. 1941), who, while not known primarily as a songwriter, projected a strong image of personal sincerity as she accompanied herself on the guitar and was the most successful of the early 1960s' folk singers; and Paul Simon (b. 1941), whose earnest, melodic anthems (which were not without a sense of humor), performed in partnership with Art Garfunkel, struck a strongly resonant note with collegiate audiences.

In the early work of Dylan and Simon, lyrics focused on personal issues in a realistic way, and songs therefore took on strong autobiographical associations. After hearing Simon sing "Kathy's Song" (on Simon and Garfunkel's *Sounds of Silence,* late 1965), one would not be surprised to learn later that Simon wrote the song about a young woman named Kathy with whom he was involved during a sojourn in England (as the story has emerged from the biographical literature on Simon). When Simon and Garfunkel were accompanied by a band, the arrangements grew not out of riffs, as in the blues-rock or psychedelic rock of the mid- to late-1960s, but, rather, out of the accompaniment patterns played by Simon on the guitar. The same tendency was true of the singer-songwriter genre in general, since band arrangements were based on the guitar or piano part played by the singer-songwriter who was accompanying herself or himself. These patterns were rhythmic arpeggiations, known as "fingerpicking" on the guitar (the style has no specific designation when originating on the piano). In terms of politics, singer-songwriters might espouse antiwar and (especially) antimaterialist views, but they tended to eschew the affiliation with specific causes that was characteristic of the 1960s folk revival.

The most prominent musicians associated with the singer-songwriter genre came from diverse backgrounds. Carole King (b. 1940) had honed her songwriting craft in the Brill Building, writing for rhythm and blues artists, such as the Drifters and the Shirelles in the early 1960s, and for bubblegum, rock, and soul artists like the Monkees, the Byrds, and Aretha Franklin in the late 1960s. Joni Mitchell (b. 1943) and James Taylor (b. 1948) wrote and performed music with clearer ties to the folk revival, while Carly Simon (b. 1945) betrayed more mainstream pop and Broadway show tune influences. Yet all these artists released influential albums between 1970 and 1972 that were recognized as introducing a new "introspective," "intimate" quality into "rock" music.[1] They were solo artists primarily, employing other musicians as necessary to amplify their own accompaniments. And their lyrics were heard as somehow referring to their own lives: Critics frequently introduced biographical elements into articles and reviews as important information that might explain the meaning of the songs. Many writers also recognized that a relatively high number of women were involved in the singer-songwriter genre and frequently attributed this to the "gentler," "prettier" quality of the music.[2]

The tone and topic of the following article on James Taylor, published in *Time* in 1971, could not form a stronger contrast with the preceding article by Lester Bangs. All the major ideas that were to dominate subsequent writing about singer-songwriters in the music press may be found here: the emphasis on autobiography and the "mature" tone of the music that positioned it as the antidote to hard rock. This generally sympathetic account reveals the continuation of a trend we saw with the *Newsweek* article in chapter 39 on *Sgt. Pepper:* the increasing acceptance of certain types of popular music by the mainstream press. Taylor is portrayed here as a soulful, sensitive fellow who converts his experiences into song lyrics and conveys the suffering and alienation that come with "plenty of money, a loving family, good schools, health, charm, and talent."

1. That these attributes have been widely accepted as exemplifying the genre can be seen from a recent blurb in the Spring 2002 *Time-Life* music catalog:

During the 1960s, thanks in large part to Bob Dylan, singers started believing they should write their own material. The singer-songwriter movement was born, and it has influenced rock ever since. This TIME-LIFE MUSIC series gathers hits from the Singer-Songwriter era: sincere, sensitive, deeply personal songs, performed by the artists who created them.

2. See, for example, Noel Coppage, "Troubadettes, Troubadoras, and Troubadines . . . or . . . What's a nice girl like you doing in a business like this?" *Stereo Review* (September 1972): 58–61. Two years later, *Time* featured an article on the same subject (with a focus on Joni Mitchell) as their cover story, "Rock 'n' Roll's Leading Lady," *Time*, December 16, 1974, 63–66 (the title on the cover is "Rock Women: Songs of Pride and Passion").

# JAMES TAYLOR: ONE MAN'S FAMILY OF ROCK
## *Time*

The decompression of rock can be traced back to 1968 and Bob Dylan's search for a simple way of saying simple things in *John Wesley Harding*. Among the groups, the gentling process was carried to mellow new highs and lows by The Band. The rise of rock's new solo poets is a natural extension. Often they are talented offshoots from famous groups, the most notable examples being all four Beatles. Characteristically, they make the new sound but leave explanations to musicologists and sociologists. Occasionally, however, one will fall prey to the seductions of historic hindsight. "The dream is over," John Lennon has lately observed. "I'm not just talking about the Beatles, I'm talking about the generation thing. It's over, and we gotta—I have personally gotta—get down to so-called reality."

Whether or not the dream is over for good, the man who best sums up the new sound of rock—as well as being its most radiantly successful practitioner—is a brooding, sensitive 22-year-old rich man's son who sings, he says, "because I don't know how to talk." James Taylor's first album came out only two years ago on the prestigious Apple label. It sold only 30,000 copies its first year. Today Taylor is one of the best and steadiest national record sellers since the loudest days of Beatlemania. *Sweet Baby James*, his second album, has already sold 1,600,000 copies and, along with his single *Fire and Rain*, has been nominated for five Grammy Awards. A third album, *Mud Slide Slim*, will be released next month. Last month, Taylor was included in the predominantly classical Great Performers series at New York City's Lincoln Center. He has just finished a movie, *Two-Lane Blacktop*, for late spring release, and last week he began a sell-out national concert tour of 27 cities.

These and other abundant signs of commercial achievement measure, but do not begin to explain, James Taylor's peculiar hold on the ear and imagination of youthful Americans. A good deal of his success is based on the kind of personal magnetism that has been making baritones and matinee idols rich and famous for generations, a particular masculine presence. Lean and hard (6 ft. 3 in., 155 lbs.), often mustachioed, always with hair breaking at his shoulders, Taylor physically projects a blend of Heathcliffian inner fire with a melancholic sorrows-of-young-Werther look that can strike to the female heart—at any age. Half explaining, half apologizing for her delight in *Fire and Rain*, a University of Michigan coed who is also a trained musician admits: "I don't know why I love it. I know I shouldn't, because he doesn't really sing. He just sort of intones."

What Taylor intones is far more artful than it seems at first. For if his voice is spare and strangely uninflected, his guitar fingering lends sudden lights and shadows to the barest melody. Musically, Taylor is a fusion of the three black and white mainstreams of pop: the lonely twang of country, the pithy narrative of folk and the rhythmic melancholy of the blues. Beyond that, Taylor's use of elemental imagery—darkness and sunlight, references to roads traveled and untraveled, to fears spoken and left unsaid—reaches a level both of intimacy and controlled emotion rarely achieved in purely pop music. He can, says one of his campus admirers, "turn an arena into a living room."

Listeners do not need to know anything about him to enjoy his music. Taylor is a master of many styles and subjects. The song *Sweet Baby James* is simply one of the best lullabies ever composed. In *Suite for 20 G*, he can ease into a cool, rock-'n'-roll-flavored parody of the 1950s, or do wailing variations on old-fashioned blues (*Oh Baby Don't You Loose Your Lip on Me*).

Yet much of the time Taylor sings about himself, and most of his fans feel instinctively that the anguished outlines of his private life—as well as those of his two brothers,

---

*Source:* "James Taylor: One Man's Family of Rock," *Time*, March 1, 1971, pp. 45, 48. © 1971 Time, Inc., reprinted by permission.

Livingston, 20, and Alex, 23, and his sister Kate, 21, all now launched on singing careers—could be their own. The four singing Taylors, in fact, run some risk of becoming a sort of *One Man's Family* of rock.

Like so many other troubled, dislocated young Americans, Taylor may at first seem self-indulgent in his woe. What he has endured and sings about, with much restraint and dignity, are mainly "head" problems, those pains that a lavish quota of middle-class advantages—plenty of money, a loving family, good schools, health, charm and talent—do not seem to prevent, and may in fact exacerbate. Drugs, under-achievement, the failure of will, alienation, the doorway to suicide, the struggle back to life—James Taylor has been there himself.

It seems to add something to the impact of a song like *Fire and Rain* to know that the lyric is really a mini-trilogy dealing with three bad times in the singer's life. Part I goes back to a moment of sadness—and a sense of failure—when he was making his first record in London in 1968. A girl he knew died at the time, but his friends did not tell him until the record was finished because they thought he was "too strung out" to handle the news:

> *I've seen lonely times when I could not find a friend,*
> *But I always thought I'd see you again.*

Part II finds Taylor bottoming out in the New York drug-scene abyss:

> *Won't you look down upon me Jesus?*
> *You've got to help me make a stand,*
> *You've just got to see me through another day.*

The song's final stanza is a footnote to 1968, when James left New York trying to escape heroin and personal squalor, and thus brought to an end The Flying Machine, a struggling group started by his friend Danny Kootch:

> *There's hours of time on the telephone line*
> *To talk about things to come,*
> *Sweet dreams and flying machines in pieces on the ground.*

Taylor's voice is mercifully free of the whiny self-pity that haunts most singers of lovelorn pop lyrics. Even his most self-revealing effort, *Knocking 'Round the Zoo*, which tells what it was like in a mental hospital, where James spent nine months, comes out heavily armed with witty, riffy musical irony—at least until the end, when Taylor tacks a chilling descant of bedlamite sounds onto the following stanza:

> *Now my friends all come to see me, they point at me and stare,*
> *Said he's just like the rest of us so what's he doing in there?*
> *They hide in their movie theaters drinking juice—keeping tight*
> *'Cause they're certain about one thing, that zoo's no place to spend the night.*

Today Taylor's experiences seem frighteningly in tune with the troubles of his age. "Right now," remarks Danny Kootch, who first met James in the late 1950's and now not only plays guitar with Taylor but leads his own group Jo Mama, "if you're not alienated, you're weird. All you have to do is grow your hair long and everybody talks to you. But in those days you felt, 'What's the matter with me that I can't exist in this world?' Either you ended up very neurotic and screwed up, or you got strength from it." James eventually ended up doing a little of both.

Offstage, James seems in many ways to be the average rock-'n'-roll musician. He wears regulation T shirts, regulation Levi's, regulation cowboy boots. He crosses living rooms or recording studios with the same ten-league strides he would use heading up a country road. He eats—and drinks—anything and everything that is put before him. Like his songs, he is also much turned in upon himself, rarely talkative, sometimes edgy, always haunted by the precariousness of human joy.

## Easing the Guilt

He is fully aware that a pop star can be destroyed by his fond public. Interviews seem to threaten him tremendously. "With all that feedback of ideas and memories and resonances from the past," he says, "an interview can be like an epileptic fit. People come at me as though they had a coloring book and ask me to fill in the colors." The false rumors that accrue to fame are exasperating. "One day," he told a reporter, "my brother Alex got ten calls consoling him about my suicide, my reinstitutionalization, and my split with Joni Mitchell." Chatter about Taylor's very real romance with Joni is currently the gossip rage of the teeny-bopper set. Now that his face and name are nationally known, Taylor ponders the effects of his record as a junkie. "I don't want some kid out in Nebraska to read about me and say, 'Well, I'm gonna pick up some smack just like James did.'"

Though he arrived at his present feelings and scruples before they became fashionable, he is driven by many contemporary idealistic concerns—about nature and its misuse, about wealth, about manipulation of people. "Nothing is wrong in making as much bread as you need," he says, "but there are things wrong in making more bread than you need." To help ease that guilt, he has lately taken to giving away some of the proceeds from his public concerts—to, among others, the Hopi Indians. "I wish I were really part of the environment, part of the land," he says, "instead of a successful Caucasian." He is proud of his accomplishments, though, and will admit that "I like success almost as much as I dislike it." Aware of these mixed feelings, he is concerned about the very real problem of maintaining a proper perspective between the private James Taylor he and his friends know and the public James Taylor who sometimes seems to be coming in the windows. Taylor may perhaps derive some comfort from the division of public attention, which is certain to grow more pronounced as the individual reputations of his fellow rock troubadours grow. There are, for example, such famous ex-group soloists as the individual Beatles, Neil Young and Stephen Stills (of Crosby, Stills, Nash & Young). Elton John is an English one-man music industry whose songs range panoramically from country rock to blues. Leon Russell, the presiding master of gospel rock, invokes the Lord Jesus with piano playing that has a touch of Fatha Hines and a voice that has a touch of bayou frog. Nashville's Kris Kristofferson, an ex-Rhodes scholar, sings bluntly sensual protest songs that have made him the most controversial country songwriter-singer of the day. Van Morrison, an Irishman late of Them, flavors his blues-gospel-folk broth with a salty pinch of jazz. In the wings are two virescent newcomers. One is Carole King, a soul blues singer who plays piano on James's records and has written a song for his new album. The other is English Folk Minstrel Cat Stevens, who sounds like an off-the-moors Harry Belafonte.

## A Special Kind of Salvation

In pop music no fashion lasts for long. Though now is predominantly the moment of the solo trip and the modulated musical message, group think could easily come back strong. For that matter, it is still around with varying degrees of excellence in the work of Chicago and Led Zeppelin. Yet just as individuals like Ray Charles and Chuck Berry influenced the major groups of the 1960s, so today's soloists are bound to affect the future. If so,

tomorrow's rock could well be more religious and pastoral in tone, more intricate and ambitious in style. Because of the increasing influence of Miles Davis, jazz is bound to be an
added ingredient. Intriguingly complex forms, exemplified by the rock passion *Jesus Christ,
Superstar,* have yet to be explored adequately and may one day engage collective talent, perhaps even the Taylors.

# 52. Joni Mitchell Journeys Within

Although never attaining quite the same level of commercial success as
James Taylor and Carole King, Joni Mitchell (b. 1943) became an archetype for future singer-songwriters. Like Taylor, she recorded her first
album in 1968, but unlike him, she was already known to the surviving
remnants of the folk music audience through recordings of her early work
by artists such as Tom Rush, Dave van Ronk, and Ian and Sylvia. Judy
Collins's Top 10 hit with her version of Mitchell's "Both Sides Now" (1968)
added to awareness of Mitchell as a songwriter. Mitchell did not experience a similar level of success herself, however, until 1974 with her sixth
album, *Court and Spark,* and the first single from it "Help Me."[1]

Mitchell's music was distinguished from the start by unusual guitar
tunings that produced unique and complex harmonies; in addition to
being a skillful performer on guitar, piano, and dulcimer, her elaborate
vocal ornamentation of her already complex melodies revealed a technical ability far beyond that ordinarily associated with folk music.[2] Her
fourth album, *Blue* (1971), exhibited the growing influence of jazz, an influence that would peak with her association with Charles Mingus from
1979, entitled *Mingus.* Mitchell continues up to the present to be reluc-
tant to repeat herself musically.

---

1. For an excellent account of her early career, see William Ruhlmann, "Joni Mitchell: From Blue to
Indigo," *Goldmine,* February 17, 1995; reprinted in *The Joni Mitchell Companion: Four Decades of Commentary* (New York: Schirmer Books, 2000), 21–40.

2. For an analysis of Mitchell's music, see Lloyd Whitesell, "Harmonic Palette in Early Joni Mitchell,"
*Popular Music,* 21, no. 2 (May 2002): 173–94; and Jeffrey Pepper Rodgers, "My Secret Place: The Guitar
Odyssey of Joni Mitchell," in *The Joni Mitchell Companion,* 219–30.

Of all the early 1970s' singer-songwriters, Joni Mitchell best exemplifies what might be called the "autobiographical effect": the impression that the songs are directly relaying events from her life (along with her psychologically acute reflections upon them). This quote from a review of *Blue* in *Rolling Stone* typifies this perception of Mitchell's work: "Her primary purpose is to create something meaningful out of the random moments of pain and pleasure in her life."[3] This is not to say that her lyrics are without humor; nevertheless, the main persona that emerges in her work from *Song to a Seagull* (1968, sometimes called *Joni Mitchell*) through *Don Juan's Restless Daughter* (1977) is that of a restless romantic torn between adventurousness and stability. And as noted by the interviewer in the piece that follows, the words "free" and "freedom" probably occur more often than any others in her lyrics from this period.

The following conversation with the Israeli folksinger, Malka, comes from the height of her fame in 1974. Mitchell touches on the autobiographical nature of her work and on the importance of introspection and analysis, but also gives a nuanced view of the interaction of these autobiographical elements with values that she shares with musicians working in other genres.

## Joni Mitchell: Self-Portrait of a Superstar
### *Malka*

**Malka:** *You're on the road performing again. Why the silence of two full years?*

**Joni Mitchell:** I like to retire a lot, take a bit of a sabbatical to keep my life alive and to keep my writing alive. If I tour regularly and constantly, I'm afraid that my experience would be too limited, so I like to lay back for periods of time and come back to it when I have new material to play. I don't like to go over the old periods that much; I feel miscast in some of the songs that I wrote as a younger woman.

**Malka:** *How do you feel, then, about listening to your records?*

**Joni:** I don't enjoy some of the old records; I see too much of my growing stage; I've changed my point of view too much. There are some of them that I can still bring life to, but some that I can't. Let's take the *Ladies of the Canyon* album; there are good songs on there which I feel still stand up and which I could still sing. There's a song called "The Arrangement" which seemed to me as a forerunner and I think has more musical sophistication than anything else on the album. And the *Blue* album, for the most part, holds up. But there are some early songs where there is too much naïveté in some of the lyrics for me to be able now to project convincingly.

3. Timothy Crouse, "Review of *Blue*," *Rolling Stone*, August 5, 1971; reprinted in *The Rolling Stone Record Review, Volume II*, by the editors of *Rolling Stone* (New York: Pocket Books, 1974), 471.

*Source:* Malka, "Joni Mitchell: Self-Portrait of a Superstar," *Maclean's*, June 1974. Reprinted in Stacy Luftig, ed., *The Joni Mitchell Companion: Four Decades of Commentary* (New York: Schirmer Books, 2000), 66–74.

**Malka:**   *Your name has been linked to some powerful people in the business, James Taylor and Graham Nash, for instance. Do you feel that your friends have helped your career in any way?*

**Joni:**   I don't think so, not in the time that James and I were spending together anyway. He was a total unknown, for one thing—maybe I helped his career? . . . But I do think that when creative people come together, the stimulus of the relationship is bound to show. The rock and roll industry is very incestuous, you know; we have all interacted and we have all been the source of many songs for one another. We have all been close at one time or another, and I think that a lot of beautiful music came from it. A lot of beautiful times came from it, too, through that mutual understanding. A lot of pain too, because, inevitably, different relationships broke up.

**Malka:**   *But isn't there a certain amount of danger, when you surround yourself with musicians and troubadours doing the same kind of work you are doing, that you really create your own special world and are not so open to what's happening in the rest of the world?*

**Joni:**   A friend of mine criticized me for that. He said that my work was becoming very "inside." It was making reference to roadies and rock 'n' rollers, and that's the very thing I didn't want to happen, why I like to take a lot of time off to travel some place where I have my anonymity and I can have that day-to-day encounter with other walks of life. But it gets more and more difficult. That's the wonderful thing about being a successful playwright or an author: you still maintain your anonymity, which is very important in order to be somewhat of a voyeur, to collect your observations for your material. And to suddenly often be the center of attention was . . . it threatened the writer in me. The performer threatened the writer.

**Malka:**   *Many of your songs are biographical—do you think that the change in your lifestyle now has affected your songs?*

**Joni:**   I don't know. I had difficulty at one point accepting my affluence, and my success and even the expression of it seemed to me distasteful at one time, like to suddenly be driving a fancy car. I had a lot of soul-searching to do as I felt somehow or other that living in elegance and luxury canceled creativity. I still had that stereotyped idea that success would deter creativity, would stop the gift, luxury would make you too comfortable and complacent and that the gift would suffer from it. But I found the only way that I could reconcile with myself and my art was to say this is what I'm going through now, my life is changing and I am too. I'm an extremist as far as lifestyle goes. I need to live simply and primitively sometimes, at least for short periods of the year, in order to keep in touch with something more basic. But I have come to be able to finally enjoy my success and to use it as a form of self-expression, and not to deny. Leonard Cohen has a line that says, "Do not dress in those rags for me, I know you are not poor," and when I heard that line I thought to myself that I had been denying, which was sort of a hypocritical thing. I began to feel too separate from my audience and from my times, separated by affluence and convenience from the pulse of my times. I wanted to hitchhike and scuffle. I felt maybe that I hadn't done enough scuffling.

**Malka:**   *On your new album,* Court and Spark, *for the first time you've recorded a song that isn't yours, "Twisted." Why did you decide to record something that is not your own?*

**Joni:**   Because I love that song, I always have loved it. I went through analysis for a while this year, and the song is about analysis. I figured that I earned the right to sing it. I tried to put it on the last record, but it was totally inappropriate. It had nothing to do with that time period, and some of my friends feel it has nothing to do with this album either. It's added like an encore.

**Malka:**  *I hope I'm not encroaching on your privacy, but why the analysis now?*

**Joni:**   I felt I wanted to talk to someone about the confusion which we all have. I wanted to talk to someone and I was willing to pay for his discretion. I didn't expect him to have any answers or that he was a guru or anything, only a sounding board for a lot of things. And it proved effective because simply by confronting paradoxes or difficulties within your life several times a week, they seem to be not so important as they do when they're weighing on your mind in the middle of the night, by yourself, with no one to talk to, or someone to talk to who probably will tell another friend, who will tell another friend, as friends do. I felt that I didn't want to burden people close to me, so I paid for professional help. And I went through a lot of changes about it, too. It's like driving out your devils—do you drive out your angels as well? You know that whole thing about the creative process. An artist needs a certain amount of turmoil and confusion, and I've created out of that. It's been like part of the creative force— even out of severe depression sometimes there comes insight. It's sort of masochistic to dwell on it, but you know it helps you to gain understanding. I think it did me a lot of good.

**Malka:**  *When I listen to your songs I notice that there are certain themes that keep appearing; one theme that comes up often is loneliness.*

**Joni:**   I suppose people have always been lonely but this, I think, is an especially lonely time to live in. So many people are valueless or confused. I know a lot of guilty people who are living a very open kind of free life who don't really believe that what they're doing is right, and their defense to that is to totally advocate what they're doing, as if it were right, but somewhere deep in them they're confused. Things change so rapidly. Relationships don't seem to have any longevity. Occasionally you see people who have been together for six or seven, maybe 12 years, but for the most part people drift in and out of relationships continually. There isn't a lot of commitment to anything; it's a disposable society. But there are other kinds of loneliness which are very beautiful, like sometimes I go up to my land in British Columbia and spend time alone in the country surrounded by the beauty of natural things. There's a romance which accompanies it, so you generally don't feel self-pity. In the city when you're surrounded by people who are continually interacting, the loneliness makes you feel like you've sinned. All around you you see lovers or families and you're alone and you think, why? What did I do to deserve this? That's why I think the cities are much lonelier than the country.

**Malka:**  *Another theme I think is predominant in your songs is love.*

**Joni:**   Love . . . such a powerful force. My main interest in life is human relationships and human interaction and the exchange of feelings, person to person, on a one-to-one basis, or on a larger basis projecting to an audience. Love is a peculiar feeling because it's subject to so much . . . change. The way that love feels at the beginning of a relationship and the changes that it goes through and I keep asking myself, "What is it?" It always seems like a commitment to me when you said it to someone, "I love you," or if they said that to you. It meant that you were there for them, and that you could trust them. But knowing from myself that I have said that and then reneged on it in the supportive—in the physical—sense, that I was no longer there side by side with that person, so I say, well, does that cancel that feeling out? Did I really love? Or what is it? I really believe that the maintenance of individuality is so necessary to what we would call a true or lasting love that people who say "I love you" and then do a Pygmalion number on you are wrong, you know. Love has to encompass all of the things that a person is. Love is a very hard feeling to keep alive. It's a very fragile plant.

**Malka:**   *I sometimes find myself envying people that seem to be able to handle love, people who have found a formula for marriage. You were married at one point yourself; how do you feel about marriage now?*

**Joni:**   I've only had one experience with it, in the legal sense of the word. But there's a kind of marriage that occurs which is almost more natural through a bonding together; sometimes the piece of paper kills something. I've talked to so many people who said, "Our relationship was beautiful until we got married." If I ever married again, I would like to create a ceremony and a ritual that had more meaning than I feel our present-day ceremonies have, just a declaration to a group of friends. If two people are in love and they declare to a room of people that they are in love, somehow or other that's almost like a marriage vow. It tells everybody in the room, "I am no longer flirting with you. I'm no longer available because I've declared my heart to this person."

**Malka:**   *Do you think you'll get married again?*

**Joni:**   I really don't know. I wouldn't see a reason for marriage except to have children, and I'm not sure that I will have children, you know. I'd like to and I have really strong maternal feelings, but at the same time I have developed at this point into a very transient person and not your average responsible human being. I keep examining my reasons for wanting to have a child, and some of them are really not very sound. And then I keep thinking of bringing a child into this day and age, and what values to instill in them that aren't too high so they couldn't follow them and have to suffer guilt or feelings of inadequacy. I don't know. It's like I'm still trying to teach myself survival lessons. I don't know what I would teach a child. I think about it . . . in terms of all my talk of freedom and everything.

**Malka:**   *Freedom, and in particular the word "free," is another theme in your music. What does freedom mean to you?*

**Joni:**   Freedom to me is the luxury of being able to follow the path of the heart. I think that's the only way that you maintain the magic in your life, that you keep your child alive. Freedom is necessary for me in order to create, and if I cannot create, I don't feel alive.

**Malka:**   *Do you ever envision or fear that the well of creativity might dry up?*

**Joni:**   Well, every year for the last four years I have said, "That's it." I feel often that it has run dry, you know, and all of a sudden things just come pouring out. But I know, I know that this is a feeling that increases as you get older. I have a fear that I might become a tunesmith, that I would be able to write songs but not poetry. I don't know. It's a mystery, the creative process, inspiration is a mystery, but I think that as long as you still have questions the muse has got to be there. You throw a question out to the muses and maybe they drop something back on you.

**Malka:**   *Sitting from the outside, it seems that as a creative person you have attained quite a lot: you have an avenue in which to express your talent, affluence, recognition. What are your aims now?*

**Joni:**   Well, I really don't feel I've scratched the surface of my music. I'm not all that confident about my words. Thematically I think that I'm running out of things which I feel are important enough to describe verbally. I really think that as you get older life's experience becomes more; I begin to see the paradoxes resolved. It's almost like most things that I would once dwell on and explore for an hour, I would shrug my shoulders to now. In your twenties things are still profound and being uncovered. However, I think there's a way to keep that alive if you don't start putting up too many blocks. I feel that my music will continue to grow—I'm almost a pianist now, and the same thing with the guitar. And I also continue to draw, and that also is in a stage of growth, it hasn't stagnated yet. And I hope to bring all these things together. Another thing I'd like to do is to make a film. There's a lot of things I'd like to do, so I still feel young as an artist. I don't feel like my best work is behind me. I feel as if it's still in front.

# 53. Sly Stone

## "The Myth of Staggerlee"

The phenomenal popularity of Aretha Franklin, the ongoing success of James Brown along with the grittiest practitioners of Southern Soul, and the continued ubiquity of the pop-oriented productions of Motown attested to soul music's continued relevance to a broad cross-section of the U.S. audience in the late 1960s. However, the activity and popularity of many of the first wave of soul practitioners declined after 1968. Producer/songwriters Holland-Dozier-Holland, who had been responsible for the bulk of the hits for the Supremes and the Four Tops during the peak 1964–67 period left Motown, while Stax, following the death of Otis Redding, underwent administrative reorganization and became increasingly inconsistent in both artistic and commercial terms (by 1975, the company filed for bankruptcy).

Nevertheless, soul music was far from finished; instead it split in two directions: a "sweet" soul style taking its cue from Motown and balladeers, such as Curtis Mayfield, and a "funky" soul style, taking its cue from James Brown, the "Southern Soul" practitioners, and Aretha Franklin. The discussion of funk rightfully began in chapter 34 with the excerpts from James Brown's autobiography. Brown's innovations and their adoption by other artists in the late 1960s also had an explicit political component, since these musical innovations coincided with a shift in African American politics from the integrationist stance of the civil rights movement (associated with the rise of soul music) to the more radical stance of the black power movement, a shift heralded by Brown's recording, "Say It Loud, I'm Black and I'm Proud" (1968).[1] These shifts

1. The fullest (and most entertaining) account of funk to date may be found in Rickey Vincent, *Funk: The Music, the People, and the Rhythm of the One* (New York: St. Martin's Griffin, 1996).

were discussed in Part 3 in conjunction with artists like Aretha Franklin, and songs such as "Respect."

Concurrent with the developments in Brown's band, other bands created their own forms of funky soul music, including Booker T. and the MGs, the Bar-Kays, the Meters, and Charles Wright and the Watts 103rd Street Rhythm Band. In an important contrast to earlier rhythm and blues and soul performers, these bands were self-contained, writing their own material and producing all vocal and instrumental parts. The first band to absorb Brown's rhythmic approach and extend it was Sly and the Family Stone. The San Francisco Bay Area–based aggregation joined Brown's rhythmic and textural innovations with a fragmented doo-wop vocal style featuring rapidly alternating voices and with aspects of psychedelic rock, a fusion evident in their first successful single, "Dance to the Music" (1968). The psychedelic influence (particularly that of Jimi Hendrix) was felt by other funk bands as well, most notably Funkadelic ("Maggot Brain," 1971) and the Isley Brothers ("Who's That Lady," 1973).

Sly and the Family Stone played a significant role in another important development in funk: The role of the bass expanded as Larry Graham of Sly and the Family Stone created an innovative thumb-popping technique particularly evident in an early 1970 release, "Thank U Falettin Me Be Mice Elf Agin." Brown's new bass player, William "Bootsy" Collins, was another crucial influence on subsequent bassists in recordings such as "Sex Machine" and "Superbad" from 1970–71.

Greil Marcus's piece on Sly Stone (b. 1944) documents how Sly's stylistic blend satisfied a particular need within the white counterculture, as well as within the soul music audience. In Marcus's words, the music of Sly and the Family Stone "fill[ed] a vacuum" in which "the racial contradictions of the counterculture" were worked out.[2] Marcus's overriding concern, here as in the rest of Mystery Train (the book from which this essay was taken), is to illuminate how Sly articulates "shared unities in the American imagination" through the connections between his music and certain American myths.[3] In this case, Marcus relates Sly Stone's public persona to the myth of Staggerlee, the archetypal "bad man." Marcus spends much of the chapter discussing Sly's dystopian album, Riot (1971), a recording that underscored the self-destructive nature of Sly's attachment to the Staggerlee character.

By the time of Mystery Train, Marcus was already well known to readers as a critic for Rolling Stone and its close competitor, Creem. In addition to exemplifying Marcus's music criticism, which displays an unusual talent for making music come alive with prose, the essay that follows conveys vividly the history of an extraordinary wave of black popular music during the early 1970s. In providing a broader context for the

2. Greil Marcus, Mystery Train: Images of America in Rock 'n' Roll Music, 3rd rev. ed. (New York: Plume, [1975] 1990), 69.

3. Ibid., p. xvii.

understanding of Sly Stone's brand of funk and the reception of *Riot*, Marcus details the relationship of black popular music of the time to social changes; to the emergent black cinema known as "blaxploitation"; and to political developments, such as black nationalism as embodied by the Black Panther Party, all of which are tied together by their connection to the myth of Staggerlee.

## *from* MYSTERY TRAIN: IMAGES OF AMERICA IN ROCK 'N' ROLL MUSIC
### *Greil Marcus*

## Sly Versus Superfly

The best pop music does not reflect events so much as it absorbs them. If the spirit of Sly's early music combined the promises of Martin Luther King's speeches and fire of a big city riot, *Riot* represented the end of those events and the attempt to create a new music appropriate to new realities. It was music that had as much to do with the Marin shootout and the death of George Jackson as the earlier sound had to do with the pride of the riot the title track of this album said was no longer going on.

"Frightened faces to the wall," Sly moans. "Can't you hear your mama call? The Brave and Strong—Survive! Survive!"

I think those faces up against the wall belonged to Black Panthers, forced to strip naked on the night streets of Philadelphia so Frank Rizzo and his cops could gawk and laugh and make jokes about big limp cocks while Panther women, lined up with the men, were psychologically raped.

A picture was widely published. Many have forgotten it; Sly probably had not. This again is why *Riot* was hard to take. If its spirit is that of the death of George Jackson it is not a celebration of Jackson, but music that traps what you feel when you are shoved back into the corners of loneliness where you really have to think about dead flesh and cannot play around with the satisfactions of myth.

The pessimism of *Riot* is not the romantic sort we usually get in rock 'n' roll. Optimistic almost by definition, pop culture is always pointing toward the next thing and sure it is worth going after; rock 'n' roll is linked to a youthful sense of time and a youthful disbelief in death. Pop culture pessimism is almost always self-indulgent; not without the power to move an audience, but always leaving the audience (and the artist) a way out. In retrospect, records made in this spirit often seem like reverse images of narcissism. *Riot* is the real thing: scary and immobile. It wears down other records, turning them into unintentional self-parodies. The negative of *Riot* is tough enough to make solutions seem trivial and alternatives false, in personal life, politics, or music.

Rock 'n' roll may matter because it is fun, unpredictable, anarchic, a neatly packaged and amazingly intense plurality of good times and good ideas, but none save the very youngest musicians and fans can still take their innocence for granted. Most have simply seen and done too much; as the Rolling Stones have been proving for ten years, you have to

*Source:* Greil Marcus, "Sly Stone: The Myth of Staggerlee," from *Mystery Train: Images of America in Rock 'n' Roll Music*, 3rd rev. ed. (New York: Plume, an imprint of Dutton Signet, a division of Penguin Books USA, Inc., [1975] 1990), pp. 78–83, 84–86. © 1975, 1997 by Greil Marcus. Used by permission.

*work* for innocence. You have to win it, or you end up with nothing more than a strained naïveté.

Because this is so pop heeds an anchor, a reality principle, especially when the old ideas—the joy of the Beatles, the simple toughness of the Stones—have run their course and the music has begun to repeat its messages without repeating their impact. Rock 'n' roll may escape conventional reality on a day-to-day level (or remake it, minute-to-minute), but it has to have an intuitive sense of the reality it means to escape; the audience and the artists have to be up against the wall before they can climb over it. When the Stones made "Gimmie Shelter," they had power because their toughness had taken on complexity: they admitted they had doubts about finding even something as simple as shelter, and fought for it anyway. But because the band connected with its audience when they got that across, and because the music that did it was the best they ever made, the song brought more than shelter; it brought life, provided a metaphor that allowed the Stones to thrive when Altamont proved toughness was not the point, and gave them the freedom to go on to sing about other things—soul survivors, suffocation, a trip down a moonlight mile.

*Riot* matters because it doesn't just define the wall; it makes the wall real. Its sensibility is hard enough to frame the mass of pop music, shuffle its impact, jar the listener, and put an edge on the easy way out that has not really been won. It is not casual music and its demands are not casual; it tended to force black musicians to reject it or live up to it. Some months after *Riot* was released—from the middle of 1972 through early 1973—the impulses of its music emerged on other records, and they took over the radio.

I don't know if I will be able to convey the impact of punching buttons day after day and night after night to be met by records as clear and strong as Curtis Mayfield's "Super-fly" and "Freddie's Dead," the Staple Singers' "Respect Yourself" and the utopian "I'll Take You There," the O'Jays' "Back Stabbers," War's astonishing "Slipping into Darkness" and "The World Is a Ghetto," the Temptations' "Papa Was a Rolling Stone," Johnny Nash's "I Can See Clearly Now," Stevie Wonder's "Superstition," for that matter the Stones' *Exile on Main Street* (the white *Riot*)—records that were surrounded in memory and still on the air as recent hits, by Marvin Gaye's deadly "Inner City Blues," by the Undisputed Truth's "Smiling Faces Sometimes (Tell Lies)," by the Chi-Lites' falsetto melancholy, by *Riot* itself. Only a year before such discs would have been curiosities; now, they were all of a piece: one enormous answer record. Each song added something to the others, and as in a pop explosion, the country found itself listening to a new voice.

To me, the Temptations took the prize. Imagine—or simply remember—the chill of driving easily through the night, and then hearing, casually at first, then with interest, and then with compulsion, the three bass patterns, repeated endlessly, somewhere between the sound of the heart and a judge's gavel, that open "Papa Was a Rolling Stone." The toughest blues guitar you have heard in years cracks through the building music like a curse; the singer starts in.

More than one person I knew pulled off the road and sat waiting, shivering, as the song crept out of the box and filled up the night.

Four children have gathered around their mother to ask for the truth about their father, who has been buried that very day. They don't know him; he was just another street-corner Stagolee. So they ask. Was he one of those two-faced preachers, mama— "Stealing in the name of the Lord?"* A drunk? A hustler? A pimp? With another wife, more kids? They slam the questions into their mother, and all she can give them is one of

---

*A reference to Paul Kelly's single of the same name, which, along with Jerry Butler's "Only the Strong Survive," had opened up the new territory the Tempts were exploring.

the most withering epitaphs ever written, for them, as well as for him "When he died, all he left us was alone."

Some thought "Back Stabbers" hit even harder. It moved with a new urgency, heading into its chorus with an unforgettable thump; it was like hearing the Drifters again, but the Drifters robbed of pop optimism that let them find romance even in the hard luck of "On Broadway." The O'Jays sounded scared when they climaxed the song with an image that was even stronger than the music: "I wish somebody'd take/Some a' these *knives* outta my back!"

Stevie Wonder reached number one with "Superstition"—his first time on top in ten years. It was the most ominous hard rock in a long while, a warning against a belief in myths that no one understood; Wonder made the old chicka-chicka-boom beat so potent it sounded like a syncopated version of Judgment Day.

All these records were nervous, trusting little if anything, taking *Riot's* spirit of black self-criticism as a new aesthetic, driven (unlike *Riot*) by great physical energy, determined to get across the idea of a world—downtown or uptown, it didn't matter—where nothing was as it seemed. These black musicians and singers were cutting lose from the white man's world to attend to their own business—and to do that, they had to tell the truth. And so they made music of worry and confinement that, in their very different way, the Chi-Lites took to even greater extremes.

The Chi-Lites—like all the artists discussed here—had been around for many years, but they broke into the Top 40 in the seventies, with a dark chant called "(For God's Sake) Give More Power to the People." Stylistically, this was an old kind of record, but it was a new kind of politics; instead of a demand, or an affirmation, it was a plea, and a desperate one at that. The Chi-Lites' persona was open and vulnerable, the antithesis of machismo (something they explicitly dismissed with the great "Oh, Girl"). Other hits—"A Lonely Man," "Have You Seen Her," and "The Coldest Day of My Life"—undercut the high-stepping burst of mastery on which Wilson Pickett and so many other black artists of the sixties had based their careers; the Chi-Lites made Pickett's old bragging music sound fake. Pickett had told his audience that ninety-nine and a half won't do and made them believe it, but the Chi-Lites seemed ready to settle for a lot less—or to beg for something else altogether. The key to any black singer is in that old catch phrase about the way you talk and the way you walk; the Chi-Lites spoke softly and moved with great care.

This new music was a step back for a new look at black America; it was a finger pointed at Staggerlee and an attempt to freeze his spirit out of black culture. On many levels—direct, symbolic, commercial, personal—this music was a vital, conservative reaction to the radical costs Sly had shown that Staggerlee must ultimately exact. And since Stack was roaming virtually unchallenged in the new black cinema, this musical stance amounted to a small-scale cultural war.

All the new black movies—from *Hit Man* to *Trouble Man* to *Detroit 9000* to *Cleopatra Jones*—were cued by the reality behind one very carefully thrown-away line from *The God-father* (a movie, it is worth remembering, that attracted millions of black Americans, even though it had no black characters, let alone any black heroes).

"They're animals anyway," says an off-camera voice, as the Dons make the crucial decision to dump all their heroin into the ghettos. "Let them lose their souls."

The Mafia may have missed the contradiction in that line, but Francis Coppola certainly did not; neither did the black men and women in the theaters. They suffered it; in *Lady Sings the Blues*, Diana Ross was stalking screens all over the country showing just what it meant. The audience had a right to revenge.

And so the fantasy went to work again. If that line had opened up the abyss, the old black hero shot up from the bottom and pushed in the white man instead. Stack slipped through the hands of the white sheriff, won his fight, got his girl, and got away.

*Superfly* summed up the genre; perhaps its first scene did, more than it was meant to. The hero, cocaine dealer Priest (played by Ron O'Neal, who looked uncomfortably like a not-very-black Sean Connery) stirs in the bed of his rich white mistress. Some black fool has made off with his stash. Priest chases him through the alleys, up the side of a building, and traps him in a tiny apartment. There, in full view of the man's family, Priest beats him half to death.

Still, Priest is nervous. Hustling's all the Man has left us, he tells his partner, who thinks that's just fine; Priest wants out of the Life, but the invisible whites who run the show want him in—or dead. He bets everything on one last big deal. He turns on the pressure; one of his runners, Freddie, can't take it, and he panics and gets himself killed. Another man, a sort of father figure (who started Priest out peddling reefers when just a lad) is talked into the game, and he too loses his life to Priest's bid for freedom. Priest's partner weighs the odds and sells him out.

Moving fast, Priest penetrates the white coke hierarchy, takes out a first-class Mafia contract on Mr. Big to cover his bet, unmasks Mr. Big as a queer, and, with his money and his strong black woman, gets away clean. He turned up one movie later as a crusader for social justice in Africa, where life was simpler.

It was a fairy tale; but like most of the Staggerlee movies, *Superfly* had a soundtrack by an established soul singer, and in this case Curtis Mayfield's songs were not background, but criticism. (Mayfield had appeared in the picture singing in a dealers' bar, grinding out an attempted parody of his audience—but they thought it was a celebration.) His music worked against the fantasy, because to him one incident in the movie counted for more than all its triumphs: Freddie's dead. "Pushin' dope for *the Man!*" he sang, incredulous and disgusted. The movie hadn't even slowed to give Freddie an epitaph, but Mayfield clearly aimed his song at the hero as well.*

*Superfly* had a black director, Gordon Parks, Jr.; there was a surface ghetto realism, and there were touches of ambiguity, but the movie had Hollywood in its heart, and that was enough to smother everything else. Most of the pictures that followed simply shuffled *Superfly* clichés, but they kept coming.

One movie was different, but it never found its audience, not among blacks, or whites either. *Across 110th Street* (directed by Barry Shear, who earlier made *Wild in the Streets*, the most paradoxical youth exploitation picture; written by Luther Davis) looked enough like all the others to make it easy for nearly all critics to dismiss it. The film was almost unbelievably violent, which gave reviewers license to attack it. It began with the same clichés everyone else used, but intensified them mercilessly. It pumped so much pressure into the world of the new black movies that it blew that world apart.

Three black men—Jamaica, Superflake, and Dry Clean—murder a pack of black and white Mafia bankers and make off with the week's take for all of Harlem. They don't steal because they hate the mob; they steal because they want the money. A Mafia lieutenant—played by Tony Franciosa—is sent out to bring back the money and execute the thieves, knowing full well he can forget his future if he fails. Anthony Quinn plays a bought cop caught in the middle. He has to take the case straight to make his pension, and a new black cop is keeping an eye on him, but he has to do it without losing his payoff—or his life—to

---

*Interestingly, these lyrics were not in the movie, even though the backing track was. Mayfield held off until the film was in the theaters, then wrote the words, released the record, and so took on the picture on his own turf: the radio. You could say he chickened out, and you could also say he was very smart.

the Mafia hirelings who control his district: a black man who runs a taxi company and looks like Fats Domino risen from the swamp of evil, and his bodyguard, a Staggerlee who watches over the entire film with the cold eyes of someone who sold his soul to the devil the day he was old enough to know he had one.

You paid for every bit of violence, perhaps because the film refused its audience the pleasures of telling the good guys from the bad guys, and because the violence was so ugly it exploded the violence of the genre. It wasn't gratuitous, but it wasn't "poetic" either. Every character seemed alive, with motives worth reaching for, no matter how twisted they might turn out to be; every character (save for Taxi Man and his gunman) fled through the story scared half out of his wits, desperate for space, for a little more time, for one more chance.

The thieves speed away from the litter of corpses, divide up the money, and go into hiding. Superflake is too proud of himself to stay holed up; good times are what it was all for, right? His best hustler's clothes—tasteless Sly Stone, but gaudy—have been hanging for this moment. Down at the best whorehouse in Harlem Superflake has a dozen women and he's bragging.

Franciosa picks up the scent, and with Taxi Man's Staggerlee at his side, his eyes glazing over with a sadism that masks his own terror, he rips Superflake out of the whorehouse bar. When Quinn finds Superflake crucified, castrated, and skinned alive, you realize that along with no heroes, this movie may offer no way out. It was made to take your sleep.

Jamaica and Dry Clean pass the word and panic; they know that Superflake had to finger them. Dry Clean shoves his money into a clothes bag from his shop and hails a cab for Jersey. The driver spots the markings on the bag, radios back to Taxi Man, and delivers Dry Clean straight to Franciosa at 110th Street—the border of Harlem and the one line the movie never crosses. Dry Clean breaks away; Franciosa traps him on a roof, ties a rope to his leg, and hangs him over a beam, dangling him into space. Staggerlee holds the rope; his eyes show nothing as he watches the white man torture the black. If Dry Clean talks, they say, they won't kill him; he is so scared he believes them. He talks, and the rope shoots over the side.

Jamaica and his girl meet in his wretched apartment (there is a little torn-out picture of Martin Luther King taped to the wall, a gray reminder of some other time) to plan an escape, or a better hideout. And in one of the most extraordinary scenes in any American movie, a death's-head reversal of every warm close-up you have every seen, Jamaica begins to talk—about green hills and a blue sky; about quiet, rest, peace of mind; about going home. He has only killed nine men to get there. His face is scarred by smallpox; his eyes try hard to explain. Jamaica goes on; you don't hear him; the camera stays tight. Every few seconds his whole face shudders, seems almost to shred, as a ghastly, obscenely complex twitch climbs from his jaw to his temple, breaks, and starts up again.

It is the visual equivalent of that last song on *Riot*, "Thank you for talkin' to me Africa," another reach for a home that isn't there. Like Sly's music, the scene is unbearable long, it makes you want to run, but each frame like each note deepens the impact, until everything else in the world has been excluded and only one artistic fact remains. Jamaica's twitch traces the fear of every character in the movie; it is a map of the ambiguities the other movies so easily shot away; and in this film, it is most of all the other side of Staggerlee's face, which never moves.

Finally, Franciosa, Quinn, and their troops converge on the abandoned tenement where Jamaica and his girl are hiding. Taxi Man gets word of the showdown. "Wanna watch," says Staggerlee. "No," says Taxi Man. "I know how it's gonna turn out."

A bullet cuts through the girl's forehead and pins her to the wall behind Jamaica. She stays on camera, standing up dead, a blank ugliness on her face. When Jamaica turns to see her you can feel the life go out of him, but he keeps shooting. Franciosa is killed; the cops take over. Jamaica flees to the roof with his gun and his bag of money, still firing. He kills more. Staggerlee, sent to cover for Taxi Man, watches from another rooftop. Jamaica falls, and in the only false moment in the picture, flings his money down to children in a playground. Staggerlee sets up a rifle, takes aim on Quinn, who has proved himself too weak to be worth the mob's time, and kills him.

In one way, then, this movie was like all the others: Staggerlee wins. But this time, the audience was not given the benefit of any masks; they had to take him as he came, and they were not about to pay money to see that.

# 54. Not-so-"Little" Stevie Wonder

Stevie Wonder (b. 1950) blended funk, jazz, reggae, rock, African and Latin rhythms, and electronic experimentation with old-fashioned songwriting craft to create a fusion that made him the most popular black musician of the early- to mid-1970s.

Wonder's career has superficial similarities to that of another Motown artist, Marvin Gaye. Like Gaye, Wonder's music became noticeably more eclectic and his lyrics more personal and political as his career progressed. Unlike Gaye, who came to Motown in his early 20s, Wonder's first success came at age 13: Billed as "Little Stevie Wonder," his novelty instrumental hit, "Fingertips, Pt. 2" in 1963 hit the top of *Billboard*'s pop chart. By the late 1960s, Wonder was recording jazz-influenced ballads like "My Cherie Amour" (1969) and uptempo songs with an almost manic vocal intensity, such as "I Was Made to Love Her" (1967). This variety only hinted at the transformation in style that would occur after his 21st birthday in 1971. In a development that paralleled the release of Gaye's creative breakthrough *What's Going On* (1971), Wonder signed a new contract with Motown that gave him vastly increased artistic autonomy. The albums that followed—*Where I'm Coming From* (1971), *Music of My Mind* and *Talking Book* (both 1972), *Innervisions* (1973), *Fulfillingness' First Finale* (1974), and *Songs in the Key of Life* (double album, 1976)—all displayed an increased social awareness and utopianism in his lyrics, as well as an adventurousness as a performer of both the synthesizer and conventional instruments (he played almost all the instruments on the albums just listed). Wonder's use of the synthesizer was particularly innovative, since he introduced many experimental timbres and techniques to popular music.

The following profile and interview by Ben Fong-Torres appeared early in
1973, when it became clear that *Talking Book* was becoming an unprecedented critical and commercial success for Wonder. This article, as did
others from this period, addresses the notion that Wonder's audience
has expanded to include a greater number of white, countercultural listeners without losing his core fan base of African Americans.[1] The publication of this interview in *Rolling Stone* is at least partly responsible
for the focus on Wonder's "new audience." This article-interview also
provides additional background on Motown in the 1960s (discussed in
chapter 33) from the perspective of Wonder's career with the company
and again calls attention to the important role played by Motown's
mostly unheralded studio musicians.

# THE FORMERLY LITTLE STEVIE WONDER
## *Ben Fong-Torres*

[Stevie Wonder:] I had a dream about Benny Benjamin [Motown's first studio drummer,
who died of a stroke in 1969]. I talked to him a few days before he died; he was in the hospital. But in my dream I talked to him, he said, "Look man, I'm . . . I'm not gonna make it."
"What, you kiddin'!" The image . . . he was sitting on my knee, which means like he was
very weak. And he said, "So, like I'm leavin' it up to you." That was like a Wednesday, and
that following Sunday I went to church and then to the studio to do a session; we were
gonna record "You Can't Judge a Book by Its Cover," and they said, "Hey, man, we're not
gonna do it today. Benny just died."

*He died without notice. I mean, nobody really knew who he was.*
Man, he was one of the major forces in the Motown sound. Benny could've very well been
   the baddest—like [Bernard] Purdie. He was the Purdie of the Sixties. But unknown.

*Why unknown?*
Well, because for the most part these cats'd be in the studios all day and as musicians they
   weren't getting that recognition then, you know. People weren't really that interested in
   the musicians.

*Couldn't they also have had jobs with performing groups?*
They'd do clubs, but they all were basically . . . Benny would be messin' up all the time.
   Benny'd be late for sessions, Benny'd be drunk sometimes. I mean, he was a beautiful
   cat, but. . . . Benny would come up with these stories, like [in an excited, fearful voice]
   "Man, you'd never believe it man, but like a goddamn *elephant*, man, in the middle of

---

1. For a lengthy profile of Wonder from two years later that rehabilitates this theme, albeit in a pater-
nalistic manner, see Jack Slater, "A Sense of Wonder," *New York Times Magazine*, February 23, 1975, 18,
21–23, 26–32. In one telling passage, Slater compares the effect of Wonder's synthesis to that of Bob
Dylan in the mid-1960s (pp. 30–32).

the road, stopped me from comin' to the session so that's why I'm late, baby, so [clap of hands] it's cool!" But he was *ready* man. He could play drums, you wouldn't even need a bass, that's how bad he was. Just listen to all that Motown shit, like "Can't Help Myself" and "My World Is Empty Without You Babe" and "This Old Heart of Mine" and "Don't Mess with Bill." "Girl's All Right with Me," the drums would just *pop*!

*Did Benny teach you a lot about drumming?*
Yeah, you can hear it, you know, I learned from just listening to him.

*Is it true that you put out a drum album once?*
Well, I put out an album that I played drums on, called *The Jazz Soul of Little Stevie.* I did an-other album which was called *Eivets Rednow* about '68, an instrumental with "Alfie" and a few other things . . . "Eivets Rednow" being "Stevie Wonder" spelled backwards.

*Everybody knew who it was right away. . . .*
Some people did, some didn't. As a matter of fact there was a cat in the airport that came up and said, "Hey, man" [laughs], he said, "Man, these whites takin' over everything," he says, "Look, I heard a kid today, man, played 'Alfie' just *like* you, man!" "O yeah, this cat named Rednow?" "Yeah, that's it!" I said, "Ooooh, man, that cat is—well, don't worry about *him!*" [laughs]

*You've said that the first song you ever wrote was "Uptight," but the credits were given to Sylvia Moy, Henry Cosby and a "S. Judkins." Was that you?*
Well, Judkins is my father's name. But it's crazy to explain it. Morris was on my birth cer-tificate and everything, but Judkins was the father. I took his name when I was in school. We just signed the song contract like that.

*Why didn't you sign Stevie Wonder?*
I don't know.

*You signed "Wonder" on songs like "I'm Wondering" and "I Was Made to Love Her."*
Well, that was later; I decided I wanted people to know that I wrote those songs.

*How did you get the name Wonder?*
It was given to me by Berry Gordy. They didn't like "Steve Morris" so they changed it.

*Were there some alternatives?*
"Little Wonder". . . "Wonder Steve. . . ." I think we should change it to Steveland Morris [laughs], That would put a whole different light on everything.

*You weren't an immediate hit, were you? You put out a record called "I Call It Pretty Music."*
It was a thing that Clarence Paul wrote . . . an old blues thing . . . The first thing I recorded was a thing called "Mother Thank You." Originally it was called "You Made a Vow," but they thought that was too lovey for me, too adult.

*How did the first records do?*
They started after we did "Contract on Love." That made a little noise. "Fingertips" was after that. That was a biggie.

*The first production credit you were given was on the "Signed Sealed and Delivered" album, but that wasn't the first producing you did.*
Well, that was the first that was *released.* I also did a thing with the Spinners, "It's A Shame," and the follow-up, "We'll Have It Made." I wanted that tune to be big. I was so hurt when it didn't do it.

*You also produced Martha once?*
Yeah, they never released it. Called [sings, snapping fingers], "Hey, look at me, girl, can't
  you see. . . ."

*And one on David Ruffin.*
Yeah, [sings] "Lovin' you's been so wonder-ful. . . ." In the midst of all that, I was in the
  process of getting' my thing together and decidin' what I was gonna do with my life.
  This was like I was 20, goin' on 21, and so a lot of things were left somewhat un-
  followed-up by me. I would get the product there and nobody would listen and I'd say,
  "Fuckit". . . . I wouldn't worry about it.

*This was around "Signed Sealed and Delivered". . . .*
It was a little after that. "Signed Sealed and Delivered" was like the biggest thing I'd had.

*Then you went into a lull.*
Yeah, we did *Where I'm Coming From*—that was kinda premature to some extent, but I
  wanted to express myself. A lot of it now I'd probably re-mix. But "Never Dreamed
  You'd Leave in Summer" came from that album, and "If You Really Love Me". . . . but
  it's nothing like the things I write now. I love getting' into just as much weird shit as
  possible. I'll tell you what's happening. Syreeta's album is better than my last two
  albums, man, shit! [laughs] No, but it's cool.

*But the public Stevie Wonder is a lot of ideas and images that people have of you, regardless of what
  you actually are.*
I know there are thousands of images of me. There was a guy one time, I heard: "Hey, uh,
  Stevie Wonder told me to come and get this grass from you, so where is it?" He said,
  "Stevie Wonder told you? He didn't man, 'cause I'm his guitar player, and he doesn't
  even smoke grass. He doesn't even get high." I guess people expect or figure me to be
  a lot of different things.

*You've actually said that you considered your blindness to be a gift from God.*
Being blind, you don't judge books by their covers; you go through things that are relatively
  insignificant, and you pick out things that are more important.

*When did you discover that there was something missing, at least according to other people's stan-
  dards?*
I never really knew it. The only thing that was said in school, and this was my early part of
  school, was something that made me feel like because I was black I could never be or
  would never be.

*So being black was considered to be more a weight. . . .*
I guess so. [laughs] This cat said in an article one time, it was funny: "Damn! He's black!
  He's blind! What else?!" I said, "Bull*shit*, I don't wanna *hear* that shit, you know."

*So you wouldn't even bother having people describe things to you. Colors and. . . .*
Well, I have an idea of what colors are. I associate them with the ideas that've been told
  to me about certain colors. I get a certain feeling in my head when a person says "red"
  or "blue," "green," "black," "white," "yellow," "orange," "purple"—purple is a *crazy*
  color to me. . . .

*Probably the sound of the word . . .*
Yeah, yeah. To me brown is a little duller than green, isn't it?

*In school, what subjects did you like best?*
History, world history, but it got kind of boring. And science. The history of this country
  was relatively boring—I guess because of the way it was put to us in books. The most

interesting to me was about civilizations before ours, how advanced people really were, how high they had brought themselves only to bring themselves down because of the missing links, the weak foundations. So the whole thing crumbled. And that's kind of sad. And it relates to today and what could possibly happen here, very soon. That's basically what "Big Brother" is all about.

I speak of the history, the heritage of the violence, or the negativeness of being able to see what's going on with minority people. Seemingly it's going to continue to be this way. Sometimes unfortunately violence is a way things get accomplished. "Big Brother" was something to make people aware of the fact that after all is said and done, that I don't have to do nothing to you, meaning the people are not power players. We don't have to do anything to them 'cause they're gonna cause their own country to fall.

"My name is Secluded; we live in a house the size of a matchbox." A person who lives there, really, his name *is* Secluded, and you never even know the person, and they can have so many things to say to help make it better, but it's like the voice that speaks is forever silenced.

I understand that when you don't hear anything and you hear this very high frequency, that's the sound of the universe.

*Or a burglar alarm, which takes some of the mystery out of it. . . . Tell me about your experiments with electronic effects and music. First have you listened to Beaver and Krause, or Pink Floyd, Emerson Lake and Palmer, or Walter Carlos?*
Walter Carlos, yes, but for the most part I've listened to just what's in my head, plus Bob Margoloff and Malcolm Cecil—they just built a new synthesizer you should see—they have their own company, Centaur, and they did an album, *Tonto's Expanding Headband*. They are responsible for programming and I just tell them the kind of sound I want.

I hadn't got tired of strings or horns or anything, it's just another dimension. I'd like to get into doing just acoustic things, drums, bass, no electronic things at all except for recording them.

*What else are you checking out these days?*
There's this string instrument made in Japan. You tune it like a harp to a certain chord scale. It takes you somewhere else that's sort of earthy and in the direction where my head is slanting—like going to Africa. Maybe I'll take a tape recorder over there and just sit out and write some stuff.

*In concert, your opening number includes African scatting.*
I got that from this thing called *The Monkey Chant* that we used in different rhythms, and we came up with [chop-chants, in speedtime} *ja-ja-ja-jajajajajaja*. . . .

*And there are three pairs of drumsticks going.*
It's like fighting. I'd love to go to Ghana, go to the different countries and see how I'd like to live there.

*Do you know Sly Stone?*
I've seen him a couple of times. I haven't heard too much about him lately, just rumors. . . .

*He influenced you to a degree.*
Ah . . . I think there's an influence in some of things I've done, like "Maybe Your Baby." But I can hear some of the old Little Stevie Wonder in a lot of his early things [Stevie sings a bit of "Sing a Simple Song"]. It used to tickle me. . . .

*You've said that your writing was influenced by the Beatles.*
I just dug more the effects they got, like echoes and the voice things, the writing, like "For the Benefit of Mr. Kite."

*Did it make you feel that you could be more loose yourself?*

Yeah, I just said, "Why can't I?" I wanted to do something else, go other places. Same thing abut keys. I don't want to stay in one key all the time.

*I understand that in the old days at Motown, groups had to compete for tracks. Writers would come up with a song and a track, and artists would all sing over it, and the best would get a single released.*

I could see why that would happen though. It's kind of crazy. But then again you think the writer, whoever the writer is—the music, the sound wasn't really Motown as much as the writer. I think for the most part they should listen in advance and know the artists. Holland-Dozier-Holland usually would sing the melodies themselves and say, "This is how I want you to do it."

*What about you? Did you always have more independence?*

I had the independence because I was somewhat distant, because I was in school, and I would just come back home sometime and do some singing.

*"Blowing in the Wind" and "Alfie" were unusual songs for a Motown artist to be doing back when you did them.*

Most of them came about from doing gigs and wanting certain kinds of tunes. Clarence Paul, who was my arranger and conductor when we had the big group—we would work out doing tunes, ridin' in cars like in England around '65. We'd think of different songs like "Funny How Time Flies Away" or "Blowin' in the Wind."

Writers are so important. I think a lot of our artists could have been more sustained if they had other writers, besides Holland-Dozier-Holland, because then they would have found their identity—and that's what everybody needs.

*So you can understand why groups like Gladys and the Pips, Martha and the Vandellas, the Tops, the Spinners, left.*

I do, when you become just one of the others, it's difficult to be a sustaining power for a long period of time. It's like a person comes out with a beat, and you keep on doing it and doing it and driving it to the ground.

# 55. Parliament Drops the Bomb

Funk as a genre really came into its own during the early 1970s. Bands as diverse as the Latin-influenced War; the jazz-influenced Tower of Power and Kool and the Gang; the earthy Ohio Players; the utopian, Afro-centric Earth, Wind, and Fire; and the adjective-defying Parliament-Funkadelic, all began to achieve success during this period. Parliament, with master-mind George Clinton (b. 1940), began a string of recordings with "Up for the Down Stroke" that succeeded on the R&B charts for the duration of the 1970s, including "Tear the Roof Off the Sucker" (1976), "Flash Light" (1977), "One Nation Under a Groove—Part 1" (by Parliament alter-ego, Funkadelic), and "Aqua Boogie (A Psychoalphadiscobeta-bioaquadoloop)" (both 1978). Clinton created a striking form of funk: emphasizing a clear backbeat (often reinforced with electronic hand claps), Clinton thickened the texture with a wealth of contrasting, overlapping parts, featuring "Bootsy" Collins's (following his tenure with James Brown) extroverted bass lines, Bernie Worrell's innovative synthesizer work (including the use of the "synthesizer bass" on "Flashlight"), horn players from Brown's band, and gospel-rooted group vocals. Clinton expanded the Parliament stage show into a spectacle that set new standards for grandiosity in black popular music. Beginning with the album *Mothership Connection* (1975), Clinton developed a cosmological narrative that proselytized the redemptive power of funk. Concerts would enact the landing of the "Mothership" while Clinton and up to 50 performers would hold forth in outlandish garb. Clinton's utopian vision of a Black "Nation [United] Under a Groove" and his commitment to undiluted funk have continued to influence numerous hip-hop musicians.

---

George Clinton's popularity and influence were at their peak in the late 1970s, the period from which the following interview comes. The epigraph by Sun Ra underscores the continuity between the science fiction-inspired visions of Sun Ra's interplanetary "Arkestra" and Clinton's various intergalactic projects; both point to a continuing African American fascination with the possibility of a society beyond the reach of racism, and one that can be imagined only in outer space. The article-interview also adopts the language of Clinton and of funk music in general and provides background on Clinton in a fanciful manner while outlining a basic history of funk. Clinton's empire of bands, which arose as a creative response to elude music industry control, is described here, as are Clinton's views on the relationship between his music and a socially responsible politics.

## GEORGE CLINTON: ULTIMATE LIBERATOR OF CONSTIPATED NOTIONS
### *W. A. Brower*

If you are not a reality whose myth are you?
                                                    —*Sun Ra*

A concept can just be thrown in the air around the funk and before it hit the ground you got two albums. You know? What I am saying is that a mafunkah will shoot holes in that bad boy 'fore it hits the ground, like you do in the ghetto.
                                                    —*George Clinton*

---

*Source:* W. A. Brower, "George Clinton: Ultimate Liberator of Constipated Notions," *Down Beat*, April 5, 1979, pp. 16–18, 44.

George Clinton (a.k.a. the Long Haired Freaky Sucker, Star Child, Dr. Funkenstein, just plain Dr. Funk, and now Mr. Wiggles the Worm—"ultrasonic, semi-bionic clone of Dr. Funkenstein," who was specially grafted for Clinton's latest on-stage extravaganza and recording *Motor Booty Affair*, Casablanca 7125) is no one's myth. Although the lineup from his newest production, which includes Queen Freakalene, Monkey Sea and Monkey Woo, Minus Mouf, Howard Codsell, Octave Pussy, Rita Mermaid and P-Nut Booty Jellyfish sounds like a cast of renegade cartoon characters from a Motor Bugged Out Affixation, George Clinton is *fo' real, allllllll* the way, live and in 3-D, Dig—

Clinton walks around dressed like it's Halloween 365 days a year. He is Head Funkentelecktual-In-Charge of P-Funk Labs from which such uncontrolled substances as the Bomb, the P. Funk, the Uncut Funk, the Pee, Supergroovalisticprosifunkstication, Flash Lights, DooDoo Chasers and Liquid Sunshine originate. Dr. Clinton told me, in an unguarded moment, that his work is dedicated to ego reduction and the eradication of mental ghettos. Clinton is also Head Referee of the Funk-Mob, a voluntary association of barnstorming funkateers, who get their hard core jollies off funkin' with folks' heads. Through the Dr.'s own funkreative mitosis, the First Family of Funk has grown to include Parliament, Funkadelic, Bootsy's Rubber Band, Brides of Funkenstein, Parlet, the Horny Horns, and Bernie Worrell's Woo. George Clinton is the main purveyor of the funk which, along with rock and disco, dominates the popular music market.

Recently, George Clinton has also become a wizard of finance and a big reality in the record business. Everythang he touches turns funky. The P. Funk Earth Tour made 30 million funky dollar bills in two years. A few months ago, Funkadelic's album *One Nation Under A Groove* (Warner Bros. 3209) went platinum funk.

The success of *One Nation* put Clinton in a funkified dilemma. For sure, *One Nation* was the Pee, a monstrous hit, but it came right on the heels of three years of touring with such huge productions as the Mothership Connection. The Mothership, an Apollo 15 lookalike from which the Dr. disembarked on stage, cost a stankin' quarter of a million all by his lonesome.

Clinton's problem was mounting a stage show that could outfunk the last two. His response to the situation says a bunch about how his mind funktions. "We had just come off that [major tour] one month before *One Nation* came out, which meant we had to do somethang. We *had* to go back out on the road and we couldn't go back in them same places. And the Brides was comin' out so they had to have some place to play.

"So we said, 'We'll take a tour of small joints where we can play three or four hours and we'll call it the *anti-tour*, which will de-program our heads from that big 20,000 seats. Let all the young members see what it's really like to have to play a *gig*,' you know, where you have to play fo' real. And they could get off on it because they can play their shit. And best of all, in going to these cities under *One Nation*, playin' small places, we could get down with the people.

"The people that get in, the *real* fans, will say, 'Them mathahfunkahhhaas played three hours and turned that mathahfunkah out!' With no props, no nothing." In Washington, D.C. (which he has dubbed a Chocolate City encircled by a Vanilla Suburbia) Clinton took the anti-tour into the legendary Howard Theatre. Instead of three hours the show ran nearly five. At 1:30 a.m. 2000 militants of the funk were damn near tearin' the roof off the sucker, hyperventilating to *One Nation* for the umpteenth time.

P-Funk was mega-funk that night. The Dr. was decked out in red beret and fatigues, and looked more like Captain Zero, the Sandinista guerilla, than the Star Child, as he pumped the audience with stuff like, "Get funky . . . get loose . . . free your mind . . . let your ass follow . . . let your booty do its duty." The anti-tour was typical of Clinton's "anti-logic or expanded framework for logic." Instead of shooting for an even bigger production and possibly reaping a diminished return he did just the opposite and funked better.

The Dr. is big fun to talk to, being that he is an advanced student of mentalcourse—which is to say mindfunkin' and gamin' on ya as necessary. He studied signifying for ten years in a Plainfield, New Jersey barbershop which he ended up owning. In the process he specialized in conking heads. ". . . pre-Superfly . . . just scorchin' heads in the name of the cool."

When the bloods put the torch to Plainfield Ave. during the '67 riots, George Clinton's barbershop was the only thang left standing. By then Clinton had a Master's in street rhythms and consense, the highest form of game. He survived the '60s and went on to get his doctorate in poetic licentiousness from the Universal Corner . . . hanging out and eating reality sandwiches from Harvard Square to the Motor City. George Clinton is a deep dude. Dig.

The Dr. is from Cannapolis, North Carolina—if they've got olfactory glands strong enough to claim him. He spent his early years funkin' up in the Chocolate City and in Chase City, Virginia, before his family settled in Plainfield. That's where he started Parliament in '55, lifting their name from a still-popular oral fixation.

"It was ego," says Clinton. "I was a little Leo. If I couldn't have a baseball team I wanted a singing group. You know that was our only out . . . out of the ghetto . . . if you could sing, dance, or some shit." Ego is okay with the Dr. if it motorvates you to some goal beyond yourself. But, in itself, ego will "do-loop," that is to say, self-destruct. Self-destruction through dysfunktional ego rhythms is something Clinton manages to avoid by diggin' on the One.

He runs it down like so: "No one person can do it. No philosophy, no religion, no scientist, no state. This shit takes a *whole* mathahfunkin' band and singers and everythang. To actually get out there takes planets because they are all connected . . . magnetic . . . revolving around. All this shit is connected. So any one mafunker sayin', 'Hey, I'*m* going to do it myself.' You know? Let the *sun* stop shinin' on that mafunkah. He be a dull mathah-funkah and that's all it is to it. He'll need a dynamite Flash Light. . . . I'll put it that way. Ain't no one mafunkah can do this shit. And no one species . . . no one state . . . no one nothin'. 'Cause it's all on the One. I mean I am not one. I am *part* of one. We are all part of one.

"All this shit put together . . . all life . . . it takes it all. I mean anybody thinking that he is deep enough to be One is truly trippin'. You know what I mean? Truly trippin'. I mean, we ego trip on stage. We got a spaceship. But we park that mafunker when it's snowing cause it ain't got no snow tires."

Believe it. If you don't feel this funk one way *or* the other you better get your family physician to check your bottom inside out because it just may be false, phony as play money, devoidoffunk and other et ceterasses. This is dancing music, be it the Freak, the Rock or the Wiggle. The Dr.'s funk is, first of all, plenty of feet in the bass drums and thumping ostinatos in the bass guitars. The sock cymbal is steady against them bootin' feet. The Dr.'s idea of bottom is to find a groove, even it out, and hold it dead, as they say, in the pocket. At base the funk is rhythmic, and being in the pocket is a rhythmic concept analogous to the classical idea of swing. Once time is in the pocket, the funk is ready to roll.

Funk is the rawest rhythm and blues happening today. It is minimalist gutbucket in the space age. It descends from the jump band school that spawned r&b, with doses of sock hop doowop and street corner harmonizing. It asscends directly from the sound of Papa James Brown, Godfather of Soul and precursor of funk. It incorporates the innovations of Sly Stone and Jimi Hendrix, who between them foreshadowed the liberation of r&b from its song form limitations and introduced freer instrumental styles. The funk, to a large extent, represents the assimilation of Hendrix and Sly's influences into the r&b mainstream. Funk is the antithesis of its main contender in the r&b world, disco.

The Dr. has two basic brands of the funk. The number one selling funk is Parliament, which draws heavily from the James Brown style. The current edition of Parliament nods in JB's direction, featuring the Horny Horns, led by JB alumni, Fred Wesley and Maceo Parker, and their punching, brass-heavy riffs. The Funkadelic, on the other hand, is basically a guitar band bordering black rock with its own cult-like following. Funkgeetarists Gary Shider and Mike "Kid Funkadelic" Hampton lay down supercharged heavy metal in the tradition of Hendrix. Whichever way the funk is going, the Dr. calls upon two of the finest keyboard players in pop music—Bernie "DaVinci" Worrell, a Funk Mob veteran, and Walter "Junie" Morrison, formerly of the Ohio Players. Clinton is a master at layering each collaborator's contribution into a series of massive crescendos aimed at *Tearin' The Roof Off The Sucker.*

Like most all of what the Dr. knows, the concept of diversifunkation was born of cold realities. When Parliament ventured to Detroit in '67 it was basically a doo-wop group, aspiring to success in the Motown mold. They cut a mini-hit called *I Wanna Testify* and seemed on their way to plenty of that golden chicken scratch. Then came what the Dr. likes to call the "big blow."

"Dig," the Dr. says, "the label we was with, that had *I Wanna Testify* out, went out of business. And they had our name and we couldn't use it because the court wouldn't clear it. The problem was immediate. We had to survive. So the only thing to do was to take the musicians that we had and put them up front and the singers became backup. We just said that the musicians are the Funkadelic and the singers sing *with them* as opposed to *them* playing with the singers. They were friends of ours from Jersey; they came with us. The only shift we had to make was one of ego. Could we stand our brothers to be up front? It was just who's singing lead and who's not. That was easy to say because it was basically my group.

"So they couldn't stop us from doing that. In the meantime Parliament became free from that record thang. We had records out as Funkadelic by then. So we had two names because the Parliament was known. It made sense to me to get a separate deal on a separate label for them, not with any person's name on it, just the name Parliament. We had to do it for survival because a group gets shelved when it's only one group and they funk up or they don't get no hits. The companies just automatically think, 'Well, they thang ain't happenin'.' When you got two names you got a better chance. I have know that since '68. The only way to justify having two groups was to have different personalities."

With the emergence of funk as a real power in the market, Clinton began generating contracts for members of the Mob as solo acts or groups as the major labels bid for their piece of the funk. Thus there are five female singers playing various characters and popping in and out of a Parliament-Funkadelic show. Two of them open the evening as Brides of Funkenstein while the other three (who back them) are billed as the Bridesmaids. The Brides record for Atlantic while the Bridesmaids have become Parlet when recording for Casablanca. To manage his funky conglomerate Clinton employs Leber and Krebs, the people who handle Aerosmith, Ted Nugent and Beatlemania . . . all biggies. Yes, the Dr. and his family are a big reality in the record business.

The Dr. has it in his head to be even bigger. Parliament-Funkadelic returned stateside in December from three months in France, Holland and Germany, and now the Dr. talks about the possibility of "one planet under a groove." Moreover, Clinton claims, "We are negotiating higher—I mean *higher*—than any thang that's ever been done, black or white.

We are negotiating from the point of view that we are the biggest thang ever happened. But we know we have to do it five times bigger than anybody, just to be equal."

Does the Dr. worry about the inherent personal vulnerabilities that come with that kind of power? Will he become a target? "Not really," he grins, "because again, it ain't me, you know, it's the funk, and I am careful not to let it get into *that* rhythm. It only self-destructs you when it's personality . . . dominant personality. Right now it's all flattery and amazement and shit. But that'll wear off and it'll just be the funk. I ain't gon' provoke it, is what I am saying. And that's not a dangerous position. It's a good position to be in as long as you don't do it really out of rhythm and you can back up what you say with some good funk.

"It's the same concept that Muhammad Ali used, 'I am the baddest mafunkah around.' You know what I am saying? When you knock out enough people you can even get knocked out yourself and people still say, 'Cool.' But you got to know when to back off, when you did a thing enough, 'cause the novelty wear offa anythang."

Clinton is way ahead of the game when it comes to keepin' the novelty from wearing offa *his* thang. Many of the major groups in pop music augment their performances with fantastic special effects and props. Players appear and disappear in large clouds of pastel colored smoke, or play their axes suspended in air. The Dr. takes multi-media dramatization to its logical conclusion, creating his own funky operettas. Every Parliament-Funkadelic recording is programmatic in concept. His themes include: *Standing On the Verge Of Gettin It On, Maggot Brain, America Eats Its Young, Funkenteleckty* vs. *The Placebo Syndrome, Chocolate City, the Mothership Connection, The Clones Of Dr. Funkenstein, Hard Core Jollies, One Nation Under A Groove,* and now, the *Motor Booty Affair.* On stage, the First Family perform these themes with the aide of rather graphic scatological and sexual imagery, special effects, costumes and scenarios.

The *Motor Booty Affair* takes the funk underwater. "It's basically the same themes that we have been doing for a while," he explained: "Two meanings. One is that Sir Nose and Dr. Funkenstein is rivalring. And the other is Psychoalphadiscobeta-bioaquadoloop, which is a rhythm that is compatible to dancing in the streets and not getting funked up. It's the same rhythm you can have under water and not get wet. That's about how deep you have to be in this world and not really get funked up.

On stage, Clinton leaves most of the singing to the five ladies, Gary Shider and the Funkateer of longest tenure, basso-profunkdo Ray Davis. Clinton's funktion is to run down the rap, the rhythm, the onomatopoeia. The Dr. cuttin' loose with the funk is poetic licentiousness on the bizarre side, and that aspect of his "rhythm and business" has caused consternation in some quarters of the black community. The Rev. Jesse Jackson, whose organization, People United to Save Humanity (PUSH) has launched a national self-improvement campaign, "Push for Excellence," among inner city youth, has raised questions about the impact of Clinton's lyrics on the impressionable, youthful segment of the audience. But the Dr. sees himself as a deprogrammer in a culture that is telling its youth, particularly black youth of the urban underclass, that they can't handle themselves, that they are dysfunctional, and that the system is their solution. Rather than exploiting sex, Clinton defetishizes, satirizing an already demeaned subject. He views his slogans (e.g., "Get off your ass and jam") as exhorting youth, in language they can clearly understand, to burn down the ghettos in their minds. Thus each production portrays blacks in an alternative reality—dealing in space, underwater, or whatever. Apparently the impetus to project alternative realities is an imperative in black culture. The analogies to be found in Sun Ra and the Nation of Islam are too uncanny to be coincidental.

"The language," Clinton says, "helps deprogram you, too—*and* it's marketable. It's really the rhythm. Actually, the only communication that can penetrate the sematics and the structure, the straightjacket of what's happening with the logic and language of today, is to do it the way we do it, which is the same language but with our own rhythm and a few words Xed out because certain words have emotional value. This other shit is cold and calculated and no emotion. So when you say 'shit'. . . no matter if you sayin' it to be funny, it penetrates."

It's the same attitude toward language that permits "nigger," which has its own odious history, to be a term of endearment when uttered by the proper party with the proper rhythm. The sense of double entendre which pervades Clinton's lyrics, like the various vocalisms with which they are delivered, are as old as the blues.

"So," Clinton reasons, "I try to give them something interesting, give them what they want. I just don't be up there, talkin' about, 'I'm into my music . . . I'm for peace and happiness and there is a message in my music and I hope the brothers and sisters . . .' That one has a patent on it and people don't even hear it. But when you say 'Promentalshitback-washpsychosis Enema Squad (The Doodoo Chasers) comin' to tidy the bowl of your brain, giving you music to get your shit together by,' muthafunkahs have to say what the funk?—and just that *what* is cool. That's enough, 'cause then they have got to think about it. It's not telling you what to think. All we do is say, *'think.'* We don't preach and we don't guru, other than, 'Hang loose for the night.' It's that basic mother wit shit. It's a party tonight and if they don't get nothin' else out of it but the party, that's cool. And the rest of it they talk about until they get something else out of it. It's multi-sided."

George Clinton puts his money where his motor mouth is. Dig: "When you think about it, it's another thing when groups come in the community and take all the money and keep moving. And just to make sure we ain't gettin' absorbed into the *they,* we dedicate from now on, throughout the rest of our career, 25¢ on every ticket we sell to the United Negro College Fund. All our groups gonna do it and gonna challenge all the other groups to do it. Those people are the ones that buy our records and come to our concerts and *they* trying to phase out black colleges anyway—too much vibes and rhythm in it. We think we *should,* because the only people that's gonna be able to do anything about what is happening is the young people. And the *thang* for them to do is think. We can't tell them what to do. We don't know no answers. But giving them a chance to think is one thang that *we can* do.

"It's all relative, you know, 'cause I have found so much about the funk that I had no idea of. It's got such heavy meaning. In a German dictionary it's got the rhythm of life from the heartbeat, of amoebas coming out of the water. So that's a definition of the shit of the funk. 'Cause I had it as a good excuse after I did the best I could do. The next best thing to saying funk it. Now I done the best I could do and I ain't jumpin'. And to me that's a rhythm and I guess that's the rhythm of life. Cause if you got a funk, a good one, you ain't goin' commit suicide."

# 56. Heavy Metal Meets the Counterculture

The thriving London blues-rock scene; the riff-oriented songs of the Kinks, the Who, and the Yardbirds; and the improvisatory flights of psychedelic rock gradually coalesced into a genre forming the antithesis of the "soft rock" of the singer-songwriters. Jimi Hendrix, Cream, and the Jeff Beck Group stand as the main intermediaries-progenitors of the new genre, retrospectively named "heavy metal."[1] What separated bands, such as Led Zeppelin, Black Sabbath, and Deep Purple, from their blues revival antecedents was not a lesser reliance on the blues but, rather, a less reverent attitude toward the form. These new bands were not so interested in faithful re-creation as in taking certain elements—the tonality, riff-orientation, sexual imagery, sense of aggression—found in some blues songs and heightening or refashioning them for an audience that was less interested in folklore and more interested in visceral power.[2] In metal, the peace-loving idealism of folk-rock and psychedelia also diminished in favor of darker visions and expressions of crude sexuality that spoke to another aspect of the countercultural experience.

The "power chord"—the root and fifth of a chord sounded without the third, but magnified by distortion in a sonic emblem of transgressive masculinity—joined forces with riffs played in unison by guitar and bass and a heavy "bottom" (bass and bass drum mixed up front, memorialized by Spinal Tap in their anthem "Big Bottom"), to create a genre of unparalleled volume, and one that found a large audience of working- and middle-class white youths. The initial rumblings from England were aided and abetted by sheets of noise from late 1960s' American aggregations, such as Blue Cheer and the highly political MC5.

The early 1970s witnessed a dispersion of a hard rock style, as writers of the time lumped bands like Alice Cooper, Grand Funk Railroad,

---

1. This genealogy is borne out by *Hit Parader's Top 100 Metal Albums* (Spring 1989) and *Hit Parader's* "Heavy Metal: The Hall of Fame" (December 1982) reprinted in Robert Walser, *Running with the Devil: Power, Gender, and Madness in Heavy Metal Music* (Hanover, N.H.: Wesleyan University Press and University Press of New England, 1993), 173–74. The account here is also indebted to Steve Waksman's in *Instruments of Desire: The Electric Guitar and the Shaping of Musical Experience* (Cambridge, Mass.: Harvard University Press, 1999), esp. p. 263; and Walser's in *Running with the Devil.*

2. Walser, in fact, focuses on the concept of "power" as a defining feature of the heavy metal genre and traces this connection in the historical usage of the term dating back two hundred years (pp. 1–3).

and Iggy and the Stooges together with Black Sabbath and Led Zeppelin.[3] New attitudes toward showmanship emerged in the mid-1970s with Kiss, and hard rock reached a peak of pop stylization with one-word bands—Journey, Foreigner, Boston, and Toto. Of these bands, the crown for longevity goes to Aerosmith, a band whose hard rock (and lead singer's lips) owed more to the Stones than to anybody else (note: critics often used "hard rock" and "heavy metal" interchangeably at this time).

Heavy metal spoke to class and age divisions in the audience: lower and lower-middle class versus bourgeois and college students versus high school students. The following entry features a record review of Led Zeppelin's first album that appeared in *Rolling Stone* and the response of some readers to this review. This exchange reveals early public recognition of divisions in the rock audience and a divide between part of the audience and the aesthetic of *Rolling Stone*'s rock critics. John Mendelsohn, the reviewer, compares Led Zeppelin's album unfavorably to the first album by the Jeff Beck Group, which had received positive reviews a short time before.

# REVIEW OF *LED ZEPPELIN*
## *John Mendelsohn*

## Led Zeppelin

*Led Zeppelin (Atlantic SD 8216)*

The popular formula in England in this, the aftermath era of such successful British bluesmen as Cream and John Mayall, seems to be: add, to an excellent guitarist who, since leaving the Yardbirds and/or Mayall, has become a minor musical deity, a competent rhythm section and pretty soul-belter who can do a good spade imitation. The latest of the British blues groups so conceived offers little that its twin, the Jeff Beck Group, didn't say as well or better three months ago, and the excesses of the Beck group's *Truth* album (most notably, its self-indulgence and restrictedness), are fully in evidence on Led Zeppelin's debut album.

---

3. Lester Bangs wrote several essays exploring these interconnections; see the following: "Heavy Metal," in Anthony DeCurtis and James Henke with Holly George-Warren, eds., *The Rolling Stone Illustrated History of Rock and Roll* (New York: Random House, [1976] 1992), 459–463; "Bring Your Mother to the Gas Chamber" (part 1), *Creem*, 4, no. 1 (June 1972): 40ff; "Bring Your Mother to the Gas Chamber: Black Sabbath and the Straight Dope on Blood-Lust Orgies, Part 2," *Creem* (July 1972): 47ff.

Jimmy Page, around whom the Zeppelin revolves, is, admittedly, an extraordinarily proficient blues guitarist and explorer of his instrument's electronic capabilities. Unfortunately, he is also a very limited producer and a writer of weak, unimaginative songs, and the Zeppelin album suffers from his having both produced it and written most of it (alone or in combination with his accomplices in the group).

The album opens with lots of guitar-rhythm section exchanges (in the fashion of Beck's "Shapes of Things" on "Good Times Bad Times," which might have been ideal for a Yardbirds' B-side). Here, as almost everywhere else on the album, it is Page's guitar that provides most of the excitement. "Babe I'm Gonna Leave You" alternates between prissy Robert Plant's howled vocals fronting an acoustic guitar and driving choruses of the band running down a four-chord progression while John Bonham smashes his cymbals on every beat. The song is very dull in places (especially on the vocal passages), very redundant, and certainly not worth the six-and-a-half minutes the Zeppelin gives it.

Two much-overdone Willie Dixon blues standards fail to be revivified by being turned into showcases for Page and Plant. "You Shook Me" is the more interesting of the two—at the end of each line Plant's echo-chambered voice drops into a small explosion of fuzz-tone guitar, with which it matches shrieks at the end.

The album's most representative cut is "How Many More Times." Here a jazzy introduction gives way to a driving (albeit monotonous) guitar-dominated background for Plant's strained and unconvincing shouting (he may be as foppish as Rod Stewart, but he's nowhere near so exciting, especially in the higher registers). A fine Page solo then leads the band into what sounds like a backwards version of the Page-composed "Beck's Bolero," hence to a little snatch of Albert King's "The Hunter," and finally to an avalanche of drums and shouting.

In their willingness to waste their considerable talent on unworthy material the Zeppelin has produced an album which is sadly reminiscent of *Truth*. Like the Beck group they are also perfectly willing to make themselves a two- (or, more accurately, one-and-a-half) man show. It would seem that, if they're to help fill the void created by the demise of Cream, they will have to find a producer (and editor) and some material worthy of their collective attention.

JOHN MENDELSOHN
3-15-69

SIRS:
Mendelsohn's review of Led Zeppelin was a 100% lie. Pure bullshit. Never has there been such a great band since Winwood's departure from Traffic.

Eric Charles
Brooklyn, N.Y.

SIRS:
If I used your record reviews as a guide to my personal record purchases, I would have the worst pile of garbage in the history of record collecting.

A few issues back, your unbelievably fucked review of Led Zeppelin. This, plus past reviews of Creedence Clearwater, Cream, etc.

I don't know where the musical taste of San Francisco is at, but if your magazine is an indicator—perhaps you all ought to come east on your vacation this summer.

Charles Laquidara
WBCN-FM
Boston, Massachusetts

# 57. Led Zeppelin Speaks!

The following interview of Jimmy Page by Dave Schulps originally appeared in *Trouser Press* over three successive issues in 1977. While several years had passed since the critical disdain that greeted Led Zeppelin's early albums, this interview is littered with references to the gap between their success with audiences and the negative response from critics. Numerous interviews with Led Zeppelin were published in the mid-1970s (usually with Robert Plant), but Schulps's piece is unusual in its focus on Zeppelin's music.[1] Other interviews tended to obsess about Plant and Page's mystical predilections or about other aspects of Zeppelin's image, such as their reputation for destroying hotel rooms and ravaging groupies. This interview covers the entirety of Page's career, including his background in art school and London-area blues bands, his experiences as a session guitarist, his stint with the Yardbirds, and his friendship with Jeff Beck. Page comes across as thoughtful and humble—a far cry from the public perception of heavy metal guitarists as craven wild men. In passages that may be responding directly to Mendelsohn's review, Pages answers charges about a lack of originality in relation to the Jeff Beck group and discusses another somewhat controversial issue: Led Zeppelin's use of traditional blues lyrics and tunes on their early albums without attribution.[2]

---

1. This interview was not alone in this approach, however; for an interview that goes to great lengths to convince readers of Page's seriousness as a musician from earlier in his career, see Chris Welch, "Jimmy Page, Part Three," *Melody Maker* (February 28, 1970): 10. For another interview that gives both Page and Plant space to talk about music, see Cameron Crowe, "Jimmy Page and Robert Plant Talk," *Rolling Stone* (March 13, 1975): 33–37. Perhaps the strangest interview, and one that does dwell on Page's interest in the occult, is his interview with William Burroughs (Beat-associated author of *Naked Lunch*, a hallucinatory chronicle of a junkie), "Rock Magic: Jimmy Page, Led Zeppelin, and a Search for the Elusive Stairway to Heaven," *Crawdaddy* 49 (June 1975): 34–35, 39–40.

2. For a musicological defense of Led Zeppelin against charges of appropriation and plagiarism, see Dave Headlam, "Does the Song Remain the Same? Questions of Authorship and Identification in the Music of Led Zeppelin," in *Concert Music, Rock, and Jazz Since 1945: Essays and Analytical Studies*, ed. Elizabeth West Marvin and Richard Hermann (Rochester, N.Y.: University of Rochester Press, 1995), 313–63. For the most thorough and sophisticated scholarly study of Led Zeppelin to date, see Susan Fast, *In the Houses of the Holy: Led Zeppelin and the Power of Rock Music* (New York: Oxford University Press, 2001).

# THE CRUNGE: JIMMY PAGE GIVES A HISTORY LESSON
## Dave Schulps

*Were you into the blues as much as the Stones or was it more rock 'n' roll for you?*
I was an all-arounder, thank God.

*Do you think that's helped your career?*
Immensely. I think if I was just labeled a blues guitarist I'd have never been able to lose the tag. When all the guitarists started to come through in America—like Clapton, Beck, and myself—Eric, being the blues guitarist, had the label. People just wanted to hear him play blues. I saw the guitar as a multifaceted instrument and this has stayed with me throughout. When you listen to the various classical guitarists like Segovia and Julian Bream, brilliant classical players, and Manitas de Plata doing flamenco, it's two totally different approaches to acoustic. Then there's Django Reinhardt and that's another approach entirely.

In those early days I was very interested in Indian music, as were a lot of other people too. Most of the "textbook" of what I was forced to learn was while I was doing sessions, though. At that point you never knew what you were going to be doing when you got to the session. In America, you were a specialist. For example, you would never think of Steve Cropper to do a jazz session or film session or TV jingles, but in Britain you had to do everything. I had to do a hell of a lot of work in a short time. I still don't really read music, to be honest with you. I read it like a six-year-old reads a book, which was adequate for sessions, and I can write it down, which is important.

*What got you into guitar playing? You listened to a lot of music being a collector, so was it just hearing it on record?*
Exactly. I've read about many records which are supposed to have turned me on to want to play, but it was "Baby, Let's Play House" by Elvis Presley. You've got to understand that in those days "rock 'n' roll" was a dirty word. It wasn't even being played by the media. Maybe you'd hear one record a day during the period of Elvis, Little Richard, and Jerry Lee Lewis. That's why you were forced to be a record collector if you wanted to be part of it. I heard that record and I wanted to be part of it; I knew something was going on. I heard the acoustic guitar, slap bass, and electric guitar—three instruments and a voice—and they generated so much energy I had to be part of it. That's when I started. Mind you, it took a long time before I got anywhere, I mean any sort of dexterity. I used to listen to Ricky Nelson records and pinch the James Burton licks, learn them note for note perfect. I only did that for a while, though. I guess that after one writes one's first song you tend to depart from that. It's inevitable.

*How old were you when you left Neil Christian[3] and started going heavily into sessions?*
I left Neil Christian when I was about 17 and went to art college. During that period, I was jamming at night in a blues club. By that time the blues had started to happen, so I used to go out and jam with Cyril Davies's Interval Band. Then somebody asked me if I'd like to play on a record, and before I knew where I was I was doing all these studio

---

3. "Neil Christian" is a reference to Page's first band, Neil Christian and the Crusaders.

*Source:* Dave Schulps, "The Crunge: Jimmy Page Gives a History Lesson," *Trouser Press* (September–November 1977), pp. 21–23. Reprinted by permission of Dave Schulps.

dates at night, while still going to art college in the daytime. There was a crossroads and you know which one I took.

*You mentioned you were good friends with Beck before the Yardbirds. How did your friendship come about? Did you see the Yardbirds often when Beck was with them?*

When I was doing studio work I used to go see them often, whenever I wasn't working. I met Beck through a friend of mine who told me he knew this guitarist I had to meet who'd made his own guitar. Beck showed up with his homemade guitar one day and he was really quite good. He started playing this James Burton and Scotty Moore stuff; I joined in and we really hit it off well.

    We used to hang out a hell of a lot when he was in the Yardbirds and I was doing studio work. I remember we both got very turned on to Rodrigo's Guitar Concerto by Segovia and all these sorts of music. He had the same sort of taste in music as I did. That's why you'll find on the early LPs we both did a song like "You Shook Me." It was the type of thing we'd both played in bands. Someone told me he'd already recorded it after we'd already put it down on the first Zeppelin album. I thought, "Oh dear, it's going to be identical," but it was nothing like it, fortunately. I just had no idea he'd done it. It was on *Truth* but I first heard it when I was in in Miami after we'd recorded our version. It's a classic example of coming from the same area musically, of having similar taste. It really pissed me off when people compared our first album to the Jeff Beck Group and said it was very close conceptually. It was nonsense, utter nonsense. The only similarity was that we'd both come out of the Yardbirds and we both had acquired certain riffs individually from the Yardbirds.

*Under what circumstances did you finally join the Yardbirds when Paul Samwell-Smith quit in late summer of 1966?*

It was at a gig at the Marquee Club in Oxford which I'd gone along to. They were playing in front of all these penguin-suited undergraduates and I think Samwell-Smith, whose family was a bit well to do, was embarrassed by the band's behavior. Apparently Keith Relf had gotten really drunk and he was falling into the drum kit, making farting noises into the mike, being generally anarchistic. I thought he'd done really well, actually, and the band had played really well that night. He just added all this extra feeling to it. When he came offstage, though, Paul Samwell-Smith said, "I'm leaving the band. Things used to be so final back then. There was no rethinking decisions like that. Then he said to Chris Dreja, "If I were you, I'd leave too." Which he didn't. They were sort of stuck.

    Jeff had brought me to the gig in his car and on the way back I told him I'd sit in for a few months until they got things sorted out. Beck had often said to me. "It would be really great if you could join the band." But I just didn't think it was a possibility in any way. In addition, since I'd turned the offer down a couple of times already, I didn't know how the rest of them would feet about me joining. It was decided that we'd definitely have a go at it; I'd take on the bass, though I'd never played it before, but only until Dreja could learn it as he'd never played it before either. We figured it would be easier for me to pick it up quickly, then switch over to a dual guitar thing when Chris had time to become familiar enough with the bass.

*What about your own desire for stardom, did that have any role in your quitting sessions to join the Yardbirds in the first place?*

No. I never desired stardom, I just wanted to be respected as a musician.

*Do you feel the extent of your stardom now has become a burden for you in any way?*

Only in relation to a lot of misunderstandings that have been laid on us. A lot of negative and derogatory things have been said about us. I must say I enjoyed the anonymity that was part of being one fourth of a group. I liked being a name but not necessarily a face to go with it. The film, *The Song Remains the Same*, I think, has done a lot to put faces to names for the group.

*And after Relf and McCarty said they were quitting the Yardbirds, you planned to keep the group going with Chris Dreja and bring in a new drummer and singer, is that right?*

Well, we still had these dates we were supposed to fulfill. Around the time of the split John Paul Jones called me up and said he was interested in getting something together. Also, Chris was getting very into photography; he decided he wanted to open his own studio and by that time was no longer enamored with the thought of going on the road. Obviously, a lot of Keith and Jim's attitude of wanting to jack it in had rubbed off on him, so Jonesy was in.

I'd originally thought of getting Terry Reid in as lead singer and second guitarist but he had just signed with Mickie Most as a solo artist in a quirk of fate. He suggested I get in touch with Robert Plant, who was then in a band called Hobbstweedle. When I auditioned him and heard him sing, I immediately thought there must be something wrong with him personality-wise or that he had to be impossible to work with, because I just could not understand why, after he told me he'd been singing for a few years already, he hadn't become a big name yet. So I had him down to my place for a little while, just to sort of check him out, and we got along great. No problems. At this time a number of drummers had approached me and wanted to work with us. Robert suggested I go hear John Bonham, whom I'd heard of because he had a reputation, but had never seen. I asked Robert if he knew him and he told me they'd worked together in this group called Band of Joy.

*So the four of your rehearsed for a short time and went on that Scandinavian tour as the New Yardbirds.*

As I said, we had these dates that the Yardbirds were supposed to fulfill, so we went as the Yardbirds. They were already being advertised as the New Yardbirds featuring Jimmy Page, so there wasn't much we could do about it right then. We had every intention of changing the name of the group from the very beginning, though. The tour went fantastically for us, we left them stomping the floors after every show.

*What were the original ideas behind Zeppelin when the band first got together? Was it immediately decided to be a high energy thing?*

Obviously, it was geared that way from the start. When Robert came down to my place the first time, when I was trying to get an idea of what he was all about, we talked about the possibilities of various types of things, "Dazed and Confused," for example. Then I played him a version of "Babe I'm Gonna Leave You." It was the version by Joan Baez, the song is traditional, and I said, "Fancy doing this?" He sort of looked at me with wonder and I said, "Well, I've got an idea for an arrangement," and started playing it on acoustic guitar. That's indicative of the way I was thinking with regards to direction. It was very easy going.

*There was a bit of a fuss made at one point because on the first couple of albums you were using a lot of traditional and blues lyrics and tunes and calling them your own.*

The thing is they were traditional lyrics and they went back far before a lot of the people that one related them to. The riffs we did were totally different, also, from the ones that had come before, apart from something like "You Shook Me" and "I Can't Quit You," which we attributed to Willie Dixon. The thing with "Bring It on Home," Christ, there's only a tiny bit of that taken from Sonny Boy Williamson's version and we threw that in as a tribute to him. People say, "Oh, 'Bring It on Home' is stolen."

Well, there's only a little bit in the song that relates to anything that had gone before it, just the end.

*Your next album, Led Zeppelin III, presented a very different image of Led Zeppelin from the first two albums. Most importantly, it was predominantly acoustic. It was a very controversial album. How and why did the changes that brought about the third album take place?*

After the intense touring that had been taking place through the first two albums, working almost 24 hours a day, basically, we managed to stop and have a proper break, a couple of months as opposed to a couple of weeks. We decided to go off and rent a cottage to provide a contrast to motel rooms. Obviously, it had quite an effect on the material that was written.

*Did you write the whole album there?*

Just certain sections of it. "That's the Way," "Bron-Y-Aur Stomp," quite a few things. It was the tranquility of the place that set the tone of the album. Obviously, we weren't crashing away at 100 watt Marshall stacks. Having played acoustic and being interested in classical guitar, anyway, being in a cottage without electricity, it was acoustic guitar time. It didn't occur to us not to include it on the album because it was relative to the changes within the band. We didn't expect we'd get thrashed in the media for doing it.

*Was there a rethink by the band about the stage act, since you were faced with having to perform material from a predominantly acoustic LP?*

It just meant that we were going to have to employ some of those numbers onstage without being frightened about it. They were received amazingly well.

*Had you wanted to bring in more of the English folk roots to Zeppelin or was it just the influence of living in the cottage that gives the album a pastoral feeling?*

It has that because that's how it was. After all the heavy, intense vibe of touring which is reflected in the raw energy on the second album, it was just a totally different feeling. I've always tried to capture an emotional quality in my songs. Transmitting that is what music seems to be about, really, as far as the instrumental side of it goes, anyway. It was in us, everything that came out on *Zeppelin III* can still be related to the essence of the first album when you think about it. It's just that the band had kept maturing.

*Were you surprised when the critical reaction came out?*

I just thought they hadn't understood it, hadn't listened to it. For instance, *Melody Maker* said we'd decided to don our acoustic guitars because Crosby, Stills and Nash had just been over here. It wasn't until the fourth LP that people began to understand that we weren't just messing around.

*You did take a lot of stock in the criticism of the third record. Personally, you seemed to be hit hard by it at the time*

To pave the way for 18 months without doing any interviews, I must have. Silly, wasn't I? That was a lot of the reason for putting out the next LP with no information on it at all. After a year's absence from both records and touring, I remember one agent telling us it was professional suicide. We just happened to have a lot of faith in what we were doing.

*Was the cover of the fourth album meant to bring out the whole city/country dichotomy that had surfaced on the third record?*

Exactly. It represented the change in the balance which was going on. There was the old country man and the blocks of flats being knocked down. It was just a way of saying that we should look after the earth, not rape and pillage it.

*Do you think the third record was good for the band, regardless of the critical reaction, because it showed people that the band was not just a heavy metal group, that you were more versatile than that?*

It showed people that we weren't going to be a stagnant group. There were some people who knew that already and were interested to see what we'd come up with; there were others who thought we were just an outright hype and were still living back in the '60s. They just didn't take anything we did seriously. A lot of them have since come around. You should read that *Melody Maker* review, though, it's absolutely classic. I felt a lot better once we started performing it, because it was proving to be working for the people who came around to see us. There was always a big smile there in front of us. That was always more important than any proxy review. That's really how the following of the band has spread, by word of mouth. I mean, all this talk about a hype, spending thousands on publicity campaigns, we didn't do that at all. We didn't do television. Well, we did a pilot TV show and a pilot radio show, but that's all. We weren't hyping ourselves. It wasn't as though we were thrashing about all over the media. It didn't matter, though, the word got out on the street.

*Once a band is established it seems to me that bad reviews can't really do anything to a band.*

No, you're right. But you've got to understand that I lived every second of the albums. Whereas the others hadn't. John Paul and Bonzo would do the tracks and they wouldn't come in until needed. And Robert would do the vocals. But I'd be there all the time and I'd live and cringe to every mistake. There were things that were right and wrong on a subjective level.

*The fourth album was to my mind the first fully realized Zeppelin album. It just sounded like everything had come together on that album.*

Yeah, we were really playing properly as a group and the different writing departures that we'd taken, like the cottage and the spontaneity aspects, had been worked out and came across in the most disciplined form.

"Rock and Roll" was a spontaneous combustion. We were doing something else at the time, but Bonzo played the beginning of Little Richard's "Good Golly Miss Molly" with the tape still running and I just started doing that part of the riff. It actually ground to a halt after about 12 bars, but it was enough to know that there was enough of a number there to keep working on it. Robert even came in singing on it straight away.

I do have the original tape that was running at the time we ran down "Stairway to Heaven" completely with the band. I'd worked it all out already the night before with John Paul Jones, written down the changes and things. All this time we were all living in a house and keeping pretty regular hours together, so the next day we started running it down. There was only one place where there was a slight rerun. For some unknown reason Bonzo couldn't get the timing right on the twelve-string part before the solo. Other than that it flowed very quickly. While we were doing it Robert was penciling down lyrics; he must have written three quarters of the lyrics on the spot. He didn't have to go away and think about them. Amazing, really.

"Black Dog" was a riff that John Paul Jones had brought with him. "Battle of Evermore" was made up on the spot by Robert and myself. I just picked up John Paul Jones's mandolin, never having played a mandolin before, and just wrote up the chords and the whole thing in one sitting. The same thing happened with the banjo on "Gallows Pole." I'd never played one before either. It was also John Paul Jones's instrument. I just picked it up and started moving my fingers around until the chords sounded right, which is the same way I work on compositions when the guitar's in different tunings.

*When did Sandy Denny come in to sing on "Gallows Pole"?*

Well, it sounded like an old English instrumental first off. Then it became a vocal and Robert did his bit. Finally we figured we'd bring Sandy by and do a question-and-answer-type thing.

"Misty Mountain Hop" we came up with on the spot. "Going to California" was a thing I'd written before on acoustic guitar. "When the Levee Breaks" was a riff that I'd been working on, but Bonzo's drum sound really makes the difference on that point.

*You've said that when you heard Robert's lyrics to "Stairway to Heaven" you knew that he'd be the band's lyricist from then on.*

I always knew he would be, but I knew at that point that he'd proved it to himself and could get into something a bit more profound than just subjective things. Not that they can't be profound as well, but there's a lot of ambiguity implied in that number that wasn't present before. I was really relieved because it gave me the opportunity to just get on with the music.

*Did you know you'd recorded a classic when you finished?*

I knew it was good. I didn't know it was going to become like an anthem, but I did know it was the gem of the album, sure.

*Was the idea of the symbols on the cover of the fourth album yours?*

Yeah. After all this crap that we'd had with the critics, I put it to everybody else that it'd be a good idea to put out something totally anonymous. At first I wanted just one symbol on it, but then it was decided that since it was our fourth album and there were four of us, we could each choose our own symbol. I designed mine and everyone else had their own reasons for using the symbols that they used.

*Do you envision a relationship between Zeppelin cover art and the music on the albums?*

There is a relationship in a way, though not necessarily in a "concept album" fashion.

*Does Robert usually come into sessions with the lyrics already written?*

He has a lyric book and we try to fuse song to lyric where it can be done. Where it can't, he just writes new ones.

*Is there a lot of lyric changing during a session?*

Sometimes. Sometimes it's more cut and dried, like on "The Rain Song."

*There are a few tracks on the fifth album that seemed to exhibit more of a sense of humor than Zeppelin had been known for. "The Crunge" was funny and "Dyer Mak'er" had a joke title which took some people a while to get.*

I didn't expect people not to get it. I thought it was pretty obvious. The song itself was a cross between reggae and a '50s number, "Poor Little Fool," Ben E. King things, stuff like that. I'll tell you one thing, "The Song Remains the Same" was going to be an instrumental at first. We used to call it "The Overture."

*You never performed it that way*

We couldn't. There were too many guitar parts to perform it.

*But once you record anything with overdubs, you end up having to adapt it for the stage.*

Sure. Then it becomes a challenge, a tough challenge in some cases. "Achilles" is the classic one. When Ronnie Wood and Keith Richard came to hear us play, Keith said, "You ought to get another guitarist; you're rapidly becoming known as the most overworked guitarist in the business." Quite amusing. There are times when I'd just love to get another guitarist on, but it just wouldn't look right to the audience.

# 58. "I Have No Message Whatsoever"

The stars of glam (or glitter) rock in the early 1970s—David Bowie, T-Rex, Slade, Gary Glitter, and Sweet—all hailed from the United Kingdom, and all (with the eventual exception of Bowie) achieved greater success there than in the United States Part of the resistance in the United States stemmed from how glam artists emphasized the artificial at the expense of the authentic passion so carefully cultivated by other genres of the era. However, campiness and androgyny gradually became hip in the United States in the mid- to late 1970s, as evidenced by the success of a film, such as the *Rocky Horror Picture Show,* and of some of the later new-wave bands like the B-52s. Not accidentally, this development coincided with the mass acceptance of Bowie in the United States.

In the early 1970s, however, when he first became a phenomenon in the United Kingdom, Bowie (David Jones, b. 1947), along with the other glitterati just mentioned, shared a style founded on a riff-based, hard rock, with rather exaggeratedly stiff rhythms. While the actual heyday of glam was brief, its emphasis on androgyny and on campy posing influenced many other rock stars of the time, such as Mick Jagger, Rod Stewart, Elton John, and Lou Reed. Although not necessarily glam, Alice Cooper emerged during the early 1970s with a sound that is sometimes described as the prototype for a kind of American heavy metal. In addition to a hard-rock sound, Cooper shared with glam an emphasis on the theatrical, at first with gender-bending androgyny, then with an act that relied on images gleaned from horror movies and pulp magazines.

The following interview with Bowie, conducted by teenage phenom reporter Cameron Crowe,[1] highlights Bowie's unabashed acknowledgment that his performances present him as an actor playing a part. This apparent distance from his persona places him at the opposite end of the authenticity spectrum from singer-songwriters, who had made self-revelation the cornerstone of their art. Within the flow of his exaggerated egocentricity, Bowie touches on different perceptions about gender and sexual identity on opposing sides of the Atlantic, glories in his

---

1. Crowe may well be better known to readers as a writer and/or director of many films, including *Fast Times at Ridgemont High* (1982) and *Almost Famous* (2001), his semiautobiographical account of coming of age as a rock critic in the early- to mid-1970s.

superficiality and lack of depth, takes a jab at Elton John for allegedly ripping off aspects of his persona, and expresses pride in artistic theft and
lack of originality. Calculated to offend the rock establishment of the day,
Bowie presents an antidote to the pompousness and self-seriousness
pervading other rock genres and anticipates the media machinations of
later stars, such as Madonna.

# DAVID BOWIE INTERVIEW
## Cameron Crowe

**Playboy:**  Let's start with the one question you've always seemed to hedge: How much of
your bisexuality is fact and how much is gimmick?

**Bowie:**  It's true—I am a bisexual. But I can't deny that I've used that fact *very* well. I suppose it's the best thing that ever happened to me. Fun, too. We'll talk all about it.

**Playboy:**  Why do you say it's the best thing that ever happened to you?

**Bowie:**  Well, for one thing, girls are always presuming that I've kept my heterosexual vir-
ginity for some reason. So I've had all these girls try to get me over to the other side
again: "C'mon, David, it isn't all that bad. I'll show you." Or, better yet, "We'll show
you." I always play dumb.

 On the other hand—I'm sure you want to know about the other hand as well—
when I was 14, sex suddenly became all important to me. It didn't really matter who or
what it was with, as long as it was a sexual experience. So it was some very pretty boy
in class in some school or other that I took home and neatly fucked on my bed upstairs.
And that was it. My first thought was, Well, if I ever get sent to prison, I'll know how to
keep happy.

**Playboy:**  Which wouldn't give much slack to your straighter cellmates.

**Bowie:**  I've always been very chauvinistic, even in my boy-obsessed days. But I was
always a gentleman. I always treated my boys like real ladies. Always escorted them
properly and, in fact, I suppose if I were a lot older—like 40 or 50—I'd be a wonderful
sugar daddy to some little queen down in Kensington. I'd have a houseboy named
Richard to order around.

**Playboy:**  How much of that are we supposed to believe? Your former publicist, the celebrated ex-groupie Cherry Vanilla, says she's slept with you and that you're not gay at
all. She says you just let people *think* you like guys.

**Bowie:**  Oh, I'd love to meet this impostor she's talking about. It sure ain't me. That's
actually a lovely quote. Cherry's almost as good as I am at using the media.

**Playboy:**  Why, at a time when nobody else in rock would have dared allude to it, did you
choose to exploit bisexuality?

**Bowie:**  I would say that America forces me into it. Someone asked me in an interview
once—I believe it was in '71—if I were gay. I said, "No, I'm bisexual." The guy, a writer
for one of the English trades, had no idea what the term means. So I explained it to him.
It was all printed—and that's where it started. It's so nostalgic now, isn't it? 'Seventy-one

was a good American year. Sex was still shocking. Everybody wanted to see the freak. But they were so ignorant about what I was doing. There was very little talk of bisexuality or gay power before I came along. Unwittingly, I really brought that whole thing over. I never, ever said the word gay when I first got over here to America. It took a bit of exposure and a few heavy rumors about me before the gays said, "We disown David Bowie." And they did. Of course. They knew that I wasn't what they were fighting for.

Nobody understood the European way of dressing and adopting the asexual, androgynous everyman pose. People all went screaming, "He's got make-up on and he's wearing stuff that looks like dresses!" I wasn't the first one, though, to publicize bisexuality.

**Playboy:**   Who was?

**Bowie:**   Dean. James Dean did, very subtly and very well. I have some insight on it. Dean was probably very much like me. Elizabeth Taylor told me that once. Dean was calculating. He wasn't careless. He was not the rebel he portrayed so successfully. He didn't want to die. But he did believe in the premise of taking yourself to extremes, just to add a deeper cut to one's personality.

James Dean epitomized the very thing that is so campily respectable today—the male hustler. It was part of his incredible magnetism. You know, that he was . . . a whore. He used to stand in Times Square to earn money so he could go to Lee Strasberg and learn how to be Marlon Brando. He had quite a sordid little reputation. I admire him immensely—that should take care of any question you may have about whether or not I have any heroes.

**Playboy:**   Thanks. Now what about you posing in drag for the cover of the English album of *The Man Who Sold The World*?

**Bowie:**   Funnily enough, and you'll never believe me, it was a parody of Gabriel Rossetti. Slightly askew, obviously. So when they told me that a drag-queen cult was forming behind me, I said, "Fine, don't bother to explain it; nobody is going to bother to try to understand it." I'll play along, absolutely *anything* to bring me through. Because of everybody's thirst for scandal—look at how big *People* is—they gave me a big chance. All the papers wrote *volumes* about how sick I was, how I was helping to kill off true art. In the meantime, they used up all the space they could have given over to true artists. That really is pretty indicative of how compelling pretension is, that it commanded that amount of bloody writing about what color my hair was gonna be next week. I want to know why they wasted all that time and effort and paper on my clothes and my pose. *Why?* Because I was a dangerous statement.

The follow-up to that, now that I've decided to talk a little more—if only to you— was, "How dare he have such a strenuous ego?" That, in itself seemed a danger to some people. Am I, as a human being, worth talking about? I frankly think, Yes, I am. I've got to carry through with the conviction that I am also my own medium. The only way I can be effective as a person is to be this confoundedly arrogant and forthright with my point of view. That's the way I am. I believe myself with the utmost sincerity.

**Playboy:**   But aren't you having trouble getting *other* people to believe you? Take, for example, your well-publicized farewells to showbiz. You've retired twice, swearing you'd never have another thing to do with rock 'n' roll. Yet you've just finished a six-month world concert tour, promoting your newest rock-'n'-roll album, *Station to Station*. How do you rationalize these contradictions?

**Bowie:**   I lie. It's quite easy to do. Nothing matters except whatever it is I'm doing at the moment. I can't keep track of everything I say. I don't give a shit. I can't even remember how much I believe and how much I don't believe. The point is to grow into the person you grow into. I haven't a clue where I'm gonna be in a year. A raving nut, a flower child or a dictator, some kind of reverend—I don't know. That's what keeps me from getting bored.

**Playboy:** In the song *Station to Station*, though, you do refer to cocaine—

**Bowie:** Yes, yes. The line is, "It's not the side effects of the cocaine. . . . I'm thinking that it must be love." Do the radio stations bleep it out?

**Playboy:** None that we've heard. Did you have any reservations about using the line in the song?

**Bowie:** None whatsoever.

**Playboy:** One might easily construe it as advocating the use of cocaine. Or is that the message?

**Bowie:** I have no message whatsoever. I really have nothing to say, no suggestions or advice, nothing. All I do is suggest some ideas that will keep people listening a bit longer. And out of it all, maybe *they'll* come up with a message and save me the work. My career has kind of been like that. I get away with murder.

**Playboy:** Do you have trouble deciding which is the real you?

**Bowie:** I've learned to flow with myself. I honestly don't know where the real David Jones is. It's like playing the shell game. Except I've got so many shells I've forgotten what the pea looks like. I wouldn't know it if I found it. Being famous helps put off the problems of discovering myself. I mean that. That's the main reason I've always been so keen on being accepted, why I've striven so hard to put my brain to artistic use. I want to make a mark. In my early stuff, I made it through on sheer pretension. I consider myself responsible for a whole new school of pretensions—they know who they are. Don't you, Elton? Just kidding. No, I'm not. See what I mean? That was a thoroughly pretentious statement. True or not. I bet you'll print that. Show someone something where intellectual analysis or analytical thought has been applied and people will yawn. But something that's pretentious—that keeps you riveted. It's also the only thing that shocks anymore. It shocks as much as the Dylan thing did 14 years ago. As much as sex shocked many years ago.

**Playboy:** You're saying sex is no longer shocking?

**Bowie:** Oh, come on. Sorry, Hugh. Sex has never *really* been shocking, it was just the people who performed it who were. Shocking people, performing sex. Now nobody really cares. Everybody fucks everybody. The only thing that shocks now is an extreme. Like me running my mouth off, jacking myself off. Unless you do that, nobody will pay attention to you. Not for long. You have to hit them on the head.

**Playboy:** Is that the Bowie success formula?

**Bowie:** That's always been it. It's never really changed. For instance, what I did with my Ziggy Stardust was package a totally credible, plastic rock-'n'-roll singer—much better than the Monkees could ever fabricate. I mean, *my* plastic rock-'n'-roller was much more plastic than anybody's. And that was what was needed at the time. And it still is. Most people still want their idols and gods to be shallow, like cheap toys. Why do you think teenagers are the way they are? They run around like ants, chewing gum and flitting onto a certain style of dressing for a day; that's as deep as they wish to go. It's no surprise that Ziggy was a huge success.

**Playboy:** Is that why you said you became Ziggy at one point?

**Bowie:** Without even thinking about it. At first, I just assumed that character onstage. Then everybody started to treat me as they treated Ziggy, as though I were the Next Big

Thing, as though I moved masses of people. I became convinced I was a messiah. Very scary. I woke up fairly quickly.

**Playboy:**  Do you ever worry about your fans' giving up on you—not wanting to hear Bowie as a soul singer or whatever?

**Bowie:**  Well, they must understand what my trip was in the beginning. I've never been a musician.

**Playboy:**  What have you been?

**Bowie:**  The unfortunate thing is that I've always wanted to be a film director. And the two media got unconsciously amalgamated, so I was doing films on record. That creates your basic concept album, which becomes a bit of a slow pack horse in the end. Now I know that if I'm going to make albums, I've got to make albums that I enjoy musically, or else just make the fucking film. A lot of my concept albums, like *Aladdin Sane, Ziggy* and *Diamond Dogs,* were only 50 percent there. They should have been visual as well. I think that some of the most talented actors around are in rock. I think a whole renaissance in film making is gonna come from rock. Not because of it, though, despite it.

**Playboy:**  But you've said that you find rock depressing and sterile, even evil.

**Bowie:**  It *is* depressing and sterile and, yes, ultimately evil. Anything that contributes to stagnation is evil. When it has familiarity, it's no longer rock 'n' roll. It's white noise. Dirge. Just look at *disco* music—the endless numb beat. It's really dangerous.

So, I've moved on. I've established the fact that I am an entertainer, David Bowie, not just another boring rock singer. I've got a film out, Nicolas Roeg's *The Man Who Fell to Earth.* And I'll be doing a lot more, taking a lot of chances. The minute you know you're on safe ground, you're dead. You're finished. It's over. The last thing I want is to be established. I want to go to bed every night saying, "If I never wake again, I certainly will have *lived* while I was alive."

**Playboy:**  Let's go back to *disco* music. You say it's a dirge, yet you had the biggest *disco* hit of last year in *Fame* and you scored again this year with *Golden Years.* How do you explain that?

**Bowie:**  I love *disco.* It's a lovely escapist's way out. I quite like it, as long as it's not on the radio night and day—which it is so much these days. *Fame* was an incredible bluff that worked. Very flattering. I'll do *anything* until I fail. And when I succeed, I quit, too. I'm really knocked out that people actually dance to my records, though. But let's be honest: my rhythm and blues are thoroughly plastic. *Young Americans,* the album *Fame* is from, is, I would say, the definitive plastic soul record. It's the squashed remains of ethnic music as it survives in the age of Muzak rock, written and sung by a white limey. If you had played *Young Americans* to me five years ago and said, "This is an R&B album," I would have laughed. Hysterically.

**Playboy:**  How about if we had said, "This is going to be *your* album five years from now"?

**Bowie:**  I would have thrown you *and* the record out of my house.

**Playboy:**  How did you become a rock-'n'-roller anyway?

**Bowie:**  Truth? I was broke. I got into rock because it was an enjoyable way of making my money and taking four or five years to puzzle my next move out. I was a painter before that, studying commercial art at Bromley Technical High School. I tried advertising and that was *awful.* The *lowest.* But I was well into my little saxophone, so I left advertising and thought, Let's give rock a try. You can have a good time doing that and usually have at least enough money to live on. Especially then. It was the Mod days; nice clothes were half the battle.

**Playboy:**   What do you believe in?

**Bowie:**   Myself. Politics. Sex . . .

**Playboy:**   Since you put yourself first, do you consider yourself an original thinker?

**Bowie:**   Not by any means. More like a tasteful thief. The only art I'll ever study is stuff that I can steal from. I do think that my plagiarism is effective. Why does an artist create, anyway? The way I see it, if you're an inventor, you can invent something that you hope people can use. I want art to be just as practical. Art can be a political reference, a sexual force, any force that you want, but it should be usable. What the hell do artists want? Museum pieces? The more *I* get ripped off, the more *flattered* I get. But I've caused a lot of discontent because I've expressed my admiration for other artists by saying, "Yes, I'll use that," or, "Yes, I took this from him and this from her." Mick Jagger, for example, is scared to walk into the same room as me even *thinking* any new idea. He knows I'll snatch it.

**Playboy:**   Is it true that Jagger once told you he was hiring the French artist Guy Peellaert for the jacket of a Rolling Stones album and you ran right off to hire Peellaert for your own album, *Diamond Dogs,* which was released first?

**Bowie:**   Mick was silly. I mean, he should never have shown me anything new. I went over to his house and he had all these Guy Peellaert pictures around and said, "What do you think of this guy?" I told him I thought he was incredible. So I immediately phoned him up. Mick's learned now, as I've said. He will never do that again. You've got to be a bastard in this business.

**Playboy:**   You stated in *Rolling Stone* that you'd like to use your music to "rule the world . . . subliminally." Would you care to elaborate?

**Bowie:**   I think subliminal advertising is great. If it hadn't been outlawed, it would have gone out of advertising very quickly and straight into politics. I would have excelled at it. Think of it, an empty screen that people could stare at for an hour and a half and not actually see anything but leave with an entire experience in their heads.

   Of course, *Rolling Stone* got hate mail. So did Dali in his day. He knew exactly what he was doing when he painted his paintings. He knew what all the objects meant. Should his work have been destroyed and he forced to paint a vase of flowers? The attitude that says the artist should paint only things that the proletarian can understand, I think is the most destructive thing possible. That sounds a little like Hitler's going around to museums and tearing modern paintings down, doesn't it?

   You mustn't be scared of art. Rock 'n' roll is only rock 'n' roll. People hold it so sacred—mustn't tamper, in case you find out that it really does govern kids. Those old Fifties antirock movies were right. Rock-'n'-roll records are dangerous to the moral fiber. But then, records are a thing of the past now, so who knows?

**Playboy:**   We're not quite sure how you made the leap from subliminal advertising to reporting the death of the record industry, but since you have, what do you propose will happen to music in the future?

**Bowie:**   It will return to the sensitivities of the working class. That excites me. Sound as texture, rather than sound as music. Producing noise records seems pretty logical to me. My favorite group is a German band called Kraftwerk—it plays noise music to "increase productivity." I like that idea, if you have to play music.

**Playboy:**   Do you feel *you've* been taken advantage of over the years?

**Bowie:**   Not taken advantage of. Exploited.

**Playboy:**   Are you suggesting you haven't made all that you should have?

**Bowie:**   What, moneywise? Oh, Lord no—we made nothing. All I've made is an impact and a change, which of course, is worth a lot. I keep telling myself that. The best thing to say about it all is that it's archetypal rock-'n'-roll business. Read the reports of the Beatles, the Stones and a lot of other big entertainers and take some kind of amalgamation of all that; it's a pretty accurate picture of my business. John Lennon has been through it all. John told me, "Stick with it. Survive. You really go through the grind and they'll rip you off right and left. The key is to come out the other side." I said something cocky at the time like, "I've got a great manager. Everything is great. I'm a *Seventies* artist." The last time I spoke to John, I told him he was right. I'd been ripped off blind.

**Playboy:**   You're not a rich man? After five gold albums?
**Bowie:**   *Now*, yes, exceedingly. No! Wait, America! Not at all. Haven't got a penny to my name. I'm pleading poverty at the moment, but I'm *potentially* very rich. Theoretically rich but not wealthy.

**Playboy:**   Are you as bitter about the music business as Lennon and Jagger have said they are?
**Bowie:**   No, no, no. You see, I needed to learn about it. You've got to make mistakes. It's very important to make mistakes. Very, very important. If I glided through, I wouldn't be the man I'm not today.

**Playboy:**   Last question. Do you believe and stand by everything you've said?
**Bowie:**   Everything but the inflammatory remarks.

# 59. Rock Me Amadeus[1]

The spawn of psychedelic rock and European art music ("classical" music), progressive rock (alternately known as "art rock," "prog rock," or simply "prog") emerged from a complex of genres (including heavy metal and glam) that formed in the late 1960s–early 1970s and owed various debts to blues-rock and psychedelic rock. What distinguished prog from other contemporary genres with similar influences was the tendency to

---

1. I stole the title of this section from the 1986 hit single of that name by Austrian pop star Falco. The song has nothing to do with the subject of the chapter, progressive rock, but then my title of choice, "Rocking the Classics," was already taken by Edward Macan's book on prog-rock, which is, by the way, the most systematic history of the genre; see Macan, *Rocking the Classics: English Progressive Rock and the Counterculture* (New York: Oxford University Press, 1997).

include overt references to classical music in terms of form and texture. Occasionally, the melody and harmony of a particular piece of art music might influence a specific song.

Mostly a British phenomenon, several stages of classicizing influence can be observed in the genre as it developed.[2] The first of these influences was the incorporation of orchestral instruments, not in the manner of pre–rock 'n' roll background filler, but as active participants in the texture. The Beatles' use of a string quartet in "Yesterday" (1965) and the Baroque-influenced harpsichord break in "In My Life" (1965) may have initiated this phenomenon, which was echoed by other "Baroque"-influenced pop hits in the mid-1960s, like the Left Banke's "Walk Away Renee" (1966) and Procul Harum's "A Whiter Shade of Pale" (1967).[3] Another phase involves the use of complex forms: suites, multimovement works, and so forth. While the Beatles' *Sgt. Pepper's Lonely Hearts Club Band* (1967) arguably inaugurated this trend with its recapitulation of the title track and its overall framework of a "show," works, such as King Crimson's *In the Court of the Crimson King* and side two of the Beatles' *Abbey Road,* extended the idea to more complex notions of musical unity.[4] The Who also contributed to this direction, first with a miniopera "A Quick One" (1966); then with a concept album, *The Who Sell Out* (1967); and, finally, with the first "rock opera," *Tommy* (1969).

Eventually, Emerson, Lake, and Palmer, as well as other bands, rearranged classical pieces, basing their new "works" on themes taken from the classical canon. Finally, in the apotheosis of the progressive rock style as realized by groups like Yes and Gentle Giant, one finds rock instrumentation and sections featuring improvisation embedded within complex multimovement forms alternating with carefully worked-out contrapuntal textures. Progressive rock bands might also incorporate other influences, such as jazz, avant-garde electronic sounds, and musical processes borrowed from 1960s minimalism.

An interesting point of departure between progressive rock musicians and other rock or soul artists of the period is the emphasis on artifice. The "authentic" baring of the soul, so important to the aesthetics of other genres at this time, is avoided in favor of technical prowess that

---

2. John Rockwell, in an excellent overview of the genre, ascribes the British domination of prog rock to the more overt persistence and awareness of class difference in the United Kingdom versus the United States; see "The Emergence of Art Rock," in Anthony DeCurtis and James Henke with Holly George-Warren, eds., *The Rolling Stone Illustrated History of Rock and Roll* (New York: Random House [1976] 1992), 493. Greg Lake (the "Lake" of "Emerson, Lake and Palmer") explains it thusly: "I think it's a question of heritage. European musicians tend to come from a classical heritage. American bands tend to come from a blues-based heritage see Eric Gaer, "Emerson, Lake & Palmer: A Musical Force," *DownBeat* 41 (May 9, 1974), p. 14.

3. The connection in these songs with European art music may be felt as much or more in the classically influenced voice-leading and harmonic progressions as in the instrumentation.

4. And as I stated in Part 3, *Freak Out!* by the Mothers of Invention, and *Pet Sounds,* by the Beach Boys (both 1966) are both sometimes put forward as the first concept album.

does not necessarily emphasize spontaneity. This is not to say that prog rock fans necessarily eschewed "authenticity" as an aesthetic criterion; rather, "authenticity" in prog is earned by the display of mastery over the materials and in lofty intellectual ambitions projected through formal manipulation and "deep," cosmic lyrics (another legacy from psychedelic rock).

---

The majority of articles and interviews with musicians associated with progressive rock took place in a new form of publication that began to prosper in the 1970s: magazines, such as *Guitar Player* and *Contemporary Keyboard*, that catered to the aspiring rock musician and were filled with articles about playing techniques, practice regimens, and equipment. The seriousness of the prog rockers made them obvious subjects for these magazines, which paid far more attention to them than did publications that were directed more toward the lay rock audience, such as *Rolling Stone* or *Creem*. Thus, the following interview with Keith Emerson (of Emerson, Lake, and Palmer) concentrates on the gigantism of his band's stage show, his equipment (not included here), and on his approach to adapting classical music. I've also included a statement from Aaron Copland about the band's adaptation of his "Fanfare for the Common Man."

# KEITH EMERSON
## *Domenic Milano*

In late 1969, Keith met bassist/vocalist Greg Lake, then of King Crimson, in San Francisco where the two were playing on the same bill. Both were dissatisfied with the bands they were in, and each liked the other's playing. The two joined musical forces and began their search for the proper drummer. Carl Palmer of Atomic Rooster was their choice, and so was formed Emerson, Lake & Palmer—ELP for short.

*Works, Vol. 1* [their most recent album] has been the subject of much talk among the followers of ELP, because of the extensive use of an orchestra throughout the album. Many feel that the band is smothered behind the lavish strings and brass, while others find those elements pleasant additions to the ELP sound. Another radical move on the album was Emerson's forsaking his Hammond organ and modular Moog synthesizer, the latter of which he had been the first to use in a live performance situation. Instead he chose to use Yamaha's mammoth $50,000 polyphonic synthesizer, the GX-1, and a Steinway grand piano.

In the early spring of 1977, the group mounted a tour which included a 59-piece orchestra, 6 vocalists, 19 technicians, 6 roadies, and others, for a total of 115 people. It was the largest touring production ever attempted in a rock context. However, by mid-summer the group was forced to drop the orchestra for financial reasons.

---

*Source:* Domenic Milano, "Keith Emerson," *Contemporary Keyboard* (October 1977), pp. 22–25, 30.

*How do you go about re-arranging tunes by classical composers?*

I sit down with the score. As far as Aaron Copland's "Fanfare for the Common Man," on
    *Works*, goes, it needed transposing, so I did that first. I wanted to improvise in a key
    that was sort of bluesy. It ended up in *E*. The rest of it was straightforward, really. You
    know, in order to get the shuffle sound, the timing needed to be changed, but it was
    common sense.

*What about earlier things like "The Barbarian"?*

That was taken from Bartok's *Allegro Barbaro*. There were a few timing things that needed to
    be changed to fit what we were doing there. Ginastera's *First Piano Concerto*, fourth
    movement, which we called "Toccata" on *Brain Salad Surgery*, was about the most
    complicated piece we did. I had to go through the whole thing and condense it, to bring
    out the parts of it that I thought were the most important. Of course, we couldn't do it
    exactly the way Ginastera had written it because all of it uses the whole keyboard on
    the piano. So those bits I got the synthesizer to do. Ginastera loved it when I took it
    along to him. He made some comment that that was exactly how his music should al-
    ways sound. And the same with Copland. In fact, I've got a tape of what Copland
    thinks of our version of "Fanfare for the Common Man." [*Ed. Note:* For a transcription
    of that tape see page 286.] This always pleases me, because I don't want to adulterate
    the music or anything.

*How do you orchestrate your keyboard parts?*

You mean what music is to played on what instrument? I don't know. I invariably start with
    the piano. From there on it'll go out either to the organ or to another instrument. It de-
    pends on how it sounds and on what the original intention is for the piece. If I'm pretty
    convinced it is going to be, say, a piano concerto, or it's going to be for ELP, then that
    will determine what instruments I'll use. Sometimes I've got that in mind before I start.
    I swap around for variety. I may have been playing one line on the organ for a long time
    and just by way of a change I'll play it on the Yamaha.

*Where did your interest in arranging other people's music come from?*

Simple reason—I like the tunes. I want to play these tunes, but I want to play them in a way
    that's acceptable to our audience. And stimulate new interest in the original. You know
    I started doing this back in the Sixties, and that was my intention. But obviously since
    that time, audiences have become far more perceptive—intelligent. One doesn't really
    have to do that now. I think people are going for classical music as much as for any
    other form. You wouldn't have had your Chick Coreas five years ago. Chick Corea
    doesn't have to really dress up in blazer gear to get a wide following. It just goes to
    show you that it's not a question of image these days. It's more a question of the actual
    music. So I don't mean to be insulting the public's intelligence by saying the reason I'm
    playing "Fanfare for the Common Man" is because I want them to listen to the original.
    That may have been the case six years ago, but since then it's become part of what peo-
    ple expect of me. I still occasionally enjoy other people's music. If a piece comes out
    which lends itself to a particular situation, a particular meter, then I use it. If it doesn't,
    I don't force the issue. My music has been tagged with the label "classical rock," which
    I guess is okay. Broadly speaking, I guess that's true, but it's not a term that I want to
    really like.

*What would you call it?*

I guess it *is* classical rock [laughs], mainly because I can't think of anything else to call it. It's
    playing classical music with a definite meter behind it. That sounds nicer. It's like call-
    ing a guy who collects rubbish a waste disposal officer instead of a dustman. It sounds

far more polite. Like, how would you term what you call your music? I call it playing classical music with the focus on the meter, a straight, rigid meter—one that's different from what the composer originally intended. Or, rudely speaking, dustman—classical rock.

*What made you want to write a piano concerto?*
I said, "Look, I'm gonna write a piano concerto. That's my biggest wish." And I went to John Mayer for technical advice. He said, "Fine. What form would you like it to be in?" And I said, "Sonata form." And we went from there. He'd tell me what I need here and there and this is what has to come next to make it work. It's all instinctive with me. Often there were times he'd say, "Well, look. It's stuck. We have to . . . *You* have to make a movement there that's fast." And I'd invariably come up with something on the spot. We always worked together, either at my house or at his. Then I'd be listening to it and it just seemed to work. And he'd say, "Well, of course it works, because. . . ." And then he'd reel off the formula for why it worked.

*Can you play just about anything you can hear?*
No. I mean the "Fugue" on the *Trilogy* album was literally written out on paper before I ever played it. I couldn't work a fugue any other way. Some people are very clever and can improvise them. It's great to be able to do that. But as for me, I have to write it down, look at it, and work it out. I don't write things that are easy for me. Everything that I write is a new step forward. Sometimes I hear it in the back of my mind and know the effect that I want, but I can't get it. I work at it for days and days and days.

*Do you write out all of the music for the band to learn?*
Now I do in order to get the orchestrations down, but the earlier stuff like *Tarkus* wasn't written out. I'm very aware of what Carl and Greg like to do, and in the case of *Tarkus* Carl was very struck by different time signatures. He told me that he'd like to do something in 5/4, so I said I'd keep that in mind and started writing *Tarkus* from there. Greg wasn't too sure about it at the beginning. It was too weird. But he agreed to try it, and afterwards he loved it. Listening back to those things, I think they just scratch the surface. It moves too quickly from one idea to another. One thing I manage to do now is expand more on an idea. I get more out of it than doing just little bits and pieces. I think if I did *Tarkus* again today, I'd orchestrate it and it would sound marvelous.

# Aaron Copland on the ELP Version of "Fanfare for the Common Man"

"Of course it's very flattering to have one's music adapted by so popular a group as Emerson, Lake & Palmer. A lot depends on what they do with what they take. And naturally, since I have a copyright on the material, they're not able to take it without my permission. In each case where I have given my permission there was something that attracted me about the version that they perform which made me think I'd allow them to release it. Of course, I always prefer my own version, but what they do is really *around* the piece, I'd say, rather than a literal transposition of the piece. They're a gifted group. In that particular case I allowed it to go by because when they first play the "Fanfare," they play it fairly straight, and when they end the piece they play it fairly straight. What they do in the middle—I'm not sure how they connect that to my music, but they do it somehow, I suppose. But the fact that at the beginning and at the end it is 'Fanfare for the Common Man' gave me the feeling I ought to allow them to do with it as they please."

These excerpts from interviews with the members of Yes discuss two of their best-known recordings: the single "Roundabout" (1971) and the album *Close to the Edge*. Of particular interest here is Yes's ad hoc process of assembling their most ambitious tracks, which turn out to result from an extensive trial-and-error method of collective composition, rather than from the master plan of a single composer (as in the writing of art music).[5]

## *from* YESSTORIES: YES IN THEIR OWN WORDS
### *Tim Morse*

## "Roundabout"

**Steve [Howe, guitarist] (1987):**   When we recorded "Roundabout" we thought we had made one of the all-time epics. Jon Anderson and I wrote that in Scotland. It was originally a guitar instrumental suite. You see, I sort of write a song without a song. All the ingredients are there—all that's missing is the song. "Roundabout" was a bit like that; there was a structure, a melody and a few lines. When the Americans wanted us to edit it for a single we thought it was sacrilege. Here the song was so well-constructed and quite over the top—but in the end we did have to edit it. The song did very well. In fact Jon and I won an award for it in 1972.

**Jon [Anderson, vocalist] (1989):**   We were traveling from Aberdeen through to Glasgow and we'd started this song . . . me and Steve were singing it in the back of the van on the way down. One of the things you'll drive through is a very winding small road that goes through this incredible valley and the mountains are sheer from both sides of the road—they just climb to the sky. And because it was a cloudy day, we couldn't see the top of the mountains. We could only see the clouds because it was sheer straight up. . . . I remember saying, "Oh, the mountains—look! They're coming out of the sky!" So we wrote that down: Mountains come out of the sky and they stand there. And we came to a roundabout right at the bottom of this road and within twenty-four hours we were back in London. We'd been on tour then for about a month. So it was sort of twenty-four hours before I'll be home with my loved one, Jennifer. So the idea as twenty-four before my love and I'll be there with you. In around the lake—just before you get to Glasgow there's a lake—a very famous one—the Loch Ness. So we were driving in around the lake—mountains come out of the sky—they stand there.

**Steve (1982):**   [The intro is] the easiest thing in the world to play. I could show anybody and they could play it. But because of sound and the intensity, so nice and strong . . . that in itself is a different kind of connection. It's not that the music or musical idea is that good. It's the come-on, the intensity. One of the secret ingredients of Yes wasn't only the sort of

---

5. For more on *Close to the Edge*, see John Covach, "Progressive Rock, 'Close to the Edge,' and the Boundaries of Style," in John Covach and Graeme M. Boone, eds., *Understanding Rock: Essays in Musical Analysis* (New York: Oxford University Press, 1997).

*Source:* Tim Morse, from *Yesstories: Yes in Their Own Words* (New York: St. Martin's Press, 1996), pp. 28–29, 33–37. Copyright © 1996 by Tim Morse. Reprinted by permission of St. Martin's Press, LLC.

material we were using, it was the intensity of the color. Maybe the beginning of "Round-about" without the backward piano wouldn't have been so dramatic. People don't even know it's a backward piano, all they hear is "mmmmmweeng!" But it really intensified that idea and I think that's a good side to the music that I have been involved in.

**Chris [Squire, bassist] (1994):**   I overdubbed my entire part an octave higher on one of Steve's old Gibson hollow-body jazz guitars. We just miked it acoustically and mixed it in with the bass. That's what gave the part such a bright sound.

(1985): "Roundabout" was done in a series of edits. That was the time when we started getting into that idea. Although we'd already played the song in rehearsal, we'd go in the studio and get the first two verses really good.

**Jon (1989):**   We always tried to make sure we had a lot of harmony. Me, Steve, and Chris singing together had a certain texture and we worked on that all the way through that period of time. And the strong melody [was] sometimes very, very simple. On the end of "Roundabout" we sing "Da-da-da-da-duh-duh-da" a very simple melody repeated eight times. Over that there's another melody "Ba-ba-ba" . . . "Three Blind Mice!"

## Close to the Edge

*Released September 1972*

This is considered by many to be the definitive Yes album. Everything the band was trying to do was uniquely realized on this recording, so that even now it sounds as fresh as the day it came out. It was a very successful and progressive release at the time, featuring just three songs: the celestial "And You and I," the fiery "Siberian Khatru," and their first masterpiece epic, "Close to the Edge."

The making of this record was not without the loss of some blood in the process. After the laborious rehearsals and endless late nights at Advision Studios, Bill Bruford decided to leave Yes when the album was completed, to join King Crimson. His decision left his band mates in shock and desperate because an American tour was to start within a week. (Bruford did offer to do the tour, but the band decided to try to find someone else.) Luckily for the group, Alan White (of the Plastic Ono Band) agreed to climb up the drum riser and he has been with them ever since.

**Bill [Bruford, drummer] (1989):**   *Close to the Edge* had a sense of discovery for us—and presumably for the people who bought it. I'm sure it sounds trite now, but in those days it was quite a big deal. Rock musicians hadn't been capable of an arrangement of any kind of complexity at all. But now I find it's fundamentally good music, its form, its shape are timeless.

**Jon (1992):**   *Close to the Edge* is close to the edge of realization, of self-realization, that's what the theme was all about. It was based on a book I'd read called *Siddhartha* by Hermann Hesse. So there we were on the edge of learning about our potential as artists, as musicians, in order to jump into a new world of music. That's what *Close to the Edge* was all about and it did push us in a direct fashion into the limelight, one could say, of total progressive music. To the point where today, we can perform nearly twenty years later "And You and I" and it has more power now than it ever had. It's a remarkable piece of music, as though it was crafted by the heavens and we were just the vehicles to pull it together.

**Bill (1992):**   If we'd known how horrible it was going to be, we would have never done it. But it's like five guys trying to write a novel at the same time. One guy has a good begin-ning and the second guy had quite a good middle and the third guy thinks he knows what the ending is, but the fourth guy doesn't like the way the middle goes towards the ending, and the second guy who used to like the third section has changed his mind and now likes the first section.

It was torture. None of these arrangements were written and they weren't really composed. We all sat in the rehearsal room and said, "Let's have the G after the G#." And every instrument was up for democratic election, you know and everyone had to run an election campaign on every issue. And it was horrible. I mean it was incredibly unpleasant and unbelievably hard work. And Squire was always late for every rehearsal. And after about two months of this unbelievable punishment, people still say to me, "Bill, why didn't you do another one?"

People always imagine that there was this carefully structured plan. Like they do with King Crimson, they always imagine Robert Fripp enters the room and scowls at everybody and lays out sheet music, which of course is the exact opposite. And they always think that Jon Anderson somehow knew how *Close to the Edge* was going to be right from the beginning to the end. [Which is] not true at all . . . it was kind of a shambles from beginning to end, the whole thing. It was a miracle that we managed to make anything of this stuff. If we'd actually find a rehearsal room, could we actually get to it? Would Squire turn up? Would we have enough equipment to do it with? Was anyone starving? Was the band about to run out of money?

We were well served in all of this by having the ability to tape-edit. And having Eddie Offord, who would slash a two-inch master tape without even thinking about it and just glue another bit onto it. Tape editing was fundamental to this band creating this music at all. Because we couldn't play any of it through until we'd learned it. We'd play a thirty-second segment and say, "What happens now?" We'd stop the tape and write another thirty-second segment. It would go on like that, [like] climbing Mount Everest.

**Steve (1991):**   We had to hang on to our ideas and develop and arrange them and try not to forget them the next day. Because sometimes we would come in and say, "God, what did we do to this?" Many classic Yes bits of arranging have gone out the window. We actually forgot them. They were too intricate, too specialized, or one guy was the key to it and he was the guy who didn't remember it the next day. So obviously we taped things and started to have tapes of rehearsals going on all the time.

## "Close to the Edge"

**Chris (1995):**   I think it was Jon's idea to open the song with the sound effects. He got hold of a bunch of those environmental tapes and I think that's why it appeared there.

**Jon (1976):**   The lyrical content became a kind of dream sequence in a way. The end verse is a dream that I had a long time ago about passing on from this world to another world, yet feeling so fantastic about it that death never frightened me ever since. I think in the early days when I was very small I used to be frightened of this idea of not being here—where else can there be if there isn't "here"? And it just seemed a matter of course that death being such a beautiful experience for a man physically to go through as being born is. That's what seemed to come out in this song, that it was a very pastoral kind of experience rather than a very frightening and "Oh gosh, I don't want to die" kind of thing.

(1973): There are several lines that relate to the church. Churchgoers are always fighting about who's better and who's richer and who's more hip. So at the end of the middle section there's a majestic church organ. We destroy the church organ through the Moog. This leads to another organ solo rejoicing in the fact that you can turn your back on churches and find it within yourself to be your own church.

**Bill (1994):**   The thing about "Close to the Edge" is the form, I think. The shape of it is perfect. It's a real little part of history and it just fit on the side of an album perfectly. Again as we were making that I don't think anyone really knew how we were going to finish it. It felt like we were going on and on adding section after section. Lots of music in different meters and things without anybody really knowing what the conclusion to this piece of music would be. I don't think we had any idea of its length and I don't think we said, "Oh! Let's make this the side of an album." The other thing I remember was everybody saying that Simon and Garfunkel had spent three months on "Bridge Over Troubled Water" and that seemed like a record that needed to be smashed. (TMI)

# 60. Jazz Fusion

The paths of jazz and popular music in general (and rock music in particular) have crossed, intertwined, and diverged continuously. During the Swing Era, popular music and jazz overlapped considerably, and both before and after that the lines have often been murky. While the connections between jazz and pop weakened with the onset of rock 'n' roll in the 1950s, entries in earlier chapters of this book have shown how many of the musicians who played in rhythm and blues and early rock 'n' roll sessions were equally at home playing jazz. In the 1960s, Motown's famous studio band preferred to play jazz, and jazz (via John Coltrane, in particular) had a major influence on the development of psychedelic rock. Furthermore, jazz musicians, such as Cannonball Adderly, continued to chart hits well into the 1960s with recordings like "Mercy, Mercy, Mercy" (1966).[1]

However, by the late 1960s the commercial plight of jazz musicians had worsened, and even the occasional "soul-jazz" hit became increasingly rare. Avant-garde jazz, which had been viewed by the critical establishment as the next big thing, but which had failed to find a significant audience, had coincided with the massive expansion of the popular music audience in the mid-1960s, as rock and soul began to lay claim to the serious contemplation previously reserved for jazz and classical music. Many jazz musicians, frustrated by the club scene and inspired by the new complexity in recent soul and rock, decided to embrace

---

1. See David H. Rosenthal, *Hard Bop: Jazz and Black Music, 1955–1965* (New York: Oxford University Press, 1992).

electronic amplification and instruments, as well as funk-influenced rhythms and timbres. In other cases, musicians simply continued to re-fine the "funky" or "soul jazz" that they had been playing since the 1950s.

A leader in this new development, as he had been in several earlier transformations in jazz, was Miles Davis (1926–91). The furor created by Davis's use of electric guitars and pianos, of echo effects on his trumpet, and of funk-based polyrhythms has not completely subsided to this day—many jazz critics and historians remain reluctant to classify this music as "jazz."[2]

A discussion of "jazz fusion" or "jazz rock" would not be complete without noting the number of other ways that jazz intersected with popular music in the 1970s: from the smooth, sophisticated rock of Steely Dan; to the "psychedelic" group improvisations of the Grateful Dead (some of which sound remarkably close to Davis's recordings); to the instrumental jazz-flavored tracks on Jeff Beck's *Blow by Blow* (1975); to Joni Mitchell's work with jazz musicians; to groups with prominent horn arrangements, such as Blood, Sweat, and Tears and Chicago, inter-est in jazz among rock musicians was widespread. And this does not even touch on the ongoing interconnections between jazz and R&B, perhaps most obvious in an artist like Stevie Wonder (who continued to develop new wrinkles in recordings like the jazz-rock fusion "Contusion" from *Songs in the Key of Life* [1976]), but also a fundamental element in funk and even in ballads, such as Billy Paul's "Me and Mrs. Jones" (1972). When artists like Miles Davis and Herbie Hancock started playing to young audiences, the influence of jazz came full circle.[3]

In the following passage from his autobiography, Miles Davis reflects on his early fusion recordings. A phenomenal number of the musicians in-volved in these sessions (or who played with Davis immediately prior to them) eventually became some of the most celebrated and well-known exponents of the style: Herbie Hancock, with the jazz-funk Headhunters (which also included Bernie Maupin, another participant in Davis's ses-sions); Chick Corea with Return to Forever, initially a Latin-influenced band, which then developed a fusion of jazz and progressive rock; Wayne Shorter and Joe Zawinul with Weather Report; Tony Williams with Life-time; John McLaughlin with the Mahavishnu Orchestra and later with

2. For an example of two opposing views on the subject, see the exchange between Wynton Marsalis and Herbie Hancock in Rafi Zabor and Vic Garbarini, "Wynton vs. Herbie: The Purist and the Cross-breeder Duke It Out," *Musician* 77 (March 1985): 52–64; reprinted in Robert Walser, ed., *Keeping Time: Readings in Jazz History* (New York: Oxford University Press, 1999), 339–51.

3. For one of the most informative and entertaining essays on Miles Davis's recordings during this era, see Greg Tate, "The Electric Miles," *Flyboy in the Buttermilk Essays on Contemporary America* (New York: Fireside/Simon and Schuster, 1992), 68–85 (originally published in 1983).

Shakti; Keith Jarrett; Dave Holland; Jack DeJohnette, and others. Davis's
reputation and popularity called attention to the first two albums featuring this fusion style, *In a Silent Way* and *Bitches' Brew* (both 1969), both
of which featured long, loosely structured group improvisations over a
funky groove. By 1972's *On the Corner*, Davis had moved to more jagged,
fractured, dissonant funk. Davis talks about the influence on him of
James Brown, Jimi Hendrix, and Sly Stone and how his change in style
eventually led to his playing large, rock-associated venues, such as the
Fillmore auditoriums.

## *from* MILES: THE AUTOBIOGRAPHY
### Miles Davis (with Quincy Troupe)

1968 was full of all kinds of changes, but for me, the changes that were happening in my
music were very exciting and the music that was happening everywhere was incredible.
These things were leading me into the future and into *In a Silent Way.*

A lot of things were changing in music around 1967 and 1968 and a lot of new shit was
happening. One of them was the music of Charles Lloyd, who had become very popular.
When his band was really happening he had Jack DeJohnette and a young piano player
named Keith Jarrett. He was the leader, but it was those two guys who were making the
music really happen. They were playing a cross between jazz and rock, very rhythmic
music. Charles never was any kind of player, but he had a certain sound on the saxophone
that was kind of light and floating and worked with what Keith and Jack were putting
under and around it. His music was very popular for a couple of years and so a lot of people started paying attention. Our two groups shared a bill at the Village Gate at the end of
1967 or early 1968. Man, the place was packed. I knew Jack from when he filled in for Tony,
and when Charles's group was in town I would go over and listen. He started accusing me
of trying to steal his musicians from him. Charles didn't stay around for too long but made
a lot of money during the time he was hot. I hear he's rich and selling real estate today, so
more power to him.

The music I was really listening to in 1968 was James Brown, the great guitar player
Jimi Hendrix, and a new group who had just come out with the hit record, "Dance to the
Music," Sly and the Family Stone, led by Sly Stewart, from San Francisco. The shit he was
doing was badder than a motherfucker, had all kinds of funky shit up in it. But it was Jimi
Hendrix that I first got into when Betty Mabry [Davis's wife and a singer and songwriter in
her own right] turned me on to him.

I first met Jimi when his manager called up and wanted me to introduce him to the way
I was playing and putting my music together. Jimi liked what I had done on *Kind of Blue* and
some other stuff and wanted to add more jazz elements to what he was doing. He liked the
way Coltrane played with all those sheets of sound, and he played the guitar in a similar
way. Plus, he said he had heard the guitar voicing that I used in the way I played the

*Source:* Miles Davis with Quincy Troupe, from *Miles: The Autobiography* (New York: Simon & Schuster,
1989), pp. 291–300, 321–22. Reprinted with permission of Simon & Schuster Adult Publishing Group
from *Miles: The Autobiography* by Miles Davis with Quincy Troupe. Copyright © 1989 by Miles Davis.

trumpet. So we started getting together. Betty really liked this music—and later, I found out, she liked him physically, too—and so he started to come around.

So that's the way my head was as far as music was going. First, I had to be comfortable with what I was going to be playing. Then, I had to find the right musicians. It was a process of playing with different people and picking my way forward. I spent time listening to and feeling what certain people could play and give, and what they couldn't, and picking and choosing the ones who would fit, and eliminating the ones who wouldn't. People eliminate themselves when there's nothing happening—or they should.

The group [Davis's working band] disbanded sometime in late 1968. We continued to play gigs and sometimes made some concerts together—at least Herbie [Hancock], Wayne [Shorter], Tony [Williams], and I did—but for all intents and purposes the group broke up when Ron [Carter] decided to leave for good because he didn't want to play electric bass. Herbie had already recorded "Watermelon Man" and wanted to form a group of his own. Tony felt the same way. So they both left the group at the end of 1968. Wayne stayed with me a couple of years longer.

It had been a great learning experience for everyone. Bands don't stay together for ever and ever, and although it was hard for me when they left me, it was really time for all of us to move on. We left each other in a positive place and that's all you can ask for.

The changes in my band started happening in July 1968 when I replaced Ron Carter on bass with Miroslav Vitous, a young bass player from Czechoslovakia. (Ron still made a couple more studio dates with me, but he quit the working band that made club dates.) Miroslav was only a temporary replacement until I got Dave Holland. I had seen and heard Dave in June 1968, when I played a concert over in England, and he knocked me out. Since I knew Ron was going to be leaving soon I talked with Dave about joining my band. He had other commitments, so when he was through with those at the end of July, I called him in London and asked him to join us. He came over and opened with us when we played Count Basie's club up in Harlem. My interest was in finding an electronic bass player because of the sound it added to my band. I was still on the lookout for someone who would eventually play that instrument all the time in my band, because I didn't know then if Dave would want to switch to playing that instrument. But for the time being he could replace Ron on gigs I had lined up, and we could cross the other bridge when we came to it.

I had also started using both Chick Corea and Joe Zawinul on piano in some of my studio recording dates that year. I would have three piano players on some of those dates—Herbie, Joe, and Chick. On a couple of those dates I used two bass players—Ron and Dave. I also started using Jack DeJohnette on drums sometimes instead of Tony Williams, and started putting "Directions in Music by Miles Davis" on the front of my album covers so that nobody could be mistaken about *who* was the creative control behind the music. . . . I was moving more and more to using electronic instruments to make up the sound that I wanted, and I felt that saying "Directions in Music by Miles Davis" would indicate that.

I had heard Joe Zawinul playing electric piano on "Mercy, Mercy, Mercy" with Cannonball Adderley, and I really liked the sound of the instrument and wanted it in my band. Chick Corea began playing the electric Fender Rhodes piano when he started playing with me, and so did Herbie Hancock, who liked playing the Rhodes right away after he got into it; Herbie always liked electronic gadgets anyway. So he took to the Rhodes like a fish to water. But Chick wasn't sure about playing it when he first came with me, but I *made* him play it. He didn't like me telling him what instrument to play until he really got into it but then he really liked it, too, and made his reputation playing it.

See, the Fender Rhodes has one sound and that sound is itself. It has no other sound. You always know what it is. I'm crazy about the way Gil Evans voices his music, so I wanted to get me a Gil Evans sound in a small band. That required an instrument like the synthesizer, which can get all those different instrumental sounds. I could hear that you could write a bass line with the voicings that Gil did with his big band. We could get some harmony on top with the synthesizer, and that makes the whole band sound fuller. Then you double the bass when you double that; it works better than if you had a regular piano. After I got this into my head and saw how that affected the music I was doing, I didn't need a piano anymore. It didn't have nothing to do with me just wanting to go electric, like a lot of people have said, just to be having some electrical shit up in my band. I just wanted that kind of voicing a Fender Rhodes could give me that a regular piano couldn't. The same thing for the electric bass; it gave me what I wanted to hear at the time instead of the stand-up bass. Musicians have to play the instruments that best reflect the times we're in, play the technology that will give you what you want to hear. All these purists are walking around talking about how electrical instruments will ruin music. Bad music is what will ruin music, not the instruments musicians choose to play. I don't see nothing wrong with electrical instruments as long as you get great musicians who will play them right.

After Herbie left the working band in August of 1968, Chick Corea took his place. I think Tony Williams hipped me to him because they both were from Boston, and Tony knew him from up there. He had worked with Stan Getz, and when I called him to work with me he was working with Sarah Vaughan. Around the first of the year of 1969, Jack DeJohnette replaced Tony on drums, so we had a new band except for me and Wayne (although Herbie and Tony would keep making record dates with me).

In February 1969 we went into the studio: Wayne, Chick, Herbie, Dave, Tony instead of Jack on drums (because I wanted Tony's sound), Joe Zawinul, and I added a guitarist, another young Englishman, named John McLaughlin, who had come over here to join Tony Williams's new group, Lifetime (it had Larry Young on organ). Dave Holland had introduced Tony and me to John when we were over in England where we first heard him. Then Dave loaned Tony a tape of John playing, and Tony let me hear it. I heard him play with Tony up at Count Basie's and he was a motherfucker, so I asked him to make the date. He told me had been listening to me for a long time and that he might be nervous going into the studio with one of his idols. So I told him, "Just relax and play like you did up at Count Basie's and everything will be all right." And he did.

This was the *In a Silent Way* recording session. I had called Joe Zawinul and told him to bring some music to the studio because I loved his compositions. He brought me a tune called "In a Silent Way," and it became the album's title tune. (The other two tunes on the album are mine.) I had recorded some of Joe's other tunes like "Ascent" and "Directions" in the November 1968 recording sessions we did together. "Ascent" was a tone poem very similar to "In a Silent Way," only it wasn't as compelling. When Joe brought "In a Silent Way," I saw what he was doing, only this time he had put it together better. (With the tunes I wrote for the November 1968 session, like "Splash," you can hear that I'm moving toward a more rhythmic, blues-funk sound.)

We changed what Joe had written on "In a Silent Way." Cut down all the chords and took his melody and used that. I wanted to make the sound more like rock. In rehearsals we played it like Joe had written it, but it wasn't working for me because all the chords were cluttering it up. I could hear that the melody that Joe had written—which was hidden by all the other clutter—was really beautiful. When we recorded I just threw out the chord sheets and told everyone to play just the melody, just to play off that. They were surprised to be working in this way, but I knew from when I had brought in music that nobody had ever heard for *Kind of Blue* that if you've got some great musicians—and we did, both then and now—they will deal with the situation and play beyond what is there and above where they think they can. That's what I did with *In a Silent Way*, and the music on there came out beautiful and fresh.

Joe never did like what I did with his composition, and I don't think he likes it even today. But it worked and that's all that really matters. Today many people consider Joe's tune a classic and the beginning of fusion. If I had left that tune the way Joe had it, I don't think it would have been praised the way it was after the album came out. *In a Silent Way* was a collaborative thing that Joe and I did. Some people don't like the way I work. Some musicians feel sometimes I don't give them enough credit. But I have always tried to credit people who did things for me. People were walking around mad because I took credit for arranging *In a Silent Way*, but I *did* arrange the music by changing it like I did.

After we finished *In a Silent Way*, I took the band out on the road; Wayne, Dave, Chick, and Jack DeJohnette were now my working band. Man, I wish this band had been recorded live because it was really a bad motherfucker. I think Chick Corea and a few other people recorded some of our performances live, but Columbia missed out on the whole fucking thing.

We toured through the spring and up until August, when we went back into the studio again and recorded *Bitches Brew*.

Nineteen sixty-nine was the year rock and funk were selling like hotcakes and this was put on display at Woodstock. There were over 400,000 people at the concert. That many people at a concert makes everybody go crazy, and especially people who make records. The only thing on their minds is, How can we sell records to that many people all the time? If we haven't been doing that, then how can we do it?

That was the atmosphere all around the record companies. At the same time, people were packing stadiums to hear and see stars in person. And jazz music seemed to be withering on the vine, in record sales and live performances. It was the first time in a long time that I didn't sell out crowds everywhere I played. In Europe I always had sellouts, but in the United States, we played to a lot of half-empty clubs in 1969. That told me something. Compared to what my records used to sell, when you put them beside what Bob Dylan or Sly Stone sold, it was no contest. Their sales had gone through the roof. Clive Davis was the president of Columbia Records and he signed Blood, Sweat and Tears in 1968 and a group called Chicago in 1969. He was trying to take Columbia into the future and pull in all those young record buyers. After a rough start he and I got along well, because he thinks like an artist instead of a straight businessman. He had a good sense for what was happening; I thought he was a great man.

He started talking to me about trying to reach this younger market and about changing. He suggested that the way for me to reach this new audience was to play my music where they went, places like the Fillmore. The first time we had a conversation I got mad with him because I thought he was putting down *me* and all the things I had done for Columbia. I hung up on him after telling him I was going to find another record company to record for. But they wouldn't give me a release. After we went back and forth in these arguments for a while, everything finally cooled down and we got all right again. For a while, I was thinking about going over to Motown Records, because I liked what they were doing and figured that they could understand what I was trying to do better.

What Clive really didn't like was that the agreement I had with Columbia allowed me to get advances against royalties earned, so whenever I needed money, I would call up and get an advance. Clive felt that I wasn't making enough money for the company to be giving me this type of treatment. Maybe he was right, now that I'm looking back on all of it, but right from a strictly business proposition, not an artistic one. I felt that Columbia should live up to what they had agreed to. They thought that since I sold around 60,000 albums every time I put out a record—which was enough for them before the new thing came around—that wasn't enough to keep on giving me money.

So this was the climate with Columbia and me just before I went into the studio to record *Bitches Brew*. What they didn't understand was that I wasn't prepared to be a memory yet, wasn't prepared to be listed only on Columbia's so-called classical list. I had seen the future with my music, and I was going for it like I had always done. Not for Columbia and their record sales, and not for trying to get to some young white record buyers. I was going for it for myself, for what I wanted and needed in my own music. *I* wanted to change course, *had* to change course for me to continue to believe in and love what I was playing.

When I went into the studio in August 1969, besides listening to rock music and funk, I had been listening to Joe Zawinul and Cannonball playing shit like "Country Joe and the Preacher." . . . I had been experimenting with writing a few simple chord changes for three pianos. Simple shit, and it was funny because I used to think when I was doing them how Stravinsky went back to simple forms. So I had been writing these things down, like one beat chord and a bass line, and I found out that the more we played it, it was always different. I would write a chord, a rest, maybe another chord, and it turned out that the more it was played, the more it just kept getting different. This started happening in 1968 when I had Chick, Joe, and Herbie for those studio dates. It went on into the sessions we had for *In a Silent Way.* Then I started thinking about something larger, a skeleton of a piece. I would write a chord on two beats and they'd have two beats out. So they would do one, two, three, da-dum right? Then I put the accent on the fourth beat. Maybe I had three chords on the first bar. Anyway, I told the musicians that they could do anything they wanted, play anything they heard but that I had to have this, what they did, as a chord. Then they knew what they could do, so that's what they did. Played off that chord, and it made it sound like a whole lot of stuff.

I told them that at rehearsals and then I brought in these musical sketches that nobody had seen, just like I did on *Kind of Blue* and *In a Silent Way.* We started early in the day in Columbia's studio on 52nd Street and recorded all day for three days in August. I had told Teo Macero, who was producing the record, to just let the tapes run and get everything we played, told him to get *everything* and not to be coming in interrupting, asking questions. "Just stay in the booth and worry about getting down the sound," is what I told him. And he did, didn't fuck with us once and got down everything, got it down real good.

So I would direct, like a conductor, once we started to play, and I would either write down some music for somebody or I would tell him to play different things I was hearing, as the music was growing, coming together. It was loose and tight at the same time. It was casual but alert, everybody was alert to different possibilities that were coming up in the music. While the music was developing I would hear something that I thought could be extended or cut back. So that recording was a development of the creative process, a living composition. It was like a fugue, or motif, that we all bounced off of. After it had developed to a certain point, I would tell a certain musician to come in and play something else, like Benny Maupin on bass clarinet. I wish I had thought of video taping that whole session because it must have been something and I would have liked to have been able to see just what went down, like a football or basketball instant replay. Sometimes, instead of just letting the tape run, I would tell Teo to back it up so I cold hear what we had done. If I wanted something else in a certain spot, I would just bring the musician in, and we would just do it.

That was a great recording session, man, and we didn't have any problems as I can remember. It was just like one of them old-time jam sessions we used to have up at Minton's back in the old bebop days. Everybody was excited when we all left there each day.

Some people have written that doing *Bitches Brew* was Clive Davis's or Teo Macero's idea. That's a lie, because they didn't have nothing to do with none of it. Again, it was white people trying to give some credit to other white people where it wasn't deserved because the record became a breakthrough concept, very innovative. They were going to rewrite history after the fact like they always do.

What we did on *Bitches Brew* you couldn't ever write down for an orchestra to play. That's why I didn't write it all out, not because I didn't know what I wanted; I knew that what I wanted would come out of a process and not some prearranged shit. This session was about improvisation, and that's what makes jazz so fabulous. Any time the weather changes it's going to change your whole attitude about something, and so a musician will play differently, especially if everything is not put in front of him. A musician's attitude *is* the music he plays. Like in California, out by the beach, you have silence and the sound of waves crashing against the shore. In New York you're dealing with the sounds of cars honking their horns and people on the streets running their mouths and shit like that. Hardly ever in California do you hear people talking on the streets. California is mellow, it's about sunshine and exercise and beautiful women on the beaches showing off their bad-ass bodies and fine, long legs. People there have color in their skin because they go out in the sun all the time. People in New York go out but it's a different thing, it's an inside thing. California is an outside thing and the music that comes out of there reflects that open space and freeways, shit you don't hear in music that comes out of New York, which is usually more intense and energetic.

I was getting interested in seeing the black sound develop and that's where my head was moving toward, more rhythmic stuff, more funk rather than white rock. I had met Sly and he had given me one of his albums; I liked it. He also gave me that album of Rudy Ray Moore's, who was a real funny comedian back then, raunchy, you know, out there. The people at Columbia who own Epic—the label Sly was on—wanted to see if I could get Sly to record quicker. But Sly had his own way of writing music. He got his inspiration from the people in his group. When he wrote something he would write the music to be played live, rather than for a studio. After he got big he always had all these people around his house and at his recording sessions. I went to a couple and there were nothing but girls everywhere and coke, bodyguards with guns, looking all evil. I told him I couldn't do nothing with him—told Columbia I couldn't make him record any quicker. We snorted some coke together and that was it.

But when I first heard Sly, I almost wore out those first two or three records, "Dance to the Music," "Stand," and "Everybody Is a Star." I told Ralph Gleason, "Listen to this. Man, if you know a promoter you better get him to get Sly, because he's something else, Ralph." This was before Sly got real big. Then he wrote a couple of other great things, and then he didn't write nothing because the coke had fucked him up, and he wasn't a trained musician.

It was with Sly Stone and James Brown in mind that I went into the studio in June 1972 to record *On the Corner*. During that time everyone was dressing kind of "out street," you know, platform shoes that were yellow, and electric yellow at that; handkerchiefs around the neck, headbands, rawhide vests, and so on. Black women were wearing them real tight dresses that had their big butts sticking way out in the back. Everyone was listening to Sly and James Brown and trying at the same time to be cool like me. I was my own model, with a little bit of Sly and James Brown and the Last Poets. I wanted to videotape people coming into a concert who were wearing all those types of clothes, especially black people. I wanted to see all those different kinds of outfits and the women trying to hide them big bad asses, trying to tuck them in.

I had gotten into the musical theories of Karlheniz Stockhausen, a German avant-garde composer, and an English composer who I had met in London in 1969, Paul Buckmaster. I was into both of them before I did *On the Corner* and, as a matter of fact, Paul stayed with me during the time I was recording. He was also in the studio. Paul was into Bach and so I started paying attention to Bach while Paul was around. I had begun to realize that some of the things Ornette Coleman had said about things being played three or four ways, independently of each other, were true because Bach had also composed that way. And it could be real funky and down. What I was playing on *On the Corner* had no label, although people thought it was funk because they didn't know what else to call it. It was actually a combination of some of the concepts of Paul Buckmaster, Sly Stone, James Brown, and Stockhausen, some of the concepts I had absorbed from Ornette's music, as well as my own. The music was about spacing, about free association of musical ideas to a core kind of rhythm and vamps of the bass line. I liked the way Paul Buckmaster used rhythm and space; the same thing with Stockhausen.

# 61. Get On Up Disco

From an underground phenomenon at the outset of the 1970s, disco grew to dominate popular music by the end of the decade. In its heyday, "disco" referred to at least three distinct phenomena: a musical style, a performance site, and a mode of participation and of musical fandom. While the rock music embraced by the counterculture increasingly made dancing difficult (if not impossible), clubs catering to gay, African American, and Latino subcultures in New York City began relying on music featuring a blend of Motown soul, Latin-inflected funk, and a new, sophisticated type of uptown soul associated with Philadelphia-based producers (discussed earlier in Greil Marcus's essay; see chapter 53). Artists, such as Harold Melvin and the Blue Notes, Barry White, White's Love Unlimited Orchestra, and Cameroonian jazz-pop artist Manu Dibango, had national hits that "crossed over" from dance clubs to pop radio. The genre name "disco" was applied first to such "rockin'" dance hits as The Hues Corporations' "Rock the Boat" and George McCrae's "Rock Your Baby," both from 1974, while another important early disco recording, Van McCoy's "The Hustle" (early 1975), launched the most popular dance step of the era. Disco's impact extended beyond its musical style, challenging prevalent notions in popular music criticism about authorship and creativity.

The central figure in this challenge to the critical status quo was the disc jockey or "DJ." Because DJs were responsible for selecting and sequencing songs, it was their taste that dictated disco's sense of style, rather than the singers and instrumentalists of soul and rock musics, and successful DJs could acquire their own following in much the same way as a recording artist. DJs shared the creative locus of the disco scene with the audience itself, since the focus on dancing stressed social interaction (this is vividly portrayed in Andrew Kopkind's article, reprinted here).

During 1975–76, disco began to concentrate on three main tendencies. The first, "R&B disco," was derived more directly from previous
styles of soul and funk, often retained gospel-oriented vocals and syncopated guitar and bass parts, and was sometimes recorded by self-
contained bands associated with funk, such as the Ohio Players, Kool
and the Gang, the Commodores, and KC and the Sunshine Band. A second trend, "Eurodisco," tended to feature simple, chanted vocals, less-
syncopated bass parts, and thicker arrangements filled with orchestral
instruments and synthesizers and relied on a producer who directed
anonymous studio musicians. Eurodisco recordings often filled entire
album sides and attempted to usurp some of the DJ's creative role by sequencing a series of contrasting episodes over an unvarying tempo. The
style could be said to have arrived with Donna Summer's "Love to Love
You Baby," in which producers Pete Bellote and Giorgio Moroder embedded Summer's suggestive moaning in a 17-minute orchestrated epic. A
third variant, "pop disco," was represented by mainstream pop artists,
such as the Bee Gees, an Australian trio who had hopped on the disco
bandwagon in 1975 to revive their dormant careers; pop disco's importance grew throughout the decade.[1]

The final transformation of disco from a genre associated with
gays, blacks, and Latinos to one embraced by straight, white Americans
occurred with the success of the film, *Saturday Night Fever,* released
late in 1977. The film's soundtrack featured new songs by the Bee Gees
and an assortment of songs from the preceding two years by the Bee
Gees, Kool and the Gang, Walter Murphy, and the Trammps. The soundtrack yielded four Number One singles and became the best-selling
album up to that time. The most popular disco clubs, such as Studio 54
in New York City, became celebrity-studded hangouts where high society and a gay sense of style intertwined.[2] The Eurodisco and pop disco
styles had clearly superseded R&B disco in the public notion of what
constituted the genre, although a few artists on the borderline between
funk and disco continued to succeed. The most important of these
artists was Chic, whose last major hit, "Good Times" (1979), is notable
for providing the musical basis for the first rap hit, "Rapper's Delight,"
by the Sugarhill Gang (1979).

Andrew Kopkind addresses the broader cultural significance of disco at
the height of its popularity in the wake of *Saturday Night Fever.* Writing

1. This typology-taxonomy is used by Stephen Holden in his article "The Evolution of a Dance Craze,"
*Rolling Stone* (April 19, 1979): 29. *Rolling Stone* dedicated its August 28, 1975, issue to disco, just as disco
was becoming more than an underground phenomenon. Of special note in that issue is Vince Aletti's discussion of early disco's history, aesthetics, and musical influences; see Vince Aletti, "Dancing Madness:
The Disco Sound," *Rolling Stone* (August 28, 1975): 43, 50, 56.

2. For an account of Studio 54 that paints a portrait of corruption, celebrities, and Steve Rubell's obnoxious chutzpah during the club's high point from April 1977 to March 1978, see Henry Post, "Sour
Notes at the Hottest Disco," *Esquire* (June 20, 1978): 79–86.

at the end of the 1970s, he uses disco as a way of discussing shifts in popular music, the music industry, and the relationship of popular music to politics and lifestyle. Most strikingly, he sees the rise of disco as representing the triumph of artifice over the authenticity so valued by the 1960s counterculture (a quality that underscored a not-so-obvious link among glam, disco, and some new wave). An important point in this article is how the popularity of disco marks the acceptance (albeit somewhat unconsciously) of a kind of gay sensibility into the mainstream. As Kopkind notes, however, that the heightened visibility of gay subcultures also occasioned a backlash among rock fans.[3]

## THE DIALECTIC OF DISCO: GAY MUSIC GOES STRAIGHT
### *Andrew Kopkind*

Disco is the word. It is more than music, beyond a beat, deeper than the dancers and their dance. Disco names the sensibility of a generation, as jazz and rock—and silence—announced the sum of styles, attitudes, and intent of other ages. The mindless material of the new disco culture—its songs, steps, ballrooms, movies, drugs, and drag—are denounced and adored with equal exaggeration. But the consciousness that lies beneath the trendy tastes is a serious subject and can hardly be ignored: for it points precisely where popular culture is headed at the end of the American '70s.

Disco is *phenomenal*—unpredicted and unpredictable, contradictory and controversial. It has spawned a new $4 billion music industry, new genres in film and theatre, new radio stations, a new elite of promoters and producers, and a new attitude about the possibilities of party going. It has also sparked major conflicts: "Death to Disco" is written on SoHo walls and "Disco Sucks!" rises from the throats of beleaguered partisans of rock, punk, or jazz who find their cultural identity threatened by disco's enormous commercial power.

Scenes from disco wars erupt across the landscape. Gangs of rockers and hustlers (the dancing kind) fight furiously in the streets outside disco clubs in provincial cities. When Mick Jagger or Rod Stewart "goes disco" (with "Miss You" and "Do You Think I'm Sexy?" respectively), their cultural conversion is debated in hip salons as well as in the *New York Times*. The rock critical establishment still treats disco music as an adolescent aberration, at best; many cultural commentators look on the whole sensibility as a metaphor for the end of humanism and the decline of the West.

The sense of the '60s provided coherence, contest, and validity to rock, when the critics of an earlier era proclaimed such sounds to be junk. Rock was "our music": only "we"—whoever we were—knew that it was good and what parts of it were best. The music was riding an historical tide; it was the sound of the politics, the expectations, the

---

3. This led most infamously to a riot in Chicago's Comiskey Park during the intermission of a White Sox doubleheader; see Don McLeese, "Anatomy of an Anti-Disco Riot," *In These Times* (August 29–September 4, 1979): 23.

*Source:* Andrew Kopkind, "The Dialectic of Disco: Gay Music Goes Straight," *The Village Voice*, February 12, 1979, pp. 1, 11–14, 16, 25.

explorations, and the institutions of an era. It was the background music as well as the marching melody for civil disobedience, sexual liberation, crunchy granola, and LSD. The Buffalo Springfield's "For What It's Worth" was perfect music-to-avoid-the-FBI-by. "Street Fighting Man" was made for trashing draft boards. "Mr. Tambourine Man" was for smoking dope. "Up the Country" was for dropping out of the city. "Let It Be" was for letting it be.

History hardly stops. Disco in the '70s is in revolt against rock in the '60s. It is the antithesis of the "natural" look, the real feelings, the seriousness, the confessions, the struggles, the sincerity, pretensions and pain of the last generation. Disco is "unreal," artificial, and exaggerated. It affirms the fantasies, fashions, gossip, frivolity, and fun of an evasive era. The '60s were braless, lumpy, heavy, rough, and romantic; disco is stylish, sleek, smooth, contrived, and controlled. Disco places surface over substance, mood over meaning, action over thought. The '60s were a mind trip (marijuana, acid); Disco is a body trip (Quaaludes, cocaine). The '60s were cheap; disco is expensive. On a '60s trip, you saw God in a grain of sand; on a disco trip, you see Jackie O. at Studio 54.

In describing "camp" in her influential essay 15 years ago, Susan Sontag remarked that "a sensibility (as distinct from an idea) is one of the hardest things to talk about." It is "not only the most decisive, but also [the age's] most perishable, aspect. To name a sensibility, to draw its contours and to recount its history, requires a deep sympathy modified by revulsion."

The performance and production of disco music creates a technical and economic foundation on which the intangible aspects of culture and sensibility develop. The ways in which the sounds are chosen, the records produced, the performers packaged, and the cultural artifacts marketed will profoundly influence the styles we see.

Disco, first of all, is not a natural phenomenon in any sense. It is part of a sophisticated, commercial, manipulated culture that is rooted exclusively in an urban environment. Disco music is produced in big cities and its fashions are formed in big cities, at considerable expense, by high-priced professionals. Almost as an afterthought is the product then disseminated to the provinces. All the sparkle, speed, cynicism, and jaded irony associated with metropolitan life is attached to disco. It is far from wholesome. Provincials may either envy or abhor it. But it belongs to the city.

"Disco is a New York thing. It happened here," says Kenn Friedman, the 26-year-old promotion wizard of Casablanca Records. "And it still happens here." Of a weekend evening in the city, Friedman may commandeer the label's limo—or slip out on his own—and make the rounds of the hottest New York clubs: Infinity, Flamingo, Les Mouches, Studio 54, 12 West. He holes up with the disc jockeys in their sound booths, then quickly moves out onto the dance floors, soaking up the spirit of the music and catching the response of the crowds. He and his crew are eminently successful (Casablanca is the new miracle mogul in the disco record business) because he can feel the hits.

"I *know* what will be number one, what the hottest record is going to be on the street this weekend," Friedman told me matter-of-factly. At the time we spoke he predicted it would be James Wells's "My Claim to Fame"; and sure enough, when I went round to the clubs the next Saturday, it was the song that provoked the peak excitement of the night. "I can't tell you exactly how I know, but it's because I'm part of the culture, I love to dance, I love the music."

Dancing is what does it. Last week at Casablanca's "Casbah"—the company's New York digs in an arabesque townhouse on 55th Street—I found Casablanca's top disco director, Marc Simon, boogying excitedly in Friedman's cramped office. Just back from the world record industry's annual congress in Cannes, Simon was effusive about the "completely new sound" his label will introduce as its 1979 line later this month. The first group making this as-yet unknown music is called Nightlife, and Simon says he's banking his business ($100 million last year) on his intuitions.

"I heard a different producer's sound every 15 minutes, five hours a day, all the time I was in Cannes," Simon said coolly, "and I picked the ones I felt were going to be the *dance* hits. While the sounds of disco are highly synthesized, the hits cannot be completely determined. Nobody dreamed up the whole disco promotion campaign in the first place. "In the beginning we used to dance to the best rhythms from Motown and other rhythm-and-blues records," Simon recalled. "There was nothing called 'disco' back in the '60s—just Diana Ross, Freda Payne, the Temptations." Then the producers in Philadelphia—Gamble and Huff—started making a specific disco sound, with the familiar heavy beat and the modified samba rhythm.

By reckonings, the first big disco hit—as *disco*—was Gloria Gaynor's 1974 top-of-the charts "Never Can Say Good-bye." Others pick "Love's Theme," by Love Unlimited Orchestra. But the record companies seemed bewildered by what they had, and promo people continued their quirky disregard of the disco category in their portfolios. Instead, they inflated passing fancies into seismic cultural events: Peter Frampton, reggae, and punk, for example. Not that some of those sounds or stars lacked merit; certainly Springsteen, Bob Marley, and the best of the New Wave deserve seats high in rock and roll heaven. But disco would soon swamp them all, and nobody was watching.

There are real differences in disco numbers that those who have learned to appreciate the music—and dance to it—can easily distinguish but may be missed by others. "All disco sounds alike" is commonly heard among rock fans; it is a bit like Caucasians saying, "All Chinese people look alike." Certain features of disco songs hardly vary from one tune to another (compare: flat noses or epicanthic folds). If you look for continuous changes in beat or for nuances of poetry in the lyrics, you will find few differences among disco songs. But the lengthy *construction* of a disco record (more than a "song") and its emotional *intensity* are highly changeable aspects, and may account for success or failure.

Or they may not. The fact is that while disco is racing to new levels of sophistication and elaboration at high speed, there is yet no reliable test for a hit. The reason is that the disco phenomenon has turned the pop industry upside-down, as no development has since the advent of '60s rock.

First, the disco wave crashed on unseen shores, catching producers and musicians without adequate cultural or commercial bearings. There were few critics to say what was good or bad—that is, what their readers or listeners should buy. There were no researchers to test the market; no one knew what questions to ask. The one or two music writers who dove into disco—notably the *Voice's* frequent contributor, Vince Aletti—often felt overwhelmed by the legitimacy and power wielded by the rock establishment, and they hid their opinions under barrels or in closets.[4]

Second, the primary sales medium of popular records changed, from radio for rock to dance clubs for disco. The shift entailed no small change: billions of dollars had come to rest on the "airplay" system of marketing music. Consumers heard their tunes on the air and rushed to their dealer for the vinyl version. Now, there were no stations, AM or FM, playing disco music as a regular feature of their format.

The third major change that disco wrought in the industry was the concentration of performance. For all its New York and L.A. stars, rock was a decentralized popular form. It

---

4. Aletti, cited earlier for his insightful early article on disco, eventually became involved in running RFC records, a label devoted to disco.

carried provincial and suburban values with it as it came up the river from Mississippi, or down the slopes from Colorado, or down the pike from Greenwich. Any four young people with axes and amps could start a band in the hinterlands, playing local clubs with a repertoire of original songs and "covered" hits of national stars. Some groups would work their way up to regional fame (J. Geils in Boston, the Allman Brothers in Atlanta) and then make it big in the continental markets.

But disco must be produced in a few studios in the urban centers—here and abroad. If there is talent in the small towns it must travel to the big city *before* that process begins; and in so doing, the performers must shed their innocent attitudes and naïve notions before they open their mouths. Donna Summer began in Boston and in Germany and Austria (singing pop and folk opera, as well as other genres) before Casablanca launched her record career as a cosmopolitan sex siren.

"People don't want local bands anymore," says John "T.C." (for Top Cat) Luongo, an impresario in MK Promotions, one of the country's leading disco promotional companies (it is largely responsible for the success of the *C'est Chic* album). "They'd rather hear the stars on records over sensational sound systems than listen to the local rock band play third-rate versions of old hits.

Many of the disco "stars," of course, are nonpeople—interchangeable studio musicians who shuttle between group names, from one album to the next. MFSB, Love Unlimited, and many of the Philadelphia bands of the mid-'70s were composed of the same people, give or take the odd sideman. Salsoul, the Ritchie Family, and other current hot groups are wholes that add up to less than the sum of their parts. Only recently have genuine musicians broken through disco anonymity into stardom: Donna Summer and the Bee Gees, for better and worse, are the best example of the new personalized wave.

Fourth, disco facilitated the birth of a lucrative subcategory of record sales—the new 33 rpm 12-inch "disco mix" or "long version." The Salsoul group, originally an Hispanic manufacturer of ladies' lingerie, made a more substantial fortune by turning from *schmatas* to the sounds of the Latin Hustle; Salsoul brought out some of the first big disco-mix 12-inches six years ago. The industry yawned. Now a 12-inch disco single can sell 17,000 copies in New York City alone, and the companies carefully regulate the availability of the various versions of a hit song to maximize sales. For example, Atlantic put 200,000 copies of the "Le Freak" disco mix on sale to stimulate interest in the *C'est Chic* album—then withdrew the long 12-inch single to eliminate competition for the high-priced package and the mass-volume 45 rpm versions.

Finally, the music business has been jolted by the sudden prominence of the record *producer* which the technical requirements of disco now entails. The European producers of the suave, lush "Eurodisco" sounds are perhaps the brightest lights: Giorgio Moroder, Cerrone, Alex Costandinos, Roger Tekarz. Many of them use their own names instead of their performers' to identify albums; thus, the latest album produced by Cerrone is called, simply, "Cerrone IV." Moroder uses the name "Giorgio" both as an album title and also as an advertisement for his productions; a sticker slapped on the new Three Degrees album announces "Produced by Giorgio," as rock albums feature the most familiar cut.

Today, the disco record industry is a mammoth $4 billion enterprise—bigger than television, movies, or professional sports in America. "Disco accounts for about 40 percent of all the 'chart activity,'" Friedman estimated. By the end of the decade, half the top 100 songs on *Billboard's* lists will be disco numbers. Disco radio stations are sweeping the country. New York's WKTU is a story in itself: in nine months of disco programming (it used to send out "mellow rock") it has gone from the dregs of stations too low to rate to the number one broadcaster in the country, either AM or FM—beating out the gargantuan WABC. Boston's WBOS was miniscule before it went all-disco; it now tops the biggest FM rock stations in

America's hottest "youth market." And there are 20,000 disco clubs in the U.S., earning $6 billion annually.

What all this means is that a sizable hunk of capital in the entertainment industry is now in the hands of the disco elite—a mixed breed of newcomers, switchovers and fast dancers who had the sense to accommodate themselves to the sensibility of the '70s.

The new disco elite has its own vocabulary and its own values, and they are quite different from those of the rock entrepreneur. For one thing, the disco people have to feel like dancing—not autistic, explosive fits of movement but the more controlled, stylized dancing of the disco clubs. And for another, they have to be able to mingle and mix in gay discos as well as straight ones, for the locus of the emerging disco culture is pointedly in urban male homosexual society.

"There *is* a big cultural difference between rock and disco," Kenn Friedman said firmly, "and it's gayness. Some people don't like to talk about it, but it's true. Disco began in gay clubs. At first, it was just a case of speeding up the gap between records on the juke box. But that's how the concept of continuous music began. The disco club was the first entertainment institution of gay life, and it started in New York, as you would expect."

Disco promoter John Luongo agrees. "In the beginning, there was the gay audience for disco. The 'primo' disc jockeys were gay. Gays couldn't find any rock bands to play in their clubs, so they had to make records their own form of entertainment.

Not long ago, Kenn Friedman took John Brody around to several clubs on his Saturday night rounds, and Brody gave me this report:

"The intensity was different at Infinity, which is predominantly straight, and at 12 West, which is mostly gay. At Infinity the energy was lower, there was less emphasis on dancing. At 12 West everybody was dancing, and it was a kind of sexual thing. It was very powerful. There was a strong smell of poppers—amyl nitrate—in the air, and I guess a lot of people were high on whatever. That must be part of the mood. But the gays seemed a lot less hung up in their environment than the heterosexuals seemed in theirs. At 12 West, I looked at these people dancing at four in the morning; it looked like the last night of their lives."

Even so, Friedman did not take Brody to Flamingo, the most intense and emotionally powerful gay disco in New York. "I didn't think he could handle it," Friedman joked.

What Brody would have seen was this:

Flamingo is an enormous loft on the edge of SoHo, undistinguished by signs or lights. Members (who pay $75 a year plus a substantial fee for each visit) start wandering in well after midnight on Saturday nights, the only day of the week the club is regularly open. By 3 A.M., several thousand people, almost entirely men, mostly shirtless and universally stoned, are dancing feverishly to the most imaginatively mixed, most persistently powerful music ever assembled in one continuous set. One wall of the danceroom is paneled with colored lights, which flicker and race at appropriate intervals in harmonious correlation to the music. Along another wall, a dozen or so men dance by themselves on a raised banquette, acting as erotic cheerleaders to the swirling crowd. The fume of poppers is overpowering.

Many Saturday night dances at Flamingo have a theme like a senior prom. Late last month there was a "Western/Tattoo" night, which featured a raised platform in the lobby where party-goers could be tattooed in their moments of relaxation from dancing. Another annual feature is the "Black Party"—named not for the race of the customers but for the suggested color of attire, the decorations, and the mood of the evening. Last spring's black party was one of the final Saturdays of the season—before Flamingo closes for the summer while its thousands of members repair to Fire Island for whatever adventures await them in dunes. Now this was some senior prom. In the entrance hall there were cages, platforms, and theatrical sets where various happenings were in progress, all in accordance with a vaguely S&M, "black," leather-gear theme. Some of the goings-on were semimentionable:

people (actors?) were in chains, under the whip, groveling and groping, disheveled. Other attractions were unmentionable, and getting more so as the evening wore on. There were more people in the loft at 6 a.m. than there were at 1. When *do* these people sleep?

A strange fascination kept me at Flamingo past my bedtime, and I have returned many times in the months since then. Most often, the mood is lighter than on that black night (the "White Party" is coming up later this month), but the extravagant sense of theatricality is maintained. The throbbing lights, the engulfing sound, the heightened energy, and the hyperbolic heat of Flamingo gives me the sense (which I have heard that others share) that the world is enclosed in this hall, that there is only *now*, in this place and this time. It can be extraordinarily assaultive; I have felt trapped forever in a theater of sound, of flesh, like a character in Bunuel's *The Exterminating Angel,* unable to leave a party even after its positive appeal has fled. But what is worse is the prospect of a chill gray Manhattan dawn outside. Leaving is more depressing than staying: the disco beat is like a life rhythm, and to stop would be to create a killing thrombosis.

Danae—it's his *nom de disco*—is a well-known disc jockey on the New England and New York circuit. I asked him what he does to make the special blend of music that distinguishes the disco club sound from just "playing records":

"The mix starts at a certain place, builds, teases, builds again, and then picks up on the other side. The break is the high point. It's like asking a question, repeating and repeating it, waiting for an answer—and then giving the answer. That is the great, satisfying moment."

In practice, a "hot" disco mix in a dance club is a sexual metaphor; the deejay plays with the audience's emotions, pleasing and teasing in a crescendo of feeling. The break is the climax.

"That's the rush," Danae says. "The dancers cheer, they pump the air with their fists, they wave and shout. It's very exciting. I played at 12 West last Christmas, and it was one of the best nights I've ever had. After a while, someone came up to me, all excited, and said, 'You were fucking me with your music! Do me a favor, fuck me again with your music.' I took it as a great compliment."

"There's gay disco and straight disco, although there's overlap between the two," Danae continued. "Straight disco is heavy-duty funk, the driving sound, that has all the power without much of the emotion. Gays like to hear black women singers; they identify with the pain, the irony, the self-consciousness. We pick up on the emotional content, not just the physical power. The MFSB sound was gay; Barry White was a gay sound, so is Donna Summer, Gloria Gaynor. We knew the Trampp's 'Disco Inferno' was a great song years before it got into the *Saturday Night Fever* soundtrack. To me, the epitome of gay disco this year is Candi Staton. She's all emotion, you can feel it when she says, 'I'm a victim of the very song I sing.'"

There are contradictions within contradictions in the sexual implications of disco. Consider The Village People, the singing group that claims to hail from Greenwich Village and parodies the macho styles of its homosexual culture. One of the members is dressed as a leather biker, another as a construction worker, a third as an Indian, a fourth as a cowboy, and so on. They perform songs that extend the parody—notably "Macho Man" and "YMCA." For gays, the line "I want to be a macho man" from the mouths of these butch impersonators is a bit like "I want to be white" if it were sung by Stevie Wonder for a black audience.

Gays are amused by The Village People, but the group is finding its biggest fans among straights. "YMCA" is never heard at Flamingo. Kenn Friedman, whose Casablanca label produces the group (one of the most profitable in his stable) agrees:

"'Macho Man' did not happen in gay clubs but in straight ones. The Village People is the first gay-to-straight 'crossover' group, a group with an originally gay image and following that's made it in straight discos. The funny thing is that straights don't really believe the group is gay. They love 'em in Vegas and in tacky suburban dinner theaters in Midwestern shopping centers. Did straights ever catch on with Paul Lynde? With Liberace? People will protect their identity at all costs, they'll pretend to the last possible minute that it's all an act."

Gay activists have protested that Casablanca is deliberately closeting The Village People to make the act "safe" for straights. A Casablanca PR functionary says that producer Jacques Morali (who reportedly picked all the members except possibly the accomplished lead singer because of their tough good looks rather than their musical talent) became visibly upset when a *Newsweek* interviewer began probing into the gay issue. But the group is coming out, as it were, with ever more outrageous lyrics and postures. Their biggest hit to date is "YMCA," which concerns a young boy who comes into the big city, looks around for a place to hang out, and lands in a hostelry that is legendary in the gay community as a cruising spot. What did Middle America think it all meant when The Village People sang that number, with all the appropriate gestures, at the height of the Macy's Thanksgiving Day parade on national television?

There are two levels on which The Village People's campiness works: the first is with the "knowing" gay audience, the listeners who are in on the joke, the images, the allusions (Fire Island, the bushes, Castro Street, Key West, the Y). The other is with the "naive" straight audience, the listeners who either don't know (or mind) what's going on in the lyrics, or else think it is all theatrical drag.

In much the same way, disco music as a whole appeals to a "knowing" audience that sees what Friedman calls the "cultural gayness" in it, and a naive audience that simply likes the fashion and the beat.

"The straights don't see the gay culture, they've only seen what they've made—the styles," Friedman says. Just before Casablanca's disco movie, *Thank God It's Friday,* opened across the country last year, Friedman took a short segment of it to several cities and showed it on videotape to selected audiences. Casablanca boss Bogart was worried that straight Americans would be offended if they detected the goings-on in the background of one sequence on the tape: two men were dancing together and sniffing amyl nitrate.

"I interviewed hundreds of people, showed it to thousands, and as far as I know not one straight person ever saw the men dancing, even after I showed the segment to them two or three times," Friedman reported. "And yet the gay viewers saw it immediately."

One more example: Paul Jabara's song, "Disco Queen," on the TGIF soundtrack, concerns a "queen" who is "known from L.A. to San Francisco to the Fire Island shore." She "even sleeps with her tambourine." She flirts with a handsome young marine. The chorus asks: "Where does she get her energy? Where does she get her energy?" *Really.* The images in the song are all attached to male homosexual styles. This queen is certainly a queen. But I'll bet heterosexuals never even consider the possibility that the disco queen is not a woman. To them, it's just another nice dance tune; which it is.

Disco became the theme music of gay culture in the '70s (not only in America but in Europe and Latin America as well). Of course, the straight audience now far outnumbers the gay one, but the music still has a special meaning for gays: if '60s freaks could say that rock was "our music," gays now say the same for disco. It is the background music for the activities and institutions of the burgeoning urban gay culture—for the shops, the bars, the restaurants, and the offices where gays go about their business. It is music for sex, for dancing, and for looking at the straight world go by. It is reassuring and supportive; in an important way, it is the sensational glue that unites a community.

But disco has deep roots and strong attachments in other cultural groups as well. Disco is, after all, a mixture of certain black rhythm-and-blues sounds, Latin forms, and an African beat.

New York's first major disco station was WBLS, a "black" radio outlet. Many of the best disco performers are black—while rock is bleached and white. For years disco suffered several disadvantages to total acceptance: major disco artists were black or Latin, many were women, the principal white audience was gay, and the nongay white audience was located in the urban ethnic working class—all reasons for cultural disability.

*Saturday Night Fever* illustrated the class aspect of disco for urban whites. While rock was infused with middle-class attitudes (although often downwardly mobile in its aspirations), disco was originally proletarian. One clue: the "weekend" theme reappears in disco lyrics, as in "Thank God It's Friday," "I Just Can't Wait for Saturday," "Funky Weekend," and, of course, in the film title *Saturday Night Fever* itself. Working-class kids toil all week and wait for their one big shot at fun, escape, and dreams on the weekend; they dress up, get drunk, and play out sexual fantasies in a community context.

Quite the other way with the rock culture: hippies hang out all week and can't tell Saturday night from Tuesday afternoon. They don't do much dancing, and when they do, they do not care much for dressing up, spending money, having dates, and controlling their movements on the dance floor.

There are certain immutable characteristics of rock culture: it is white, straight, male, young, and middle class. The exceptions to those rules prove them. For example, female stars and their songs must conform to male sexual fantasies—Linda Ronstadt, Christine McVie. Black musicians must be chlorinated to make it up the rock charts—Jimi Hendrix, Stevie Wonder, Chubby Checker. What may appear to be lower-class images in rock usually turn out to be middle-class myths and fantasies: punk violence, "Working Class Hero" radicalism, dropout dreams. And performers who tinker with sexual stereotypes must remain determinedly "ambiguous" or turn up with partners of the opposite sex from time to time, to beard their offensive nakedness: Bowie with Angie, Jagger with Bianca, Elton John, Alice Cooper, the Kinks. Jagger may French kiss Ron Wood on *Saturday Night Live,* but it's fortunate that he can lose a paternity suit with, figuratively, the same breath. Sexual deviation (like gender, class, and race aberrations from the norms) must be playful and let's pretend: it cannot seriously threaten straight identity.

For a time, it appeared that disco culture might change those rules to a degree, particularly in the case of sexual identity. It now looks as if the dominant demands of American society will prevail, to no one's great surprise. The past year has seen several disco stars or groups achieve the necessary "cross-over" effect, bringing the music out of the subcultural ghettoes into mainstream life. The Bee Gees were crucial to that passage; they made disco safe for white, straight, male, young, and middle-class America. What Elvis Presley did for black rhythm and blues, and Diana Ross did for soul, and Elvis Costello did for punk, the Brothers Gibb have done for disco. Now all Nassau County is lining up for disco lessons. '60s survivors who steadfastly resisted disco because it was apolitical, or dehumanized, or feminine, or homosexual, or too Bay Ridge, are suddenly skipping to the beat. They have found what Gladys Knight calls out, in one of the best songs of the season: "It's *better* than a good time."

The rise of disco music occurred alongside the decline of rock, but whether there is connection between these two aesthetic events is not at all clear.

"Rock and roll is at an all-time low in creativity," promoter John Luongo fretted. "It's all rehashed material, there's no freshness. I love rock," he insisted, "and it's where I started. But the music has let people down. There was a big hole, and disco filled it. There's no other form of music that offers the power, the excitement, the party atmosphere of disco."

Disco is the word, as grease was the word. It is a handle on the '70s, as the other was a metaphor for the '50s, for in the extraordinary cultural and commercial success of disco several of the new elements of this generation can be identified. Disco has many functions, but one of the most essential may be as a drug: it feeds artificial energy, communal good feelings, and high times into an era of competition, isolation, and alienation. As drugs go, it is not egregiously harmful, but it is easily abused, quickly tolerated, and naggingly addictive.

Sensibility is dialectical—which is to say that it grows from the material of history and the experience of society. It does not descend from the heavens of invention or corporealize out of thin air. The '70s sensibility emerged from the achievements and excesses, the defeats and triumphs of the years before. Our end is *always* in our beginning, and we are, as Candi Staton croons, the victims of the very songs we sing.

# 62. Punk

## The Sound of Criticism?

At the end of the preceding article, promoter John Luongo decried the creative stasis that had overcome rock music during the 1970s. Many musicians working in rock (and critics devoted to it) could not have agreed more. While Kopkind's essay mentions punk and new wave in passing, these genres arose as rock musicians' response to the same crisis that spurred the popularity of disco.

Punk, a favorite subject of rock critics,[1] is one of the few genres in the history of rock 'n' roll in which the people who read about it may have outnumbered the people who heard it (at least during its initial heyday in the late 1970s). The genre may also be the first to have followed the aesthetic imperatives of rock criticism, rather than the reverse. We need only think back to the impassioned manifestos of Lester Bangs and his colleagues at *Creem* magazine in the early 1970s, many of which anticipated the style of mid-1970s punk as represented, in particular, by the Ramones. The self-consciousness of the participants (musicians and audience members alike) about style—in musical, sartorial, and political terms—made it a rich field for sociologists as well as critics.[2]

The critics and musicians who either identified with or took an interest in punk in the mid-1970s were also aware of the legacy of the Velvet

---

1. For an excellent discussion of rock criticism from this period, and one to which the following discussion is much indebted, see Bernard Gendron, *Between Montmartre to the Mudd Club* (Chicago: University of Chicago Press, 2002), chaps. 10–13.

2. For a classic academic study dating from this period, see Dick Hebdige, *Subculture: The Meaning of Style* (London: Methuen, 1979).

Underground, the band established by Bangs as the sine qua non of punk in his early writings.[3] A genealogy gradually evolved that gained tacit acceptance by most other writers:

> (ca. 1966) Velvet Underground (+ 60s garage bands + "rave-ups"
> of Yardbirds and Kinks) →
> (ca. 1969) Stooges/MC5 →
> (ca. 1973) Modern Lovers/New York Dolls →
> (ca. 1975) Ramones/Patti Smith/Talking Heads →
> (ca. 1976) Sex Pistols/Clash.

In musical terms, this genealogy emphasizes a deliberately simplistic, "do-it-yourself" amateur aesthetic; many writers referred to this quality with the term "minimalism," by which they meant the stripping of rock music down to its most basic elements (not to be confused with the music of Terry Riley, Philip Glass, Steve Reich et al.). By 1975, the term "punk" included a great diversity of musical styles under its rubric, held together by a common attitude toward the growing gentrification of rock and the common use of a performance venue in New York City, CBGB's. Writing in 1977, Robert Christgau provided a pithy summary of punk:

The underlying idea of this rock and roll will be to harness late industrial capitalism in a love hate relationship whose difficulties are acknowledged, and sometimes disarmed, by means of ironic aesthetic strategies: formal rigidity, role-playing, humor.[4]

James Wolcott was one of the first critics to recognize the historical and potential theoretical importance of punk rock as it developed in New York City. The following article describes a festival presented at CBGB's in the summer of 1975, and gives an overview of the scene at that moment. Wolcott uses the term "underground" (i.e., unrecorded bands) to describe the music and calls the festival "the most important event in New York rock since the Velvet Underground played the Balloon Farm." Like other writers of the time, he views punk as opposed to the "baroque theatricality of rock" and observes the stagnant quality of rock music, sensing that dance music is where "the scenemakers" are.[5] Wolcott's usage of "conservative" here means "to carry on the rock tradition," and he approves of the manner in which the CBGB's bands are accomplishing it.

The article also mentions the use of past styles in punk, not as parody or homage, but as pastiche, somewhat in the manner of the camp

---

3. In addition to Bangs, the connection between the Velvet Underground and punk was explicitly addressed by James Wolcott in "Lou Reed Rising" (entitled "The Rise of Punk Rock" on the inside), *Village Voice,* March 1, 1976, back page, 87–88.

4. Robert Christgau, "A Cult Explodes—and a Movement Is Born," *Village Voice,* October 24, 1977, 57, 68–74.

5. For an earlier example that discusses the New York Dolls in these terms, see Lorraine O'Grady, "Dealing with the Dolls Mystique," *Village Voice,* October 4, 1973, 52.

sensibility found in Andy Warhol's "pop art."[6] This is particularly prominent in bands, such as Television and the Talking Heads, and Wolcott
captures well their affectless presentation with phrases like "banal
façade" and a "a sense of detachment." Tina Weymouth, bassist for the
Talking Heads, sums up the attitude behind such self-presentation when
she states: "Rock isn't a noble cause."[7]

# A Conservative Impulse in the New Rock Underground
## James Wolcott

Arabian swelter, and with the air-conditioning broken, CBGB resembled some abbatoir of a kitchen in which a bucket of ice is placed in front of a fan to cool the room off. To no avail of course, and the heat had perspiration glissading down the curve of one's back, yeah, and the cruel heat also burned away any sense of glamour. After all, CBGB's Bowery and Bleeker location is not the garden spot of lower Manhattan, and the bar itself is an uneasy oasis. On the left, where the couples are, tables; on the right, where the stragglers, drinkers and love-seekers are, a long bar; between the two, a high double-backed ladder which, when the room is really crowded, offers the best view. If your bladder sends a distress signal, write home to your mother, for you must make a perilous journey down the aisle be-tween seating area and bar, not knock over any mike stands as you slide by the tiny stage, squeeze through the piles of amplifiers, duck the elbow thrust of a pool player leaning over to make a shot . . . and then you end up in an illustrated bathroom which looks like a page that didn't make *The Faith of Graffiti.*

Now consider the assembly-line presentation of bands, with resonant names like Movies, Tuff Darts, Blondie, Stagger Lee, the Heartbreakers, Mink de Ville, Dancer, the Shirts, Bananas, Talking Heads, Johnny's Dance Band and Television; consider that some nights as many as six bands perform, and it isn't hard to comprehend someone declining to sit through a long evening. When the air gets thick with noise and smoke, even the most committed of us long to slake our thirst in front of a Johnny Carson monologue, the quin-tessential experience of bourgeois cool.

---

6. Since the preceding article by Kopkind already referred to a camp sensibility as one of the aspects of disco's appeal, the mention of that term here may suggest an unsuspected affinity between disco and punk. Interested readers are encouraged to seek out Susan Sontag's influential essay on the subject, "Notes on 'Camp,'" in *Against Interpretation* (New York: Anchor Books, 1990), 275–92. Originally published in 1964.

7. For a later discussion of the Talking Heads that further discusses their music and the impact of their art school background, see John Rockwell, "The Artistic Success of Talking Heads," *New York Times*, September 11, 1977, D14, 16. Rockwell, longtime music critic for the *New York Times*, is certainly as well positioned as anyone to discuss the artistic aspirations of rock music. His *All-American Music: Composition in the Late Twentieth Century* (New York: Vintage Books, 1984), in its inclusion of rock music, salsa, jazz, Broadway, and a wide range of classical music, presciently anticipates the crossing of musical categories that has since become more common for music critics and academics. *All-American Music* also contains an in-depth examination of the Talking Heads (pp. 234–45).

*Source:* James Wolcott, "A Conservative Impulse in the New Rock Underground," *Village Voice*, August 18, 1975, pp. 6–7.

So those who stayed away are not to be chastised, except for a lack of adventurousness. And yet they missed perhaps the most important event in New York rock since the Velvet Underground played the Balloon Farm: CBGB's three-week festival of the best underground (i.e. unrecorded) bands. The very unpretentiousness of the bands' style of musical attack represented a counter-thrust to the prevailing baroque theatricality of rock. In opposition to that theatricality, this was a music which suggested a resurgence of communal faith.

So this was an event of importance but not of flash. Hardly any groupies or bopperettes showed up, nor did platoons of rock writers with their sensibilities tuned into Radio Free Zeitgeist brave the near satanic humidity. When the room was packed, as it often was, it was packed with musicians and their girlfriends, couples on dates, friends and relatives of band members, and CBGB regulars, all dressed in denims and loose-fitting shirts satorial-style courtesy of Canal Jeans. The scenemakers and chic-obsessed were elsewhere.

Understandable. Rock simply isn't the brightest light in the pleasure dome any longer (my guess is that dance is), and Don Kirschner's *Rock Awards* only verifies the obvious: rock is getting as arthritic, or at least as phlegmatic, as a rich old whore. It isn't only that the enthusiasm over the Stones tour seemed strained and synthetic, or that the Beach Boys can't seem able to release new material until Brian Wilson conquers his weight problem, or that the album of the year is a collection of basement tapes made in 1967. "The real truth as I see it," said the Who's Pete Townshend recently, "is that rock music as it was is not really contemporary to these times. It's really the music of yesteryear."

He's right and yet wrong. What's changed is the nature of the impulse to create rock. No longer is the impulse revolutionary—i.e., the transformation of oneself and society—but conservative: to carry on the rock tradition. To borrow from Eliot, a rocker now needs a historical sense; he performs "not merely with his own generation in his bones" but with the knowledge that all of pop culture forms a "simultaneous order." The landscape is no longer virginal—markers and tracks have been left by, among others, Elvis, Buddy Holly, Chuck Berry and the Beatles—and it exists not to be transformed but cultivated.

No, I'm not saying that everyone down at CBGB is a farmer. Must you take me so literally? But there is original vision there, and what the place itself is doing is quite extraordinary; putting on bands as if the stage were a cable TV station. Public access rock. Of course, not every band which auditions gets to play, but the proprietor, Hilly, must have a wide latitude of taste since the variety and quality of talent ranges from the great to the God-condemned. As with cable TV, what you get is not high-gloss professionalism but talent still working at the basics; the excitement (which borders on comedy) is watching a band with a unique approach try to articulate its vision and still remember the chords.

Television was once such a band; the first time I saw them everything was wrong—the vocals were too raw, the guitar work was relentlessly bad, the drummer wouldn't leave his cymbals alone. They were lousy all right but their lousiness had a forceful dissonance reminiscent of the Stones' *Exile on Main Street*, and clearly Tom Verlaine was a presence to be reckoned with.

He has frequently been compared to Lou Reed in the Velvet days, but he most reminds me of Keith Richard. The blood-drained bone-weary Keith on stage at Madison Square Garden is the perfect symbol for Rock '75, not playing at his best, sometimes not even playing competently, but rocking, swaying back and forth as if the night might be his last and it's better to stand than fall. Though Jagger is dangerously close to becoming Maria Callas, Keith, with his lanky grace and obsidian-eyed menace, is the perpetual outsider. I don't know any rock lover who doesn't love Keith; he's the star who'd always at the edge and yet occupies the center.

Tom Verlaine occupies the same dreamy realm, like Keith he's pale and aloof. He seems lost in a forest of silence and he says about performing that "if I'm thinking up there, I'm not having a good night." Only recently has the band's technique been up to Verlaine's reveries and their set at the CBGB festival was the best I've ever seen; dramatic, tense, tender ("Hard On Love"), athletic ("Kingdom Come"), with Verlaine in solid voice and the band playing as a band and not as four individuals with instruments. Verlaine once told me that one of the best things about the Beatles was the way they could shout out harmonies and make them sound intimate, and that's what Television had that night: loud intimacy.

When Tom graduated from high school back in Delaware, he was voted "most unknown" by his senior class. As if in revenge, he chose the name Verlaine, much as Patti Smith often invokes the name Rimbaud. He came to New York, spent seven years writing fiction, formed a group called Neon Boys, then Television. The name suggests an aesthetic of accessibility and choice. It also suggests Tom's adapted initials: T.V.

"I left Delaware because no one wanted to form a band there," he says. "Then I came to New York and no one wanted to form a band here either." Verlaine came to New York for the same reason every street-smart artist comes to New York—because it's the big league—even though he realizes "New York is not a great rock & roll town."

Still, they continue to arrive: Martina Weymouth, bassist, born in California; Chris Frantz, drummer, in Kentucky; David Byrne, singer and guitarist, in Scotland. All attended the Rhode Island School of Design, and according to their bio, are "now launching careers in New York"—a sonorous announcement, yes?

These people call themselves Talking Heads. Seeing them for the first time is transfixing: Frantz is so far back on drums that it sounds as if he's playing in the next room; Weymouth, who could pass as Suzi Quatro's sorority sister, stands rooted to the floor, her head doing an oscillating-fan swivel; the object of her swivel is David Byrne, who has a little-boy-lost-at-the-zoo voice and the demeanor of someone who's spent the last half-hour whirling around in a spin-drier. When his eyes start ping-ponging in his head, he looks like a cartoon of a chipmunk from Mars. The song titles aren't tethered to conventionality either: "Psycho Killer" (which goes, "Psycho killer, qu'est-ce c'est? Fa-fa-fa-fa-fa-fa-fa"), "The Girls Want To Be With The Girls," "Love is Like A Building On Fire," plus a cover version of that schlock classic by ? and the Mysterians, "96 Tears."

Love at first sight it isn't.

But repeated viewings (precise word) reveal Talking Heads to be one of the most intriguingly off-the-wall bands in New York. Musically, they're minimalists: Byrne's guitar playing is like a charcoal pencil scratching a scene on a note pad. The songs are spined by Weymouth's bass playing which, in contrast to the glottal buzz of most rock bass work, is hard and articulate—the bass lines provide hook as well as bottom. Visually, the band is perfect for the cable-TV format at CBGB; they present a clean, flat image, devoid of fine shading and colour. They are consciously anti-mythic in stance. A line from their bio: "The image we present along with our songs is what we are really like."

Talking to them, it becomes apparent that though they deny antecedents—"We would rather advance a 'new' sound rather than be compared to bands of the past"—they are children of the communal rock ethic. They live together, melting the distinction between art and life, and went into rock because as art it is more "accessible." They have an astute sense of aesthetic consumerism, yet they're not entirely under the Warholian sway, for as one of them told me, "We don't want to be famous for the sake of being famous." Of all the groups I've seen at CBGB, Talking Heads is the closest to a neo-Velvet band, and they represent a distillation of that sensibility, what John Cale once called "controlled distortion." When the Velvets made their reputation at the Balloon Farm, they were navigating through a storm of multi-media effects; mirrors, blinking lights, strobes, projected film images. Talking Heads works without paraphernalia in a cavernous room projecting light like a television located at the end of a long dark hall. The difference between the Velvets and Talking Heads is the difference between phosphorescence and cold gray TV light. These people understand that an entire generation has grown up on the nourishment of television's accessible banality. What they're doing is presenting a banal façade under which run ripples of violence and squalls of frustration—the id of the vid.

David Byrne sings tonelessly but its effect is all the more ominous. The uneasy alliance between composure and breakdown—between outward acceptance and inward coming-apart—is what makes Talking Heads such a central seventies band. A quote from ex-Velvet John Cale: "What we try to get here [at the Balloon Farm] is a sense of total involvement." Nineteen sixty-six. But what bands like Television and Talking Heads are doing is amelio-rating the post-'60s hangover by giving us a sense of detachment. We've passed through the Dionysian storm and now it's time to nurse private wounds. Says Tina Weymouth, quite simply: 'Rock isn't a noble cause.'

The Ramones recently opened at a Johnny Winter concert and had to dodge flying bottles. During one of their CBGB sets, they had equipment screw-ups and Dee Dee Ramone stopped singing and gripped his head as if he were going to explode and Tommy Ramone smashed the cymbal shouting, "What the FUCK'S wrong?" They went off-stage steaming, then came back and ripped into "Judy Is A Punk." A killer band.

"Playing with a band is the greatest way of feeling alive," says Tom Verlaine. But the pressures in New York against such an effort—few places to play, media indifference, the compulsively upward pace of city life—are awesome. Moreover, the travails of a rock band are rooted in a deeper problem: the difficulty of collaborative art. Rock bands flourished in the sixties when there was a genuine faith in the efficacious beauty of communal activity, when the belief was that togetherness meant strength. It was more than a matter of "belonging"; it meant that one could create art with friends. Playing with a band meant art with sacrifice, but without suffering. Romantic intensity without Romantic solitude.

What CBGB is trying to do is nothing less than to restore that spirit as a force in rock & roll. One is left speculating about success: will any of the bands who play there ever amount to anything more than a cheap evening of rock & roll? Is public access merely an attitude to be discarded once stardom seems possible, or will it sustain itself beyond the first recording contract? I don't know, and in the deepest sense, don't care. These bands don't have to be the vanguard in order to satisfy. In a cheering Velvets song, Lou Reed sings: "A little wine in the morning, and some breakfast at night. Well, I'm beginning to see the light." And that's what rock gives: small unconventional pleasures which lead to moments of perception.

# 63. Punk Crosses the Atlantic

Punk's musical style, do-it-yourself attitude, and disdain for the bour-geois hedonism of rock superstars resonated strongly among sectors of British youths. With pub-rock, older styles of rock 'n' roll, and the Ramones forming the immediate musical backdrop, the stage was set for a distinctive British punk to emerge. Punk in the United Kingdom was felt to have more social and political relevance than U.S. punk because of the identification of British working-class youths with punk's nihilism, an identification facilitated by rampant unemployment and a depressed economy.[1] While a band like the Sex Pistols emphasized the nihilist as-pects of punk, the Clash pursued a more overt political agenda.

Another major difference between U.S. and U.K. punk was the amount and type of attention they received in the press. As early as 1976, near-hysterical reports surfaced in Britain, some of them appearing before any recordings had even been released. As a writer for the British pub-lication, *Melody Maker,* Caroline Coon was well positioned to observe the burgeoning punk scene from close range. Coon's sympathetic ac-count focuses as much on what British punk was reacting against as it does on punk itself. While some might quibble with claims of British punk's autonomy from New York City punk, this belief was widespread at the time, and it is certainly true that the British punks were free of the "retro" influences favored by some of the New York bands. In addi-tion to describing the music, Coon captures the distinctive sartorial ap-proach and "subcultural style" of the British scene.[2] For Coon, the dy-namic fulcrum of this scene revolves around the most notorious band of the era, the Sex Pistols, and its equally notorious lead singer, Johnny Rotten.

---

1. Robert Christgau was drawn to British punk for its projection of a greater sense of political engage-ment; see his "A Cult Explodes—and a Movement Is Born," *Village Voice,* October 24, 1977, 57, 68–74. Simon Frith explores the political contradictions of British punk in "Beyond the Dole Queue: The Politics of Punk," *Village Voice,* October 24, 1977, 77–79. For the first in-depth portrait of the Sex Pistols to appear in *Rolling Stone,* and one that conveys some of the shock felt by certain sectors of the rock establishment, see Charles M. Young, "Rock Is Sick and Living in London: A Report on the Sex Pistols," *Rolling Stone* (October 20, 1977): 68–75.

2. From roughly the same period, see Caroline Coon, "Punk Alphabet," *Melody Maker* (November 27, 1976), 33, in which she gives more space to the interconnections between British and American punk and stresses the increased role of women in punk relative to other genres.

# REBELS AGAINST THE SYSTEM
## *Caroline Coon*

Johnny Rotten looks bored. The emphasis is on the word "looks" rather than, as Johnny would have you believe, the word "bored." His clothes, held together by safety pins, fall around his slack body in calculated disarray. His face is an undernourished grey. Not a muscle moves. His lips echo the downward slope of his wiry, coat-hanger shoulders. Only his eyes register the faintest trace of life.

This malevolent, third generation child of rock & roll is the Sex Pistols' lead singer. The band play exciting, hard, basic punk rock. But more than that, Johnny is the elected generalissimo of a new cultural movement scything through the grass-roots disenchantment with the present state of mainstream rock.

You need look no further than the letters pages of any *Melody Maker* to see that fans no longer silently accept the disdain with which their heroes, rock giants, treat them.

They feel deserted. Millionaire rock stars are no longer part of the brotherly rock fraternity which helped create them in the first place.

Rock was meant to be a joyous celebration; the inability to see the stars, or to play the music of those you can see, is making a whole generation of rock fans feel depressingly inadequate.

Enter Johnny Rotten. Not content to feel frustrated, bored and betrayed, he and the Sex Pistols, Glen Matlock (bass), Paul Cook (drums), and Steve Jones (guitar), have decided to ignore what they believe to be the elitist pretensions of their heroes who no longer play the music they want to hear. The Pistols are playing the music they want to hear. They are the tip of an iceberg.

Since January, when the Sex Pistols played their first gig, there has been a slow but steady increase in the number of musicians who feel the same way—bands like the Clash, the Jam, Buzzcocks, the Damned, the Subway Sect and Slaughter and the Dogs. The music they play is loud, raucous and beyond considerations of taste and finesse. As Mick Jones of the Clash says: "It's wonderfully vital."

These bands' punk music and stance is so outrageous that, like the Rolling Stones in the good old days, they have trouble getting gigs. But they play regularly at the 100 Club, which is rapidly becoming the venue at which these bands cut their teeth.

The musicians and their audience reflect each other's street-cheap, ripped-apart, pinned-together style of dress. Their attitude is classic punk: icy-cool with a permanent sneer. The kids are arrogant, aggressive, rebellious. The last thing any of these bands make their audience feel is inadequate.

Once again there is the feeling, the exhilarating buzz, that it's possible to be and play like the bands on stage.

We're back where we were in 1964. The Beatles, Stones, Kinks, Who, Them, Animals and the Yardbirds—in effect, a new wave—blasted out of the national charts the showbiz pop of Adam Faith, Bobby Vee, Cliff Richard and Paul Anka, which had replaced the initial vibrant explosion triggered by Bill Haley's "Rock Around The Clock" and Elvis's "Heartbreak Hotel" in 1956.

The last five years of rock can be compared to the early sixties when the rock stars of the fifties were wiped out. Buddy Holly's plane crashed. Elvis was drafted into the army, Chuck Berry was jailed. Car crashes killed Eddie Cochran and hospitalized Gene Vincent and Carl Perkins. The field was left open to the businessmen.

*Source:* Caroline Coon, "Rebels Against the System," *Melody Maker*, August 7, 1976; reprinted as "Rock Revolution: 28th July 1976," in *1988: The New Wave Punk Rock Explosion* (London: Omnibus Press, 1977), 10–22. Reprinted with permission of Caroline Coon.

The parallels with today are uncanny.

What happened to the rock stars—the new wave—who revolutionized the scene from 1964–7? Jimi Hendrix, Jim Morrison, Brian Jones and Janis Joplin are dead. Clapton retired, and is only just returning, Dylan rested up for several years with a broken neck. Those who are left—the ex-Beatles, Stones, Who, Kinks, have become businessmen. OK, some are still playing rock & roll—but aren't they a little more motivated by making money than making music?

When these bands first shook the foundations of the established musical order they reveled in their image as *rebels:* misfits, outcasts. The Beatles played in Hamburg with toilet seats around their necks, the Who smashed expensive equipment they could ill afford every night, the Rolling Stones, with their long hair and tieless shirts, were chucked out of hotels and restaurants wherever they went.

These rock & rollers were the heroes of their generation because they rejected and broke through the restrictions which had kept teenagers bound to the outdated authority of their parents. Their music was loud, the clothes outrageous.

Most important of all, they were anti-elitist, voices from and of the people—or so we believed. They spoke our language. Every kid who sang along to "My Generation," "All Day And All Of The Night" and "Let's Spend The Night Together" felt that he was as involved with the music as the musicians.

And the bands tried to keep it that way. When the Beatles felt they were becoming the acceptable face of rock with songs like "Michelle," "Norwegian Wood" and "Yesterday," they zapped it back to the true believers with a mind-blowing concoction of backward tapes, multi-tracking and psychedelic weirdness that only youth could really understand.

The trouble is, in the last five years, the rock stars have become "adults"; they have forgotten that crucial to their appeal was their rebellious stance. Instead they are bending over backwards to become acceptable.

Mick Jagger, once the arch-deacon of iconoclasm, now couldn't be farther removed from his fans. It's no longer possible to imagine him as a man of the people, if he ever was—his yobbo accent doesn't wash any more. He's elitist, the aristocracy's court jester, royalty's toy. How long before his name appears on the Queen's honours list?[3]

The Who are becoming Pete Townshend's private nightmare—trotting out their musical history, the seventies' Chuck Berry.

The Beach Boys and the Byrds, America's initial reply to the British eruption, haven't been a vital force in rock for eight years.

The Beatles are the fastest-expanding nostalgia industry yet conceived. On an individual level Paul McCartney and Wings is the only one to have maintained the tradition of an artist consistently performing for an audience, and he speaks mainly to the generation he grew up with.

To his credit, although Lennon is now a quiet family man, he, with Yoko, was the only rock giant to attempt to bring the rebellious protest of his generation to a political level which transcended the rhetoric of rock.

With few exceptions, the interim bands, the ones who sprang up while the old wild men were moving from cellar to penthouse, never transcended their music to become cultural heroes. The psychedelic bands like Jefferson Airplane, Grateful Dead, Soft Machine and Pink Floyd were musically important until they disintegrated with the underground, or disappeared into their own insularity.

Basically middle class, affluent or university academics, they set the stage for bands like Genesis, Jethro Tull, ELP, Yes, Rick Wakeman, Roxy Music and Queen, whose

---

3. Coon's worst fears were realized in December 2003 when Jagger was knighted.

"progressive rock" uses an increasing amount of technical apparatus, has become increasing quasi-orchestral and quotes liberally from the classics.

All these bands have been acclaimed by the critics, sometimes justifiably. But the crucial element is missing. These musicians have always been gentlemen rockers and their music can only be played by people with similar academic temperaments. The music, although inspired, is far beyond what the average teenager, without expensive equipment, can reproduce in his own front room.

David Bowie is the one person the growing wave of third-generation rock fans seem to identify with. Although a musical stylist rather than an innovator, he's captured their imagination with a film and stage persona creating him as a mutant alien from another planet.

Thus he has brilliantly detached himself from the conventional jet set, rock star establishment. Unlike other stars whose private lives are totally disparate with their rock stance, Bowie's private life seems freaky enough, weird and secret enough to get him elected the first Punk Space Cadet.

There was a time when it looked as though Led Zeppelin and Bad Company might have carried the torch for raw, raunchy rock & roll but they became multi-national corporations, casualties of the business ethic.

The present state of rock came to a dramatic climax in May and June of this year, at the series of businessmen's conventions held at Wembley, Earls Court and Charlton.

The Who, the Stones, Elton John, David Essex, Steve Harley, David Bowie, Uriah Heep, all put on shows which, whatever they may have said and whatever attempts they may have made to overcome their self-imposed problems, had little to do with music and everything to do with the kind of gestures these stars think is all that's needed to keep their fans happy.

The fans, wanting to give their heroes the benefit of the doubt, weren't as angry as they had the right to be. But a great many were heartsick, disillusioned and bored rotten.

Of course, thousands of people, especially those who grew up with Rock Giants, were still loyal fans, still buying the albums and having a good time. But this is simply not the atmosphere in which the new generation of rock musicians can thrive or have any desire to carry on from where the old guard has left off.

There is a growing, almost desperate, feeling that rock music should be stripped down to its bare bones again. It needs to be taken by the scruff of its bloated neck and given a good shaking, bringing it back to its sources and traditions.

The time is right for an aggressive infusion of life-blood into rock.

It's no coincidence that the week the Stones were at Earls Court, the Sex Pistols were playing to their ever-increasing following at London's 100 Club. The Pistols are the personification of the emerging British punk rock scene, a positive reaction to the complex equipment, technological sophistication and jaded alienation which has formed a barrier between fans and stars.

Punk rock sounds simple and callow. It's meant to.

The equipment is minimal, usually cheap. It's played faster than the speed of light. If the musicians play a ballad, it's the fastest ballad on earth. The chords are basic, numbers rarely last longer than three minutes, in keeping with the clipped, biting cynicism of the lyrics.

There are no solos. No indulgent improvisations.

It's a fallacy to believe that punk rockers like the Sex Pistols can't play dynamic music. They power through sets. They are never less than hard, tough and edgy. They are the quintessence of a raging, primal rock-scream.

The atmosphere among the punk bands on the circuit at the moment is positively cutthroat. Not only are they vying with each other but they all secretly aspire to take Johnny

Rotten down a peg or two. They use him as a pivot against which they can assess their own credibility.

It's the BSP/ASP Syndrome. The Before Or After Sex Pistols debate which wrangles thus: "We saw Johnny Rotten and he *changed* our attitude to music" (the Clash, Buzzcocks), or "We played like this *ages* before the Sex Pistols" (Slaughter and the Dogs), or "We are *miles* better than the Sex Pistols" (the Damned). They are very aware that they are part of a new movement and each one wants to feel that he played a part in starting it.

All doubt that the British punk scene is well under way was blitzed two weeks ago in Manchester, when the Sex Pistols headlined a triple, third-generation punk rock concert before an ecstatic capacity audience.

Participation is the operative word. The audiences are reveling in the idea that any one of them could get up on stage and do just as well, if not better, than the bands already up there. Which is, after all, what rock & roll is all about.

When for months, you've been feeling that it would take ten years to play as well as Hendrix, Clapton, Richard (insert favourite rock star's name), there's nothing more gratifying than the thought: Jesus, I could get a band together and blow this lot off the stage!

The growing punk rock audiences are seething with angry young dreamers who want to put the boot in and play music, regardless. And the more people feel "I can do that too," the more there is a rush on to that stage, the more cheap instruments are bought, fingered and played in front rooms, the more likely it is there will be the "rock revival" we've all been crying out for.

There's every chance (although it's early days yet) that out of the gloriously raucous, uninhibited melee of British punk rock, which even at its worst is more vital than most of the music perfected by the Platinum Disc Brigade, will emerge the musicians to inspire a fourth generation of rockers.

The arrogant, aggressive, rebellious stance that characterizes the musicians who have played the most vital rock and roll has always been glamorized. In the fifties it was the rebel without a cause exemplified by Elvis and Gene Vincent, the Marlon Brando and James Dean of rock. In the sixties it was the Rock & Roll Gypsy Outlaw image of Mick Jagger, Keith Richard and Jimi Hendrix. In the seventies the word "rebel" has been superseded by the word "punk." Although initially derogatory it now contains all the glamorous connotations once implied by the overused word—"rebel."

Punk rock was initially coined, about six years ago, to describe the American rock bands of 1965–8 who sprung up as a result of hearing the Yardbirds, Who, Them, Stones. Ability was not as important as mad enthusiasm, but the bands usually dissipated all their talent in one or two splendid singles which rarely transcended local hit status. Some of the songs, however, like "Wooly Bully," "96 Tears," "Psychotic Reaction," "Pushin' Too Hard," have become rock classics.[4]

In Britain, as "punk rock" has been increasingly used to categorize the livid, exciting energy of bands like the Sex Pistols, there has been an attempt to redefine the term.

The new British bands emerging have only the most tenuous connections with the New York punk rock scene which has flourished for the last four years. Bands like the New York Dolls, the Ramones, Patti Smith, Television and the Heartbreakers are much closer, musically, to the Shadows of Knight, the Leaves and other punk rock bands of the sixties.

---

4. This is a reference to articles, such as the one by Lester Bangs reprinted in chapter 50; or to other early classics, such as Greg Shaw's "Punk Rock: The Arrogant Underbelly of Sixties Pop," *Rolling Stone* (January 4, 1973): 68–70.

And they dress almost exclusively in the classic punk uniform. Those not in Levis, sneakers, T-shirts and leather jackets are still pretending to be English rock stars circa 1965.

On the other hand, the British punk scene, far from glorifying, is disgusted by the past. Nostalgia is a dirty word. The music's only truck with yesterday's rock is an affection for one or two classics, "Substitute," "What'cha Gonna Do About It," "Help," "I Can't Control Myself," "Stepping Stone": all vitriolic outbursts mirroring the spirit of the bands' own songs, which have titles like "Pretty Vacant," "No Feelings," "Anarchy In The UK," "You're Shit!" or "I Love You, You Big Dummy."

While New York cultivates avant-garde and intellectual punks like Patti Smith and Television, the British teenager, needing and being that much more alienated from rock than America ever was, has little time for such aesthetic refinements.

British punk rock is emerging as a fierce, aggressive, self-destructive onslaught.

There's an age difference too. New York punks are mostly in their mid-twenties. The members of the new British punk band squirm if they have to tell you they are over eighteen. Johnny Rotten's favourite sneer is: "You're too old." He's twenty.

British punk rock garb is developing independently too. It's an ingenious hodgepodge of jumble sale cast-offs, safety-pinned around one of the choice, risqué T-shirts especially made for the King's Road shop, Sex.

Selling an intriguing line of arcane fifties cruise-ware, fantasy glamour-ware, and the odd rubber suit, this unique boutique is owned by Malcolm McLaren, ex-manager of the New York Dolls, now the Sex Pistols' manager.

His shop has a mysterious atmosphere which made it the ideal meeting place for a loose crowd of truant, disaffected teenagers. Three of them were aspiring musicians who, last October, persuaded McLaren to take them on. They wanted to play rock & roll. They weren't to know what they were about to start and even now no one is sure where it will lead. All Steve, Glen and Paul needed then was a lead singer.

A few weeks later Johnny Rotten strayed into the same murky interior. He was first spotted leaning over the jukebox, looking bored. . . .

# 64. Punk to New Wave?

"New wave" began to be used as a complementary term to "punk" during 1976 and 1977. The term did not originate in order to supplant "punk" or to provide a competing category, but, rather, in the words of Bernard Gendron, "to capture in punk bands what the designator 'punk' left out—the arty, avant-gardish, studied, and ironic dimension that accompanied the streetwise, working-class and raucously 'vulgar' dimension."[1] Initially, the terms were used interchangeably, or, when distinctions were attempted, confusingly. Gradually, by 1978, consistent usages developed whereby the "punk" label was affixed retroactively to bands that had fit the definition as developed by Bangs: loud, fast, crude, angry or pseudo-angry, while "new wave" began to be used exclusively for bands that tended toward the ironic, cool, and distant.[2] Of the original CBGB bands, the Talking Heads most clearly fit the "new wave" label.

By the time the punk-new wave labeling crisis began to subside, musicians and critics in New York City shared a growing sense that the scene was stagnating. Among rock critics, this sense was fueled by the fact that punk represented the first critically acclaimed genre not to find a large audience. Several new directions arose that constituted a "second" wave of new wave bands. One branch was represented by the decidedly noncommercial turn of "no wave," led by Lydia Lunch, the Contortions, and the D. N. A., which became a new underground and shared much with the downtown avant-garde art scene. Another aspect of this second wave was directed toward a wider audience, had more in common with the Talking Heads than the Ramones, and was best represented by bands, such as Devo and the B-52s (from Ohio and Georgia, respectively).

Stephen Holden's article on the B-52s focuses on the "retrotrash" aesthetic of the band, one that was most clearly anticipated by a "first wave" new wave band like Blondie (who, curiously enough, belatedly achieved popularity around the same time as the B-52s). The "historicist" approach of the band has much in common with aspects of what cultural theorist Fredric Jameson later labeled "postmodernism," but perhaps more responsible for the B-52s' impact was their sense of fun and the danceability of the music.[3]

---

1. *Between Montmartre and the Mudd Club* (Chicago: University of Chicago Press, 2002), 270. Also see Gendron's chapter on "no wave" (pp. 275–97).

2. An article from early 1978 begins with a discussion of this dilemma of terminology: "One of the more interesting aspects of the current popular music scene is the discussion surrounding the admittedly hairsplitting distinction between punk and new wave. . . . taken as two sides of a constantly fluctuating and dynamic equation, these terms help describe what is so fascinating about the current renaissance in rock 'n' roll. . . . What has distinguished the local scene, of course, are the ties that join the N.Y. art community with the rock 'n' roll world." The implication here being that this is also what distinguishes new wave from punk; see Roy Trakin, "Avant Kindergarten [Sturm and Drone], *Soho Weekly News, Inc.*, January 26, 1978, 31.

3. The classic formulation of Jameson's theory may be found in "Postmodernism, or the Cultural Logic of Late Capitalism," *New Left Review* 146 (July–August 1984): 59–92; reprinted in *Postmodernism, or the Cultural Logic of Late Capitalism* (Durham, N.C.: Duke University Press, 1991), 1–54.

# THE B-52S' AMERICAN GRAFFITI
## Stephen Holden

Though they've arrived some 15 years after Andy Warhol made the cover of *Time*, the B-52's strike me as the ultimate pop art rock band. Urbane, funny, and sharp, they use *American Graffiti*–era trash with the precision and purpose of "serious" artists. Yet the actual content of their lyrics is defiantly nonserious. If 15 years ago the Velvet Underground-Fugs art/rock nexus nudged rock & roll along the road to literary respectability, the B-52s nudge it back toward silliness. I haven't seen them perform, but their first album is the most likable New Wave debut since Talking Heads. You can spend hours sifting through its trivia, but you can also frug to it. They may have a New York sensibility, but that sensibility is so ubiquitous in 1979 that they could develop their sound in southern Georgia, a locale which probably accounts for their funkwise rhythm section.

Through a scrupulous compilation of kitsch, the B-52s lovingly reconstruct the sounds and attitudes of post-Sputnik, pre-Vietnam pop America within a New Wave context. Their mining of the past is so thorough that it becomes the basis of a rock style—one that implies almost as much by what it omits (literary sense, adult emotion) as by what it enshrines (nonsense). If I got on my critical high horse, I could mount an argument about how their music consciously reflects a media-disintegrated environment, an electronically blitzed-out culture in which all values have been leveled. But I won't, because the B-52s' music is too much fun. It's not the slightest bit polemical, and they have a great time making it. Clearly, the group cherishes all the detritus—the cultural backdrop of their collective adolescence—that's gone into the album. At their best, they're awesomely convincing in their assertion of the positive side of culture shock, by pointing out the democracy of pop culture. Among dozens of references, some subliminal but most deliberate, they treat early Kinks, *Peter Gunn*, the Shangri-Las, *Star Trek*, early Motown, Duane Eddy, "Telstar," "Pipeline," Petula Clark, and *Beach Blanket Bingo* all with equal respect and humor. No rock group has made me so aware that pop culture, even its dregs, has had a lot more to do with shaping my fantasy life than the "high" culture I was brought up to revere.

Their song lyrics seem consciously McLuhanist in their post-literate allusiveness. The language is fractured, reduced to telegraphic popisms. "This is the Space Age/Just don't worry/This is the Space Age/Others like you," they proclaim in the robot chorus that winds up "There's a Moon in the Sky (Called the Moon)." The rest is a confused catalog of pseudo-sci-fi catch-phrases that jumble reality and fantasy so casually you begin to question not only if there's a difference between kiddie-show space travel and the real thing, but also if it matters whether there's a difference. Gamma rays and kryptonite—aren't they finally the same thing, catch words to the stars in a child's garden of TV trash? If the TV screen literally shrinks everything to the same size and degree of reality, don't the transistor radio and even the walkie-talkie do the same thing? In the B-52s' world, all these communications devices are operating at once. Mediums and styles are scrambled together, so that one's time sense finally collapses under the barrage, and all modern culture becomes as simultaneous as the rerun of an instant replay—20 years of trash compacted into a 40-minute docudrama.

And the very least, The B-52's is a superb exercise in camp nostalgia. But I think it's more than that. The best cuts burst with a spirit of real celebration. "Dance This Mess Around," in which they invent wonderful dance names like the Shy Tuna and the Aquavelva, is an affectionate tribute to the Mashed Potato-Frug era and also a killer boogie cut

*Source:* Stephen Holden, "The B-52s American Graffiti," *Village Voice*, August 13, 1979, p. 60.

that's eager to compete with "Stop! In the Name of Love," which it proudly quotes. The quintet's tense, post-primal vocals brim with excitement; Fred Schneider sounds like a Devo-ed Ringo Starr finally "getting back," while Kate Pierson, pleading that she "ain't no limburger," does Patti Smith doing Yoko Ono just about perfectly. "Lava" is a hot, funny, sexual anthem that gets hilarious mileage out of its lava-love-Mauna Loa alliteration. It's also a beautifully constructed call-and-response rock song—terse, catchy, with a knockout punchline (Schneider: "I'm gonna jump in a crater." Girls, gleefully: "See ya later.") "Planet Clare" is a deft exercise in '60s sci-fi kitsch with an absurdist satiric edge ("She drove a Plymouth Satellite/Faster than the speed of light"). "Rock Lobster" conjures up a surrealistic '60s beach party where bikini-clad mermen frug with warbling manta-rays and narwhales. The instrumentation is transcendently tacky, a rollicking farce of guitar and Farfisa.

Is it "great" rock? Maybe. The three major charges that could be leveled against the B-52s are that they're hopelessly arty, hopelessly New Yorky, and hopelessly silly. But for all its arty precision, their music is totally accessible. It may lack classic American roots, but in the endless garbage heap of modern pop culture, the band has found a tradition—and an American one at that. To me, their silliness shows considerable courage. They recapture rock & roll innocence—or at least this 38-year-old writer's idea of innocence—in the only way that seems possible nowadays, by reconstructing it. Their trash rock anthem squirming with animated sea creatures belongs squarely in the tradition of "Tutti Frutti."

# 65. UK New Wave

Emerging during the same period in the United Kingdom as the Sex Pistols were artists who bore roughly the same relationship to the Sex Pistols that the Talking Heads and the B-52s had to the Ramones. And while Elvis Costello, Graham Parker, and Joe Jackson all recycled models from pop music's past, they also all featured an angry edge that put them in accord with the "vulgar" side of punk. As described vividly by Caroline Coon, these musicians were all rebelling against the slick professionalism of contemporary rock superstars. Elvis Costello (b. 1954), in addition to employing musical pastiche, extended the notion of pastiche to his appearance (which resembled a nerdish, yet defiant Buddy Holly) and, of course, to his name—born Declan MacManus, his first record was released, by a strange coincidence, almost simultaneously with the announcement of Elvis Presley's death on August 16, 1977.

The following interview-profile comes from early in Costello's career. The interviewer, Allan Jones, is clearly in Costello's camp, as he waxes enthusiastically about a solo performance and the two singles that Costello had released thus far, while eagerly anticipating the first album, which was due out shortly. While Jones seems a bit frustrated by Costello's reluctance to explain himself (a tendency decisively reversed in later interviews[1]), Jones observes (or succeeds in getting Costello to observe) Costello's originality and emotional range as a songwriter, and his avoidance of clichés. Costello's comments clarify his links with punk: projecting an antiromantic persona, he presents what is virtually a manifesto advocating a return to a "core" ideal of rock that had been lost in the 1970s, and rejecting the trappings of fame and celebrity, along with grandiose displays of musical virtuosity that rock stars had increasingly embraced. As he says toward the end of the interview, "The songs are the most important thing."

# THE ELVIS (COSTELLO, THAT IS) INTERVIEW
## *Allan Jones*

*Let's talk about the future now, we'll put the past away.*
*—Elvis Costello, "Less Than Zero"*

Elvis Costello was emphatic: he would volunteer no information about his past. "I don't," he said, adjusting his shades impatiently, "really think that the past—my past—is all that interesting.

"I don't see any point in talking about the past. I don't want to get into that. I mean, I haven't just learned the guitar in the last ten minutes, but I'm not going to get talking about what I've done in the past.

"Nobody showed any interest in me then. If you weren't there, you missed it and that's it. It's gone. The people who were there then either appreciated it or they didn't. The past would only be relevant to them. As far as I'm concerned, it's pointless talking about the past. F_____it. I'd just rather talk about the future, you know."

There, I told you he was emphatic didn't I?

Elvis Costello and I are bickering this sundrenched Tuesday afternoon in an office above Stiff Records' London HQ because I had, accidentally, seen and been enthralled by his performance a week earlier at the Nashville Rooms.

Friday, May 27, it was: I'd tubed over to West Kensington to catch the Rumour that night. The presence at the bar of the Nashville, of Stiff executive Jake Riviera, accompanied by an assorted crew of Stiff hirelings and lackeys, seemed, initially, to be of no profound consequence.

---

1. See, for example, Bill Flanagan, "The Last Elvis Costello Interview," *Musician* (March 1986): 40, 42, 44. In this interview, Costello explains how he wanted to create a space free of either macho posturing (as in hard rock or heavy metal) or soul-baring autobiography (as in the singer-songwriters) and reveals a rarely discussed connection between the discourse of music critics and musicians' own ideas about creativity.

*Source:* Allan Jones, "The Elvis (Costello, That Is) Interview," Melody Maker, June 25, 1977, p. 14. Allan Jones/ Melody Maker/IPC Syndication.

There exist, after all, several connections between Stiff, Graham Parker and the Rumour; and, anyway, Jake ain't the kind of cat who'd miss out on a decent lig should one appear on the horizon as it had that evening.

Jake's appearance, however, was not on this occasion relegated to the pursuit of hedonistic adventures. He announced casually that one Elvis Costello, a recent Stiff protege, was to make a previously unscheduled debut as supporting attraction for the Rumour.

This information I received with considerable interest: Elvis Costello, though not yet a name on the lips of the nation, had released two singles ("Less Than Zero" and, more recently, "Alison") of rare distinction.

To see this enigmatic charmer in action was, unquestionably, a proposition not to be overlooked. Well, I dragged myself away from the bar as a brief whisper of applause signalled El's appearance. And there he stood, alone on the stage: black cropped hair swept back, the inevitable shades shielding his eyes, slickly cut Harry Fenton jacket, blue jeans and Fender guitar.

His attitude and performance were both characterised by an aggressive conviction and, as the applause between songs intensified, a clear and thrilling confidence.

Elvis Costello, let me tell you, bowled me out of my breeches that night.

Why, I even swore that if a platter containing such Costello meisterwerks as "(The Angels Wanna Wear) My Red Shoes," "Mystery Dance," "I'm Not Angry" and "Waiting For The End Of The World," was not in the vicinity of my Dansette turntable by the end of the month I'd be around to Stiff looking for the head of Jake Riviera.

The fact that Jake's head remains unsevered would suggest that the platter for which I yearned has been delivered: and so it has, to my immense delight. Trouble is that Stiff, after falling out with Island, are without a distribution organisation. El's album has been temporarily suspended—it was originally due for release this very week, actually. Fear not, however. It will be with you soon: in the meantime, I thought I'd bring you a despatch from the Elvis Costello front . . .

Here we go: Elvis Costello is 22. He's been writing songs for eight years. Since he first negotiated three juvenile chords on a battered guitar, in fact. He reluctantly admits to listening to the likes of the Beatles, Cliff Bennett and Georgie Fame as an adolescent; "Standard stuff. Whatever was on the radio."

Elvis, though he elsewhere proves to be refreshingly honest and forthright in the opinions he expresses, remains defiantly vague about the songs he was composing during this early period of his career: "I've written hundreds of songs," he says. "I write at least a song a week. That doesn't necessarily mean I keep them all.

"They're not all classics. I mean, I've discarded songs I wrote last month because I thought they were inept or didn't match up to the best of what I've written. I wouldn't talk about them, let alone songs I wrote eight years ago."

I had been interested in these earlier songs, I explain, simply because I wanted to form some idea of the pattern and evolution of his writing. The songs collected on his forthcoming album, "My Aim Is True," for instance, are marked by a precocious maturity.

Costello may deal principally with themes familiar in rock—the majority, in fact, are concerned with fiercely detailed accounts of romantic encounters and failures—but he introduces a ruthless honesty to these themes and invests his observations and scenarios with perceptive insights and astonishingly vivid images.

The insecurities and infidelities of relationships, adolescent attempts to attain a personal identity and independence, are examined with sensitive compassion and wit (often quite acerbic, but equally as often, as on the classic "Alison," with an exquisite tenderness).

Always, Costello retains his originality as a lyricist: he avoids conclusively the obvious and tiresome teendream preoccupations of comparative writers like Nils Lofgren (the midget Yank's recent work, at least), Elliott Murphy and Springsteen.

No, Elvis' songs possess the cutting clarity of the best of Graham Parker and Van Morrison: indeed, like this latter pair, Costello's music refers constantly to the classic pop/rock standards of the last decade, each song being sharply defined and full of irresistible hooks and delightful instrumental phrasing (for the verve and incisiveness of the album's sound, some considerable credit must be attributed to Nick Lowe, Elvis' producer).

"This influence stuff," says Costello, when several of the aforementioned musicians are mentioned, "is really irritating, 'cos people are always trying to pin you down to sounding like somebody else. I appreciate the comparison you drew with Graham Parker. I suppose that it's because he's currently maybe the only person that's doing anything like me.

"If there's a general musical area that he's working in, then I accept that I'm working in a similar area and the comparison is validly drawn. And I'd rather be compared to Graham Parker than Tom Jones. If someone came along and said that I sounded like John Denver then I'd f_____worry. It's better to be compared to somebody good; but it still doesn't mean that I sit at home trying to think of ways to re-write songs from 'Heat Treatment.'

"Anyway, if I'd had a record out before Graham Parker, it would all be reversed . . . 'cos, you know, the people who're saying that I sound like Graham Parker are the same people who said that Graham Parker sounded like Bruce Springsteen, who are the same people who said that Bruce Springsteen sounded like Van Morrison, who are the same people who said that Van Morrison sounded the same as Bobby Bland or whoever. You know, the people who NEVER listen to the f_____music."

The prospect of being compared to Springsteen, whose panavision scenarios—replete with so much obvious romantic, rock-mythology imagery of a kind quite antithetical to Costello's writing—fills Elvis with anguish and dread.

"Springsteen always romanticizing the f_____street," he complains, with no little justification. "I'm bored with people who romanticize the f_____street. The street isn't f_____attractive. I mean, I don't pretend to live in the heart of one of the worst areas of the world, right.

"I live near Hounslow. It's a very boring area. It's a terrible place. Awful, Nowhere, Nothing happens.

"There's nothing exciting or glamorous or romantic about it.

"There's nothing glamorous or romantic about the world at the moment. There is no place for glamour or romance. Romance, in the old pop song sense, has gone right out of the f_____window for the moment. Nobody's got the time or the money. It's gone beyond all that. But, please remember, I don't sit around wondering how people see the world, or how they feel about things.

"I don't attempt to express their feelings. I only write about the way I feel. I mean, I'm not arbitrator of public taste or opinion. I don't have a following of people who are waiting for my next word. I hope I never have that kind of following. People should be waiting for their own next word, not mine."

Elvis approached Stiff Records last August: he arrived at their office in West London with a tape of his songs and the response of Jake Riviera and Dave Robinson (also manager of Graham Parker) was immediate and enthusiastic.

They signed him to the label, in fact.

"There was no phenomenal advance," he laughs. "They've bought me an amp and a tape recorder. I'm glad that they're not subsidizing me to any greater extent. I don't want to be put on a retainer and spend my time ligging around record company offices like a lot of other musicians.

"I don't want any charity. I want to be out gigging, earning money. I don't want anything for nothing. I'm not askin anybody for their f_____ charity. I went to a lot of record companies before I came to Stiff. Major record companies. And I never asked them for charity. I didn't go in with any servile attitude.

"I didn't go in and say, 'Look, I've got these songs and, well, with a bit of patching up and a good producer I might make a good record.' I went in and said, 'I've got some great f_____ songs, record them and release them.' Stiff were the only ones that showed that kind of faith in me.

"They let me do it. I'm still working, right. I'll only give up the job when I start working with a band."

Elvis mentions, mischievously, that none of the musicians that contributed their services to his album are credited on the sleeve (Nick Lowe gets a production credit on the label, though). It transpires that this was El's idea of a caustic comment upon the contemporary state of the music business—an industry for which Elvis has very little admiration or respect.

He had a caption, in fact, prepared for the sleeve of his album, which would have read: "No thanks to anybody." Unfortunately, the Damned got there first when they had printed on the sleeve of their album: "Thanks to no one." El didn't want anyone to think he'd copped the idea so it was abandoned.

"The people who were directly involved with the album know who they are," El explains, "and they're not the kind of people who'd be worried about credits and namechecks. Equally, the people who were instrumental in stopping me from recording before know who they were, and I wanted to remind them that I hadn't forgotten them.

"Like, I went around for nearly a year with demo tapes before I came to Stiff, and it was always the same response. 'We can't hear the words.' 'It isn't commercial enough.' 'There aren't any singles.' Idiots. Those tapes were just voice and guitar demos. I didn't have enough money to do any thing with a band. It was just a lack of imagination on the part of those people at the record companies. I felt as if I was bashing my head against a brick wall, those people just weren't prepared to listen to the songs.

"It's a terrible position to be in. You start thinking you're mad. You listen to the radio and you watch the TV and you hear a lot of f_____ rubbish. You very rarely turn on the radio or TV and hear anything exciting, right? And, all the time, you know that you're capable of producing something infinitely better.

"But I never lost faith. I'm convinced in my own talent, yeah. Like I said, I wasn't going up to these people meekly and saying, 'Look, with your help and a bit of polishing up, and with all your expertise and knowledge of the world of music we might have a moderate success on our hands.'

"I was going in thinking." 'You're a bunch of f_____ idiots who don't know what you're doing. I'm bringing you a lot of good songs, why don't you go ahead and f_____ well record them.' They didn't seem to understand that kind of approach.

"No, it didn't make me bitter. I was already bitter. I knew what it would be like. I had no illusions. I have no illusions at all about the music business. It was no sudden shock to be confronted by these idiots. I didn't ever think that I was going to walk into a record company to meet all these fat guys smoking big cigars who'd say something like. 'Stick with me son, I'll make you a STAR.'

"I'm not starry-eyed in the slightest. You can tell what all these people are like instinctively. You just have to look at them to tell that they're f_____ idiots. But, I don't want to come off sounding like I'm obsessed with the music business.

"I couldn't give a s_____ about the music business. They just don't know anything. That's all you've got to remember. They're irrelevant. I don't give any thought to any of those people. They're not worth my time."

Elvis, who by this time seems to be metamorphising before my very eyes into the superhuman guise of Captain Verbals, is telling me about his album. It was recorded, he says, on his days off from work (he is a computer analyst in Acton), over a very brief period.

He was fortunate, he readily admits, that Nick Lowe was so sympathetic a producer: their respective ideas were entirely compatible and there were few arguments about the sound and instrumentation employed. All the songs were written within weeks of the first session; "Less Than Zero," his first single, was written three days before it was recorded, for instance.

Elvis just says he felt inspired and excited. The hits just kept on coming ("My Aim Is True," incidentally, is the first album I've heard for ages that sounds as if it is essentially a collection of Top Ten singles), as it were.

"I just love the sound of the album," Elvis enthuses. "'Cos I love things that sound great on the radio. 'Less Than Zero,' I thought sounded great on the radio. The record isn't for people with f_____great hi-fis. I'm not interested in those people, or that kind of mentality. I don't want my records to be used to demonstrate f_____stereos in Lasky's. I just want people to listen to the f_____music.

"I don't want to be successful so that I can get a lot of money and retire to a house in the f_____country. I don't want any of that rock and roll rubbish. I don't want to go cruising in Hollywood or hang out at all the star parties. I'm not interested in any of that. It's the arse end of rock and roll. I'm just interested in playing.

"I want to put a band together as soon as possible and get out on the f_____road. We're auditioning people this week. We're looking for young people. People that want to get out and play. Putting a band together is the most important thing at the moment.

"I think it might be difficult getting the right kind of people and I can imagine us wading through a right bunch of idiots. The group sound I want will be a lot sparser than the album sound. I just want bass, drum, guitar—my guitar—and for keyboards we'll probably go for a Vox or Farfisa sound.

"I want to get away from the conventional group sound. I'd say that I want a kind of pop group line-up, but people might take that as something lightweight or trivial. But it will be a pop line-up in the sense that it won't be a rock band.

"I hate hard-rock bands. I hate anything with f_____extended solos or bands that are concerned with any kind of instrumental virtuosity. I can listen to maybe 15 seconds of someone like the Crusaders, say, before I get very bored. I know how good they are because everybody keeps telling me how f_____marvellous they are. But I get bored.

"There are going to be no f_____soloists in my band. The songs are the most important thing. I want the songs to mean something to people. I don't mean by that that I want them to be significant. It's just that too much rock has cut itself off from people. It's become like ballet or something. Ballet is only for people who can afford to go and see it. It's not for anybody else. You don't get ballet going on in your local pub.

"There's a lot of rock music that's become exclusive and it's of no use to anyone. Least of all me. Music has to get to people. In the heart, in the head. I don't care where, as long as it f_____gets them. So much music gets thrown away. It's such a f_____waste.

"That's why I like and write short songs. It's a discipline. There's no disguise. You can't cover up songs like that by dragging banks of f_____synthesizers and choirs of angels. They have to stand up on their own. With none of that nonsense. Songs are just so f_____effective. People seem to have forgotten that.

"Like, people used to live their lives by songs. They were like calendars or diairies. And they were pop songs. Not elaborate f_____pieces of music. You wouldn't say, like, 'Yeah, that's the time I went out with Janet, we went to see the LSO playing Mozart.' You'd remember you went out with Janet because they were playing. 'Summer In The City' on the radio."

You will have gathered by now that Elvis is committed to success: he's not, however, altogether sure when that success will be achieved.

"There are lot of people," he says, "who should be successful. If ability had anything to do with success then there would be a whole lot of obscure people who'd be famous and there would be a whole lot of famous people who'd be lingering in obscurity."

Was there anyone, I wondered, that he would like to see becoming famous?

"Yeah," he replied "Me."

# 66. A "Second British Invasion," MTV, and Other Postmodernist Conundrums

The twin prongs of critical attention in late 1970s' pop music—disco and punk—became strangely irrelevant as the 1980s began. Punk, the darling of rock writers and sociologists of popular culture, never attained any sort of widespread commercial success, although it did receive a burst of mainstream media attention in 1977 owing to the antics of the Sex Pistols. Disco flamed out, a victim of overexposure and resentment among rock and R&B fans whose music had been all but obliterated from Top 40 and black radio. Neither punk nor disco actually disappeared, but punk remained underground minus the media exposure, and disco temporarily retreated to dance clubs, emerging from seclusion periodically with the occasional pop hit.

In the void left by the temporary demise of disco, album-oriented rock or album-oriented radio (AOR), a radio format developed in the early 1970s, began to assert a stronger presence in the mainstream.[1] A formulaic outgrowth of late-1960s "progressive" radio (in that it used a rigidly limited playlist of album cuts), AOR featured the one-name hard rock outfits mentioned in Part 4 (e.g., Boston, Journey, Foreigner, and Styx), along with "rootsy" rockers, such as Bruce Springsteen and Bob Seger. AOR fans formed the most virulent strain of the antidisco backlash, and the increasing importance of AOR relative to AM-based Top 40 led to a growing monochromaticism (i.e., a lack of African American popular music), thus reducing the number of crossover hits between black radio and the mainstream. At the same time, mid-1970s AOR favorites, such as the Eagles, Linda Ronstadt, and Fleetwood Mac, began to lose steam, taking with them some of the melodic pop sensibility of that era.

The declining fortunes of AOR were not occurring in a vacuum—the crash of disco, an increasing "blockbuster" mentality in the music

---

1. For an extensive overview of radio formats in the 1980s, see Ken Barnes, "Top 40 Radio: A Fragment of the Imagination," in Simon Frith, ed., *Facing the Music* (New York: Pantheon Books, 1988), 8–50. See also Greg Tate's humorously critical reference to the format as "apartheid-oriented rock" in chapter 44.

industry following *Saturday Night Fever*,[2] and the economic recession of the early 1980s in the United States, all contributed to a slump in the music industry. Two new and related developments arose to shake the industry from its doldrums: On August 1, 1981, the Music Television channel, better known as MTV, began broadcasting, introducing both a new way of disseminating pop music and a new way for audiences to experience it. A group of aspiring musicians capitalized on the new medium. Filling the void in music videos created by the relative paucity and lack of quality of, videos made by American bands, a number of British artists emerged who combined the ironic detachment of punk with the heightened fashion sense, danceable beat, and synthesized instrumentation of disco. This new genre, dubbed alternately "blitz," "New Romantic," "new wave," "new music," "synth-pop," "electro-pop," or "techno-pop" (and this list does not exhaust the monikers), made a strong impact on both sides of the Atlantic in the early 1980s and featured a visual style that made other videos seem drab—what Parke Puterbaugh tellingly termed "pop modernism with a British bias."[3]

We encountered Robert Christgau first back in chapter 47 in a pair of short articles on the Monkees. A prolific critic (primarily) for the *Village Voice,* his essay reprinted here on the music industry and large-scale shifts in the cultural position of popular music in the early 1980s is particularly incisive.[4] Christgau recounts media reports that were circulating about the music industry at the time and enumerates the two factors that are usually cited for the industry's problems in the early 1980s: the collapse of disco, and home taping. The argument about the impact of home taping may sound familiar to contemporary readers who are acquainted with current debates around file sharing, the Internet, and downloading. Although his article is framed by sections focusing on the music industry, he uses that focus as an opening through which to analyze the most significant musical trends of the period, including the "Second British Invasion" of techno-pop groups and the impact of MTV. Christgau questions the glibness with which certain aspects of these trends were currently being discussed, especially the idea of the Second British Invasion and the notion that music videos were nothing more than advertisements (which does not mean that he was not critical of music videos). One of his most original moves in the context of criticism of the time is to show how the success of Michael Jackson's *Thriller* connects to both these trends.

---

2. Other mega-hits of the mid- to late-1970s included Peter Frampton's *Frampton Comes Alive* (1976–10 million copies sold), the Eagles' *Hotel California* (1976–11 million copies sold), and Fleetwood Mac's *Rumours* (1977–25 million copies sold).

3. Parke Puterbaugh, "Anglomania: American Surrenders to the Brits—But Who Really Wins?" *Rolling Stone* (November 10, 1983): 31–32.

4. This is an edited version of the original article, which Robert Christgau cut by about one third. The complete article is available at <www.robertchristgau.com>.

Yet the significance of this article for our understanding of popular music history goes beyond the insightful analysis of these specific trends. Christgau describes a general transformation in the role of "rock culture," especially the loss of its sense of being "cutting edge." This was not a claim that "rock was dead" but, rather, an observation that rock was now doomed to be one genre among many. Christgau's point is supported by the current constitution of the rock canon, focused as it is in the 1960s and 1970s.[5] This transformation in the status of rock was further reflected in the changing relationship between the popular music audience and musicians and in the types of cultural meanings that different genres might claim. While such a discussion could easily turn nostalgic, this one does not: Christgau may be pessimistic about the long-term effects of capitalism on art, but he remains a populist and skeptical about claims for value that are not connected to popularity on a broad scale.

# Rock 'n' Roller Coaster: The Music Biz on a Joyride
## Robert Christgau

### Woe Is Us

Because only those willing to suspend their disbelief in eternal youth invest any real confidence in the staying power of rock and roll, premature obituaries have been as much a tradition of the music as teen rebellion and electric guitars. Ever since the '60s—in fact, ever since the '50s—I've scoffed at them. The nasty rumors of 1982, however, proved so persistent, pervasive, and persuasive that by the fall of that year I was half a believer myself. And now that they've vanished as utterly as Peter Frampton, I find it difficult to shake that bad feeling. Teen rebellion and electric guitars aren't looking particularly eternal themselves these days.

As often happens, 1982's rumors surfaced at the top of the information pyramid—it was major stories in *Time* and *Newsweek* that seemed to crystallize general unease into near panic. In February and April, Jay Cocks and Jim Miller filed trend pieces reflecting the gloom that first gripped the record industry after the Great Disco Disaster of 1979 and took another turn for the worse after the Bad Christmas of 1981. Essentially, both were laments for what used to be called rock culture, but Miller, who is less sentimental than Cocks, got the scoop in the process. Rather than indulge in blanket critical condemnations of a music that had made successes out of the Police, Rick James, and X, he concentrated on the slump in the music business and the dubious utility of marketing strategies designed to combat it. His conclusion was grim: "Rock 'n' roll has a future all right. But whether it can ever

---

5. In a December 11, 2003, *Rolling Stone* feature on the "500 Greatest Albums of All Time" albums from the 1960s and 1970s account, for 64 percent, while albums since the 1980s account for 31 percent. Of the Top 10, 9 were from the period 1965–75. The voters were largely critics, musicians, and others working in the music industry.

*Source:* Robert Christgau, "Rock 'n' Roller Coaster: The Music Biz on a Joyride," *Village Voice*, February 7, 1984, pp. 37–45. © Robert Christgau. Used by permission.

recapture its cutting edge and resume a leading role in defining the frontiers of America's popular culture is another matter entirely."

As 1982 slogged on, the music business was analyzed in major dailies and the consumer music press and bewailed week after week in the trades. The story was there, too. Right on time for Robert Palmer's August feature in the *Times*, CBS closed 10 of Columbia's branch offices and laid off 15 percent of its total staff—300 jobs. Other companies also retrenched. In arenas and auditoriums, concerts were fewer and more sparsely attended. By year's end record sales, off 11.4 percent in 1981, were rumored (somewhat hyperbolically) to have dipped 15 percent more. Gold albums were reported down from 153 to 128, platinum from 60 to 54. Where REO Speedwagon's *Hi Infidelity* had moved six million copies in 1981, 1982's apparent pacesetters, *Asia* and John Cougar's *American Fool*, hadn't sold half that many. And the first casualty of this lost revenue was venture capital—money for new and marginal talent.

The official explanation for these misfortunes concentrated on that well-known social evil, home taping. The audiocassette industry is still fighting off a Recording Industry Association of America (RIAA) campaign that seeks legislation to control record rentals and institute a hefty surcharge on blank tape sales—despite the Supreme Court's recent Betamax decision, which holds that home taping doesn't violate copyright law. In the beginning the theory that such consumer "theft" was costing the record business upwards of $1 billion a year looked fishy to most observers, but eventually it gained some converts—last spring, with recovery already in the air, the *Chicago Tribune* quoted with apparent equanimity RIAA president Stan Gortikov's remarkable claim that for every record bought another is home taped. Although a suspiciously unspecific October 1983 RIAA study asserts that 425 million hours of prerecorded music were home taped annually (1982 blank tape sales were barely half that), detached analysis of the more detailed 1982 Warners survey which kicked off the furor suggests a maximum annual loss of around $350 million, much of it absorbed by distributors and retailers. Though this isn't chicken feed, it no more accounts for a billion-dollar slump than that other slant-eyed bogeyman, videogames. But if leisure activities cut into each other that mechanistically, the sports equipment boom of the late '70s would have done music in.

The no-nonsense social science analysis is that the "recession-proof" music industry simply wasn't—that in tandem with the demographic dip that always awaited rock and roll as the baby boomers grew up, the near depression of the early '80s was just too much for it to take. Without doubt the much-bruited Reaganomic "recovery" occasioned a mood shift that helped bring record buyers back into the stores. But the biz earned its recession-proof rep by surviving several recessions, and it got beat in the latest one for the most fanciful reason of all: quality. By this I hardly mean that if only the big labels had promoted Blood Ulmer or the Human Switchboard or Southside Johnny or Black Flag, the world would now be safe for rock and roll. I've never sung that old song. But I'll settle for the follow-up, popularly known as "Nobody Loves You When You're Bored and Bland." One thing about cults—they do *love* what they like, enough to seek it out and if necessary pay a premium for it. All of the industry's payola and market research and super-group status-mongering couldn't instill that kind of enthusiasm in the passive audience shaped by radio's cowardice and conservatism—its consultancies, its racism, its fear of tuneouts. Whatever excitement people are once again finding in music begins with content—or anyway, with form/content. As bizzers like to say, it's in the grooves—or anyway, that's half the story. And if there were hypes at work too, well, they damn near hit the record business upside its pointy little head.

## New Technology, MTV, MR, "New Music," and Michael Jackson

So many accounts of rock and roll's recovery dwell on new technology—business analysts always prefer machines, which can be owned, to human beings, who (according to enlightened capitalist theory) can't. But in fact bizzers progressed with science only after first clambering headlong in the opposite direction. It took years of ghetto blasters and walkmen, both far more stimulating to the public appetite for music than high-end hi-fi, before the tape crusaders had the bright idea of lowering the price of prerecorded cassettes. The digitally recorded super-fidelity laser discs now causing such a tizzy are much more to their taste in toys—high per-unit profit, perhaps even with music that's already in the can. Indeed, laser playback may eventually be as big as stereo. But it may also die like quad, or (more likely) wind up almost as specialized as vinyl audiophile discs.

A similar pattern is evident in video. Before their misreading of disco ate up all that venture capital, forward-looking record execs used to dream about producing and selling consumer videos, which five years later is still risky business. But even Warners, half of MTV's parent corporation, had little inkling of the vast hype potential of the 24-hour rock-video cable service. For all its infinite venality, MTV provided a breath of proverbial fresh air for the rock audience and a shot in the proverbial arm for record sales. Of course, if the majors had been prepared with Linda Ronstadt and REO Speedwagon videos when the channel went on the air in 1981, it's conceivable it would have flopped, or meant very little. Instead, bizzers handed the ball to mostly British "new wave" longshots. Appearance-obsessed art-school types who were eager to stake some of their Eurodollars on the state-side profits rock and rollers dream of, these young musicians came up with lots of snazzy clips. Thus MTV was the making of such bands as Men at Work, whose debut eventually outsold both *Asia* and *American Fool* in 1982; the Stray Cats, London-trained Massapequa-billies whose midline-priced compilation is now double platinum; A Flock of Seagulls, with their high-IQ haircuts and dumb hooks; and let us not forget Duran Duran.

Much as I hate typing with my fingers crossed, I'm willing to venture that MTV won't ever be as conservative a cultural force as AOR. The circumstances that thrust it briefly into the commercial forefront of "new wave" were temporary, and that was never the whole story—the rampaging "new" heavy metal has also been a major beneficiary, as have "Puttin' on the Ritz" and Linda Ronstadt's Nelson Riddle album. But because visual information is so specific that people quickly get bored with it, the channel craves novelty by nature. And thus, inexorably, it has shaken radio up. MTV was certainly in Lee Abrams's AOR mastermind, when he took a quick look at KROQ, which had jumped to the top of the Los Angeles Arbitron ratings after switching to a new wavish format in 1981, and ordered his faltering Super-Stars consultancy network to double the new music it played. Although Abrams reserved special praise for "techno stuff," he apparently can use a dictionary. So he defined new as recently released, which often turned out to mean Huey Lewis and Quiet Riot rather than "Free Bird" and "Stairway to Heaven."

For many younger bizzers, of course, the innocent words "new music" resonate with significance, and the annual New Music Seminar, launched by Rockpool and *Dance Music Report* in July 1980, is their very own industry confab. The term "new music" was apparently appropriated from the downtown minimalist avant-garde just as "new wave" was taken over from the French auteurist avant-garde, and no one knows exactly how to define it—the *Wall Street Journal* has called it "futuristic 'technopop'" and "a blend of rock, soul and reggae" in the same sentence. I'd suggest that, as with "postmodernism," the sweeping yet abjectly relative vagueness of the term signifies above all a fervent desire to deny antecedents which are in fact inescapable. Having once defined "rock," an equally amorphous category, as "all music derived from the energy and influence of the Beatles," I would now define "new music" as "all music deriving primarily from the energy and influence of the

Ramones and the Sex Pistols." Then I would hope against hope that two qualifications were understood: first, that "energy and influence" refer more to sociological movement than to formal musical development, and second, that I'm making fun.

The New Music Seminar began as a mildly bohemian one-day affair in a friendly recording studio, and it was still pretty bohemian in 1982, when it attracted 1100 to the Sheraton Centre. In 1983 it was at the Hilton, enrollment had more than doubled, and bohemian it wasn't. "Everyone realizes that they are the future of the industry, so there is less rowdiness," opined organizer Joel Webber, and with the Police, Eddy Grant, Kajagoogoo, David Bowie, Culture Club, and Madness in the top 10 and Duran Duran, Naked Eyes, the Eurythmics, Prince, the Human League, and Men at Work bubbling up from 30, this sense of destiny was understandable. Not that some bohemian stragglers didn't hoot at the chasm between the Sex Pistols and Kajagoogoo, and not that all the skepticism came from disillusioned punks—"It's our business to give the audience what they want," announced Ocean City, Maryland, deejay Brian Krysz, who clearly didn't think these New Yorkers had any idea what that might mean where he was from. But somewhere in between the old bohos and the old pros there was a comfortable consensus that the ailing music industry had pulled itself back from the brink by finally coming to terms with the progress it had resisted so pigheadedly for so long.

One factor was missing from this analysis, however: Michael Jackson. "New music" is such an all-encompassing concept that an enthusiast could claim it subsumes all others. But there's no way it subsumes Michael. The overwhelming success of *Thriller*, which has long since surpassed *Bridge Over Troubled Water* as CBS's biggest album of all time, is the fulfillment of the blockbuster fantasy that has possessed the industry ever since *Saturday Night Fever.* For years retailers argued that if only the nudnicks over in production could suck people into the stores with another piece of product like that, they'd take care of the rest. And there are those who believe—cynically, in my judgment—that *Thriller* is the whole secret of the recovery.

The thing is, *Thriller* couldn't have happened in a vacuum. Insofar as new music is basically Anglodisco, its rapprochement between the white rock audience and dance music worked to the enormous advantage of *Thriller*: for all its whiteskin provincialism, its defanged funk and silly soul, the world of new music is somewhat more open to black artists than the world of AOR. (What isn't?) Certainly neither Prince nor Eddy Grant could have crossed over without first proving themselves in the white dance clubs, and while Michael Jackson didn't need this more hospitable atmosphere—not with Paul McCartney and Eddie Van Halen on his side—he benefited from it. But here too it was MTV that made the biggest difference. Once again indulging in disgraceful if not unconstitutional reluctance to air black music, MTV at first turned down Jackson's videos and only after CBS president Walter Yetnikoff threatened to withdraw CBS clips from the channel—the story is denied on both sides, but it's clear some heavy muscle was applied—did MTV capitulate. Soon thereafter the $200,000 production number Jackson contrived around "Beat It" turned into the channel's most widely popular item ever. With MTV fallen, AOR jumped in and a hit album was transformed into an unprecedented megacrossover.

The triumph of *Thriller* makes an edifying record-biz fable. A heroic tale of music marketers moving the news from the grooves to the yearning masses, it would seem to refute my brave assertion that the recovery owes more to art than it does to hype. But I did hedge, because just like the neat binary opposition between form and content, the division of hype and art is a middlebrow convenience, useful in obscuring the vulgar details of the pop process, which needn't be deep to be enduring or meaningful. With Michael Jackson or the Stray Cats or Culture Club, it's hard to say where art leaves off and hype begins, because all three devote unmistakable aesthetic energy to the promulgation of image as well as to the invention of music. Now, as we learned in the '60s, image promulgation is tricky business and trickier art, but I'm proud to admit that after a dull gray decade of grind-it-out professionalism I'm rather enjoying the current flashstorm. My pleasure is sure to diminish as the most cunning of the ignorant young posers currently overrunning the London video industry dig in for the careerist haul. But if hype it's gotta be, I'll take mine tacky, thanks.

## Kajagoogoomania

All descriptions of the current pop moment invoke the British Invasion hook sooner or later, so why not. But let's get one thing straight. Unless you favor the formulation in which the second British wave began Hollies-Donovan-Cream circa 1967 (making the current incursion number seven or so), the so-called Invasion was more like an occupation, or an endless parade. Granting a fair share of misses—most significantly T. Rex and Slade, two seminal singles bands who were huge in England by 1971 but scored one real hit between them here—it lasted from 1964 all the way till 1977, when Malcolm McLaren, who didn't invent punk but did do his damnedest for his nation's economy, set about revitalizing the troubled U.K. branch of an industry that was marching off a cliff without knowing it.

Many armchair promo men, ignoring the stylistic precedents of T. Rex and Slade as well as the Sex Pistols' unseemly politics, actually professed surprise when this latest London phenomenon failed to conquer America, where disco and AOR were reaching sizable new markets. This besmirched Britannia's image among the captains of America's music capital for half a decade. Which is why all this talk of a "second" British Invasion is basically bullshit. What we have here is a reactive return to normalcy, with conveniently prepackaged Brits regaining their customary advantage in the musical balance of trade. I insist on this not to beef up my pitch for American music, a worthy cause that's turning into one more pious cliché, but to take the barb off the British Invasion hook, the hidden intent of which is to make this pop moment seem altogether more . . . *gear* than it actually is. Oh, it's *different*, sure; times change. Still, all the headline-writers hope to intimate, isn't it kind of like Swinging London all over again?

I should remind my more mature readers that in 1964 most new music fans were still in diapers if that. They may be acquainted with the music of the "first" British Invasion, but its excitement comes to them secondhand. British punk was a great pop moment, but it was also a great antipop moment, excluding potential listeners far more antagonistically than any generation gap. When it didn't put new clothes on the old radical fallacy that youth is sitting out there eagerly (if passively) awaiting an Alternative, it worked off the supposed truism that rock and roll thrives on shock—just outrage the Establishment and every teenager in the NATO alliance will throw money at you. It would have been wonderful if some synthesis of these ideas had reunified the pop world, and in fact it was wonderful anyway. But it's hardly a surprise that unity didn't ensue, because punk's antagonisms weren't aimed solely at the Establishment; they were also aimed at the complacent or self-deluded or indifferent or just plain different rock fans who failed to get the message. Some of these were converted, others quickly became very pissed off, others remained indifferent, and still others changed their minds a little. Very roughly speaking you could say that Swinging London II comprises most of the people who changed their minds plus many indifferents and a significant admixture of re-converted converts. And for all its backbiting, infighting, and ridiculously sectarian trendiness, its pop impulse—which in this case means nothing more noble than its craving for commercial success—is more wholehearted, though not more idealistic, than punk's ever was.

Yet, avant-garde polemicism notwithstanding, 1977 does stand as a great pop moment, and reconciliations notwithstanding, 1983 remains a dubious one. That's because 1977 held out a promise far more radical and far more realistic than that of Elvis or the Beatles or the hippies. Where the myth of rock culture had vitiated rock and roll's rebel strain by glamorizing it, punk amplified it by focusing it, and though it despised all '60s-style utopian folderol, it refused to surrender its idealism-in-the-negative. In contrast, all 1983 could offer was 15 minutes of pleasure in the limelight. Or make that three minutes. Punk's populist strategy was to reclaim the quick hooky virtues of the then-moribund pop single, and though "new music" could be quicker, it's definitely taken over that punk idea. In the process it's also inherited two kinds of burnout—not only the no-future cynicism affected by 1977's cynosures and penny-rockets, but the flash-in-the-pan one-shotism of the pre-"rock" era. There's nothing more British Invasion about it than the bewildering profusion of new names on the charts.

Nevertheless, I can't go along with McLaren, who claims that the new Brit wave broke because American bizzers "don't want black music taking over." It's not just that he's oversimplifying with an ulterior motive as usual. Nor is it that Michael J. has rendered further race war superfluous—sure it was *Thriller*'s year, but Afrika Bambaataa and Blood Ulmer and the perennial George Clinton did great work in 1983 too, and none of them has cracked MTV quite yet. My skepticism has more to do with the sometimes useful, often unavoidable, but here merely obfuscatory vagueness of the term "black music" itself. Insofar as Anglomania kept conciliatory, professional black *pop* down in a strong year for the genre, it did so in fairly open competition; James Ingram may be a nice fellow, but Boy George has more to tell the world. And there's no reason to believe that if every fop in England were suddenly to expire of synthesizer poisoning, hard, eccentric black *funk* would fill the vacuum. Like punk, funk is an avantish style that articulates megapolitan street values. If they've failed to change middle America, that's largely middle America's fault, and choice: hegemony is subtle and not altogether undemocratic stuff.

If this seems like a retreat from my traditionally staunch affirmative action stand, I'm sorry, but it isn't. Of course black music would be more popular if it got the exposure it's denied by the manipulatively racist assumptions of AOR and MTV. But that doesn't mean those assumptions have no basis in white listeners' actual tastes—tastes that don't necessarily reduce to race, and tastes they have a right to even though they live worse for them. Anyway, current music is too multifarious to justify any kind of single-genre campaign. Always craning their necks at the next big thing, opportunists like McLaren make pop music happen, but their perspective is screwy by definition. Even in the heady punk years of 1977 and 1978, there was great work from old farts like Fleetwood Mac and the Stones and Pete Townshend and oddballs like the McGerrigles and Joe Ely and Ronnie Lane, not to mention all the soul and funk and disco and blues and folk and country professionals who rolled merrily along as if Johnny Rotten didn't exist, which for them he didn't. More often, several promising-to-exciting things will go on at once. And then there are times that throw up no markers at all. This patternlessness doesn't have to mean there's no significant action. But it can be a bitch to figure out.

## Wha?

Perhaps my dismay merely reflects an awareness that the skeptical but positive picture of the recovery I outlined was nowhere near skeptical enough. For instance, it may have given the impression that I can watch MTV for an hour without gastric distress. It's a distortion to label rock videos commercials; at worst they're promos, which is not the same thing, and if they borrow advertising techniques, that's an inevitable consequence of their brevity, their lyric structure, and their roots in rock and roll's hook aesthetic. But to excuse the directors a little is only to blame the music more. Great exceptions and pleasant surprises notwithstanding, most rock videos diminish the second-rate songs they're supposed to enhance; however circumscribed rock artistes may be musically, their literary and dramatic endowments are usually even narrower. Because videos visualize lyrics and compel contemplation of the artists' mugs, they bring home how slick, stunted, smug, self-pitying, and stupid rock culture has become. Even more offensive than the racism the channel promulgates by omission is the way sexism that's only implicit in words and live performance is underlined again and again by the vaguely sadie-maisie mannequins who sing backup or play their mute roles in male jackoff and/or revenge fantasies. The clips make it all but impossible to reimagine songs you like—Billy Idol's fake-gothic misogyny and adolescent fear of commitment have ruined "White Wedding" for me forever. And they replace participation with spectatorism on the physical level as well—fans watch raptly instead of dancing or at least boogieing in the aisles.

True, whenever I think such thoughts I remind myself that early media-brainwash theorists once leveled similar charges at talkies. Because pop culture evolves like anything else, there's a chance that great exceptions and pleasant surprises—"Atomic Dog" and "Burning Down the House" and "Thriller" and "Atlantic City" and "TV Dinners" and "One on One" and even (Phil Collins's) "You Can't Hurry Love"—will eventually prevail, enabling rock video to escape its current box, the one with genre movies, film school dream sequences, Helmut Newton and *Midnight Special* at the corners. Who knows, maybe it will turn into a Genuinely Innovative Art Form that melds technological flash with aesthetic insouciance over a beat that makes it all happen.

But even in this best instance the little matter of capital would make MTV one of the bad guys. Clips cost $15,000 for technically acceptable concert footage, with 40 or 50 grand about par for concept videos and $200,000 not unheard of. As an accepted part of promotion, videos raise the ante for struggling artists even more inescapably than high-tech audio; eight years after the first Ramones album seemed to harbinger a new era of rock and roll access because it cost $6400 to record, they put the game squarely back into the hands of the money boys. And while I don't buy the Mass Culture 1 fantasy of a nation of suburbanized adolescents lulled into a passive, consumerist pseudo-community by their television sets, I do believe that every popular form has its optimum audience size, and that rock and roll climbs above five million or so at its (occasionally invigorating) peril. In the stagnant information system of AOR, MTV provided liberating alternative input—pluralism has always been one secret of good rock and roll. But MTV's tuneout-sensitive national programming cut the roots of that secret.

Nor has MTV moved radio to the left. On the contrary, the latest shake-up has come in the form of a "new music backlash" already rumored at the Hilton in July. In a typically visionary memo, Lee Abram's SuperStars HQ warned its stations that "progressive music is out." Artists such as Elvis Costello, Graham Parker, and Joan Armatrading (as well as many heavy metal acts) had "no business being on the radio" because the nation's tastes had turned "horizontal"—consultant talk for top 40, music that crosses demographic boundaries, which under the initials CHR (Contemporary Hits Radio) is the new hot programming idea. In New York, AOR bellwether WPLJ set tongues wagging a year ago when it added "Little Red Corvette" (performed by a black person, you know) and by June was playing nothing but hits, which in current radio parlance is not the same thing at all as "rock," which designated all popular music except country and disco five years ago but is now considered too "vertical." Soon WPLJ was joined and vanquished by the smarmier (if more integrated) Z-100, which is momentarily tops among the city's music stations.

There's something comic about all this commotion—just imagine, maybe people actually *want to listen to hit records*. But in fact the pop single had become almost theoretical during the slump—if it weren't for MTV, its attendant Anglomania, and let us not forget a reintegrated black pop, the format mightn't have come back at all. And insofar as it brings down bastions of white power like WPLJ, CHR is incontrovertibly a good thing. You can listen to it, too. But this in no way justifies eager comparisons to top 40's Beatlemaniac glory years by bright-eyed populists old enough to know better. Top 40 commands neither the consensus nor the excitement it did in the middle '60s. It can't, because that excitement was bound up in a sense of imminent social possibility, with rock and roll more reflection than source, that for the moment is effectively dead.

And one more thing—horizontal radio ain't necessarily so great for the record business. One survey indicates that for every CHR fan who buys six LPs a year there are three AOR faithful, and while CHR can't be the root cause of such deplorable penny-pinching (the younger, predominantly female audience it attracts has never been all that long on music dollars), it's not helping any. The phenomenal growth of the album market was predicated on the passionate, committed, "vertical" myth of rock culture; pop commitments aren't as steady and wide-ranging. So perhaps it shouldn't be surprising that, just as the slump was never as severe as the tape-obsessed doomsayers in an emotional industry said it was, the current recovery doesn't qualify as any sort of boom. When the tally was in, it turned out that the great comeback of 1983 had been good for only 111 gold albums while the great slump of 1982 had produced 130, with platinum albums down from 55 to 49. Not there hasn't really been a recovery of sorts, though even in the unlikely event of a final gain of 10 percent, more will still have been lost between 1981 and 1982. The dollar volume of four albums—*Thriller*, *Flashdance*, Def Leppard's *Pyromania*, and the Police's *Synchronicity*, all reportedly well over five million—made up most of it.

This is inauspicious, because it commits venture capital to a blockbuster mentality. Experience has shown that blockbusters can't be predicted positively—except maybe for *Synchronicity*, nobody knew for sure that any of the albums I've named would sell a quarter of what they did. But they can be predicted negatively, and they will be: it's going to get even harder for marginal artists with zero-plus platinum potential to find backing. Because make no mistake, folks, the big problem with the music business is capitalism. What did you think it was—the natural order of things?

## Eternal Youth

I'm aware that such rhetoric is apt to exasperate many readers, especially when I fail to lay out an alternative. Because make no mistake about this either: rock and roll is capitalist in its blood. Its excitement has always been bound up in the individualistic get-up-and-go of ambitious young men who looked around their land of plenty and decided that they deserved—hell, just plain wanted—a bigger piece, and it would never have reached its constituency or engendered its culture without the entrepreneurial derring-do of countless promoters, hustlers, petty criminals, and other small businessmen. But though there are still more than enough young rock and rollers to go around, the most ambitious are rarely as likable or as visionary as they were 20 and 30 years ago. Where the pursuit of an audience was once a fair equivalent to the education of a community, in a self-proclaimed scarcity economy any kind of marketing smacks of exploitation. And the derring-do of the big businessmen involved is often on a grandly international scale. Like the man says, it's a jungle out there, and for those who aspire to a musical vocation what might have seemed like a dream or a lark in 1967 or even 1977 now feels more like a gamble—all-or-nothing, go-for-broke.

The obvious alternative attracts many gifted musicians: avant-gardism, pop or renegade. Devolving into three-chord clamor or forging toward total cacophony, recombining root musics or traversing alien structural and improvisational concepts, these artists put the limits of their acquiescence in boldface and let the fans fall where they may. Inaccessibility both formal and physical assures that their audiences won't be passive, and sometimes they make music galvanizing enough to jar some free-floating complacency loose as well. But by definition avant-gardists sacrifice the unique political purchase of popular form— the way it speaks to and for the populace. The charm of a walking tolerance advert like Boy

George or a raving idealist like U2's Bono Vox is that their refusal to make that sacrifice evinces the kind of willful provisional naïveté that these days is rarer and wiser than irony. The enduring beauty and pleasure of black music from pop to rap likewise inheres in its will to keep on keeping on—nowhere are the material satisfactions of living in the U.S.A. evoked more seductively, and nowhere do they sound more earned.

Nor did punk destroy the rock faith among those it moved most directly, so that now two otherwise adverse youth populations—AOR's 12–24 white male demographic and the tiny core of perhaps 50,000 (?) postpunk clubgoers and record collectors who send their elected representatives to hoot at functions like the New Music Seminar—continue to make music the measure of things. We veterans are loathe to pass the flame to either side because in rock and roll populists and avant-gardists are supposed to work together, keep each other honest—on our kind of cultural frontier, you need both numbers and acuteness. But if that hasn't happened, the reason isn't the music's breakdown as a cultural organism so much as capitalism's breakdown as a nexus of social possibility.

I mean, just exactly what frontier is it supposed to take? In the present go-for-broke environment, all the arts are fucked. Those popular forms that remain cheerful avoid making stringent demands on themselves, as in the rich but complacent neoclassicism enjoyed by jazz musicians and Hollywood folk. Network television is network television, and while video artists are bursting with technological imperative, their visions of a public-access future are tinged with utopian folderol. It's also worth noting that video artists are rarely disdainful of rock and roll—or rather, of the capital that will be ventured if rock video opens up a little. And among poets and visual artists, for instance, the punk and funk subcultures that seem so truncated to participant-observers like me are viewed more positively, as a means to the "vitality" of their fitful dreams. There's still a profusion of good rock and roll coming down, of every conceivable description and in a state of continual superpluralistic international cross-fertilization. In fact, the music's shapeless quality these days sometimes seems a virtue—a metaphor redolent with democratic fecundity. It pleases me to remember that the myth of the Great Artist has become a quintessential capitalist hype.

And if I then conclude that for all that the current situation really won't do, it's not because I pine for rock culture; it's because I refuse to suspend my disbelief in eternal youth. That theme has been turning sour for a decade now, but the older I get the surer I am that it carries meaning—something like what Bob Dylan called busy-being-born before life got to him. Rather than a simple matter of age, it's an idealism-in-the-negative that might conceivably foster the kind of cross-generational alliances that have always been too rare among white Americans. Even after you factor in America's inferiority complex and dead-ass bizzers, what puts the U.K.'s young rock and rollers in the chips and ours in day jobs boils down to style, by which I do not mean haircuts. The good young rock and rollers here still partake of enough of our tattered national optimism to act as if youth rebellion is a real-life possibility, complete with a hearty fuck-you-if-you-can't-take-the-heat that as always I could do without, but also with a depth of commitment that seems to come naturally. In London, on the other hand, youth rebellion looks like a desperate game, a flamboyant and probably fleeting masquerade. What fascinates the new Brits about youth is that like everything else it'll betray you eventually, and unless I'm mistaken their fans everywhere find comfort in that. Expectations are such a burden these days.

It will be said that like rock culture itself, eternal youth is an illusion worth discarding—that kids today are realistic and good for them. But that kind of realism is exactly what the neoconservative thrust of capitalist culture means to inculcate, and I'm against it. Of course I believe people should grow up, and yes, I think it's the better part of grace to accept the inevitable decline of body-pride, the purely physical exuberance behind rock and roll's fabled energy. But the fact that people grow up doesn't mean they have to stop growing, and if that sounds like some Marin County bromide, well, I learned it from

Chuck Berry and John Lennon and George Clinton and, indirectly, Karl Marx too. Only people who insist on changing themselves are liable to end up changing the world around them, and although it would be nice to think rock and roll could change the world all by itself, I've never had much use for that fallacy. All I expect from rock and roll is what rock and roll taught me to expect: more.

# 67. *Thriller* Begets the "King of Pop"

We already encountered Michael Jackson (b. 1958) briefly in Berry Gordy's account of Motown in the 1960s (see chapter 33). Jackson was arguably the greatest child prodigy in the history of post-1955 popular music, and his early recordings with the Jackson Five intrigued adults as much for their maturity (and uncanny absorption of James Brown's vocal style) as they did teenagers and preteens with their visceral excitement.

Jackson's first records as a solo artist in 1971, like those of the Jackson Five, were remarkably successful. However, Jackson's solo career did not really take off until the late 1970s. In 1978, while starring in the film musical, *The Wiz*, as the Scarecrow, Jackson met producer Quincy Jones. The two collaborated on Jackson's next album, *Off the Wall*, which outsold his previous solo efforts and garnered favorable critical notices. Jones and Jackson successfully updated Jackson's sound, presenting Jackson as a mature artist capable of appealing to dancers and Top 40 radio programmers alike. *Off the Wall* only hinted at what was to come. *Thriller*, Jackson's next album (again produced by Jones), released late in 1982, became an international phenomenon, breaking all sales records and selling approximately 45 million copies to date. *Thriller* did not so much create a new style as it successfully synthesized aspects of preexisting ones: On it, one hears soulful, middle-of-the-road ballads ("The Girl Is Mine," sung with Paul McCartney), slick funk-disco ("Billie Jean"), and funky heavy metal ("Beat It"). This stylistic blending enabled Jackson to transcend boundaries between audiences that music industry experts believed were unassailable. In chapter 66, Robert Christgau offered an alternate explanation when he argued that synth-pop had helped prepare and create an audience for the album through "its rapprochement between white rock and dance music."[1]

---

1. "Rock 'n' Roller Coaster," p. 40. For an account in a music trade publication, see Paul Grein, "Michael Jackson Cut Breaks AOR Barrier," *Billboard* (December 18, 1982), 1, 58.

Videos provided another key to Jackson's success, since he began conceiving of his songs as soundtracks. The videos for "Billie Jean," "Beat It," and "Thriller" were more than mere promotional vehicles for the recordings—they were "minifilms," small narratives with budgets that dwarfed those of previous videos. Jackson's understanding of how to employ his singing and dancing skills within the rhetoric of video enabled him to exploit his abilities as a *performer*, rather than as a *musician* per se. Viewed in this way, the magnitude of his success is inextricable from the age of music video.

Jackson's next two albums following *Thriller*, *Bad* (1987) and *Dangerous* (1991), saw him struggling to match the critical and commercial success of *Thriller*. Both albums sold upward of 20 million copies, which would rank them among the most popular albums of all time, but there was a sense in which Jackson was repeating himself (the formulaic funk of *Bad*) or groping for new ideas (the attempts to incorporate aspects of New Jack Swing with the help of producer Terry Riley in *Dangerous*). Although Jackson had devoted much effort to humanitarian causes throughout the 1980s and early 1990s (most famously in the recording of "We Are the World," cowritten with Lionel Ritchie for U.S.A. for Africa in 1985), by the mid-1990s, his career was in danger of being overshadowed by tabloid-style scandals and his brief marriage to Lisa Marie Presley (daughter of Elvis).

For many listeners and viewers, Jackson's physical transformation gave a new inflection to the concept of "crossover," and these cosmetic changes constitute the focus of Greg Tate's review of *Bad*. Tate revisits the idea of Jackson's precocity and discusses the relationship of Jackson's 1980s recordings to the legacy of Berry Gordy and the Motown recordings of the 1960s. Similar to his article on Santana (reprinted in chapter 44), albeit in a less fanciful fashion, Tate considers the relationship of black identity to the process of middle-class acculturation, an approach that cautions against the easy dismissal of Motown or *Thriller* as a racial "sellout." Yet, at the same time, Tate implies some connection between the aesthetic disappointment of *Bad* and Jackson's ongoing physical repudiation of his racial heritage. Tate is not alone: Many other cultural critics have taken up the subject of Jackson's fluctuating physical appearance, which generates so much attention that it threatens to obscure appreciation of his musical achievements.[2]

---

2. See, for example, Michele Wallace, "Michael Jackson, Black Modernisms and 'The Ecstasy of Communication," in *Invisibility Blues: From Pop to Theory* (London: Verso, 1990), 77–90; Kobena Mercer, "Monster Metaphors: Notes on Michael Jackson's *Thriller*," *Screen*, 27, no. 1 (1986) reprinted in Simon Frith, Andrew Goodwin, and Lawrence Grossberg, eds., *Sound and Vision: The Music Video Reader* (London and New York: Routledge, 1993), 93–108; and Susan Willis, "I Want the Black One: Is There a Place for Afro-American Culture in Commodity Culture," in *A Primer for Daily Life* (London: Routledge, 1991), 108–32.

# I'M WHITE! WHAT'S WRONG WITH MICHAEL JACKSON

## *Greg Tate*

There are other ways to read Michael Jackson's blanched skin and disfigured African features than as signs of black self-hatred become self-mutilation. Waxing fanciful, we can imagine the-boy-who-would-be-white as a William Gibson-ish work of science fiction: harbinger of a trans-racial tomorrow where genetic deconstruction has become the norm and Narcissism wears the face of all human Desire. Musing empathetic, we may put the question, who does Mikey want to be today? The Pied Piper, Peter Pan, Christopher Reeve, Skeletor, or Miss Diana Ross? Our Howard Hughes? Digging into our black nationalist bag, Jackson emerges a casualty of America's ongoing race war—another Negro gone mad because his mirror reports that his face does not conform to the Nordic ideal.

To fully appreciate the sickness of Jackson's savaging of his African physiognomy you have to recall that back when he wore the face he was born with, black folk thought he was the prettiest thing since sliced sushi. (My own mother called Michael pretty so many times I almost got a complex.) Jackson and I are the same age, damn near 30, and I've always had a love-hate thing going with the brother. When we were both moppets I envied him, the better dancer, for being able to arouse the virginal desires of my female schoolmates, shameless oglers of his (and Jermaine's) tenderoni beefcake in *16* magazine. Even so, no way in those say-it-loud-I'm-black-and-I'm-proud days could you not dig Jackson heir to the James Brown dance throne. At age 10, Jackson's footwork and vocal machismo seemed to scream volumes about the role of genetics in the cult of soul and the black sexuality of myth. The older folk might laugh when he sang shake it, shake it baby, ooh, ooh or teacher's gonna show you, all about loving. Yet part of the tyke's appeal was being able to simulate being lost in the hot sauce way before he was supposed to know what the hot sauce even smelt like. No denying he *sounded* like he knew the real deal.

In this respect, Jackson was the underweaned creation of two black working-class traditions: that of boys being forced to bypass childhood along the fast track to manhood, and that of rhythm and blues auctioning off the race's passion for song, dance, sex, and spectacle. Accelerated development became a life-imperative after slavery, and R&B remains the redemption of minstrelsy—at least it was until Jackson made crossover mean lightening your skin and whitening your nose.

Slavery, minstrelsy, and black bourgeoisie aspirations are responsible for three of the more pejorative notions about blacks in this country—blacks as property, as ethnographic commodities, and as imitation rich white people. Given this history, there's a fine line between a black entertainer who appeals to white people and one who sells out the race in pursuit of white appeal. Berry Gordy, Bürgermeister of crossover's Bauhaus, walked that line with such finesse that some black folk were shocked to discover via *The Big Chill* that many whites considered Motown *their* music. Needless to say, Michael Jackson has crossed so way far over the line that there ain't no coming back—assuming through surgical transformation of his face a singular infamy in the annals of tomming.

The difference between Gordy's crossover dream world and Jackson's is that Gordy's didn't preclude the notion that black is beautiful. For him the problem was his pupils not being ready for prime time. Motown has raised brows for its grooming of Detroit ghetto kids in colored genteel manners, so maybe there were people who thought Gordy was trying to make his charges over into pseudo-Caucasoids. Certainly this insinuation isn't foreign to the work of rhythm and blues historians Charles Keil and Peter Guralnick, both of whom write of Motown as if it weren't hot and black enough to suit their blood, or at least

*Source:* Greg Tate, "I'm White! What's Wrong with Michael Jackson," *Flyboy in the Buttermilk*, pp. 95–99 (originally published in 1987). © Greg Tate. Used by permission.

their conception of bloods. But the intermingling of working-class origins and middle-class acculturation are too mixed up in black music's evolution to allow for simpleminded purist demands for a black music free of European influence, or of the black desire for a higher standard of living and more cultural mobility. As an expression of '60s black consciousness, Motown symbolized the desire of blacks to get their foot in the bank door of the American dream. In the history of affirmative action Motown warrants more than a footnote beneath the riot accounts and NAACP legal maneuvers.

As a black American success story, the Michael Jackson of *Thriller* is an extension of the Motown integrationist legacy. But the Michael Jackson as skin job represents the carpetbagging side of black advancement in the affirmative action era. The fact that we are now producing young black men and women who conceive of their African inheritance as little more than a means to cold-crash mainstream America and then cold-dis—if not merely put considerable distance between—the brothers and sisters left behind. In this sense Jackson's decolorized flesh reads as the buppy version of Dorian Gray, a blaxploitation nightmare that offers this moral: Stop, the face you save may be your own.

In 1985 black people cherished *Thriller's* breakthrough as if it were their own battering ram against the barricades of American apartheid. Never mind how many of those kerzillon LPs we bought, forget how much Jackson product we had bought all those years before that—even with his deconstructed head, we wanted this cat to tear the roof off the all-time-greatest-sales sucker bad as he did. It's like *Thriller* was this generation's answer to the Louis-Schmeling fight or something. Oh, the Pyrrhic victories of the disenfranchised. Who would've thought this culture hero would be cut down to culture heel, with a scalpel? Or maybe it's just the times. To those living in New York City and currently witnessing a rebirth of black consciousness in protest politics, advocacy journalism (read *The City Sun!* read *The City Sun!*) and the arts, Jackson seems dangerously absurd.

Proof that God don't like ugly, the title of Michael's new LP, *Bad* (Epic), accurately describes the contents in standard English. (Jackson apparently believes that *bad* can apply to both him and L.L. Cool J.) No need to get stuck on making comparisons with *Thriller*, *Bad* sounds like home demos Michael cut over a long weekend. There's not one song here that any urban contemporary hack couldn't have laid in a week, let alone two years. Several of the up-tempo numbers wobble in with hokey bass lines out of the Lalo Schifrin fakebook, and an inordinate number begin with ominous science fiction synthnoise—invariably preceding an anti-climax. *Bad* has hooks, sure, and most are searching for a song, none more pitifully than the fly-weight title track, which throws its chorus around like a three-year-old brat.

The only thing *Bad* has going for it is that it was made by the same artist who made *Thriller*. No amount of disgust for Jackson's even newer face (cleft in the chin) takes anything away from *Thriller*. Everything on that record manages a savvy balance between machine language and human intervention, between palpitating heart and precision tuning. *Thriller* is a record that doesn't know how to stop giving pleasure. Every note on the mutha sings and breathes masterful pop instincts: the drumbeats, the bass lines, the guitar chicken scratches, the aleatoric elements. The weaving of discrete details into fine polyphonic mesh reminds me of those African field recordings where simultaneity and participatory democracy, not European harmony, serve as the ordering principle.

*Bad*, as songless as *Thriller* is songful, finds Jackson performing material that he has absolutely no emotional commitment to—with the exception of spitefully named "Dirty Diana," a groupie fantasy. The passion and compassion of "Beat It," "Billie Jean," and "Wanna Be Startin' Somethin'" seemed genuine, generated by Jackson's perverse attraction to the ills of teen violence and teen pregnancy. There was something frightful and compelling about this mollycoddled mama's boy delivering lapidary pronouncements from his Xanadu like "If you can't feed your baby, then don't have a baby." While the world will hold its breath and turn blue in the face awaiting the first successful Michael Jackson paternity suit, he had the nerve to sing, "This kid is not my son." Not even David Bowie could create a subtext that coy and rakish on the surface and grotesque at its depths.

Only in its twisted aspects does *Bad*, mostly via the "Bad" video, outdo *Thriller*. After becoming an artificial white man, now he wants to trade on his ethnicity. Here's Jackson's sickest fantasy yet: playing the role of a black preppie returning to the ghetto, he not only offers himself as a role model he literally screams at the brothers "You ain't nothin'!" Translation: Niggers ain't shit. In Jackson's loathsome conception of the black experience, you're either a criminal stereotype or one of the Beautiful People. Having sold the world pure pop pleasure on *Thriller*, Jackson returns on *Bad* to see his own race hatred. If there's 35 million sales in that, be ready to head for the hills ya'll.

# 68. Madonna and the Performance of Identity

Along with Michael Jackson, Madonna (b. 1958) was one of the first stars to truly understand and exploit the potential of music video and MTV. Even more than Jackson, she relied less on conventional musical chops than on creative visual self-presentation, choreography, and dancing. Both Michael Jackson's hits from his *Thriller* album and Madonna's early hits proved that a significant audience existed for dance-oriented recordings. In fact, Madonna's early recordings found success in dance clubs before they were played on mainstream pop radio and before she ever made a video. Her early videos projected a kind of ironic pastiche, playing off well-known cinematic sequences; this occurred most strikingly in her video for "Material Girl" (1985) in which Madonna presented herself as a Marilyn Monroe-type character in a scene based on the performance of the song, "Diamonds Are a Girl's Best Friend" (from *Gentlemen Prefer Blondes*, the 1954 film featuring Monroe).[1] Madonna's early image also made much of her thrift-store attire, a look that had a lot in common with another female star from this period who figured prominently on MTV: Cyndi Lauper

Madonna subsequently proved herself adept at manipulating her image and in maintaining media interest in her career—Jon Pareles

---

1. See E. Ann Kaplan's analysis in *Rocking Around the Clock: Music Television, Postmodernism and Consumer Culture* (London: Methuen, 1987), 117–27.

memorably described her as a "virtuoso of the superficial."[2] Her flaunting of her sexuality while presenting herself as being "in control" (i.e.,
consciously choosing to flaunt her sexuality) provided a particularly potent model for young female fans (dubbed "wannabes") and fueled debate about whether the Madonna persona represented a new form of
feminism or the repudiation of it. Because of her obvious delight and skill
in publicly manipulating this persona, Madonna has become a favorite of
cultural critics.[3]

---

The following essay by Camille Paglia presents a good overview of
Madonna's career up through the early 1990s, with a particularly strong
focus on her videos. While Paglia's views on feminism provoked a storm
of controversy in the early 1990s, her enthusiasm for Madonna is related
to her ideas about the importance of instinctual sexuality, which, in turn,
formed part of her critique of feminism. Since Madonna's presentation of
her sexuality constituted an undeniable part of her fascination, Paglia's
account illuminates Madonna's enormous impact in ways that a more
conventional, "distanced," academic account could not.

## VENUS OF THE RADIO WAVES
### Camille Paglia

I'm a dyed-in-the-wool, true-blue Madonna fan.

It all started in 1984, when Madonna exploded onto MTV with a brazen, insolent, in-
your-face American street style, which she had taken from urban blacks, Hispanics, and her
own middle-class but turbulent and charismatic Italian American family. From the start,
there was a flamboyant and parodistic element to her sexuality, a hard glamour she had
learned from Hollywood cinema and from its devotees, gay men and drag queens.

Madonna is a dancer. She thinks and expresses herself through dance, which exists in
the eternal Dionysian realm of music. Dance, which she studied with a gay man in her home

---

2. Jon Pareles, "Madonna's Return to Innocence," *New York Times,* October 23, 1994, sec. 2, pp. 1, 38.

3. For an examination of Madonna as feminist and a musicological analysis of how her recordings en-
code empowering messages for women, see Susan McClary, "Living to Tell: Madonna's Resurrection of
the Fleshy," in *Feminine Endings* (Minneapolis: University of Minnesota Press, 1991), 148–66. For a contrasting view, see bell hooks, "Madonna: Plantation Mistress or Soul Sister?" in *Black Looks: Race and Representation* (Boston: South End Press, 1992), 157–64. For collections of essays by cultural studies scholars,
see Paul Smith, ed., *Madonnarama: Essays on Sex and Popular Culture* (Pittsburgh, Penn.: Cleis Press, 1993);
and Cathy Schwichtenberg, *The Madonna Connection: Representational Politics, Subcultural Identities, and
Cultural Theory* (Boulder, Colo.: Westview Press, 1993).

*Source:* Camille Paglia, "Venus of the Radio Waves," in *Sex, Art, and American Culture* (New York: Vintage
Books, 1992), pp. 6–13. Originally published in *The Independent Sunday Review*, London, July 21, 1991.
© Camille Paglia. Used by permission.

state of Michigan, was her avenue of escape from the conventions of religion and bourgeois society. The sensual language of her body allowed her to transcend the over-verbalized codes of her class and time.

Madonna's great instinctive intelligence was evident to me from her earliest videos. My first fights about her had to do with whether she was a good dancer or merely a well-coached one. As year by year she built up the remarkable body of her video work, with its dazzling number of dance styles, I have had to fight about that less and less. However, I am still at war about her with feminists and religious conservatives (an illuminating alliance of contemporary puritans).

Most people who denigrate Madonna do so out of ignorance. The postwar baby-boom generation in America, to which I belong, has been deeply immersed in popular culture for thirty-five years. Our minds were formed by rock music, which has poured for twenty-four hours a day from hundreds of noisy, competitive independent radio stations around the country.

Madonna, like Venus stepping from the radio waves, emerged from this giant river of music. Her artistic imagination ripples and eddies with the inner currents in American music. She is at her best when she follows her intuition and speaks to the world in the universal language of music and dance. She is at her worst when she tries to define and defend herself in words, which she borrows from louche, cynical pals and shallow, single-issue political activists.

Madonna consolidates and fuses several traditions of pop music, but the major one she typifies is disco, which emerged in the Seventies and, under the bland commercial rubric "dance music," is still going strong. It has a terrible reputation: when you say the word *disco*, people think "Bee Gees." But I view disco, at its serious best, as a dark, grand Dionysian music with roots in African earth-cult.

Madonna's command of massive, resonant bass lines, which she heard in the funky dance clubs of Detroit and New York, has always impressed me. As an Italian Catholic, she uses them liturgically. Like me, she sensed the buried pagan religiosity in disco. I recall my stunned admiration as I sat in the theater in 1987 and first experienced the crashing, descending chords of Madonna's "Causing a Commotion," which opened her dreadful movie *Who's That Girl?* If you want to hear the essence of modernity, listen to those chords, infernal, apocalyptic, and grossly sensual. This is the authentic voice of the *fin de siècle.*

Madonna's first video, for her superb, drivingly lascivious disco hit "Burnin' Up," did not make much of an impression. The platinum-blonde girl kneeling and emoting in the middle of a midnight highway just seemed to be a band member's floozie. In retrospect, the video, with its rapid, cryptic surrealism, prefigures Madonna's signature themes and contains moments of eerie erotic poetry.

"Lucky Star" was Madonna's breakthrough video. Against a luminous, white abstract background, she and two impassive dancers perform a synchronized series of jagged, modern kicks and steps. Wearing the ragtag outfit of all-black bows, see-through netting, fingerless lace gloves, bangle bracelets, dangle earrings, chains, crucifixes, and punk booties that would set off a gigantic fashion craze among American adolescent girls, Madonna flaunts her belly button and vamps the camera with a smoky, piercing, come-hither-but-keep-your-distance stare. Here she first suggests her striking talent for improvisational floor work, which she would spectacularly demonstrate at the first MTV awards show, when, wrapped in a white-lace wedding dress, she campily rolled and undulated snakelike on the stage, to the baffled consternation of the first rows of spectators.

I remember sitting in a bar when "Lucky Star," just out, appeared on TV. The stranger perched next to me, a heavyset, middle-aged working-class woman, watched the writhing Madonna and, wide-eyed and slightly frowning, blankly said, her beer held motionless halfway to her lips, "Will you look at this?" There was a sense that Madonna was doing something so new and so strange that one didn't know whether to call it beautiful or grotesque. Through MTV, Madonna was transmitting an avant-garde downtown New York sensibility to the American masses.

In "Lucky Star," Madonna is raffish, gamine, still full of the street-urchin mischief that she would portray in her first and best film, Susan Seidelman's *Desperately Seeking Susan* (1984). In "Borderline," she shows her burgeoning star quality. As the girlfriend of Hispanic toughs who is picked up by a British photographer and makes her first magazine cover, she presents the new dualities of her life: the gritty, multiracial street and club scene that she had haunted in obscurity and poverty, and her new slick, fast world of popularity and success.

In one shot of "Borderline," as she chummily chews gum with kidding girlfriends on the corner, you can see the nondescript plainness of Madonna's real face, which she again exposes, with admirable candor, in *Truth or Dare* when, slurping soup and sporting a shower cap over hair rollers, she fences with her conservative Italian father over the phone. Posing for the photographer in "Borderline," Madonna in full cry fixes the camera lens with challenging, molten eyes, in a bold ritual display of sex and aggression. This early video impressed me with Madonna's sophisticated view of the fabrications of femininity, that exquisite theater which feminism condemns as oppression but which I see as a supreme artifact of civilization. I sensed then, and now know for certain, that Madonna, like me, is drawn to drag queens for their daring, flamboyant insight into sex roles, which they see far more clearly and historically than do our endlessly complaining feminists.

Madonna's first major video, in artistic terms, was "Like a Virgin," where she began to release her flood of inner sexual personae, which appear and disappear like the painted creatures of masque. Madonna is an orchid-heavy Veronese duchess in white, a febrile Fassbinder courtesan in black, a slutty nun-turned-harlequin flapping a gold cross and posturing, bum in air, like a demonic phantom in the nose of a gondola. This video alone, with its coruscating polarities of evil and innocence, would be enough to establish Madonna's artistic distinction for the next century.

In "Material Girl," where she sashays around in Marilyn Monroe's strapless red gown and archly flashes her fan at a pack of men in tuxedos, Madonna first showed her flair for comedy. Despite popular opinion, there are no important parallels between Madonna and Monroe, who was a virtuoso comedienne but who was insecure, depressive, passive-aggressive, and infuriatingly obstructionist in her career habits. Madonna is manic, perfectionist, workaholic. Monroe abused alcohol and drugs, while Madonna shuns them. Monroe had a tentative, melting, dreamy solipsism; Madonna has Judy Holliday's wise-cracking smart mouth and Joan Crawford's steel will and bossy, circus-master managerial competence.

In 1985 the cultural resistance to Madonna became overt. Despite the fact that her "Into the Groove," the mesmerizing theme song of *Desperately Seeking Susan,* had saturated our lives for nearly a year, the Grammy Awards outrageously ignored her. The feminist and moralist sniping began in earnest. Madonna "degraded" womanhood; she was vulgar, sacrilegious, stupid, shallow, opportunistic. A nasty mass quarrel broke out in one of my classes between the dancers, who adored Madonna, and the actresses, who scorned her.

I knew the quality of what I was seeing: "Open Your Heart," with its risqué peep-show format, remains for me not only Madonna's greatest video but one of the three or four best videos ever made. In the black bustier she made famous (transforming the American lingerie industry overnight), Madonna, bathed in blue-white light, plays Marlene Dietrich straddling a chair. Her eyes are cold, distant, all-seeing. She is ringed, as if in a sea-green aquarium, by windows of lewd or longing voyeurs: sad sacks, brooding misfits, rowdy studs, dreamy gay twins, a melancholy lesbian.

"Open Your Heart" is a brilliant mimed psychodrama of the interconnections between art and pornography, love and lust. Madonna won my undying loyalty by reviving and re-creating the hard glamour of the studio-era Hollywood movie queens, figures of mytho-logical grandeur. Contemporary feminism cut itself off from history and bankrupted itself when it spun its puerile, paranoid fantasy of male oppressors and female sex-object victims. Woman is the dominant sex. Woman's sexual glamour has bewitched and destroyed men since Delilah and Helen of Troy. Madonna, role model to millions of girls worldwide, has cured the ills of feminism by reasserting woman's command of the sexual realm.

Responding to the spiritual tensions within Italian Catholicism, Madonna discovered the buried paganism within the church. The torture of Christ and the martyrdom of the saints, represented in lurid polychrome images, dramatize the passions of the body, re-pressed in art-fearing puritan Protestantism of the kind that still lingers in America. Playing with the outlaw personae of prostitute and dominatrix, Madonna has made a major contri-bution to the history of women. She has rejoined and healed the split halves of woman: Mary, the Blessed Virgin and holy mother, and Mary Magdalene, the harlot.

Madonna's inner emotional life can be heard in the smooth, transparent "La Isla Bonita," one of her most perfect songs, with its haunting memory of paradise lost. No one ever men-tions it. Publicity has tended to focus instead on the more blatantly message-heavy videos, like "Papa Don't Preach," with its teen pregnancy, or "Express Yourself," where feminist cheerleading lyrics hammer on over crisp, glossy images of bedroom bondage, dungeon torture, and epicene, crotch-grabbing Weimar elegance.

"Like a Prayer" gave Pepsi-Cola dyspepsia: Madonna receives the stigmata, makes love with the animated statue of a black saint, and dances in a rumpled silk slip in front of a field of burning crosses. This last item, with its uncontrolled racial allusions, shocked even me. But Madonna has a strange ability to remake symbolism in her own image. Kitsch and trash are transformed by her high-energy dancer's touch, her earnest yet over-the-top drag-queen satire.

Madonna has evolved physically. In a charming early live video, "Dress You Up," she is warm, plump, and flirty under pink and powder-blue light. Her voice is enthusiastic but thin and breathy. She began to train both voice and body, so that her present silhouette, with some erotic loss, is wiry and muscular, hyperkinetic for acrobatic dance routines based on the martial arts. Madonna is notorious for monthly or even weekly changes of hair color and style, by which she embodies the restless individualism of Western personality. Children love her. As with the Beatles, this is always the sign of a monumental pop phenomenon.

Madonna has her weak moments: for example, I have no tolerance for the giggling baby talk that she periodically hauls out of the closet, as over the final credits of *Truth or Dare*. She is a complex modern woman. Indeed, that is the main theme of her extraordinary achievement. She is exploring the problems and tensions of being an ambitious woman today. Like the potent Barbra Streisand, whose maverick female style had a great impact on American girls in the Sixties, Madonna is confronting the romantic dilemma of the strong woman looking for a man but uncertain whether she wants a tyrant or slave. The tigress in heat is drawn to surrender but may kill her conqueror.

In "Open Your Heart," Madonna is woman superbly alone, master of her own fate. Off-stage at the end, she mutates into an androgynous boy-self and runs off. "What a Tramp!" thundered the *New York Post* in a recent full-page headline. Yes, Madonna has restored the Whore of Babylon, the pagan goddess banned by the last book of the Bible. With an instinct for world-domination gained from Italian Catholicism, she has rolled like a juggernaut over the multitude of her carping critics. This is a kaleidoscopic career still in progress. But Madonna's most enduring cultural contribution may be that she has introduced ravishing visual beauty and a lush Mediterranean sensuality into parched, pinched, word-drunk Anglo-Saxon feminism.

The sheer longevity of Madonna's career (20 years and counting) attests to her creative understanding of the rules of post-MTV celebrityhood. Through many musical changes, however, she has remained grounded in dance-oriented music. Following some uncharacteristically uncertain moves in the early-to-mid-1990s, Madonna's 1998 release, *Ray of Light*, showed her enthusiastically embracing the then-current vogue for electronic dance music (or "electronica," discussed in more depth in chapter 92). The following review of *Ray of Light* by Jane Dark casts Madonna in a more critical light than did the preceding essay. Dark's criticisms do not suggest, however, that Madonna's music is without value, only that its power comes from its embrace of the visceral, rather than through "serious" lyrics, that remainder of late 1960s' rock accreditation.

# MADONNICA
## *Jane Dark*

Imagine *The Wizard of Oz* but with Madonna in each of the climactic roles: she is the infinitely mighty Wizard, oohing and awing her subjects; she is the flawed, human-sized figure revealed behind both the curtain and the vast machinery of her own projection; and finally she is the girl redelivered from the profound Technicolor fantasy into her real life—now with a woman's wisdom.

This is, more or less, the narrative leading up to and incorporating *Ray of Light*, all of it meant to establish the new Madonna as older and wiser, human sized and recovered from grandiose mania. She's dishing up Sanskrit coffeetalk on her new album, and speaks these days of capital-K Karma and her Zen yoga practice. It makes sense, sort of. Buddhism's about effacing the self, and she's been chipping away at her primal self—Madonna the Pop Singer—all decade.

Her five '90s records have been left-handed projects: the pointedly indifferent *Bedtime Stories*; a ballad compilation; and the troika of *Erotica*, *I'm Breathless*, and *Evita*, each the soundtrack to an outside text. Okay, it's not exactly achieving No Mind, but at least she's not erecting colossal Madonna statues in the Third World. Nor merely marking time, plutonium clock-style, by the decay rate of her own fame. So instead she's an author, she's a mogul, she's an actress, she's a mom.

But if the fictional public, of which we're all a part, might have yearned to buy the allegory of Dorothy and the Wiz back in the day, in '98—with big radio and bigger video, with pure fame beamed real time into every home on the range—it's the sort of okeydoke no one goes for. There is no return of the real, really.

Still, you can't blame a girl for trying. There is no way to compete against the Eighties Pop Singer. Madonna's carefully post-shameless these days: the glossies capture her as "immaculately understated" with a haircut that says "don't notice me." She swears she'll never ever perform "Like a Virgin" again. On the new record, she just wants "to deal with my truth right now."

The problem is, she still has to compete in the marketplace—she can run from True Blue, but she can't hide from Celine Dion, whose cyborg bombast will crush *Ray of Light* like

a bug. We know this; for the first time, we expect it. Madonna returns as the most successful underdog imaginable. Hey look, it's Single Working Mom vs. the Celinator!

In the dream of rehumanizing, boredom also is on her side. She took self-referential
stardom to realms that would turn Andy Warhol's hair white, but by now she's pretty much
played: Madonna, sexual politics, discourse of fame, yawn. Never mind that Lourdes kid—
the Spice Girls are her true daughters, laughing at themselves all the way to the bank:
feminism, girl power, blah blah blah.

Madonna once wore the audience's fanaticism and the crit/cult hysteria like a wedding
dress and veil; now she's naked on the radio. Well, not really—she's never gonna get to the
magic zero of context-neutral, of a bunch of sounds we can freely love or hate or ignore. But
we can at least try to hear it, sitting in the listening room she's cleared out against the vast
architectural ruins of her own phenomenon.

And the first thing we hear—almost inevitably, given her self-effacing vibe—is the
stunning but ultimately misguided production of William Orbit. An early player in the ambient techno game, Orbit's served as Madonna's 12-inch mechanic on and off since "Justify
My Love." Here he gets the keys to the jeep—there are almost no other musician credits—
and proves that size counts, at least in budgets. *Ray of Light* sounds fathoms deeper than his
own albums (recorded under 43 different noms d'electronica). It's musical mercury: inhu-
manly reflective surface over restless pools of swoon and swoop, shimmery and tempera-
tureless. For the objectivist soundhead, the processed acoustic guitar at the beginning of
"Swim" is worth the ticket alone; one of the three great guitar tones in memory (along with
Mudhoney, "Touch Me I'm Sick," and the sampled riff in N2Deep's "Back to the Hotel").
Similarly thrilling touches pop up all over the disc: the Dopplered tom'n'snare in the lead
single "Frozen"; the building and beguiling charts for "Drowned World (Substitute for
Love)." That song is a production wonderland: drum 'n' bass drowning in a river of Valium,
while a different ultrasheen six-string sweetens the mix with digitized arpeggio. And hey,
you get a vocal track too!

Ay, there's the rub. While it's true that Madonna's voice carries more depth and a richer
timbre than in the past, the new sincerity is sort of a disaster. Back when she made fake so
big there was no beyond, she could survive dopey lyrics. They were part and parcel of the
moneymakin' pop/art joke, balanced over the lowest common denominator of the dancefloor. That was then. Nineteen ninety-eight's politics of meaning, her "truth right now,"
weighs heavier on the ear, wavering between therapy chitchat and Kahlil Gibranisms:
"Never forget who you are, little star. Never forget how to dream, butterfly." Stop, you're
hurting me. I suppose now's a good time to mention that Rod McKuen has a writing credit
in here somewhere.

Yet it can't be true that there's no room in the musical universe for a serious Madonna.
That argument's always been hooey; I take "Like a Prayer" as serious FM preaching and it
moves me unfailingly. Hoodwinking the Andrae Crouch Choir into recording what a holy
fuck ought to sound like may be over the top—but where else do you go when your idea is
not that "2 become 1" but that two become all? A Madonna record that thinks the thought-
fulness lives in the lyric sheet is born into a semi-doomed life; and William Orbit's elegantly
under-the-top sonics miss the point. Someone needs to remind her that she's a gospel
singer.

She's never had the pipes of the great crossover gospelists, of Aretha, or Chaka Khan,
or Dolly Parton. But Tramaine Hawkins also sings circles around Ms. Ciccone; I'll take the
latter's platters. Gospel shouting in and of itself isn't very interesting. It's all about the tension in playing churchy abandon against the secular grain. Madonna's dancefloor gospel,
bridging sexual and religious shamelessness, derives most directly from Chaka's, by way of
Donna Summer: orgasm as a joyful noise unto the Lord. It's the jubilation that sold "Lucky
Star" but is now too trashy for "Little Star"; the ecstasy that oughta be selling "Skin."

"I close my eyes, I need to make a connection," she says in that song. It's boilerplate and she knows it: "Why do all the things I say sound like the stupid things I said before?" Gosh, Madonna, maybe because they are: "I hear your voice, feels like flying," she sang once. "I close my eyes." But "Like a Prayer" was mysterious and sweaty and ecstatic, all about union. "Skin" just hangs around sounding shiny and pretty, and polite to the depths—a soundtrack nearly dissociated from the twice-told tale it's meant to accompany. Despite a vocal hook or two (for which we're grateful), the same dissonance renders "Frozen" a non sequitur: no matter how much she swears "You're frozen when your heart's not open," the music never wavers from absolute zero at the bone.

Such a chasm between sound and vision mirrors exactly the no-woman's-land the world provides for 39-year-old pop singers—lost to the hormonal urgency of youth, still a way from the mortal keening that lands you gigs at the Vatican. And it would be pleasing to end in suggesting that she's found something new in that wasteland, or conveyed its wastedness. But finally, she's at her best when she sneaks back into the old house for a few minutes in the title cut. She sells herself utterly to the big beat, like for now she's forgotten about introspection, the problem of the self, credibility, motherhood, Pre-Raphaelite coiffures—everything not currently rocking the disco cathedral. This one's between her and heaven: "Got herself a universe," she says, or maybe "goddess of a universe"—we'll believe either way. For the moment we'll believe anything, and we can hear the sound of her belief; for the only time on the record, she breaks into wails, loses language altogether. Then it comes back to her: "And I feel," she hollers, "and I feeeeel like I just got home."

# 69. Bruce Springsteen

## Reborn in the USA

Hailed as the latest in a series of "New Dylans" upon the release of his first albums in 1973 and 1975, lauded by critic Jon Landau (who later become his manager and producer) by a review that exclaimed "I saw rock & roll's future and its name is Bruce Springsteen,"[1] Bruce Springsteen (b. 1949) had to wait for the beginning of the video era in the early 1980s to achieve superstar status. Springsteen's early success relied as much as on his epic-length performances as on his early recordings, which ranged from the Spector-esque "Born to Run" (1975), to early rock 'n' roll à la Gary "U.S." Bonds and Roy Orbison, to bleak acoustic ballads of resignation. The subjects of his songs vacillated between sensitive portraits

---

1. Jon Landau, "I Saw Rock and Roll's Future . . . ," *The Real Paper* (May 23, 1974); reprinted in Clinton Heylin, ed., *The Da Capo Book of Rock & Roll Writing* (New York: Da Capo Press, [1992] 2000), 227–28.

of working-class people stuck in dead-end lives, to rousing, celebratory rockers.

A yearning for a return to rock's roots (that may have been related to the critical manifestos leading to punk) ran through the ecstatic responses to Springsteen in the mid- to late-1970s. References to rock 'n' roll's past also figure in Springsteen's aesthetic; and it is this nostalgic, or "retro," aesthetic, in which pastiche as a strategy is never far away, that links successful early 1980s' artists that may be as stylistically disparate as Springsteen and Madonna. Can it be a coincidence that Springsteen's first two albums, *Greetings from Asbury Park, N.J.*, and *The Wild, the Innocent and the E Street Shuffle* both appeared in 1973, the same year as that cinematic evocation of the innocence of the pre-1964 era, *American Graffiti*?

---

David Marsh came to prominence as a rock critic in the early 1970s on the staff of *Creem*. He wrote the first biography of Springsteen, *Born to Run: The Bruce Springsteen Story* (1979), which he followed with a second volume in 1987, *Glory Days: Bruce Springsteen in the 1980s*. The following may be Marsh's first article on Springsteen—it appeared in 1975 immediately prior to the release of Springsteen's album *Born to Run*—and it represents well the enthusiasm expressed by critics over Springsteen's early efforts. Marsh's predictions of breakthrough success proved to be on the money, since *Born to Run* and the single bearing the same title became Springsteen's first hits.

## LITTLE EGYPT FROM ASBURY PARK—AND BRUCE SPRINGSTEEN DON'T CRAWL ON HIS BELLY, NEITHER
### *David Marsh*

Bruce Springsteen sits cross-legged on his half-made bed, and surveys the scene. Records are strewn across the room, singles mostly, intermixed with empty Pepsi bottles, a motley of underwear, socks and jeans, half-read and half-written letters, an assortment of tapes, and a copy of Richard Williams's *Out of His Head*, the biography of Phil Spector.

"Here," he says, "I'll play ya something else." He puts on a tape of he and the E Street Band at the Main Point in Philadelphia. Suddenly, out of the speakers booms his own voice, cracking up at what he's singing. ("That song has some of the best lines," he says shaking his head, "and some of the *dumbest*.") "Stan-din' on a mountain lookin' down at the city, the way I feel t'nite is a dawgawn pity." When the band comes in, the room is charged. The playing and the singing is rough, even ragged, but it is alive, sparked with the discovery of something vital in an old, trashy song. It has been a long time since I heard anyone get this

---

*Source:* David Marsh, "Little Egypt from Asbury Park—and Bruce Springsteen Don't Crawl on His Belly, Neither," *Creem*, 7, no. 5 (October 1975), pp. 29–30, 77–78. Used by permission of David Marsh.

interested in rock and roll, even classic old rock and roll. It has been a lot longer since any-one has gotten me so interested.

Song done, Springsteen snaps the tape recorder off. "There," he says, with the charac-teristic delinquent twinkle in his eye, "If that don't get a club goin', *nothin'* will."

Bruce Springsteen is determined to get 'em going. The magic is that he doesn't have to be so determined to get himself going. Without being constantly "on," like a performer, Springsteen is constantly on, like someone who knows how good he is. He is full of himself, confident without being arrogant, almost serene in his awareness of what he is doing with his songs, his singing, his band. . . . Unlike say, Roxy Music, which makes very exciting music out of a nearly desperate sense of boredom, Springsteen makes mesmerizing rock out of an inner conviction that almost everything is interesting, even fascinating.

Take the three songs which, at this point, form the focus of the long awaited third Springsteen album. "Born to Run" is almost a rock opera. But, rather than building his con-cept piece around a derivative European anti-funk motif, Springsteen has built his master-work around a guitar line ripped straight from the heart of "Telstar." It may be too long (4:30) and too dense (layer upon layer of glockenspiel, voice, band, strings) to be a hit, but it does capture the imagination with its evocation of Springsteen's usual characters—kids on the streets and 'tween the sheets—and its immortal catch-line: "Tramps like us, baby we was born to run."

The sense that he is special has begun to pervade even Springsteen's semi-private life. When he showed up at a party for label mates Blue Oyster Cult, Springsteen completely dominated the room. So much so that Rod Stewart and a couple of the Faces, no slouches at scene-stealing themselves, were all but ignored when they made a brief appearance. Yet he has yet to lose his innocence. Going to visit the Faces later that night, at the ostentatiously elegant Plaza Hotel, Springsteen feigned awe—although you wondered if it were entirely feigned—at the mirrored, plushly carpeted lobby.

Fragments of a legend have begun to build. There are the stories about school—in high school, the time when he was sent to first grade by a nun, and, continuing to act the wise-ass, was put in the embarrassing position of having the first grade nun suggest to a smaller child: "Johnny, show Bruce how we treat people who act like that down here." Johnny slapped Springsteen's face. Or in college, the story of how the student body petitioned the adminis-tration for his expulsion, "because I was just too weird for 'em, I guess." The news that his fa-ther was a bus driver, which gives added poignancy to "Does This Bus Stop at 82nd Street?" (Which begins, "Hey, bus driver, keep the change.") Aphorisms are not beyond him: On Led Zeppelin: "They're like a lot of those groups. Not only aren't they doing anything new, they don't do the old stuff so good, either." On marriage: "I lived with someone once for two years. But I decided that to be married, you had to write married music. And I'm not ready for that." On the radio: "I don't see how anyone listens to [the local progressive rock station]. Every-thing's so damn long. At least if you listen to [the local oldies station] you know you're gonna hit three out of five. And the stuff you don't like doesn't last long."

All of this goes only so far, of course. A record, a *hit* record, is a crucial necessity. Sales of the first two albums are over 100,000 but that's nothing in America. There are still large areas of the country where Springsteen hasn't played—even important large cities such as Detroit have been left out—and though the word travels fast, and frequently, articles like this ultimately seem like just the usual rhetoric without something to back them up. As one Californian put it, "I've heard enough. It's like having everyone tell me I'm really missing something by not seeing Egypt. When's he going to come out here?"

Presuming he has the hit he deserves, Springsteen should be hitting most of America over the rest of the year. After an abortive arena journey with Chicago, he is, he says, reluc-tant to play large halls ever again. But he is one of the few rockers who would have any idea of what to do—except blast—in a room the size of a hockey rink. (Mick Jagger is about the only example who comes to mind, though Rod Stewart and Elvis do pretty well now that I think of it.)

Suppose that he does hit the big time. Even, suppose that he really is, as the ads have it, "rock and roll future." What happens then?

Since I believe that all of the above is true, and is going to happen, I have been at some pains to try to figure it out. Certainly, not a new explosion, à la Beatles and Elvis. Those phenomena were predicated upon an element of surprise, of catching an audience unaware, that is simply no longer operative. Not with rock on nationwide TV too many times a week. And not the kind of quiet, in-crowd build-up that propelled Dylan into the national eye. What Springsteen is after—nothing less than everything—has to be bigger than that, in mass terms, though it obviously cannot exceed Dylan in influence, his biggest achievement.

Springsteen's impact may very well be most fully felt as a springboard, a device to get people to do more than just pay attention. He can, potentially, polarize people in the way that Elvis, the Beatles, the Stones, Dylan—all the great ones—initially did. (Already, some early Springsteen fans feel alienated by his ever more forceful occupation with his soul influences.) The key to the success of those four is that as many hated them as loved them—but everyone had to take a position. God knows who he'll drag into the spotlight with him—it might have been the N.Y. Dolls, whose passion for soul oldies was equal to his, or Loudon Wainwright, whose cool, humorous vision parallels Bruce's in a more adult (sort of) way—but that ought to be something like what will happen. Sort of the way Carl Perkins, Jerry Lee Lewis and the other rockabilly crazies followed Elvis.

He's smart though. He said it all, one night, introducing "Wear My Ring Around Your Neck," the Presley oldie. "There have been contenders. There have been pretenders. But there is still only one King."

But no king reigns forever.

> Springsteen's second album of the 1980s, the introspective *Nebraska* (1982), was recorded at home on a four-track tape recorder, after which he radically reversed directions with *Born in the U.S.A* (1984). On that album Springsteen retooled the populist themes of his earlier work in anthemic settings, while placing an American flag on the album cover and using the flag on his stage sets. The inherent political ambiguity of populism meant that Springsteen's message could be appropriated by people with whose political stance he was not necessarily sympathetic: Ronald Reagan cited the title song approvingly during his presidential reelection campaign in 1984. The singles taken from *Born in the U.S.A.* also marked Springsteen's successful entry into the video arena with his newly buffed-up bod. No fewer than seven Top 10 singles were released from the album in 1984–85, attesting to new legions of fans, and his videos were constant features on MTV.

> Simon Frith's 1987 article followed the release of Springsteen's immensely successful box set, *Live/1975–85*. Frith documents well the contradictions of mass-market populism and analyzes several of the myths attached to the Springsteen image, one of which asserts that his disdain for commerce renders him impervious to charges of commercialism. Frith uses the discussion of these myths to take up the issue of authenticity,

an issue that he has addressed many times in other writings (and an issue that, as we have seen, has been central to rock criticism since it began in the mid-1960s).[2] Springsteen's authenticity springs from both his image and his storytelling technique: a "refusal to sentimentalize social conditions, a compulsion to sentimentalize human nature," a celebration "of the ordinary, not the special." Frith is not necessarily insisting that Springsteen is a sham, but rather that "Music can not *be* true or false, it can only refer to *conventions* of truth and falsity." Frith voices a European counterweight to the celebratory tones of many American critics, remaining skeptical about divisions between "democratic populism" and "market populism."[3]

# THE REAL THING—BRUCE SPRINGSTEEN
## *Simon Frith*

## Introduction

My guess is that by Christmas 1986 Bruce Springsteen was making more money per day than any other pop star—more than Madonna, more than Phil Collins or Mark Knopfler, more than Paul McCartney even; *Time* calculated that he had earned $7.5 million in the first *week* of his *Live* LP release. This five-record boxed set went straight to the top of the American LP sales charts (it reputedly sold a million copies on its first day, grossing $50 million "out of the gate") and stayed there throughout the Christmas season. It was the nation's best-seller in November and December, when more records are sold than in all the other months of the year put together. Even in Britain, where the winter charts are dominated by TV-advertised anthologies, the Springsteen set at £25 brought in more money than the tight-margin single-album compilations. (And CBS reckon they get 42% of their annual sales at Christmas time). Walking through London from Tottenham Court Road down Oxford Street to Piccadilly in early December, passing the three symbols of corporate rock—the Virgin, HMV and Tower superstores—each claiming to be the biggest record shop in the world, I could only see Springsteen boxes, piled high by the cash desks, the *safest* stock of the season.

Whatever the final sales figures turn out to be (and after Christmas the returns of the boxes from the retailers to CBS were as startling as the original sales), it is already obvious that *Bruce Springsteen and the E Street Band Live* is a phenomenal record, a money-making

---

2. Frith's most thorough explorations of this issue may be found in *Sound Effects* (New York: Pantheon Books, 1981); and *Performing Rites: On the Value of Popular Music* (Cambridge, Mass.: Harvard University Press).

3. Daniel Cavicchi noted in book on Springsteen fandom how arguments about the constructedness of Springsteen's authenticity are bound to have little weight for fans of the Boss; for them, "authenticity is about Springsteen as a real person." See *Tramps Like Us: Music and Meaning Among Springsteen Fans* (New York: Oxford University Press, 1998), 65.

*Source:* Simon Frith, "The Real Thing—Bruce Springsteen," in *Music for Pleasure: Essays in the Sociology of Pop* (New York: Routledge, 1988), pp. 94–101. Originally published in 1987 in *Musica E Dossier*. © Simon Frith. Used by permission.

achievement to be discussed on the same scale as *Saturday Night Fever* or Michael Jackson's *Thriller*. Remember, too, that a live record is cheaper to produce than a new studio sound (and Springsteen has already been well rewarded for these songs from the sales of previous discs and proceeds of sell-out tours). Nor did CBS need the expensive trappings or promo videos and press and TV advertising to make this record sell. Because the Springsteen box was an event in itself (the only pop precedent I can think of is the Beatles' 1968 *White Album*), it generated its own publicity as "news"—radio stations competed to play the most tracks for the longest times, shops competed to give Bruce the most window space, newspapers competed in speculations about how much money he was really making. The Springsteen box became, in other words, that ultimate object of capitalist fantasy, a commodity which sold more and more because it had sold so well already, a product which had to be *owned* (rather than necessarily used).

In the end, though, what is peculiar about the Springsteen story is not its marks of a brilliant commercial campaign, but their invisibility. Other superstars put out live sets for Christmas (Queen, for example) and the critics sneer at their opportunism; other stars resell their old hits (Bryan Ferry, for example) and their fans worry about their lack of current inspiration. And in these sorry tales of greed and pride it is Bruce Springsteen more often that not who is the measure of musical integrity, the model of a rock performer who cannot be discussed in terms of financial calculation. In short, the most successful pop commodity of the moment, the Springsteen Live Set, stands for the principle that music should not be a commodity; it is his very disdain for success that makes Springsteen so successful. It is as if his presence on every fashionable turntable, tape deck and disc machine, his box on every up-market living-room floor, are what enables an aging, affluent rock generation to feel in touch with its "roots." And what matters in this post-modern era is not whether Bruce Springsteen *is* the real thing, but how he sustains the belief that there are somehow, somewhere, real things to be.

## False

Consider the following:

*Bruce Springsteen is a millionaire who dresses as a worker*. Worn jeans, singlets, a head band to keep his hair from his eyes—these are working clothes and it is an important part of Springsteen's appeal that we do see him, as an entertainer, working for his living. His popularity is based on his live shows and, more particularly, on their spectacular energy: Springsteen works *hard*, and his exhaustion—on our behalf—is visible. He makes music physically, as a *manual* worker. His clothes are straightforwardly practical, sensible (like sports people's clothes)—comfortable jeans (worn in) for easy movement, a singlet to let the sweat flow free, the mechanic's cloth to wipe his brow.

But there is more to these clothes than this. *Springsteen wears work clothes even when he is not working*. His off-stage image, his LP sleeves and interview poses, even the candid "off duty" paparazzi shots, involve the same down-to-earth practicality (the only time Springsteen was seen to dress up "in private" was for his wedding). Springsteen doesn't wear the clothes appropriate to his real economic status and resources (as compared with other pop stars), but neither does he dress up for special occasions like real workers do—he's never seen flashily attired for a sharp night out. It's as if he can't be seen to be excessive or indulgent except on our behalf, as a performer for an audience. For him there is no division between work and play, between the ordinary and the extraordinary. Because the constructed "Springsteen," the star, is presented plain, there can never be a suggestion that this is just an act (as Elvis was an act, as Madonna is). There are no other Springsteens, whether more real or more artificial, to be seen.

*Springsteen is employer-as-employee.* It has always surprised me that he should be nicknamed "the Boss," but the implication is that this is an affectionate label, a brotherly way in which the E Street Band honor his sheer drive. In fact "boss" is an accurate description of their economic relationship—Springsteen *employs* his band; he has the recording contracts, controls the LP and concert material, writes the songs and chooses the oldies. And whatever his musicians' contributions to his success (fulsomely recognized), he gets the composing/performing royalties, could, in principle, sack people, and, like any other good employer, rewards his team with generous bonuses after each sell-out show or disc. And, of course, he employs a stage crew too, and a manager, a publicist, a secretary/assistant; he has an annual turnover now of millions. He may express the feelings of "little" men and women buffeted by distant company boards but he is himself a corporation.

*Springsteen is a 37-year-old teenager.* He is 20 years into a hugely successful career, he's a professional, a married man old enough to be the father of adolescent children of his own, but he still presents himself as a young man, waiting to see what life will bring, made tense by clashes with adult authority. He introduces his songs with memories—his life as a boy, arguments with his father (his mother is rarely mentioned)—but as a performer he is clearly *present* in these emotions. Springsteen doesn't regret or vilify his past; as a grown man he's still living it.

*Springsteen is a shy exhibitionist.* He is, indeed, one of the sexiest performers rock and roll has ever had—there's a good part of his concert audience who simply fancy him, can't take their eyes off his body, and he's mesmerizing on stage because of the confidence with which he displays himself. But, for all this, his persona is still that of a nervy, gauche youth on an early date.

*Springsteen is superstar-as-friend.* He comes into our lives as a recording star, a radio sound, a video presence and, these days, as an item of magazine gossip. Even in his live shows he seems more accessible in the close-ups on the mammoth screens around the stage than as the "real" dim figure in the distance. And yet he is still the rock performer whose act most convincingly creates (and depends on) a sense of community.

*Springsteen's most successful "record" is "live."* What the boxed set is meant to do is reproduce a concert, an *event*, and if for other artists five records would be excessive, for Springsteen it is a further sign of his album's truth-to-life—it lasts about the same length of time as a show. There's an interesting question of trust raised here. I don't doubt that these performances were once live, that the applause did happen, but this is nevertheless a false event, a concert put together from different shows (and alternative mixes), edited and balanced to sound like a live LP (which has quite different aural conventions than an actual show). Springsteen fans know that, of course. The pleasure of this set is not that it takes us back to somewhere we've been, but that it lays out something ideal. It describes what we *mean* by "Springsteen live," and what makes him "real" in this context is not his transparency, the idea that he is who he pretends to be, but his art, his ability to articulate the right *idea* of reality.

## True

The recurring term used in discussions of Springsteen, by fans, by critics, by fans-as-critics is "authenticity." What is meant by this is not that Springsteen is authentic in a direct way—is simply expressing himself—but that he represents "authenticity." This is why he has become so important: he stands for the core values of rock and roll even as those values become harder and harder to sustain. At a time when rock is the soundtrack for TV commercials, when tours depend on sponsorship deals, when video promotion has blurred the line between music-making and music-selling, Springsteen suggests that, despite everything, it still gives people a way to define themselves against corporate logic, a language in which everyday hopes and fears can be expressed.

If Bruce Springsteen didn't exist, American rock critics would have had to invent him. In a sense, they did, whether directly (Jon Landau, *Rolling Stone*'s most significant critical theorist in the late sixties, is now his manager) or indirectly (Dave Marsh, Springsteen's official biographer, is the most passionate and widely read rock critic of the eighties). There are, indeed, few American rock critics who haven't celebrated Springsteen, but their task has been less to explain him to his potential fans, to sustain the momentum that carried him from cult to mass stardom, than to explain him to himself. They've placed him, that is, in a particular reading of rock history, not as the "new Dylan" (his original sales label) but as the "voice of the people." His task is to carry the baton passed on from Woody Guthrie, and the purpose of his carefully placed oldies (Guthrie's "This Land Is Your Land," Presley and Berry hits, British beat classics, Edwin Starr's "War") isn't just to situate him as a fellow fan but also to identify him with a particular musical project. Springsteen himself claims on stage to represent an authentic popular tradition (as against the spurious commercial sentiments of an Irving Berlin).

To be so "authentic" involves a number of moves. Firstly, authenticity must be defined against artifice; the terms only make sense in opposition to each other. This is the importance of Springsteen's image—to represent the "raw" as against the "cooked." His plain stage appearance, his dressing down, has to be understood with reference to showbiz dressing up, to the elaborate spectacle of cabaret pop and soul (and routine stadium rock and roll)—Springsteen is real *by contrast*. In lyrical terms too he is plain-speaking; his songwriting craft is marked not by "poetic" or obscure or personal language, as in the singer/songwriter tradition following Dylan, folk-rock (and his own early material) but by the vivid images and metaphors he builds from common words.

What's at stake here is not the authenticity of experience, but authenticity of feeling; what matters is not whether Springsteen has been through these things himself (boredom, aggression, ecstasy, despair) but that he knows how they work. The point of his autobiographical anecdotes is not to reveal himself but to root his music in material conditions. Like artists in other media (fiction, film) Springsteen is concerned to give emotions (the essential data of rock and roll) a narrative setting, to situate them in time and place, to relate them to the situations they explain or confuse. He's not interested in abstract emotions, in vague sensation or even in moralizing. He is, to put it simply, a story-teller, and in straining to make his stories credible he uses classic techniques. Reality is registered by conventions first formulated by the nineteenth-century naturalists—a refusal to sentimentalize social conditions, a compulsion to sentimentalize human nature. Springsteen's songs (like Zola's fictions) are almost exclusively concerned with the working-class, with the effects of poverty and uncertainty, the consequences of weakness and crime; they trawl through the murky reality of the American dream; they contrast utopian impulses with people's lack of opportunity to do much more than get by; they find in sex the only opportunity for passion (and betrayal). Springsteen's protagonists, victims and criminals, defeated and enraged, are treated tenderly, their hopes honoured, their failure determined by circumstance.

It is his realism that makes Springsteen's populism politically ambiguous. His message is certainly anti-capitalist, or, at least, critical of the effects of capitalism—as both citizen and star Springsteen has refused to submit to market forces, has shown consistent and generous support for the system's losers, for striking trade unionists and the unemployed, for battered wives and children. But at the same time, his focus on individuals' fate, the very power with which he describes the dreams they can't realize (but which he has) offers an opening for his appropriation, appropriation not just by politicians like Reagan but, more importantly, by hucksters and advertisers, who use him to sell their goods as some sort of *solution* to the problem he outlines. This is the paradox of mass-marketed populism: Springsteen's songs suggest there is something missing in our lives, the CBS message is that we can fill the gap *with a Bruce Springsteen record.* And for all Springsteen's support of current causes, what comes from his music is a whiff of nostalgia and an air of fatalism. His stories describe hopes-about-to-be dashed, convey a sense of time passing beyond our control, suggest that our dreams can only be dreams. The formal conservatism of the music reinforces the emotional conservation of the lyrics. This is the way the world is, he sings, and nothing really changes.

But there's another way of describing Springsteen's realism. It means celebrating the ordinary not the special. Again the point is not that Springsteen is ordinary or even pretends to be, but that he honors ordinariness, making something intense out of experiences that are usually seen as mundane. It has always been pop's function to transform the banal, but this purpose was to some extent undermined by the rise of rock in the sixties, with its claims to art and poetry, its cult-building, its heavy metal mysticism. Springsteen himself started out with a couple of wordy, worthy LPs, but since then he has been in important ways committed to common sense. Springsteen's greatest skill is his ability to dramatize everyday events—even his stage act is a pub rock show writ large. The E Street Band, high-class professionals, play with a sort of amateurish enthusiasm, an affection for each other which is in sharp contrast to the bohemian contempt for their work (and their audience) which has been a strand of "arty" rock shows since the Rolling Stones and the Doors. Springsteen's musicians stand for every bar and garage group that ever got together in fond hope of stardom.

His sense of the commonplace also explains Springsteen's physical appeal. His sexuality is not displayed as something remarkable, a kind of power, but is coded into his "natural" movements, determined by what he has to do to sing and play. His body becomes "sexy"—a source of excitement and anxiety—in its routine activity; his appeal is not defined in terms of glamour or fantasy. The basic sign of Springsteen's authenticity, to put it another way, is his sweat, his display of *energy.* His body is not posed, an object of consumption, but active, an object of exhaustion. When the E Street Band gather at the end of a show for the final bow, arms around each other's shoulders, drained and relieved, the sporting analogy is clear: this is a team which has won its latest bout. What matters is that every such bout is seen to be real, that there are no backing tapes, no "fake" instruments, that the musicians really have played until they can play no more. There is a moment in every Springsteen show I've seen when Clarence Clemons takes center-stage. For that moment he is the real star—he's bigger than Springsteen, louder, more richly dressed. And he's the saxophonist, giving us the clearest account all evening of the relationship between human effort and human music.

To be authentic and to sound authentic is in the rock context the same thing. Music can not *be* true or false, it can only refer to *conventions* or truth and falsity. Consider the following.

Thundering drums in Springsteen's songs give his stories their sense of unstoppable momentum, they map out the spaces within which things happen. The equation of time and space is the secret of great rock and roll and Springsteen uses other classic devices to achieve it—a piano/organ combination, for example (as used by The Band and many soul groups), so that melodic-descriptive and rhythmic-atmospheric sounds are continually swapped about.

The E Street Band makes music as a group, but a group in which we can hear every instrumentalist. Our attention is drawn, that is, not to a finished sound but to music-in-the-making. This is partly done by the refusal to make any instrument the "lead" (which is why Nils Lofgren, a "lead" guitarist, sounded out of place in the last E Street touring band). And partly by a specific musical busy-ness—the group is "tight," everyone is aiming for the same rhythmic end, but "loose," each player makes their own decision as to how to get there (which is one reason why electronic instruments would not fit—they're too smooth, too determined). All Springsteen's musicians, even the added back-up singers and percussionists, have individual voices; it would be unthinkable for him to appear with, say, an anonymous string section.

The textures and, more significantly, the melodic structures of Springsteen's music make self-conscious reference to rock and roll itself, to its conventional line-up, its cliched chord changes, its time-honoured ways of registering joys and sadness. Springsteen himself is a rock and roll star, not a crooner or singer/songwriter. His voice *strains* to be heard, he has to shout against the instruments that both support and compete with him. However many times he's rehearsed his lines they always sound as if they're being forged on the spot.

Many of Springsteen's most anthemic songs have no addresses (no "you") but (like many Beatles songs) concern a third person (tales told about someone else) or involve an "I" brooding aloud, explaining his situation impersonally, in a kind of individualised epic. Listening to such epics is a public activity (rather than a private fantasy), which is why Springsteen concerts still feel like collective occasions.

## Conclusion

In one of his monologues Springsteen remembers that his parents were never very keen on his musical ambitions—they wanted him to train for something safe, like law or accountancy: "they wanted me to get a little something for myself; what they did not understand was that I wanted *everything*!"

This is a line that could only be delivered by an American, and to explain Springsteen's importance and success we have to go back to the problem he is really facing: the fate of the individual artist under capitalism. In Europe, the artistic critique of the commercialization of everything has generally been conducted in terms of Romanticism, in a state of Bohemian disgust with the masses and the bourgeoisie alike, in the name of the superiority of the *avant-garde*. In the USA there's a populist anti-capitalism available, a tradition of the artist as the common man (rarely woman), pitching rural truth against urban deceit, pioneer values against bureaucratic routines. This tradition (Mark Twain to Woody Guthrie, Kerouac to Credence Clearwater Revival) lies behind Springsteen's message and his image. It's this tradition that enables him to take such well-worn iconography as the road, the river, rock and roll itself, as a mark of sincerity. No British musician, not even someone with such a profound love of American musical forms as Elvis Costello, could deal with these themes without some sense of irony.

Still, Springsteen's populism can appeal to everyone's experience of capitalism. He makes music out of desire aroused and desire thwarted, he offers a sense of personal worth that is not determined by either market forces (and wealth) or aesthetic standards (and cultural capital). It is the USA's particular account of equality that allows him to transcend the differences in class and status which remain ingrained in European culture. The problem is that the line between democratic populism (the argument that all people's experiences and emotions are equally important, equally worthy to be dramatized and made into art) and market populism (the argument that the consumer is always right, that the market defines cultural value) is very thin. Those piles of Bruce Springsteen boxes in European department stores seem less a tribute to rock authenticity than to corporate might.

"We are the world!" sang USA for Africa, and what was intended as a statement of global community came across as a threat of global domination. "Born in the USA!" sang Bruce Springsteen, on his last great tour, with the Stars and Stripes fluttering over the stage, and what was meant as an opposition anthem to the Reaganite colonization of the American dream was taken by large sections of his American audiences as pat patriotism (in Europe the flag had to come down). Springsteen is, whether he or we like it or not, an American artist—his "community" will always have the Stars and Stripes fluttering over it. But then rock and roll is American music, and Springsteen's *Live—1975–1985* is a monument. Like all monuments it celebrates (and mourns) the dead, in this case the idea of authenticity itself.

# 70. R&B in the 1980s
## To Cross Over or Not to Cross Over?

*Thriller* opened the door to blockbuster, "crossover" hits by black artists. In addition to Jackson's album, the increasingly visible mainstream success of Prince and Lionel Richie in the mid-1980s owed something to the end of apartheid policies on MTV. Changes in the music industry and in the number of small black-owned record stores, however, raised the question of whether these crossover artists, in the process of reaching a large audience, had somehow forsaken the black community or were "selling out" to white commercial dictates in some other fashion (we already read Greg Tate's criticism of Michael Jackson along those lines in chapter 67).

During the 1980s, Nelson George was one of the music critics who was the most consistently devoted to articulating the links between African American popular music and arguments about black economic self-sufficiency. George advanced his views in a column on black music from a perch on *Billboard*'s staff throughout much of the decade.[1] His 1988 book, *The Death of Rhythm and Blues*, presented the most cogent version of a recurring argument in his writing: Looking at the history of African American popular music through the prism of the opposition between early 20th-century views advanced by W. E. B. DuBois on economic self-determination and by Booker T. Washington on assimilation, George contended that R&B in the 1980s lost much of its expressive power

---

1. For a more in-depth discussion and analysis of George's *Billboard* articles and of the issues involved in crossover in the early 1980s, see David Brackett, "(In Search of) Musical Meaning: Genres, Categories, and Crossover," in David Hesmondhalgh and Keith Negus, eds., *Popular Music Studies* (London: Arnold, 2002), 65–82.

because of its separation from the black community. In this excerpt, George looks at the well-known crossover artists just mentioned, as well as artists, such as Anita Baker (b. 1957) and Frankie Beverly (b. 1946), whom he terms "retronuevo": musicians who celebrate the history of rhythm and blues by remaining true to previous standards of musicianship and soulfulness.

## *from* THE DEATH OF RHYTHM AND BLUES
### *Nelson George*

Sometimes it seems really funny, but it's also quite sad that in surveying black America through its music in the eighties, much of the discussion revolves not around music but skin color, cosmetic surgery, and the rejection of Negroid features. Case in point: Compare current photographs of George Benson with pictures from early in his career. You will be confronted with facial alterations that have nothing to do with age. Surgery has reshaped him into a commercial product for mass consumption. It's as simple and, I think, as frightening as that. Change your face to sell a hundred thousand more units, to do the movies, to make more money. Stop looking like your mother and father, in the name of commerce. Maybe, like Whoopi Goldberg, Oprah Winfrey, and the otherwise sweet Janet Jackson, wear blue or green contact lenses. After all, it might help you achieve that most tempting symbol of eighties assimilation: an MTV video.

The two greatest black stars of the decade, Michael Jackson and Prince, ran fast and far both from blackness and conventional images of male sexuality (and their videos got on MTV). Michael Jackson's nose job, often ill-conceived makeup, and artificially curled hair is, in the eyes of many blacks, a denial of his color that constitutes an act of racial treason. Add to that a disquieting androgyny and you have an alarmingly un-black, unmasculine figure as the most popular black man in America.

Prince is similarly troublesome. Where Jackson's androgyny was like that of an innocently unaware baby, Prince preached sex as salvation in explicit and often clumsy terms. "Head" (oral sex), "When You Were Mine" (sexual ambiguity), and "1999" (sex as resignation in the face of nuclear war) were just a few of the songs in which Prince expressed his funky yet fanciful fascination with physical engagement. Onstage, he went from wearing black bikini, g-strings, and leg warmers to taking seductive pseudobaths and dry-humping his piano, all with a wink and shimmy that suggested his lover could be of any sexual persuasion. No black performer since Little Richard had toyed with the heterosexual sensibilities of black America so brazenly.

Prince's more irksome trait was that, like Jackson, he aided those who saw blackness as a hindrance in the commercial marketplace by running from it. Unlike the many black stars who altered their face to please "the mass market," Prince didn't have to; his features suggested he was a product of the interracial marriages so popular in Minneapolis. But he really wasn't. Both his parents were black. Yet in the quasi-autobiographical film *Purple Rain,* Prince presented his mother as white, a "crossover" marketing strategy as unnecessary as Jackson's tiresome claims to "universality." In fact, it can be argued that Prince's consistent use of mulatto and white leading ladies convinced many black male (and some female)

---

*Source:* Nelson George, from *The Death of Rhythm and Blues* (New York: Pantheon Books, 1988), pp. 173–75, 177–78, 181–83, 186–88, 194–96. © 1998 by Nelson George. Used by permission.

artists to use romantic interests of similar shading in their videos, hoping to emulate Prince's success. The resulting videos seem to reinforce the stereotypic idea that dark-skinned black women are not as attractive as their lighter sisters. As icons of style, Jackson and Prince were assimilation symbols as powerful as Bill Cosby. But thankfully, there was more to them than image. There was music, but we'll deal with that a bit later. . . .

On November 18, 1982, I wrote a story for the front page of *Billboard*, "Times Tough for Black Retailers," that revealed the social schism found between the assimilated and unassimilated in the R&B world and in the larger black society. "Black-oriented mom-and-pop retailers are going out of business in increasing numbers, and are not being replaced by new enterprises. At the same time, black music is holding its own in the depressed sales environment and is generating a slew of popular new performers. This dichotomy emerges from a *Billboard* survey of black retailers, label executives, and other industryites. As reasons for the problems of the small operator, they cite unemployment, poor management, locations in declining inner-city neighborhoods, and competition from stores in active city centers. General market retail chains are said to be increasing their awareness and sales of black music."

## Counting the Losses

The Commodores' black manager, Benny Ashburn—"the sixth Commodore"—who died of a heart attack in 1982, was one of the few black managers to build and hold on to a mainstream rhythm & blues group capable of million-selling albums. It was not unexpected that after Ashburn's death, Richie split from the Commodores and signed with Kenny Rogers's manager, Ken Kragen. But it was surely disheartening to those who hoped he'd give a brother or sister a shot at managing one of the industry's most promising careers.

Richie went for a manager who had turned a country singer, for a time, into America's most popular male vocalist. Richie wanted the same thing, and Kragen, if not for the incredible ascendence of Michael Jackson into pop heaven, would have accomplished it. However, Richie's acceptance by Middle America didn't mean he had escaped the turmoil of the rhythm & blues world. Richie, like Jackson, Prince, and other crossover stars, was a target of verbal abuse and boycott threats from black concert promoters, as the bitterness revealed at the 1979 BMA conference continued into the next decade.

[The lack of talented songwriter-producers in R&B] played a role in the growing difficulty black artists found reaching the pop charts. Musically the songs weren't as good as in the sixties and early seventies. As dance records, the grooves were still inventive, but they were hampered by a disco backlash at pop radio. As a cultural force, the term "disco" went out as quickly as it had come in. Unfortunately, all black dance music was for a time labeled "disco." It was stupid. It was racist. It revealed again how powerful a force semantics can be in the reception of pop music. Just as rock & roll came to mean white music, disco came to represent some ugly amalgam of black and gay music. The Bee Gees went straight down the tubes because of such labeling. They were, after all, disco's biggest white group.

As for the decline in black crossover, you can look it up.[2] Of the fourteen records to reach number one on the black chart in 1983, only one reached the pop top-ten. "She Works Hard for the Money" by Donna Summer, the only disco-bred artist to escape the genre's career-deflating stigma. In contrast, some of that year's great number one black singles—Mtume's

---

2. Perhaps George meant to precede this sentence with "Excluding recordings by Michael Jackson and Lionel Richie . . . ," since recordings by Jackson and Richie released during 1983 made both the pop and R&B Top 10, in several cases going to Number One. George implies as much in his comments later in this paragraph.

sensual "Juicy Fruit," the hard-core funk of Rick James's "Cold-Blooded" and George Clinton's "Atomic Dog," the melodic and danceable "Candy Girl" by New Edition, the soulful boogie songs "Get It Right" by Aretha Franklin and "Save the Overtime for Me" by Gladys Knight and the Pips—only went to number forty or lower on the pop chart. That of course was the same year that Michael Jackson's *Thriller* sold 20 million copies in the U.S. and Lionel Richie's singles "All Night Long" and "Can't Slow Down" sold over 10 million, only confirming the feast-or-famine cycle in popular music. A black who crossed over could sell a humongous number of records. And the fact that so few succeeded didn't stifle the dream.

For many black entertainers, chasing that dream was a fixation, and one that could destroy a career. Peabo Bryson, a smooth, soulful vocalist and distinctive, if limited, songwriter, began his career in the early seventies as a songwriter-vocalist with a number of bands on independent labels. In 1977, he signed with Capitol and immediately became one of the best-loved singers in black America. Deep in the heart of disco he recorded ballads like "Reaching for the Sky," "I'm So Into You," and one of the rare soul classics to be written and recorded in the 1975–85 period, "Feel the Fire." With its devotional lyrics, dramatic piano chords, and wonderful arrangement by coproducer Johnny Pate, a former Curtis Mayfield collaborator, "Feel the Fire" was one of the most respected and covered R&B compositions of the period.

From 1977 to 1983, every new album released by Bryson sold at least half a million copies, and he became a major concert attraction. However, in the age of crossover, Bryson wanted what Lionel Richie and Michael Jackson had, a white audience, and he attempted to get it. A duet with Roberta Flack on the Barry Manilow-like ballad "Tonight I Celebrate My Love" in 1984 gave him his first taste of pop success. In 1985, he jumped to Elektra and had another top-ten hit with "Whenever You're in My Arms Again," another mushy mainstream ballad. Bryson did not see the drop-off in his album sales during this transition as a bad omen. Sure that a pop audience awaited him, Bryson changed his image: gone were the white suits and modest Afro of his Capitol years. He draped himself in ultratrendy English threads and had his low Afro styled into a "fade" cut, high on top, low on the sides. His Elektra debut was synthesized, uptempo, and contemporary, and it was received with all the enthusiasm of a broken computer chip. His old audience hated it, and without a breakthrough single, whites paid no attention. It was clear that the whites who had bought his hit singles had liked the record but didn't know who Bryson, the artist, was. As a result, this album sold a meager 200,000 copies and his concert bookings dwindled. Peabo Bryson, once a staple of what was left of the old R&B world, had tried to leap the barrier and stumbled. It remains to be seen whether he can pick himself back up.

## Retronuevo

It was in studying the history of rhythm & blues that I came to admire those in the eighties who have been able to break away from, ignore, or battle the crossover consciousness and remain true to the strength of R&B, while not conceding that that approach left them unacceptable to white America. Inspired by that attitude and the music it produced, I created in 1986 the term "retronuevo," which can be defined as an embrace of the past to create passionate, fresh expressions and institutions. It doesn't refer just to music. The willingness of broadcaster Percy Sutton to revive the Apollo Theater in New York and of black haircare kingpin Robert Gardner to do the same in Chicago for the Regal Theater showed that some black businesspeople possessed the heart and moxie to understand how much symbolic importance and economic potential these once grand R&B showcases hold for now downtrodden inner city neighborhoods. With *She's Gotta Have It* and *Hollywood Shuffle*, Spike Lee and Robert Townsend used hustle and comedy to create non-Hollywood, profoundly black

films that partially realized the ambitious dreams of Booker T. Washington in the 1920s and
Melvin Van Peebles in the 1970s.

But mostly retronuevo means black music that appreciates its heritage. Until the eighties, R&B never emphasized looking back—one reason for its ongoing creativity, as I've said
in earlier chapters. But as too much of the music became as enticing as a ripped diaphragm
and not nearly as dangerous, artists emerged to bring back some of the soul and subtlety its
audience deserves.

Maze, featuring Frankie Beverly, had been retronuevo from record one. From 1977 to
1985, this Bay Area band released five albums on Capitol, each selling half a million but
never breaking the million mark. Many a black artist would have been frustrated by this
inability to crack the magical million mark, and Beverly often complained about Capitol's
inability to cross him over. But, crucially, Beverly wasn't willing to sell his soul to cross over.
He just continued with an idiosyncratic sound that balanced the street feel of his native
Philadelphia with the relaxed mood of his Bay Area home. He'd been signed by Larkin
Arnold after touring as an opening act for Marvin Gaye. Arnold was a black attorney who'd
been brought in to mastermind the expansion of Capitol's black music. Coming on the heels
of the jazzy Earth, Wind and Fire and the raunchy Parliament-Funkadelic, Beverly's Maze
established itself as a less frantic, less abrasive alternative. Moreover, Maze had the kind of
cross-generational appeal that eluded most other young black acts of the time. The 1981 *Live
in New Orleans* double album was classic Beverly, with all but one of the twelve songs
featuring slow to medium tempos with arrangements rich in glowing electric pianos, humming organs, and tasteful synthesizer figures. The rhythm section—drummer Billy Johnson, bassist Robin Duhe, and percussionists McKinnley William and Roame Lowery—
interlocked as smoothly as the keyboards, never pushing the beat, a discipline vital to the
aura of Beverly's soothing compositions.

With these sultry grooves as the frame, Beverly paints his wholesome pictures on top
with voice and pen. In his phrasing, I hear echoes of his benefactor, Marvin Gaye, and his
idol, Sam Cooke. But Beverly's voice has an understated, more working-class quality that
differentiates him from those love men. Instead, he sounds like a dedicated husband still
madly in love with his wife after all these years. His love songs exist in a world where one-
night stands are spurned and real affection is sought, appreciated, returned.

Beverly also has a real gift for nonspecific protest songs in the tradition of the Isley
Brothers' "Fight the Power"—songs that refer to the troubles of black America without the
nuts-and-bolts rhetoric of an overtly political songwriter like Gil Scott-Heron. In addition to
"We Need to Live," a tribute to Atlanta's murdered children, *Live* includes two inspirational
numbers with the upbeat sixties flavor of Mayfield's "People Get Ready" and Cooke's eloquent "A Change Is Gonna Come." "Changing Times" assures us, "We'll get through these
changing times," while "Running Away" preaches, like Booker T. Washington, that "the
things you want are the things you have to earn."

Just as Beverly grew stronger by swimming against the tide, so did the radio format
originated by WHUR in 1976 called "the Quiet Storm." Ten years later, stations in every
major market and in many of the secondary markets made three- to five-hour blocks of mellow music a crucial part of their programming day. Some stations, like Los Angeles' KUTE
went totally Quiet Storm, while others utilized the format, if not the title, from late evening
into the morning. The program gave new life to the title of one of Smokey Robinson's last
great compositions and proved a comfortable home, not just for Beverly, but for singers
more interested in ballads than boogie. My favorite example is the woman who originally
inspired the retronuevo idea: Anita Baker.

Baker's brilliant *Rapture* album, one of the surprise hits of 1986, was an album of contemporary intelligence and old-fashioned pipes. The intelligence was primarily Baker's. As
executive producer, Baker made an eight-cut album with no uptempo songs, a complete

reversal of the norm for black female vocalists in the post-disco era. In making that decision she displayed an understanding of her voice as instrument and demonstrated why more women should demand control of their recordings. The pipes were Baker's, too. Wrapping her voice in supportive arrangements and using real live bass players and drummers, Baker shone with the maturity of a Dinah Washington. It is unashamedly adult music that, as did her 1982 Beverly Glen hit "Angel," sounds progressive despite its old-fashioned values.

Baker's impact was profound because it exposed how superficially so many vocal divas had pursued their crossover dreams, diluting the power of their voices in the process, and because in *Rapture*'s wake the industry allowed some of its most gifted young voices (Miki Howard, Regina Belle) to record with a minimum of production overkill.

Yes, Baker made music for assimilated black Americans, though unlike that of crossover artists, her work tapped into the traditions of jazz and blues with a feeling that suggested being middle class didn't make your taste the musical equivalent of a Big Mac.

Considering my earlier comments, the following conclusion may be a surprise, but the two most important retronuevo artists have been Michael Jackson and Prince. Despite the unfortunate impact of their imagery, this dynamic duo proved to be the decade's finest music historians, consistently using techniques that echoed the past as the base for their superstardom.

During his epochal 1983 performance on *Motown 25*, Jackson suggested Jack Wilson's athleticism, James Brown's camel walk, the intensity of the Apollo amateur night, and the glitter of Diana Ross. In *Purple Rain*, Prince with the sensitivity of a poet, made historical allusions to Hendrix, Little Richard, Patti LaBelle, and Brown, while his employee, the Time's Morris Day, was molded into a modern-day Louis Jordan. Both Jackson (on "Beat It") and Prince (on "Let's Go Crazy" and "Purple Rain") made rock & roll for black folks while injecting their own idiosyncratic perspective into black dance music. Jackson's "Billie Jean" and "Wanna Be Startin' Something" raise superstar paranoia to a high art over grooves just as technologically assured as they were funky. "Don't Stop Til You Get Enough" is an incredible dance record, an anthem of spiritual and physical liberation in a wonderful synthesis of disco, the Philly sound, and Quincy Jones's own understanding of the drama in musical arrangement.

Prince, the auteur of the Minneapolis sound and himself a major talent scout, created the only competition to hip hop in the eighties, injecting fresh musical ideals into black music. Vanity, Morris Day, Jesse Johnson, the production team of Jimmy Jam Harris and Terry Lewis, Alexander O'Neal, Monte Moir, Andre Cymone, Sheila E., and quite a few others were ripples that came to our attention when Prince hit the shore. Not all these folks have great affection for Prince, but either their image or their music owes a debt to his fertile, cunning mind. Prince says that when he was a kid he didn't hear much black radio or music, but if his Brownesque 1986 *Parade* tour and the dancing in the film, *Sign "O" the Times*, is any indication, this retronuevo innovator had done a lot of catching up.

More, if we look at Jackson and Prince from the perspective of economic self-sufficiency, there is no question that this duo exercise a control over their careers and business that neither James Brown nor Sam Cooke, as ambitious as they were, could have envisioned. All major decisions, and even a great many minor ones, involving their money and artistic direction are determined personally by these performers. In Jackson's case this has meant, most significantly, the multimillion-dollar acquisition of the song catalogues of Sly Stone and the Beatles, two of his major influences, and the willingness to pay major directors like John Landis and Martin Scorsese big-budget money to expand the scope of music videos.

Where most of Jackson's business activities have been designed to promote and perpetuate his larger-than-life persona (much as with James Brown), Prince has used his energy to build and direct a multi-media empire that has spawned a slew of artists, launched a record label (Paisley Park), and led to the production of three feature films (*Purple Rain, Under the Cherry Moon,* and *Sign "O" the Times*), two of which he's directed himself.

Also as with James Brown, of course, there are disagreeable elements in the way that they each manifest their power and in the images of themselves they choose to project to both black and white audiences. However, to ignore their power, artistically and within their own organizations, solely because of their cosmetics would be ignorant. By using star clout to further their own interests (and, yes, whims) in unprecedented directions, Michael Jackson and Prince have set new standards of autonomy for black musicians—and for black-music businesspeople, too.

> In contrast to George, Steve Perry sees crossover in terms of a narrative of increasing racial equality in the United States. In something of a Marxist framework, Perry prefers to think in terms of economic, rather than racial, uplift, and he criticizes the idea of black economic self-determination because he sees it as mainly helping the black middle class. As an example of the benign character of crossover, he explores the specific conditions in Minneapolis that influenced the development of R&B/pop fusion artists there, most notably Prince (b. 1958), as well as Terry Lewis and Jimmy Jam. Perry brings the argument full circle to the discussion in chapter 5 when he discusses the contrasting views of Leroi Jones and Ralph Ellison in light of the politics of crossover.

## AIN'T NO MOUNTAIN HIGH ENOUGH: THE POLITICS OF CROSSOVER
### *Steve Perry*

Though almost all of the anticrossover criticism in the eighties is cast in terms of a debate about "authentic" black music versus "fake" black music, that doesn't mean the real issue is always aesthetic. One of the most vocal critics in recent years has been Nelson George, *Billboard*'s black music columnist and author of the Motown history *Where Did Our Love Go?* In his work, a black nationalist agenda is never far from the surface, though he rarely mentions it by name; rather, it's there to be inferred from the sum of his views.

George has described crossover as the product of "black American singers [who] want to be Barry Manilow," and the symbolism evoked by his analogy to the supreme purveyor of banal white pop is emphatic: not only does crossover amount to a kind of cultural treason, blacks who have consistent pop hits necessarily sacrifice their racial identity. What's the alternative, George? Well, he points favorably toward 1973, when such "intrinsically black songs" as Marvin Gaye's "Let's Get It On" and the Isley Brothers' "Who's That Lady" cracked the pop Top 10. "And that," he adds, "was before disco, and before record labels got interested in black music." He also mentions the example of Frankie Beverly and Maze, whose records have frequently gone gold without much attention from white audiences. And he says this about radio: "It's a fallacy that you need a big [pop] single to reach white people. Plenty of white people listen to black radio."

*Source:* Steve Perry, "Ain't No Mountain High Enough: The Politics of Crossover," in Simon Frith, ed., *Facing the Music* (New York: Pantheon Books, 1988), pp. 57–59, 78–83, 86–87. Reprinted by permission of Steve Perry.

If it seems curious to assert that "record companies" weren't interested in black music in 1973, if it seems misleading to claim you can reach the white pop audience to a significant degree through black radio—if it's hard to find any consistent aesthetic thread running through his commentary about music—that's because the real issue is more economic than musical. It's of more than passing interest to note that George's examples of authentic black music from 1973 were both released on black-owned record labels (Gordy's Motown, and the Isley's own T-Neck), and that what he finds inspirational about Maze is the group's ability to have gold records with an almost all-black audience. Conversely, one reason George disdains crossover is that the creeping integration of record charts and major label artist rosters threatens to undermine the interests of black entrepreneurs by gnawing simultaneously at their traditional markets and their productive resources.

It's a serious issue and—in American capitalism more generally—an old one. But it's highly disingenuous of George to conceal this agenda in a series of harangues about musical standards; it lets him circumvent the tough questions. His remark about black radio is symptomatic. When he points out that you can reach some white listeners through black radio, what he's really suggesting between the lines, of course, is that black radio is the proper home for black records. Yet as *The Discordant Sound of Music*, the NAACP's 1987 report on racism in the music industry, indicates, "Of the more than 9,000 radio stations in the country, fewer than 400 target their programming to black listeners, so that the market for black artists is limited to less than 30 million people in a country of over 230 million people."

The manifest appeal of George's argument to black capitalism is clear, but so is the extent to which his vision would harden the lines that keep black artists and black audiences in segregated economic ghettos. For every black artist who becomes a crossover success, he elaborates, "there are many more who fail. Everyone wants to be Michael Jackson. But very few people understand the nature of record companies—that there are very few people who reach that [level of success]."

If George were commenting generally on the record industry's version of late capitalism, in which fewer and fewer products are released to more and more hype, he'd have a point. But he's speaking in specifically racial terms, and his implicit point—which can hardly be made explicit since it isn't true—is that black artists would stand a better chance of succeeding with small labels, or with record divisions that appeal to principally black markets. Small independent labels are very often undercapitalized, which makes them less able to pay and promote artists. It is no accident that artists tend to flee these smaller labels for larger ones as soon as the opportunity presents itself; the chances to make money and gain exposure are that much greater (even if, in absolute terms, they still aren't that great). As crossover possibilities opened up in the 1980s, a number of black independent labels—most notoriously, Sylvia Robinson's Sugar Hill Records—saw their artists migrate to major labels.

The interracial complexity of pop music's roots defies the black nationalist vision of culture, which dictates that black culture has thrived not despite blacks' institutional separation from dominant society, but because of it. To the nationalist, a separate black community with its own economic infrastructure is a necessary precondition of black culture. And though this can make for strange bedfellows aesthetically—Nelson George has championed derivative white rappers the Beastie Boys on the grounds that they contribute to the cause by recording for black-controlled Def Jam—it's hardly surprising, since nationalists almost always elevate economics over the music itself. In the terms of an old proverb, nationalists locate the cultural significance of black music in neither the singer nor the song, but in the publishing company.

It isn't difficult to see why the black professional and entrepreneurial class might embrace this view, but it inverts the real significance black music has for most of its consumers, black and white. For them, the greatest impact is right there in the grooves, not in the means by which the music is produced. (Nor is that impact just aesthetic: It's not entirely coincidental that the civil rights movement gained its greatest white support in the 1960s, the decade following the infusion of black culture into white households through rock 'n' roll and R&B.) Besides, it's impossible to claim that an economically separatist black community is a precondition to powerful black music. History doesn't bear it out, and neither does the contemporary Minneapolis scene, which has become a focal point of black pop in the late eighties.

One way to understand Minneapolis is by contrast to Detroit, the most far-ranging and influential northern center of black pop since World War II. The source of Detroit's musical strength lay in its large and varied black population, much of which migrated en masse from the rural South during and after the war. These people brought with them a set of established musical traditions, and they settled by necessity into poor, mostly segregated neighborhoods, which ensured that those traditions would take root; consequently, it's possible to follow the development of the blues and R&B in a relatively straight line from the acoustic blues of the Mississippi Delta to the electrified music that later took shape in cities such as Detroit and Chicago. Moreover, Detroit blacks were a diverse enough group to encompass not only blues and R&B; there was also a nascent middle class to support the growth of jazz, which was actually the young Berry Gordy's first love.

Minneapolis could hardly be more different. Never exactly a center of heavy industry, it didn't offer migrating blacks the same opportunities as other major northern cities. As of the 1980 census, blacks constituted roughly 2.4 percent of the Minneapolis–St. Paul metro area population; despite the presence of a few ethnic enclaves (most notably, Irish and Slavic) in St. Paul and on Minneapolis's north side, the predominance of German and Nordic elements may well make it the most homogeneous major urban area in the country. If Prince's racially and sexually mixed bands have given some people the impression that Minneapolis is an integrationist mecca, it's important to remember some of the city's other prominent exports, including the Twins, an organization that continually vies with the Mets and the Red Sox for the title of whitest team in baseball, and the ultrawhite pastoral fantasies of Garrison Keillor's *Prairie Home Companion*.

Besides their small numbers, the blacks who do live in the area didn't move there in the same concentrated influx as in Detroit, which has made for a less pronounced black culture. Nor do most of them have any direct connection to the southern heritage that produced most of the major movements in earlier black pop. By the 1980s, almost all the local black musicians were Midwest born and bred: Jesse Johnson grew up in Rock Island, Illinois, where he came of age playing Led Zeppelin covers in a biker bar; Morris Day likewise moved to Minneapolis from a small city in Illinois. Terry Lewis spent his early years in Omaha before his family moved north; Prince and Jimmy (Jam) Harris were born in Minneapolis. Of the major talents to emerge from the city in the eighties, only Alexander O'Neal—born in Natchez, Mississippi—had extensive roots in southern R&B.

This is not to suggest there was no black music happening in Minneapolis before the 1980s explosion; critic David Adams has sketched the historical outlines in his "Roots of a Revolution" essay. But the musical movers of the eighties were less influenced by their local antecedents than by what they heard on radios and turntables, and that was a mixed lot indeed. Prince once told an interviewer he heard more country music as a child than any other kind, and a friend of mine who clerked at a downtown record shop in the early eighties confirms the tales of his eclecticism. Prince, he says, would pop up at the shop every couple of weeks, and might buy anything from James Brown to Dolly Parton to Molly Hatchet. By this time, of course, Prince could finally afford all the records he wanted, but tastes as catholic as his weren't uncommon among young blacks in Minneapolis, and they resulted from practical considerations more than ideological choices. As Terry Lewis put it, "To an extent, the music we're making today is the result of white rock 'n' roll radio and black music station static. None of *our* radio stations would come in as good as the mainstream stations. You could hear the beat and the rest was noise." (Ironically, this remark—made to writer Martin Keller in 1984—prefigured the formula that gave Flyte Tyme Productions its first crossover blockbuster two years later in Janet Jackson's *Control*, a wedding of accessible pop melodies and funky electronic beats.)

What all these men share is a disrespect for the lines drawn by white racists and black separatists alike. As Lewis's observation implies, this attitude was born of need; the only culture available to them was a polyglot mass culture. But it also expresses the enormous ambition of talented young men and women—ambition shaped in an environment where the very idea of succeeding meant reaching outside the black community as they knew it. In Minneapolis, owing to the small black population and to a goodly dollop of genteel northern racism, black culture has always been all-but-invisible from the outside. There were never more than two or three local clubs where black musicians could play. (That's one reason the *studio* is the preferred métier of nearly every black act that's emerged from there.) And so, said Jimmy Jam, "Black musicians were going, 'We can't get a job, we better make a demo tape or something and try to get up out of here.' Prince did it; Rocky Robbins [one of the first major label signees from the city] did it. That's why we made it out here. Not that we had more talent [than the white musicians]; nothing like that. We just had more initiative, because there was nothing here for us."

According to the terms of black nationalist ideology, the Minneapolis scene ought to have been impossible in the first place; instead, it became a germinating center of pop music in the eighties. Its achievement hasn't been a triumph over assimilationism, as some critics insist that black music should be, but a triumph of integrationist impulses. The best Minneapolis has had to offer—*Dirty Mind, Purple Rain* (the album), *Sign of the Times* (album and movie), *Control,* Alexander O'Neal's excellent Flyte Tyme-produced albums, the Time albums, Jesse Johnson's *Shockadelica*—mixes up funk, rock, soul, jazz, and high-tech adventurism, skewing musical categories with a self-assurance and accessibility more and more at odds with pop music's growing fragmentation.

But being a successful black person in a racist society can hardly fail to have its complications. Of the Minneapolis musicians, Prince especially has been singled out by critics of crossover, who wax contemptuous over his exotic clothing and imagery, his ambiguous sexuality, and the advantages he derives from having light skin. There is no doubt that these factors have made it easier for Prince to cross over than, say, Alexander O'Neal, a man who is bigger, darker, and more unmistakably heterosexual; but to scrutinize Prince rather than the society that raises the barriers he got around is just another way of blaming the victim, and to presume (as the separatist ideologue almost always does) that O'Neal's expression of blackness is more "authentic" than Prince's is an awfully monolithic and condescending view of what it means to be black.

Terence Trent D'Arby, the most outspoken and talented new black artist to surface in the late 1980s, has blasted his contemporaries for pulling punches:

Black male acts are far, far too apologetic. . . . Look, any black act in the States who has been [a] massive quote-unquote crossover success has had to emasculate himself to some degree. Prince has had to play the bisexual image, cast aspersions as to his dominant heterosexuality, Jackson's had to be asexual, Vandross couldn't possibly offend anybody, George Benson . . . it's like in the contract, it certifies them to a free plastic surgeon visitation, guarantees them a makeup artist at all times to lighten 'em up for photographs if you sell more than two million albums, and these guys wouldn't do or say anything which would lose them one record sale.

D'Arby obviously abhors these perceived accommodations to the dominant society, and that may be why he neglects to mention his own: He, like Jimi Hendrix before him, moved to Britain (where the racial equation is different, at least for American blacks) to launch his career.

What's disturbing about the whole notion of compromising, of making accommodations, is not compromise itself, but the implication—dating all the way from 19th-century black minstrelsy to Michael Jackson's multiple nose jobs—that the compromises are motivated by racial self-hatred. This specter has haunted the whole history of integrationism, most pointedly in the entertainment field; it figures in Prince's bizarre 1986 film, *Under the Cherry Moon*, whose subtext is really the psychology of crossover.

If *Under the Cherry Moon* carries the crossover impulse too far, to the point where it begins to be a denial of blackness itself, it is hardly more errant than the black nationalist rhetoric that stands as its counterpoint in a polarized racial climate—a rhetoric which, as Ralph Ellison pointed out, presumes that blacks alone among all the American peoples "remain unaffected by the climate, the weather, the political circumstances—from which not even slaves were exempt—the social structures, the national manners, the modes of production and the tides of the market, the national ideals, the conflicts of values, the rising and falling of national morale, or the complex give and take of acculturalization which was undergone by all others who found their existence [in America]." These remarks appeared in Ellison's review of Leroi Jones's *Blues People*, an ambitious and temperamentally separatist treatise on black music; of its author, Ellison continued, "Jones has stumbled over that ironic obstacle which lies in the path of any who would fashion a theory of American Negro culture while ignoring the intricate network of connections which binds Negroes to the larger society. To do so is to attempt a delicate brain surgery with a switchblade."

However bogged down the struggle for integration has become in the twenty-five years since Ellison wrote those words, popular music is still in the vanguard. By any reasonable measure, black music continues to be underrepresented on pop charts and CHR radio; nonetheless, it presents black people and black art on a larger scale and in more humanizing terms than any other facet of mass culture. The popularity of black music also exposes to anyone with eyes and ears just how profoundly black experience has shaped the cultural mainstream. To deny blacks their rightful place in the heart of American culture is not only a gross political injustice, but a denial of reality, which, so long as it prevails, makes it impossible for anyone to understand the lifeblood of the culture.

# 71. Heavy Metal Thunders On!

Chapter 56 discussed the dispersion of heavy metal approaches in genres such as hard rock, glam, and punk. Heavy metal persisted in its own right, however, becoming more stylized with bands like Judas Priest, Iron Maiden, and AC/DC focusing on a riff-oriented approach while emphasizing guitar heroics and high-pitched vocals. A uniquely American form of metal developed in the United States in the late 1970s with bands, such as Van Halen, recording catchy, hook-laden material that eschewed the more arcane lyrics of their British counterparts. The guitarist for the band, Eddie Van Halen, developed the most significant addition to rock guitar playing since Hendrix with his mastery of the two-handed "tapping" technique, enabling him to slur rapid-fire arpeggios that would have been physically impossible using conventional guitar technique.[1] "Tapping" would soon become standard practice among metal guitarists.

If during the mid- to late 1970s heavy metal had been a very popular "underground" phenomenon (in terms of media attention and radio play), the early 1980s saw the genre emerge into the bright light of the mass media. During the time that mainstream outlets were ignoring heavy metal, metal bands were nonetheless filling arenas and selling millions of records. As the sound of metal became associated with lower- and lower-middle-class white youths and suburban ennui, bands from both sides of the Atlantic began to build on Van Halen's blend of pop hooks with guitar virtuosity. The result? "Lite-metal" or "hair-metal" bands, such as Def Leppard and Mötley Crüe, began to cross over to the pop charts, inflecting the legacy of Foreigner-Boston et al. with a harder edge and a fashion sense derived from glam via Queen.

The following article by J. D. Considine was published in 1984 at a time when media attention documenting the widespread appeal of heavy metal grew more common. The two bands discussed in the article, Judas Priest and the Scorpions (the section on the Scorpions is largely deleted), do not hail so much from the pop end of the heavy metal spectrum, although both bands nudged their way onto MTV during the early- to mid-1980s. Instead, what this article captures is the emphasis on visceral power and excitement and on an unironic seriousness about technique that Priest's lead singer, Rob Halford, compares to that of Western classical music (much to the amusement of Considine).[2] We also hear a description of why heavy metal caught on in Britain from Priest guitarist K. K. Downing and a few ideas about the appeal of metal to its audience.

---

1. See Robert Walser's chapter analyzing Eddie Van Halen's solo guitar *tour de force*, "Eruption," and its influence on subsequent heavy metal guitarists (Walser, *Running with the Devil: Power, Gender, and Madness in Heavy Metal Music* [Hanover, N.H.: Wesleyan University Press and University Press of New England, 1993], 67–107).

2. This connection is not as ridiculous as it seemed to some critics, and it is the focus of the chapter just cited from Walser's *Running with the Devil*.

# Purity and Power—Total, Unswerving Devotion to Heavy Metal Form: Judas Priest and the Scorpions

## J. D. Considine

No doubt about it, heavy metal is the Music Which Gets No Respect. Oh, sure, the fans like it. For some of them, metal is the very marrow of their cultural existence. And there are even a few broad-minded critics who are willing to let the music, like any other dog, have its day, even if their appreciation is more sociological than musical.

But for most folks, heavy metal is a musical moron joke, fodder for frustrated teens and dominion of dim-witted devil-worshippers. At best, the phrase conjures up the likable lunkheads of Rob Reiner's satiric *This is Spinal Tap;* at worst, the mind turns to Ozzy Osbourne, biting the heads off dead bats in Des Moines or pissing on the Alamo. In all, not exactly what you'd call positive images.

"You get narrow-minded critics reviewing the shows, and all they think about heavy metal is that it is just total ear-splitting, blood-curdling noise without any definition or point," complained Judas Priest's Rob Halford. "This is a very, *very* professional style of music. It means a great deal to many millions of people. We treat heavy metal music with respect."

Halford paused to gaze out the window at the passing Texas countryside. It was a bright Saturday afternoon. Judas Priest were en route from Houston to San Antonio, smack in the middle of a nine-month American tour which had found the band playing to both narrow-minded critics and adoring heavy metal fans, the latter being in the distinct majority. Nevertheless, the question of heavy metal's aesthetic worth is one which Halford takes very much to heart. Heavy metal, he insisted, was genuine *art.*

"This might sound like a bizarre statement," he said, leaping back into the fray, "but I don't think playing heavy metal is that far removed from classical music. To do either, you have to spend many years developing your style and your art, whether you're a violinist or a guitarist, it still takes the same belief in your form of music to achieve and create. It is very much a matter of dedication."

As a herd of cattle receded in the distance, I tried to imagine Halford, in white tie and tails, standing center-stage in a New York recital hall to sing the celebrated art song "Eat Me Alive," while somewhere in the Midwest, a leather-clad Robert Mann of the Julliard String Quartet is screaming into a microphone, asking a rowdy coliseum crowd if they're "ready for some Beethoven?" Somehow the image refused to come.

No, heavy metal isn't exactly serial composition, but then again, art isn't always a matter of complexity. Sometimes, getting and keeping things simple takes as much or more skill.

"A funny story," said Judas Priest's Glenn Tipton, backstage one night, "When we were recording *Defenders Of The Faith* in Spain, this guy from South America came up, a friend of mine. He plays guitar—amazing things, rhythms, phrases, strange South American-type beats, stuff I couldn't begin to play, much more complex than those Police things. Real sambas and stuff, and difficult as hell. All he wanted off me was to learn how to play things with rock accents.

"He couldn't play 'em," Tipton laughs. "An entirely different feeling."

*Source:* J. D. Considine, "Purity and Power—Total, Unswerving Devotion to Heavy Metal Form: Judas Priest and the Scorpions," *Musician* (September 1984), pp. 46–50. Used by permission of J. D. Considine.

It's that bone-headed simplicity, the art of knowing what *not* to play, that Tipton feels makes heavy metal so ultimately British.

"To me, and I can say this honestly, there are not very many American heavy metal bands. There are some great rock bands, the best rock bands in the world. But it's not heavy metal. The American bands are too sophisticated. And I think that's it—English bands, like ourselves, have that lack of sophistication which, I suppose, has to do with upbringing, the fact that we were born and raised poverty-struck. I think you can lose that out of your music, if you're not careful."

In other words, great heavy metal turns its limitations into assets, its insularity into a sense of community, and ends up doing everything art is expected to do. True, heavy metal is often musically limited, culturally reactionary and too damned loud, but at its best, it is *transcendently* so. Which is why, ludicrous as it may seem, Rob Halford's analogy between heavy metal and classical music contains a grain of truth: both disciplines ultimately aim for the triumph of emotion over form.

It's Saturday night in San Antonio, the last night of the city's annual Easter Fiesta. There's a buzz of excitement throughout the city and a roar inside the Civic Arena. When the lights go down for Judas Priest's set, 12,000 kids are on their feet, fists in the air, screaming. As a taped synthesizer growl drones ominously, the curtains part to reveal "the Metallian," a twenty-foot high aluminum gargoyle who holds the drum kit in its left claw. Fog wafts across the stage as the Metallian's vari-light eyes scan the audience: then, in a blinding burst of flashpots, the members of Priest materialize, leaping headlong into the hyper-adrenal pulse of "Love Bites."

As spectacle, it's pretty impressive. With the Metallian looming above like a malevolent building, Halford's macho strut and the rest of the band's leather-clad choreography seem less a matter of vainglorious posturing than an assertion of will, a dance against the demons of the city. Even at the end of the set, as the Metallian breathes fire through the final, crashing chords to "The Green Manalishi (With The Two-Pronged Crown)," it wields its menace almost in defeat, a vanquished dragon.

Granted, that's a lot of meaning to read into an elaborate prop, but it would be foolish to overlook the resonances of such devices. As Halford puts it, "When we use those props, people see them and they say, 'Oh, what is *this?*' But when they suddenly connect with the props, it's a total unification, music and material object working together."

The night before, in Houston, guitarist K. K. Downing had begun to explain his theory of heavy metal. "in certain parts of Great Britain, some bands started taking progressive blues and playing them in their own way. Heavy metal is our own blues, actually."

This "white man's blues," as Downing is fond of calling it, worked because it translated the emotional impact of American blues into a form that young musicians in Britain's industrial heartland could more easily understand. "It was more aggressive," Downing said. "It's a way of getting rid of your blues by expending energy. And it's a way for the audience to expend energy as well."

This makes sense if you look at the music's structure. "All the licks that we play," explained Glenn Tipton, who shares the lead guitar role with Downing, "form around the blues. You get something like the lead break in 'Another Thing Comin',' it's all blues stuff, all the same runs. Even the fast stuff." Grabbing a guitar and practice amp, he plugged in. "Something like this," he said, spinning off a fast splatter of notes, "is just from cadences like this." He began to play a typical blues riff—up from the 7th to the tonic, up again to the minor 3rd, and back down to the tonic—and slowly sped it up, letting the syncopation bleed out as the figure turned into insistent eighth-notes, moving the pattern up the neck by half-steps. Pure metal, "and it's all blues stuff."

Except, of course, that the rhythm is completely different. Where American blues, whether country acoustic or urban electric, maintain an easy rhythmic bounce, heavy metal surges with almost mechanical regularity, pushing the downbeat instead of laying behind the backbeat. It's not a party energy, certainly not dance music; it's more like a football cheer, group aggression focused through rhythm and sheer volume.

Of course, no football crowd could ever hope to muster a sound like Judas Priest's (much to the relief of Pete Rozelle). Despite the volume, Priest's sound isn't noisy or brittle, but sits comfortably in the midrange with a presence so great you could immerse yourself in it. "A total wallow," Halford cheerfully admitted. And during the three Priest shows I attended, the fans did almost seem to be floating, reacting to shifts in dynamics like toy boats in a bathtub.

"A lot of the access and understanding of our music for so many people is that they're able to relate to what we're singing about," Halford continued. "Beyond the vocals, it's the way a guitar makes you feel when someone hits a particular chord, the way a snare drum is cracked."

Flashing back to Halford's classical analogy, I suddenly realized that the difference between the kid playing air guitar in his bedroom to "Rock Hard, Ride Free" and his father in the family room, conducting the last movement of the *Symphonie Fantastique* along with Herr von Karajan, is not much more than a matter of props. That's not to say that classical music and heavy metal are necessarily equivalents, just that the listener's experience can be, because for both father and son, it's a matter of release through pure sound. So it wasn't hard to nod appreciatively when Halford concluded by remarking, "I just hope that, after seeing us for the first time, people go away from a show fulfilled by what they've experienced."

I'll bet Herr von Karajan feels the same way.

Call it another side-effect to adolescent glandular mayhem, or just call it zit cream for the soul. In any case, both Priest and the Scorps agree that the key to the heavy metal's popularity is the power transfer between performer and audience. "We have a high energy level," says Scorpion Matthias Jabs, "and when the audience is great, they feel that and give it back to you."

"You can't analyze it much beyond the fact that there are 11,000 separate individual human beings getting off on what you're doing," concludes Priest's Halford, "each of them experiencing an emotional vibe and throwing it back at you. I mean, that's what art is all about. We all need each other."

# 72. Metal in the Late Eighties
## Glam or Thrash?

The popularity of heavy metal could not remain underground forever: Top 40 hits by Def Leppard, Quiet Riot, Ratt, Mötley Crüe, and the Scorpions and the growing ubiquity of metal-influenced guitar solos in the early- to mid-1980s presaged a full-scale breakthrough. One of the clearest signs of the change of status was the addition to MTV's schedule in 1986 of a show devoted entirely to metal, "Headbanger's Ball." This show reflected a change in MTV's format as the video channel moved away from continuous 24-hour video flow into a schedule broken down into specialized time slots, as well as the recognition that heavy metal was now acceptable to the demographic represented by MTV's audience.

This development in the realm of music video was paralleled by increased radio play for metal bands, not only for the ever-expanding progeny of "lite-metal" bands, such as Poison and Warrant, but for bands that followed from the "harder" Judas Priest/Iron Maiden approach. Earlier distinctions between British and American metal began to erode, and a band like Guns 'n' Roses (probably the most popular metal band of the late 1980s) successfully combined several different strands of the genre.

Many of the bands of the "hard" heavy metal school were influenced not only by earlier metal bands, but by hardcore punk, and they developed new subgenres of metal, dubbed "speed metal," "thrash metal," and (even) "death metal." Within the heavy metal subculture, these latter bands represented the "purer," "non-commercial" strain of metal in contrast to the "glam metal" bands. If one of the best examples of a pop-metal band in the late 1980s was Bon Jovi, then the clearest example of a band that seemed to follow its own inclinations and respond to a core audience of metal fanatics was Metallica (which, by the way, went on to become wildly popular themselves).[1] Another important issue related to heavy metal in the late 1980s was the public discussion of lyric themes: Heavy metal lyrics had become a *cause célèbre* for their focus on teenage

---

1. For a profile of Metallica on the cusp of mass popularity as they struggle with the contradictions engendered by their shifting status, see David Fricke, "Heavy Metal Justice," *Rolling Stone,* January 12, 1989, 42–49.

problems and had come under attack by groups, such as the Parents
Music Resource Center (PMRC), which claimed that heavy metal lyrics
were responsible for teenage suicide.[2]

In the following piece, Richard Gehr portrays Metallica on the verge of
moving from an extremely popular cult band to a band with mass
popularity, a topic that comes to the fore in the band's comments about
their "outsider" status. Particularly fascinating is the description of
Metallica's songwriting process, one of the factors responsible for song
structures that were unusually complex within the context of other metal
of the time. Gehr also describes how the content of Metallica's lyrics was
one of the factors separating their brand of "thrash" from "pop-metal."
The highpoint of heavy metal's popularity in the late 1980s and
early 1990s created a situation in which bands like Metallica could
simultaneously maintain "underground" status and experience mass
popularity, a balancing act taken over by grunge after 1991. Gehr begins
the article writing in the voice of the two members of Metallica who are
profiled in this piece, James Hetfield and Lars Ulrich.

# METALLICA
## *Richard Gehr*

Ulrich has recently risen from the sleep, dreamless or otherwise, of the very successful. His
band, billed fourth (between Led Zep wannaboys Kingdom Come and metal morons
Dokken) on the Monsters or Rock tour—a.k.a. the "Fucking Monsters of Fucking Rock"
tour, a.k.a. the "weekend" tour—has garnered *at least* as much critical oom-pah as their
co-"Monsters," even Van Fucking Halen.

  During their non-touring weekdays, Metallica was ensconced in the bucolic environs
of Woodstock, New York, feverishly mixing tracks for their fourth LP, . . . *And Justice for All!*
Ulrich doesn't remember that the studio where they're working is named Bearsville; he
only knows that it's several miles from the nearest watering hole. But when bleary-eyed
singer/guitarist James Hetfield joins us a little later, he'll helpfully add, "It's out in the middle of the forest up there. I heard something about The Band."

---

2. For more on censorship and the PMRC, see Robert Walser, *Running with the Devil: Power, Gender, and
Madness in Heavy Metal Music* (Hanover, N.H.: Wesleyan University Press and University Press of New
England, 1993), 137–45; and Reebee Garofalo, "Setting the Record Straight: Censorship and Social Re-
sponsibility in Popular Music," *Journal of Popular Music Studies* 6 (1994), 1–37. The transcript of Frank
Zappa's comments to Congress on the issue are as edifying as they are entertaining; see Frank Zappa,
"Statement to Congress, 19 September 1985," in Clinton Heylin, ed., *The Da Capo Book of Rock and Roll
Writing* (New York: Da Capo Press, [1992] 2000), 501–08.

*Source:* Richard Gehr, "Metallica," *Music Sound and Output* (September 1988). © Richard Gehr. Used by
permission.

Ulrich and Hetfield formed Metallica in Los Angeles in 1981 as a hard-edged response to late-Seventies mainstream rock. Inspired in equal parts by the so-called "new wave of British heavy metal" and by the Southern California hardcore scene, Metallica stripped away the gothic excesses of the former and expanded the shortform song structures of the latter to produce five- to eight-minute mini-epics of ear-shattering volume and mind-boggling speed. They compounded multiple riffs within single tunes, linking them with subject matter that rejected "gonna-rock-ya-all-night-long" HM cliches (not to be confused with "gonna-love-ya-all-nite-long" HM cliches) in favor of darker meditations on power, violence, aggression and death.

Young and hungry, Metallica evinces absolutely no influence prior to, say, 1976. For example: an AOR "oldies" station plays quietly in the background as we talk. At one point, a strange expression passes across Hetfield's face. He looks at the radio and, almost complaining, asks, "What's this?!" The scrap that caught his attention was Leigh Stevens's guitar solo on "Help Me Doctor" from Blue Cheer's first LP, *Vincebus Eruptum*—arguably the finest heavy metal album ever recorded.

Rather than subsisting as just another metal band from L.A., the group, which included lead guitarist Kirk Hammett and bassist Cliff Burton, moved to New York in 1983. After signing with Megaforce, they released their first LP, *Kill 'Em All*, whose leather-roots popularity kept them on the road in the United States and Europe for the next nine months. The band's second Megaforce LP, a post-adolescent death trip titled *Ride the Lightning*, was quickly snatched up by Elektra and went on to sell more than half a million copies. As to the record's morbid theme, Ulrich says, "around then we were talking about capital punishment and had a lot of fucking thoughts about dying and death."

"We were putting ourselves in various situations," adds Hetfield, "like the electric chair and cryonics."

Both make a big deal about how none of their records, including *Lightning*, is a concept album. "I think records reflect whatever shit you're going through at that point in time," noted Ulrich sagely.

With the success of *Lightning*, Metallica's stock quickly ascended. They were still a cult band, but they were a cult band like Pee-Wee Herman is a cult comedian. By the time Elektra released *Master of Puppets* in 1986, Metallica had welded shut their position in the metal pantheon, despite the fact that virtually no radio station dared to air their savagely sophisticated megawattage and they made no music videos.

Collectively, Metallica's members thrive on their independence and outsider status, scorning anything short of total musical and personal autonomy. Ulrich describes *Puppets*, for example, as being about the dangers of "drugs, manipulation, anything that takes you over." The lyrics' syntax may scan in the most bizarre of fashions—just try and parse lines like "Not dead which eternal lie/Stranger eons death may die"—but the impact and emotion is unmistakable. What do you expect from a metal band, after all. Cole Porter?

An American tour with Ozzy Osbourne following the release of *Puppets* nailed their appeal. The album has since sold more than 750,000 copies domestically and penetrated *Billboard's* Top 30.

Sadly, bassist Cliff Burton was killed in Scandinavia when the band's tour bus crashed that summer. Rather than fade into oblivion, however, the band resuscitated itself in his honor and added bass player Jason Newsted (of Flotsam & Jetsam fame). After touring Japan, they even returned to Europe and made up the dates they'd missed.

For Metallica, writing and recording an album is an extremely piecemeal, even abstract process. Their songwriting begins literally in a garage, which Ulrich and Hetfield sift through riff tapes compiled by the four band members.

"We've got riffs from years and years," explains Hetfield. "On the road we constantly riff and write it down."

"The riffs have *feels*," says Ulrich. "First we start separating the riffs into . . . "

". . . Categories. . . . ." says Hetfield.

"Like, some shit is strong enough to be the main idea of a tune. Then we go through the tapes and try to find possible bridges, choruses, middle bits or whatever. After we have the skeleton of a song, we start getting a feel for what the song's really like. Then we search for a title from a list of titles that fits with the riffing's mood."

After assembling the song, the group works it out on a demo.

Hetfield: "Then Lars and I sit with the demos and go, Well, this is a little too fast here, and this is little too slow. We'll play it live and see if it really grooves. If not, we'll try it a little faster."

Ulrich and Hetfield next assemble a click track that schematizes the song's various tempos.

Hetfield: "First I'll lay down a scratch rhythm, then he'll go in and do his drums. I think our click track situation is something unique from what other bands do because some songs have between 10 and 15 click-track samples, which really freaks people out. They can't understand it. Usually clicks keep the time steady, but we have many moods and grooves within each eight- or nine-minute song. So for every riff we figure out what tempo it sounds best at, to make it fit better with the whole thing's overall feel.

"Putting down the clicks for a couple of songs on *Justice!* took two days each. But when I tell that to other people they think I mean two hours or something."

After completing the click track, the group is ready to record. Here again Metallica differ from standard procedure by going after a full, "live" sound in the most roundabout of ways.

"We record about as nonlive as possible," says Ulrich. "There's never more than one guy in the studio at any one point in time."

Building the click track, says Hetfield, takes "a lot longer, probably, than it would to actually do it live." The recording procedure goes something like this: Hetfield lays down his scratch rhythm, Ulrich records his drum tracks, Hetfield returns and completes his final rhythm-guitar parts, Newsted adds the bass, then Hetfield and Hammett alternate leads and vocals, "so we don't burn ourselves out."

Metallica's last two LPs were recorded in Copenhagen's Sweet Silence Studios. One of the differences between most studios in Los Angeles and their European equivalents, says Ulrich, is how "all that shit's included. You don't have to fucking *rent* anything." Another difference is the tendency of European studios to employ an in-house engineer, which is how the group discovered Flemming Rasmussen.

During their '84 European tour, the band decided to concentrate their energies on an extended stay on the continent, where they could tour, record an album, blitz the press and "really spread a lot of shit around."

They met the man with whom they would record their next three albums during their first day in Sweet Silence Studios. "Flemming had done some Rainbow stuff that sounded pretty good and he was supposedly a really happening engineer," recalls Ulrich. "At that point in time we had had a really bad experience with an I-use-the-term-loosely 'producer' on the first album [Paul Curcio on *Kill 'Em All*], and we were glad to have two more weeks of studio time instead of spending $10 or $15 thousand on someone who really didn't know anything about the band. So we went in and did it with Flemming, and instantly there was some sort of happening vibe there. There still is, and it's been growing stronger, really. He's like the fifth member when it comes to recording."

Unfortunately, Rasmussen wasn't immediately available after Metallica began recording . . . *And Justice for All!*, so the band hooked up with Guns N' Roses producer Mike Clink for their first sessions at One on One. On *Master of Puppets,* according to Ulrich, "we booked studio time and fucking got all the decisions together way too early in the songwriting. But when it came time to go into the studio, we weren't really ready." With *Justice!,* however, the situation was exactly the opposite.

"This time around we didn't want to make any recording decisions until we had all the songs written. So we started writing in October and it only took eight or nine weeks to write the songs. It went a lot quicker than we thought it would." By January, they were ready to record, but Rasmussen wasn't, having been unavoidably detained by a prior commitment to a band amusingly called Danish Pregnant Woman. But Metallica wanted him bad, and did everything in their power to snare him, but to no avail.

"We fucking tried everything, but there was no fucking way to get this fucking Danish Pregnant Woman to fucking give Flemming up. We offered to fucking fly engineers in at our expense, pay for studio time, anything, right? No. See ya.

"So basically we were faced with the situation of whether we wanted to sit around and *dwell* for fucking three months, let the fuckin' songs get burned out, and kind of fuckin' start hating things. We're all sitting around on our couch going flump, we've gotta fuckin' start doing something with our time."

The decision was made to go into the studio with Mike Clink, get comfortable by wailing on a couple of Diamondhead and Budgie chestnuts, work out some B-sides and prepare for Rasmussen's availability. But, according to Ulrich, "The Clink situation emphasized that we really can't work, or at least record, with anyone other than Flemming."

"Well, we can." Adds Hetfield, "but it's a slow process."

"We'd still be in there right now doing drum tracks," moans Ulrich.

Rasmussen finally came to the rescue, and the drummer and guitarist acknowledge that their time with Clink wasn't totally wasted. Rather, it was just enough to loosen the group up and enable them to start recording within a couple of days of Rasmussen's arrival six weeks into their studio block. "If we'd started from scratch it probably would have taken us three weeks," says Ulrich.

Metallica mixed . . . *And Justice for All!* with Michael Barbiero and Steve Thompson, whose credits include Whitney Houston, Madonna, the Rolling Stones, Prince, Cinderella, Tesla and Guns N' Roses. Ulrich and Hetfield are optimistic about the collaboration.

"Looking back," opines Ulrich, "I don't think we've been too comfortable with any of the mixes we've ever done."

Hetfield agrees, adding, "I think the problem with a lot of people who specialize in mixing is they set up the mix the way they're used to mixing bands, and everyone ends up sounding like those mixes. What's great about these guys is they go out of their way to keep the band's identity completely together."

How does *Justice* differ from *Puppets?*

"It's a lot . . ." begins Ulrich.

"Drier," continues Hetfield.

"A lot drier, and a lot more . . ."

"In your face," Hetfield pipes in again. "Everything's way up front and there's not a lot of 'verb or echo. We really went out of our way to make sure that what we put on the tape was that we wanted, so the mixing procedure would be as easy as possible and not like the old saying, 'We'll save it in the mix.'"

"*Puppets* was very well recorded," says Ulrich, "and had a very huge sort of sound, but didn't really fuckin' come out of the speakers and hit you in the face."

"Compared to *Ride the Lightning* it did," Hetfield reminds him.

"I don't want to listen to *Ride the Lightning,*" groans Ulrich.

"Flemming was in a reverb daze," explains Hetfield.

Did the experience of recording *The $5.98 EP* affect *Justice's* sound?

"I think we were pretty pleased with the way it was so upfront and raw," reckons Hetfield.

"We learned something from that mix," says Ulrich.

"We learned that the bass is too loud," says Hetfield.

"And when is the bass too loud?" chants Ulrich.

Together: "When you can hear it!"

Upon completion, . . . *And Justice for All!* will be another Metallica mouthful of super-charged riffs and vaguely upsetting lyrics just this side of deeply disturbing. Although they joke flippantly about its content, Ulrich and Hetfield obviously place much greater existential stock in their work than your typical metal numbskulls.

What's it about? I inquire.

"Walking your dog in the park," quips Ulrich.

"And not wanting to clean up after it," continues Hetfield, as usual. "But there's a law, so you have to. It's basically about independence and freedom, and how they are stopped in certain ways."

"How they're very surfacey things," adds Ulrich. "At a certain point they really start shoving those words in your face, but when you really start thinking about a lot of shit . . ."

". . . how free is it?" concludes Hetfield.

Ulrich goes on. "You have freedom of choice, but how many choices do you have? It's easy to say you can make up your own mind, but you can only make up your mind about two or three different things."

Like, for example, between Dokken, the Scorpions, Kingdom Come, Poison, Venom, Van Fucking Halen, and a skidillion other munsters of rock. Metallica prove it that Sunday afternoon in Foxboro, where they play an abbreviated, probably even mediocre set for several thousand curious complexions. No matter. It's clear that Metallica embody an electrically overamped power and passion that rings a hundred times truer than their monster mates. Like free jazz, New York noise or even composer Krystof Penderecki, Metallica are original dynamos, weekend warriors outstanding in a very loud field of their own. And that's the fucking truth.

# 73. Postpunk Goes Indie

As stated earlier, the critical attention given to the initial wave of New York and British punk in the late 1970s surpassed its popular appeal. Punk, as both musical and subcultural style, nevertheless continued to spread, branching out into a variety of subgenres. As we have already seen, the most commercial of these branches resulted in the synth-pop "New Romantic" movement. A variety of underground genres, based on different regional scenes and supported by a loose network of fanzines, independent record labels, college radio stations, and clubs in urban areas and college towns, gradually earned the label "indie rock." The many "scenes" that developed were one of the ways that college-age, post-baby boomers created a distinction between themselves and the long shadow cast by the musical dispositions of their boomer parents and older siblings.[1] Indies scenes sprang up in college towns as far flung as Athens, Georgia, Austin, Texas, and Champaign, Illinois.[2]

The liveliest scene most directly descended from Ramones-style punk was the Los Angeles–based hardcore movement. Memorialized in Penelope Spheeris's documentary, *The Decline of Western Civilization*, this scene featured bands, such as X, Black Flag, and the Minutemen, who gloried in life on the margins while their songs focused on speed, anger, and aggression. That being said, the Los Angeles bands were hardly of a piece; X combined the quasi-folk harmonizing of husband-wife team John Doe and Exene Cervenka with the rockabilly flavored antics of guitarist Billy Zoom; Black Flag could be humorous ("TV Party"), as well as scabrous ("Fuck the Police"); and the Minutemen showed what could be done in a rock song lasting 60 seconds or less. In Minneapolis, an active club scene developed around bands like the Replacements and Hüsker Dü, who added a melodic edge to their distorted guitars and up-tempo songs.

---

The following article, by Al Flipside (copublisher of the fanzine, *Flipside*), presents a brief history of punk's transformation into hardcore. Flipside makes an important connection between the policies of then-President Ronald Reagan and the emergence of hardcore, and he observes how in some ways the new political realities of the early 1980s parallel those in the United Kingdom five years earlier. The latter part of the article presents a survey of hardcore scenes around the United States, but I include here only the section on Los Angeles because that is the area that developed the most widely known scene; this section provides a taste of the thorough cataloguing provided by Flipside in the rest of the article.

## WHAT IS THIS THING CALLED HARDCORE?
### *Al Flipside*

What is this "hardcore" movement anyway? Doesn't it mean slam dancing like there's no tomorrow? Is it beating people violently on the dance floor and doing a back flip off the p.a. column? Is it loud as you can go, fast as you can play? Is it beach punks, surf punks or skate

---

1. This is one of the conclusions drawn by Holly Kruse in "Subcultural Identity in Alternative Music Culture," *Popular Music*, 12, no. 1 (January 1993): 33–41.

2. For an in-depth examination of the scene in Austin, see Barry Shanks, *Dissonant Identities: The Rock 'n' Roll Scene in Austin, Texas* (Hanover, N.H.: Wesleyan University Press and University Press of New England, 1994). The Holly Kruse article cited in note 1, focuses on the scene in Champaign. On the scene in Athens, see Anthony DeCurtis, "The Athens Scene," in *Rocking My Life Away: Writing About Music and Other Matters* (Durham, N.C.: Duke University Press, 1998), 21–27 (written in 1981).

*Source:* Al Flipside, "What Is This Thing Called Hardcore," *Trouser Press*, August 1982, pp. 22–24.

punks? An excuse for excessive drug and alcohol imbibition? Does it mean you hate your parents, teachers and the police? Is it kids too young to know any better or too frustrated to want anything else? Is it the youth of the nation speaking up for what they believe in and what they see is wrong with today's world? Is it just another fad? Is it another name for "punk rock"?

Hardcore is all of the above, in various combinations and proportions. To some of us it is simply punk by another name. The term "punk" is still acceptable in England, and the English rallying cry, "punk's not dead" refers to the same music as the American expression "hardcore." The recent explosion of hardcore punk comes after years of development. It is the work of many dedicated people and was inspired (directly and indirectly) by America's decaying social, political and economic situation.

Let's start by looking where "punk" came from in the first place. Cities have always had their own music scenes. In the late '60s and early '70s, local activity dwindled as "stadium rock" reigned. By the mid-'70s, though, rock musicmaking again became a more personal concern. Local groups emerged playing original music and clubs emerged to showcase them.

Around 1976 punk rock sprang up simultaneously in New York, London and Los Angeles. Each area developed an individual style while being influenced by the others. London borrowed the Ramones' guitar style and leather jackets, but developed the pogo dance, safety pin look and political grounding. Los Angeles sped up the basic sound, adding its own dress, dances, political twists, etc. This exciting and energetic new punk scene was alive and kicking by 1977. However, with the breakup of the Sex Pistols in 1978 the media declared punk rock dead. Disco became the next fad, and for the most part that's what teenage America was all about. But the media were wrong about punk. It hadn't died, it just went underground.

Most of the London punk bands put out great first albums and then sold out with shitty second releases; many disbanded. New York's so-called punk rockers turned out to be just plain flakes. The Los Angeles punk bands (those of San Francisco too) never got anything going, and most disappeared or were incorporated into other projects. The original attitude, however, was firmly established. Punk would not die; the seeds were sown.

All was not lost as the pioneering punk bands disappeared. "New wave" came along to gloss over any remaining sore spots, but the scars were too deep to heal. Out of this new music rage came many important independent record labels and distributors, in America as well as England.

Where does hardcore fit into this ancient history? I first saw the word used as a noun on a poster announcing a new tour by Vancouver band D.O.A. The term signified dedication and defiance, and at the same time named the new breed.

This new breed developed on a foundation that the early punks had no idea they had set up. In 1977 there were almost no independent record labels in the US willing to sign a new act, let alone a network to distribute such a record. Today there are literally hundreds of labels willing to take the chance and a handful of distributors eagerly awaiting any new releases. The pattern has repeated itself all over the country: One band forms a label as its only means to release its own material. That label then offers the opportunity for other bands to be heard. A distribution network set up once can work again and again. Where there was one single, now there are EPs, LPs and compilation albums. Although new labels spring up all the time, the older labels find themselves with growing catalogues.

The machinery, then, is waiting. But I would have to think an entire scene could develop out of sheer opportunity—and this wasn't the case.

London's punk scene re-emerged in a big way with bands like Crass, Discharge and Exploited. They had a new look (mohawk haircuts) and new seriousness to their pro-anarchy, anti-war stance. In America the remaining hardcore bands, in an amazing act of faith, were making cross-country tours. Their records were out there, but the record-buying public still wasn't aware of them and radio stations (except for a few) were hopeless. Black Flag, D.O.A., the Dead Kennedys and others screamed their messages to anyone who would listen and inspired more than they could imagine.

Who was inspiring the bands themselves? Time now to pay tribute to hardcore's chief impetus: President Ronald Reagan.

Listen to any hardcore band's lyrics: recession, depression, WWIII, nuclear war, the arms race, unemployment—Reagan brainstorms every one. There are probably more "I hate Reagan" songs around than on any other topic. As federal aid cutbacks hit close to home, political theories become frighteningly real, just as they did for English punks five years ago. Most hardcore bands are dead serious.

On the other hand, there are opportunists and hordes of hardcore recruits who are into the scene only because it's cool to be a punk in their high school. As with any movement, these imbeciles can only ruin hardcore for its sincere fans. There's always hope the new punks will listen to what the bands are saying and be enlightened. They're obvious at every gig, with their mindless fighting, drug abuse and peer pressure that punk never stood for.

The hardcore scene is full of people with ideals who have healthy things to say (like the Washington, DC bands). There are also people—sometimes I think in the majority—who are just plain assholes out to exploit punk's reckless reputation. Everyone and every place has to be judged individually. The second half of this article is a rundown on the American hardcore punk scene based on reading and talking to fanzine editors and bands themselves.

## Los Angeles

We'll start on the west coast, just as American hardcore did. Los Angeles, of course, is at the heart of the movement. The LA punk scene has remained strong, although underground at times, since its beginnings. Clubs open and close but there's always somewhere to play. The vast suburbs, stretching for at least 100 miles from one end of the San Fernando valley to the edge of Orange County, supply new faces and room for individual development. There are undoubtedly more hardcore bands and gigs here than in any city in the US.

The LA hardcore scene started around 1980 with the beach punks and the Fleetwood club at Redondo Beach. But not everyone lives at the beach. Today's hardcore bands come from all over the giant suburb that is Los Angeles.

Black Flag is probably America's best and best known hardcore band. They've been around for quite a while in many forms, and are admired for their hardcore stance in both music and lifestyle. Few LA groups come close to matching Black Flag's dedication.

Los Angeles has many hardcore bands who have been around for several years, among them Fear, Circle Jerks, Social Distortion, Red Cross—even the Dickies. The Fleetwood/beach punk era saw bands rise to prominence like TSOL, Adolescents, Bad Religion, Channel 3, China White and Saccharine Trust. Most of these bands have released records and now headline at smaller clubs. The hardcore club Godzillas has hosted a new crop, including Circle One, Sin 34, Symbol Six, Suicidal Tendencies, Public Nuisance, Social Dismay, Modern Protest, Moral Decay and Lost Cause.

Other bands, like Wasted Youth, the Dischords and RE7, have just begun gaining popularity from gigs and records. There's also a "horror band" contingent that some consider hardcore. TSOL used to be among them: these bands have names like Christian Death, Super Heroines, Voodoo Church and 45 Grave. The Sins are a hardcore band from Riverside, not far from LA although it might as well be another country.

# 74. Indie Brings the Noise

Underground groups did not simply disappear in New York City at the end of the 1970s. The fruitful union of art school bohemian attitudes with a rebellious, no-frills approach to music making continued in the "no wave" movement and the Downtown avant-garde. No wave (mentioned in chapter 64) incorporated a more explicit relationship with avant-garde tendencies while rebelling against what no wavers viewed as the institutionalized quality of punk. The Downtown scene featured musicians, such as John Zorn, with credentials in the art gallery, jazz improvisation, or art music scenes, who adopted punk's embrace of noise and combined it with approaches derived from classical music. Another notable participant in this scene, Glenn Branca, created noisy, minimalist manifestoes with an orchestra of electric guitars. Two members of one of Branca's ensembles, Lee Ranaldo (b. 1956) and Thurston Moore (b. 1958), brought the dissonant textures of Branca's (and no wave's) music to a more conventional rock-group format with the formation of Sonic Youth. Eventually Sonic Youth applied this avant-garde approach to songs with more obvious connections to pop structures, alternating extended textural instrumentals with vocal passages led by Moore or bassist, Kim Gordon (b. 1953), singing-speaking in a style recalling that of Lou Reed and Ur-punkers, the Velvet Underground.

Kim Gordon's account of life on the road with Sonic Youth is instructive for several reasons. First, it provides an insider's view of touring on the indie circuit in the 1980s and shows how tours were built on shows in small clubs in college towns, relying on personal connections to set up the show and make local arrangements. Second, her journal tells us something about the still somewhat unusual perspective of the female rock musician, including her motivation for playing rock music, and about some of the issues raised by being the only female in a band.

## Boys Are Smelly: Sonic Youth Tour Diary, '87
### *Kim Gordon*

Before picking up a bass I was just another girl with a fantasy. What would it be like to be right under the pinnacle of energy, beneath two guys crossing their guitars, two thunderfoxes in

*Source:* Kim Gordon. "Boys Are Smelly: Sonic Youth Tour Diary, '87," *The Village Voice Rock & Roll Quarterly*, Fall 1988. Reprinted in *Rock She Wrote: Women Write About Rock, Pop, and Rap*, ed. Evelyn McDonnell and Ann Powers (New York: Delta Trade Paperbacks, 1995), pp. 66–73.

the throes of self-love and male bonding? How sick, but what desire could be more ordinary? How many grannies once wanted to rub their faces in Elvis's crotch, and how many boys want to be whipped by Steve Albini's guitar?

In the middle of the stage, where I stand as the bass player of Sonic Youth, the music comes at me from all directions. The most heightened state of being female is watching people watch you. Manipulating that state, without breaking the spell of performing, is what makes someone like Madonna all the more brilliant. Simple pop structures sustain her image, allowing her real self to remain a mystery—is she really that sexy? Loud dissonance and blurred melody create their own ambiguity—are we really that violent?—a context that allows me to be anonymous. For my purposes, being obsessed with boys playing guitars, being as ordinary as possible, being a girl bass player is ideal, because the swirl of Sonic Youth music makes me forget about being a girl. I like being in a weak position and making it strong.

## We're the Archies!

People who can't even believe we have an audience are always curious about who they are. Maybe half the crowd who shows up in New York are *real* fans: noise buffs, death rockers, yuppies who have never heard a Sonic Youth record but know who Lydia Lunch is, rock writers, fanzine moguls, and sexual misfits, each and every one of them dressed in black. In L.A. everyone is more power-shag. In other cities audiences are younger, mostly fourteen- and fifteen-year-olds from areas that have cable (MTV's *120 Minutes*), get exposed to us, and unlike college students, have nothing better to do. New Yorkers familiar with Sonic Youth never consider us a teenybopper band, but that just goes to show how provincial New Yorkers really are. They should get out of the city more often and see the world.

A lot has changed, though, since Sonic Youth began in '81. Cofounder and guitarist Thurston Moore named a show he was booking *Noisefest*. That's where we met guitarist Lee Ranaldo and the band came together. The festival's name was a joke, inspired by the owner of Hurrah, who had said he was gonna close the club because all the bands just sounded like a bunch of noise. Nobody even knew what a noise band was. I wondered if people would be disappointed in Europe, the easiest place for New York bands to get gigs, because we didn't fit the image. Next to our friends the Swans, who were very loud and had a percussionist who pounded metal, we were total wimps.

## Every Night, a Different Gig

Lyle Hysen, drummer for Das Damen, a New York band with a Deep Purple-like zest for guitar curdle and intricate song structures that frame a tragicomic persona (if comedian Richard Lewis were a band, they'd be it), told me about this vision he had that would change the face of indie rock. Instead of the band going on the road, from city to city, the audience would tour. For instance, they could do the Midwest. Head out to Minneapolis and see the Replacements, Soul Asylum, and Run Westy Run. Get back on the bus and drive to Madison to Killdozer, Die Kreuzen, and the Tar Babies. Just think, every night a different gig.

You'd be better off than the typical small touring band. There'd be no endless bickering about where-what-when to eat, all the draining decision-making. The tour manager would take care of everything, so you could just concentrate on watching the bands play. If the bus broke down, well, maybe you'd miss a gig, but it's *not your responsibility*.

Personally, I like to know that a band has suffered by the time they get onstage. Like the first time Redd Kross toured. Out of some thirty dates they did six. They drove out of L.A. in some crappy station wagon they bought with a record company advance, and they had big suitcases filled with their gear—high heeled sneakers, spangled bell-bottoms, poly-coated blouses—and everything got all messy and wrinkled, but a half dozen times they shimmied onstage and played their hearts out.

## Richmond, 9/14

I never feel like we're really on tour till we hit Richmond. The wide streets feel different, slow and empty, and then I know we've left NYC/New Jersey/Philly/Baltimore/D.C. That turnpike shit is the ugliest anywhere.

"Mom, I Gave the Cat Some Acid" was the funny industrial rock song by Happy Flowers we covered tonight when we played with them. They covered Sonic Youth's "Catholic Block" and wailed all over us, 'cause they're so fucking cute. There were a couple guys from Fishbone hanging out, trying to be funnier than anyone else. One guy was trying to impress me, telling me what neighborhood he comes from in L.A. He said that he could be making a lot of money selling crack, but he preferred to play music. I really felt like saying to him, "Yeah, so fucking what, I'm a girl and here's my ghetto pal."

## Chapel Hill, 9/15

The Cat's Cradle was packed and too hot to remember anything. The last time we played in Chapel Hill, '82, it was the old Cat's Cradle, which was filled with the kind of dreariness that comes from redneck bars.

That was our first tour, us and the Swans. Yeah, we thought we were hot shit. (We had a record out and had played CBGB, the Mudd Club, and Danceteria.) It was raining and sad as hell, and the headlining Swans played their set to six jeering cowboys. Chapel Hill is one of the hippest places on earth to play, but in 1982 we were too underground or something. Mike Gira, the leader of the Swans, introduced a song amid giggles and chants for "Freebird" by saying, "This next song is about getting butt-fucked by a cop," or something to that effect. We stood around waiting to see if Harry Crosby, then the English bass player for the Swans, who was as drunk as anyone, would feel the need to defend their honor. But nothing happened, a fitting end to a stupid evening.

All ten of us piled into the van, and the Swans fought among themselves. Morale was very low, tempers short, and our expectations not as high as Mike's, which is why they scream at one another. One night Mike and his drummer started strangling each other and calling each other "dickhead" and "asshole." Meanwhile everyone else is crammed around them trying to mind his or her own business, being really cool.

## Atlanta, 9/16

On the drive from Athens to Atlanta there's this great Sno-Kone stand run by a six-year-old who offers a million different flavors—poppy seed or corn dog, for instance. We've totally given up on Athens, where we played twice and nobody came. The first time was the night Gira jumped off the stage and pushed someone who was pogoing. Mike thought the guy was a poser who was making fun of him. In reality he was a nerd, and Mike had never seen a nerd before.

We played at the Metroplex in Atlanta. As wholesome as Athens likes to think it is, Atlanta is self-consciously decadent. For instance, when my bass amp broke during the set, I felt pressured to go through the motions, pretending that sound was still blasting out, dry-humping as it were. Someone in the audience shouted, "Play some fucking noise, that's what it's all about, isn't it? Stop complaining that the PA isn't loud enough." This is the kind of expert who will later review the show, complaining that no one stuck a drill up his butt.

Anyhow, Atlanta used to have a super bad reputation as an evil punk scene, lots of kids hanging out and slashing the tires of touring bands, a real pit. Thurston tried to discourage his sister, Susan, from coming to the Metroplex. He must've thought we were gonna suck, or that he had to protect her. Thurston is really hung up about having to protect women, must be his upbringing. (Thurston and I even had a Catholic wedding.) He told Susan she'd be raped and murdered if she came. A handsome redhead, thirty, the mother of four, she ignored him and appeared at the club with a camera around her neck, gasping to their cousins, "God, I'm the only nerd here!" Someone asked Susan for her autograph.

We stayed at her house and awoke to food flying around the room and babies crawling all over us. I know many people think we indulge in twisted sex and ingest massive amounts of drugs on tour, and of course we do. But I'll always remember Susan, standing in the driveway with the kids and waving good-bye.

## Texas, 9/17

On our way to Dallas, we just melt, sleep, and nag our drummer Steve Shelley about driving too slow and Thurston for driving too much like he plays guitar. Lee Ranaldo is holding his movie camera out the window again, and Terry Pearson, our sound man, is ripping through another rock 'n' roll autobiography. He can read one in ten minutes. Suzanne Sasic is also with us.

Suzanne is our T-shirt vendor and runs the lighting board. Tomboyish, but with long red hair, she wears spurs and keeps her money in her boots. Her penchant for wearing glitter and silver, combined with her almost translucent skin, are other reasons we call her our goddess of light. Suzanne and I sit in the last row of the van and complain about something or other or just voice our opinions in general. No one ever listens to us. It's so far back, what with the windows open and stereo blasting, that we have to shout to be heard. "Turn that shit off." "Stop the car, I have to pee." Thurston complains that we're always mumbling.

Suzanne has a diet that's a challenge to accommodate. She won't eat anything green, except guacamole, and will only eat *the middle* of various foods like pancakes and cheese omelettes. (She hates the egg part.) Spaghetti, chocolate, and orange juice are staples. I'm writing this as a warning for all the boys across the country who write to ask who the vixen with the devastating eyes is. Does she care? No, she's a heartbreaker. Just send obscure vinyl, After Eights, and forget the rest.

## Boston, 10/18

There was a point when I started getting sickened by the violence onstage. Thurston's fingers would swell up all purple and thick from banging his guitar. Usually, I never know what's happening onstage, I would just see guitarlike objects whizzing through the air out of the corner of my eye. A couple of times Thurston pushed Lee into the audience, as the only way to end a song, but that was harmless fun.

At our first gig in Boston about four years ago, *Conflict* editor Gerard Cosloy, *Forced Exposure*'s Jimmy Johnson, and this drunken fan-boy were just about the only ones there. During the first song the fan-boy picked up this broken drumstick that had flown onto the floor and threw it back. It speared into my forehead. At first I thought it had bounced off Thurston's guitar. Shocked, I didn't know whether to cry or keep playing, but then I just felt incredibly angry. It took a long time to resolve that incident, 'cause it really made me feel sick, violated, like walking to the dressing room after a set, having some guy say, "Nice show," then getting my ass pinched as I walk away.

I blamed it on the music for a while, because it did draw fans who really want to see you hurt yourself. It's not that I don't share similar expectations; there's beauty in things falling apart, in the dangerous (sexual) power of electricity, which makes our music possible. But what was once a hazy fantasy has since clarified itself. I don't want my blood to be entertainment.

When we most recently played the Channel in Boston, some kid threw a handful of firecrackers in my face. I threw down my bass and left the stage, and so did the rest of the band. We figured out what happened and went back on to finish the set, while bouncers were throwing the kid out. I was actually beginning to feel sorry for him, probably a misplaced Aerosmith fan.

## Naugatuck, Connecticut, 10/24

There's nothing like Naugatuck on a Saturday night. It was just about the last gig on the tour. The club is next to a Chinese restaurant in a shopping plaza. *River's Edge* could have been filmed here. I've never seen so many metalheads cruising the roads. They make perfect sense, though, when you look at the barren trees, the discount store, all this desolation and quietness—you want to crank up something really loud and ugly. I couldn't help wondering what the girls did while the boys were off playing with Satan. Maybe they also crave electricity, swirling around their heads, through their legs.

I know what they feel like. When Iggy Pop came onstage in Naugatuck (or was it London?) to sing "I Wanna Be Your Dog," Lee and Thurston were ready to rock. I was amazed that he was so professional. He expressed the freakiness of being a woman and an entertainer. I felt like such a cream puff next him. I didn't know what to do, so I just sort of watched.

## Secret Message

This guy writes me letters. He tells me up front he's been hospitalized for mental disturbances several times and asks that I stop sending messages to him through our music. Guys like this take over your whole life if you give them even a smidgen of attention. So if you read this baby, stop sending those letters.

# 75. Hip-Hop, Don't Stop

"Rap" had been around for years in African American neighborhoods in the New York City area before the first hit recording appeared in 1979 with "Rapper's Delight" by the Sugarhill Gang. Rap music existed as part of a larger complex of cultural practices known as "hip-hop," which, in addition to rap, included breakdancing, graffiti writing, and a distinct fashion sense. However, rap, like rhythm and blues in the 1950s, did not initially elicit much public disapproval because it was (in the words of the 1955 *Variety* editorial included in chapter 19) "restricted to special places" and "off in a corner by itself. . . . [as part of] the music underworld—not the main stream."

The history of hip-hop has been voluminously detailed since its debut in the South Bronx during the 1970s, and the story gives new meaning to the idea of "making the best of a bad situation." On the one hand, the South Bronx post-1970 qualifies as one of the most disastrous examples of "urban renewal" in recent U.S. history: A combination of declining manufacturing jobs and affordable housing, along with decreased funding for public education, left a whole generation without the resources that had sustained decades of optimism about upward mobility. On the other hand, rap arose from the combination of people thrown together by adversity and the happy collusion of DJ'ing practices from disco; of the sound systems and "toasting" of recent Jamaican émigrés, such as the legendary Kool DJ Herc; and of centuries of African American rhyming lends credence to the notion of rap as the product of an overarching "Afrodiasporic" cultural background.[1]

The following two articles on hip-hop may have been the first to appear in print. In the first article, published in the summer of 1978, *Billboard* writer Robert Ford, Jr., reported on an unusual phenomenon in the Bronx: young DJs, led by Kool Herc (Clive Campbell, b. 1955), were seeking out obscure records with hot rhythm breaks. Herc describes the emergence of a new aesthetic, one more attuned to rhythm than to singing or lush textural enhancements, such as string tracks. The second article, also by Ford from a year later, documents the rise of rapping as a popular practice that was being joined to spinning records in black clubs in the Bronx and Manhattan. This article also attests to the circulation of self-produced rap tapes before the release of "Rapper's Delight" and, as a point of curiosity, points to how the roles of DJ and MC were not yet defined as separate entities.

## B-Beats Bombarding Bronx: Mobile DJ Starts Something with Oldie R&B Disks

### *Robert Ford, Jr.*

NEW YORK—A funny thing has been happening at Downstairs Records here.

The store, which is the city's leading disco product retailer, has been getting calls for obscure R&B cutouts, such as Dennis Coffy's "Son Of Scorpio," on Sussex, Jeannie Reynolds' "Fruit Song" on Casablanca, and the Incredible Bongo Band's "Bongo Rock" on Pride.

The requests, for the most part, come from young black disco DJs from the Bronx who are buying the records just to play the 30 seconds or so of rhythm breaks that each disk contains.

1. My account is most indebted to Tricia Rose's in *Black Noise: Rap Music and Black Culture in Contemporary America* (Hanover, N.H.: Wesleyan University Press and University Press of New England, 1994). For another excellent history of rap up to 1991, see David Toop, *Rap Attack 2: African Rap to Global Hip Hop* (London: Serpent's Tail, 1991).

*Source:* Robert Ford, Jr., "B-Beats Bombarding Bronx: Mobile DJ Starts Something with Oldie R&B Disks," *Billboard*, July 1, 1978, p. 65. © 1978 VNU Business Media, Inc. Reprinted with permission.

The demand for these records, which the kids call B-beats, has gotten so great that Downstairs has had to hire a young Bronxite, Elroy Meighan, to handle it.

According to Meighan the man responsible for this strange phenomenon is a 26-year old mobile DJ who is known in the Bronx as Cool Herc. It seems Herc rose to popularity by playing long sets of assorted rhythm breaks strung together.

Other Bronx DJs have picked up the practice and now B-beats are the rage all over the borough and the practice is spreading rapidly.

Herc, who has been spinning for five years, says that his unique playing style grew from his fascination with one record, "Bongo Rock." "The tune has a really great rhythm break but it was too short so I had to look for other things to put with it," Herc relates.

Since Herc was not completely satisfied with the new disco product coming out at the time, he started looking in cutout bins for tunes with good rhythm breaks.

Herc's intensive searching for tunes has now even come up with a new remake of "Bongo Rock." The '73 tune has been covered by a group called the Arawak All-Stars on an apparently Jamaican-based label, Arawal records.

Herc has also found that some of the rhythm breaks get better response when they are played at a faster speed. Herc plays tunes such as the Jeannie Reynolds record at 45 rather than the 33 1/3 at which it was recorded.

Herc thinks the popularity of B-beats stems from the kids' dissatisfaction with much of today's disco product. "On most records, people have to wait through a lot of strings and singing to get to the good part of the record," Herc believes. "But I give it to them all up front."

Herc hopes that someday he will be able to produce an entire B-beat album featuring "Bongo Rock" and other obscure numbers. Till then he plans to keep packing them in at the clubs and dances he works in the Bronx.

## JIVE TALKING N.Y. DJS RAPPING AWAY IN BLACK DISCOS
### *Robert Ford, Jr.*

NEW YORK—Rapping DJs reminiscent of early R&B radio jocks such as Jocko and Dr. Jive are making an impressive comeback here—not in radio but in black discos where a jivey rap commands as much attention these days as the hottest new disk.

Young DJs like Eddie Cheeba, DJ Hollywood, DJ Starski and Kurtis Blow are attracting followings with their slick raps. All promote themselves with these snappy show business names.

Many black disco promoters now use the rapping DJs to attract young fans to one-shot promotions and a combination of the more popular names have filled the city's largest hotel ballrooms.

The young man credited with reviving the rapping habit in this area is DJ Hollywood, who started gabbing along with records a few years ago while working his way through school as a disco DJ.

Hollywood is now so popular that he has played the Apollo with billing as a support act. It is not uncommon to hear Hollywood's voice coming from one of the countless portable tape players carried through the city's streets. Tapes of Hollywood's raps are considered valuable commodities by young blacks, here.

*Source:* Robert Ford, Jr., "Jive Talking N.Y. DJs Rapping Away in Black Discos," *Billboard,* May 5, 1979, p. 3. © 1979 UNV Business Media, Inc. Reprinted with permission.

A close friend and disciple of Hollywood's, Eddie Cheeba, has been working as a mobile jock for five years and talking over the records for the last two. He now travels with an entire show, which includes seven female dancers and another DJ, Easy Gee, who does most of the actual spinning. Cheeba and his Cheeba Crew are now booked two months in advance.

Cheeba says the rapping craze grew out of a need for something more than records.

"These people go to discos every week and they need more than music to motivate them," Cheeba observes. "I not only play records, but I rap to them and they answer me."

Though they often work before crowds in the thousands, Cheeba and most of the popular rapping DJs do not get records from labels or from pools. Most of them buy their own product and do so without complaining.

As DJ Starski puts it, "Most of the records the labels send us won't go up here anyway, so I'd rather buy what I want."

Starski is one of the most popular DJs with high school and college age blacks in the Bronx and Manhattan. He has played almost every major black club and ballroom in the area. He generally works with Cool DJ AJ, who does not rap but is a master of B-beats. B-beats are series of short rhythm breaks strung together to sound like one song.

Starski is proud of his ability to excite a crowd with his rapping. "It's a beautiful thing to see a dance floor full of people dancing to your music and answering your rap," Starski says.

Kurtis Blow, the most popular rapping DJ in Queens, hopes disco will be a springboard into broadcasting for him. Blow, a student at CCNY, has been working about a year and got his first break at the now defunct Small's Paradise. Blow built a following at Small's and is now booked solid for weeks.

Cheeba already had a shot at radio during a fill-in run last summer at Fordham's WFUV-FM.

> Following the commercial success of "Rapper's Delight," rap continued to transform rapidly, albeit still as a largely underground phenomenon. In the wake of Kool Herc came the further exploitation of "break beats" (i.e., the repeating of a drum break taken from the middle of a recording), led by virtuosi of the turntable, such as Grandmaster Flash (Joseph Saddler, b. 1958), who developed those staples of hip-hop craft— scratching (moving the needle rapidly back and forth across the grooves of a record) and backspinning. Breakdancers, many of them Puerto Rican residents of the South Bronx, also formed an integral part of the scene, as nearly every early account attested to.[2]
>
> Subsequent developments included the electro-funk and social activism of Afrika Bambaataa (Kevin Donovan, b. 1960), especially in his "Planet Rock" (1982), the political protest and social realism of Grandmaster Flash and the Furious Five featuring Melle Mel in "The Message" (1982), and the emergence of commercially savvy Def Jam records with stars like Run-DMC. Instrumental tracks were largely collages, built up from fragments of previous recordings, synthesizer riffs, drum machines, and the efforts of skilled studio funk musicians.
>
> Run-DMC developed the first successful crossover strategy for rap by explicitly incorporating rock elements into their music. Videos for

---

2. For an example, see Tim Carr, "Talk That Talk, Walk That Walk," *Rolling Stone,* May 26, 1983, 20–25.

recordings like "The King of Rock" (1985) presented the group entering a "Rock and Roll Hall of Fame" (only two years before the actual Rock and Roll Hall of Fame opened) and commenting on the racial politics involved in the construction of conventional rock histories. The recording itself uses a heavy metal guitar riff throughout, backed by a thunderous drum machine track. "Walk this Way" (1986) adopted an even bolder strategy, using the 1970s hit by the rock band Aerosmith as the backing track, newly rerecorded by members of Aerosmith with Run-DMC for the occasion. The video also included members of both bands; the narrative climaxes with Run-DMC breaking through the barriers that separate them from Aerosmith and, by implication, from the larger record-buying public of white consumers of rock music.

　　In another sense, however, the use of rock music had been a part of hip-hop from the beginning. Many rap DJs discuss how they delighted in getting a crowd of hip-hop fans to get down to the drum break from the Monkees' "Mary, Mary," and heavy metal riffs had long formed a staple of the DJ's repertoire.[3] Def Jam records was also home to the first successful white rap act, the Beastie Boys, who projected jokey-punky personas while taking a few pages out of Run-DMC's musical playbook.

---

The next article was published in the wake of "Walk This Way," the success of which seems to have been enough to awaken a sense of moral panic in the mass media. The focus on gang violence at rap concerts was a constantly recurring theme as the public became aware of rap's increasing popularity. This article offers a rebuttal to that theme, even as it leaves the general impression that rap and criminality are somehow connected.

## BAD RAP

### *Time*

Its driving beat and chanted lyrics echo the pulse and pitch of inner-city streets. But rap music also draws out a meaner side of ghetto life: gang violence. When some 14,500 fans poured into Long Beach Arena near Los Angeles last week for a concert featuring the popular rap group Run-D.M.C., more than 300 members of black and Hispanic street gangs swarmed through the crowd, attacking everyone around them. Audience members struck back with metal chairs and whatever else came to hand, until police armed with batons broke up the concert. Forty-five people were injured, including a man who was stabbed. The rioting was the fourth major outbreak of violence on Run-D.M.C.'s "Raising Hell" tour this summer, following earlier incidents in Pittsburgh, New York City and St. Louis that left 39 injured.

　　The next day, fearing another bloody melee, officials at the Hollywood Palladium canceled a Run-D.M.C. concert. The band, however, blamed lax security for the riot. Joseph

---

3. For an account of this playful approach to source material, see the interviews with Grandmaster Flash and Afrika Bambaataa in *The History of Rock and Roll* (PBS/BBC video series), "The Perfect Beat."

("Run") Simmons, 21, who with Partner Daryll ("D.M.C.") McDaniels became the first rap artist to produce a platinum album (1 million copies sold), defended his group. "Rap music has nothing to do with crack or crime," he said. "Check my lyrics. I'm a role model for kids, and I go out of my way to give them a positive message."

Indeed, rappers have produced songs that urge kids to stay in school and avoid crime and drugs. The majority of rap lyrics are concerned with nothing more volatile than partying and macho boasting. Yet since rap became popular several years ago, many performances have been marred by brutality. Says Public Safety Commissioner John Norton of Pittsburgh, where teenagers went on a window-smashing rampage after a Run-D.M.C. concert in June: "There is absolutely no doubt in my mind that rap music spurs violence."

Many figures in the entertainment industry contend that rap is no more aggressive than heavy metal, punk and other types of highly charged rock 'n' roll. Rejecting the notion that rap is inherently violent, Psychiatrist Alvin Poussaint of Harvard explains that "rap music really comes from inner-city street kids, some of whom are gang members immersed in antisocial behavior." Promoters have found that when guards are trained to spot gang colors and bar potential troublemakers, rap concerts are trouble free. Meanwhile, Run-D.M.C. is proceeding with the final week of its tour, hoping to raise a little less hell.

# 76. "The Music Is a Mirror"

The invention and commercial accessibility in the mid-1980s of the digital sampler was quickly exploited by hip-hop musicians. Samplers, which make possible the manipulation of recorded sounds (or "samples"), played right into the collage aesthetic of hip-hop, greatly easing the looping of grooves previously accomplished through backspinning. Sampling also made it easier to use fragments of previous recordings as historical references or as homages that could place a recording within a lineage of African American popular music. This greater control over sonic sources and the enhanced ability to manipulate them also led to new possibilities for the musical use of what might have previously been considered "noise."[1] Eric Sadler of the Bomb Squad, the production team responsible for the instrumental tracks of Public Enemy's recordings, put it this way:

Turn it all the way up so it's totally distorted and pan it over to the right so you really can't even hear it. Pan it over to the right means put the sound only in the right side speaker, and turn it so you can't barely even hear it—it's just like a noise in the side. Now, engineers . . . they live by certain rules. They're like, "You can't do that. You don't want a distorted sound, it's not right, it's not correct." With Hank (Shocklee) and Chuck (D) it's like, "Fuck that it's not correct, just do this shit." And engineers won't do it. So

---

1. For more on the use of "noise" in rap, see David Brackett, "Music, " in Bruce Horner and Thomas Swiss, eds., *Key Terms in Popular Music and Culture* (Malden, Mass.: Blackwell, 1999), 124–40; and Robert Walser, "Rhythm, Rhyme, and Rhetoric in the Music of Public Enemy," *Ethnomusicology* 39 (1995): 193–217. See Part 6 of this volume for more on the media debates about whether rap was "noise" or "music."

if you start engineering yourself and learning these things yourself—[get] the meter goin' like this [he moves his hand into an imaginary red zone] and you hear the shit cracklin,' that's the sound we're lookin' for.[2]

Indeed, Public Enemy's "Bring the Noise" (1988), with its densely layered, noisy backing track, sounds almost like a credo for this aesthetic, calling into question received notions of both music and musicianship (with lines like "Run-DMC first said a deejay could be a band"). On this and other recordings' the band's frequent use of samples of James Brown's recordings emphasized the linkage between the grooves of rap and those of the Godfather.

While bands like Public Enemy extended the use of political content pioneered in "The Message," women began to take a greater role in the genre, with Salt 'n' Pepa becoming the first female hip-hop superstars. These developments were part of the increasing inclusion of rap in the mainstream initiated by Run-DMC. By 1989, recordings, such as "Wild Thing" by Tone Loc, had entered heavy rotation on MTV, and the cable channel had made the ultimate concession to hip-hop by creating a show devoted entirely to the genre, "Yo! MTV Raps."

The growth of rap's popularity forms the immediate backdrop for the following article by Harry Allen, which appeared in *Essence*, the "preeminent lifestyle magazine for today's African-American woman." Allen's article provides a history of hip-hop, placing it within other African American cultural practices, and raises such issues as the relationship of rap to black identity, the appropriate terms for the criticism of rap, and the growing commentary about misogyny. Allen started writing about hip-hop in 1983 and has continued to be involved with hip-hop since the publication of this article, acting as the "Media Assassin" for Public Enemy, and even uttering the title line in the PE recording "Don't Believe the Hype." More recently, Allen created the newsletter, *rap dot com,* and is developing a Larry King Live–style talk show with Chuck D under the aegis of their multimedia production company, Scramjet.

## HIP HOP MADNESS: FROM DEF JAMS TO COLD LAMPIN', RAP IS OUR MUSIC
### *Harry Allen*

The young, brown-skinned woman stood in the middle of the group, patting out a beat on the ground with her feet, at the same time beating out a rhythm on her chest and legs with her hands. People crowded closer, caught by the quiet, distinct, funky sound. Suddenly she

2. Tricia Rose, *Black Noise: Rap Music and Black Culture in Contemporary America* (Hanover, N.H.: Wesleyan University Press and University Press of New England, 1994), 74–75.

*Source:* Harry Allen, "Hip Hop Madness: From Def Jams to Cold Lampin', Rap Is Our Music," *Essence* (April 1989): 78–80, 114, 117, 119.

began to rhyme, fast and furiously. As people listened, swayed and swung to the beat, she shot poetic insults at friends nearby, to their chagrin and the crowd's delight. She rhymed about her experiences, things that both she and her audience had seen and experienced. She kept that same funky rhythm as the dancing crowd went crazy with loud screams and shouts.

Basement party beat-box in the Bronx? L.A. street-corner performer? Neither. A description of "pattin' juba," circa 1850, from historian Eileen Southern's revelatory work *The Music of Black Americans*.

Nearly 140 years later, over the sound of a drum machine and one eerily repeating, mournful, four-note horn riff, 20-year-old Mike G matter-of-factly drops science on the Jungle Brothers's recording "In Time": *"In time this rhyme will be more than just a fantasy/A Black man will be the man to claim presidency/Is it hard to see? So try to see as I see/In time I see a better Black reality/It took one man to open the door/He let in one million more/And I don't think/That this country knows/What the hell that it's in for. . . ."*

You won't hear lyrics like that from 50,000 of today's R&B artists. Such frank talk will only be found in hip-hop music, or "rap," to use a term that we invented and whites coopted to rename, defame or claim the music. If sales, influence and visibility are any indication, hip-hop is now runnin' thangs; it's the dominant African-American music. It's about time. Hip-hop is youthful, strong. It exhibits none of the creative listlessness with which much of R&B is currently burdened. Nor does it have the hands-off, gloves-on reverence with which jazz often finds itself draped. Rather than pretending to bourgeois standards of style, or attempting musically to evoke a time dead and gone, as many jazz and R&B artists are wont to do, rappers instead sling the rawest, most realistic insights at your car. Deejays take your favorite records, cut 'em up, mix 'em around and serve 'em to you on a record platter. Meanwhile their crowds move and shake their bodies in ways that Grandmother once said would definitely get you pregnant or arrested. It all comes together in a whole: funky. Youknowhumsayin?

*"Rats in the front room, roaches in the back/Junkies in the alley with the baseball bat/I tried to get away, but I couldn't get far/ 'Cause a man with a tow truck repossessed my car. . . ."*

"To me, hip-hop's always been around," says Melvin Glover, aka Melle-Mel, lead vocalist for Grandmaster Flash & the Furious Five, who gave us "The Message," above, and are no doubt the most important crew in the music's short history. "It's the same shit that Black people was chantin' on the chain gang, and that they was sayin' when they was slaves. 'Hi-de-ho!'—all that shit is rap. Pigmeat Markham and 'Heah Comes De Judge'. . . . That's rap! Rap always been out there. It was just waitin' for somebody to claim it."

Pigmeat Markham, Muhammad Ali, Cab Calloway, Isaac Hayes, Moms Mabley, Millie Jackson, Joe Tex, Malcolm X. As Mel says, "That's always been *our* essence—just to talk, you know what I'm sayin'?"

*"Now what you hear is not a test/I'm rappin' to the beat/And me, the groove, and my friends/Are gonna try to move your feet. . . ."*

When many people think of the beginnings of hip-hop, they head back to the Sugarhill Gang's "Rapper's Delight," a 15-minute jam quoted above whose "Ho-tel, mo-tel, Holiday Inn" refrain drove dancers wild back in September 1979. That wasn't the first "rap" record, however. The honor goes to Fatback Band's "King Tim III," which was released earlier that same year. Says Pebbles Riley, aka Pebblee-Poo, one of hip-hop's first female vocalists, "I started in '78, and I was definitely hearing people rapping at block parties in '76, '77." And, according to Ralph Blandshaw, aka Van Silk, who was one of the music's earliest, most ardent party promoters, you could hear mobile deejays, the rhythmic founders of hip-hop, in New York City parks as early as 1974. Hmm. Trying to pin down a start time for hip-hop is, as RUN-D.M.C. would say, tricky.

Andrei L. Strobert, a Brooklyn-based scholar, musician and artist, says that to get to the real roots of hip-hop, you have to go back even farther than "King Tim III," mobile deejays,

Pigmeat Markham, or slavery—say, to the Yoruba people of Nigeria, or the Nago of Dahomey (now Benin). "The scratch that you hear in hip-hop is similar to the African *sekere*," says Strobert, "A *sekere* is a big gourd with beads around it. If you think about scratching, you see how it connects. 'Cause, see, the scratch is *shk shk-shk shk-shk*. The *sekere* sound is basically the same thing. Rappers come to my studio to record rhythms that they want to use to their rhymes. A lot of the rhythms that they use are Ibo rhythms, from the Ibo tribe of Nigeria."

For all African music, including African-American music, rhythm is the key, the point of entry. The only way you could get us to pay attention to and love something as fundamentally antimusical as a turntable scratch was to make it funky, and in this is hip-hop's genius. I believe that this concept of "funky" is the dividing line between people of African descent, people of non-African descent, and our respective traditions. That is to say, Picasso copied West African art, but couldn't make his painting "guitar" *nowhere* near as funky as a Dogon mask. The difference between the late Jimi Hendrix and an acre of white rock guitarists was funk. Elvis was loud, but he was never funky. Little Richard's "Rip It Up" still does. Knowhumsayin?

*"Cause the 'D' is for 'dangerous'/You can come and get some of this/I teach and speak so when it's spoke it's no joke/The Voice of Choice; the place shakes with the bass/Go one for the treble/The rhythm is the rebel!"*

To get from the Yoruba Nation to Public Enemy's "Louder Than a Bomb," quoted above, you have to jet through 400 not-so-hot years in America. Stop just long enough to hear early forms of rapping from Douglas "Jocko" Henderson, the Last Poets and Parliament/Funkadelic. Eventually you'll wind up in a place where three Black guys called RUN-D.M.C. sell more than 3 million copies of *Raising Hell* . . . and four white guys called the Beastie Boys, after being coached by those three Black guys, sell 4 million copies of *Licensed to Ill.* You've entered . . . the twilight zone, the point where this very African art "is being accepted by middle America," in the words of Hurby Azor, producer of million-selling crew Salt-n-Pepa. "That's one of the biggest developments. The white people are gettin' into it now. Which is funny. The music business is always interested in the white people."

And vice versa. White music critics and cultural historians are talking about hip-hop and find themselves tossing long, funny words into the air to describe it. Words like *deconstruction, appropriation, iconography* and *recontextualization.* But those words have little to do with the way African-American people live or make music, and hip-hop is no more or less than Black life on black vinyl. Whatever one finds in the community, they'll find in the records. This has a lot to do with why it's so attractive to some people and repulsive to others.

For African-Americans, especially young people, the music is a mirror. "These aren't cheap records," says Nat Robinson, president of MC Lyte's label, First Priority Music. "These are natural records." Hip-hop talks like us; it's rooted in African-American wordplay, like "snapping" or "the dozens." It moves like us. It homes in like radar on our "musicultural" values. Rhythm. Call and response. Repetition. Reinterpretation of original ideas via improvisation. The voice as instrument, and as rhythmic and tonal ideal. And other values . . .

*"Rappers take a step back or you will soon regret that you ever had to confront me and you can bet that I come correct perfect in full effect/Disconnect dissect eject as I wreck/Shop/Stand in command with the clan/Caravan or band/We go man for man. . . ."*

Hip-hop speaks to a view of life that is expressly communal in nature. In Africa, there are cultures with musical categories solely for *the praise of friends,* for instance. When Big Daddy Kane ends the elastic "Set It Off," quoted above, by naming more than 30 friends one at a time, when Kool Moe Dee turns the names of his neighborhood crew into exultant, defiant poetry on "Wild Wild West," when Public Enemy thanks 240-plus people and groups on the crew's liner notes, that's African. That's "posse," "brotherhood," "community" being expressed on the terms of African-American young people. "I say the names of my posse to look out for 'em, to acknowledge that they do exist," admits 19-year-old Dana Owens, aka Latifah, who thanks the R.E. (Ram Enterprise) Posse on her fluid, funky single, "Wrath of My Madness/Princess of the Posse," quoted below. "Had it not been for them, I probably wouldn't have even started in this. You know what I'm saying?"

*"I-ray/The lesson of today/You have to listen to each and every single word I have to say because/The Ruler Lord Ramsey is on my side/And I'm the Princess of the Posse so, yo . . . take it light. . . ."*

So, yo. Why is hip-hop so hype? What are those millions of rappers and record buyers really getting out of it? Fab 5 Freddy, cohost of MTV's (Ooh! Now it's hip) hip-hop video show *Yo! MTV Raps!*, puts it like this: "There's sum'n in hip-hop that makes it good, that you can't even really *record*, because a lot o' hip-hop is about attitude, feeling and style, as opposed to musical virtuosity as we know it, dealing with Western forms of music. Like L. L. Cool J said, when you hear a good hip-hop record, you make that *face*, youknowhum-sayin'? You hear a regular record, you just go, 'Yeah, that's pretty good.' But when you hear a good hip-hop record, you make that face like, '*Yeeeah!*'"

*"Flowin' in file with the new style/Barrels are cleaned then loaded for salute/Chanters with the choice standing steady like my mouthpiece/Paragraph preacher is now introduced/Drums are heard sounding off in each and every person/Vocal confetti is thrown at top stage/Roses and violets aren't proper for throwing for showing in appreciation (why?)/This is the D.A.I.S.Y age!"*

Listen to "Plug Tunin'," above, by the trio De La Soul, or to almost any cut from their *3 Feet High and Rising*. You'll make that face all album long. But some think that when people hear a good hip-hop record, they do other things. Like stick chemicals up their noses, snatch gold chains, rampage and even kill, if you're talking about the murder of Julio Fuentes at Long Island's Nassau Coliseum on September 10, 1988. Ask the usually serene Latifah what the most common misconception about hip-hop is, and you touch a nerve. "Definitely that it's violent, that it's a bunch of hoodlums and nondescripts making records about bullshit. That we can't put out a goddamn positive message. If they took a second to listen to the words, then they would know that wasn't the case."

Word. The fact is that drugs and crime live in our communities. Their habitation there predates the music called hip-hop. These ills have less to do with Schoolly D calling his album *Smoke Some Kill* than they do with the government drug-jogging with Manuel Noriega. They have less to do with beeper-carrying brothers than they do with the U.S. banks and other multinationals for which we work. These corporations know that drug money is the only thing that'll keep a flow of American dollars going into the debt-ridden Latin American countries they lend to.

To say that hip-hop is surrounded by violence and drug use sounds like a captive African blaming work songs and field hollers for the perpetuation of slavery, don't you think? Hip-hop is descriptive and often attempts to be prescriptive. African-American people are, again, using music to make sense of and mediation for our circumstances.

However, there is certainly one real problem. Hip-hop has taken a rap for being sexist. It is. When Ice-T releases a record called "Girls, Let's Get Butt Naked and Fuck" ("Girls, L.G.B.N.A.F." on the album cover), when 2 Live Crew on a cut called "S & M" calls to women to bring their "d- -k-sucking friends," when Ultramagnetic M.C.'s Kool Keith on "Give the Drummer Some" talks about smacking up his bitch in the manner of a pimp, sisters understandably scream. Hip-hop is sexist. It is also frank.

As I once told a sister, hip-hop lyrics are, among other things, what a lot of Black men say about Black women when Black women aren't around. In this sense, the music is no more or less sexist than your fathers, brothers, husbands, friends and lovers, and, in many cases, more up-front. As an unerringly precise reflection of the community, hip-hop's sexist thinking will change when the community changes. Because women are the ones best able to define sexism, they will have to challenge the music—tell it how to change and make it change—if change is to come. Only then will record companies cease the release of cuts that call for bitch-smacking.

*"How could I keep my composure/When all sorts of thoughts fought for exposure?"*

Hip-hop is here to stay. As Eric B. & Rakim note in their "Musical Massacre" above, the music is bursting with ideas. It is, says Kay Gee The All from the seminal crew Cold Crush Brothers, "up-to-date music," and it speaks to a change in the way we socialize and get our music. When *Billboard,* the bible of the music industry, began its charts in the 1940's, they tallied sales of sheet music. Today they tally records-by-ethnicity, compact discs and videos. That reflects a huge change in the way we get music and think about it. So do cassettes, almost nonexistent 20 years ago. So does a Walkman, non-existent ten years ago. Music we choose goes where we do. Says master percussionist and composer Max Roach in *New York Newsday* music used to go where we did in another way. "When I was growing up in Bedford-Stuyvesant [Brooklyn], there was always an instrument a student could take home from school; if a student wanted to study rhetoric, he could. That's all been wiped out; our urban centers are in shambles."

How are you going to get kids to read music if they can't read? "These kids were never exposed to poets or playwrights in school," continues Roach. "They had all this talent, and they had no instruments. So they started rap music. They rhymed on their own. They made their own sounds and their own movements."

I couldn't have said it any better. Why hasn't this hip-hop "fad" died out? The same reason we haven't. If nothing else, hip-hop speaks most directly to African-American pride and sense of self, failures of the American mess, our history, the things we lack and, ultimately, hope. Hope that people without the benefit of a common musical language, articulated by bars, staffs and bass clefs, will come up with one on their own, made from the stuff of their lives. Hope that, for at least a moment, an average Joe-Ski from around the way will have his place in the spotlight. Hope that we survive and prosper as a people into the twenty-first century and beyond. We will. It promises to be a ferocious, funky future.

> In the same issue of *Essence* that published Harry Allen's article, Carol Cooper looks at the gender-specific obstacles faced by female rappers and at the progress made by them in the late 1980s. By detailing the institutional obstacles to females' access to creative roles in rap recordings, she offers an implicit riposte to Allen's assertion that it is up to female rappers to challenge misogyny in rap. Like Allen, Cooper had already been active writing about hip-hop for several years before this article appeared. She has continued since that time writing for a wide range of publications, as well as occasionally working for the music industry in positions like East Coast director of black music artists and repertoire for A&M Records.

## GIRLS AIN'T NOTHIN' BUT TROUBLE
### *Carol Cooper*

For all its immense popularity, rap music is still very much a man's world. Women are buying the records, but by and large they aren't on them nor are they producing them—though as the music progresses, that's beginning to change. Women rap artists such as Princess

(Criminal/WTG), Salt-n-Pepa (Next Plateau) and The Real Roxanne (Select) are excited about getting on the mike and on vinyl; for the moment, issues of creative and financial autonomy are taking a backseat. Don't expect these women to address sexism directly. Much as we might like them to, that's not happening—yet.

As a popular art form that, like standup comedy, draws inspiration from "outlaw" oral traditions such as pimp toasts, prison doggerel and urban childhood's "dirty dozens," rap is accepted by its practitioners—male and female—as the most brutally honest form of self-expression possible.

"Rap is cultural," says Princess, whose first records came out on Arthur Baker's Criminal/WGT label only this winter, despite the fact that she has been writing and producing her own raps for three years. "I grew up with it, and it's here to stay. But when I started making and shopping my own tapes as a teen, because I thought the things other people wanted to produce on me were too commercial, the male label owners were very unreceptive. I spoke to people at Uptown Enterprises, at Next Plateau, Sleeping Bag, Reality . . . I made the rounds. Only when I led them to believe that a man had written or produced my stuff did they show interest."

Along the same lines, when Roxanne Shante defended the skeezer's (groupie's) low-slung lifestyle on Rick James's "Loosey's Rap," she was just doing a job. Female rappers are often invited to participate in a statement devised by a male artist and expected to contribute "something appropriate." As professionals, these girls deliver what is asked, get paid and get credit—relatively oblivious to how that participation might be perceived by others.

"There are a lot of rhymes we write on our album, but we don't go for the credit," admits Cheryl James (Salt), of platinum rap duo Salt-n-Pepa. "And I guess we should, because people are on this kick about why we don't write. It doesn't bother *us*, but it bothers us that it bothers other people. Most singers don't write all their own lyrics, either, and nobody cares about that. I guess because Hurby Azor is our producer, manager and one of our songwriters, it gives the impression that he has total control. But we all got into this business together, it's like a family. And if he ever came up with a song or a video concept we didn't want to do, we wouldn't do it."

Most contemporary rap women (coming along in a time when rap is so much more profitable than it was for their sister pioneers of five or six years back) are philosophical about the internecine name-calling and cross-gender "dissing" that sometimes make it into the grooves. None of them seem to think that "explicit" or sexist lyrics are harmful in and of themselves, and all of them are aware that there is a definite cash-money fandom out there for dirty talk. The Puerto Rican rapper, The Real Roxanne, co-wrote her single "Respect" around that very dilemma. The Real Roxanne has felt pressure toward "propriety" both from within and as the young mother of an articulate first-grader: "Girls disrespecting each other on stage is just not me; not the image I want to promote. But at the beginning, with all the Roxanne answer records and all these girls coming onstage to challenge me and each other, my production company back then who'd had the original 'Roxanne' concept had to show them what time it was!" Roxanne laughs.

"Now, with my first album out, I hear that [fellow rapper] MC Lyte has started in on me. I hear that she has a girl dressed like me in one of her videos and has something to say. "Oh boy," she grins wryly, "sounds like fun."

Because rap prides itself on staying thematically true to the African-American experience in America today, it stands to reason that every issue—good or bad—that manifests itself in our communities will eventually be exposed in a rap forum. In the case of normally touchy subjects such as sex, sexism, racism, crime, VD, homophobia and light-skin privilege, a rap dialogue may be the only discussion certain youngsters ever have on these subjects. If so, perhaps we ought to take advantage of rap's daring to start the discussion, so that we, as knowledgeable adults, can finish it.

# 77. Where Rap and Heavy Metal Converge

The sense of panic over rap in the mass media grew in proportion to its increased visibility on outlets, such as MTV, and its increased audibility on the radio. This reaction was further exacerbated by the fact that MTV was widely watched in the suburban hinterlands, previously believed to be hostile to rap, and by the emergence of an angrier, more militant style spearheaded by Public Enemy and N.W.A. (Niggas with Attitude). The following article by Jon Pareles makes clear, however, that it was public statements made by Public Enemy's "minister of information" Professor Griff that attracted attention, rather than the political statements in Public Enemy's songs.[1] Yet, as Pareles notes, while they may have received more attention than other entertainers, rap artists were not alone in projecting volatile messages via mass cultural products. And Pareles also raises interesting points about the *amount* of attention received by Public Enemy for controversial statements in relation to bigoted statements made by white heavy metal band Guns N' Roses and white comedian, Andrew Dice Clay. Pareles has been the main pop music critic at the *New York Times* since the late 1980s and was one of the first critics at a major daily to write sympathetically about hip-hop (much to the chagrin of many stodgy readers of the *Times*).[2]

## THERE'S A NEW SOUND IN POP MUSIC: BIGOTRY

### *Jon Pareles*

Has hatred become hip? From isolated spots in pop culture, racial and sexual prejudice have slithered back into view. Andrew Dice Clay, a comedian whose Nassau Coliseum performance on Saturday sold out immediately, mixes dirty-word jokes with vicious

---

1. Public Enemy continued to attract attention both for their militant messages critiquing racism and advocating African American economic self-determination, and for their anti-Semitic references, which they have never fully retracted. For more on the debate, fueled in particular by the release of "Welcome to the Terrordome" shortly after the Pareles article reprinted here, see Robert Christgau, "Jesus, Jews, and the Jackass Theory," *Village Voice* (January 16, 1990): 83–86. Chuck D's fullest account may be found in his autobiography; see Chuck D (with Yusuf Jah), "Black and Jewish Relationships," in *Fight the Power: Rap, Race, and Reality* (New York: Delacorte Press, 1997), 205–39.

2. Some of these other articles by Pareles, and readers' responses to them, are discussed at the beginning of Part 6.

*Source:* Jon Pareles, "There's a New Sound in Pop Music: Bigotry," *New York Times*, September 10, 1989, Sec. 2, pp. 1, 32, 33. Copyright © 1989 by the New York Times Co. Reprinted with permission.

put-downs of women, homosexuals, blacks and Japanese. During a sketch on "The Tonight Show" Aug. 11, Johnny Carson, as his yokel character Floyd R. Turbo, invoked "baseball the way it was meant to be played, on real grass, with no designated hitter and all white guys"; the studio audience gasped, then tittered nervously.

In a recent *Rolling Stone* magazine cover story, Axl Rose of the heavy metal band Guns N' Roses, whose debut album sold nine million copies, defends his song "One in a Million," which includes the verse: "Immigrants and faggots/They make no sense to me/They come to our country/And think they'll do as they please/Like start some mini-Iran or spread some [expletive] disease." He also savors the word "niggers" in a verse that continues, "Get outta my way/Don't need to buy none/Of your gold chains today."

Across the color line, the rap group Public Enemy fired, then rehired Richard (Professor Griff) Griffin, who as its "minister of information" said in a May interview with the *Washington Times:* "The Jews are wicked. And we can prove this." He went on to say that Jews are responsible for "the majority of wickedness that goes on across the globe." Mr. Griffin was made the group's liaison to the black community and local youth programs, but no longer gives interviews. In a statement announcing the rehiring, Public Enemy's leader, Carlton (Chuck D.) Ridenhour, said, "Please direct any further questions to Axl Rose."

Meanwhile, numerous rappers include homophobic asides in the course of an album. For example, Heavy D. and the Boyz, whose album "Big Tyme" recently reached No. 1 on Billboard's black-music chart, boast that with their rhymes, "you'll be happy as a faggot in jail."

It's ugly stuff, and, as the sticker on Mr. Clay's album package puts it, "offensive." While those examples are vastly outnumbered by nonracist, nonhomophobic cultural messages, they are like cockroaches in a clean kitchen, signaling more trouble to come.

Ethnic stereotyping runs deep in American popular culture. Blacks have been caricatured since the days of slavery; during World War II, the Japanese were portrayed as evil incarnate. Ethnic jokes have always been comedians' staples. But the triumphs of the civil rights movement of the 1960's, and the feminist and homosexual-rights movements that followed, made prejudicial statements less tolerable in mainstream society, almost taboo. Now, that taboo is cracking.

"On the one hand, it seems like a new openness," said Alvin Poussaint, associate professor of psychiatry at Harvard Medical School and a consultant to "The Cosby Show." "But on the other, it shows a new acceptance, a license to say derogatory things about other people. The argument is that the people making these statements are being for real and not covering anything up, and they have a point. Young kids, particularly kids from working-class backgrounds, have had these racist attitudes for a long time. But until recently, it was not publicly acceptable to say so."

Popular culture, like the regulator that jiggles atop a pressure cooker, vents tensions in the society it addresses. "One in a Million" and Mr. Clay's comedy suggest not only deep resentment but an attempt to reassert white male heterosexual power over others. Whether it is a last gasp backlash or a new majoritarianism remains unclear. Meanwhile, minorities battle one another.

Prejudice against and among minorities isn't confined to popular culture, where it is still relatively rare. But culture shifts with politics. Surveys have shown renewed prejudice in the United States across all income levels and classes in recent years, not least among young people—who, experts in race relations point out, face competition for entry-level jobs and may resent newly franchised, visibly distinguishable minorities. Another factor they cite has been the Reagan Administration's opposition to affirmative-action programs, a signal that minority rights were vulnerable.

Joel Kovel, a social science professor at Bard College who teaches a course on ideology in mass culture, said, "The need in our society to express identity by excluding others has always been very, very strong. With the decline of the cold war, demonizing the Soviets doesn't carry the symbolic weight it used to, and there's a resurgence of more old-fashioned nativism and racism."

Racial divisions have made headlines in recent politics. This week's mayoral primary in New York takes place under the shadow of a racial killing in Bensonhurst. David Duke, a former Ku Klux Klan official, was elected to the Louisiana Legislature; George Bush's Presidential campaign was accused of stirring racial fears with its Willie Horton commercial about a black convicted murderer who raped a white woman while on furlough from prison.

"That commercial legitimized prejudicial speech, and the Bernhard Goetz case legitimized it," Dr. Poussaint said, "And the Reagan Administration set the tone. They were openly militant against affirmative action and for giving Federal money to segregated, church-related schools. Reagan didn't even make any symbolic gestures toward the black community. He set a tone that you can keep blacks shut out and they can't do anything about it."

## Increasing Prejudice in the Age of AIDS

Another longstanding prejudice, homophobia, has been rekindled by fear of AIDS, which was at first stigmatized as the "gay disease." The offhand virulence of homophobia in music with a largely teen-aged audience is particularly telling. "Male teenagers generally go through a period of fear that they're going to be homosexual," Dr. Poussaint said. "Some teenagers, especially those with a lot of conflict, go through a very homophobic stage to reinforce their heterosexuality." Heavy D.'s rap, Guns N' Roses's heavy metal and Mr. Clay's comic universe are all overwhelmingly male clubhouses; they flaunt homophobia.

Randy Shilts, author of "And the Band Played On," a book about the AIDS epidemic, sees resurgent homophobia as a political backlash. "Whenever you have a group that begins to assert itself, you're going to have a reaction. Something like Guns N' Roses is obviously emblematic of the alienation that some younger people feel from what they presume to be a reigning liberal morality—it's a way of rebelling against authority. But to me, it's an incredibly unsophisticated analysis that sees gay people as part of the power structure. Nobody can look at what's gone on around AIDS and gay people in the United States and think that gay people are in power."

As power relationships are re-drawn and an us-against-them mentality sets in, sexual and ethnic lines make convenient divisions. "For young men growing up," said Peggy R. Sanday, an anthropologist at the University of Pennsylvania, "their manhood seems to be based on expressing their rights, but with those rights phrased in terms of power over others."

Prejudicial statements have slipped through the mass media. Many radio stations, especially in the South and Middle West, broadcast "One in a Million," with its four-letter word bleeped out; rappers, however, generally save their homophobic lines for album tracks rather than more widely broadcast singles. Mr. Clay had his own Home Box Office special, and he serves up his milder material on talk shows. Mr. Carson's line came out of the mouth of a comic character, and in that context was approved for broadcast after discussion between programming and network standards executives, said Pat Schultz, and NBC spokeswoman. In context, she added, the line, "clearly did not represent the opinion of Johnny Carson or of 'The Tonight Show.'"

Record companies' main concerns are commercial. Although they regularly work with performers on everything from packaging to song choices, they obviously didn't expect Heavy D.'s homophobia or Mr. Rose's scapegoating to hurt their prospects. Most popular music steers away from divisiveness in order to garner larger audiences; rock has a tradition of embracing (or exploiting) the contributions of racial and sexual outsiders. Yet in an increasingly fragmented pop market, it is also possible to succeed by rallying a single constituency against outsiders.

Mr. Rose in his interview indicated that to him, racial epithets represent artistic freedom, a position echoed by his recording company, Geffen Records. According to Bryn Bridenthal, Geffen Records' director of media and artist relations, "There were a lot of discussions about 'One in a Million,' and if it were totally a label decision, the decision would probably have been not to release it. But if you're going to start censoring your artists, it's going to damage your relationship. There's always somebody who's going to release it, and if you've got an artist like Guns N' Roses, you want to keep the relationship with the company. In the end, Geffen Records just does not support censorship of the artist's creative desires.

"Guns N' Roses have a lot of power because they've sold a lot of records," she added. "But if they hadn't sold a lot of records, no one would have paid any attention to that song." Interestingly, Geffen also released Mr. Clay's album, "Dice," produced by its Def American subsidiary—but the album was deemed so controversial that no Geffen information appears on the package. Mr. Clay's next album is tentatively titled "No Tolerance."

Censorship of popular culture would not eliminate prejudice, although censorship efforts are rising. Universities are trying to regulate prejudicial statements published by students; pressure groups are battling what they see as permissiveness on television; the United States Senate recently moved to restrict public support of controversial art. (The Parents' Music Resource Center in Washington, which monitors rock lyrics, has concerned itself with violence, sexual explicitness, drug references and blasphemy, not bigotry.)

Racist and sexist statements are a byproduct of societal tensions, and they belong well within constitutionally defined free speech. They're worth allowing because the alternative, the imposition of governmental regulations—like Senator Jesse Helms's guidelines for government financed arts programs—could hobble virtually all controversial expression. Politically correct art, under any definition of political correctness, tends to be strangulated art.

## Free Speech Allows Denunciation of Bigotry

But legal tolerance need not mean acceptance. Free speech allows those who are disgusted by prejudicial conduct to denounce it, as Jewish groups did after Public Enemy's actions; the Anti-Defamation League of B'nai Brith called Mr. Griffin's firing and rehiring a "repugnant charade." Yet Guns N' Roses, 10 times as commercially successful as Public Enemy, have generated hardly a peep. According to Ms. Bridenthal, Mr. Rose's comments to *Rolling Stone* brought not protests but requests for more interviews, which he has refused.

"Axl does not believe that what he said was a horrible racist thing," she said. "I think he's reflecting a whole stratum of our society that feels the same way. That may be a scary thing, but part of what art is supposed to do is to make people look at things, and that's how it changes the world."

There are differences between Public Enemy and Guns N' Roses. The rap group's overall message is one of self-determination for blacks. Mr. Ridenhour's lyrics are angry—one song describes Public Enemy as "prophets of rage"—and on stage he performs surrounded by what the group calls a "security force," young men in uniform who hold plastic Uzis. (Mr. Griffin used to lead them through quasi-military maneuvers; now his successor does.) The stance is militant, confrontational.

But Mr. Ridenhour kept racism out of Public Enemy's songs. While he calls himself a "follower of Farrakhan," referring to the Nation of Islam leader Louis Farrakhan, who has made inflammatory, anti-Semitic statements, he does not include such sentiments in his songs. His adversaries are the likes of "the media" and "the government," not targeted groups. In "Party for Your Right to Fight," mostly about the history of the Black Panther Party, he uses the phrase, "grafted devils," alluding to black-supremacist Nation of Islam theories that consider whites the end result of a diabolical genetic bleaching process. But the lyrics charge the "devils" with specific offenses.

Yet Public Enemy's actions outside its music send a different message. When Mr. Griffin's statements led to a public outcry, Mr. Ridenhour fired him and issued public apologies. But he effectively annulled those apologies when he rehired Mr. Griffin. Although Mr. Ridenhour has said Mr. Griffin apologized to him for his statements, Mr. Griffin has made no public apology, and in his final interview on Aug. 3, with the *Kansas City Jewish Chronicle*, he called his statements "100 percent pure."

## Caving in to Pressure

Public Enemy is clearly torn privately (Mr. Griffin and Mr. Ridenhour are longtime friends) and publicly; Mr. Ridenhour does not want to be seen within the black community as caving in to pressure from whites. But in his actions self-contradiction reigns. A group that intends to fight racism should distance itself decisively from all forms of bigotry, including anti-Semitism. Public Enemy may already have been penalized for its actions; it was negotiating a new recording contract with MCA Records, but the deal collapsed during the controversy.

Guns N' Roses, meanwhile, addresses a white majority and remains unrepentant. While 1980's rock has had an obscure fringe of white-supremacist "skinhead" and, in Britain, "oi" bands, none has had major-label support or concert and radio exposure like Guns N' Roses, although standard heavy-metal boasting and sexism, not racism, is the band's main message. (On stage, Guns N' Roses goes through the motions of strutting narcissism and macho camaraderie.) Mr. Rose spewed his racism in a song on a Top 10 recording, the two-million-selling "G N' R Lies," and he considers himself brave and forthright.

"Why can black people go up to each other and say, 'nigger,' but when a white guy does it all of a sudden it's a big put-down?" Mr. Rose complains in the *Rolling Stone* interview. "I used the word 'nigger' to describe somebody that is basically a pain in your life, a problem. The word 'nigger' doesn't necessarily mean black."

Mr. Rose ascribed the "immigrants" verse to his being harassed at a convenience store run by immigrants, and to "very bad experiences with homosexuals"—inadvertently supplying classic examples of bigoted illogic, which extrapolates from individuals to demonize whole groups. Although the Gay Men's Health Crisis dropped Guns N' Roses from a June benefit concert for AIDS research, the band has been otherwise unscathed. Its record company is still solicitous about their "relationship."

In popular culture's market system, it is up to listeners to repudiate messages they dislike, passively or actively—and to disabuse bigots of any claim to the mainstream. Rock and comedy have a mandate to probe taboos, and they should be expected to go too far now and then. But what's pitiable about the current outbursts is how timid they are. They don't break new artistic ground—or, as Public Enemy chant, "fight the powers that be"—they scapegoat groups perceived as weaker. While the promise of American popular culture is its willingness to defy conventional wisdom and established hierarchies, performers who spew prejudice offer only their own ignorance and cowardice.

# 78. Hip-Hop into the 1990s

## Gangstas, Fly Girls, and the Big Bling-Bling

*hip-hop without wit is like sushi without wasabi*

Greg Tate[1]

The surge of mainstream popularity experienced by rap at the close of the 1980s continued into the 1990s. One of the most curious aspects of this, because it was so unexpected at the time, was the commercial ascendance of "gangsta rap." Gangsta rap, although pioneered by Northeast rappers, such as Schoolly D and Boogie Down Productions, achieved its broadest early circulation as a product of South Central Los Angeles and the nearby black communities of Long Beach and Compton. With lyrics featuring raw language in an unprecedented description of graphic violence, sex, and anger, N.W.A. (or Niggas with Attitude—mentioned briefly at the start of chapter 77) brought a new sense of urban, quasi-cinematic realism to popular music. The majority of mass media reportage focused on the sensationalistic aspects of the recordings, thereby missing two important components of N.W.A.'s approach: the driving, noisy, hard-edged, and funk-inflected grooves of the instrumental tracks produced by Dr. Dre (Andre Young, b. 1965), accentuated by the rhythmic declamations of the group's rappers (especially Ice Cube and Easy-E), and the way in which N.W.A.'s depictions of violence criticized how social institutions (especially law enforcement) perpetuated systemic racism.[2]

While the "hardcore" aspects of gangsta rappers and some other flamboyantly *outré* groups, such as 2 Live Crew, seized media attention for flaunting public taboos, the late 1980s and early 1990s witnessed some other, less controversial developments in rap that were every bit as notable. Prominent among them was what the music press later dubbed "alternative" or "progressive" hip-hop, represented by groups like De La

---

1. "Above and Beyond Rap's Decibels," *New York Times* (March 6, 1994), Sec. 2, 36.

2. Robin D. G. Kelley presents a thorough and sympathetic scholarly account of gangsta rap in "Kickin' Reality, Kickin' Ballistics: 'Gangsta Rap' and Postindustrial Los Angeles," in *Race Rebels: Culture, Politics, and the Black Working Class* (New York: Free Press, 1994), pp. 183–227.

Soul and A Tribe Called Quest. Greg Tate defined progressive hip-hop as "hiphop praxis wherein lyric content and raising the art form to the next level outweighs the profit margin."[3] Albums, such as De La Soul's *Three Feet High and Rising*, used the flow of radio variety shows from the pre-TV era to reinvent the album format (an innovation that was soon widely adopted), but with material that could only come from growing up in the post-TV era.[4] Combining skits that were takeoffs on TV game shows and witty, insightful and (above all) nonviolent lyrics with samples taken from all over the pop music spectrum, De La Soul and other progressive hip-hop groups became critical darlings. Another development, the politically oriented rap initiated by Public Enemy, was extended by female artists, such as Queen Latifah, who also received much favorable critical attention at the time.[5]

Nevertheless, mainstream media coverage of hip-hop almost single-mindedly conveyed a sense of moral outrage and panic, focused on the most lurid examples of hardcore rap. Articles in not-so-new publications, ranging from *Newsweek* to the *New Republic*, deplored what the authors viewed as the mindless glorification of violence and misogyny. Many of the writers directed their attention toward the "anger" that such writers heard in the music, although these accounts rarely seemed aware of how this anger was often politically motivated by a critique of white privilege (especially in recordings by Public Enemy and Boogie Down Productions/KRS-One). The growing appeal of gangsta rap to young, white listeners caused the writer of a 1991 article in the *New Republic* to claim that rap music was neither "music" nor "black."[6] In contrast, Jon Pareles wrote a series of sympathetic articles in the *New York Times*, which, however, invariably elicited a round of letters to the editor protesting that hip-hop should not be included in the music section of Arts and Leisure, since rap, after all, was not really music.[7]

---

3. Greg Tate, "Diatribe," *Village Voice*, September 3, 1996, 46.

4. Jon Pareles explores the TV-hip-hop connection in "How Rap Moves to Television's Beat," *New York Times* (January 14, 1990), Sec. 2, 1–2.

5. See, for example, Michelle Wallace, "When Black Feminism Faces the Music, and the Music Is Rap," July 29, 1990, *New York Times*, Sec. 4.

6. The title says it all: David Samuels, "The Rap on Rap: The 'Black Music' That Isn't Either," *New Republic* (November 11, 1991): 24–29. The articles referred to in *Newsweek* were David Gates et al., "The Rap Attitude," *Newsweek* (March 19, 1990): 56–63; and John Leland, "Rap and Race," *Newsweek* (June 29, 1992): 47–52. Although this type of criticism has lessened in recent years, it has not disappeared entirely, as evidenced by the following statement in my local newspaper: "Rap consists, in large part, of people ranting and cursing to a monotonous beat. It is now America's most popular music"; see Peter Carlson, "Uncivil Discourse: The Breathless Harangue Is All the Rage," *Binghamton Press & Sun Bulletin*, March 2, 2003, 9A. Originally published in the *Washington Post*.

7. See Pareles, "How Rap Moves to Television's Beat"; letters to the editor, *New York Times*, February 4, 1990, Sec. 2; idem., "Rap: Slick, Violent, Nasty and, Maybe, Hopeful," *New York Times* (June 17, 1990), Sec. 4; idem., "On Rap, Symbolism and Fear," *New York Times*, February 2, 1992, Sec. 2, 1, 23; letters to the editor, *New York Times*, February 16, 1992, Sec. 2.

We already heard from J. D. Considine in chapter 71 in the article on Judas Priest and the Scorpions. Displaying impressive critical range, Considine turns his attention to many of the issues (described earlier) that dominated media discussions about hip-hop in the early 1990s. Considine uses interviews with Chuck D (Carlton Ridenhour, b. 1960) and Ice Cube (O'Shea Jackson, b. 1969, who left N.W.A. to embark on a successful solo career in 1990) to rebut many of the criticisms directed toward hip-hop, while paying particular attention to the "is it music?" question (posed here by nonrap musicians, Al DiMeola, Lita Ford, and Ozzy Osbourne) and to the social context for the violent imagery found in much rap.

## FEAR OF A RAP PLANET

### *J. D. Considine*

In the 12 years since "Rapper's Delight" bum-rushed the Top 40, it would seem that rap has developed an unshakeable grip on popular culture. It's heard everywhere—on MTV, in movies, in advertising, even in Saturday morning cartoons, where Hammerman just replaced Kid 'N Play as the networks' favorite animated rapper.

Granted, a lot of people don't particularly *like* rap. They aren't down with "O.P.P.," have no memories of bliss concerning P.M. Dawn, and don't want to talk about sex—or anything else with Salt-N-Pepa.[8] These are the folks for whom rap is just noise with a beat, and they feel the same things their parents felt about rock 'n' roll: disinterest, distaste and disgust.

But fear? Who could possibly be afraid of rap?

Well, Bob Greene, for one. In his Chicago *Tribune* column last month, he wrote about a mugging in New York which happened to have been videotaped by the perpetrators themselves. Although he reports that police, who eventually arrested two teens, were "puzzled" by the event, what sparked this not-ready-for-prime-time crime was no mystery to Greene—rap music made them do it. Or, to be specific, rap videos, which, writes Greene, "are purposely glorifying armed violence and criminality. Most Americans probably have not seen these rap videos. But they are broadcast day and night by various cable channels, and they are frightening."

But not as frightening as the rap audience itself. Just ask all those radio stations that not only refuse to play rap records, but actually boast about it, courting listeners with slogans like "All the Best Music—And No Rap." Some are so petrified that they'll even excise rap-like passages from recordings by non-rap acts, as WLLZ-FM in Detroit did recently when it cut a few bars of unsung rhyming from "Roll the Bones" by Rush.

If you really want a sense of how deep this fear of a rap planet goes, however, check out the mass media, for whom rap seems to be a never-ending source of scare stories. When a white New York investment banker was beaten, raped and left for dead in the celebrated Central Park "wilding" incident, it was widely (and, apparently, erroneously) reported that the suspects after their arrest were happily chanting Tone-Loc's "Wild Thing"—the

---

8. This sentence refers to then-recent hits by those artists.

*Source:* J. D. Considine, "Fear of a Rap Planet," *Musician* (February 1992), pp. 34–43, 92. Used by permission of J. D. Considine.

implication being that the rap had somehow inspired the rampage. Indeed, when *Newsweek* published its 1990 cover story lambasting rap culture, the magazine made sure it was Tone-Loc's face that was framed by the "Rap Rage" headline.

Then, after N.W.A.'s *Efil4zaggin* entered the *Billboard* album charts at number one (the first rap album ever to do so), the *New Republic* ran a cover story suggesting that rap, described in a subhead as "The 'black music' that isn't either," isn't even listened to by blacks. According to the *TNR* story, rap's primary audience is suburban white kids, and N.W.A.'s sex-and-violence posturing is little more than minstrelsy, cartoonish blacks doing their best to entertain thrill-seeking Caucasians.

And now there's the controversy over Ice Cube's *Death Certificate*, which has been denounced by anti-defamation activists, Korean citizen groups, syndicated columnists and even the editors of *Billboard*. Granted, Ice Cube has provided his critics with plenty of ammunition, what with lyrics that characterize Korean store owners as "Oriental one-penny-countin' motherfuckers," that insist "true niggas ain't gay," and that suggest his former bandmates in N.W.A. dispose of manager Jerry Heller:

> *Get rid of that devil real simple*
> *Put a bullet in his temple*
> *Because you can't be a Niggaz 4 Life crew*
> *With a white Jew telling you what to do.*

It's ugly, sure. Angry, too. But Ice Cube refuses to consider the quatrain quoted above to be anti-Jewish. "I'm really surprised that people would take that record so out of proportion," he says. "The record is not geared towards Jerry Heller or the Jewish community; the record is geared towards the group who attacked me. In most cases I felt that Jerry Heller attacked me—in the *Rolling Stone* interview, and the *Spin* articles.

"They even attacked me on the record, and said that when they caught me, they was going to cut my hair and fuck me with broomstick. Now, I've seen them a couple of times after that record—they haven't cut my hair, and they definitely haven't fucked me with a broomstick." In other words, it's all just "woofing," with both sides making outrageous verbal threats they have no intention of following through on.

"So why are you taking rap music literally?" he asks, rhetorically. "It's stupid to take anything that literally, other than news. This is a form of *entertainment*. People keep forgetting that. I'm not a schoolteacher or a professor at any university. I'm a rapper. I entertain."

The question is, are you amused? Or are you afraid?

## It's a Black Thing, You Wouldn't Understand

Ask Public Enemy's Chuck D why people are afraid of rap, and at first he just shakes his head. "That's ridiculous," he says, "Because we don't tear up hotels, we don't tear up arenas." It isn't, after all, as if he and his fellow rappers are inciting youths to riot on a nightly basis.

Chuck D's no dummy, though, and it doesn't take him long to come up with real answer. "Anything that comes from a black point of view that the establishment doesn't have full control over or understanding of, they view as being offensive," he says. "And now even more so, since that point of view is coming across to white kids."

That's not to say Public Enemy's audience is entirely white, mind you. The crowd of young Baltimoreans he plays to this evening, for example, is almost 95 percent black (don't they read the *New Republic?*) But overall, the audience P.E. attracts is as broad as it is big, and that, as the establishment sees it, makes the group doubly dangerous.

"I look at this country as being a predominantly white male-dominated society," Chuck says. "It has never even given a black male his chance or his due, because we are seen as being not even part of that whole structure. It's a white male structure versus everything else.

"Now, some of the frustration is coming across. This stuff is coming out from all different angles, but the media have been built by white men, and the first maneuver when you can't control the play is to attack it."

If that seems a little paranoid from where you're sitting, it makes perfect sense from Public Enemy's perspective. After all, this group has spent much of its recording career articulating the black community's anger and taking flak for its efforts. First it was lambasted for endorsing Louis Farrakhan in "Bring the Noise," then for anti-Jewish remarks Professor Griff, its former Minister of Information, made in an interview with the Washington *Times*. The current controversy, for those keeping score at home, stems from a gay-bashing rhyme uttered by Flavor Flav in "A Letter to the New York Post"—"ask James Cagney / He beat up on a guy when he found he was a fagney."

Chuck shrugs off the "Letter" controversy. "I mean, you really can't take it that serious on Flavor," he says, "because he just found something that rhymes." Beyond that, though, he says he's more concerned with the motives behind these attacks than with what his attackers have to say. "I don't judge criticism, I judge the critic," he says, adding that as far as he can see, the only thing these anti-rap diatribes are meant to do is maintain the status quo.

"You have certain defense mechanisms up to keep things the way they are supposed to be and maintain order in this structure," he says. "That's because you have a lot of people who are paranoid, with no really full grasp of what they believe in, and they feel that they have something to lose. They lose belief in themselves and in their structure. They feel like they'll lose a grip on their future.

"In our view, that's not necessarily so. The black race is just trying to get a grip on itself to survive. I mean, the thing with black people in this country is they're real beat-down people. And it's really more serious than a lot of white people take to heart, because we have everything to lose—and we lost a lot. I try to tell our people, 'There's no time for making excuses, we've got to make the best of it.' But many of them are damaged goods, you know what I'm saying?

"To make a long story short, white people have to understand that black people already have respect for [them], because we've been trained to do so. We just don't have respect for ourselves. When a level of self-respect comes, then you'll see that it gets better. But self-respect has never been taught, so right now, black people are still slaves to that."

Unfortunately, what some rappers see as their efforts to uplift the race, their critics take as attacks on others. Ice Cube, for instance, explains in the liner notes to *Death Certificate* that the album is divided into two parts, with the "Death Side" being "a mirrored image of where we are today," while the "Life Side" pictures "where we need to go." But it's disturbingly easy to translate that message as "Let's stop destroying ourselves, and start destroying others."

Which, Cube says, is dead wrong. "They figure when you're pro-black, you've got to be anti-whatever," he says. "But see, that's guilt from the pain that they inflicted on blacks. We aren't pro-black to be anti-white or anti-Korean, anti-Jewish. We're pro-black so we can look back at history and make sure that it doesn't repeat itself."

Being pro-black doesn't necessarily mean articulating your ideas as violently as Ice Cube does. Take the Afrocentric movement. Although the Allan Blooms of the world consider it a threat to the very foundations of Western Civilization, Afrocentricity as expressed by the likes of Queen Latifah is simply a means for young blacks to learn who they are, and have some pride in that knowledge.[9]

"It's very hard, because we're brainwashed in this country in a lot of ways," she says. "It's like when a little black kid grows up, what do they see on TV? They see so much white. What are they supposed to connect to? They connect to what this white thing is. So they think their hair is supposed to be long and their eyes are supposed to be light and their skin is supposed to be light and it's not, and they feel low about it. When they go out with the girls, all the guys want to talk to the light ones, or the one with long hair.

"We have a lot of stereotypes to fight, a lot of barriers to break down. And it's hard, because nobody's perfect. Nobody can just change all this stuff in one day. It's going to take years and years of barrier-breaking for things like this to change."

## Rap Isn't Music

"I have a problem with rap," admits Guitarist Al Di Meola. "It's not music. It's not like I'm hearing an instrumentalist play, with some harmony and a good vocalist. Where are the people who've learned to play their instrument?"

"I'm really bored with this rap music," says fellow fretboarder Lita Ford. "I think it's about time that it was on its way out. It sounds like gang music to me."

"I'm a believer in melody," says singer Ozzy Osbourne. "Rap I can appreciate, but it drives me nuts after about an hour. I mean, if you haven't got a melody. . . ."

When musicians talk about what they don't like about rap, the points that come up rarely concern racial politics; instead, it's the rap musical value they question. *It hasn't got a melody. They don't play instruments, they don't have any ideas, they steal everything. It's just not music.*

Rappers, naturally, counter that such talk is just so much sour grapes. "It's not *their* instrument [on the record], so it's not music," laughs Russell Simmons, president of Def Jam Records. "Drummers are the same—they say there's no live drummers on it, so it's not real, it's not a record. 'Course, now that live drums are back, drummers think those same records are fine. I think they're ridiculous."

"A lot of people don't like that we could take a song that's been done before and probably sold 300,000, and do 1.3 million with it," adds Ice Cube. "Like Hammer took 'Super Freak,' and made it into a bigger hit than Rick James did. That's why I think people get mad at us. They've got to understand that we took something and just made it better. The talent we put on top of it was better than the talent that was on it originally."

Not that it takes a sampler to steal a groove. A decade ago, the pioneering rappers at Sugar Hill all recorded with a live rhythm section. But as Matt Dike, whose production credits include Tune-Loc's "Wild Thing," points out, "What they were doing was playing grooves from other records, that they had stolen. Like the bass in 'White Lines' was from a song by Liquid Liquid, this underground New York band. They were ballsier than anybody! They just replayed the whole thing, and acted like they wrote it."

Besides, if it takes no talent to make rap records, Ice Cube has a simple question: "I say, 'Why don't *you* try to do a hit rap record?'

"They'd be lost, in most cases."

Maybe so, but rap's critics do raise some valid questions. For instance, given that rap vocals rarely change pitch (and certainly aren't "sung" in any conventional understanding of the term), is it fair to say that rap records don't have any melody?

---

9. Allan Bloom (author of a conservative diatribe against late 20th-century mass culture), *The Closing of the American Mind* (New York: Simon and Schuster, 1987), which was widely discussed during this period.

No way, answers producer Bill Laswell. "That's just people who have been conditioned into thinking a certain chord sequence ending on middle C is the absolute concept of melody," he argues. "If you're familiar with Asian or African music, you realize that a lot of the melody is inherent in the drumming. In African drumming, you hear all kinds of melodies and phrases, and there's as much melody in hip-hop and rap as in African drumming—and that's a lot of melody. You just have to listen."

True enough. Even a seemingly simple rap record, like Naughty By Nature's "O.P.P.," reveals unexpected complexity if you know where to look. Sure, it has the "ABC" piano hook, looped right off the original, which is probably the only "melodic" element anyone noticed when it first came up on the radio. But there's also a reggae-style bassline churning up a nice rhythmic cross-current with the syncopated kick drum, a fair amount of percussive interplay (check out the parallelism between the two-note piano part that sets up each two-bar phrase and the two-beat cowbell accent that leads into three each measure), and, of course, the raps themselves, which spin clever variations on the bassline's cadence—sometimes stretching across the bar, sometimes double-timing the beat, sometimes pulling up short to add to the track's rhythmic tension.

Even though they use samplers, sequencers and drum machines instead of guitars, bass and drums, rap acts orchestrate their rhythm frameworks as thoughtfully as any rock act would. Take Public Enemy, for example. "They're the only rap group I know of that can take five or six snippets of a record, put it together and make it sound like one band," said Branford Marsalis after contributing a tenor solo to "Fight the Power."

"They're not musicians, and don't claim to be—which makes it easier to be around them. Like, the song's in A minor or something, then it goes to D7, and I think, if I remember, they put some of the A minor solo on the D7, or some of the D7 stuff on the A minor chord at the end. So it sounds really different. And the more unconventional it sounds, the more they like it."

On the latest Public Enemy album, *Apocalypse 91 . . . The Enemy Strikes Black*, the group extends that approach. "We've taken a lot of instruments and processed them through computers," says Chuck D, who explains that the P.E. approach often relies on playing the samples on a keyboard to lend more of a live feel to the tracks. "The only difference between sampling and live sound is change," he says. "When a bass player plays bass, he makes mistakes sometimes. But he fixes the mistake so quick that it's just a change in the pattern, an ad-lib. But your programming is not going to program a mistake. So what we try to do is, we don't program it so much. We play the keys. Like 'Homey Don't Play That' from the *Terminator X* record. I played the bass on keys."

Then there's the rap itself. Those who don't rap often assume that rap lyrics are little more than simply metered rhyming doggerel—which, to be honest, a certain amount of them are. But the best rappers take as much care with their cadences as they do with the rhythm beds, so that the words flow along with the music instead of just hammering home the beat.

Chuck D, for instance, won't even start writing until he has a groove to work from, and often sketches out his rhythmic ideas with nonsense syllables before filling out his raps. "I'll have a groove that inspires me, do my vocals in a certain way and then fill it with words," he says. "And if it doesn't fit the groove, I'm not going to fuck with it."

Ironically, once he's finished recording, Chuck then has to go through the laborious process of relearning what he has written. "I have a bad memory for remembering words," he laughs. "People say, 'Didn't you write it?' I say, 'Yeah, I wrote it, and it's on a piece of paper. Is it in my head? It came out of my head, but now I have to relearn it.' A lot of people don't understand that.

"You know who's got a crystal-clear memory? Ice-T. Ice-T recites records from back in 1981, line for line. He can recite every single one of his records line for line, word for word. Ice Cube is the same thing. They're like Michael Jordan or Magic Johnson. I guess I'm like [Charles] Barkley—I gotta work for everything I got.

"The only thing that might be natural about me is my voice. But a voice doesn't mean nothing if you don't know how to use it."

"It all comes with style," explains Ice Cube. "A lot of raps that come straight on the beat were written without a beat, know what I'm saying? They put a beat in their head and just write from that. Then they get the music and the music isn't exactly what they had in their head, but they can come down on every beat and make it work. I choose to have my music first. I'll write a rap that fits it like a glove, or at least try to. I can take breaths here, I can slow down here, I can speed up here, and just try to throw some style and flavor on it without sounding so robotic."

As for material, Ice Cube says there's never any shortage of things for him to write about. "Living just gives me records to do," he says. "I just finished *Death Certificate*, and I've thought of three topics that I might want to write on for my new album.

"I just live life, man, however it comes. When things come up that I think need to be talked about, then I do it. I just start writing."

# 79. Nuthin' but a "G" Thang

In the wake of the successes of N.W.A. and Ice Cube, gangsta rap became the dominant form of hip-hop in the early 1990s. The level of censorship and political attention that rap received rose correspondingly. Political militancy assumed heightened levels of confrontational violence in tracks, such as N.W.A.'s "Fuck tha Police" (1988); Public Enemy's "Arizona" (1991, criticizing Arizona's failure to recognize Dr. Martin Luther King's birthday); Ice-T with Body Count's "Cop Killer" (1992); and Dr. Dre's (now recording on his own) "Deep Cover" (1992). Many of the songs emanating from Southern California seemed eerily to anticipate or comment upon the May 1992 uprising following the exoneration of Los Angeles police officers in the beating of Rodney King. With the PMRC's rating system already in place (and with the recordings just mentioned all receiving "parental advisory" stickers), pressures mounted on recording companies to limit such confrontational recordings. Time-Warner, in response to the pressure, first dropped "Cop Killer" from the *Body Count* album and then released Ice-T (a Los Angeles rapper who had recorded an album called *O.G. Original Gangster* in 1991) from his contract.

Dr. Dre's *The Chronic* became the best-selling hip-hop album of 1992 (the title is a reference to test-grade marijuana). Dre had modified his sound from N.W.A., producing a smoother form of funk that featured high-pitched, whiny synthesizers and (frequently) sung choruses. Now recording with soon-to-be-notorious Death Row records, Dre introduced rapper Snoop Doggy Dogg (Calvin Broadus, b. 1972) on *The Chronic* and "Deep Cover," the single that preceded it. Dre and Snoop shared rapping duties on about half the tracks on *The Chronic,* the lyrics of which were written mainly by Snoop. The critique of racist institutional policies that had featured prominently in early N.W.A. recordings became increasingly implicit in *The Chronic'*s detailed depictions of sex and violence, which fans appreciated because of their humorous language and apparent fidelity to experience. The notion of "keeping it real" thus assumed greater importance in the evaluation of hip-hop.

Snoop Doggy Dogg's solo album, *Doggystyle,* repeatedly described in the press of the time as the "most anticipated rap album of all time," was released in late 1993 and quickly became the best-selling rap album ever. As described in the following article by Touré, the notion of "keeping it real" took on a macabre cast when Snoop was arrested in conjunction with a shooting while finishing the album. Yet, as he notes here (echoing the words of Ice Cube in chapter 78), the words of his songs should not be taken literally, but rather as entertainment. Clearly, the line was blurring between the way in which the words "should be taken," and how rappers and listeners were actually taking them. Also of interest here are Snoop's comments on his delivery and approach to rhythm, which, again, confirm the statements by Chuck D and Ice Cube in the previous article.[1]

## Snoop Dogg's Gentle Hip Hop Growl
### *Touré*

It's past midnight on a cool Friday in September, and a photo shoot for a beer ad is breaking up. The photographer's lights still illuminate a small parking lot in West Hollywood, Calif., which is empty save for a few Mercedes-Benzes, Jeeps and low-riders and a handful of young black men.

At the center of the group, looming over all, is the shoot's subject, a thin, dark-skinned 6-foot-4 rapper with sunken cheeks and a razor-sharp nose. He leans at what appears a 45-degree angle, surveying the scene around him out of the corners of his eyes. Hours ago he had turned himself in to the police on the charge of murder and was released on $1 million bail; in minutes he will return to the studio to work on his debut album, "Doggystyle," the most anticipated hip-hop album ever. His name is Snoop Doggy Dogg.

---

1. For a more in-depth portrait of Snoop around this time, see dream hampton, "Snoop Doggy Dogg: G-Down," *The Source* 48 (September 1993): 64–70. Particularly interesting in this article are Snoop's comments about the early stages of the West Coast–East Coast rivalry and his connections with the Crips and Bloods—rival African American gangs in Southern California.

*Source:* Touré, "Snoop Dogg's Gentle Hip Hop Growl," *New York Times,* November 21, 1993, p. 32.
Copyright © 1993 by the New York Times Co. Reprinted with permission.

Over this past year the 22-year-old rapper has been the most ubiquitous man in hip-hop. His voice has flowed from Walkmans, DJ turntables and Jeep stereos as his face graced MTV and the cover of Rolling Stone, all thanks to his featured role on Dr. Dre's album, "The Chronic," which has sold more than three million copies, becoming the fifth-biggest-selling rap album.

On Tuesday, Death Row Records will release "Doggystyle," from the man born Calvin Broadus in Long Beach, Calif., and nicknamed Snoop by his mother. The album follows the first single and video, "What's My Name?" and is expected to enter Billboard's pop album chart at No. 1, a first for a debut album. "This is the biggest buzz I've ever seen," says Chris Lighty, president of Rush Management, which handles many of the top rappers. "The last time there was anything close was probably Jimi Hendrix, no, N.W.A.'s *Niggaz4Life*. People are going to the store asking, 'Is it in yet? Is it in yet?'"

Snoop's music is gangster rap, a genre marked by rhymes that describe the violent challenges of urban living. Gangster rap is probably hip-hop's best-known subset, but it is no more the definitive expression of hip-hop than fusion is of jazz. Like jazz, all hip-hop may sound the same to the inexperienced ear, but beneath the posturing and booming beat lies one of pop's most complex forms. With its collagist ethic, hip-hop pulls from all of popular culture, from old television shows to up-to-the-minute slang, to inform the rapper's often autobiographical presentation. But just as jazz celebrates mastery, hip-hop prizes originality; in (now dated) hip-hop parlance, the word fresh meant excellent. At the moment, "dope" means great.

There are rappers with greater rhythmic flexibility and tonal dynamism than Snoop, but where newness is the virtue, Snoop matters, because his vocal approach is, in every sense, fresh. "Snoop ain't the dopest," says Jermaine Dupri, the producer of the platinum-selling rap group Kris Kross, "but he's king right now."

Snoop's vocal style is part of what distinguishes him: where many rappers scream, figuratively and literally, he speaks softly. Compare the treatment of the murder of a police officer in the song "Deep Cover," from the soundtrack of the 1992 movie of that name, with that of Ice-T's "Cop Killer." Both songs gained popularity in the summer of 1992, but "Deep Cover" did not provoke the controversy "Cop Killer" did because of Snoop's subtlety: to understand "Deep Cover's" refrain—"'cuz it's one eight seven on a undercover cop"—one has to know that in Los Angeles police terminology the number 1-8-7 means homicide.

"It's the way you put it down," Snoop explains. "I put it down with a twist. Everybody in the whole world knew 'Cop Killer' meant kill a cop. And every policeman knows the municipal code is 187, but everybody in the whole world didn't know that."

Soft tones mark Snoop as vocal descendent of the soul vocalists Al Green and Curtis Mayfield. His voice is a nasal tenor, especially distinct because of his Southernish twang (derived from his Mississippi-born parents and grandparents) and the considerable restraint of his delivery. It all projects the aura of a man who is ultra-cool.

"It's a basic conversation," Snoop says of his style. "I don't rap, I just talk. I don't like to get all pumped up and rap fast 'cause that ain't me. I want to be able to relax and conversate with my people. It's a distinction between Steven Seagal and Clint Eastwood. Seagal ain't laid back. Eastwood is."

Laid-back cool places Snoop in the African-American tradition of making light of personal horror. From the same emotional source from which bluesmen found the grace to understate the weight of their pain comes Snoop's nonchalance in the middle of warring gangs and the police.

Snoop Doggy Dog sounds even cooler when that conversation is juxtaposed against the ominous, sinister, funk-inspired music of his producer, Dr. Dre, an innovator as important in hip-hop as Quincy Jones has been in jazz. Unlike most hip-hop producers who create tracks by sampling from original sources, Dr. Dre uses a band. It's led by T-Green, a one-time George Clinton collaborator and a longtime member of the funk band the Dramatics.

"You know how you would be real sensitive and delicate with a newborn baby," Snoop asks. "That's how I treat the beat when I'm rapping: like a newborn baby. Even if it's a hard track, what I'm saying will move you, because I'm delicately putting it down."

Rage, a female rapper who appears on "The Chronic" and "Doggystyle," says Dr. Dre has contributed much to Snoop's success. "I don't know if Snoop would be as big, because Dre's production plays a big part," she says. "If you don't have good beats, then you might not get as much recognition."

While Snoop delivers rhymes delicately, the content is anything but. Growing up poor, often surrounded by violence, and having served six months in the Wayside County jail outside of Los Angeles (for cocaine possession) gave Snoop experiences upon which he draws: "My raps are incidents where either I saw it happen to one of my close homies or I know about it from just being in the ghetto," he says. "I can't rap about something I don't know. You'll never hear me rapping about no bachelor's degree. It's only what I know and that's the street life. It's all everyday life, reality."

It's all reality is the most-repeated refrain in hip-hop, a proclamation of integrity in a world where it's cool to be from the inner city with a checkered past and many lie about their background. Hip-hop fans prefer artists who are honest, but, in fact, the argument over "realness" may be pointless: they are entertainers. As Rakim, widely considered one of the best rappers, puts it: "You got groups that come out saying they're killing, but in all reality, they're just rappers."

It is important that the rapper's voice and stories be realistic, but must they be the author's own? To thoughtful fans, what's important is how credible the lyrics sound. Here again Snoop stands out: his attention to detail makes him sound extremely credible. According to Mr. Dupri, the producer, "The details in Snoop's writing makes people think, 'Damn, he must've really seen that.'"

For example, in Snoop's favorite song on "The Chronic"—whose title is laden with obscenities—he describes a hot day, when, minutes after completing six months in prison, the protagonist is driven to his girlfriend's house, bursts in brandishing a Glock pistol and finds her having sex with his cousin. He considers shooting her but does not, deeming women not worth killing.

Snoop may sound—and be—more honest than most, but that does not mean he is as tough as his gangster posture or his handlers would suggest. Snoop began rapping in the sixth grade, sang in the choir of Golgotha Trinity Baptist Church in Long Beach and graduated from Long Beach Polytechnic High School. He maintains that he never joined a gang, though he hung out with gang members. Watching them gave Snoop his subject matter; imprisonment focused him.

"I started thinking about my life," he says. "Do I want to keep coming back to this place, or do I want to elevate myself and make my mother proud of me? At Wayside I listened to all the stories people told, wrote them down on my note pad and turned them into raps. That's the first time I really started getting serious about rapping. The older inmates would take me aside and say, 'Youngster, you don't need to be inside this place. God gave you some talent, and you ought to use it.'"

The assertion that lyrics are drawn from reality is also hip-hop's biggest excuse for not passing judgment on what it describes. Rappers routinely discuss violent and obscene situations without taking responsibility for the implications, like reporters from the street willfully lacking a worldview.

Snoop contends he does take a stand against what he describes. "I feel like it's my job to play the backup role for parents who can't get it across to their kids," he says. "For little kids growing up in the ghettos, it's easy to get into the wrong types of things, especially gangbanging and selling drugs. I've seen what that was like, and I don't glorify it, but I don't preach. When my momma would whoop me and tell me, 'You can't do this,' it made me want to go do that; I bring it to them rather than have them go find out about it for themselves."

It takes very critical listening to hear Snoop's implicit message. Far easier is losing oneself in his accounts of renegade days and nights. He may not intend to, or want to admit it, but Snoop adds epic gloss to his life with the skill of a Hollywood movie star.

Yet soon, all of Snoop's talent may be overshadowed. On Aug. 25, Snoop's bodyguard, Malik (McKinley Lee), shot a man named Philip Woldermariam twice—once in the back—from the passenger seat of the Jeep that Snoop was driving. Other details surrounding the event are in dispute. Snoop says the shooting was in self-defense and pleaded not guilty at his arraignment on Oct. 1; his next hearing is set for Nov. 30.

Back in the parking lot, Snoop speaks of his dream. "After I take care of my album," he says, "I'm going to try to eliminate the gang violence. I'll be on a mission for peace." If the trial is on his mind, it does not appear so as he speaks of the future, neglecting to note that on Aug. 25 he could not prevent the 187 that may destroy his life. "I know I have a lot of power," Snoop says. "I know if I say, 'Don't kill,' niggers won't kill."

# 80. Keeping It a Little Too Real

Gangsta rap and the notion of "keeping it real" continued to dominate hip-hop music following *Doggystyle*. New rappers emerged in the New York City area who modified elements of the West Coast style, either by emphasizing partying and material acquisitions, as in the recordings of Biggie Smalls (Christopher Wallace, a.k.a. the Notorious B.I.G., 1972–97), or through heightened obscurantism and bizarrely imaginative humor and music, as in the Wu Tang Clan. Wu Tang Clan, which boasted up to nine members, illustrated the tendency toward increasingly large posses or crews among rap artists. Touré, writing in 1995, describes the development as a move from the late 1980s–early 1990s emphasis on Afro-Centrism to "blockism," this being

the idea that your neighborhood block is the center of the world, the people there the most important audience to impress. It's also the directive that if you get off the block, your peeps come too. . . . it's led to the family-like structure behind the three biggest entities in hiphop today: the Wu-Tang Clan, Death Row, and the Biggie Smalls clique.[1]

---

1. Touré, "The Family Way: The Hiphop Crew as Center of the World," *Village Voice*, October 10, 1995, 49.

The contradictions and ambiguity embedded in notions of "keeping it real" and rap as "only entertainment," which the arrest of Snoop in 1993 had begun to expose, intensified with the arrest of 2Pac (Tupac Shakur, 1971–96) late in 1994 on sexual assault charges, followed by the shooting of Shakur (from which he recovered) under mysterious circumstances before the trial began. Tensions began to build between West Coast rappers, centered on Death Row records, and East Coast rappers, many of whom recorded for Bad Boy records (the "Biggie Smalls clique" referred to earlier, which included Sean "Puff Daddy" Combs). A crisis point was reached in the murder, first of 2Pac, in September 1996, and then of Biggie Smalls, in March 1997. The following articles provide background on the West Coast–East Coast feud and show a range of reactions to the murders. While many decried how mass media accounts misrepresented the victims by implying that everyone involved with hip-hop was a criminal, even committed fans could not ignore the relationship between the deaths of two of hip-hop's biggest stars and the increasing rate of black-on-black violence.[2]

# Rap Sheet

## Sam Gideon Anso and Charles Rappleye

The murder of Brooklyn rapper Notorious B.I.G. early Sunday morning in Los Angeles cast a pall over a rap industry that had for weeks basked in the glow of a declared truce in the so-called East Coast/West Coast wars—an outbreak of peace that infused the festivities of the annual Soul Train Awards the night before.

Instead, the shooting recalled the scene at the 1996 Soul Train Awards, an event marred by a guns-drawn confrontation between delegations including Tupac Shakur of L.A.'s Death Row Records, and Biggie Smalls, who'd sold platinum for New York's Bad Boy Entertainment. Shakur was gunned down in September in Las Vegas; now B.I.G., whose real name was Christopher Wallace, is dead as well.

Kevin Kim, who was on the scene providing security for Faith Evans, Wallace's estranged wife, said he believes the shooting was a planned attack on Wallace. "They knew who they were shooting at," Kim said in an interview Sunday afternoon. "Look at the shot pattern—tight shots, not like a regular West Coast drive-by where gang members are spraying bullets all over the place."

However, Kim cautioned against speculation that Wallace's murder was linked to the much publicized rivalry between Wallace, Shakur, and the respective companies. "The East Coast/West Coast thing is all blown up," Kim said. "At the party that night, everybody was dancing together, artists hugging each other. . . . They squashed that beef, and it is still squashed."

Kim is referring in part to the truce, memorialized last month in an episode of the sitcom *The Steve Harvey Show*, in which Death Row's Snoop Doggy Dogg and Sean "Puffy"

---

2. Particularly moving on this account was Touré's eulogy for hip-hop in the form of a letter to a cousin, "It Was a Wonderful World," *Village Voice*, March 18, 1997, 41.

*Source:* Sam Gideon Anso and Charles Rappleye, "Rap Sheet," *Village Voice*, March 18, 1997, p. 40.

Combs, CEO of Bad Boy Entertainment, publicly laid aside the dispute that has been simmering between rap's leading labels for more than two years.

In the twisted logic of the rap game, even the coziness between Snoop and Puffy, who had been seen together in recent weeks in New York, raised eyebrows and fueled talk that Puffy—and by extension B.I.G.—was disrespecting Death Row and its chief Marion "Suge" Knight, who'd been sentenced to nine years in state prison the week before. "Puffy and Biggie thought with Suge put away it was all good," said one West Coast rap insider. "But it's not all good. There is still a lot of tension out there. And Snoop and Puffy hanging out like they are best friends—that shit ain't right."

The chronology of the feud begins with gunfire in the building lobby of a Manhattan recording studio, where Tupac Shakur, then on trial for the rape of a fan, was shot five times and robbed of $40,000 worth of jewelry. In a jailhouse interview with *Vibe* following his conviction, Shakur left no doubt that he suspected Wallace, who was upstairs in the studio at the time of the shooting, had set him up. Wallace and Combs denied any involvement in the shooting.

From there the events unfold in rapid succession. In August 1995, Knight "disrespected" Combs from the podium of The Source Awards at Manhattan's Paramount Theater. A month later, Knight accused Combs of having a hand in the shooting death of Death Row employee (and reputed member of a Compton Blood set) Jason "Big Jake" Robles at an industry party in Atlanta. Combs again denied involvement, but Knight was sufficiently suspicious that he allegedly assaulted an independent record promoter named Mark Anthony Bell at yet another party—this one following an MTV awards show in Los Angeles in December 1995—in an effort to get information about Combs, including his home address.

While Knight and Combs issued repeated denials that a beef existed at all, their albums and videos were peppered with incendiary remarks directed coast to coast, most notoriously Shakur's boast, "I fucked your bitch, you fat motherfucker," on last year's "Hit 'Em Up." All of which helped sell millions of records and magazines, and all of which made fertile ground for speculation when Shakur was slain in Las Vegas.

Las Vegas police have named a suspect in Shakur's murder—a Compton resident and reputed member of the Southside Crips gang named Orlando Anderson, who fought with Shakur and his entourage in the lobby of the MGM hours before the shooting. According to a search warrant affidavit made public last month, the fight at the MGM grew out of an earlier incident in which Anderson and a group of seven or eight Southside Crips stole a Death Row Records medallion from Travon Lane, a Death Row associate and reputed member of the MOB Piru Blood set, at a Foot Locker store in the Lakewood Mall. Anderson denies any involvement in the Shakur killing. Police detained him for questioning in September, but have made no arrests.

While this would seem to lay to rest any East Coast connection in Shakur's killing, the affidavit also suggests a link between Wallace's label and Anderson's Southside Crip set. Bad Boy Entertainment, according to the affidavit, "employed Southside Crips gang members as security."

The Compton connection figures prominently in some informed speculations on the killing. According to one source, the hit on Wallace was pulled off by Compton Bloods, who came to the party in the entourage of a well-known Compton rap artist, and coordinated the shooting over cell phones. Another report put an individual dressed in red standing outside the party with a cell phone saying "Biggie is here now."

"This was a hit, something pre-planned," said one Blood from Compton. "And there's going to be a few more hits."

The killing is harder to swallow coming in the midst of a reduction of hostilities in the hip hop nation. At last year's Soul Train Awards, says one source, "Biggie had half a dozen or so bodyguards and they were very conscious of looking over their shoulders." With the exception of a smattering of boos from the balcony as Wallace and Combs came onstage to present an award, this year's festivities were marked by positive vibes. Which may have something to do with the fact that Suge Knight was cooling his heels in the L.A. County jail.

"For the next six months no one is going to feel comfortable," says Kevin Kim. "Can I trust this person? Or is he setting me up?"

## PARTY OVER
### *Selwyn Seyfu Hinds*

As with Tupac, much has been made of the self-prophetic element in Big's passing. *Ready To Die*, his classic debut, was an organic mesh of Brooklyn bad boy narratives and the flossy party aesthetic, all tinged by no meager dose of suicidal musings—a phenomenon encapsulated by a frighteningly realistic video that featured a screaming Puff, a depressed Biggie dying from a self-inflicted gunshot wound, and the pound of a reverberating, eventually stilling heartbeat.

Big's pending album, *Life After Death . . . 'Til Death Do Us Part*, is very different, although certain elements remain consistent. Part cinematic (and calculated) tie-in to the debut, it is the creation of a once desperate, now well-paid baller negotiating the pitfalls endemic to rap success—jealousy, envy, and the like. It is celebratory and triumphant at some junctures, remorseful and contemplative in others.

*Life After Death* also possesses no small degree of tragic irony—the intro, which picks up where *Ready to Die* left off, with a morose Puffy mourning the passing of his man: "Damn/We was supposed to rule the world baby/We was unstoppable/The shit can't be over"; the enthusiastic "Going Back to Cali": "Y'all niggas is a mess/Thinkin' I'm gon stop/Giving L.A. Props"; an interlude where an anonymous caller threatens to kill Big and urges him to "watch his fucking back"; and "You're Nobody 'Til . . ." ("somebody kills you"), a piece of metaphoric tough talk that now packs a heartbreak.

Big's gone and this album is his last artistic testament. An MC who felt that he'd never received his due props *Life After Death* would have allowed Big to witness the 'cross-the board affirmation he so desired. And although it's too late to pour this sentiment out, maybe Christopher Wallace can still feel it somewhere and rest satisfied: you were the best, baby baby.

## TOWN CRIERS
### *Natasha Stovall*

Radio station Hot 97 acted as town crier and community center, just as they did after Tupac. In one of the most painful moments of the day's broadcast, Biggie protégé Delvico, from Junior M.A.F.I.A., called in from Brooklyn, in tears and waiting for the call to go to the West Coast. "I don't believe it, yo. I just don't believe it's real." The DJs let him know, "Y'all are our family, on the air, off the air, we're here for you. Ain't nothing fake going on here."

*Source:* Selwyn Seyfu Hinds, "Party Over," *Village Voice*, March 18, 1997, p. 42.

*Source:* Natasha Stovall, "Town Criers," *Village Voice*, March 18, 1997, p. 42.

"I'm turning on the news and that's really what's getting me upset," the Fugees' Wyclef told 97 DJ Dr. Dre. "Let's get one thing straight. Biggie Smalls was an inspiration to us MCs and the whole hip hop community. Every time it's hip hop they're trying to bring us down." "I look at it this way," said Public Enemy's Chuck D, also on Hot 97. "When the magazines and the newspapers and the radio shows all come out and go 'Whoop! Whoop! East Coast/West Coast,' it becomes a big story. It becomes a hysteria. If you add hype and hysteria to a situation, it can bring craziness from any direction."

Chuck D spoke at length about the larger picture, in which Biggie Smalls's death is only a puzzle piece. "It's bigger than rap. Until black people control our reality, not only will art imitate life, but life will start to imitate art." The fact that Biggie's and Tupac's deaths were just larger manifestations of the staggering number of black men under 30 who are murdered each year loomed large in the minds of Brooklyn residents. Back in front of Baker's, Janice's friend Tasha sighed, "It was just a murder, not a West Coast/East Coast thing."

Ultimately, the most numbing thing about Biggie's death is its proximity to Tupac's. "I feel like I just hung up with you about Tupac," Roxanne Shante told Hot 97. Brooklyn lost another son way too early, but next week another death will eclipse his. "I loved the brother. He was a good brother, a righteous young man," a man selling pictures of Biggie for $2 outside KFC put it. "Now I'm a capitalist, and I've got two of these left. Do you want to buy one?"

# 81. Sample-Mania

It may be that the death of gangsta rap's stars hastened its demise or that the genre had simply run its course; whatever the reasons, gangsta rap seemed to fade from view following the shootings of Biggie and 2Pac. In its place came rap that emphasized partying and material opulence. As I mentioned earlier, the recordings/videos of Biggie Smalls, while depicting gang life and violence, had also featured grandiose displays of wealth. Biggie's producer, Sean "Puff Daddy" (later "P-Diddy") Combs, heightened this trend in many of the songs and videos for his first solo album, *No Way Out,* which followed closely on the heels of Biggie's *Life After Death* (both 1997). Combs, while a weak rapper, was a great judge of talent and an astute reader of the audience. His image, in both his appearances in *Life After Death* and his own album, attempted to project hipness via association with material success, rather than with the "hardness" associated with gangsta rap and, as such, demonstrated the increasing importance of "image" relative to the MCing skills that defined "old-school" artists of the 1980s.

Neil Strauss addresses another aspect of some of the songs on *No Way Out and Life After Death:* the use of large sections of previous songs, which inaugurated a new era in sampling and quotation. Strauss's account, though laced with humor, is largely critical, noting how acceptance of this practice contrasted with previous disdain among hip-hop fans. His critique raises a pressing question: Does this new development in sampling differ from the types of creative reuse of materials that have characterized previous forms of African American music? Strauss points out the diverging receptions of Puff Daddy's work and the recordings of MC Hammer and Vanilla Ice, but what about the value of Sugarhill Gang's "Rapper's Delight" and Run-DMC's "Walk This Way," which were also constructed almost entirely around preexisting recordings?

## SAMPLING IS (A) CREATIVE OR (B) THEFT?
### *Neil Strauss*

It was early 1991, and two songs ruled the radio airwaves: "U Can't Touch This" by M. C. Hammer and "Ice Ice Baby" by Vanilla Ice. The popularity of both songs was not necessarily due to the rapping skills of their performers. It was due to the fact that both melodies were sampled from familiar pop tunes, "Superfreak" by Rick James and "Under Pressure" by Queen and David Bowie, respectively. At the time, these derivative hits seemed to threaten the legitimacy of rap, which had always prided itself on its street credibility and a refusal to pander to popular taste. Consequently, the artists, justly or not, were soon mocked out of existence.

This summer, however, songs based on samples of previous hits are not only back but so pervasive that they deserve to be re-evaluated. The issue is not just sampling, the now standard music-making tool of using digital excerpts of sounds and songs. The issue is making a sample the song itself, so that a chorus lifted wholesale from an earlier hit becomes the basis of a new hit. There are two ways of looking at the practice: Is taking pieces of a well-known song and incorporating them into a personal musical vision the equivalent today of remaking a pop standard? Or are these hits evidence of a creative slump, a sign that pop musicians have lost their ability to write effective melodies and songs?

The king of sampled hits is Sean (Puffy) Combs, better known as Puff Daddy, whose "I'll Be Missing You," "No Way Out" and "Mo' Money, Mo' Problems" (a collaboration with the Notorious B.I.G.) were three of the summer's most popular songs.

All are based on excerpts from hits, including ones by the Police, Grandmaster Flash and Diana Ross.

Meanwhile Will Smith looks to Patrice Rushen's "Forget Me Not" for "Men in Black," Lil' Kim uses Kool and the Gang's "Ladies' Night" for the chorus of "Not Tonight," and Wyclef Jean of the Fugees leans on the Bee Gees for "We Just Trying to Stay Alive." The difference between 1997 and 1991, however, is that unlike M. C. Hammer and Vanilla Ice, these artists are respected in their fields. And, more so than their predecessors, they are repeat offenders when it comes to plundering pop's collective memory.

Since its inception, sampling has offered its practitioners myriad new ways of remaking a song in their own image—to slice and dice a song so drastically that they don't even have to call it by its original name—and talented artists from Public Enemy to the Chemical Brothers have emerged in this genre. But musicians are no longer content just to pilfer a drumbeat, a bass line or a vocal snippet. They want huge chunks, unchanged from the original. After all, asks the pragmatic producer, why mess with something that already works.

Consider Wyclef Jean's "We Just Trying to Stay Alive." Listening to his eclectic solo album, it's clear that "We Just Trying to Stay Alive" was added because the record needed a hit single. So, inspired by the success of "Killing Me Softly," the Roberta Flack hit that put the Fugees on the pop-music map, he snatched the chorus and bass line of the Bee Gees' disco classic "Stayin' Alive" and sandwiched a few irrelevant raps between the choruses.

When he sings along with the Bee Gees, his hit simply sounds like a karaoke version of "Stayin' Alive." Nostalgia, not creativity, made the song a success.

Only when plundering and originality come together to create something new does sampling become reminiscent of pop's pre-rock days, when new and vital music came out of the intersection between a good song, a good interpreter and perhaps a good arranger.

The same cliché that applies to any remake applies to sampled songs: in a valid, worthwhile version, an artist makes the song his or her own. Examples range from John Coltrane playing "My Favorite Things" to Frank Sinatra singing "I've Got You Under My Skin."

Somewhere between interpretation and quotation is Janet Jackson's new single, "Got Till It's Gone," which uses Joni Mitchell's "Big Yellow Taxi" as part of its chorus but doesn't rely on it to carry the entire song.

An even better example involves the English groups Portishead and Tricky, each of which released a song that samples the same Isaac Hayes melody. Both songs use that sample to anchor different musical interpretations of desperation, but if you removed it from the songs, they would still stand up.

In future months, expect to see newcomers breaking into the pop charts riding a stolen song. It's a clever way for pop singers to remake a classic and keep some of the writer's royalties for themselves.

If you get tired of the formula, you can always try it yourself. Just program a drum machine with any 4/4 rhythm with a strong back beat. Now grab a pop song that is no longer current but still recognizable, like Survivor's uplifting "Eye of the Tiger." Let your beat run for a few bars to create a groove, then drop in the chorus of "Eye of the Tiger" completely unchanged from the original. Follow it with a vapid rap along the lines of: "It's the eye of the tiger/The tiger of the eye/I'm working hard just to get by/Got more moves than Rocky/I'll sip a glass of sake/Pay some royalty checks/Cause Survivor's on the decks." Then go back to your "Eye of the Tiger" chorus (sing along or scratch a record over it if you like) and you've got your hit.

Just make sure you send me a portion of the proceeds after it's on the charts. Survivor has reunited to cash in on the revival, and with the blessing of the Rolling Stones, you're on to your next hit, "(I Still Can't Get No) Satisfaction."

# 82. Women in Rap

The new pluralism in hip-hop in the mid-1990s also expanded the role for women. Rappers, such as Foxy Brown and L'il Kim emerged who used their sexuality aggressively, often presenting men in their songs as important only for how they might satisfy their (the rappers') needs.[1] This development might be viewed as resurrecting the classic blues singer's persona: a strong woman who knows what she wants and isn't afraid to demand it, while refusing to be defined by her relationship with a man. In another vein, Lauryn Hill (b. 1975) broke through with the Fugees in *The Score,* which became the hip-hop smash of 1996—an album viewed as "progressive hip-hop" and a critical fave by some, while being dismissed as inauthentic fluff by others. Hill impressed with her verbal skills and rapping dexterity, as well as with her R&B singing chops: The biggest hit on the album, a remake of Roberta Flack's "Killing Me Softly," featured Hill's alto in a faithful re-creation of Flack's vocal.

The following year Missy "Misdemeanor" Elliot (Melissa Elliot, b. 1971) released her first solo album after writing songs for, as well as performing on, many other people's recordings. Her wacky, surreal, and decidedly nonglamorous (in the conventional sense) persona/image has proved remarkably durable, and her subsequent releases, aided and abetted by the innovative production of Timbaland, continue to earn her critical and commercial success.

Although the careers of many female rappers thrived in the late 1990s, it was Lauryn Hill who became the first big crossover female superstar in hip-hop. Her solo album, *The Miseducation of Lauryn Hill,* received five Grammy awards in 1999, and her photo appeared on the February 8, 1999, cover of *Time* next to the caption, "Hip-Hop Nation: After 20 Years— How It's Changed America." Hill's crossover (and the largely favorable *Time* article) signaled a new level of acceptance of hip-hop by the mainstream audience, and it was safe to say that, in terms of recording sales at any rate, hip-hop had *become* the mainstream. Hill seemed to be the perfect figure to accomplish this: Multitalented, a philosophy major at Columbia, attractive, articulate, and adamantly religious, she was a far cry from the denizens of Death Row. The rest of the *Time* article and the portrait of Hill, which are reprinted here, revisit some ideas presented in

---

1. See "Nuthin' but a G String," a forum featuring two articles: Robert Marriot, "Starring Lil' Kim as the Posthiphop Hussy," and Kweli I. Wright, ". . . and Foxy Brown as the Moschino Macktress," *Village Voice*, December 24, 1996, 63.

earlier entries, especially the turn in hip-hop toward the glorification of materialism and the withering of political content. In discussing figures, such as Hill and Puff Daddy, it becomes clear that the popularity of hip-hop had largely transcended racial boundaries and that the influence of hip-hop had spread to other genres. Whether this symbolized a break-through in race relations or new opportunities for white voyeurism of African Americans remained an open question. Although this change in status raised worries about whether hip-hop could maintain its creativity and "underground" credibility, changes in recording technology meant that an increasing number of people who were not successful enough to worry about such issues could create their own high-quality demos. The contrast between the generally favorable tone of this article and a number of articles that appeared in mass circulation publications in the 1980s and early 1990s (cited in chapters 75 and 78) reveals how rapidly the social position of hip-hop had changed. Of course, a lot of this change may have been due to hip-hop's increasing slice of the music industry pie, as noted in the beginning of the article that follows.

# HIP-HOP NATION

## Christopher John Farley

How will we remember the last days of the '90s? Most likely, to the rough-hewn beat of rap. Just as F. Scott Fitzgerald lived in the jazz age, just as Dylan and Jimi Hendrix were among the rulers of the age of rock, it could be argued that we are living in the age of hip-hop. "Rock is old," says Russell Simmons, head of the hip-hop label Def Jam, which took in nearly $200 million in 1998. "It's old people's s_____. The creative people who are great, who are talking about youth culture in a way that makes sense, happen to be rappers."

Consider the numbers. In 1998, for the first time ever, rap outsold what previously had been America's top-selling format, country music. Rap sold more than 81 million CDs, tapes and albums last year, compared with 72 million for country. Rap sales increased a stunning 31% from 1997 to 1998, in contrast to 2% gains for country, 6% for rock and 9% for the music industry overall. Boasts rapper Jay-Z, whose current album, *Vol. 2 . . . Hard Knock Life* (Def Jam), has sold more than 3 million copies: "Hip-hop is the rebellious voice of the youth. It's what people want to hear."

Even if you're not into rap, hip-hop is all around you. It pulses from the films you watch (Seen a Will Smith movie lately?), the books you read (even Tom Wolfe peels off a few raps in his best-selling new novel), the fashion you wear (Tommy Hilfiger, FUBU). Some definitions are in order: rap is a form of rhythmic speaking in rhyme; hip-hop refers to the backing music for rap, which is often composed of a collage of excerpts, or "samples," from other songs; hip-hop also refers to the culture of rap. The two terms are nearly, but not completely, interchangeable.

Rap music was once called a fad, but it's now celebrating a 20th anniversary of sorts. The first hip-hop hit, *Rapper's Delight* by the Sugar Hill Gang, came out in 1979. Hip-hop got its start in black America, but now more than 70% of hip-hop albums are purchased by whites. In fact, a whole generation of kids—black, white, Latino, Asian—has grown up

*Source:* Christopher John Farley, "Hip-Hop Nation," *Time,* February 8, 1999, pp. 55–58, 59–64; and Christopher John Farley, "Lauryn Hill," *Time,* February 8, 1999, p. 59. © 1999, TIME Inc., reprinted by permission.

immersed in hip-hop. "I'm hip-hop every day," declares 28-year-old Marlon Irving, a black record-store employee in Portland, Ore. "I don't put on my hip-hop." Says Sean Fleming, a white 15-year-old from Canton, Ga.: "It's a totally different perspective, and I like that about it." Adds Katie Szopa, 22, a white page at NBC in New York City: "You do develop a sense of self through it. You listen and you say, 'Yeah, that's right.'"

Hip-hop represents a realignment of America's cultural aesthetics. Rap songs deliver the message, again and again, to *keep it real*. The poet Rainer Maria Rilke wrote that "a work of art is good if it has sprung from necessity." Rap is the music of necessity, of finding poetry in the colloquial, beauty in anger, and lyricism even in violence. Hip-hop, much as the blues and jazz did in past eras, has compelled young people of all races to search for excitement, artistic fulfillment and even a sense of identity by exploring the black underclass. "And I know because of [rapper] KRS-1," the white ska-rap singer Bradley Nowell of Sublime once sang in tribute to rap. Hip-hop has forced advertisers, filmmakers and writers to adopt "street" signifiers like cornrows and terms like player hater. Invisibility has been a long-standing metaphor for the status of blacks in America. "Don't see us/but we see you," hip-hop band the Roots raps on a new song. Hip-hop has given invisibility a voice.

But what does that voice have to say?

*Now tell me your philosophy*
*On exactly what an artist should be.*
—Lauryn Hill, "Superstar"

It's a Friday night, early December 1998, and you're backstage at *Saturday Night Live.* You're hanging out in the dressing room with Lauryn Hill, who is sitting on the couch, flipping through a script. The 23-year-old rapper-singer-actress is the musical guest on this week's show. It's her coming-out party, the first live TV performance she's done since releasing her critically acclaimed and best-selling album *The Miseducation of Lauryn Hill.* She might also do a little acting on the show—*SNL* staff members have asked her to appear in a skit. But as Hill reads, her small rose-blossom lips wilt into a frown. She hands you the script. It's titled *Pimp Chat*—it's a sketch about a street hustler with a talk show. Hill's role: a 'ho. Or if she's uncomfortable with that, she can play a *female pimp*. Hmmm. Now, being in an *SNL* sketch is a big opportunity—but this one might chip away at her image as a socially conscious artist. What's it going to be?

*It's all about the Benjamins, baby.*
—Sean ("Puffy") Combs, "It's
   All About the Benjamins"

You are in a recording studio in midtown Manhattan, hanging out with hip-hop superproducer Sean ("Puffy") Combs. It's 1997, and Puffy is keeping a low profile, working on his new album, his first as a solo performer. This album will be his coming-out party. He's eager to play a few tracks for you. People have him all wrong, he says. He majored in business management at Howard. He's not just about gangsta rap. Sounds from his new album fill the room. One song is based on a bit from the score to *Rocky.* Another, a sweeping, elegiac number, uses a portion of *Do You Know Where You're Going To?* That's what he's about, Combs says. Classic pop. "I'm living my life right," he says. "So when it comes time for me to be judged, I can be judged by God."

*You're mad*
*because my style*
*you're admiring*
*Don't be mad—UPS is hiring.*
—The Notorious B.I.G., "Flava in Your Ear (Remix)"

Hip-hop is perhaps the only art form that celebrates capitalism openly. To be sure, film-makers pore over weekend grosses, but it would be surprising for a character in a Spielberg film to suddenly turn toward the camera and shout, "This picture's grossed $100 million, y'all! Shout out to DreamWorks!" Rap's unabashed materialism distinguishes it sharply from some of the dominant musical genres of the past century. For example, nobody expects bluesmen to be moneymakers—that's why they're singing the blues. It's not called the greens, after all. As for alternative rockers, they have same relationship toward success that one imagines Ally McBeal has toward food; even a small slice of the pie leaves waves of guilt. Rappers make money without remorse. "These guys are so real, they brag about money," says Def Jam's Simmons. "They don't regret getting a Coca-Cola deal. They brag about a Coca-Cola deal."

Major labels, a bit confused by the rhythms of the time, have relied on smaller, closer-to-the-street labels to help them find fresh rap talent. Lauryn Hill is signed to Ruffhouse, which has a distribution deal with the larger Columbia. Similar arrangements have made tens of millions of dollars for the heads of these smaller labels, such as Combs (Bad Boy), Master P (No Limit), Jermaine Dupri (So So Def), and Ronald and Bryan Williams (Co-CEOs of Cash Money, home to rising rapper Juvenile).

"I'm not a role model," rapper-mogul-aspiring-NBA-player Master P says. "But I see myself as a resource for kids. They can say, 'Master P has been through a lot, but he changed his life, and look at him. I can do the same thing.' I think anyone who's a success is an inspiration."

Master P introduced something new to contemporary pop: shameless, relentless and canny cross-promotion. Each of the releases on his New Orleans-based No Limit label contains promotional materials for his other releases. His established artists (like Snoop Dogg) make guest appearances on CDs released by his newer acts, helping to launch their debuts. And his performers are given to shouting out catchphrases like "No Limit soldiers!" in the middle of their songs—good advertising for the label when the song is being played on the radio.

Madison Avenue has taken notice of rap's entrepreneurial spirit. Tommy Hilfiger has positioned his apparel company as the clothier of the hip-hop set, and he now does a billion dollars a year in oversize shirts, loose jeans and so on. "There are no boundaries," says Hilfiger. "Hip-hop has created a style that is embraced by an array of people from all backgrounds and races." However, fans are wary of profiteers looking to sell them back their own culture. Says Michael Sewell, 23, a white congressional staff member and rap fan: "I've heard rap used in advertising, and I think it's kind of hokey—kind of a goofy version of the way old white men perceive rap."

But the ads are becoming stealthier and streetier. Five years ago, Sprite recast its ads to rely heavily on hip-hop themes. Its newest series features several up-and-coming rap stars (Common, Fat Joe, Goodie Mob) in fast-moving animated clips that are intelligible only to viewers raised on Bone-Thugs-N-Harmony and Playstation. According to Sprite brand manager Pina Sciarra, the rap campaign has quadrupled the number of people who say that Sprite is their favorite soda.

Hollywood too is feeling the rap beat. After Lauryn Hill passed on a role in *The Cider-House Rules* (an adaptation of the John Irving book), filmmakers cast hip-hop soul singer Erykah Badu. Ice Cube, who has appeared in such movies as *Boyz N the Hood* and *Fridays,* will soon star with George Clooney in the Gulf War thriller *Three Kings.* Queen Latifah, featured in the recent film *Living Out Loud,* is now set to be the host of a TV talk show. And the former Fresh Prince, Will Smith, has become one of the most in-demand actors around. Ice Cube—who performed a song with Public Enemy titled *Burn Hollywood Burn* in 1990—says Tinseltown wants rapper actors because "we add a sense of realism where sometimes a trained actor can't deliver that reality the way it needs to be done."

Warren Beatty, who directed and starred in *Bulworth*, a comedy about a Senator who becomes possessed by the spirit of hip-hop, became interested in the subject because "it seemed to have a similar protest energy to the Russian poets of the 1960s. The Russian poets reigned in Moscow almost like rock itself reigned in the U.S. Ultimately it seemed to me that hip-hop is where the voice of protest is going in the inner city and possibly far beyond because the culture has become so dominated by entertainment."

Even Tom Wolfe, who documented the counterculture in the '60s and greed in the '80s, found himself buying a stack of hip-hop records in order to understand Atlanta in the '90s for his best-selling book *A Man in Full.* In several sections of his novel, Wolfe offers his own sly parodies of today's rap styles: "How'm I spose a love her/Catch her mackin' with the brothers," Wolfe writes in a passage. "Ram yo' booty! Ram yo' booty!" Most of the characters in *A Man in Full* are a bit frightened by rap's passion. It's Wolfe's view that "hip-hop music quite intentionally excludes people who are not in that world." That world, however, is growing.

*We in the '90s*
*And finally it's looking good*
*Hip-hop took it to billions*
*I knew we would.*
—Nas, "We Will Survive"

All major modern musical forms with roots in the black community—jazz, rock, even gospel—faced criticism early on. Langston Hughes, in 1926, defended the blues and jazz from cultural critics. Hard-core rap has triumphed commercially, in part, because rap's aesthetic of sampling connects it closely to what is musically palatable. Some of the songs hard-core rappers sample are surprisingly mainstream. DMX raps about such subjects as having sex with bloody corpses. But one of his songs, *I Can Feel It,* is based on Phil Collins' easy-listening staple *In the Air Tonight.* Jay-Z's hit song *Hard-Knock Life* draws from the musical *Annie.* Tupac's *Changes* uses Bruce Hornsby. Silkk the Shocker samples the not-so-shocking Lionel Richie.

The underlying message is this: the violence and misogyny and lustful materialism that characterize some rap songs are as deeply American as the hokey music that rappers appropriate. The fact is, this country was in love with outlaws and crime and violence long before hip-hop—think of Jesse James, and Bonnie and Clyde—and then think of the movie *Bonnie and Clyde,* as well as *Scarface* and the *Godfather* saga. In the movie *You've Got Mail,* Tom Hanks even refers to the *Godfather* trilogy as the perfect guide to life, the I-Ching for guys. Rappers seem to agree. Snoop Dogg's sophomore album was titled *The Doggfather.* Silkk the Shocker's new album is called *Made Man.* On his song *Boomerang,* Big Pun echoes James Cagney in *White Heat,* yelling, "Top of the world, Ma! Top of the world!"

Corporate America's infatuation with rap has increased as the genre's political content has withered. Ice Cube's early songs attacked white racism; Ice-T sang about a *Cop Killer;* Public Enemy challenged listeners to "fight the power." But many newer acts such as DMX and Master P are focused almost entirely on pathologies within the black community. They rap about shooting other blacks but almost never about challenging governmental authority or encouraging social activism. "The stuff today is not revolutionary," says Bob Law, vice president of programming at WWRL, a black talk-radio station in New York City. "It's just, 'Give me a piece of the action.'"

Hip-hop is getting a new push toward activism from an unlikely source—Beastie Boys. The white rap trio began as a Dionysian semiparody of hip-hop, rapping about parties, girls and beer. Today they are the founders and headliners of the Tibetan Freedom Concert, an annual concert that raises money for and awareness about human-rights issues in Tibet.

Last week Beastie Boys, along with the hip-hop-charged hard-rock band Rage Against the Machine and the progressive rap duo Black Star, staged a controversial concert in New Jersey to raise money for the legal fees of Mumia Abu-Jamal, a black inmate on death row for killing a police officer. Says Beastie Boy Adam Yauch: "There's a tremendous amount of evidence that he didn't do it and he was a scapegoat."

Yauch says rap's verbal texture makes it an ideal vessel to communicate ideas, whether satirical, personal or political. That isn't always a good thing. "We've put out songs with lyrics in them that we thought people would think were funny, but they ended up having a lot of really negative effects on people. [Performers] need to be aware that when you're creating music it has a tremendous influence on society."

In Mill Valley, Calif., in a one-bedroom apartment above a coin-operated laundry, Andre Mehr, a white 17-year-old with a crew cut, and Emiliano Obiedo, a ponytailed 16-year-old who is half white and half Hispanic, are huddled over a PC. A beat spirals up. Obiedo offers some advice, and Mehr clatters away at the keyboard. They are making music. Once they settle on a beat, Obiedo will take a diskette bearing a rhythm track home and lay down some rhymes. Soon they hope to have enough for a CD. Boasts Obiedo: "I'm going to change rap."

Across the country, similar scenes are playing out as kids outside the black community make their own hip-hop or just listen in. Some say they don't pay much attention to the lyrics, they just like the beat. "I can't relate to the guns and killings," says Mehr. Others are touched more deeply. Says 15-year-old Sean Fleming: "I can relate more and get a better understanding of what urban blacks have to go through."

Todd Boyd, a professor of critical studies at the University of Southern California, says rap can bring races together: "It's a little more difficult to go out and talk about hate when your music collection is full of black artists. That is not to say that buying an OutKast record is the same as dealing with real people, but it is reason to hope." Ice Cube is a bit more cynical: "It's kinda like being at the zoo. You can look into that world, but you don't have to touch it. It's safe."

Nonblack performers are increasingly drawing from rap. Beck expertly combined folk and hip-hop. Hanson's hit *MMMBop* included deejay scratching. Portishead refashioned hip-hop into ethereal trip-hop. Singer Beth Orton, whose enchantingly moody album *Central Reservation* is due out in March, blends folksy guitars with samples and beats. Doug Century, author of *Street Kingdom: Five Years Inside the Franklin Avenue Posse,* studied hip-hop culture as he documented the lives of gang members; he predicts white acts will eventually dominate rap, just as white rockers pushed out rock's black forerunners. "It's possible that in 15 years all hip-hop will be white," Century says. "[Then] black youth culture will transform itself again."

Already the white b-boy has become an iconic figure—ridiculed in movies like *Can't Hardly Wait* and the forthcoming *Go,* and in songs like Offspring's *Pretty Fly (for a White Guy).* In *Pretty Fly* the punk band Offspring mocks whites who adopt hip-hop styles, singing, "He may not have a clue/And he may not have style/But everything he lacks/Well he makes up in denial." Irish-American rap-rocker Everlast, whose new CD, *Whitey Ford Sings the Blues,* has proved to be a commercial hit, says the song makes him laugh: "They ain't talking about me, 'cause I'll beat the s_____ out of every one of those guys." In fact, Everlast feels confident enough about his standing in the rap world to take a verbal swipe at Puffy Combs: "I don't think Puffy really cares about what he's doing. He's a brilliant businessman, but he's no different from the Backstreet Boys or the Spice Girls because he's just creating a product."

Wu-Tang Clan producer-rapper RZA is also concerned about maintaining standards. He believes many performers are embracing the genre's style—rapping—but missing its essence, the culture of hip-hop. "I don't think the creativity has been big. I think the sales have been big, and the exposure has been big," says RZA. "Will Smith is *rap*. That's not hip-hop. It's been a big year for rap. It's been a poor year for hip-hop."

Underground rap is available for those industrious enough to seek it out. At New York City's Fat Beats record store, you can pick up vinyl editions of independently released songs by such promising new acts as the Philadelphia-based Maylay Sparks (call 215-492-4257 for more information) and the all-female antimisogyny hip-hop collective Anomolies (917-876-0726). Maylay Sparks' spirited *I Mani* and the New York City-based Anomolies' raucous tune *Blacklisted* (a collaboration with the group Arsonists) are two of the best songs to come out this year.

Other groups, signed to major labels, are trying to perpetuate rap's original spirit of creativity. The rapper Nas's forthcoming album *I Am . . . the Autobiography* promises to be tough, smart and personal. And the Atlanta-based duo OutKast's Bib Boi: "We're not scared to experiment."

One of the most ambitious new CDs is the Roots' *Things Fall Apart* (named after the book by the Nigerian Nobel laureate Chinua Achibe). The CD features live instrumentation, lyrics suitable for a poetry slam and a cameo from Erykah Badu. Roots drummer Ahmir hopes, in the future, the more creative wing of performers in hip-hop will form a support network. "There are some people in hip-hop that care about leaving a mark," he says. "There are some of us that look at *Innervisions* as a benchmark, or *Blood on the Tracks* or *Blue* or *Purple Rain*. Leaving a mark is more important than getting a dollar. I think Lauryn's album is one of the first gunshots of hip-hop art the world is gonna get."

> *You could get the money*
> *You could get the power*
> *But keep your eyes on the final hour.*
> —Lauryn Hill, **"Final Hour"**

It's Puffy's 29th birthday party, and the celebration is being held on Wall Street. Inside the party, women in thongs dance in glass cages. Above the door a huge purple spotlight projects some of Puffy's corporate logos: Bad Boy (his record company) and Sean John (his new clothing label). But where's Puffy?

The music stops. The crowd parts. Muhammad Ali arrives. He's only the appetizer. The score to *Rocky* booms over the speakers. Only then does Puffy enter, in a light-colored three-piece suit. Forget being street. He's Wall Street, he's Madison Avenue, he's le Champs Elysées. Donald Trump is at his side. It's Puffy's moment. His album *No Way Out* played on some familiar gangsta themes, but it's a smash hit. Puffy is a household name, a brand name. In fact his name comes up again and again, in gossip columns and other people's rap songs. He has transformed himself into a human sample. He is swallowed by the crowd.

You are at the Emporio Armani store on Fifth Avenue in downtown Manhattan. There's a benefit here tonight for the Refugee Project, a nonprofit organization Lauryn Hill founded to encourage social activism among urban youth. Hill is here, and the cameras are flashing. Her musical performance on *Saturday Night Live* has boosted her album back to the upper reaches of the charts. In a few days she will receive 10 Grammy nominations, the most ever by a female artist.

She never did do that *SNL* skit about the hooker. She says she feels too connected to hip-hop to do a movie or TV role that compromise the message in her music. She addresses the crowd. "I'm just a vehicle through which this thing moves," she says. "It's not about me at all." You think back to some of the rappers you've talked to—Jay-Z, Nas, the Roots, Grandmaster Flash. A record cues up in your mind: "Ain't no stopping us now . . ."

# Lauryn Hill

Strange that something so alive now could have begun in a museum. In late 1997, Lauryn Hill was visiting Detroit to produce a song that she wrote for her childhood hero, Aretha Franklin. On the way to the airport, she stopped at the Motown Museum. The Supremes, Stevie Wonder, the Jackson 5—these were the performers she was reared on. She could picture their 45s scattered across her bed. "It was incredible to me and really inspiring," says Hill. Now she was ready to push forward on her own solo album.

Looking back, looking back, Hill grew up in South Orange, N.J.; her father was a management consultant, her mother a grade-school English teacher. From an early age, Lauryn (she has an elder brother Malaney) was into singing and performing. When she was in middle school, she was invited to sing the national anthem at a high school basketball game. "People went wild," says LuElle Walker-Peniston, Hill's guidance counselor at Columbia High School. "I don't think we had a winning team, but *she* was inspiring." Fans liked her rendition so much that recordings of it were played at subsequent games.

While still in high school, Hill landed a recurring role as the troubled runaway, Kira, on the TV soap *As The World Turns*. In 1993 she was cast as a difficult teen in *Sister Act 2*. There's a scene in that film in which Hill's character reels off a rap as her classmates look on. "None of that was scripted," says director Bill Duke. "That was all Lauryn. She was amazing." While in high school, she formed the rap trio the Fugees (short for refugees) with classmate Prakazrel ("Pras") Michel and Wyclef Jean, who went to a nearby school. The group's debut album, *Blunted on Reality,* sold poorly. Hill spent about a year at Columbia University but left school when the Fugees' second album, *The Score,* took off. It has sold more than 17 million copies worldwide.

But Hill wasn't satisfied. In the studio, she and Jean were "innocently competitive," gently sparring to see who could spin off the wittiest rhymes. Hill was eager to see what she could do solo. She booked a recording studio in New York City and gathered up every instrument she could think of—a harpsichord, a timpani, a trombone, a Hammond B-3 organ. She wanted to create hip-hop with live instruments.

She still needed another spark. So she flew to Jamaica. Hill is engaged to Rohan Marley, the son of reggae superstar Bob Marley and the father of her two children, one-year-old Zion and three-month-old Selah. ("We haven't been in front of a minister yet, but we will be soon," says Hill. "Our marriage right now is more a spiritual one.") As part of the extended Marley clan, she was allowed to record in the studio in the Bob Marley Museum. She says she could feel Marley's spirit as soon as she arrived. The first day there she wrote *Lost Ones.* As she began to rap, the various young Marley grandchildren who happened to be wandering around that day joined in, chanting the last word of every line. Everyone could feel the energy.

Hill says that before Rohan, she had "dysfunctional" relationships. She tried to channel the pain of those experiences into her music. "It wasn't someone writing for me; it wasn't someone telling me what I felt," says Hill, who wrote and produced the songs on *Miseducation.* "It was exactly how I felt the moment I felt it." Her maverick vision hasn't been without controversy. Late last year a group of four musicians who worked on *Miseducation* filed a suit claiming they deserved additional songwriting credits. Hill denies the allegations. Gordon Williams, who worked as the sound engineer on every song says, "Definitely the driving force behind that record was [Hill]."

Her colleagues worry about Hill's frantic pace. "She's a workaholic," says Williams. "She doesn't stop. To be a mother, two times, and then have all this stuff going on is crazy. Sometimes I just look at her and go, 'Lauryn, take it easy.'"

But Hill plans to push ahead. She says the Fugees "definitely aren't broken up," though the members have to "sit down and see where all our heads are at." She has her own production company, and she might steer it in a unique direction: "I'm looking to produce black science-fiction films." Then there's her tour. She'll perform her first solo show in the U.S. on Feb. 18 in Detroit. But she'll take time out to attend the Grammys in Los Angeles on Feb. 24, for which she has received 10 nominations. "There are kids in the audiences now who weren't born when there wasn't hip-hop," says Hill. "They grew up on it; it's part of the culture. It's a huge thing. It's not segregated anymore. It's not just in the Bronx; it's all over the world. That's why I think it's more crucial now that we, as artists, take advantage of our platform."

# 83. The Beat Goes On

Since the late 1990s, subgenres have continued to proliferate in hip-hop. While artists, such as Ja Rule and the irrepressible P-Diddy, continue to rap about diamonds, cars, and women's physical features, the bar for achieving "real" gangsta-hood floats ever higher and the utility of thuglife stories for promotional purposes remains strong, as witnessed by the recent emergence of 50 Cent. A *Rolling Stone* article entitled "No. 1 with a Bullet" described 50 Cent with the following anecdotes: "After being shot nine times, Eminem protégé 50 Cent wisely decided to invest in protection," and "When 50 signed his contract, his first purchase was crack."[1] In other developments, Nelly has put St. Louis on the rap map with his devastating (and chanted rather than rapped) party jams; Jay-Z presents a blend of bling-bling with gangsta bravado with music relying on lots of lush, old school R&B samples; and Outkast has updated the zany psychedelia of P-Funk and added a new sophistication to "progressive" rap.

The most successful and controversial turn-of-the-millennium rapper has been, however, also the first white rapper to earn some measure of respect from the "hip-hop community." Mentioned in the preceding paragraph as the mentor of 50 Cent, Eminem's career took off when Dr. Dre took him on as *his* protégé (with Dre reviving his own moribund career in the process). Despite his undeniable originality and verbal skills, Eminem (Marshall Mathers, b. 1972) has been the focus of (and

---

1. Mark Binelli, "No. 1 with a Bullet," *Rolling Stone*, February 6, 2003, 31–32. Perhaps even more chilling is the continuation of actual violence, as in the murder of Jam Master Jay (of Run-DMC) in October 2002. Rumor has it that Jay was murdered because of his association with 50 Cent.

has probably benefited from) some of the most intense media scrutiny in years, and not only because of his race. Many of his songs feature virulent homophobia and a macabre form of misogyny.[2] He has been involved repeatedly in conflicts with other pop stars, in public fights and confrontations, and in ongoing suits involving his mother and ex-wife.

---

Renee Graham's brief article appeared near the end of 2003 and addressed the latest controversy to confront Eminem. Unlike previous controversies embroiling the rapper, this one centered on an event with implications that were more difficult for Eminem to dismiss: the discovery of a tape made (probably) in 1993 in which he made racist comments about African Americans. While, in spite of their offensiveness to many, his homophobic and misogynist lyrics had actually strengthened the connections between his work and some of his hip-hop contemporaries, Eminem had foresworn use of the "N-word" because of sensitivity about his position as a white rapper. The potential revelatory force of the new tape was weakened, however, owing to the vehemence with which it was pushed by the hip-hop magazine, the *Source*. The motivations of this publication, long notable for the way in which it eschewed conventional notions of reportorial distance, were suspect in this case and were quite possibly driven by the *Source*'s own questionable agenda.

## EMINEM'S OLD WORDS AREN'T HIP-HOP'S BIGGEST PROBLEM
### *Renee Graham*

When his Grammy-winning, multimillion-selling CD, "The Marshall Mathers LP," was vilified by some as homophobic and misogynistic, Eminem responded by abusing an inflatable doll (in the guise of his then-wife, Kim) in concert and flipping off the audience after performing a duet with Elton John at the 2001 Grammy Awards.

Defiant and unapologetic, Eminem racked up sales and awards. Accusations of hatred toward women and gays only enhanced his reputation as a rebel who, as he claimed on "The Real Slim Shady," was "only giving you things you joke about with your friends inside your living room, the only difference is I got the [expletive] to say it in front of y'all, and I don't gotta be false or sugarcoat it at all."

Yet Eminem's reaction has been markedly different since being branded a racist by the hip-hop magazine the *Source*.

---

2. For a well-measured critique, see Elizabeth Keathley, "Eminem's Murder Ballads," *Echo*, 4, no. 2 (Fall 2002); available on-line at <http://www.humnet.ucla.edu/echo/volume4-issue2/keathley/index.html>

Last week, a federal judge granted Eminem's request for an injunction against the magazine, preventing its editors from releasing with its February issue a CD featuring an old recording of the then-unknown rapper making derogatory remarks about black women. Monday, however, the judge authorized the *Source* to publish as much as 20 seconds of the recording on a CD. The tape was aired at a November news conference with the *Source's* owners, David Mays and Ray "Benzino" Scott. On an untitled song, Eminem drops N-bombs and disses black women.

Eminem quickly admitted that he had made the tape, but in a statement added the song was "made out of anger, stupidity and frustration when I was a teenager," after breaking up with a black girlfriend. Then the rapper did something he never did when he was called a homophobe and misogynist—he apologized.

"So while I think common sense tells you not to judge a man by what he might have said when he was a boy, I will say it straight up: I'm sorry I said those things when I was 16." (The *Source's* editors maintain the tape was made in 1993, when Eminem was 21.)

If Eminem never showed an ounce of remorse for his anti-woman, anti-gay rhymes, that's because he knew such vitriol was so commonplace in hip-hop lyrics that it would have no effect on his seemingly bulletproof career. But as a white rapper accused of racism, Eminem, probably for the first time in his career, is worried about negative public perceptions.

Without question, Eminem, 31, is one of the best rappers in hip-hop history. With a nasal Midwestern flow as outrageous as his lyrics, Eminem's considerable talent as a rapper cannot be denied, even if his lyrics are sometimes bullying and hateful.

But being called a racist in a musical culture that remains overwhelmingly African American could shake Eminem's career. Since his 1999 major-label debut, "The Slim Shady LP," put him on the hip-hop map, he has studiously avoided racial epithets that could alienate black fans. When asked several years ago why he never used the N-word, a staple of many mainstream hip-hop recordings, in his songs, Eminem told *Rolling Stone's* Anthony DeCurtis, "That word is not even in my vocabulary. And I do black music, so out of respect, why would I put that word in my vocabulary?" Eminem has always understood that making it in hip-hop meant more than clever lyrics and juicy beats—without the acceptance of black fans, he would be as dissed and dismissed as Vanilla Ice.

In the hip-hop industry, so far only Irv Gotti, head of the Inc. (formerly Murder Inc., label home of Ja Rule and Ashanti), has publicly criticized Eminem. But hip-hop entrepreneur and patriarch Russell Simmons defended the rapper, calling his apology "sincere and forthright." And the accusations haven't hurt Eminem with the Grammy folks; he received several nominations this month for his song "Lose Yourself."

The hip-hop community's apparent reluctance to address the tape is due to the fact that the *Source's* motives are suspect. Everyone knows Benzino is an Eminem archnemesis and seems spurred only by the notion that having a white rapper gain widespread success is somehow bad for hip-hop. (He has called Eminem "the rap Hitler" and a "culture stealer.") Benzino and Mays claim to be concerned with exposing "influences corrupting hip-hop," but there are far more serious issues—such as a lack of creativity, obsessions with wealth, and yes, anti-woman, anti-gay rhetoric—facing the community than the contents of a scratchy old tape.

Eminem has acknowledged the tape's veracity and has apologized. It's time to move on. Perhaps when the *Source* becomes as concerned with the state of rap music as with playing out a strange, personal vendetta with its own racist undertones, then the magazine may be more successful in exposing and ridding hip-hop of its corrupting influences.

# 84. From Indie to Alternative to . . . Seattle?

At the close of the 1980s, no earth-shattering developments appeared to be on the horizon for indie rock. The "indie" genre label was proving increasingly capacious, including everything from the "goth" of the Cure to the "dream pop" of My Bloody Valentine to bands bearing a more obvious allegiance to punk. In fact, articles attempting to explain and identify the almost bewildering multiplication of subgenres appeared frequently throughout the 1990s.[1] Yet, in the late 1980s and early 1990s, an indie scene that had been developing in Seattle around the local label Sub Pop displayed a new fusion of musical styles and a new alliance of social groups and subcultural symbols that would ultimately remap and reorient the entire idea of indie rock. Around this time, a new term, "alternative," was increasingly substituted for "indie," indicating a turn toward populism and a rapprochement with non-indie rock practices, both musically (through more obvious "pop" music influences) and institutionally (through bands moving from indie record labels to majors).

The caption under the title of a 1990 report on Seattle by Dave DiMartino—"Record companies are flocking to the Great Northwest, signing bands like crazy and hoping to find the Next Big Thing"—sums up the article fairly well. While addressing the questions, "Why here? Why now?," DiMartino captures a moment of transition in the Seattle scene, as bands formerly affiliated with Sub Pop began to sign with major record companies. This article reveals that the term "grunge" had already entered circulation, describing both the overdriven guitar sound characteristic of Seattle postpunk bands and the dress style of faded flannel and torn jeans. Amusing in retrospect are the passages that ponder whether local bands like Nirvana will "make it." In the course of such ponderings, DiMartino introduces his readers to Soundgarden, Alice in Chains, and Mother Love Bone (which contained two members who would later form part of Pearl Jam)—groups that would achieve

---

1. See, for example, Jim Sullivan, "The Age of Hyphen-Rock," *Chicago Tribune* (October 13, 1991), Sec. 13, 26–27 (a good overview of the splintering of rock genres); David Browne, "Turn that @#!% Down," *Entertainment Weekly* (August 21, 1992): 16–25 (describes the many varieties/subgenres of alternative); Neil Strauss, "Forget Pearl Jam: Alternative Rock Lives," *New York Times*, March 2, 1997 (a brief introduction to the many subcategories that function as alternatives to alternative); and Ben Ratliff, "A New Heavy-Metal Underground Emerges," *New York Times*, February 15, 1998 (a taxonomy of metal subgenres).

national prominence in less than two years—as well as bands, such as the Young Fresh Fellows, who have now been swallowed by the sands of time.[2]

# A SEATTLE SLEW
## *Dave DiMartino*

San Francisco moved to Oregon and Washington," says Bob Pfeifer, director of A&R of Epic Records. "The whole thing is psychedelic. You can see it in the T-shirts and the tie-dye. It's all hippies. These are the hippies' kids or something."

That's just one of several theories making the rounds these days about Seattle, a city that until recently was famous for its rainy weather and inexpensive real estate. But in the past two years, Seattle has become a regular music mecca—a haven for record-company executives who regularly fly in from Los Angeles and New York to compete for the privilege of signing such bands as Soundgarden, the Posies, Alice in Chains, Mother Love Bone and the Screaming Trees. And the labels are coming because amid the city's lush greenery, they smell money.

"I talked to somebody at CBS in New York last October," says one woman who works for a Seattle artist-management firm, "And he said, 'You're from Seattle. Just find me *any* Seattle band. I'm *dying* to sign a Seattle band—I'm so mad I didn't sign Alice in Chains.'"

It's a situation that is hardly unprecedented in rock's trend-ridden history—remember San Francisco, Detroit, Boston, New York, Cleveland, Athens, Austin, Minneapolis. But the big question in Seattle at the moment is: *Why here? Why now?*

Producer Terry Date—who has had a hand in the careers of most of Seattle's better-known bands, starting with Metal Church in 1984 and continuing to the most recent albums by Soundgarden and Mother Love Bone—believes one reason local groups are attracting so much attention is that they are unique. "They're not in a major music market, so they don't follow any sort of formula at all," Date says. "They don't look at something on MTV and say, 'We're gonna look like that.' They pretty much find their style from the records they listen to—which are typically very underground.

"On top of that" Date adds, "the weather isn't always that great, and they sit in their garages a lot."

For such a hotbed of talent, Seattle doesn't offer its artists much choice. Aside from garage-land, only a handful of small clubs—the Vogue, the Central and the Backstage—are options open to bands itching to play live. "The funny thing is," says Charles Cross, editor and publisher of the local music paper *The Rocket*, "if you go to New Orleans, you go to Tipitina's. If you go to New York, I guess you have CBGB. And in Los Angeles there's Club Lingerie. There isn't that kind of club in Seattle. Our club scene has been horrible for years."

Instead, the driving force behind the Seattle scene has been a record label, Sub Pop. With a roster that includes Mudhoney, Nirvana and Tad, Sub Pop has defined the Seattle

---

2. For views of the Seattle scene after grunge broke nationally, see Michael Azzerad, "Grunge City," *Rolling Stone*, April 16, 1992, 43–48; and John Book, "Seattle Heavy," *Goldmine* (April 17, 1992): 46–54.

sound—loud, fast, grungy rock & roll. "And all these people were friends," Sub Pop co-owner Jonathan Poneman says of the bands on his label. "This is a small community of people, and when one person got into Scratch Acid, everybody got into Scratch Acid. When one person got into Big Black, everybody got into Big Black."

Two former Sub Pop bands, Soundgarden and Screaming Trees, have been snapped up by major labels (A&M and Epic, respectively), and CBS Records has reportedly been negotiating a pressing-and-distribution deal that would put Sub Pop acts Mudhoney and Tad in the same Sam Goody racks holding the latest by Fleetwood Mac and New Kids on the Block. "We want it to happen," says Poneman. "We're trying to make it happen, because we want to be able to get the records out there." But, he adds, "whether or not there will be full cooperation in terms of our agenda, and whether or not we will be able to acquiesce to the things they're asking for are still things that remain to be seen."

Indeed, one has to wonder whether such key label artists as Mudhoney or Nirvana could cross over into the Nineties mainstream without seriously compromising their sound. "I don't think we're really easy enough for a lot of people to swallow," says Mudhoney's Mark Arm, a former member of Seattle's legendary (and now defunct) Green River. "Motorhead never made it beyond a certain point, and they're one of the greatest bands on Earth."

But Bob Pfeifer, who signed both Metal Church and Screaming Trees to Epic Records, thinks some Seattle bands have long-term potential. "Screaming Trees are capable of selling 100,000 records," says Pfeifer. "Whether they will or not is another question. Three albums from now, I don't know *how* many albums they'll be able to sell—maybe a million. That's not the pressure I put on the band or the way I structured the deal. Everybody will be happy at a certain level, which allows the band to have the freedom and time to grow."

But major-label interest in Seattle hasn't been limited to one very hip record label that has so far seen great press coverage but less-than-great overall sales. Nastymix Records, the local label that features the best-selling rapper Sir Mix-a-Lot, has been approached by all the majors regarding a potential buy-in, according to Ramon Wells, the label's national promotion director. "Even [Island Records chairman] Chris Blackwell flew in to talk with us," Wells says. But with one platinum and one gold album already, Wells adds, "we're perfectly content with where we are now."

Then there's PopLlama Products, a label helmed by Conrad Uno that has released the work of Seattle's Young Fresh Fellows and the Posies, among others. Both bands are now on different labels, both are miles away from the grunge that Sub Pop has glorified, and both are essential components of the Seattle scene.

The Fellows, as they're called, are enormously talented and extremely unfocused. Together, the two attributes are likely to confuse any market-conscious A&R person. The Fellows' most recent records for Frontier are now getting major-label distribution, thanks to a deal the California label signed with RCA Records last year. But so far, that linkup has been of little benefit to the Fellows, and they are pursuing other options.

"I guess we're finally making an effort to get signed to a major label," says vocalist Scott McCaughey. "I hate to say that, because it's always been totally anti-everything the Fellows were about. But I guess it's gotten to the point where we've been doing it for six or seven years, I've got a kid now, and we're thinking a little bit more about how rough it is to make a living. We're trying to figure out a way that we can be musicians and make a little bit more money, so we can live comfortably, because for the last three years we've just been musicians. We quit our jobs because we went on tour too much."

The Fellows recently hired former Concrete Blonde manager Frank Volpe to help them firm up a deal with a major and are now ready to "seriously try to step up" their career.

At the same time, the Fellows' former manager, Terry Morgan, recently inked a lucrative deal with Geffen Records' new label DGC for the Seattle popsters the Posies. And in the end, the city's more accessible bands—like the Posies, Alice in Chains and Mother Love Bone—may prove to be more attractive to the major labels than Sub Pop's unique brand of metallic grunge. All three of those bands have recently released their major-label debuts, and you don't have to be an A&R man to imagine their music getting played on the radio.

Meanwhile, one of the best-selling albums in Seattle's hipper record stores these days is a compilation called *Here Ain't the Sonics*. The album tells the story of the first wave of great Northwest rock—the Sonics, the Kingsmen, "Louie Louie." But the artists who perform on the album—the Young Fresh Fellows, Screaming Trees, the Mono Men—are part of the city's new generation.

Terry Date sees many parallels between the Seattle of 1990 and the one to which *Here Ain't the Sonics* pays tribute. "These bands are coming from all over the state," Date says, "and they're all playing a fairly similar type of music, attitude-wise. Especially the Sub Pop stuff. It's all real *garagey*, just like 'Louie Louie,' the perfect example of that era.

"It's really cool," continues Date, "because these guys do whatever they want—and the labels don't really know what they're trying to get, they just know people are buying it. And it leaves it wide open for us."

# 85. Riot Girl

The Riot Girl (or "Riot Grrrl") movement developed from indie-punk institutions, such as fanzines; indie record companies; and the do-it-yourself attitude toward performance, recording, and promotion developed in the post-punk hardcore scenes. To this foundation was added a second-wave feminist critique of the limits of patriarchy for females who would rock or otherwise participate in aspects of popular music formerly assumed to be male preserves. With music based in hardcore punk, the musicians associated with Riot Grrrl adopted an "in-your-face" approach to expressions of femininity and a confrontational attitude toward presumed male intransigence (though it must be added that the musicians most commonly considered to be part of the Riot Girl movement often resisted being characterized as "Riot Girls" or as part of any movement).[1]

The following written statements come from the fanzine *Bikini Kill* and provide background about the involvement of band members from

---

1. See, for example, the liner notes to *Bikini Kill: The C.D. Version of the First Two Records* (1994), especially the section written by Tobi Vail.

Olympia, Washington, and Washington, D.C., in groups, such as Bikini Kill and Bratmobile, while illustrating the manifesto-like approach of much of the writing in the fanzine. The opening essay of the fanzine, entitled "Lame Lame So Very Lame," lists 10 typical sayings that men use "in order . . . to maintain the unequal power distribution of male over female." To do this "without looking like assholes . . . they must find more subtle ways of discounting and discouraging you." These sayings include

1. You take things too seriously. You are paranoid.
2. You are exclusionary and alienating to men.
3. You know, some women manage to "go beyond" sexism.
4. You are not *really* a feminist because . . .
5. You are just bored. You are inventing the problem by talking about it so much.
6. You are just trying to be political.
7. What you are doing is sexist to men.
8. Don't worry—be happy!!!!!!
9. But I know a girl who lied about being raped . . .
10. Complain, complain, complain. . . . At least you don't have it as bad as

    a. women used to
    b. people of color
    c. women in other countries[2]

Although it isn't evident from this list, one of the more interesting aspects of the Riot Grrrl critique is how it links gender oppression to the operations of capitalism, a critique that features prominently in the brief excerpts that follow. While recordings of musicians associated with the Riot Grrrl movement never achieved the sales figures of some of the male alternative bands, their militant approach did heighten awareness of how limited female participation in rock music had been until that time and of how these limits were linked to broader, institutionalized manifestations of patriarchal authority.

## RIOT GRRRL
### Bikini Kill

---

RIOT GRRRL . . . Believe in me!

"Once upon a time . . ." last spring ('91), Molly and Allison (Girl Germs, Bratmobile) went to Washington DC, shook things up and got shook up, and connected with this radsoulsister Jen Smith who wanted to start this girl network and fanzine called Girl Riot. (This was also inspired by the Cinco de Mayo riots occurring in her neighborhood at the time.) So that summer a bunch of us Olympia kids (Bratmobile and Bikini Kill) lived in D.C. to make something happen with our friends there. Tobi (Bikini Kill, Jigsaw) had been talking about doing weekly zines in the spirit of angry grrrl zine-scene, and then one restless night, Molly

---

2. "Lame Lame So Very Lame," *Bikini Kill* (July 1991).

*Source:* "riot grrrl," *Bikini Kill* (July 1991).

made this little fanzine stating events in the girl lives of the Oly-D.C. scene connection—and Riot Grrrl was born. Kathleen (Bikini Kill) took it a step further in that she wanted to have weekly D.C. grrrl meetings too, to connect with and see what's up with the grrrls in D.C. With a lot of effort and organizing on the part of Kathleen and other D.C. and Oly grrrls, weekly Riot Grrrl meetings started happening at the Positive Force house. It was great, like 20 girls came and we talked about female scene input (or lack of it) and how we could support each other, etc. And the fanzines kept coming out each week with certain contributors like Jen Smith, Kathleen, Molly, Allison, Tobi, Tiffany, Christina, Ne Sk8 Rock and Billy. And the coolest thing is that even though many of us went back to Olympia, the meetings and zines are still happening. (Soon Bikini Kill are moving to D.C. and Molly and Allison will be back and forth between Olympia and D.C. til forever.)

Now Kathleen and Allison (and anyone else who wants to) are starting Riot Grrrl records and press. Allison is gonna do the records/tapes and Kathleen is gonna do the press/mail order stuff, which will include grrrl fanzines. We want to distribute fanzines by girls all over the country. So if you're a girl and you make a fanzine, you can send Kathleen (in D.C.) a good *flat* unstapled copy of your zine so she can xerox it, list it in the mail order catalogue and mail it to whoever orders it. We don't really have much cash so we can't pay you for your zine, but we plan to give each contributor copies of other girls' zines. Cool deal. This can be a way to support and participate in a cool girl network nationwide (or internet?)

With this whole Riot Grrrl thing, we're not trying to make money or get famous; we're trying to do something important, to network with grrrls all over, to make changes in our own lives and the lives of other girls. There is no concrete vision or expectation. We Riot Grrrls aren't aligning ourselves with any one position or consensus, because in all likelihood we don't agree on everything. One concrete thing we do agree on so far is that it's cool/fun to have a place where we can safely and supportively confront, express ourselves, and bring up issues that are important to us.

So if you want to be on the mailing list, please send a postcard (or your fanzine flat copy) with your address on it to:

RIOT GRRRL
c/o The Embassy
3217 19th St. NW
Washington DC 20010

Riot Grrl is . . .

BECAUSE us girls crave records and books and fanzines that speak to US, that WE feel included in and can understand in our own ways.

BECAUSE we wanna make it easier for girls to see/hear each other's work so that we can share strategies and criticize-applaud each other.

BECAUSE we must take over the means of production in order to create our own meanings.

BECAUSE viewing our work as being connected to our girlfriends-politics-real lives is essential if we are gonna figure out how what we are doing impacts, reflects, perpetuates, or DISRUPTS the status quo.

BECAUSE we recognize fantasies of Instant Macho Gun Revolution as impractical lies meant to keep us simply dreaming instead of becoming our dreams AND THUS seek to create revolution in our own lives every single day by envisioning and creating alternatives to the bullshit christian capitalist way of doing things.

BECAUSE we want and need to encourage and be encouraged, in the face of all our own insecurities, in the face of beergutboy rock that tells us we can't play our instruments, in the face of "authorities" who say our bands/'zines/etc are the worst in the U.S. and who attribute any validation/success of our work to girl bandwagon hype.

BECAUSE we don't wanna assimilate to someone else's (Boy) standards of what is or isn't "good" music or punk rock or "good" writing AND THUS need to create forums where we can recreate, destroy and define our own visions.

BECAUSE we are unwilling to falter under claims that we are reactionary "reverse sexists" and not the truepunkrocksoulcrusaders that WE KNOW we really are.

BECAUSE we know that life is much more than physical survival and are patently aware that the punk rock "you can do anything" idea is crucial to the coming angry grrrl rock revolution which seeks to save the psychic and cultural lives of girls and women everywhere, according to their own terms, not ours.

BECAUSE we are interested in creating non-hierarchical ways of being AND making music, friends, and scenes based on communication + understanding, instead of competition + good/bad categorizations.

BECAUSE doing/reading/seeing/hearing cool things that validate and challenge us can help us gain the strength and sense of community that we need in order to figure out how bullshit like racism, able-bodieism, eyeism, speciesism, classism, thinism, sexism, anti-semitism and heterosexism figures in our own lives.

BECAUSE we see fostering and supporting girl scenes and girl artists of all kinds as integral to this process.

BECAUSE we hate capitalism in all its forms and see our main goal as sharing information and staying alive, instead of making profits or being cool according to traditional standards.

BECAUSE we are angry at a society that tells us Girl = Dumb, Girl = Bad, Girl = Weak.

BECAUSE we are unwilling to let our real and valid anger be diffused and/or turned against us via the internalization of sexism as witnessed in girl/girl jealousies and self defeating girltype behaviors.

BECAUSE self defeating behaviors (like fucking boys without condoms, drinking to excess, ignoring truesoul girlfriends, belittling ourselves and other girls, etc. . .) would not be so easy if we lived in communities where we felt loved and wanted and valued.

BECAUSE I believe with my holeheartmindbody that girls constitute a revolutionary soul force that can, and will, change the world for real.

# 86. Grunge Turns to *Scrunge*

While the move of postpunk music toward mainstream popularity excited rock fans who longed for an "oppositional" quality in their music, as well as music critics who welcomed music that highlighted interesting sociological issues, it also occasioned a crisis within the remnants of the indie scene itself. This mainstreaming of bohemianism threatened the

indie-punk notion that certain kinds of consumerism might somehow resist commodification. If this reaction of indie fans sounds suspiciously
reminiscent of that old modernist credo "if it's popular, it must be bad,"
then that's because the arguments about authenticity versus commerce
that developed in the wake of Dylan's "going the rock & roll route" were
never fully vanquished. As Eric Weisbard states in the article that follows
(in a section not reprinted here)

> On some basic level, the fundamental unresolved issue here—one that artists and fans
> alike have to work out individually—is not major labels versus indies, but the extent to
> which rock gains in glory by seeking or attaining popularity.[1]

The signs in the transformation of indie include (as was indicated
earlier) the signing of an increasing number of bands by major record
companies, the airing of indie-alternative videos on MTV, and the emergence of *scrunge*—music by bands that took elements of grunge-
alternative's sound, but left its indie values behind.[2]

Eric Weisbard, for many years a critic with *Spin*, the *Village Voice*, and
other publications, is now senior program director in the education department at the Experience Music Project in Seattle. The article of his
that is reprinted here describes a moment three years after the release of
*Nevermind* by Nirvana during which time numerous alternative acts
reached a large audience of rock fans. The question "alternative to
what?" arises (both for Weisbard and other critics) when the idea of a
style's marginality (and oppositionality) remains central to its appeal
even as the style has been accepted by the mainstream. The strength of
this essay lies in the historical perspective and broad view that Weisbard
brings to his discussion of alternative rock and the specificity provided by
several anecdotes of what happens when bands move (or contemplate
moving) from indie to major record labels. Weisbard clarifies the links to
prior bohemian movements while not being uncritical, noting the privileged place within alternative music of what he calls "white guy angst"
even though many critics (and fans) included certain types of hip-hop
within the category. This article also captures a moment when major
record companies had begun to grant alternative acts the same type of
creative freedom allowed to rock bands in the late 1960s, hiring young
experts in much the same fashion that companies in the 1960s hired
"house hippies." In other ways, though, 1990s alternative represents the
inverse of 1960s rock: As Weisbard notes,"Alternative strives clunkily for
the massification of hip, as boomer rock was the hipification of mass."[3]
This moment was doomed to be short-lived: In a year-end report for *Spin*
magazine reflecting on developments in popular music for 1995 (only a

---

1. Eric Weisbard, "Over & Out: Indie Rock Values in the Age of Alternative Million Sellers," *Village Voice Rock & Roll Quarterly* (Summer 1994): 19.

2. Eric Weisbard, "The Year in Music: The Great Pretenders," *Spin* (January 1996): 50.

3. "Over & Out," 17.

year later), Weisbard echoed the sentiments of many critics when he pronounced the "indie" part of the "indie-alternative" movement all but
dead.[4]

## OVER & OUT: INDIE ROCK VALUES IN THE AGE
## OF ALTERNATIVE MILLION SELLERS
### *Eric Weisbard*

*Indier Than Thou*, a New Jersey zine is called, and it's an attitude I can tell you all about.
Where'd I learn to care and sneer at the same time? From [Alex] Chilton, Lou Reed, the
Feelies, Paul Westerberg, and dozens more, some brimming with energy and hope like
Hüsker Dü and the Pixies, others prematurely jaded, like Dinosaur Jr. and Sonic Youth.
Indie rock, it was called, though some of the heroes, like R.E.M. and X, had major-label
deals or distribution from very near the beginning, and many of the ancestors, like the Velvet Underground and the Stooges, were never on small or "independent" record labels at
all. Then too, these were the '80s, rock's postpunk interregnum. Smart, nonmetal guitar
bands were a corporate taboo, at best signed, pressured to "broaden" their sound with an
outside producer for that crucial mainstream appeal, then left to flop with no promo bud-
get. In retrospect, the independence of a Big Black was about as coveted as the Gaza Strip.

But for those who were part of the indie rock network in those years—the musicians,
label staffs, college radio DJs, zine writers, club workers, Drunks With Guns collectors—
both pride and scars remain. Pride in creating a form of rock that could thrive on volun-
tarism, subsistence, and obscurity, where the distance between fanship and participation
was no distance at all, so one could be a consumer without the traditional associations of
gross commodification, audience passivity, and massness. Indie rockers essentially formed
a cultural community, people whose attitudes toward consumption give them an oppositional identity similar (if weaker and less widely recognized) to that provided for others by
race, gender, class, or sexuality.

In many ways indie resembled '80s radical movements, especially in its ingrained conviction that real power over the mainstream was unattainable, so the only workable model
for resistance had to be small-scale change and self-transformation—the personal as political. Putting out a record by a friend's band that you loved but knew ordinary people would
never like was indie's neighborhood recycling project. And such attitudes changed the nature of rock. Punk still required major labels so the Sex Pistols could at least spit in EMI's
face. But indie rockers were content to discover a garage obscurity like "The Hunch" by
Mad Mike & the Maniacs, or feud with Gerard Cosloy in the college-radio trade magazine
*CMJ*, or yell out a request for a b-side at a hipster shrine like Maxwell's and briefly convince
the band struggling onstage it was legendary.

---

4. Weisbard, "The Year in Music," 48–54. By late 1997, Weisbard could offer a more definite eulogy:
"Ultimately American postpunk insisted on rock at a human scale; that's why it dissolved when major-
label muscle was put behind it" (Eric Weisbard, "The Me, Myself, and I Decade," *Spin* (December 1997):
157). Of course, the physical demise of grunge-alternative's biggest star, Kurt Cobain (1967–94), did nothing to slow the dissolution of the indie ethos. For an exploration of the relationship between Cobain's
suicide and indie ideology, see Dave Marsh, "Live Through This," *Rock 'n' Roll Confidential* (May 1994).

*Source*: Eric Weisbard, "Over & Out: Indie Rock Values in the Age of Alternative Million Sellers," *Village
Voice Rock & Roll Quarterly*, Summer 1994, pp. 15–19. Used by permission of Eric Weisbard.

The best account of these years to date is Gina Arnold's *Route 666: On the Road to Nirvana*, a book whose subtitle explains what happened next. R.E.M.'s rise had convinced indie to believe in itself; Nirvana's explosion onto the charts convinced the rest of the world to believe in indie. Artists who've never made any pretense of accessibility, from Daniel Johnston to the Boredoms, get signed by Atlantic and Warner Bros., who, reversing the assumptions of the postpunk interregnum, presume that fanzine followings indicate a basis for wider popularity, not hopeless obscurantism. The same labels hire A&R people with indie label and college radio backgrounds. MTV proves enormously willing to give "Buzz Clip" exposure to artists like the Breeders or Green Day, who would previously have been dismissed as too subtle or obnoxiously adolescent.

Rock, these last couple of years, has in effect been revised. A new canon now gives marginal bohemians like Big Star equal status with long popular favorites. Rock stars no longer make a pageant of their power, as modesty and constant allusions to little-known underground bands become required decorum. At the level of *ideology* as much as music, today's alternative marketplace now offers a large-scale, corporate-sponsored version of indie rock. Green Day appears on Letterman the night Belly does Leno; Lollapalooza's the only sure money-making ticket in the business, apart from boomer nostalgia tours like the Eagles, who sold out five nights in San Francisco the week Big Star played. The word *mainstream* has virtually disappeared, even if the mainstream hasn't.

But as a result, the scars of the indie-only years have started to manifest themselves. In a recent issue of Chicago's indier-than-thou zine *The Baffler* headlined "Alternative To What?" Tom Frank writes: "Now we watch with interest as high-powered executives offer contracts to bands they have seen only once, college radio playlists become the objects of intense corporate scrutiny, and longstanding independent labels are swallowed whole in a colossal belch of dollars and receptions. Now *Rolling Stone* magazine makes pious reference to the pioneering influence of bands like Big Black and Mission of Burma whose records they ignored when new." Can the indie values of smallness, marginality, antipop as a basis for community formation and everything else, really serve as a blueprint for '90s mainstream rock? Isn't that a contradiction in terms, or something even worse—a betrayal of values?

Such questions are starting to seem inescapable. Kurt Cobain kills himself in a manner that indicts his own celebrity. *Maximumrocknroll*, bible to the hardcore punk scene that's always been indie's dumber big brother, runs a cover with an image of a man putting a gun in his mouth and the caption "Major Labels: Some Of Your Friends Are Already This Fucked." *Sassy*, which has been giving glossy coverage to the riot grrrl movement since practically before riot grrrl existed, gets an angry letter from Bratmobile's Molly Neuman. "Did you actually think the majority of your readers would know many indie labels or zines? . . . I think I speak for many girl bands (I'm in one) and punks when I say we don't want your attention or support. Stick to exploiting models." And [in] the next issue, Jenny Toomey of Tsunami responds to Neuman with a letter denouncing "an alternative community that claims to be inclusive and yet remains so enamored of the 'fringes' . . . that its main concern is not communication or accessibility but, ultimately cliquishness."

To give Frank credit as more than a subcultural purist, his *Baffler* piece recognizes a crucial dialectic at work. "Consumerism's traditional claim to be the spokesman for our inchoate disgust with consumerism was hemorrhaging credibility, and independent rock, with its Jacobin 'authenticity' obsession, had just the things capital required." Is this brave new alternative world creepy, even for those of us who understand that we're all better off that Elvis Presley got signed to a major from Sun Records after a few promising indie singles? (Today RCA would have Sam Phillips keep producing Elvis, then publicize his refusal to compromise.) Of course. I think the indie credo of fatalistic marginality is badly outdated in a Clintonian era where power is there for the taking. I was rooting for Big Star to seize the day on Leno. And I still resented having to share the live reunion with a crowd of neo-phytes. Was I being elitist?

## Alternative Nation

Trent Reznor of Nine Inch Nails is bored with the grunge look. "I guess the statement was, 'Look this is honest; we don't need to pretend we're rock stars and all this shit,'" he told Moon Unit Zappa in a recent issue of *Raygun*. "I think that mindset is a good one . . . it killed off the Bon Jovis and those type of bands with our new earnest attitude. But that's become contrived now. . . . [W]hen I see a show, I want to be entertained. I'd rather see David Bowie/Ziggy Stardust on stage than that guy that just pumped gas for me."

Reznor is reenacting an almost hallowed argument, the sort of thing Depeche Mode might have said about R.E.M. clones 10 years ago; that is, the rock/pop split that drove primarily English bands in the New Wave era in the direction of dance rhythms, polished production, and visual style, while American outfits by and large clung belligerently to their street clothes and guitars. It went without saying, throughout the 1980s, that bands who went the former route would sign to major labels and, escaping the postpunk media ghettoes, be seen on MTV and heard on radio stations that called the music "modern rock." Indie bands on SST or Homestead, on the other hand, mostly got to claim the mantle of rock integrity; opposition to mass culture and unbridled experimentalism if you bought into the rhetoric; a space for privileged white guy angst to reign unchecked if you didn't.

In truth, a variety of stylish outfits found idiosyncratic ways to flourish during the postpunk interregnum with one foot in indie's door—New Order, Joan Jett, Violent Femmes, the Beastie Boys, R.E.M., and the Smiths, to name a few. By the time of 1991's first Lollapalooza, conceived by the leader of one such band, Jane's Addiction, and a break-through moment for another, Nine Inch Nails, such artists were cementing a new genre, "alternative," that seemed destined to heal the rock/pop split. (At the same time, a generation of former speed metal bands on indie labels, led by Metallica, staged a coup in the metal world, dooming the big hair and spandex crowd.) Even today, the indie guitar bands in pop abundance are only one musical subculture among many, especially if you set aside groups like Green Day, Bad Religion, and the Offspring, whose allegiances are to the separate hard-core set. Kurt Cobain, Sub Pop, K, and the appropriation of the indie aesthetic are hardly the only story in alternative 1994.

Nevertheless, it's Henry Rollins, once of Black Flag, and Sonic Youth's Thurston Moore who are MTV's favorite alternative faces. U2 act more like Negativland and less like Springsteen with every new album, realizing that the essence of rock's moral leadership has shifted. Lollapalooza '94, looking to regain its credibility, first begs Nirvana to appear, then in their absence features an indie-identified lineup including Smashing Pumpkins, the Breeders, L7, Nick Cave, and the Boredoms. *Sassy* would rather write about Fugazi than the Cure. Kurt Cobain is deemed the John Lennon of his generation. Why? Because of indie's status as the emblem of integrity, its ownership of rock's new yardstick: resistance to mass culture. Thus, it wasn't until "Smells Like Teen Spirit," when (mostly former) indie rockers started receiving media exposure without being pressured to revise their sound or stance, and the walls of the post-punk ghetto came down, that the interregnum ended and alternative came to be fully accepted as the new rock.

In trying to fuse modern rock's cynicism about traditional rock sounds and imagery with indie rock's commitment to modesty and a notion of the underground, alternative has discovered that you can't get by without that most traditional and immodest of animals: the rock star. Only given that selling records, exerting power, and reveling in stardom are all etiquette no-no's now, celebrity can only be seen as an aesthetic embarrassment—when the Pet Shop Boys sang "How Can You Expect To Be Taken Seriously?" did they have any idea how much further the kill rock star creed would take it? The role of the rock star is one of many crucial questions that alternative's emergence has left unanswered. What does the indie onslaught of new guitar bands do to modern rock's perfectly valid efforts to push the music away from sounding like the umpteenth version of AOR? Why are seemingly all the new gods of alternative white men? Must our integrity heroes be so cartoonish?

As an oppositional movement grounded in the tension between small-scale consumption and mass culture, indie has proven unable to articulate a cause that goes beyond remaining pure of outside influence—a nearly impossible position for a megastar to maintain. Yet, without megastars able to translate indie values into something socially meaningful, alternative loses whatever shred of justification it had left. All that remains is to wince as the process turns indie rhetoric into the worst possible parody of itself. Like the Bud Dry "reach for an alternative—Bud Dry" radio commercials, heard on modern rock stations, where an alternative musician spouts "some bands strive for artistic integrity and expressing their free creative identities. Us, hey, we just want free beer."

Eddie Vedder, Rollins, Perry Farrell, Cobain, Michael Stipe, and yes, Trent Reznor if he'd like, ultimately became sacrificial lambs for alternative's failure of self-definition. Their ability to hold up the tent allows dozens of other bands to flourish within, but what sort of a movement can survive by so thoroughly ripping apart its leaders? Mike Dirnt of Green Day said of Cobain: "To some extent he's like Jesus to me. He died for my sins, so I could get signed to a major label?"

Still, alternagods can't help seeming desperately ridiculous. They've become mass men. Vedder ostentatiously refuses to shoot a video for the new Pearl Jam album. Rollins is invited to *The Tonight Show*, not to perform "Liar" but to sit on the couch and talk with Jay. Hardly the sort to chicken out like Alex Chilton, he shows and the two cover Black Flag, Rollins's free-jazz fanship and poetry readings (is the guy a beatnik or what?) and then the big question: "So you haven't compromised at all?" "Zero."

## Major or Minor?

Back in Indieland, Steve Albini starts another *Baffler* essay imagining major labels as a big long trench "filled with runny, decaying shit" that bands desiring contracts have to swim across. Then back. Mac, from Superchunk, is a little more reasonable, though his conclusion is exactly the same. "It just makes you feel that the bands are there to be used by someone else. Their bottom line is not the music." On Merge, his own label, of late grown large enough to employ full-time staff, "you're totally in control of everything. You know where your money's going, because it's you and not some far-reaching department of a company you don't know how big it really is." Why should he take an advance that's a loan, not a gift, spend more money to record than he needs to, and ultimately face the prospect of being dropped? Even the traditional reason for signing to a major—better distribution—makes less sense now that the chain stores have started to stock product from independent distributors like Merge's Touch and Go.

Major labels could supply the promotional capital to help Superchunk sell five or 10 times what they do already—a more than respectable 30,000 copies of the new *Foolish* in its first two months out. But then, to Mac, "the popular bands have usually been the crappiest bands." I wonder, though: let's say Mac did sign, took the advance, burned his bridges to the indie world, recorded with an outside producer, worried about getting dropped, thought about how to make Superchunk translate to the people outside his secure constituency. Isn't it possible that after five nearly identical albums he'd start making the best music of his life? Worked for Green Day.

A few days later, I'm talking all this over with Kim Deal, who made a similar jump between the first and second Breeders albums. She explodes into laughter at Mac's reticence. "Fucking turn up your vocals, please! I hate it when people make things so difficult that they actually don't work 'cause they're being so *indie*. That was one of the things recording *Last Splash*. I had to constantly remind myself, turn up the fucking vocals. I tried to do that so I wouldn't sound like this wimp indie band. Really, I thought it was cowardly not to." For Deal, a gold album has changed little in her life. "We're not that big." She contrasts herself to Hammer, whose album marketing plans once included Saturday cartoons and ads for Kentucky Fried Chicken. "With the Breeders it's like, 'Here's an article in *Spin*, do you want to do it?'"

Eddie Roeser of Urge Overkill, a band that started tweaking the indie rock staidness Trent Reznor hates, caused serious bad feelings when it left Touch and Go for Geffen, basically concurs that signing to a major isn't necessarily stepping in shit. "At this stage of the game, if you have something that has some merit, the record company is not going to say well, we're not releasing it, it's not polished enough. You have to go back and record it again. They're not stupid. They're not going to fuck with us. And they haven't, at all. The real worrying starts when you've sold a million records, and they want you to sell a million records again, and maybe the band doesn't." Roeser knows what he's talking about—Urge Overkill spent time touring with Pearl Jam.

The Breeders and Urge Overkill are in the closest thing to an ideal position the alternative age has to offer. They've met the artistic challenge of reaching outside the hipoisie, while avoiding the point where artists are forced into the role of public figures. With their indie backgrounds, neither Deal nor Roeser, it's clear, feels comfortable aspiring to more. It's as if Grand Funk Railroad, instead of hoping to supplant the Rolling Stones, expressed a desire to remain cool like the New York Dolls. Roeser may play the star onstage and in videos, but he's careful to mention that he was just talking to Spiral Stairs of Pavement about how embarrassing it is to meet "these kids who really think you're a rock star. And in your own mind you're definitely not one. And you don't know how to treat someone who thinks that about you." "Who wants to wear spandex?" says Deal. "To communicate in a festival setting, you've got to do those moves and things. You just feel dumb. 'All right everybody, let's rock and roll!' No way. I'll do something if I think it makes sense musically."

## Power? Pop?

Indie rock's cultural community most closely resembles two earlier eras when even smaller groups of musicians and consumer cultists developed subcultures that would eventually be diverted away from them. The hot jazz fans of the 1930s and 1940s maintained a rigorous distinction between "true" and "commercial" jazz, favoring small combo jams and Dixieland arrangements, even after their comrade Benny Goodman brought the mainstream a lot closer to the real thing by ushering in swing. The beat generation, who emerged in the later 1940s and early 1950s, later found themselves unexpectedly spawning beatniks—the six years *On the Road* waited to be published (to enormous media onslaught, from which Kerouac never recovered) is not unlike the gap between *New Day Rising* and *Nevermind*.

The fate of these predecessors offers interesting lessons. Jazz cultists, mostly white, would eventually be challenged by beboppers who could supplement their consumption-based ethic of oppositionality with the politics of race—much as women and queers seem to be doing within indie rock today. The beats, demoralized and fragmented by commercialization, watched hippies willingly use the media to gain social influence. Will a new wave of alternative, sufficiently distanced from its indie rock sources, eventually achieve the same mediated flamboyance?

It would be specious to argue that the last few years have shown that indie rock's qualities cannot survive on major labels. Even a cursory list of emergent artists—Nirvana,

P.M. Dawn, My Bloody Valentine, A Tribe Called Quest, P. J. Harvey, Pavement—shows how, if anything, "alternative" has opened up possibilities within rock to women, blacks, the English, and others mostly left out of the Homestead/SST years, without in the least penalizing bands of determinedly indie sensibilities. Ironically, many of the more close-minded indie types, like former Amphetamine Reptile acts Helmet and Surgery, have proven the most irresistible to the majors, since as arrogant metallic white boys they're hardly a huge divergence.

But the clash between indie values and the realities of an alternative-rock obsessed pop world are real—and almost impossible to resolve. Why should Mac risk mutilating his fan base so I can hear a better record? How do we want our Eddie Vedders to behave, anyway? (For what it's worth, I think he's a terrible musician but a great star—for initiating antitrust inquiries against Ticketmaster he deserves the thanks of everyone.) And anyway, why should alternative fans be expected to work out questions of politics, art, consumption, and commodification that the left in general falls over itself trying to deal with? The only commentary on Cobain's death as pigheadedly determined to blame major labels as *Maximumrocknroll* ran in, no surprise, *The Nation*.

The tragedy here is that rock has lost its cultural populism, a sense that the most popular *can* be the best. Without that, rock will produce challenging and sophisticated works, some of them again on major labels. It will unite groups of people who aren't anybody's Generation X but share symbolic hipster affiliations. But it won't upset the applecarts of cultural hierarchy the same way it did with Presley or the Stones. It won't be the king of the popular arts. It won't be as powerful.

Power. That's what this all about, isn't it? Indie, a genre bred out of powerlessness over mainstream rock, nevertheless, through the triumph of alternative, ended up reinscribing a certain notion of power back into rock. By prefiguring, at the level of cliques and individuals, the kind of unbridled rock culture that wasn't being tolerated at a corporate level, indie set a standard for how seriously rock needed to be taken. It provided a necessary counterbalance to modern rock's rejection of "rockism," the Depeche Mode/Cure argument that spins on fashion and style matter just as much as the frontier individualism of a distorted guitar. In pop art terms, Depeche Mode were right. But socially, they always seemed like market accomodationists, further proof that, as a legacy of their class system, the English inevitably rend popular culture trivial and ineffective.

Indie rock gave the notion that rock should speak truth to power, or at least offer the powerless a way to speak, a safe hiding place during the postpunk interregnum. (Go back and listen to songs like Hüsker Dü's "It's Not Funny Anymore" and "In a Free Land" and you'll see exactly what I mean.) Yet, interregnums end. The reshuffling of rock's elite has more than commenced. (To make one last Fillmore reference, when the place reopened this April, Smashing Pumpkins, not a '60s holdover, headlined the first night.) And it's time to see whether alternative can find enough power within itself to push rock's new momentum back into the culture at large. Because there, the positive aspects of alternative's bohemian-hipster legacy—a love for the diverse and eclectic, hostility to established sexual and gender norms, and a politics that, like MTV, is always at least liberal—are thoroughly needed. But the conditioned reflexes—toward smallness, away from the popular, in love with power as an ideal, not a reality—that indie culture instilled in so many of us are starting to stand in the way.

My head tells me all this, then my heart sends me off to the Thread Waxing Space in lower Manhattan to see Guided By Voices, indie's latest best hope. I'm compelled to point out that they were much better when, during a previous visit, I saw them in this same location over the winter. Was the summer heat to blame? Maybe it was a crowd at least three times as large. Or a guy onstage the whole time with a camera, filming for MTV.

# 87. Two "Postalternative" Icons

While eclecticism may have figured within the indie-alternative category, individual artists' styles tended to fall within one subgenre or another, and if a band acknowledged a range of influences (such as Nirvana did with Black Flag, Black Sabbath, and the Beatles), then these influences tended to be melded into a more or less consistent, identifiable style. But what happens when a style seems to be about eclecticism itself? This is the question that artists like Beck (b. 1970) and Björk (b. 1965) seemed to be trying to answer in the mid-1990s.[1] Indie-alternative had kept alive the notion of punk "authenticity," which had added the rejection of populism to the 1960's opposition of rock to commerce. Nonetheless, indie's attitude had represented continuity with the 1960s in that it valued an idea of self-expression that could remain beyond the manipulative aspects of seeking mass popularity. Self-expression in the indie ethos still, however obscurely or angrily, represented the "real" views of the person writing and singing the songs. When an artist's style becomes so eclectic that no one source seems privileged and when the style comes to seem like an assemblage of quotations or a pastiche where the listener cannot discern parody or reverence toward what is being quoted, the notion of authentic self-expression is thrown into question.

In different ways, that is the effect produced in the recordings of Beck and Björk. Of the two, Beck is the more obvious pasticheur, bringing together a wide range of 1960s-early 1970s styles, along with allusions to 1980's–1990's industrial and hip-hop. Even more telling are the ways he mocks the conventions of the performance of sincerity.

The following article by Jon Pareles captures some of the effect of pastiche or blank irony in an early performance by Beck. These qualities are particularly clear when Pareles describes how well Beck seems to reflect "the twentysomething trademark, a mixture of self-mockery and sardonic defiance." Pareles was not alone—other critics heard Beck's song "Loser" as an anthem for "slackers"—the name given to 20-somethings whose ironic attitude also expressed the low expectations that many had

---

1. For how both these artists might be understood within a broader shift to a "postmodern aesthetic," see David Brackett, "'Where's It At': Postmodern Theory and the Contemporary Musical Field," in Judy Lochhead and Joseph Auner, eds., *Postmodern Music/Postmodern Thought* (New York: Routledge, 2002), 207–31.

about their own upward mobility.[2] But though Pareles calls Beck an "alternative rocker," he also notes how Beck's approach to recording heightens the sense of artifice: No listener could mistake the tracks on albums, such as *Mellow Gold* (1994) and *Odelay* (1996), for songs that were recorded "live."

## A DYLAN IN SLACKER'S CLOTHING
### *Jon Pareles*

### Austin, Texas

The crowd chanted, "Loser! Loser!" when Beck finished a determinedly sloppy set at Emo's here. It wasn't hostility but anticipation; Beck, a 23-year-old songwriter from Los Angeles, hadn't performed his hit, "Loser." Beck came back to demolish the song, half-heartedly rapping the verses while band members imitated drumbeats. It was pure slacker attitude; no one was going to mock his song before he did.

Beck wore 1970's detritus: a Pinto cap, a Farrah Fawcett T-shirt. But his music is fascinated with the 1960's. While everyone knows the decade is over, Beck wants to rub it in. Harking back to Bob Dylan, he started his set with a rewritten Woody Guthrie song. Songs on his debut album, "Mellow Gold" (Geffen 24634; CD and cassette), echo the Beatles, the Rolling Stones, Neil Young and lesser 60's figures. Beck's borrowings aren't sacred relics as they are for 60's idolaters like Lenny Kravitz; they're only junk he found on the cultural sidelines. And where 60's rockers set out to be beacons for a generation, Beck aspires only to be a symptom of his.

Before "Loser" conquered MTV, Beck, whose surname is Hansen, had played around New York's Lower East Side folk scene and then in Los Angeles punk clubs (still with his acoustic guitar). As an experiment with a hip-hop producer, Karl Stephenson, he sampled a slide-guitar line, added a drumbeat and casually rapped some lyrics into an eight-track tape recorder. The result, "Loser," was released as a single on the independent Bongload label. As West Coast radio stations snapped it up, Beck moved from obscurity to a recording-company bidding war. Geffen Records, the winner, released "Loser" and four other songs as an EP (Geffen 21930; CD) and then "Mellow Gold."

The sentiment of "Loser"—"I'm a loser baby, so why don't you kill me"—reflects the twentysomething trademark, a mixture of self-mockery and sardonic defiance. For generational crossover, "Loser" also has a secret ingredient; the chorus recalls the Beatles' "Hey Jude," while Beck raps like Bob Dylan talk-singing.

---

2. Reviews of Beck's 1996 release, *Odelay*, rang similar changes; see Neil Strauss, "A Sound Arranger with an Ear for Pop," *New York Times*, June 23, 1996, Sec. 2, 40. This general surfeit of critical approval led at least one writer to suspect that it was due to Beck fitting the critical profile for a "genius pop star"; see Terri Sutton, "Garbage Pail Kid," *Village Voice*, July 23, 1996, 47, 52.

*Source:* Jon Pareles, "A Dylan in Slacker's Clothing," *New York Times*, March 27, 1994, sec. 2, p. 37. Copyright © 1994 by the New York Times Co. Reprinted with permission.

In bygone days, Beck's offhand vocal tone and free-associative lyrics would have had people calling him a "new Dylan." "Shave your face with some Mace in the dark/savin' all your food stamps we're burning down the trailer park," he advises in "Loser," adding, "My time is a piece of wax fallin' on a termite who's chokin' on the splinters."

While Beck's rap roots are in Dylan's "Subterranean Homesick Blues," his splintered recordings make him a child of hip-hop. "Mellow Gold" is no folksinger's album; it's closer to the homemade hip-hop of Basehead. Beck strums an acoustic guitar and hoots on a harmonica, but the instruments don't imply virtuous sincerity.

Like other alternative-rockers, Beck has low expectations, high irony and a keen understanding of the unskilled job market. "Pay No Mind (Snoozer)" notes, "The drugs won't kill your day job, honey." "Soul Suckin' Jerk," with a lurching hip-hop bass line under chanting voices and ever-increasing guitar distortion, is the hallucinatory tale of someone whose profession is "throwin' chicken in a bucket with a soda pop can." He burns his uniform, gets arrested, steals the cop's gun and ends up "dancing on the roof, shooting holes in the moon."

On "Mellow Gold," there's no pretense that the performance is live. Noises intrude, soundscapes suddenly change, vocals are electronically warped. Beck made the album in home studios, using his few tracks shrewdly. He delivers straightforward folk-rock in the songs "Pay No Mind (Snoozer)" and "Nitemare Hippy Girl." Other songs are slowed down, made murky, surrounded in alien sounds. Birds twitter and treated voices float through "Whiskeyclone, Hotel City 1997" as Beck ruminates, "Everything we done is wrong/I'll be lonesome when I'm gone."

When Beck plugs in a guitar, it comes with fuzztone, processed vocals and a claustrophobic mix. "Mountain Dew Rock" is a sullen homage to the Rolling Stones; "Sweet Sunshine" is an electronic swamp in which Beck declares, "I wanna climb up on the wall/I wanna swing through the city on a wreckin' ball."

Yet behind the bravado is the longing of someone who feels lost. Two songs on "Mellow Gold" crawl along contemplating mortality and unnamed fears. In "Steal My Body Home," sustained sitar notes ooze around Beck's lowered voice: "You can keep yourself intact/but you know you cannot act." The album's final song, "Blackhole," concludes, "Nothing's gonna harm you," but its quasi-Indian violin and strummed guitar aren't reassuring; nor are the dissonant synthesizer swoops that end the album after a long silence.

Beck can be glib and juvenile; the "Loser" EP boasts about drinking and nitrous oxide binges. On stage, Beck threw away his songs, reinforcing suspicions that the album's production props him up. But in the studio, Beck teases at meaning. He admits, guardedly and conditionally and cryptically, that he knows he has something to say.

> In contrast to Beck, the work of Icelandic singer Björk features less of the kind of eclecticism that one might be tempted to label pastiche. This is not to say, however, that Björk's work is less eclectic, only that the stylistic diversity in her work tends to occur either between different songs or simultaneously during a single song, rather than through eclectic collage or rapid "crosscutting" of the type found in Beck's *Mellow Gold* or *Odelay*. If Beck's "default" musical setting is folk or country music, Björk's is "techno" in the broadest sense of the term. To this base she adds, or alternates, jazz, old-style musicals, contemporary art music, and a variety of non-Western influenced material. Coming first to public attention as the main singer for the Icelandic postpunk group, the Sugarcubes, her early solo albums, *Debut* (1993) and *Post* (1995) found her

collaborating with Nellee Hooper (member-producer of Afro-British club favorites Soul II Soul), who helped craft many of the dance-oriented settings for Björk's voice.

---

Björk released her third solo album, *Homogenic*, in 1997 when radio formatting and MTV had retrenched following the alternative renaissance of the early- to mid-1990s. Jonathan Van Meter devotes some space in the next article to describing the difficulties of promoting a "post-alternative" artist, such as Björk, and her reaction to the pressures felt by U.S. companies to fit her into a particular category (as the article notes, this had not been such a big issue for her in the United Kingdom). She also discusses the "rockist" critique of techno as soulless (and her music presents an even-more-forceful critique of such easy assumptions). Another interesting facet of this article is how she adapts the music of *Homogenic*, largely consisting of a string quartet and otherworldly bleeps and blops, for a live performance situation. This excerpt begins following a description of a tumultuous period in Björk's life in which she was subjected to the sensationalist scrutiny of the mass media.

# THE OUTER LIMITS
## *Jonathan Van Meter*

Björk's response to her emotional crash was to fly off to El Madroñal, a small town on the southern coast of Spain, where she spent several weeks sleeping, Jet Skiing, and making music. If we are inclined, as Björk seems to be, to find the silver lining, then her beautiful, spooky, difficult new album, *Homogenic*, appears to be it. It is a minimalist masterpiece. The extravagant disco show tunes of yore are gone, and what's left are the fuzzier musical experiments that popped up on *Debut* and *Post*, her first two solo records after leaving the punkish Icelandic band the Sugarcubes in 1992. A head-on collision of often contrary sounds—the Icelandic String Octet; the electronic, ahead-of-the-curve weirdness of coproducer Mark Bell of techno outfit LFO; and Björk's outsized, unprecedented voice—*Homogenic*, she says proudly, is her least compromised work to date. "It's the record that's closest to the music that I hear in my head. It's closest to what I am." *But.* "I don't know if people are going to like or not."

    Neither does her record label. "Björk's challenging her audience, and, more so, radio, to get beyond traditional song structure, to step outside their comfort zone," says Greg Thompson, senior vice president at Elektra. "So yeah, it's a challenge. No doubt. I liken her to Beck. They're not necessarily radio-driven, single-driven artists. They conceive great albums. Björk's concept is to combine strings and hip-hop beats, and quite frankly, from radio's standpoint, that's difficult to mix in with Sugar Ray."

    While Björk has charted 11 Top 20 singles in England, she has yet to have the same commercial impact in America (*Homogenic* debuted at No. 28 on the *Billboard* Top 200). The worldwide combined sales of *Debut*, *Post*, and *Telegram* (last year's remix album) total

---

*Source:* Jonathan Van Meter, "The Outer Limits," *Spin*, 13, no. 9 (December 1997), pp. 92–98. This article originally appeared in the December 1997 issue of *Spin*. Reprinted with permission from *Spin* and the author. All rights reserved.

around six million, with her biggest single success in America coming from "Army of Me," a song from *Post* that appeared on the *Tank Girl* sound-track. Despite the steady momentum gained from the MTV airplay of 1993's "Human Behaviour" (Björk being chased by a bear) and '95's "It's Oh So Quiet" (Björk dancing with a mailbox) and electronica's recent Stateside foot-in-the-door, chances are remote that the bizarro *Homogenic* will launch Björk beyond her cute, cuddly cult. The album's first single, "Joga," a love letter to her best friend, feels nearly a cappella, a barely detectable beat humming under Björk's soaring vocals. The stuttering, scratchy "5 Years" sounds as if it was recorded in a video arcade circa 1980. "Immature" repeats the same four lines over and over ("How extremely lazy of me!") over a church bell-laced beat. You get the idea. Unless your name is RZA, such avant-garde strivings don't do much for your bankbook. When Thompson says that the folks at alternative radio are "waiting for her to make that one gem that actually works as a radio song," you can be sure that he knows it's not on *Homogenic*.

Though Björk's loath to put down Americans and our notorious need to categorize pop music into endless charts and radio formats, she can't help herself. "It's American radio's own worst enemy," she says. "Music, to me, stands for freedom, and to be so limited is the opposite of what music is." And even within our endless sub-categories, it seems to her, we've still gotten it all wrong. "I went to New York last January and did some interviews and they were all like, 'Electronica is the next big thing,' and I'm like, '*Please.*' And they put it under the same thing as Prodigy, Kraftwerk, Massive Attack—the whole lot. To them it's this thing that was born half a year ago. *Please.*"

To Björk, the charge that techno is inherently cold and soulless—the typically rockist, typically American criticism formerly known as "disco sucks"—is patently absurd. There is no soul in a guitar, she points out; someone has to *play* it soulfully. "I saw this magazine called *Guitar*," she says, with a smirk, "and there was this comic in the back with this blues guy with a guitar, and the question was, 'Why will computers never take over the guitar?' And the final thing was, 'Well, you can never call a computer Layla.' Please! Have you heard the names all the kids give their computers?! They're like pets. *Please!*"

Settled in, at last, for band rehearsal, Mark Bell and engineer Allan Pollard are on stage fiddling with their pets: a 909 drum machine, a brand new, powerful effects unit called a Sherman—that is no bigger than a typewriter—a keyboard, and a mixer. They are gearing up for an eight-city mini-tour of nightclubs around Europe that kicks off in Munich a couple of days from now. All of the shows are low-key affairs—either barely promoted or unannounced—that will allow Björk and Bell some time to learn to play off each other before the Icelandic String Octet is brought in for the tour proper that begins in November. This is, in many ways, a new model for onstage musical performance: one person pushing buttons—remixing live, really—the other singing. "I think I can say this has never been done before," Björk announces. Many of the songs will be left "open" so that Bell "can drop things in and surprise me. And then it's just eye contact. It's all very free-form."

Bell has remixed parts of *Homogenic* for this tour, better to suit a late-night disco experience. He plays for Björk his pumped-up drum track for "Alarm Call"—it's both deafening and skittish, a nimble feat—at which point Björk joins Bell onstage and begins to dance from one end to the other, sometimes skipping, sometimes marching, sometimes standing in place and twisting her torso in a strange reverie. She's wearing an odd pants-with-a-skirt combo, a faded black T-shirt, and funny little canvas shoes that, she will tell me later, are worn by Japanese men who build houses. They make her feet appear webbed. The performance—Björk's mad dance, her improbable voice, the unlikely outfit, the schizophrenic beats—reminds me of nothing so much as *Alice in Wonderland*, a trippy little universe unto itself. When Björk sings the line "I'm no fucking Buddhist/But this is enlightenment," the track sputters out, and she and Bell matter-of-factly huddle, swapping asides on this tape loop and that string noise. Bell heads back to work. Björk comes down off the stage, yawns, and says, "I need meat."

A few blocks away from the rehearsal studio, Björk sits in front of a huge plate of crispy duck, devours it like a hungry truck driver, washes it down with red wine, and explains to me why she's titled such a weirdly eclectic new album *Homogenic*. "This album is only songs that were written last year," she says, while *Post* and *Debut* were like back catalogs of all the songs she'd always wanted to record—of all her obsessions with different sounds and ideas from different times in her life. Those records weren't as much solo projects, she says, as collections of duets with the producers who had inspired her: Nellee Hooper, 808 State's Graham Massey, Tricky, Howie B. "This is more like one flavor. Me in one state of mind. One period of obsessions. That's why I called it *Homogenic.*"

Those obsessions were, improbably, pre–*Off the Wall* Michael Jackson ("I love Michael Jackson so much. He's got a ridiculous, outrageous, stubborn faith that magic still is with us.") and 20th-century string quartets. "I went to music school in Iceland for ten years," she says, "and obviously I was introduced to a lot of music." In some ways, *Homogenic* is a return to her classical training, "going back through everything I learned," she says, "and trying to focus on where I was in that moment." With the help of Asmundur Jansson, a musicologist friend in Iceland who has been making her tapes since she was 14, Björk would sit down to compiled cassettes of, say, songs about ships or songs featuring angular, out-of-tune brass. "I went to him hoping to find a treasure," she says. "I really wanted to discover what Icelandic music is, and if there is such a thing. And in a way, there really isn't."

It is not a very big leap from this discovery, or lack thereof, to conclude that perhaps Björk herself is Icelandic music. Iceland is a country obsessed with literature and story-telling (think Viking sagas), to the exclusion of nearly all other arts. And, unlike America and Europe, countries that industrialized slowly over a period of a few hundred years, Iceland has come into the technological present fairly recently. Björk's grandfather, for example, lived in a mud house. Out of this sped-up modernization sprang both an almost mythological relationship to nature and a brand-new fixation on technology. "All the modern things/Like cars and such," Björk sings on *Post*, "Have always existed/They've just been waiting in a mountain/For the right moment . . . /To come out/And multiply/And take over." And on *Homogenic's* "Alarm Call": "I want to go on a mountain top/With a radio and good batteries."

Call it techno-nature. Or natural techno. Acoustic strings and programmed machines. Voilà! Icelandic music! Björk music!

"You know, I would tour Asia and see a very similar thing as I see in Iceland: farmers who've got really modern roads with lights and everything, but the roads have got a bend in them around a rock because they think elves live in it. And they've got a mobile telephone. It's these two extremes. People hear that in my music, but it's not so conscious with me. It's just because I come from that kind of country."

[Following a discussion of her career] I mention to Björk that all this history, both hers and her homeland's, doesn't solve the musical riddles she casually tosses out record after beguiling record. Half-jokingly, I suggest that I might like to "unravel the great Björk mystery." She stares at me, unblinkingly, and with absolute earnestness says, "Okay, I'll try."

"First of all," she begins, "I decided that my heart was with pop music because I believe in things that grannies and kids can get. If they don't get it, fuck it, you know? So even though my arrangements are quite experimental, I'm very conservative when it comes to song structure. So it's this beautiful relationship between complete discipline and complete freedom. Most people think that when I'm singing I just go, 'Wah wah wah,' and the song is finished. And I'm actually quite flattered that I get that feeling across to people.

"Usually I write about one song a month. I never write them down. The chord structure, the bass line, the lyric, the melody, it just goes around in my head when I'm in taxis or whatever. I know what instruments, I know what noises, and I could arrange these things on my own—sometimes I do—but I love working with people so much. They almost operate like my midwife—they get the song out.

"If I'm lucky, it all comes at once. With lyrics, sometimes it's a very strong feeling, then I've got to work it out, almost like a scientist. It's all these noises: *wha oui aah ooh*. It's syllables and noises. *Ahh eee ech crmpffff eeo*. First, I only sing noises, then I slowly go into Icelandic and then do hints of English. I always write in Icelandic, and when I translate it to English it adds to the song and then maybe I translate back to Icelandic and then back to English. I actually get quite a lot out of the translation."

"Your word associations are very nuanced," I say.

"Very . . . ?"

"Nuanced," I say again. "Subtle. They don't hit you over the head."

"Oh," she says, understanding. "I love nuance. I love that word so much. Me and my mate, we keep talking about nuance and nuisance. They're our favorites."

"I dare you to take me on," Björk wails from the tiny stage of the Sugar Shack in Munich as she sings "5 Years" to a firetrap-capacity crowd of sweaty, happy, twentysomething Germans. Fifteen minutes later, Björk bounces offstage and into the dressing room, all soaking wet hair and crazy eyes. The brief set—six songs from *Homogenic*—went better than anyone expected, and she is clearly relieved and thrilled. As she drums madly on a table with her hands, Mark Bell and the rest of her crew pile into the dressing room. "That was our most crowded rehearsal ever!" she says to the group, and they all laugh uproariously at what is obviously a joke at her own expense. Björk, it turns out, does not like to rehearse. She prefers, she says, "jumping off a cliff."

As everyone pairs off and recaps, Björk says to the engineer, "The best thing about the show was what you and Mark were doing. So tight. Every sound was perfect." Her sweaty hair is now clumped into little daggers all around her face. "I'm just glad I got my 'Aaaaah!' right. One-two-three, 'Aaaaah!'" Suddenly, the PA guy, who couldn't see the stage from the back of the room because the crowd stood on the furniture, shouts, "It was like setting off fireworks in the fog: 'Oh, that must have been a pretty one! Oh, that must have been a loud one!'" Everyone falls out laughing, Björk loudest and longest.

The day after the Munich show, I am waiting in the airport for my flight home. Half asleep in a coffee shop, I look up and see Björk off in the distance, walking down some far-flung ultramodern hallway. She is wearing a 21st-century, floor-length, sleeveless purple dress with a big orange circle on her stomach, and her web-footed, Japanese carpenter shoes. She is carrying a funny, furry little purse in one hand, and a cell phone in the other. She is chattering away into the cellular in Icelandic, oblivious to the fact that people are staring, not necessarily because they know she is Björk, world-famous pop star, but because she appears to be deeply strange and not so strange at all.

# 88. "We Are the World"?

Going back to at least the 1950s, a category has existed for recordings produced outside of the U.S.-U.K. axis of mainstream popular music. This category, initially dubbed "international" in the 1950s, brought the sounds of Parisian cafés and Polynesian luau orchestras into the living rooms of North American and British listeners, who might find, upon careful perusal of the liner notes, that the polka recording they just purchased was actually recorded not too far down the road from them.[1] As noted in chapter 29, an audience hankering for popular music with the allure of the noncommercial might have been tempted in the 1950s to plunk down their hard-earned cash for a Harry Belafonte "calypso" record or a "folk" recording by the Kingston Trio. During the 1960s, other sounds began emerging from beyond the Western metropole. In addition to such one-off novelties as Kyu Sakamoto's "Sukyaki," the influence of "ska" (or "bluebeat" as it was known in Britain) began to be felt outside the Jamaican sound-system parties where it had developed, both in hits by West Indian artists like Millie Small and Desmond Dekker and in the incorporation of ska rhythms in recordings by the Beatles (1964's "I Call Your Name").

However, in the early 1970s, the success of the soundtrack from *The Harder They Come*, featuring reggae star Jimmy Cliff (James Chambers, b. 1948), followed by the international triumph of Bob Marley (1945–1981), brought a new level of attention to Jamaican popular music and, in particular, to reggae. Jamaica subsequently had an impact on global popular music far out of proportion to its tiny population. The rise of what is sometimes called "second-wave ska" in Great Britain in the late 1970s, with its politically conscious "two-tone" bands is but one example. Another example is the continuation of ska-punk hybrids throughout the 1980s and 1990s (in what could be called "third-wave ska"), and the various fusions of hip-hop and reggae that continue to flourish in recordings of Jamaican dance-hall artists and U.S. hip-hop stars.

With Bob Marley's death in 1981, record companies sought to fill the void in a variety of ways. The first move by Marley's former company (Island) was to promote Nigerian jùjú star King Sunny Adé as the next Marley, an attempt that failed woefully. However, a type of sub-Saharan African music was destined to make an impact in the world of Western

---

1. Keir Keightley, "Around the World: Musical Tourism and the Globalization of the Record Industry, 1946–66," unpublished manuscript, 1998.

pop, but in a way that could not have been foreseen. Paul Simon, whose career had more or less stalled in the late 1970s, happened across some recordings of South African pop music. Simon subsequently traveled to Johannesburg to record with the musicians he heard on those recordings, and the rest, as they say, is history.[2] The resultant album, *Graceland* (1986), revived Simon's dormant career and succeeded in exposing millions of listeners to African popular music where Island's campaign had failed. Thus was born "World Music" as we now know it.

Simon's recording tapped into an urge felt by consumers of Western pop music for something new, yet familiar. Sales of other recordings from Africa and the Caribbean grew, but no one category yet existed in which to place the music (and thus no easy-to-find location in record stores), no *Billboard* chart, and no radio format. Aware of this dilemma, some 25 record industry executives met in a pub in London in 1987 and invented the name "World Music." The term has shifted since the late 1980s; from its initial emphasis on music from sub-Saharan Africa and the Caribbean (also known at the time as "World Beat"), it has increasingly included European "ethnic" musics and various new-age, dance, and ambient-fusions (which subsequently became the most successful varieties of "World Music").[3]

Much writing on the subject has focused on questions of power and economics. When Western pop stars and Western corporations record and produce recordings with non-Western musicians, who benefits? Are these Western entities exploiting Western consumers' naive fascination with the exotic for profit? If the answer to the last question is yes, is a nonexploitative involvement with non-Western music possible? How we respond to these questions will be affected by which musical projects we consider, some of which function more obviously to the advantage of the Western musicians and corporations involved than do others.[4]

In contrast to the notion of World Music, the emphasis in the following essay by George Lipsitz is on what may be termed "global music." Rather than focus on how Western-based multinational music corporations are profiting from the "raw material" of non-Western music or on famous Western musicians' interactions with non-Western musicians, Lipsitz

2. This history included a debate sparked off by the album among music critics and academics; for a sample, see Steven Feld, "Notes on World Beat" in Charles Keil and Steven Feld, *Music Grooves: Essays and Dialogues* (Chicago: University of Chicago Press, 1994), 238–46 ; Veit Erlmann, "The Aesthetics of the Global Imagination: Reflections on World Music in the 1990s," *Public Culture* 8 (1996): 467–87; Charles Hamm, "Graceland Revisited," *Popular Music* 8 (October 1989): 299–304; and Louise Meintjes, "Paul Simon's *Graceland*, South Africa, and the Mediation of Musical Meaning," *Ethnomusicology* 34, no. 1 (1990): 37–73.

3. A useful overview and analysis of these developments may be found in Timothy D. Taylor, *Global Pop: World Music, World Markets* (New York: Routledge, 1997), 1–37.

4. For a particularly tendentious critique of the World Music phenomenon, see Herbert Mattelart, "Life as Style: Putting the 'World' in the Music," *The Baffler* (1993): 103–09.

The 1990s and Beyond

focuses on how global flows of people, music, and technology have resulted in new fusions reflecting the experience of immigrants who fashion intriguing blends of tradition with sounds from the metropolis. By
emphasizing creative responses to marginalization, this account performs an important disruption of what may otherwise seem like a unified
narrative told from the perspective of dominant groups in the West (as in
many accounts of World Music). At the same time, Lipsitz is careful to emphasize that the resourcefulness of Algerians in France, West and East
Indians in the United Kingdom, and Mexican Americans in the United
States does not negate the effects of racial domination and economic exploitation. Lipsitz's work here on the "poetics of place" builds upon previous work he has done on working-class and subaltern cultural practices
and struggles in books such as *Time Passages* and *Class and Culture in
Cold War America*.[5] One of the few overtly "academic" entries in this
book, Lipsitz's clear prose and the timeliness of the issues he discusses
blur the line between academic and well-researched nonacademic
criticism.

## IMMIGRATION AND ASSIMILATION: RAI, REGGAE, AND BHANGRAMUFFIN
### George Lipsitz

During the 1980s, popular-music listeners and enthusiasts throughout Europe began to notice new musical forms that captured their fancy. In London, the band Alaap blended
bhangra music from the Indian state of Punjab with Greek, Middle Eastern, Spanish, and
Anglo-American pop styles. At the same time, Joi Bangla, made up of immigrants from
Bangladesh, mixed African-American funk sounds with traditional Bengali folk songs.* For
their part, listeners in Paris expressed enthusiasm for a techno-pop album displaying "a
faintly Moorish" sound underneath English, French, and Arabic lyrics by a Mauritanian
singer recording under the name Tahra.[†]

Soaring to popularity at the same time that immigrant populations in London and Paris
faced increasing hostility and even attacks from anti-foreign thugs, these recordings
demonstrate the complicated connections and contradictions that characterize the links between popular music and social life. Audiences and artists in these cities carried the cultural
collisions of everyday life into music, at one and the same time calling attention to ethnic
differences and demonstrating how they might be transcended. Sophisticated fusions of
seemingly incompatible cultures in music made sense to artists and audiences in part
because these fusions reflected their lived experiences in an inter-cultural society.

---

5. George Lipsitz, *Time Passages: Collective Memory and American Popular Culture* (Minneapolis: University of Minnesota Press, 1990); idem., *Class and Culture in Cold War America: A Rainbow at Midnight* (South
Hadley, Mass.: Bergin and Garvey, 1982).

*Sabita Banerji, "Ghazals to Bhangra in Great Britain," *Popular Music* vol. 7, no. 2 (May) 1988, 208, 213.
†Philip Sweeney, *The Virgin Directory of World Music* (New York: Henry Holt, 1991), 17.

*Source:* George Lipsitz, "Immigration and Assimilation: Rai, Reggae, and Bhangramuffin," from
*Dangerous Crossroads: Popular Music, Postmodernism, and the Poetics of Place* (London: Verso, 1994), pp. 119,
123–126, 127–34. Reprinted by permission of the author.

Of course, inter-cultural communication and creativity does not preclude political or even physical confrontations between members of groups fighting for a share of increasingly scarce resources. But the very existence of music demonstrating the interconnectedness between the culture of immigrants and the culture of their host country helps us understand how the actual lived experiences of immigrants are much more dynamic and complex than most existing models of immigration and assimilation admit.

Government control over the production and distribution of popular music and the peculiarities of French culture have left French citizens with far less connection to international rock 'n' roll than their neighbors in Germany, Spain, or the Netherlands. In fact, the cultural fit over the years between rock 'n' roll and French culture has been so bad that it gave rise to a saying that "*le rock français, c'est comme la cuisine anglaise*" ("French rock is to rock as English cooking is to cooking"). But with the rise of rap, French musicians of African descent have become more involved with the currents of international popular music. Members of the rap group I.A.M. come from North African neighborhoods in the southern city of Marseilles. They titled their album *From the Planet Mars*, as a pun about Marseilles, but also as a statement about how different their experiences are from those of cosmopolitan and metropolitan French citizens. I.A.M. stands for "Imperial Asiatic Men," but their music and lyrics deal mostly with Egypt, Algeria, and America.[*] The African-born Parisian rapper M. C. Solaar has immersed himself in the French hip hop subculture which he describes as "the cult of the sneaker," and "pretty much a U.S. branch office."[†]

The complicated culture mixing that has given rise to new forms of inter-cultural communication within French popular music has also had important political implications. Salif Keita of Mali recorded a powerful and popular French-language song, "Nous Pas Bouger," which championed the cause of immigrants resisting deportation.[§] Similarly, the men and women in the anti-racist folk/punk/new wave band Les Négresses Vertes base their music on French multi-culturalism. Their name means green black women, and the band's members are male and female, European and African, white and black. "It's music from the street today," explains Mathias, who plays accordion. "We all grew up with a large variety of different people who might have different roots but who are, nevertheless, French. Our musical hybrid wasn't a deliberate policy, it's the way we are. It mirrors the reality of France today."[¶]

Clearly the most important and most complicated expression of musical multiculturalism in France comes from the popularity of Algerian "rai" music. During the 1980s, political and cultural mobilizations by young people of North African origin competed with intense anti-Arab and anti-foreign organizing by French right wingers for the power to define "French" culture and citizenship.[‖] Rai music took on extra-musical importance as a visible weapon in that struggle.

Referenced by many artists including Les Négresses Vertes and I.A.M., rai music blends Arabic lyrics and instruments with synthesizers, disco arrangements, blues chord progressions, and Jamaican reggae and Moroccan gnawa rhythms. Rai originated as women's music in the Algerian port city of Oran where *meddahas* sang to other women at weddings and other private occasions and by *chiekhas* who sang for men in taverns and brothels. In a city where French, Spanish and Arabic are all spoken, the music known as

---

[*]John Rockwell, "Felicitous Rhymes and Local Roots," *New York Times*, August 23, 1992, section 2, 23.

[†]Jay Cocks, "Rap Around the Globe," *Time* (October 19, 1992), 70.

[§]Banning Eyre, "Routes: The Parallel Paths of Baaba Maal and Salif Keita," *Option* no. 53 (November–December, 1993), 45.

[¶]Jo Shinner, "Zzzzzobie!," *Folk Roots* vol. 74 (August) 1989, 35.

[‖]Azouz Begag, "The 'Beurs,' Children of North-African Immigrants in France: The Issue of Integration," *Journal of Ethnic Studies* vol. 18, no. 1, 2–4.

"Oran Modern" emerged from interactions among Spanish, French, and North African musicians.[*] Now sung by both female Chebas and male Chebs, the term "rai" comes from the Arabic phrase "Ya Rai" ("It's my opinion").[†] Reed flutes and terracotta drums provided the original instrumentation for rai, but over the years musicians added violin, accordion, saxophone, and trumpet. Bellemou Messaoud played a particularly important role in the emergence of modern rai when he added guitars, trumpets, and synthesizers to rai ensembles.[§] Disco-influenced arrangements and blues chord progressions came later to bring rai closer to the Anglo-American international style.

A product of cultural collision between Europe and North Africa, rai music has its defenders and its detractors in both places. Some factions in Algeria see rai as too French, too Western, too modern, too obscene. At the same time, there are those in France who dismiss rai as too foreign, too primitive, too exotic, too strange. It is not easy to tell if a North African immigrant to France is being assimilationist or separatist by listening to rai music. Cheb Khaled spends more time in Marseilles than in Algiers, and uses rai music to comment on "racism in France, about what's happening in Algeria, and of course, I always sing about love."[¶] Cheba Fadela created a sensation as a mini-skirted seventeen-year-old on French television in the late 1970s and helped start modern "pop rai" with her 1983 song "N'sel fik" ("You are Mine").[||] Cheb Sid Ahmed is openly homosexual and performs with a troupe of traditional female wedding singers.[°] At the other extreme, Cheba Zahouania performs mainly at women's events, does not allow herself to be photographed, and does not appear on television, reportedly because her husband threatened to take her children from her if she sang in public for men.[**]

Not surprisingly, rai has been embroiled in repeated political controversies. "The history of rai is like the history of rock and roll," explains Cheb Khaled, one of the genre's premier performers.

> Fundamentalists don't want our concerts to happen. They come and break things up. They say rai is street music and that it's debauched. But that's not true. I don't sing pornography. I sing about love and social life. We say what we think, just like singers all over the world.[‡]

The Algerian government has sporadically looked with favor on rai as a source of revenue and as a cultural voice capable of competing with Islamic fundamentalism. Its popularity in France persuaded the authorities in Algiers to sponsor international youth festivals featuring rai performers in Algiers and Oran in 1985.[§§] In France, racist attacks on Arabs led to the formation of SOS-Racisme, a massive anti-racist organization affiliated with the Socialist Party. It embraced rai as an expression of faith in France's inter-cultural future.[¶¶] They helped persuade the French government to sponsor a rai festival in a Paris suburb in 1986,

---

[*]Philip Sweeney, *The Virgin Directory of World Music*, 9.

[†]Miriam Rosen, "On Rai," *Artforum* vol. 29, no. 1 (September) 1990, 22; David McMurray and Ted Swedenburg, "Rai Tide Rising," *Middle East Report* (March–April) 1991, 39.

[§]Miriam Rosen, "On Rai," 22; Philip Sweeney, *The Virgin Directory of World Music*, 9.

[¶]Banning Eyre, "A King in Exile: The Royal Rai of Cheb Khaled," *Option* vol. 39 (July–August) 1991, 45.

[||]Miriam Rosen, "On Rai," 23.

[°]Philip Sweeney, *The Virgin Directory of World Music*, 12.

[**]Miriam Rosen, "On Rai," 23.

[‡]Banning Eyre, "A King in Exile," 45.

[§§]Miriam Rosen, "On Rai," 23; Philip Sweeney, *The Virgin Directory of World Music*, 10.

[¶¶]David McMurray and Ted Swedenburg, "Rai Tide Rising," *Middle East Report* (March–April) 1991, 42.

which seemed to mark the emergence of rai as a permanent force in French popular music.*
In fact, rai may have become more secure in France than it is in Algeria. When anti-government rioters in Algiers adopted Cheb Khaled's "El Harba Wine" ("Where to Flee?")
as their unofficial anthem in what became known as the "rai rebellion," many rai artists
hastened to disassociate themselves from the violence.†

Yet, the popularity of rai music among French and "world beat" audiences may mean
little for children of immigrants facing massive unemployment and racist attacks. In Lyons,
for example, seventy percent of the children of immigrants between the ages of 16 and 25
have no jobs and no vocational training. Even the success of an assimilationist group like
France-Plus which has managed to elect close to 400 people of North African lineage to municipal offices throughout France may increase rather than decrease the pressures on those
immigrants and their children who seem less assimilated.§

Traditional arguments about immigration, assimilation, and acculturation assume that
immigrants choose between two equally accessible cultures that are clearly differentiated
and distinct from one another. But what if immigrants leave a country that has been shaped
by its colonizers and enter one that has been shaped by those it colonized? What if immigrants leave a modernizing country that turns anti-modern and fundamentalist while they
are gone? What happens if the host country becomes deeply divided between anti-foreign
nativists and anti-racist pluralists? Which culture do the immigrants carry with them? Into
which culture do they assimilate? Rai music might be defended as either Algerian or French
music, but a more exact interpretation would establish it as a register for the changing di-
mensions and boundaries of Algerian, French, and Beur (a popular term for Arab mostly
used in Paris) identities.

Afro-Caribbean and Southwest Asian immigrants to Britain experience many of the
same dynamic changes facing North African immigrants to France. Here again, musical
syncretisms disclose the dynamics of cultural syncretisms basic to the processes of immigration, assimilation, and acculturation in contemporary societies. Immigrants leaving the
Caribbean and Asia took on new identities in Britain. If nothing else, they became "West
Indian" or "East Indian" in England instead of Jamaican or Bahamian, Bengali, or Hindi as
they had been at home. But they also became "Black" in Britain, an identity that they generally do not have in their home countries, but which becomes salient to them in England as
a consequence of racism directed at them from outside their communities as well as from its
utility to them as a device for building unity within and across aggrieved populations. Of
course, the influx of immigrants changes England too. Once immigrants from the Indian
subcontinent or the Caribbean arrive in the U.K., they transform the nature of British society and culture in many ways, changing the nature of the "inside" into which newer immigrants are expected to assimilate.

Mass migration from the West Indies to Britain began shortly after World War II. The
expanding English economy offered jobs to immigrants, but the nation's cultural institutions rarely acknowledged their presence. According to Anthony Marks, as late as 1963,
when some 15,000 records from Jamaica entered England every month, the British Broadcasting Corporation studiously ignored West Indian music and record shops rarely carried
products from the Caribbean.¶ Denied the dignity of representation in the mainstream

---

*Philip Sweeney, *The Virgin Directory of World Music*, 10.

†David McMurray and Ted Swedenburg, "Rai Tide Rising," 42; Miriam Rosen, "On Rai," 23.

§Azouz Begag, "The 'Beurs,'" 9.

¶Anthony Marks, "Young, Gifted and Black: Afro-American and Afro-Caribbean Music in Britain
1963–88," in Paul Oliver, ed., *Black Music in Britain: Essays on the Afro-Asian Contribution to Popular Music*
(Milton Keynes and Philadelphia: Open University Press, 1990), 106.

media, Afro-Caribbeans in England created spaces for themselves with neighborhood sound systems and record collections that enabled them to express their own culture and share it with others. At the heart of these new spaces was music from Jamaica.

While immigration flows included residents of all Caribbean islands, Jamaicans accounted for more than sixty percent of England's Caribbean population by the 1960s. Because of the size of the Jamaican-British community and because of the ways in which the politically-charged doctrines of Rastafarianism helped all diasporic Blacks in Britain understand and endure their treatment, Jamaican culture became the crucial unifying component in the composite Caribbean culture created in England. Differences between island identities that might be deeply felt in the West Indies, and even in England, receded in importance because of the unifying force of Jamaican music, but even more because of the uniformity of British racism against *all* West Indians. "When you're in school you all get harassed together," explained one immigrant.[*] Another adds, "I think most of my friends feel Jamaican, the English helped us do it."[†]

Popular music affirms the positive qualities of the unity forged in part by negative experiences with British racism. Through shared experiences with music, carnival celebrations, and the political activism that sometimes grows out of them, primary groups dispersed over a broad territory find themselves united by elements of a Jamaican culture that many of them had never known first hand.[§] Jazzie B of the British group Soul II Soul remembers the prominence of Jamaican "sound systems"—record players and amplified speakers—in his neighborhood as he grew up, and what they meant to him as the British-born son of immigrants from Antigua. "By the time I was 15 or 16, there was a sound system on every single street in the community. I'd guess that eight out of every 10 black kids would be involved in one way or another in a sound system."[¶] These devices offered a focal point for social gatherings, allowed disc jockeys opportunities to display their skills, and provided a soundtrack to mark the experiences and aspirations of inner-city life. But they also served as one of those sites where people made new identities for themselves as West Indians and as Black Britons.

Just as the Paris described by Simon Njami functions as an African city offering opportunities found nowhere in Africa, London and other British cities became important centers of West Indian and Jamaican cultural forms found nowhere in the Caribbean. But these forms have important uses and implications for Southwest Asians in Britain as well. The pervasive practices of British racism and occasional self-defense strategies by immigrants lead West Indians and East Indians to a shared identity as "Black" in England. Interactions between Afro-Caribbeans and Southwest Asians have a long if not completely comfortable history in the Caribbean, especially in Trinidad, but in Britain the antagonisms can be even sharper. For members of both groups, the things that divide them often seem more salient than those bringing them together. One survey showed that more than eighty percent of West Indians and more than forty percent of East Indians felt they had more in common with British whites than with each other. Almost a third of Indians and Pakistanis stated that they had nothing in common with either white Britons or West Indian Blacks. Only eight percent of West Indians and twenty percent of Pakistanis and Indians felt they had more in common with each other than they had in common with the English.[||] In few

---

[*]Winston James, "Migration, Racism, and Identity: The Caribbean Experience in Britain," *New Left Review*, no. 193 (May–June 1992), 32.

[†]Winston James, "Migration, Racism, and Identity," 28.

[§]Abner Cohen, *Masquerade Politics*, 36.

[¶]Robert Hillburn, "Tracing the Caribbean Roots of the New British Pop Invasion," *Los Angeles Times*, September 24, 1989, Calendar section, 6.

[||]Winston James, "Migration, Racism, and Identity," 45.

extremely significant cases, Afro-Asians and Afro-Caribbeans have successfully repressed their differences to defend themselves and each other from white racist attacks or judicial frame-ups, but sustained political and cultural alliances have been elusive.*

Yet, alliances between Southwest Asians and other groups that might appear unlikely in political life already exist within popular culture. Bhangra musicians fuse folk songs from the Indian state of Punjab with disco, pop, hip hop, and house music for appreciative audiences made up of people from many different groups. Like Algerian rai, bhangra originated in a part of the world characterized by extensive inter-cultural communication, but remained largely a music played for private parties, weddings, and harvest festivals before its emergence as a syncretic popular form. Bhangra brings together Punjabis of many religions (Hindu, Sikh, Muslim, Jain, and Christian) and from many countries (India, Pakistan, and Bangladesh), but in the past decade has started to speak powerfully to new audiences and interests.†

Like West Indians, East Indians came to England in the years after World War II, and like West Indians they found that their labor was more welcome than their culture in their new nation. As Sabita Banerji notes in an apt phrase, "South Asian communities in Britain have remained invisible, and their music inaudible, for a surprisingly long time."§ In the early 1980s, South Asian youths following the Jamaican example set up sound systems to play reggae, soul, jazz, and funk records during "daytimer" discos in dance halls and community centers. At first the disc jockeys and sound systems took Caribbean-sounding names, but when they started to mix bhangra with the other musical styles they used Punjabi names like "Gidian de Shingar" and "Pa Giddha Pa."¶ Almost a decade after Jamaican reggae established itself as a popular form capable of attracting audiences from every ethnic background, bhangra broke on the British scene as a viable commercial force. Alaap's 1984 album, *Teri chunni di sitare* drew an enthusiastic response from listeners for its blend of disco, pop, and Caribbean styles with bhangra. Holle Holle and Heera drew large crowds to mainstream venues including the Hammersmith Palais by adding digital sampling to the mix in their music, while bhangra groups in the Midlands blended bhangra with house music.‖ But the ultimate fusion awaited—the mixture of Jamaican "ragamuffin" and African-American hip hop with "bhangra" to create the "bhangramuffin" sound of Apache Indian.

Steve Kapur took the name Apache Indian as a reference to his Punjabi ancestry and as a tribute to the Jamaican ragamuffin star "Super Cat," sometimes known as "the wild Apache."° But he took his art from the cultural crossroads he negotiated every day. He told a reporter,

> As a young Asian in Britain, you constantly lead a double life. At home, everything is as it was—very traditional, very strict. But when you close the front door and move onto the streets everything changes. I've had so many relatives disown my family because of my love for reggae. Now, after hearing my music, and hearing the Indian influences in it, it appeals to them. But my music is first and foremost street music.**

---

*Ibid.," 34, 46.

†Sabita Banerji and Gerd Bauman, "Bhangra 1984–8: Fusion and Professionalization in a Genre of South Asian Dance Music," in Paul Oliver, ed., *Black Music in Britain*, 137–8.

§Ibid., 138.

¶Ibid., 146.

‖Ibid., 142.

°Thom Duffy, "Apache Indian's Asian-Indian Pop Scores U.K. Hit," *Billboard*, February 20, 1993, 82.

**Brooke Wentz, "Apache Indian," *Vibe* (November) 1993, 9.

For Apache Indian, the "street" is a place where Afro-Caribbean and South Asian youths learn from each other. As a teenager he wore his hair in dreadlocks, danced to the blues, and spent hours shopping for reggae records.* His first recording, "Move Over India," paid tribute to the India that he had only visited once but knew well from the Indian films that his parents watched "every time I went home."† Apache Indian knew that his music was a success when his West Indian neighbors began saying hello to him in Punjabi. His song "Come Follow Me" offers a hip hop history and travelogue of India for the edification of a West Indian friend who closes the number by telling Apache Indian that his country sounds "lovely, and next time you go send a ticket for me."§

Standing at the crossroads of Punjabi and Jamaican cultures, Apache Indian shows that Afro-Asian and Afro-Caribbean Britons share more than a common designation as Black people, that they share a common history of using culture to strengthen their communities from the inside and to attract support from the outside. Punjabis and Jamaicans both come from regions that contain diverse cultures and beliefs, and they both belong to populations that transnational capital has dispersed all over the globe. From their historical experiences at home no less from what they have learned in order to survive abroad, Punjabis and Jamaicans draw upon longstanding and rich traditions when they create cultural coalitions that transcend ethnic and political differences.

The music made by Apache Indian uses performance to call into being a community composed of Punjabis and Jamaicans, South Asians and West Indians, reggae fans and bhangra enthusiasts. But it also demonstrates the potential for all of Britain to learn a lesson from the extraordinary adaptability and creativity of its immigrant cultures. Apache Indian reads "British" culture selectively, by venerating Mahatma Gandhi and Bob Marley rather than Winston Churchill or George Frederick Handel. He assimilates into the culture of the country where he was born by proudly displaying the diverse identities that he has learned in its schools and streets. He creates problems for nation states with their narratives of discrete, homogeneous, and autonomous culture, but he solves problems for people who want cultural expressions as complex as the lives they live every day.

Yet, we should not let the brilliance and skill of Jamaican or Punjabi musicians in securing space for themselves within popular culture blind us to the harsh realities facing immigrants all over the world. Despised and degraded, they face unremitting racism and exploitation with few opportunities to communicate their condition to others. People making popular music for communities like these must address immediate issues of survival and self-respect within their group before they can think about reaching a larger audience.

For example, on the west coast of North America Los Tigres del Norte (the Tigers of the North) sing for and about migrant communities shuttling back and forth between the U.S.A. and Mexico. The five musicians in the band grew up poor in a rural family with eleven children and a disabled father. They have lived the lives they sing about in their songs, and constantly receive suggestions for new stories from farm workers who tell them about their troubles. With expressly political lyrics, they turn their listeners' lives into poignant and powerful songs. "We talk a lot about immigration," explained group leader Jorge Hernandez to a reporter, "because it has given problems to a lot of people. We talk about families who come from different countries to learn a different language and lose where they came from. We tell them it's important not to lose where you are from."¶

*Paul Bradshaw, "Handsworth Revolutionary," *Straight No Chaser*, no. 23 (Autumn) 1993, 13, 26.
†Ibid., 29.
§Brooke Wentz, "Apache Indian," 86; Apache Indian, *No Reservations*, Mango 162–539, 932–3.
¶Carolyn Jung, "S.J. Band's Rhythms Transcend Borders," *San Jose Mercury News*, March 5, 1994, 10.

Los Tigres del Norte have appeared in ten Mexican films, sold millions of albums, and regularly draw huge crowds to their live performances. Yet they have secured almost no "mainstream" commercial recognition in the U.S.A., perhaps because they sing in Spanish in a country dominated by Anglophone markets, but also perhaps because their lyrics contain values that threaten vested interests too much. In "La Jaula de Oro" ('The Gilded Cage"), an undocumented worker laments his decade of labor in the U.S.A., claiming that "even if the cage is made of gold it does not cease being a prison."[*]

The mechanisms of commercial culture that deprive Los Tigres del Norte of exposure to a broader audience also deprive Anglo listeners of needed knowledge about their country. As Jose Cuellar, Chairman of San Francisco State's La Raza Studies Department observes, "Those of us who are English-dominant would learn a great deal of the needs and aspirations of our immigrant population, of their frustrated hopes, their frustrated dreams. In these songs, it's all there."[†]

Anti-immigrant and anti-foreign sentiment plagues de-industrialized nations in the West as well as de-Stalinized countries in the East. During times of economic decline and social disintegration, it is tempting for people to blame their problems on others, and to seek succor and certainty from racist and nationalist myths. But the desire to seek certainty and stability by depicting the world solely as one story told from one point of view is more dangerous than ever before. As technology and trade inevitably provide diverse populations with common (although not egalitarian) experiences, the ability to adapt, to switch codes, and to see things from more than one perspective becomes more valuable. In the last analysis, nation states may be best served by those who refuse to believe in their unified narratives, and who insist instead on cultural and political practices that delight in difference, diversity, and dialogue. These do not need to be conjured up by political theorists, or wished into existence by mystics and visionaries. They already exist (albeit in embryonic form) in the communities called into existence by rai, ragamuffin, bhangra, and many other unauthorized and unexpected forms that people have for understanding and changing the world in which they live.

---

[*]Ibid., 10.
[†]Ibid., 10.

# 89. A Talking Head Writes

David Byrne (b. 1952) is best known as the lead singer and songwriter for the punk–new wave band Talking Heads (discussed in chapters 62 and 64). Both with the Talking Heads and as a solo artist, Byrne either incorporated non-Western influences or recorded with non-Western musicians; thus he might be vulnerable to critiques that focus on the exploitation of non-Western music and musicians by Western pop stars and music corporations. Here, Byrne, while agreeing with some aspects of such critiques, presents a defense of the idea (or spirit) of World Music, if not its practice. Why, asks Byrne, should Western consumers restrict themselves only to Western pop music? Along the way, he also presents some examples (as did Lipsitz) that call into question the possibility of ethnic/musical purity, while still criticizing the tendency of Western consumers to exoticize the unfamiliar. In addition to questioning the issue of ethnic/musical purity, Byrne also examines the flipside of this issue: how it is that listeners and musicians can enjoy and identify with types of music that come from very different circumstances than their own?

## CROSSING MUSIC'S BORDERS: "I HATE WORLD MUSIC"
### *David Byrne*

I HATE world music. That's probably one of the perverse reasons I have been asked to write about it. The term is a catchall that commonly refers to non-Western music of any and all sorts, popular music, traditional music and even classical music. It's a marketing as well as a pseudomusical term—and a name for a bin in the record store signifying stuff that doesn't belong anywhere else in the store. What's in that bin ranges from the most blatantly commercial music produced by a country, like Hindi film music (the singer Asha Bhosle being the best well known example), to the ultra-sophisticated, super-cosmopolitan art-pop of Brazil (Caetano Veloso, Tom Zé, Carlinhos Brown); from the somewhat bizarre and surreal concept of a former Bulgarian state-run folkloric choir being arranged by classically trained, Soviet-era composers (Le Mystere des Voix Bulgares) to Norteño songs from Texas and northern Mexico glorifying the exploits of drug dealers (Los Tigres del Norte). Albums by

*Source:* David Byrne, "Crossing Music's Borders: 'I Hate World Music,'" *New York Times*, October 3, 1999. Copyright © 1999 by the New York Times Co. Reprinted with permission.

Selena, Ricky Martin and Los Del Rio (the Macarena kings), artists who sell millions of records in the United States alone, are racked next to field recordings of Thai hill tribes. Equating apples and oranges indeed.

So, from a purely democratic standpoint, one in which all music is equal, regardless of sales and slickness of production, this is a musical utopia.

## So Why Am I Complaining?

In my experience, the use of the term world music is a way of dismissing artists or their music as irrelevant to one's own life. It's a way of relegating this "thing" into the realm of something exotic and therefore cute, weird but safe, because exotica is beautiful but irrelevant; they are, by definition, not like us. Maybe that's why I hate the term. It groups everything and anything that isn't "us" into "them." This grouping is a convenient way of not seeing a band or artist as a creative individual, albeit from a culture somewhat different from that seen on American television. It's a label for anything at all that is not sung in English or anything that doesn't fit into the Anglo-Western pop universe this year. (So Ricky Martin is allowed out of the world music ghetto—for a while, anyway. Next year, who knows? If he makes a plena record, he might have to go back to the salsa bins and the Latin mom and pop record stores.) It's a none too subtle way of reasserting the hegemony of Western pop culture. It ghettoizes most of the world's music. A bold and audacious move, White Man!

There is some terrific music being made all over the world. In fact, there is more music, in sheer quantity, currently defined as world music, than any other kind. Not just kinds of music, but volume of recordings as well. When we talk about world music we find ourselves talking about 99 percent of the music on this planet. It would be strange to imagine, as many multinational corporations seem to, that Western pop holds the copyright on musical creativity.

No, the fact is, Western pop is the fast food of music, and there is more exciting creative music making going on outside the Western pop tradition than inside it. There is so much incredible noise happening that we'll never exhaust it. For example, there are guitar bands in Africa that can be, if you let them, as inspiring and transporting as any kind of rock, pop, soul, funk or disco you grew up with. And what is exciting for me is that they have taken elements of global (Western?) music apart, examined the pieces to see what might be of use and then re-invented and reassembled the parts to their own ends. Thus creating something entirely new. (Femi Kuti gave a great show the other night that was part Coltrane, part James Brown and all African, just like his daddy, Fela Kuti, the great Nigerian musical mastermind.)

To restrict your listening to English-language pop is like deciding to eat the same meal for the rest of your life. The "no-surprise surprise," as the Holiday Inn advertisement claims, is reassuring, I guess, but lacks kick. As ridiculous as they often sound, the conservative critics of rock-and-roll, and more recently of techno and rave, are not far off the mark. For at its best, music truly is subversive and dangerous. Thank the gods.

Hearing the right piece of music at the right time of your life can inspire a radical change, destructive personal behavior or even fascist politics. Sometimes all at the same time. On the other hand, music can inspire love, religious ecstasy, cathartic release, social bonding and a glimpse of another dimension. A sense that there is another time, another space and another, better, universe. It can heal a broken heart, offer a shoulder to cry on and a friend when no one else understands. There are times when you want to be transported, to get your mind around some stuff it never encountered before. And what if the thing transporting you doesn't come from your neighborhood?

## Why Bother?

This interest in music not like that made in our own little villages (Dumbarton, Scotland, and Arbutus, Md., in my own case) is not, as it's often claimed, cultural tourism, because once you've let something in, let it grab hold of you, you're forever changed. Of course, you can also listen and remain completely unaffected and unmoved—like a tourist. Your loss. The fact is, after listening to some of this music for a while, it probably won't seem exotic any more, even if you still don't understand all the words. Thinking of things as exotic is only cool when it's your sister, your co-worker or wife; it's sometimes beneficial to exoticize that which has become overly familiar. But in other circumstances, viewing people and cultures as exotic is a distancing mechanism that too often allows for exploitation and racism.

Maybe it's naive, but I would love to believe that once you grow to love some aspect of a culture—its music, for instance—you can never again think of the people of that culture as less than yourself. I would like to believe that if I am deeply moved by a song originating from some place other than my own hometown, then I have in some way shared an experience with the people of that culture. I have been pleasantly contaminated. I can identify in some small way with it and its people. Not that I will ever experience music exactly the same way as those who make it. I am not Hank Williams, or even Hank Jr., but I can still love his music and be moved by it. Doesn't mean I have to live like him. Or take as many drugs as he did, or, for that matter, as much as the great flamenco singer Cameron de la Isla did.

That's what art does; it communicates the vibe, the feeling, the attitude toward our lives, in a way that is personal and universal at the same time. And we don't have to go through all the personal torment that the artist went through to get it. I would like to think that if you love a piece of music, how can you help but love, or at least respect, the producers of it? On the other hand, I know plenty of racists who love "soul" music, rap and rhythm-and-blues, so dream on, Dave.

## The Myth of the Authentic

The issue of "authenticity" is such a weird can of worms. Westerners get obsessed with it. They agonize over which is the "true" music, the real deal. I question the authenticity of some of the new-age ethnofusion music that's out there, but I also know that to rule out everything I personally abhor would be to rule out the possibility of a future miracle. Everybody knows the world has two types of music—my kind and everyone else's. And even my kind ain't always so great.

What is considered authentic today was probably some kind of bastard fusion a few years ago. An all-Japanese salsa orchestra's record (Orquestra de la Luz) was No. 1 on the salsa charts in the United States not long ago. Did the New York salseros care? No, most loved the songs and were frankly amazed. African guitar bands were doing their level best to copy Cuban rumbas, and in their twisted failure they came up with something new. So let's not make any rules about who can make a specific style of music.

Mr. Juju himself, King Sunny Ade, name-checks the country and western crooner Jim Reeves as an influence.[1] True. Rumor has it that the famous Balinese monkey chant was co-ordinated and choreographed by a German! The first South African pop record I bought was all tunes with American car race themes—the Indy 500 and the like. With sound effects,

---

1. The popularity of Jim Reeves in West Africa has long provoked curiosity among Western students of West African music; for an explanation, see Mark Schone, "Lord Jim: The African Diaspora Loves the Mellow Crooner," *Village Voice*, January 16, 1996, 55–56.

too! So let's forget about this authenticity bugaboo. If you are transported by the music, then knowing that the creators had open ears can only add to the enjoyment.

White folks needed to see Leadbelly in prison garb to feel they were getting the real thing. They need to be assured that rappers are "keeping it real," they need their Cuban musicians old and sweet, their Eastern and Asian artists "spiritual." The myths and cliches of national and cultural traits flourish in the marketing of music. There is the myth of the untutored, innocent savant whose rhymes contain funky Zen-like pearls of wisdom—the myth that exotic "traditional" music is more honest, more soulful and more in touch with a people's real and true feelings than the kid wearing jeans and the latest sports gear on Mexican television.

There is a perverse need to see foreign performers in their native dress rather than in the T-shirts and baggies that they usually wear off stage. We don't want them looking too much like us, because then we assume that their music is calculated, marketed, impure. Heaven forbid they should be at least as aware of the larger world as we are. All of which might be true, but more important, their larger awareness might also be relevant to their music, which in turn might connect it to our own lives and situations. Heaven forbid.

## La Nueva Generacion

In the last couple of years, there have been any number of articles in newspapers and magazines about how Latin music in particular was finally going to become hugely popular in the U.S. of A. Half—yes, half—of the current top 10 singles in Britain, that hot and sweaty country, are sort of Latin, if you count Geri Halliwell's "Mi Chico Latino," and why not? The others are watered-down remakes of Perez Prado's hits from the 50's and 60's. The Buena Vista Social Club record is the No. 1 selling record, in any category, in funky Germany. Les Nubians, a French-African group, is getting played on urban (translate as "black") radio in America. So is this a trend or what? Are these more than summer novelty tunes for anglos? Are we really going to learn to dance, or is this some kind of aberration?

But what about the alterna-Latino bands that are touring the United States and Europe in increasing numbers. The Columbian band Bloque (which, I confess, is on my label) was named best band of the year by a Chicago critic; Los Fabulosos Cadillacs won a Grammy last year. Both bands, and many, many others, mix the grooves of their neighborhoods with the sounds and attitudes of the North American tunes they also grew up with. They are a generation with a double heritage, and their music expresses it.

It's tough for this bunch to crack the American market: they're not always cute, safe or exotic. Their music is often more innovative than that of their northern counterparts, which is intimidating. And as cool as they are, they insist on singing in their own language, to an audience that identifies completely with them, thereby making it more difficult to gain a foothold in the States.

These bands are the musical equivalent of a generation of Latin American writers, including Gabriel Garcia Marquez, Isabel Allende, Jose Amado and Mario Vargas Llosa, that was referred to as the Boom. These musicians are defining their generation, finding a unique voice, and will influence countless others outside their home countries. Here, I believe, is where change will happen. Although they don't sell very many records yet, these and others (for things analogous to this are happening everywhere, in Africa, in Morocco, in Turkey) will plant the seeds, and while I enjoy hearing Ricky Martin's merengue on the radio, these others will change my life.

# 90. Genre or Gender?

## The Resurgence of the Singer-Songwriter

As almost any woman (and many men) who are interested in popular music will attest, a category or genre that is determined primarily by the gender of its participants is rather odd (though not necessarily any odder than one that is determined by race, a linkage that is largely taken for granted). Despite the inconsistencies of such a category, throughout the 1990s (and, into the 2000s), publications could not resist special issues with titles, such as "The Girl Issue" and "The Women of Rock," or articles with titles like "When Women Venture Forth" or "The Angry Young Woman."[1] While the female artists discussed in these articles were by no means consistent in terms of musical style, the surge of publisher and reader interest in the topic did derive from a general shift in how young women were conceiving their identities; this was reflected not only in an increased number of prominent female artists, but in the emergence of a different kind of female artist. Not limited to the "riot girl" phenomenon discussed in chapter 85, these musicians incorporated frank sexuality and some of the conventional signs of feminine attractiveness into a re-belliousness that was more aggressive than the second-wave feminism of the 1970s. Seemingly in tune with the critical perspective of books like Susan Faludi's *Backlash: The Undeclared War Against Women*,[2] many of these women merged the confessional stance of the singer-songwriter with the confrontational attitude of punk, emphasizing the importance of female desires that did not revolve around the need for male approval. A number of these musicians—"alternative" artists, such as Polly Jean Harvey, Liz Phair, and Björk—received a relatively large amount of critical acclaim and commercial success in the mid-1990s.

The release of Alanis Morissette's *Jagged Little Pill* (1995), the biggest-selling album of the 1990s, seemed to signify the triumph of a new sensibility—a successor to male-dominated alternative of the early 1990s. Morissette's success quickly occasioned its own backlash:

---

1. See "The Girl Issue," *Spin* (November 1997); "The Women of Rock," *Rolling Stone*, November 13, 1997 (*Rolling Stone* publishes a special issue with a title like this every few years); Ann Powers, "When Women Venture Forth," *New York Times*, October 9, 1994, Sec. 2, 32, 39; Jon Pareles, "The Angry Young Women: The Labels Take Notice," *New York Times*, January 28, 1996, Sec. 2, 24.

2. And, I might add, with a scholarly counterpart, such as Tania Modleski's *Feminism Without Women: Culture and Criticism in a "Postfeminist Age"* (New York: Routledge, 1991). Both Faludi and Modleski discuss the "backlash" against the gains made by feminism in the 1970s and the subsequent incorporation of feminist ideas and imagery into patriarchal narratives during the 1980s.

Despite the grunge-influenced first single, the vitriolic "You Oughta Know," those who listened to the whole album quickly realized that it had stronger links to the confessional singer-songwriter genre than to grunge. Despite this backlash, the years 1996–97 witnessed the success of numerous female artists. Sarah McLachlan (b. 1968), a singer-songwriter who had been overshadowed by Tori Amos (b. 1963) in the early 1990s, organized an all-female summer tour beginning in 1997, entitled "Lilith Fair," that presented women pop musicians in their own forum and appeared at the time to champion the triumph of a new kind of "girl culture."[3]

---

No one singer captured a more devoted following in the 1990s than Tori Amos, who released her first solo recording in 1991. A classically trained pianist and dynamic performer, Amos (according to Ann Powers) "cultivates a forthright sexuality that is more concerned with capturing what women feel than turning men on."[4] This 1996 interview with Amos finds her revisiting the issues of self-confession and autobiography that seem to appear whenever singer-songwriters are asked to talk about their music. The interview also reinvokes the ever-powerful opposition of formulaic commercialism versus authentic self-expression, an opposition with particular force in this genre, but one that Amos herself seems to call into question in her reverent discussion of the Beatles. The interview concludes with a humorous critique of one type of emotional expression that circulated widely in the 1990s: the angry despair of white, male rockers.

## Tori Amos: Pain for Sale
### Robert L. Doerschuk

*Why do you write songs?*
[Long thoughtful silence.] I remember walking down the hallways of the Peabody Conservatory and hearing the same piece being played in ten rooms, pretty much all the same. I knew that I couldn't play this piece better than any of these people. It would probably be very different: You'd know where the redhead was, you'd figure out which practice room I was in. But I'd never win any competitions, ever, because nobody was interested in my take on Debussy. I never won anything. I always got marked down. Always. I had big arguments with these people, that these guys were pushing the limits of music in their time, just like John Lennon in his time. To understand their music, you have to

---

3. Lilith Fair was seen by the press as a symbol of the triumph of female musicians; see Christopher John Farley, "Galapalooza," *Time,* July 21, 1997, 60–64; Neal Karlen, "On Top of Pop, But Not with One Voice," *New York Times,* June 29, 1997; and Ann Powers, "Wannabes: Lilith Fair," *Village Voice,* August 5, 1997, 63–64.
    4. Ann Powers, "When Women Venture Forth," *New York Times,* October 9, 1994, 39.

*Source:* Robert L. Doerschuk, "Tori Amos: Pain for Sale," *Keyboard* (November 1994), reprinted in Robert L. Doerschuk, ed., *Playing from the Heart: Great Musicians Talk About Their Craft* (San Francisco: Backbeat Books, 2002), pp. 141–46. © 2002. Used by permission of Backbeat Books.

understand the time. You have to know what's going on around them, especially when there's no lyric, when it's all music. Nobody, I thought, ever got the feel right. So I knew that if I was just gonna be playing some dead guy's music for the rest of my life, I'd probably never get a hearing, because their impression of what the dead guy should sound like was not mine at all.

*But going even further back, was there ever a time when something in you said, "I want to make my own notes and words"?*

I was seven [at Peabody]. I already knew what I was going to do. It was over when I was seven, a done deal. I was already writing. I didn't know how good or not good I could be. I knew that I could probably figure it out musically, but word-wise I was writing "The Jackass and the Toad Song." But I've always been a bit of a romantic. I'd be five years old, lying on my bed, with the afghan over me, squeezing my legs together and thinking, "Something should go here one day." I wanted to run away with all those guys, with Zeppelin and Jim Morrison and John Lennon. I [recently] told Robert Plant that I really wanted to pack my peanut butter and jelly and my teddy and my trolls and come find him.

*So even then the power of the songs being done by the people who wrote them was something you could feel.*

Yeah, I was totally conscious of that at five. It's funny, because I think I'm more affected by those writers than the ones who were happening when I was in high school. I wasn't really affected by what was going on in 1979. I had checked out; I was listening to my old records. Somebody played me the Sex Pistols after they had come and gone, and I wee'd in my pants. I said, "Shit, my father never showed me that this existed." I felt absolutely inadequate when I heard the Sex Pistols and the Clash, going, "Where was I?" I mean, I made Zeppelin and the Beatles and all those people when I was five. . . . Actually, Zeppelin didn't happen until I was nine or ten, when I started to bleed, so it was totally perfect; I was all ready for Robert.

*How did those sorts of influences affect your growth as a songwriter?*

First of all, I cannot contrive a song. I'm not nailing people who can. I know some very good writers who I respect a lot. They're called to do something for a movie, and they come up with it in two weeks. They're not schlock writers; I'm talking about people who don't do hack jobs. They've got two weeks, and they're watching the film, and they're getting inspired. And I'm like, "How do you do that?" I don't care what you offer me right now. If the fairies don't sprinkle their little wee on my head, it's not gonna happen. I can't make it happen. Now, say I'm walking down the street, eating a banana, and something happens—four bars, with a sketchy lyric. If you gave me two weeks, maybe I could develop it, just on my skills and craft alone. I'm not telling you it would be great. It might be passable. But there are certain songs I look at and say, "I would not change a breath."

*Those who can produce songs on demand tend to rely on certain formulas. Are you saying that it's best to avoid formulas in order to write more personal material?*

Well, we have to remember that hit records and good songs are not synonymous. Maybe in the old days, a little bit. But now most hit records are not great songs. I'm not saying that those formula writers cannot stumble on something. But at a certain point, it's not about formula writing. I know I'm going back to the Beatles, just because that's a big point of reference, but how consistent can you get? "Eleanor Rigby"? "Norwegian Wood"? How many great songs and hit songs do you get? I remember John Lennon talking about listening to songs that he loved, then changing them to make his own versions. He would say, "God, I love this song. I wish I'd written this song." Then it would come out totally different. You might not even know what song it is that inspired you to do something, but there is that ingredient. Sometimes I do think that we're really just rewriting songs. There are only twelve bloody notes, you know. So I'll listen to some song and say, "Why didn't I write that?"

*Because it speaks to you . . .*

. . . as if I would have written it. I could name five songs, right off the top of my head, that I would have given my right arm to write. [Joni Mitchell's] "Case of You": You don't get it any better. A better song hasn't been written. I don't care what female singer/songwriter you throw up in my face: None has done anything in the league of "Case of You," me included. For a woman to be able to say what that says, with that kind of addiction and yet that kind of grace, is just not done. Even Zeppelin and those guys listened to Joni. It kills me when the metal guys or the hard-rocking guys who are more poseurs than anything will show up and say, "You know, all the guys in my band are embarrassed to like you, because they're into Zeppelin." And I'll say, "That's kind of funny, 'cause I just did a duet with Robert." I don't think people understand that with songwriters, it's not about volume, you know?

*Commercial songwriters can be like caricaturists who scale complex emotions and issues down to bite size. You and other more personal writers are more like abstract painters.*

You're right, but my intentions for writing have changed. There's a time when you want people to sing your songs with you. If you didn't, you'd keep them in your living room. Let's not lie to ourselves; that's the truth. Even though I could tell you I'm writing because it's my form of expression, there is a need—that is a fair word, I think—to have them shared. Sometimes I'll listen to work that I've done, and I'll go, "I'm not in that place anymore. I couldn't write like that if my life depended on it. But I do understand an element of it that I would like to have in, say, this next piece." I do like that approach of, like, peeling your skin off. Although the whole concept of *Under the Pink* is about peeling the skin off, that's more of an abstract work, whereas *Little Earthquakes* is more like a diary.

*There must be a limit to how far you want to open that diary in your work.*

Funny you should say that. Since before I wrote *Little Earthquakes* I've had a pact with myself of no censorship. See, if you're a songwriter and people don't really know who you are, that's one thing. But if you're singing your own songs, it's a little different in this respect: I've found that the more known a writer gets, the less powerful and exposing their work gets, because the more they get known, the less they want to expose. I've caught myself trying to censor recently, going, "Oh, my God, they're gonna know who that is." But this is not about putting names next to things. That's irrelevant. If people want to speculate, they've missed the point.

*The paradox in this kind of writing is that the more you personalize, or Tori Amosize, your songs, the more universal they become to those who work to get inside them.*

But I don't think that these are Tori Amos songs. I translate them in such a way because of Tori's experiences that would be different from so-and-so's experiences. Emotions are very simple. I don't find them complex at all, to be quite honest. Everybody understands basic emotions: feeling like a coward, wanting to kill some cunt and having no remorse about it. It's like, "No, I don't feel guilty about this. What I feel bad about is that I don't feel bad about this." That's what I have to look at. I try and crawl into my unconscious, and it's not that different from what's inside any of us. All of us have a bit of the vampire and a bit of the nightingale. But don't tell me that the hardest cats rockin' out there right now aren't afraid of pain. I'm just saying that, whatever your lifestyle, they're all bummed out that Mom's gone.

*In his last work, John Lennon even turned domesticity into art.*
Well, who says that just because you fall in love and you open your heart to somebody that
   you're not gonna have more passion, more angst, more to look at than you ever had?
   The more you expose yourself to different feelings, the more you have to draw on. Obviously, if you're in a complacent relationship, your work might sound that way. But
   why does growing have to be synonymous with complacency? There's so much self-
   destruction on the artist's side. Not necessarily on the hack's side. Hacks aren't
   self-destructive, because they've got a business to run. But the artist will do anything to
   keep the machine going. We're so afraid to write things that won't be accepted. Well,
   I believe that audiences get bored very quickly.

*Bored with someone's output over a period of years?*
Yeah, at a certain point. Maybe you know it even before they do, because you feel it.

*How do you keep in touch with real life from within the cocoon of fame?*
Look, if my whole life was . . .

*Not your whole life.*
Wait. If most of my life was about going into the studio, making the record, doing the video,
   doing the tour, living and breathing only that, at a certain point, what would I fucking
   write about? I know that. Now, there are some very good ones out there whose work is
   still about one kind of energy. Say it's anger: That's all it is. Well, guys, hello? Can we
   have maybe a different angle on your anger today? All the angry boys out there talk
   about how they can't have this stuff. Now, I adore angry boys. I'd make 'em all apple
   pie with cinnamon ice cream. But they all talk about how they can't have this and they
   can't have that. They've got this whole movement based on what they can't have. And
   I say to them, wrong. It's a choice. They've chosen not to have certain things. And none
   of them takes any responsibility for that. Those boys are gonna get interesting when
   they start to go, "I chose not to have love." Come on, boys. Let's say something
   interesting for a change, instead of, "I can never have this or that." That's your choice,
   because you think you're shit. There's very little responsibility for their part in it. They
   don't own up to, "The reason I can't have love is because I think I'm gonna shrivel
   when I'm with this woman, because I don't think I deserve her." Let's go into the why.
   To go into that, you have to live. You're not gonna get to those answers by I-IV-V-
   fucking-I.
       And it's not just the boys. Some of the girls do it too. Ay-yi-yi, can we stop blaming
   the guys here? We can blame them for what they've done, but then we have to balance
   in what we've done. The work isn't interesting when people aren't constantly discovering. We're stopping our lives as writers because we think we won't make great art.
   Who has put this thought out there? It's like a virus.

*You're saying that there's a loss with respect to talented writers who could have said so much more
   before getting stuck on a single riff.*
Totally that's what I'm saying. It is such a sense of loss. I'm not gonna mention names, but
   I'll watch something and go, "I know that this is very calculated." Once you've been on
   the other side, you know what it is and what it isn't. You just smell it. You're like, "This
   person has so much. They could go further than they ever thought they could go in
   their pain and their darkness." I've always said that Lucifer understands love better
   than anybody. You know he's done a mean tango with Greta Garbo a few times. Really
   understanding love is the only way you get to that side of things. Otherwise, you're just
   renting videos. It's HBO. These guys and girls who write about one more torture device
   over and over again? That doesn't scare them. That's not a challenge. And that's not
   challenging those kids who really are screaming. Talk about pain: If they want to

experience pain, they should go hold hands with the Little Mermaid. Then they'll get scared shitless because they'll have to be real.

*The pain industry that you're describing . . .*
That's a great term for it. I guess I'm part of it too, in a sense.

*. . . strips real pain of its validity. When people tire of hearing songs that tell them how miserable they should be, they're robbed of the opportunity to feel real misery.*
And they become parodies of themselves. It's so theatrical. Where's the real experience, so that when you take it to theatrics the foundation is still strong? But when it's just about anger for anger's sake . . .

*. . . you're describing the fashion rather than the guts.*
It is a fashion, and it isn't really that deep. We can all be a bit seduced by it. There's a masochist in me too, but my masochist is getting a little bit bored. It's not getting satisfied by those guys anymore. It's like, "You think that's painful?" My God, Baudelaire and Rimbaud were talking about and experiencing the heart. But it's so easy to contrive something. You know, "We're marketing dismemberment this week. That seems to be what kids want, so we'll do it. No problem." The whole point is that dismemberment isn't darkness, is it? It's just dismemberment. It's like, that's why God created video, so that you don't have to do any work on yourself. It's just a good distraction, an alternative to getting to what darkness is. The music business is packaging darkness, but for the most part I think it's just a parody of darkness.

Look, I'm just saying that the writers' community has been given a drug. "Tori takes another step in her life, so she won't be able to write songs like 'Silent All These Years' anymore." Guess what? You're right. She'll never be able to write that again. So why is that a bad thing?

# 91. Public Policy and Pop Music History Collide

Although public policy in the United States has affected the radio and recording industries since their inception—most spectacularly in the 1940s with laws that first eased restrictions on playing recorded music on the radio and then encouraged the spread of nonnetwork radio broadcasting—one development in the 1990s had particularly dramatic consequences. For those who wondered what the homogeneity of U.S. radio in the late 1990s and the dominance of teen pop had in common, one need look no further than the 1996 Telecommunications Act. A law that loosened restrictions on how many radio stations could be owned by a single company led to an unprecedented concentration of programming and, hence, to the sense that all radio broadcasts were emanating from an amorphous, all-American nowhere land. After 1996, as corporate entities, such as Clear Channel, bought as many as 1,200 radio stations throughout the country, one could hear the same classic rock/modern rock/adult contemporary, etc. playlists whether driving through Maine or Montana.

The oligopolistic nature of these companies gave them enormous clout: If a new recording gained access to their playlist, it was guaranteed a huge audience; on the other hand, the lack of access created sizable barriers to large-scale success (this recalls some of the points made by Robert Christgau in chapter 66). The teen pop being produced in Orlando, Florida, with consummate skill (N'Sync, Britney Spears, Backstreet Boys, and the like) was eminently well suited to the conservative aesthetic and social vision of the programmers at media behemoths, such as Clear Channel. While teen pop had long been an important component of popular music, it had never achieved success on such a grand scale. The appearance of teen pop stars on the cover of *Rolling Stone* (a sure sign that the by-now venerable publication was experiencing an identity crisis), on college students' lists of favorite artists, and on MTV's "Total Request Live" countdown, showed teen pop boldly going into audiences and media where it had rarely gone before. This development spoke to the symbiosis between changes in consumption and the way media (especially radio) were operating.

Jenny Toomey's involvement with music is remarkably diverse: as a solo singer-guitarist and member of many bands, including Edith Frost, Tsunami, and Liquorice; as cochair of Simple Machines Records; and as director of the Future of Music Coalition, a political organization that works for the improvement of conditions for musicians. In the following article, she analyzes the impact of the 1996 Telecommunications Act, mentioning the ominous spectacle of yet further deregulation and its impact.[1]

---

1. For another view of the 1996 Telecommunications Act that details its potentially disastrous impact on the loss of local broadcasting in alerting the public in the event of emergencies (as well as on the decrease in protest music on the radio), see Brent Staples, "The Trouble With Corporate Radio: The Day the Protest Music Died," *New York Times*, February 20, 2003. Jenny Eliscu also addresses the issue in "Why Radio Sucks," *Rolling Stone*, April 3, 2003, p. 22. In another nearly contemporary editorial, Paul Krugman reveals the close links of Clear Channel to the George W. Bush administration and the role of the network in organizing pro-war rallies before and during the 2003 invasion of Iraq even as Clear Channel lobbied for further deregulation; see Paul Krugman, "Channels of Influence," *New York Times*, March 25, 2003.

# EMPIRE OF THE AIR
## Jenny Toomey

For too long, musicians have had too little voice in the manufacture, distribution and promotion of their music and too little means to extract fair support and compensation for their work. The Future of Music Coalition was formed in June 2000 as a not-for-profit think tank to tackle this problem, advocating new business models, technologies and policies that would advance the cause of both musicians and citizens. Much of the work the FMC has done in the past two years has focused on documenting the structures of imbalance and inequity that impede the development of an American musicians' middle class, and translating legislative-speak into language the musicians and citizens can understand. Our most challenging work, however, and the project of which we are most proud, is our analysis of the effects of radio deregulation on musicians and citizens since the passage of the 1996 Telecommunications Act.

Radio is a public resource managed on citizens' behalf by the federal government. This was established in 1934 through the passage of the Communications Act, which created a regulatory body, the Federal Communications Commission, and laid the ground rules for the regulation of radio. The act also determined that the spectrum would be managed according to a "trusteeship" model. Broadcasters received fixed-term, renewable licenses that gave them exclusive use of a slice of the spectrum for free. In exchange, they were required to serve the "public interest, convenience and necessity." Though they laid their trust in the mechanics of the marketplace, legislators did not turn the entire spectrum over to commercial broadcasters. The 1934 act included some key provisions that were designed to foster localism and encourage diversity in programming.

Although changes were made to limits on ownership and FCC regulatory control in years hence, the Communications Act of 1934 remained essentially intact until it was thoroughly overhauled in 1996 with the passage of the Telecommunications Act. But even before President Clinton signed the act into law in February 1996, numerous predictions were made regarding its effect on the radio industry:

- The number of individual radio-station owners would decrease. Those in the industry with enough capital would begin to snatch up valuable but under-performing stations in many markets—big and small.
- Station owners—given the ability to purchase more stations both locally and nationally—would benefit from economies of scale. Radio runs on many fixed costs: Equipment, operations and staffing costs are the same whether broadcasting to one person or 1 million. Owners knew that if they could control more than one station in a local market, they could consolidate operations and reduce fixed expenses. Lower costs would mean increased profit potential. This would, in turn, make for more financially sound radio stations, which would be able to compete more effectively against new media competitors: cable TV and the Internet.
- There was a prediction based on a theory posited by a 1950s economist named Peter Steiner that increased ownership consolidation on the local level would lead to a subsequent increase in the number of radio format choices available to the listening public. (Steiner, writing in 1952, was not talking about oligopolistic control of the market by a few firms, as we have in the United States; rather, he was basing

Jenny Toomey, "Empire of the Air," *The Nation*, January 13–20, 2003, pp. 28–30. Reprinted with permission from the January 13, 2003, issue of *The Nation*.

his predictions on an analysis of BBC radio, which is a nationally owned radio monopoly, not an oligopoly.) According to Steiner's theory, a single owner with multiple stations in a local market wouldn't want to compete against himself. Instead, he would program each station differently to meet the tastes of a variety of listeners.

But what really happened?

Well, one prediction certainly came true: The 1996 act opened the floodgates for ownership consolidation. Ten parent companies now dominate the radio spectrum, radio listenership and radio revenues, controlling two-thirds of both listeners and revenue nationwide. Two parent companies in particular—Clear Channel and Viacom—together control 42 percent of listeners and 45 percent of industry revenues.

Consolidation is particularly extreme in the case of Clear Channel. Since passage of the Telecommunications Act, Clear Channel has grown from forty stations to 1,240 stations—thirty times more than Congressional regulation previously allowed. No potential competitor owns even one-quarter the number of Clear Channel stations. With more than 100 million listeners, Clear Channel reaches more than one-third of the US population.

Even more bleak is the picture at the local level, where oligopolies control almost every market. Virtually every local market is dominated by four firms controlling 70 percent of market share or greater. In smaller markets, consolidation is more extreme. The largest four firms in most small markets control 90 percent of market share or more. These companies are sometimes regional or national station groups and not locally owned.

Only the few radio-station owners with enough capital to buy additional stations have benefited from deregulation. Station owners have consolidated their operations on a local level, frequently running a number of stations out of a single building, sharing a single advertising staff, technicians and on-air talent. In some cases, radio-station groups have further reduced costs by eliminating the local component almost entirely. Local deejays and program directors are being replaced by regional directors or even by voice-tracked or syndicated programming, which explains a marked decrease in the number of people employed in the radio industry.

Prior to 1996, radio was among the least concentrated and most economically competitive of the media industries. In 1990 no company owned more than fourteen of the more than 10,000 stations nationwide, with no more than two in a single local market. But we found that local markets have now consolidated to the point that just four major radio groups control about 50 percent of the total listener audience and revenue. Clearly, deregulation has reduced competition within the radio industry.

As a result, listeners are losing. With an emphasis on cost-cutting and an effort to move decision-making out of the hands of local station staff, much of radio has become bland and formulaic. Recall Steiner's hopeful theory that an owner would not want to compete against his own company and would therefore operate stations with different programming. We found evidence to the contrary: Radio companies regularly operate two or more stations with the same format—for example, rock, country, adult contemporary, top 40—in the same local market. In a recent *New York Times* article, "Fewer Media Owners, More Media Choices," FCC chairman Michael Powell denied this, propping up Steiner's theory by saying things like, "Common ownership can lead to more diversity—what does the owner get for having duplicative products?" But we found 561 instances of format redundancy nationwide—a parent company operating two or more stations in the same market, with the same format—amounting to massive missed opportunities for variety.

Still, from 1996 to 2000, format variety—the average number of formats available in each local market—actually increased in both large and small markets. But format variety is not equivalent to true diversity in programming, since formats with different names have similar playlists. For example, alternative, top 40, rock and hot adult contemporary are all likely to play songs by the band Creed, even though their formats are not the same. In fact, an analysis of data from charts in *Radio and Records* and *Billboard's Airplay Monitor* revealed considerable playlist overlap—as much as 76 percent—between supposedly distinct formats. If the FCC or the National Association of Broadcasters is sincerely trying to measure programming "diversity," doing so on the basis of the number of formats in a given market is a flawed methodology.

This final point may be the most critical one as we face an FCC that is poised to deregulate media even further in the next few months. (In September, the commissioners voted unanimously to open review of the FCC's media ownership rules.) It is time to put to bed the commonly held yet fundamentally flawed notion that consolidation promotes diversity—that radio-station owners who own two stations within a marketplace will not be tempted to program both stations with the same songs. There's a clear corporate benefit in "self-competition," and it's time we made regulatory agencies admit that fact.

Even in the beginning, radio was regulated to cultivate a commercial broadcast industry that could grow to serve the greatest number of Americans possible. As the decades have passed, most calls for deregulation have come from incumbent broadcasters interested in lifting local and national ownership caps that protect against the competitive pressures in other media.

While the effects of deregulation have been widely studied and discussed, scrutiny is focused on the profitability of the radio industry. But the effect of increased corporate profitability on citizens is rarely, if ever, discussed. Radical deregulation of the radio industry allowed by the Telecommunications Act of 1996 has not benefited the public. Instead, it has led to less competition, fewer viewpoints and less diversity in programming. Substantial ethnic, regional and economic populations are not provided the services to which they are entitled. The public is not satisfied, and possible economic efficiencies of industry consolidation are not being passed on to the public in the form of improved local service. Deregulation has damaged radio as a public resource.

Musicians are also suffering because of deregulation. Independent artists have found it increasingly difficult to get airplay; in payola-like schemes, the "Big Five" music companies, through third-party promoters, shell out thousands of dollars per song to the companies that rule the airwaves. That's part of why the Future of Music Coalition undertook this research. We at the FMC firmly believe that the music industry as it exists today is fundamentally anti-artist. In addition to our radio study, our projects—including a critique of standard major-label contract clauses, a study of musicians and health insurance, and a translation of the complicated Copyright Arbitration Royalty Panel proceedings that determined the webcasting royalty rates—were conceived as tools for people who are curious about the structures that impede musicians' ability to both live and make a living. Understanding radio deregulation is another tool for criticizing such structures. We have detailed the connections between concentrated media ownership, homogenous radio programming and restricted radio access for musicians. Given that knowledge, we hope artists will join with other activists and work to restore radio as a public resource for all people.

# 92. Electronica Is in the House

After its tremendous efflorescence in the late 1970s, disco assumed a lower profile during the 1980s. Yet electronically based dance music maintained a lively existence in clubs, and DJs and studio producers never ceased producing variations on grooves that would prompt listeners to shake their booties. While many pop stars, most notably Madonna, brought some of these developments to the wider pop music audience, during the 1980s, many of the changes in dance music remained out of the view of the mainstream. Frankie Knuckles in Chicago at the Warehouse Club and Larry Levan in New York City extended the embrace of purely synthesized sound initiated by Giorgio Moroder in Eurodisco. The new recordings produced for clubs like the Warehouse (largely black and mostly gay) emphasized those aspects of disco that the "disco sucks" crowd had found the most alienating, further "dehumanizing" their dance music with "tracks" that were often no more than rhythm patterns realized on drum machines. The new producers and DJs then superimposed simple synthesizer patterns and maybe a few chanted phrases sung by an African American female onto these rhythm tracks.

Concurrently during the early- and mid-1980s, DJs and record producers in Detroit, including Derrick May, Juan Atkins, and Kevin Saunderson, began producing recordings that sought to extend the futuristic techno sound of European groups, such as Kraftwerk (at around the same time as Afrika Bambaataa used Kraftwerk as the basis for electro-funk). The resultant dance genre, "techno," moved at a slightly faster tempo than house and emphasized experimental "noisy" timbres rather than the remnants of disco elegance still prominent in house. According to Jon Savage, "Derrick May once described techno as 'just like Detroit, a complete mistake. It's like George Clinton and Kraftwerk stuck in an elevator.'"[1]

Beginning in 1986–87, both techno and house (and its psychedelicized descendant, acid house) began to catch on in the United Kingdom and Europe. "Techno" the umbrella term used in the United Kingdom for electronic dance music, rapidly split off in numerous directions. One of these, "hardcore," emerged around 1990 in the context of "raves": huge, all-night dance parties in which a large number of the participants imbibed psychedelic drugs, especially MDMA, or Ecstasy. DJs achieved their reputations through their ability to produce sounds that were appealing to listeners in this particular altered state. Hardcore specialized in

---

1. Jon Savage, "Machine Soul: A History of Techno," *Village Voice Rock and Roll Quarterly* (Summer 1993): 19.

industrial "noise" and industrial-strength beats, joining the relentless four-to-the bar bass drum of techno with syncopated patterns derived from the breakbeats beloved by hip-hop DJs. Another development, "ambient" or "intelligent" techno, relied on slightly slower tempos and softer, "spacier" sounds and was designed either for listening or for "chilling out" at the end of a night-long bacchanal. Ambient techno also drew on the latent avant-garde aspect of electronic music, tracing the interest back both to Kraftwerk's interest in futurism and to Brian Eno's percussionless "ambient" music.

Raves reached the United States in the early 1990s, but the development from the United Kingdom that really attracted the attention of the music press in the States was "jungle." Developing out of hardcore, jungle speeded up the tempo to ca. 160 bpm ("beats-per-minute"—the typical house track is around 125 bpm), and sampled dance-hall reggae drum patterns, often further scrambling them with a computer once they were sampled. The most rhythmically complex form of electronic dance music, jungle joins these fast, dauntingly syncopated drum patterns with slow-moving bass lines and ethereal, sustained synthesizer parts. An important sociological factor about jungle was its connection to the black British community, leading some commentators to view it as the British corollary to gangsta rap.[2] The origins of the term "jungle" were debated, but by the end of 1995, the term "drum 'n' bass" seemed to have replaced "jungle," presumably because of its lesser racist connotations.

Another term, "electronica," began to come into play during 1996–97 as part of a larger campaign to promote electronic music as the next big thing in American popular music. Drum 'n' bass, trip hop, and big beat were all subgenres that featured prominently. While electronica never really became the next grunge, it has established itself as part of the larger field of North American popular music. Some artists, such as the Chemical Brothers (exemplars of "big beat") and Moby have achieved mainstream recognition and success, while "illbeint" and "trip hop" artists (like DJ Spooky, Tricky, and DJ Shadow) have pushed the artsy envelope. Electronic music's subgenres continue to proliferate at an amazing rate, making electronica the successor to indie-rock in terms of what it requires from its fans for insider status.[3]

The preceding offers only the barest sketch of electronic dance music in the 1980s and 1990s. For a fuller discussion, readers would have to turn to Simon Reynolds, *Generation Ecstasy: Into the World of Techno and*

2. Simon Reynolds, "Will Jungle Be the Next Craze from Britain?" *New York Times*, August 6, 1995, Sec. 2, 28.

3. This aspect of electronic dance music is the focus of Sarah Thornton's *Club Cultures: Music, Media and Subcultural Capital* (Hanover, N.H.: Wesleyan University Press and University Press of New England, 1996).

*Rave Culture*, the fullest treatment of the history presented here.[4] In the next entry, Reynolds discusses many of the factors that separate electronica from other forms of post–rock 'n' roll popular music, factors that are central to the enjoyment of its fans and the revulsion felt by its detractors. Not surprisingly, the issues that emerge bear more than a passing resemblance to those discussed in chapter 61 with reference to disco.

# HISTORIA ELECTRONICA PREFACE
## *Simon Reynolds*

Every so often, people ask me: "Why are you so into electronic music and this whole dance culture thing? What's it all about? What makes it different?" Some add a slightly combative edge to the question, pointing out that there's always been "dance music," and that anyway people will dance to any music if they like it, even a group as overtly non-funky as The Smiths or REM. If they're really sharp, these people also point out that almost all pop today is "electronic," using synthesizers, sequencers, sampling, and digital editing software like Pro Tools, or processing "natural" acoustic sounds like the human voice or drums through effects, filters, and studio sorcery of all kinds. And after all, what's an electric guitar if not an electronic instrument?

These are all good points, but the fact remains that electronic dance culture is a distinct entity. What follows here is my attempt to sketch the broad foundational principles that give electronic dance music its coherence as a defined cultural field. Not every exponent of this music, not every scene or genre, fits each single criteria, and some actively flout "the rules." But taken en masse, these parameters define a kind of "field of possibility" within which the vast, variegated sprawl of electronic dance exists. For sure, it's a terrain with porous boundaries, through which seep influences from neighbouring areas of music. Sonically, the most influential of these neighbours are hip hop, avant-garde electronic experimentalism, industrial, and dub reggae. In terms of attitudes and values, rock in all its various forms, from psychedelia to punk, has had the most impact on electronic dance culture. From full-on rave madness to self-consciously avant-garde experimentalism, electronica has become the inheritor of rock's seriousness: its belief that music can change the world (or at least an individual's consciousness), rock notions of "progression" or "subversion," the conviction that music needs to be more than entertainment. Yet at the same time, the founding principles I sketch below frequently challenge and dismantle rock ideas of how creativity works, what defines art, and where the meaning and power of music is located.

## 1. Machine Music

Dance music isn't unique in being obsessed with technology: rock has its share of songs hymning cars, while guitars are fetishized as noise-weapons. But electronica goes further

---

4. Simon Reynolds, *Generation Ecstasy: Into the World of Techno and Rave Culture* (New York: Routledge, [1998] 1999). An excellent earlier overview is provided by Jon Savage, "Machine Soul": 18–21. A more recent overview may be found in Bill Werde, "Talking Music: Sounds from the Dance Floor," *New York Times*, March 24, 2000.

*Source:* Simon Reynolds, "Historia Electronica Preface," from *Loops: Una Historia De La Musica Electronica,* ed. Javier Blanquez and Omar Morera (Barcelona; Reservoir Books, 2002). Copyright © 2001 by Simon Reynolds. Reprinted by permission of Simon Reynolds.

by defining itself as machine-music. This is upfront in the genre name "techno," and it comes through in the reverence for specific pieces of equipment: drum machines like the Roland 808 and Roland 909 to antique synths like the Moog and Wasp. You even have artists naming themselves in homage to gear: House of 909, 808 State, Q-Bass (a pun on the Cubase programming software). And you can see the cult of machinery in names that sound hyper-technical, robotic, or like models of cars or computers: Electribe 101, LFO, Nexus 21. Electronic musicians also love to describe what they do as scientific research, imagining the studio as a sound-laboratory.

Electronic music is driven by a quest to find the most radical or futuristic-sounding potential in brand-new technology. And that involves essentially (re)inventing the machines: producers are always claiming the first thing they do after acquiring new gear is to throw away the instruction manual and start messing around. Often creativity entails abusing the machines, employing them incorrectly. Mistakes—sometimes genuinely accidental, sometimes "deliberate errors"—become aestheticized. This is a pop echo of the 20th-Century classical avant-garde's project of pushing the envelope of what is conventionally regarded as "music," via the incorporation of noise-sound and environmental sonorities.

You can hear this in the contemporary genre of "glitch," where artists like Oval and Fennesz make radically beautiful music using the snaps, crackles and pops emitted by damaged CDs, malfunctioning software, etc. In dancefloor genres like speed garage and jungle, you can hear the same approach in the deliberate misuse of timestretching, a digital effect that allows a sample to be compressed or prolonged in duration without its pitch going up or down. Previously when producers speeded up a vocal sample to fit the ever-faster tempos of dance music, the effect was squeaky and cartoon-absurd, like the vocalist had inhaled helium. Timestretch was invented to enable producers to achieve pleasanter, more "musical" results, but ironically it's been seized on for the opposite effect: stretching out a vocal until the sample cracks up, creating a terrifying metallic rattle like a stuttering robot.

Even when machines aren't being used in ways never intended by the manufacturer, electronic dance music aestheticizes the mechanistic and industrial-sounding—sonic attributes opposite to the traditional musicianly premium on hand's on "feel" and nimble dexterity. In electronic music, the cold precision and uninflected regularity of drum-machine beats and sequenced basslines aren't considered unmusical or lacking in "swing." Riffs tend to be angular rather than curvaceous; timbres are blatantly synthetic and artificial-sounding (unlike in pop music, where synthesisers are mostly used to inexpensively simulate acoustic instruments like horns or strings). The very inhuman aura of electronic music is part of the culture's obsession with the future, whether that is conceived as a utopia of streamlined pleasure-tech, or a dystopia of control and automation.

A lot of electronica is not "played" in any traditional instrumental sense, but is assembled using computers. Riffs are "step-written" one note at a time on a sequencer (sometimes resulting in note-patterns that would be unplayable by human hands). With the ever-more complex "virtual studio technology" software that's available, you can "draw" the music on a computer screen as a visually represented waveform; sonic material can be endlessly edited and recombined, layered and subjected to all kinds of treatments and effects. As a result, what you hear rarely correlates with physical human actions in the way that the sounds in rock music (even heavily studio-manipulated and overdubbed rock) still correlate to recognisable manual gestures. So you rarely visualize a person or band when you hear electronic music. Some find this unnerving, an erasure of humanity, but for others it frees up the imagination: the music becomes a intricate, maze-like environment, or an abstract machine taking the listener on a journey through a soundscape.

## 2. Texture/Rhythm Versus Melody/Harmony

Another aspect of electronica's break with traditional musicality is the way that processing is more important than playing; the vivid, ear-catching textures matter more than the actual notes played. For conventionally trained musicians, the chord progressions and harmonic intervals used in electronic music can seem obvious and trite. But this misses the point, for the real function of the simple vamps and melody-lines is as a device to display timbre, texture, tone-colour, chromatics. That's why so much electronica uses naive child-like melodies that sound like a music-box's chimes. Complicated melodies would distract from the sheer lustrous materiality of sound-in-itself; the pigment is more important than the line. Recent technology like DSP (digital signal processing) and "plug-ins" (the computer age equivalent to guitar effects pedals) allow for a fantastical palette of timbral colours.

In electronic dance, every element works as both texture and rhythm. Beats are filtered to sound metallic, crunchy, spongy, shiny, wet. Melodic units are mostly simple, little vamps and riffs that work as rhythmic cogs interlocking to form a groove. And rhythm usurps the place of melody. In much of this music, it's the drum patterns—off-kilter breakbeat arrangements in drum 'n' bass, intricate hi-hat figures in house and garage—that are the hooks, the most memorable element of a track. Each year the rhythmic subdivision of time gets ever more fantastically complex: micro-syncopations, assymetrical patterns riddled with hesitations, multiple tiers of polyrhythm. Factor in DSP treatment of the beats and the spatial distribution of drums across the stereo-mix, and the result is a kind of rhythmic psychedelia.

## 3. You're So Physical

With almost everything in the music working as rhythm, electronic dance is supremely physical music, engaging the body's psychomotor reflexes and tugging at your limbs. But this doesn't make the music "mindless." Rather, electronic dance music dissolves the old dichotomy between head and body, between "serious" music for home-listening and "stupid" music for the dancefloor. As British critic Kodwo Eshun argues, at its most sophisticated electronica makes your mind dance and your body think. There is a kinaesthetic intelligence in this music that involves your muscles and nerves, and which is seen at its utmost in the extraordinary grace and fractal fluidity of the dancing style, "liquid," that's popular at American raves. Yet still you get people who uphold a dichotomy between music for listening and music for dancing. Actually, a good dancer is "listening" with every sinew and tendon in her body.

Electronic dance is intensely physical in another sense: it's designed to be heard over massive club sound systems. Sound becomes a fluid immersive medium enfolding the body in an intimate pressure of beat and bass. The low-end frequencies permeate your flesh, make your body vibrate and tremble. The entire body becomes an ear.

## 4. Against Interpretation

Electronic music appeals to the mind in a quite particular way, however. Not by engaging the listener's interpretative mechanism (the traditional rock mode of treating songs as stories or statements), but rather through heightening perception through the sheer intricacy of the music: its rhythmic detail, otherworldly textures, and spatial depth. Most of this music is devoid of lyrics, and when it does have them, they tend to be simple catchphrases or cliched evocations of celebration, hope, intensity, mystical feelings. Ultimately, this music is not really about communication but about communion: a sensory unity experienced by everybody on the dancefloor. Hence the slogan "House is a feeling," used in countless dance tracks. The word "feeling" refers both to an emotional mood (elation tinged with a hint of blues, the sense of the club space as a blissful sanctuary circumscribed by a hostile, unstable outside world) and to a physical sensation: the waves of sound caressing your body, the collective feeling of being locked in a groove, every body in the house synchronized, entrained to the same rhythmic cycle, on the same track. Dance tracks are like vehicles, taking you on a journey, a pleasure-ride; there's a reason DJs use the term "train wreck" to describe when they do a bad mix between records.

The vagueness of the saying "house is a feeling" contains its own eloquence: this sensational sensation is hard to verbalize, almost impossible to explain to those who've never felt it. It bypasses "meaning" in the rock sense but is intensely meaningful. Hence dance music's recurrent use of religious imagery, its references to a knowledge that is privy only to initiates: slogans like "you know the score," "this is for those who know." Crucial distinction: this secret knowledge isn't elitist, but it is tribal, working through a powerful inclusion/exclusion effect.

## 5. Surface Versus Depth

People coming to this music from "outside"—that's to say with no direct club experience—often complain about an "emptiness" to the music: the sense that it is superficial, lacking in real-world referents, mere escapism. One of the most radical aspects of the music, though, is the way that electronica abolishes the depth model used by most criticism (in which some art is profound, some shallow) because all its pleasures are out there on the surface. The music is a flat plane of sensuous bliss.

You can see this in the way dance music uses the human voice. House divas have always been somewhat anonymous and depersonalized, rarely being the star focus of a song but more like a technically skilled artisan playing a role in a team effort. As the music evolved, producers increasingly used vocals in a non-expressive way, treating the singer as a source of raw material, a plastic substance to be folded, snipped, recombined, processed. From the simple voice-riffs in early house music (vocal samples distributed across a sampling keyboard and played, so that the voice becomes just an instrumental color) this has evolved into the complicated "vocal science" in today's 2step garage. Here samples from R&B songs are chopped up, resequenced, and turned into percussive elements of the groove, effectively transforming the singer into an adjunct to the drum kit. "Soul" is emptied out, and the human voice becomes two-dimensional, just one of an array of special effects and sonic pyrotechnics.

This depersonalising of the voice connects to a general anxiety that many people feel about electronic music: because it is not "saying" anything, its pleasures seem vicarious, indulgent, mere empty hedonism devoid of spiritual nourishment. Often detractors use metaphors like "ear-candy" to convey this sense of something that isn't good for you but just offers an empty sugar-rush.

## 6. Drug Me

Talking of getting a rush, electronic dance music is intimately bound up with drug culture. Even when it isn't designed explicitly to enhance drugs like Ecstasy, the way the music works on the listener is drug-like, and seems to demand drug metaphors. People use the music as a mood-modifier, something that swiftly transports them into a different emotional state with no necessary connection to their life-situation.

Drugs have played a crucial role in dance music's evolution. Specific music-technology innovations have synergized with particular drugs at different points: for instance, Ecstasy meshed with the trippy bass-patterns of the Roland 303 bass-synthesiser to catalyze the acid house revolution of the late Eighties. Changing drug use patterns also propel the music's evolution: escalating Ecstasy and amphetamine use in the early Nineties caused techno to get faster and faster, leading to hyperkinetic styles like jungle and gabba. Ultimately, what has happened is that the drug-sensations get encoded into the music, abstracted. By itself, the music trips you out, stones you, gives you a speed-rush.

This drug-tech interface syndrome is not unique to dance music, of course. You can see it with psychedelic rock (LSD coincided with the arrival of 24 track studios), and even late Seventies soft rock (the endlessly overdubbed guitar lines and excessively shiny sound of The Eagles or Fleetwood Mac reflect superstar cocaine abuse—the cocaine ear likes bright treble frequencies and tiny detailed sounds, while stimulant abuse makes people obsessive-compulsive, fussy, perfectionist). Electronic dance music is unique, however, in the way it has developed an entire musical language of sounds, riffs, and effects that are explicitly designed to trigger Ecstasy rushes or accompany the aural hallucinations induced by LSD, the coma-like dissassocation caused by ketamine, etc. Moreover, because drug-states are essentially excursions outside normal consciousness, a lot of this music can be seen as involving temporary trips into insanity and schizophrenia: the paranoid rhythmic delirium of jungle, the catatonic trance of minimal techno DJs like Richie Hawtin, the psychotic fury of gabba.

## 7. This Is a Journey into Sound

Electronic dance music is all about being lost in music, whether it's being engulfed by the sonic tsunami streaming out of a gigantic rave sound system, or being meditatively absorbed by the microscopic sonic events that pervade more experimental forms of electronica. These states of ego loss and oceanic connection, of being overwhelmed or entranced, are the reason why drug imagery is central to electronic imagination. And they also explain the recourse to religious language, whether taken from the Christian mystical tradition of surrender and Gnostic grace, or Eastern spiritual notions of nirvana and kundalini.

In some Eastern religions, the universe is sounded into being; hearing is the primary sense. Electronic dance culture likewise overthrows sight in the Western hierarchy of the senses, which privileges the eye. There's a good reason why clubs take place in the dark, why some warehouse raves are almost pitch black: diminishing the visual makes sound more vivid. Retinal perception is eclipsed by the audio-tactile, a vibrational continuum in which sound is so massively amplified it's visceral. This orientation toward sound can be seen in the way that ravers will literally hug speakers stacks, sometimes even climbing inside the bass-woofer's cavity and curling up like a foetus.

Beyond this worship of sound, electronic dance culture resists the tyranny of the visual in pop culture. The electronica revolution will not be televised (at least, not without being hugely compromised). Video channels like MTV are looking for stellar faces and heavenly bodies, but electronica promos tend not to feature either (indeed the video signature of some artists—The Chemical Brothers, Fatboy Slim—is only appearing in their own promos for a few seconds!). Success in pop depends on videogenic charisma, dance moves, even acting skill (with videos increasingly like mini-movies). All this is irrevelant to electronic dance music, which is simply not in the business of selling personalities. Moreover, electronic dance music simply sounds terrible through a television's mono speakers and non-existent bass: it is mixed for big club sound systems, with panoramic stereo and seismic sub-bass. A large proportion of this record's auditory content is inaudible on a television set.

Part of electronica's "underground"-ness relates to precisely this refusal of our contemporary culture of the icon. Video is about spectatorship, whereas dance culture is about participation. And so the more underground a club is, the less there will be in terms of visual distractions: the more hardcore the scene, the less there is to be seen. Clubs will always skimp on visuals and decor before cutting back on the sound-system. Many rock fans who go to see a DJ spin or a dance outfit play "live" find it dull because there's nothing to look at: no theatrics, no performance vocabulary of flamboyant gestures as there is with rock—just a few unglamorous looking guys twiddling knobs on machines. But that misses the point, because you're not supposed to focus on the artist. The crowd is the star.

## 8. Faceless Techno Bollocks

When rave culture first took off in the UK, some diehard rock fans started to rail against "faceless techno bollocks". Soon the slogan started appearing on T-shirts, but worn by techno fans who'd flipped it around into a badge of pride. In its purest forms, electronic dance music is a revolt against celebrity culture and the cult of personality. Artists deliberately seek anonymity by adopting an array of alter-egos. Marc Acardipane, the German hardcore techno pioneer, may have the world record, having used over twenty different pseudonyms. Richard D. James illustrates how contact with the record business can conventionalize someone's career: early on, he used multiple aliases, but as he became an iconic figure with a long-term album deal, he started to release his output via only one identity, Aphex Twin.

Sometimes there are pragmatic reasons for having multiple names. The artist's primary identity may be signed to one label, but they allow him to release stuff on different labels using other names. Some artists actually have discernibly different sonic characters in their different names. But the main effect of all this is to create an effect of distancing, a break with the traditional pop impulse to connect the music to an actual human being. Along with the use of depersonalized, technical-sounding or numeric names, this intensifies the music's posthuman aura, its abstract, disembodied quality. Unlike with rock or rap, you don't identify with the music-maker, you "intensify" with the music's energy. Facelessness also has the effect of disrupting the mechanism of band or brand loyalty, the rock fan's habit of following artists through their careers. Some connoisseurs of electronic music do this, priding themselves on collecting every last item of their favorite artist's oeuvre, under all the different alter-egos. But for hardcore dance fans, producers are only as good as their latest track.

The group Underground Resistance use anonymity as part of their anti-corporate, we-are-guerrillas-of-techno aura: they are literally faceless, refusing to be photographed except wearing masks. This militant stance is all the more resonant given the rise of a dance music industry in which DJs are sold as pseudo-personalities and magazines conduct interviews that ignore the only things interesting about them (their taste in music and mixing skills) and instead talk about the DJ's career struggles, drug intake, sex lives, and VIP lifestyles.

## 9. Death of the Auteur

We look at rock music in terms of innovators: the individual artists who revolutionized music and influenced others (or, if they failed in the marketplace of their day, who were "ahead of their time"). We look always to trace things back to the trailblazing originators, and deplore the swarm of copyists following in their wake. One of the worst insults that can be directed at a rock group is "generic." In electronic dance music, things work quite differently. It is often difficult, and pointless, to strive to identify who first came up with a breakthrough in rhythm or sound. Ideas mostly emerge through anonymous processes of collective creativity. Look at the genesis of acid house in mid-Eighties Chicago or the emergence of jungle in early Nineties England, and you'll see the cultural equivalent of an ecosystem. Maybe one individual happens to stumble upon an untapped potential in a piece of music-making technology, like the weird "acid" noises inside the Roland 303 bass synthesiser. But almost immediately this idea was seized upon by other producers and instead of being diluted in the process (as usually happens with rock) the new sound was intensified. Over the course of a year, the acid tracks got weirder, fiercer, more deranging, thanks to the intense competition between producers to drive dancefloor crowds wilder, until the new effect was taken as far as it could go and became exhausted.

With jungle's chopped-up, sped-up breakbeats, it's impossible to work out who came up with the idea first, or when exactly the style crystallized. Dozens, maybe scores, of rave producers started to experiment with the idea of using sampled breakbeats instead of programmed rhythms. Through a collective musical conversation stretched across 1990–1993, "breakbeat science" (digital techniques of micro-editing and resequencing beats) emerged in an incremental process: weekly instalments of small-scale innovation, a ping-pong match of ideas going back and forth between people who never met.

Brian Eno has dubbed this syndrome "scenius," punning on the words "scene" and "genius." He argues that our old Romantic notions of the auteur as an autonomous, endlessly fertile individual were precisely that: overly romanticized, out-of-date. And he called for a more depersonalized notion of creativity influenced by cybernetic theory, ideas of self-organizing systems and feedback loops. Another way of conceptualizing "scenius" is in terms of biogenetics or virology, metaphors of mutation or cultural viruses (memes). Like a successful gene characteristic, electronic dance innovations achieve their highest success by becoming clichés: sounds so good that nobody can resist using them. (At least until they're all used up, at which point the underground abandons them to mainstream pop, and dismisses the sounds as "corny" and "cheesy." Some sounds do enjoy an afterlife, though, coming back under the sign of camp ironic nostalgia).

Ideas in dance music sometimes seem to evolve according to an immanent non-human logic of their own. It's tempting to talk mystically of machines like the 303 having their own agenda. In reality, the creativity is entirely human, it's just collective rather than auteur-driven. Because dance cultures have a very fast turnover, a track can come out and within a week another producer has picked up the baton. The life-cycles of sonic evolution are incredibly rapid. Unlike with rock music, even the rip-off artists, the clone merchants and copyists, play a role, because each replication of a sound unavoidably warps it. Indeed, in dance music, "bastardisation" is positive, productive, progressive.

Another reason "generic" isn't an insult in electronic dance discourse is that tracks exist in a context. A "generic" track is a functional track: it has the right elements to enable the DJ to mix the tune in with a bunch of similar tracks, thereby creating a flow. This play of sameness and difference is something that electronic dance music has in common with black music, where what initially seems homogenous reveals subtle inflections and shifts through concentrated immersion by the listener. From the Motown sound in the Sixties through James Brown-style funk to the stop-start rhythms in modern R&B, black American music goes through different Beat-Geists (i.e. rhythmic Zeitgeists). These innovations may originate with specific labels (Motown) or producers (like Timbaland with contemporary R&B), but they become the rhythmic template used by everybody. Jamaican music culture goes even further, being based not just on generic sounds but rhythms that are literally identical: different singers and MCs do new vocals over the same currently hot, endlessly reused riddim track.

One side effect of all this is that dance music has a different distribution of brilliance than other kinds of music. Rock's aesthetic hierarchy divides everything between the handful of visionary geniuses and a vast mass of mediocre non-originals. But in electronic dance music, there's a huge number of good (meaning useful-to-DJs) tracks, and a much smaller number of true landmark records. In a word, dance music is democratic.

## 10. We Bring You the Future

Another aspect to all this is that genres and scenes take the place of stars and artists—this is the level on which it's most productive to talk about the music. In dance culture, a huge amount of energy goes into cultural taxonomy: identifying genres and subgenres like species. This profusion of new sounds, scenes and genre names is also what is off-putting to some newcomers to the music, who understandably find it confusing, and suspect that hype or willful obscurantism is involved. Actually, the endless generic splintering is simply a result of dance culture's 20 years of existence, the huge number and diversity of people involved, and the global span of the culture. Anything that big is going to fracture, and many of the fractures are going to be worth talking about.

Mostly the names emerge for practical reasons. In the beginning (meaning the mid-Eighties) people talked about "house" and that was pretty much it. Later, different flavors of the music were distinguished, using prefix terms: deep house, hard house, tribal house. Why? More and more records were being made, and the stylistic parameters were starting to drift apart. Clubs found it useful to specify what their sound was, and people working in record stores started to get terminologically precise, to help customers find exactly what they wanted. Some of the terms achieved currency and became established throughout the culture. Eventually, stylistic dispersal increased to the point where the primacy of "house" was overthrown, and brand new words—jungle, trance, gabba—came into use (often after an intermediary phase where people talked of jungle house or gabba house).

Confusing to the uninitiated and offensive to genrephobes this may be, but these definitions become urgent and crucial once you get involved in the culture. It becomes a way of talking about the music, arguing about where it should go next. It's an expression of enthusiasm and excitement, not hairsplitting or an attempt to baffle and exclude by talking in code. Above all, the hunger for the next big thing or new sound is an expression of electronic dance culture's neophilia, its impatience for the future to arrive.

## 11. Let's Submerge

Along with "living for the future," electronic dance culture is united by a vague, open-ended ideology of "underground-ism," in which grass-roots scenes are positioned against the pop mainstream and the corporate record industry. "Underground" as a concept doesn't have a huge amount of political content, though; it's not attached to any specific revolutionary aspirations, ideas about a utopian form of social organization, or even counter-cultural ideals (beyond a libertarian attitude towards drug-taking). Anti-corporate without being anti-capitalist, "undergroundism" expresses the struggle of micro-capitalist units (independent record labels, small clubs) against macro-capitalism (the mainstream leisure-and-entertainment industry).

Electronic indie labels can be as small as a single individual making music in his bedroom and putting out the tracks himself. More often, it'll be a small gang or crew that is tightly loyal, almost communistic, and typically clustered around a central figure—an engineer/producer who owns the equipment and enables DJs to realise their ideas and become producers. Another common syndrome is independent labels that start off based around a record store. The people who work in the store, who are often aspiring DJs, develop a good sense of what is selling and what works in the clubs; they also get to know more established DJs and aspiring producers who come in to check the latest releases. The obvious next step is to take this developing A&R instinct and start releasing records by new talent. And so, to give just one example, the East London record store Boogie Times gave birth to the influential jungle label Suburban Base.

This sort of small independent tends to be unstable, though, and often doesn't survive the high turnover of dancefloor trends. Inevitably the indies that do endure are those who adopt sound business plans and managerial structures—in other words, start to behave like small corporations. Warp Records started from a record store in Sheffield, England, but watching other labels of the early rave era fall by the wayside, they developed long-term album based deals with their artists (like Aphex Twin), and evolved into a successful company specializing in "electronic listening music" (also know as IDM, short for "intelligent dance music"). For many in the hardcore underground, Warp now represents the new establishment, catering to an audience of ex-clubbers and lapsed ravers with sounds that are basically dance music for the home environment.

Electronic dance music's antagonism towards the corporate music industry isn't based on political principles but aesthetic ones: the idea that the mainstream dilutes the underground's music, blunts the music's edge, tones down its harsh futurism, turns it into mere pop. In a crucial paradox, dance scenes are populist but opposed to pop culture in the "weak," universal sense of the word. Their populism takes the form of tribal unity against what they perceive as a homogenous, blandly uninvolving mass culture. Subcultural initiates are felt to have a more committed, active, participatory relationship with the music than the desultory, passive pop consumer. Often people who believe in underground music use military rhetoric, and talk of being a "soldier" or crusader, fighting for the cause, staying hardcore.

## 12. Site-Specific

Part of the inclusive/exclusive aura of these subcultures is that the music is site-specific. You have to go to clubs to get the full experience. This doesn't apply to home-oriented IDM, obviously, but there is a vast swathe of this music that simply doesn't really make sense outside the club context. Often I'll buy a house or 2-step 12 inch single and play it at home, and it'll sound weak, the beat monotonous and numbing. Hear the same song through a huge sound system, though, and the unrelenting pump and pound of the groove becomes the whole point. Massively amplified, the kick drum becomes so thick and wide, it's a cocooning environmental pulse: you feel like you're actually inside the beat. Similarly, there are numerous genres of dance music based around floor-quaking sub-bass frequencies that are barely audible on a domestic hi-fi, let alone a boom box. And there's an entire vein of "big room" dance tracks designed for superclubs, whose dancefloors hold a thousand plus people and are surrounded by towering speaker stacks. Often these "big room" tracks contain hardly any music in the traditional sense—only the most rudimentary two-note bass-pulses, barely any melody-lines. They don't sound good at home but they work in the superclub context because they're full of effects and whooshing noises that swoop and pan across the stereo-field, sounds that are literally spectacular, designed to astonish your ears.

The more functionalist kinds of dance music can sound "flat" at home because the tracks are essentially unfinished work. They are raw material for the DJs to transform into music by mixing very minimal tracks together: superimposing or cutting back and forth, creating dynamics by using EQing effects to boost certain frequencies, and all manner of turntable tricks. These records are often described as "DJ tools." With other genres, particularly those—jungle, 2step—that have a strong influence from dancehall reggae and hip hop—the tracks really come alive through the combination of the DJ's mixing and the MC chanting over the music: hyping the crowd, ordering the DJ to do a "rewind" (i.e., stop the track mid-song and go back to the start).

Beyond this, there's a sense in which the music is like the screenplay to a movie, and is completed by "the cast"—the crowd on the dancefloor. Styles like jungle and trance are full of behavioral cues encoded in the music—breakdowns, drum builds, bass drops, climaxes—all of which trigger certain mass responses: ritualized gestures of abandonment, like hands shooting up in the air at the entrance of a certain kind of riff or noise. The music sounds diminished in the absence of such tableaux of crowd frenzy. Ultimately, most dance tracks are components in a subcultural engine—heard decontextualized and isolated, they can seem as perplexing and functionless as a carburettor outside the car. And while it might have a certain surreal appeal to keep an engine part in the middle of your living room, you'd definitely not be getting full use of that component.

"Context" can be really specific. There are some tracks that are associated with just one specific club, like the song "Twilo Thunder," made in homage to the now-defunct New York club Twilo. Its sound was tailored to the immense Twilo sound system and designed to fuel the special atmosphere generated by the crowd who religiously attended Sasha & Digweed's eight-hour DJ sets. For a culture that typically boasts of its global reach and its transcendence of geography, electronica can be disconcertingly fixated on a sense of place. What these privileged sites, these temples of sound, create is a form of postmodern tribalism: people from different backgrounds and locations gather together to experience the same "tribe-vibe."

Part of the conditions of existence for these transient communities is that people check their ideologies at the door with their coats. This isn't apolitical so much as anti-political, or perhaps pre-political: an attempt to cut through all the divisions and rediscover some primal basis of connection, even if that unity is as simple as sharing the same sonic (and often drug) sensations, occupying the same space ("Everybody In the Place," as the Prodigy titled one of their early rave anthems). Which helps explains electronic dance culture's suspicion of words, its urge to dispense with language. Because words divide. And this music is about the urge to merge, about becoming part of something larger than yourself, whether it's the dancing crowd, a sublime vastness of sound, or the cosmos.

## 13. Only Connect

One of the key words in dance culture is "mix," a term with multiple applications and resonances. Mixed crowds: most dance scenes at least pay lip service to the idea that all are welcome and that clubs with a good social/racial/gender mix are the ones with the best vibe. Mix-and-blend: the musical ethos shared by most genres of electronic dance is a belief in stylistic border-crossing—a notion of hybridity similar to mesticagem, the national ideology of Brazil which takes pride in that country's miscegenated culture and music. (Which may explain why a lot of house producers have an almost utopian vision of Brazil and are infatuated with samba and bossa nova rhythms.) Remixes: rather than a definitively complete and inviolate work of art, a dance track is treated as a provisional collection of sonic resources to be rearranged—hence the vogue for multiple remixes (sometimes as many as 10 different versions), and for remix albums where DJ/producers pay tribute to an admired artist by reworking, sometimes to the point of obliteration, their music. Mix: the art of DJing involves taking disparate tracks and connecting them into a meta-track, a potentially interminable flow. Repetition and interconnection evoke a feeling of boundless pleasure. Time is abolished ("3-AM Eternal," as one track title put it), and so is lack. The music insists "go with the flow" and "be here now," lose yourself in a never-ending present of pure sensation.

As you can see, my list of foundational principles is just a partial blueprint: culture is always messy, evading our attempts at definition.[5] The aspects I've highlighted, though, represent this music's claims to radicalism. They are the "emergent" elements, to use a concept

5. I omitted a section in which Reynolds discusses exceptions to his "foundational principles."

from cultural studies referring to tendencies that point toward future aesthetic and social formations. Any cultural phenomenon that has real impact in the present, however, must inevitably be a mixture of "emergent" and "residual" (meaning traditional). Generally speaking, music that is totally avant-garde and ahead-of-its-time subsists in the academic ghetto, depending on state subsidies or institutional support. You can see this with the most advanced forms of "sound art" or "sound design": they can't survive in the rough-and-tumble of the pop marketplace, but inhabit the world of art galleries, museums, seminars and symposiums and festivals. Which is fine, but for me the most exciting thing about electronic dance music is that you get avant-garde ideas working in a popular context, carried by groove and catchy hooks, and enlivened by a context of fun and collective celebration. One example is jungle's vibrant blend of "roots 'n' phuture" (as one early jungle track put it). The "emergent," avant-garde elements in jungle wouldn't have worked without the "residual" stuff: to have "breakbeat science," you need to have breakbeats (sweaty, human musicians playing hot funky percussive breaks) in the first place, providing the raw material to be sampled and digitally recombined.

Ultimately, electronic dance music is at its most enjoyable when it's impure: rhythm/texture colliding with songcraft, soul-less machinery fighting it out with traditional ideas of sonic beauty, avant-garde auteur impulses checked by the crowd's demand for danceable grooves. These tensions are what keep the music vital.

> As Simon Reynolds described in the preceding essay, the element of drug consumption cannot be separated from the overall experience of fandom in electronica. This brief excerpt from Scottish author Irvine Welsh's *Ecstasy* presents the point of view of a raver as the drugs begin to take effect. Many of the principals discussed by Reynolds are evident here: the impassioned preference for one type or another of electronica, the emphasis on the "cutting edge," the sense of communion experienced at dance clubs, the importance of insider knowledge, and participation in dance club culture as an apolitical form of resistance.

## LORRAINE GOES TO LIVINGSTON: A RAVE AND REGENCY ROMANCE
### Irvine Welsh

### In the Jungle

The night before his life changed, Glen had had to plead with his friend Martin,—Come on, mate, give it a try. I got good pills, those Amsterdam Playboys. The best ever.

—Exactly, Martin sneered,—and you're gonna waste them on this fuckin jungle shit. I don't go for that shit, Glen, I just can't fucking well dance to it.

—C'mon, mate, as a favour. Give it a go.

—A favour? Why you so desperate to check out this club? Keith and Carol and Eddie, they're all going down to Sabresonic and then on to the Ministry.

—Look, mate, house music's at the forefront of everything, and jungle's at the forefront of house. It's got to have a capacity to surprise, innit, otherwise it just becomes affirmation, like country-and-western, or like rock 'n' roll's become. Jungle's the music with the capacity to surprise. It's where the cutting edge is. We owe it to ourselves to check it out, Glen implored.

Martin looked at him searchingly.—There's someone you want to see at this club . . . someone from the hospital goes there . . . one of them nurses I'll bet!

Glen shrugged and smiled,—Well . . . yeah . . . but . . .

—All right, that's cool. You want to chase the girls, we'll chase the girls. Ain't got no objections on that score. Just don't give me all this cutting-edge bollocks.

They got to the club, and Glen felt despondent when they saw the size of the queue. Martin strode up to the front and talked to one of the bouncers. He then turned and gesticulated violently at Glen to come up. There were some moans of frustrated envy from others in the crowd as Glen and Martin strode through. At first Glen had been terrified that they would not get in. After Martin had blagged it so effectively, he worried that Lorraine might have been stuck outside.

In the club, they went straight to the chill-out zone. Martin hit the bar and bought two fizzy mineral waters. It was dark and Glen pulled a plastic bag out of his Y-fronts. It contained four pills with a Playboy bunny logo stamped on them. They swallowed one each and washed them down with water.

After about ten minutes, the pill kept coming back on Glen, as it tended to do, and he had dry, hiccupy wretches. He and Martin were unconcerned; Glen was just bad at taking pills.

Three girls sat down close to them. Martin had been quick to start chatting to them. Glen was equally quick to leave him and hit the dance-floor. These Es were good, but unless you started dancing straight away you would sit around talking in the chill-out zone all night. Glen had come to dance.

He skirted the already-busy dance-floor and quickly came across Lorraine and her friend. Glen danced a discreet distance away. He recognised Murder Dem by Ninjaman sliding into Wayne Marshall's G Spot.

Lorraine and her friend Yvonne were up there, going for it in a big way. Glen watched them dancing with each other, Lorraine blocking out all the world, focusing on Yvonne, giving her friend everything. God, for just a bit of that attention, he thought. Yvonne, though, was more disengaged, further away, taking in the whole scene. That was how it seemed to Glen. His pill was kicking in, and the music, which he had had a resistance to, was getting into him from all sides, surging through his body in waves, defining his emotions. Before it had seemed jerky and disjointed, it was pushing and pulling at him, irritating him. Now he was going with it, his body bubbling and flowing in all ways to the roaring bass-lines and the tearing dub plates. All the joy of love for everything good was in him, though he could see all the bad things in Britain; in fact this twentieth-century urban blues music defined and illustrated them more sharply than ever. Yet he wasn't scared and he wasn't down about it: he could see what needed to be done to get away from them. It was the party: he felt that you had to party, you had to party harder than ever. It was the only way. It was your duty to show that you were still alive. Political sloganeering and posturing meant nothing; you had to celebrate the joy of life in the face of all those gray forces and dead spirits who controlled everything, who fucked with your head and livelihood anyway, if you weren't one of them. You had to let them know that in spite of their best efforts to make you like them, to make you dead, you were still alive. Glen knew that this wasn't the complete answer, because it would all still be there when you stopped, but it was the best show in town right now. It was certainly the only one he wanted to be at.

He had looked back over at Lorraine and her friend. He couldn't tell at first, but he was dancing like a maniac, and when he glanced over at them, he realized. There were no poseurs here, they were all going crazy. This wasn't dance, that wasn't the word for what this was. And there they were: Lorraine and her friend Yvonne. Lorraine, the goddess. But the goddess had multiplied. There wasn't just one of them now, like when he came in, there was just Lorraine and her friend. Now it was Lorraine and Yvonne, in a dance of crazy, rapturous emotion which, while conducted at ninety miles an hour, slowed down to almost nothing under the onslaught of the throbbing strobes and jerky break-beats. Lorraine and Yvonne. Yvonne and Lorraine.

A mass scream went up from the crowd as the music left one crescendo and changed its tempo to build up to the next one.

# 93. R&B Divas Go Retro

As Nelson George indicated in chapter 70, old-school soul singing and R&B remained alive in the late 1970s and 1980s alongside the development of funk and disco. In addition to artists, such as Chaka Khan (b. 1954) and Aretha Franklin, younger singers like Frankie Beverly (of Maze) and Anita Baker continued the tradition of impassioned gospel-schooled vocals that addressed romantic and social concerns. Another generation of R&B "divas," typified by Whitney Houston (b. 1963) and Mariah Carey (b. 1970), emerged in the late 1980s–early 1990s and merged superb vocal technique within well-crafted (some might say "slick") productions that were unusually attuned to the current tastes of the pop marketplace.

Ann Powers (at the time a pop music critic for the *New York Times*) describes another trend that became evident in the mid- to late 1990s, as younger African American singers sought to merge the rhythms and tough attitude of hip-hop with some of the vocal technique and lyric subject matter of 1970s' soul. These arists, led by Mary J. Blige's early 1990s' recordings and D'Angelo's 1995 release, *Brown Sugar*, were predominantly female, adding a different inflection to the subject of "women in pop music" discussed earlier in chapters 85 and 90. The year 1999 represented the crest of a wave that began in 1997 with releases by Erykah Badu (b. 1972) and Missy Elliot and surged in 1998 with the *Miseducation of Lauryn Hill*. While this trend represents continuity with earlier soul music, the nostalgic or "retro" element is new and links the late 1990s soul revival with other forms of musical recycling going on concurrently in popular music.[1]

# THE NEW CONSCIENCE OF POP MUSIC
## *Ann Powers*

During "Not Lookin,'" a new duet with her former beau, the urban love man K-Ci Hailey, Mary J. Blige demonstrates how to stop a man cold. The song, from Ms. Blige's new album, "Mary," pits a woman seeking true affection against a man out for pure pleasure. The two vocalists trade diatribes over a steady rocking rhythm, their wails building as the impossibility of resolution grows clear.

Mr. Hailey soothes and cajoles in his sexy baritone. Ms. Blige cries to any women listening to stand up with her and fight such "player" nonsense. "I hear you," moans Mr. Hailey, though he obviously doesn't. Finally, Ms. Blige just snaps. "I know you're sorry!" she exclaims. The track ends, without another sound.

This abrupt dismissal is a conveniently dramatic way for Ms. Blige to win a musical cutting contest. But it also captures the mood of the rhythm-and-blues being made by young artists eager to create something more than slick background for the well-appointed bedroom. This new style has been building for a few years, but only now is it reaching full flower. And although its pioneers include men like Mr. Hailey and D'Angelo, there is no question that the fragrance of this blossom is boldly feminine.

Throughout the 1990's, most discussions of women's increased power in pop have focused on alternative-rock transgressors like Tori Amos and Courtney Love or the songbirds of Sarah McLachlan's Lilith Fair. Rhythm-and-blues artists sold albums but were rarely viewed as culture shapers. Now, though, with mainstream rock again becoming a male bastion, it is clear whose music matters within the continuing emergence of women as equal players in contemporary music.

Ms. Blige, the standard-bearer for hip-hop-inflected soul, has reached a peak in her career. She has evolved from a passionate but erratic inner-city princess to a mature artist tackling the same complexities expressed by her idols, Aretha Franklin and Chaka Khan. Lauryn Hill, a professed Blige fan who wrote and produced "All That I Can Say," the first single from "Mary" (MCA), herself exceeded all expectations with her solo debut, "The Miseducation of Lauryn Hill." The girl group TLC is at its apex, ruling the charts with two singles, "No Scrubs" and "Unpretty," that have sparked spirited public conversations about sex, money and self-respect.

These are only the most visible forces in a renaissance that includes girl groups like Destiny's Child, answering TLC's challenge with its own fresh summer single, "Bills, Bills, Bills"; Missy Elliott, an artist growing ever more influential behind the scenes as a producer; seasoned songwriters now in the spotlight, like Faith Evans, Kelly Price and Angie Stone, and left-field contenders like Macy Gray and Melky Sedeck. These artists are as carefully

---

1. Almost two years later, Powers examined the continuing pressures and contradictions faced by women in popular music, focusing on the then-current success of R&B "girl group," Destiny's Child; see Ann Powers, "In Tune with the New Feminism," *New York Times*, April 29, 2001, Sec. 2.

packaged as the elegant stars they join in the spotlight, from Whitney Houston to Toni Braxton. But they are selling a very different sensibility.

They are more individualistic, more confrontational. They grew up loving hip-hop, and in their songs they tangle with that genre's cold-blooded male pronouncements instead of merely floating past them on a cushion of strings and strummed guitars. Some find allies in brash rappers like Lil' Kim. But while the female rapper's role remains mostly that of the sexual warrior, contesting masculine power with the easily available weapon of her own body, these singers also confront the emotional costs of such battles.

The new soul queens take advantage of nostalgia's ability to conjure authenticity. Their songs invoke forebears like Ms. Khan in music thick with funk and flecked with jazz, but the mix is salted with gritty hip-hop beats. These artists' lyrics, too, resurrect old-school domestic protests within a strikingly contemporary context, as they debate proper behavior within today's seeming sexual free-for-all.

The rising stars of female soul demand attention with audacity rather than coaxing it out through prettiness. Undoubtedly sexy, they are also unapologetically human. They embody not merely the dream girls of glossy magazines but also the "unpretty" women reading those magazines. And they are earning respect, so much so that pop angels like Ms. Houston, Mariah Carey and Janet Jackson have made themselves over to look rougher and tougher in their midst—and, in the process, have made some of the best music of their careers.

This current cycle is just the latest in the rebirth of soul. Two larger commercial trends have spurred it on: the triumph of hip-hop and the return of rhythm-and-blues as the basic form of teen-age pop. After briefly being displaced by punk-flavored rock in the mid-1990's, black music is again the essence of American pop music. But the new soul queens consciously invoke a side of that music that others have avoided.

Virtually all popular music centers on romance, and historically, black music has frankly celebrated love's sexual side. But, as the historian Brian Ward points out in "Just My Soul Responding: Rhythm-and-Blues, Black Consciousness and Race Relations" (University of California, 1998), black styles from the blues to disco have not just glorified bodily pleasures.

They have given artists a way of confronting the sexual stereotypes that racism has created—what Michelle Wallace famously called "black macho and the myth of the superwoman." Through songs ranging from Wynonie Harris's "Adam, Come and Get Your Rib" to Gwen Guthrie's "Ain't Nothin' Goin' On but the Rent," rhythm-and-blues artists have encapsulated the struggles waged in every room of the black household, from the bedroom to the kitchen.

In times of political pessimism, this debate has grown more vicious. The blues painted a bleak image of love, grounded in paranoia and murderous lusts. At the height of the civil rights movement, when integration seemed possible both in public spaces and on the pop charts, romantics like Aretha Franklin gained popularity. Then, in the early 1970's, when the radical Black Power movement arose in response to social setbacks, female artists once again found themselves metaphorically embattled.

"The women of soul rejected the role of helpless victims, not by articulating a discernibly feminist program, but by giving as good as they got in the male-defined sex wars of the late 1960's and early 1970's," Mr. Ward writes. "It was the equivalent of women in the Panthers earning the respect of their male colleagues by picking up the gun—the ultimate symbol of phallocentric power—and behaving as much like men as possible."

The rhetoric of hip-hop is firmly linked to this era. Its stars constantly mimic the styles seen in blaxploitation movies of the early 1970's, and when they do venture into political speech, they most often invoke radicals like Malcolm X and the Black Panthers. Rappers like Jay-Z and Master P take an outlaw stance with overtones of social revolt, if not genuine political rebellion. Today's most successful female rappers have adopted the image of the "ho" as a feminine counterpart in criminality.

The new soul queens are taking on the often vicious representations of women in hip-hop, assessing what real strength those images may offer and when they need to be defused. They are speaking to female hip-hop fans about the contradictions facing young women in a culture that craves female power but remains deeply suspicious of it. And they are confronting the men who, in rap and in contemporary rhythm-and-blues, so often describe seduction as a theft and love as a game.

Mary J. Blige has been working on gaining equality with her male counterparts since she released her debut album, "What's the 411?" in 1992. That album posited Ms. Blige as a fingernail-flaring, Kangol cap-wearing little sister whom B-boys could dream of and ghetto girls could identify with. (The future hip-hop kingpin Sean [Puffy] Combs is listed as "stylist" on the album's credits.)

Singing with passion if not technical mastery, Ms. Blige immediately distinguished herself from stars like Ms. Carey, who possessed better instruments but little of her street credibility. With her second album, "My Life," she began writing more of her material and showed herself to be given to dark pronouncements, like her magnificent version of the Norman Whitfield–Joel Schumacher ballad "I'm Goin' Down" from the movie "Car Wash" as well as optimistic hits like "Real Love." For many fans, she became a Lady of the Sorrows, expressing their anxieties and regrets in a powerful but always vulnerable voice.

The moody Ms. Blige wore her own troubles on her sleeve. She had adversarial encounters with the press and publicly indulged in drugs and alcohol. Gradually, she grew up, and her track record of hits has turned her into her a soul matriarch by age 28. Her new album is not as obviously commercial as her previous studio efforts, nor is it as closely linked to hip-hop. With "Mary," Ms. Blige is making her case for really deserving the regal title hip-hop fans have given her from the beginning.

It is a crossover effort, with appearances by the distinctly non-ghettocentric guests Sir Elton John and Eric Clapton. Only one rapper, Jadakiss, appears; a cut featuring DMX and Nas was ultimately reserved for the B-side of "All That I Can Say." But if "Mary" gestures toward an older, non-hip-hop audience, it also makes the claim for Ms. Blige's canonization within the rhythm-and-blues hall of fame. The album's two duets enforce her status: her reunion with Mr. Hailey, who is also outrunning his bad-boy past via increasingly sophisticated recordings, and the spirited "Don't Waste Your Time," in which she receives a mentor's advice from that other queen of soul, Aretha Franklin.

The time is right for Ms. Blige to assert herself because her dramatic, direct vocal style is again soul's paradigm. Once, even the voices of Ms. Blige's imitators were heavily obscured within mixes where the producer's signature mattered more than the singer's. It was hard to find the real woman inside the work of vocally gifted artists like Ms. Braxton or Ms. Houston. The individual quirks that distinguished greats like Ms. Franklin, Ms. Khan and Patti LaBelle were processed out of most radio-ready mixes.

Gradually, though, outsiders began making commercial breakthroughs. Not only Ms. Blige, but Erykah Badu and Missy Elliott, neither of whom looked or sounded like the standard-model soul babe, became stars. Faith Evans and Kelly Price, writers who have collaborated with Ms. Blige, had hits that emphasized their unvarnished voices and dramatic range. The multiplatinum, multi-Grammy triumph of Ms. Hill, a boisterous singer and rapper whose most striking talent is for spacious vocal arrangements, cemented the change.

A shift was visible, too, among the often seemingly interchangeable girl groups of contemporary rhythm-and-blues. The trio that made the difference has progressed in much the same way Ms. Blige has. Tionne (T-Boz) Watkins, Rozonda (Chilli) Thomas and Lisa (Left Eye) Lopes, collectively known as TLC, started out as perky but artistically unremarkable teens. "Crazy sexycool," the group's 1994 sophomore effort, solidified its sound by emphasizing the internal, almost conversational singing of T-Boz and Chilli and using Left Eye's sassy raps as zest. "Crazysexycool" sold upwards of eight million copies, guaranteeing that its formula would be endlessly imitated.

Before TLC's triumph, the most successful girl group was En Vogue, a quartet with stellar vocal prowess and a taste for glamour. Like Ms. Blige, the women of TLC seemed more accessible, partly because of their connections to streetwise hip-hop. "Fanmail," this year's long-awaited follow-up to "Crazysexycool," does not totally diverge from the tried and true, but its best tracks take on soul's classic conversation about gender in adventurous ways.

The album's monster hit, "No Scrubs," is a vintage dressing-down of a financially shifty man, while the group's current single, "Unpretty," bravely considers the downside of the beauty myth most women in pop eagerly cultivate. But the most daring song on "Fanmail" is "I'm Good at Being Bad," a musical re-enactment of the conflicting stereotypes that envelop black women.

The track begins as a silky ballad, like a bubble bath with a beat, but it gives way to a huge hip-hop beat and a snarling, obscenity-laced vocal. Here is the "ho" taking on the dream girl, the woman using sex as a weapon versus the one too dependent on love. The scenario remains unresolved, and the more powerful for it.

TLC's inside view of a sexual woman's split psyche is hardly the only song to confront hip-hop's ever-present ho. Ms. Hill cautioned young girls to preserve themselves in "Lost Ones," a song that has earned her accusations of self-righteousness. Because she is openly religious, Ms. Hill is blunt about her distaste for the mercenary sexual stance of some female artists.

For all the backlash it has caused, Ms. Hill's critique of hip-hop's skewed value system reflects another element of soul's artistic revitalization. Her challenge, "How you gonna win when you ain't right within?" echoes through this new music.

New artists like Angie Stone, Melky Sedeck and Macy Gray make such questions of conscience part of their metier. These new soul queens are not moralistic; their songs toast sensuality more often than they dissect social ills. But they also consider the consequences of the hunger for sex, drugs and money, especially in the context of racism. Doing so, they invoke not only past soul queens but progenitors like Sly Stone and Marvin Gaye.

The history of rhythm-and-blues is full of unruly divas like the ones currently stealing the microphone. They are lucky that popular taste is shifting their way, saving them from the outsider status that has long afflicted soul singers who push against the stereotypes of urban style. These women are determined to give voice to their own views on the matters that shape the intimate lives of their listeners, and they are artists enough to render those perspectives in tones as vibrant as the heritage they mine. Whether tackling emotional profundities or sticking to the plain facts of woman versus man, black women are the conscience of today's pop scene.

# 94. What Have We Come To?

## (On Continuing Moral Panics in Late 1990s' Popular Music and Other Strange Developments)

In April 1999, an event captured the U.S. media's attention that suggested a link between violence and a form of popular music. The inspiration for these stories was the mass shooting carried out at Columbine High School in suburban Colorado. Only the latest in a number of public shootings, one might imagine that this would be the occasion for public figures to reconsider laws about gun ownership and possession. Instead, the immediate conclusion reached by the nation's punditocracy, in a line of reasoning reminiscent of the linking of heavy metal and teen suicide in the 1980s, was that the high school shooters were suffering from the pernicious influence of pop culture—in this case, that of "goth" music and style. As is often the case, these pronouncements came from writers who probably had never heard a Cure recording, much less one by Siouxsie and the Banshees. Later in 1999, the conjunction of rap-metal songs containing misogynist lyrics with the occurrence at Woodstock '99 of vandalism, looting, and a series of rapes and molestations again ratcheted up media scrutiny of the dangerous effects of popular music.[1]

Goth's initial heyday occurred in the early 1980s, after which it experienced a revival in the mid-1990s. Here Neva Chonin, reporting for the *San Francisco Chronicle*, interviews teenagers in the San Francisco Bay Area who clearly debunk the claims of those who would make a casual connection between those who listen to gloomy, minor-key music with depressing lyrics and those who go on mass-killing sprees.

---

1. Several articles at the time viewed the simultaneous rise of rap-metal and boy bands as a kind of backlash against the "Lilith Fair" phenomenon and antisexist male and female alternative artists. See Ann Powers, "Critic's Notebook; A Surge of Sexism on the Rock Scene," *New York Times*, August 2, 1999; and Barry Walters, "Holding Their Own Hands," *Village Voice*, November 16, 1999, 121–22.

# BAY AREA GOTHS SAY MEDIA HAS IT WRONG (MANY TEENS OFFENDED BY SNAP ASSOCIATION OF SUBCULTURE AND SUSPECTS)

## Neva Chonin

BAY AREA—A day after the massacre at Colorado's Columbine High School, Bay Area students were appalled—not only at the senselessness of the tragedy, but at media coverage they say unfairly disparaged the Goth subculture.

The media were quick to slap the Goth label on the two teenagers who are suspected of carrying out the shooting, citing the suspects' affinity for black clothing, musicians such as shock-rocker Marilyn Manson and a role-playing game called "Vampire."

But local Goths call the association misleading and just plain wrong. They say the two teens were simply mentally disturbed.

"Violence is not what Goth is about," said Karen, a 14-year-old Berkeley High School freshman with fuschia-tipped blond hair. "Those two guys were just insane."

Several Berkeley High students who gathered yesterday in Martin Luther King Jr. Park between classes accused the media of exploiting the Goth subculture for the sake of a good headline.

"It's always society's solution to blame something other than itself," said Carolyn, a 17-year-old senior. "They just want a scapegoat."

For the Berkeley High students, the two suspects in Colorado were just a lot of youth trends and fascinations gathered under a single umbrella.

Some members of the clique that called itself the Trenchcoat Mafia have worn Gothlike black clothes to school every day. Others have mixed homegrown white supremacy with a fascination with Nazism and paramilitary hardware. Still others have spent enormous amounts of time online and had their own Web pages.

Jessie, a 16-year-old Goth in black lace whose porcelain face powder could not hide her freckles, said, "Just because someone dresses in black doesn't mean that they're Goths—or that they want to murder people. The media goes crazy about this stuff because it makes good reading."

With their haunted look and other-worldly makeup, Goths may look startling, but most say their attire does not reflect a love of violence. To most Goths, their brand of rebellion is an introverted, artistic turn away from materialism and conformity, not a campaign to collect weapons and kill people.

Inspired by Gothic artists and authors from centuries ago, members of the Goth subculture turn to fashion, music, art and literature to explore themes of death, pain and isolation. The scene was born in the early '80s as a fusion of glam rock and punk, and it has undergone a national resurgence in the '90s, led by cities such as San Francisco and New York.

Mainstream rock stars from Madonna to Jewel have adopted Goth motifs. Marilyn Manson also has borrowed heavily from the Goth world, as have many prominent fashion designers and screenwriters.

"Every form of music has something violent about it, even opera and classical," said 16-year-old Roxane, a hip-hop fan in a baggy T-shirt and jeans. "And besides, Goths are not people who want to fight. They're wimps who dress scary because they have no other way to defend themselves."

"Hey, I listen to Marilyn Manson, and there's no way I'm gonna go out and start killing people," said Jane, 17, a former Goth, as she gathered her books for her next class. "Something wasn't wrong with the music—something was wrong with those two people."

The teenagers said they often have played the "Vampire" game and have never seen any violent behavior. "There are the occasional nuts who think they're vampires, but they don't hurt anyone," said Jessie, shaking her head in disgust.

Skippy, a towering but soft-spoken 18-year-old dressed in black—including a trenchcoat—called the media's generalizations "bull—."

"It's just a way of segregating people," he said. "You can always find some random way to identify anybody with anything. I could relate Jessie to a slug because their bodies are both composed primarily of water."

> Finally, how can one sum up the complexity of popular music in the early 21st century? Several scholars of popular music have recently alluded to changes in the way young listeners consume popular music.[2] For those who grew up with the continuous broadcasting of music videos, linking music with visual media has become commonplace. Changes in the way multinational entertainment corporations operate, along with mergers between what were once companies devoted to separate media, have resulted in ever-new alliances between music and a range of other media forms, including music video, video games, and cinema. Reports that DVD sales outstripped sales of CDs in 2002 may come as a surprise, but with the advent of MP3 computer files that allow virtually unlimited downloading and storage of music, combined with the continuing inflated price of retail CDs, such a shift may have been predicted.
>
> Accompanying this shift in the role of music as the privileged form of entertainment for the under-25 crowd has been a new kind of eclecticism among younger listeners of pop music. The claim "I listen to everything," familiar as a response to those who ask a student about his or her preference in music, is becoming more and more accurate. Connected to the decline in sales of the now-almost-extinct "single," compilations of recent hits, such as *NOW That's What I Call Music* and *Totally Hits,* have enjoyed runs at the top of the best-selling album charts. During the heyday of the single, such collections appeared only years after the fact and then were marketed on late-night TV, resulting in sales figures that were unlikely to earn a spot on *Billboard.* All these developments suggest a shift in the type and level of involvement with particular genres experienced by a significant part of the audience for popular music.

---

2. See Lawrence Grossberg, "Same as It Ever Was? Rock Culture. Same as It Ever Was! Rock Theory," in *Stars Don't Stand Still in the Sky: Music and Myth,* ed. Karen Kelly and Evelyn McDonnell (New York: New York University Press), 99–121; and Jason Middleton and Roger Beebe, "The Racial Politics of Hybridity and 'Neo-Electism' Contemporary Popular Music," *Popular Music,* 21, no. 2 (May 2002): 159–72.

Technology and new commercial partnerships have resulted in present-ing popular music in contexts in which it would have previously seemed incongruous. Mark Morford, a popular columnist and cultural-political critic-satirist appearing on SFGate.com, the web site for the *San Francisco Chronicle*, addresses the musical performances that occurred during halftime at the Super Bowl in January 2003. In addition to the over-the-top militarism and nationalism that have become annual fea-tures of "Super Sunday," some sort of grandiose popular music perfor-mance has climaxed the halftime show for several years. Here Morford contrasts the impact between Shania Twain's lip-synched performance with the rough and ready nonsynched performance of Sting and No Doubt. Morford's essay makes explicit one of the guiding principles of this anthology: the inseparability of contemporary politics from the func-tion of popular music in public spectacles.

# Is Shania Twain Human?

## Mark Morford

And then out Shania strutted, all perfectly timed fireworks and perfect makeup and perfect cutesy head flips and perfect stiff hip flicks and a perfect toothy smile and perfectly catchy heavily synthesized completely lip-synched lyrics non-sung to perfectly pointless pop tunes. And the crowd went, shrug.

All lukewarm and hollow enough to make you cringe and recoil and sigh and wonder why it was again you were watching this bizarre overblown spectacle, this Super Bowl half-time extravaganza thing, oh yes, that's right, for the bizarre overblown spectacle, dear God please kill me now.

But there was something very wrong about this, something a little off, and you could-n't put your finger on it right away, because Shania's eight-minute soul-molesting medley was script perfect and Vegas tacky and she hit all her stage marks and sported that godaw-ful glittery faux-goth trailer-park hotpants ensemble thing, looking like something hocked up by Liberace during a laudanum-infused Barbarella nightmare.

Too harsh? Nah. She lip-synched every word. She completely faked it. She was a walk-ing mannequin, all hair and teeth and strings pulled from above. Nothing new there, though as a culture we're probably more accustomed to such simulated performance from non-singers like Britney or J.Lo, rather than someone who professes to be an actual crossover diva "artist," but still.

But then No Doubt and Sting came onstage, immediately after Shania's perfect prere-corded fist-pumping lounge act and just after she tossed around her perfectly shellacked faux sexuality like dimestore confetti, and from the first note of the other acts, you saw it. You got it. And you understood.

They actually sang. They talked to the audience. They were genuinely into the music they wrote and their movements weren't at all scripted and their voices weren't perfect and they were breathing hard into the mics because they were running around the stage, and Gwen was moving and gyrating spontaneously like a love goddess on ecstasy and therein lies the biggest difference: They may still be pop confections, but at least they genuinely taste good.

And you can bet some Super Bowl producer somewhere said to these latter acts, hey, why not make it easy on yourselves and just lip-synch to a tape, like Shania does, no one will really care, ain't like it's Carnegie Hall or anything, not like anyone in the openly deceitful ShrubCo era expects anything more.[3] To which they probably said, screw that, this is our music, we're musicians, let us actually play.

It was night and day. It was this odd little slap, weirdly shocking, the dramatic difference in presence, in energy, artistry, musicianship, connection. Sure it's all just vapid pop music. But then again, not quite.

Gwen Stefani and Sting sang a duet to "Message in a Bottle." At one point Gwen swiveled her hips so gorgeously and so deeply that the TV cameras were forced to shoot her only from the waist up, assumedly because it was just a little too racy for the Sunday Doritos n' Bud Light football crowd.

Stefani had more genuine sex appeal and feminine power in her left eyelash than Shania has in her whole career. Yet Twain is the megastar, sixth-best-selling album of all time, current No. 1 album in the country, reaching tens of millions. Baffling, and more than a little sad. Here is why:

Because, for one thing, despite all the bare midriffs and push-up bras and coy lyrics, Shania Twain is not a sexual person. She says as much in a recent terse *Rolling Stone* interview.[4] She is not sexual or even convivial or sociable or even all that friendly. She is a workaholic, she and her superstar-producer husband focus on her pop career with a laser-beam intensity, hell-bent on pop megastardom at all costs, on propagating the image of a fiery fun-loving sexually perky independent babe, even though it has absolutely nothing to do with who she actually is. God bless America.

There she is, openly admitting in *RS* that not a single song on her new best-selling CD "Up!" means anything to her personally, not one song is the slightest bit about her or anything she really cares about, her desires or emotions or painful angst about her hair or teeth or life in a remote multimillion-dollar Swiss chalet, where she now lives.

There she is, shrugging off the fact that every single song was exhaustively, viciously, perfectly crafted in the studio to squeeze out the absolute highest quotient of commercial salability, with not a single shred of genuine integrity or even the pretense of authentic emotion or content, and of course there's not a single thing wrong with that, except that it's completely and depressingly disingenuous and hollow and sad and in an oil-drunk ShrubCo world, it feels like exactly the last thing we really need.

Here's a kicker: The music Twain cares most about, the songs that have something to do with what she's really about as a human and a woman and a Canadian and an "artist," she sings in her bathroom, with the door closed, and usually not even her husband can hear them, because she fears they're pretty much crap and have no commercial value and no catchy hooks and one would want to hear them. Yikes.

---

3. "ShrubCo" is a reference to George W. Bush, 43rd president of the United States, and other members of his administration. Critics of Bush use the nickname "Shrub" as a way of referring to his being the "younger Bush," i.e., son of George H. W. Bush, 41st president.

4. This is a reference to a feature article on Twain; see Gavin Edwards, "Global Pop Dominatrix," *Rolling Stone*, February 6, 2003, 38–43.

Maybe it's the utter shamelessness that makes this worthy of our attention, the completely spiritless and unabashed determination to simply inundate the world with vacuous pop nothingness that makes Twain such the ideal spokesmodel for exactly what's wrong with megacorporate machine-made pop-music culture.

She is, apparently, not even in it for the sheer joy of it, not for fame's swanky accoutrements, not for the love of pop songcraft, not for the rush of performing onstage, not for the sex or the drugs or the rock 'n' roll. She says she doesn't really like pop stardom, has more money than she'll ever need and doesn't even like the record biz or performing and is admittedly antisocial and mechanical and impatient and asexual and terse. Hello, role model!

Then again, maybe Shania is to be applauded. Maybe she should be openly praised for not even pretending to care about the music itself, for not bothering with even the pretense of musical integrity or emotion or connection like other stars try to, instead only caring about her music's salability, its commercial success, the bottom line. Maybe she is the ideal spokesmodel, the living motto of a new breed of American pop star: We don't even pretend to care.

And, in a broader sense, this makes Twain the perfect spokesperson for her country. No, really, it does.

Much like ShrubCo's blatant warmongering, much like Cheney barely trying to conceal the outright oily corporatization of our nation and its war interests, much like a gov't that doesn't even pretend to conceal its true draconian motives, Shania Twain, with her multimillion-selling CD and frighteningly huge reach and casually inhospitable personality and antisocial lifestyle, is just the right kind of hyperdetermined, largely unpleasant, content-free heroine. As the saying goes, a country gets exactly the kind of pop stars it deserves. What, you'd rather have Michael Jackson?

# SELECT BIBLIOGRAPHY

Aletti, Vince. "Dancing Madness: The Disco Sound." *Rolling Stone* (August 28, 1975): 43, 50, 56.

Attali, Jacques. *Noise: The Political Economy of Music.* Translated by Brian Massumi. Minneapolis: University of Minnesota Press, 1985.

Bangs, Lester. "Dead Lie the Velvet Underground." *Creem* (May 1971): 44–49, 64–67.

———. "Bring Your Mother to the Gas Chamber" (Part 1). *Creem*, 4, no. 1 (June 1972): 40ff.

———. "Bring Your Mother to the Gas Chamber: Black Sabbath and the Straight Dope on Blood-Lust Orgies, Part 2." *Creem* (July 1972): 47ff.

Baraka, Amiri. "The Changing Same (R&B and New Black Music)." In Amiri Baraka, *Black Music*, 180–211. New York: William Morrow, 1967.

Barnes, Ken. "Top 40 Radio: A Fragment of the Imagination." In *Facing the Music,* ed. Simon Frith, 8–50. New York: Pantheon Book, 1988.

Beckett, Alan, and Richard Merton. "Stones/Comment." In *The Age of Rock: Sounds of the American Cultural Revolution,* ed. Jonathan Eisen, 109–17. New York: Random House, 1969. Originally published in *New Left Review* 47 (1968).

Bodroghkozy, Aniko. *Groove Tube: Sixties Television and the Youth Rebellion.* Durham, N.C.: Duke University Press, 2001.

Book, John. "Seattle Heavy." *Goldmine* (April 17, 1992): 46–54.

Brackett, David. *Interpreting Popular Music.* Berkeley: University of California Press, [1995] 2000.

———. "Music." In *Key Terms in Popular Music and Culture,* ed. Bruce Horner and Thomas Swiss, 124–40. Malden, Mass.: Blackwell, 1999.

———. "(In Search of) Musical Meaning: Genres, Categories, and Crossover." In *Popular Music Studies,* ed. David Hesmondhalgh and Keith Negus, 65–82. London: Arnold, 2002.

———. "'Where's It At': Postmodern Theory and the Contemporary Musical Field." In *Postmodern Music/Postmodern Thought*, ed. Judy Lochhead and Joseph Auner, 207–31. New York: Routledge, 2002.

Bromell, Nick. *Tomorrow Never Knows: Rock and Psychedelics in the 1960s.* Chicago: University of Chicago Press, 2000.

Burroughs, William. "Rock Magic: Jimmy Page, Led Zeppelin, and a Search for the Elusive Stairway to Heaven." *Crawdaddy* 49 (June 1975): 34–35, 39–40.

Campbell, Michael. *And the Beat Goes On: An Introduction to Popular Music in America, 1840 to Today.* New York: Schirmer Books, 1996.

Cantwell, Robert. *When We Were Good: The Folk Revival.* Cambridge, Mass.: Harvard University Press, 1996.

Carby, Hazel V. "'It Jus' Be's Dat Way Sometime': The Sexual Politics of Women's Blues." *Radical America* 20, no. 4 (1986): 9–24. Reprinted in *Keeping Time: Readings in Jazz History,* ed. Robert Walser, 351–65. New York: Oxford University Press, 1999.

Carman, Bryan. *A Race of Singers: Whitman's Working-Class Hero from Guthrie to Springsteen.* Chapel Hill: University of North Carolina Press, 2000.

Cavicchi, Daniel. *Tramps Like Us: Music and Meaning Among Springsteen Fans.* New York: Oxford University Press, 1998.

Chang, Jeff. "Word Power: A Brief, Highly Opinionated History of Hip-Hop Journalism." In *Pop Music and the Press,* ed. Steve Jones, 65–71. Philadelphia: Temple University Press, 2002.

Chapple, Steve, and Reebee Garofalo. *Rock 'n' Roll Is Here to Pay.* Chicago: Nelson-Hall, 1977.

Charters, Samuel. *The Roots of the Blues: An African Search.* New York: Da Capo Press, 1981.

Chester, Andrew. "Second Thoughts on a Rock Aesthetic: The Band." *New Left Review* 62 (1970): 75–82.

Chilton, John. *Let the Good Times Roll: The Story of Louis Jordan and His Music.* Ann Arbor: University of Michigan Press, 1997.

Christgau, Robert. "Rock Lyrics Are Poetry (Maybe)." In *The Age of Rock: Sounds of the American Cultural Revolution,* ed. Jonathan Eisen, 230–43. (New York: Random House, 1969), First published in *Cheetah* in December 1967.

————. "A Cult Explodes—and a Movement Is Born." *Village Voice,* October 24, 1977, 57, 68–74.

————. "Jesus, Jews, and the Jackass Theory." *Village Voice,* January 16, 1990, 83–86.

————. *Any Old Way You Choose It: Rock and Other Pop Music, 1967–1973.* New York: Viking Press, 1973.

Ching, Barbara. *Wrong's What I Do Best: Hard Country Music and Contemporary Culture.* New York: Oxford University Press, 2001.

Chuck D (with Yusuf Jah). *Fight the Power: Rap, Race, and Reality.* New York: Delacorte Press, 1997.

Cleave, Maureen. "How Does a Beatle Live? John Lennon Lives Like This." *Evening Standard,* March 4, 1966.

Coleman, Ray. "Would You Let Your Sister Go With a Rolling Stone?" *Melody Maker,* March 14, 1964, 8.

Coon, Caroline. *1988: The New Wave Punk Rock Explosion.* London: Omnibus Press, 1977.

Coppage, Noel. "Troubadettes, Troubadoras, and Troubadines . . . or . . . What's a Nice Girl Like You Doing in a Business Like This?" *Stereo Review* (September 1972): 58–61.

Covach, John. "Progressive Rock, 'Close to the Edge,' and the Boundaries of Style." In *Understanding Rock: Essays in Musical Analysis,* ed. John Covach and Graeme M. Boone (New York and Oxford: Oxford University Press, 1997), 3–31.

Crowe, Cameron. "Jimmy Page and Robert Plant Talk." *Rolling Stone* (March 13, 1975): 33–37.

Crowther, Bosley. "The Four Beatles in 'A Hard Day's Night.'" *New York Times,* August 12, 1964, 41.

Davis, Angela Y. *Blues Legacies and Black Feminism: Gertrude "Ma" Rainey, Bessie Smith, and Billie Holiday.* New York: Vintage Books, 1999.

DeCurtis, Anthony. "The Athens Scene." In *Rocking My Life Away: Writing About Music and Other Matters,* 21–27. Durham, N.C.: Duke University Press, 1998. Written in 1981.

DeCurtis, Anthony, and James Henke with Holly George-Warren, eds. *The Rolling Stone Illustrated History of Rock and Roll.* 3rd rev. ed. New York: Random House, 1992.

DeVeaux, Scott. "Constructing the Jazz Tradition: Jazz Historiography." *Black American Literature Forum* 25, no. 3 (Fall 1991): 525–60.

————. *The Birth of Bebop: A Social and Musical History.* Berkeley: University of California Press, 1997.

Ellison, Ralph. "Blues People." In Ralph Ellison, *Shadow and Act,* 247–58. New York: Vintage Books, [1964] 1972.

Eisen, Jonathan, ed. *The Age of Rock: Sounds of the American Cultural Revolution.* New York: Random House, 1969.

————. *The Age of Rock 2: Sights and Sounds of the American Cultural Revolution.* New York: Random House, 1970.

Ennis, Philip T. *The Seventh Stream: The Emergence of Rocknroll in American Popular Music.* Hanover N.H.: University Press of New England, 1992.

Erlmann, Veit. "The Aesthetics of the Global Imagination: Reflections on World Music in the 1990s." *Public Culture* 8 (1996): 467–87.

Faludi, Susan. *Backlash: The Undeclared War Against Women.* New York: Crown, 1991.

Fariña, Richard. "Baez and Dylan: A Generation Singing Out." *Mademoiselle* 59 (August 1964). Reprinted in *The Dylan Companion,* ed. Elizabeth Thomson and David Gutman, 81–88. New York: Delta, 1990.

Farren, Mick, and Pearce Marchbank. *Elvis in His Own Words.* London: Omnibus Press, 1977.

Fast, Susan. *In the Houses of the Holy: Led Zeppelin and the Power of Rock Music.* New York: Oxford University Press, 2001.

Filene, Benjamin. *Romancing the Folk: Public Memory and American Roots Music.* (Chapel Hill: University of North Carolina Press, 2000.

Fitzgerald, Jon. "Motown Crossover Hits 1963–1966 and the Creative Process." *Popular Music* 14 (January 1995): 1–12.

Flippo, Chet. *Your Cheatin' Heart: A Biography of Hank Williams.* Garden City, N.Y.: Doubleday, 1981.

Floyd, Samuel. *The Power of Black Music: Interpreting Its History from Africa to the United States.* New York: Oxford University Press, 1995.

Franklin, Aretha (and David Ritz). *Aretha: From These Roots.* New York: Villard, 1999.

Fricke, David. "Heavy Metal Justice." *Rolling Stone* (January 12, 1989): 42–49.

Frith, Simon. "Beyond the Dole Queue: The Politics of Punk." *Village Voice,* October 24, 1977, 77–79.

————. "'The Magic That Can Set You Free': The Ideology of Folk and the Myth of the Rock Community." In *Popular Music 1: Folk or Popular? Distinctions, Influences, Continuities,* ed. David Horn and Richard Middleton, 159–68. Cambridge, England: Cambridge University Press, 1981.

————. *Sound Effects.* New York: Pantheon Books, 1981.

————. *Performing Rites: On the Value of Popular Music.* Cambridge, Mass.: Harvard University Press, 1996.

————, and Howard Horne. *Art into Pop.* London: Methuen, 1987.

Garofalo, Reebee. *Rockin' Out: Popular Music in the USA.* Boston: Allyn and Bacon, 1997.

————. "Setting the Record Straight: Censorship and Social Responsibility in Popular Music." *Journal of Popular Music Studies* 6 (1994): 1–37.

Gendron, Bernard. *Between Montmartre and the Mudd Club: Popular Music and the Avant-Garde* Chicago: University of Chicago Press, 2002.

George, Nelson. *Where Did Our Love Go? The Rise and Fall of the Motown Sound.* New York: St. Martin's Press, 1985.

Goldstein, Richard. "We Still Need the Beatles, but. . . ." *New York Times,* June 18, 1967, sec. 2, p. 24.

————. "Pop Eye: I Blew My Cool Through the New York Times." *Village Voice,* July 20, 1967, 14, 25–26.

Green, Archie. "Hillbilly Music: Source and Symbol." *Journal of American Folklore* 78 (July–September 1965): 204–28.

Greenfield, Robert. "Keith Richard: Got to Keep It Growing." in *The Rolling Stone Interviews, Vol. 2.* New York: Straight Arrow, 1973. First published in *Rolling Stone* in August 1971.

Grossberg, Lawrence. "Same As It Ever Was? Rock Culture. Same As It Ever Was! Rock Theory." In *Stars Don't Stand Still in the Sky: Music and Myth,* ed. Karen Kelly and Evelyn McDonnell, 99–121. New York: New York University Press, 1999.

Guralnick, Peter. *Sweet Soul Music: Rhythm and Blues and the Southern Dream of Freedom.* New York: Harper and Row, 1986.

Hajdu, David. *Positively 4th Street: The Lives and Times of Joan Baez, Bob Dylan, Mimi Baez Fariña, and Richard Fariña*. New York: Farrar, Straus and Giroux, 2001.

Hamm, Charles. *Yesterdays: Popular Song in America*. New York: W. W. Norton, 1979.

hampton, dream. "Snoop Doggy Dogg: G-Down," *The Source* 48 (September 1993): 64–70.

Harrison, Daphne Duval. *Black Pearls: Blues Queens of the 1920s*. New Brunswick, N.J.: Rutgers University Press, 1988.

Headlam, Dave. "Does the Song Remain the Same? Questions of Authorship and Identification in the Music of Led Zeppelin." In *Concert Music, Rock, and Jazz Since 1945: Essays and Analytical Studies*, ed. Elizabeth West Marvin and Richard Hermann, 313–63. Rochester, N.Y.: University of Rochester Press, 1995.

Hebdige, Dick. *Subculture: The Meaning of Style*. London: Methuen, 1979.

Hentoff, Nat. "The Playboy Interview: Bob Dylan—A Candid Conversation with the Iconoclastic Idol of the Folk-Rock Set." *Playboy* (March 1966); reprinted in *Bob Dylan: The Early Years; A Retrospective*, ed. Craig McGregor, 132–33. New York: Da Capo Press, [1972] 1990.

Heylin, Clinton, ed. *The Da Capo Book of Rock and Roll Writing*. New York: Da Capo Press, [1992] 2000.

Hill, Trent. "The Enemy Within: Censorship in Rock Music in the 1950s." *South Atlantic Quarterly* 90 (Fall 1991): 675–708.

Hirshey, Gerri. *Nowhere to Run: The Story of Soul Music*. New York: Penguin Books, [1984] 1985.

Holden, Stephen. "The Evolution of a Dance Craze." *Rolling Stone*, April 19, 1979, 29.

hooks, bell. "Madonna: Plantation Mistress or Soul Sister?" In belle hooks, *Black Looks: Race and Representation*, 157–64. Boston: South End Press, 1992.

Jackson, John A. *American Bandstand: Dick Clark and the Making of a Rock 'n' Roll Empire* (New York: Oxford University Press, 1997.

Jameson, Fredric. "Postmodernism, or the Cultural Logic of Late Capitalism." *New Left Review* 146 (July–August 1984): 59–92. Reprinted in *Postmodernism, or the Cultural Logic of Late Capitalism* (Durham, N.C.: Duke University Press, 1991), 1–54.

Jatta, Sidia. "Born Musicians: Traditional Music from the Gambia." In *Repercussions: A Celebration of African-American Music*, ed. Geoffrey Haydon and Dennis Marks, 14–29. London: Century, 1985.

Jones, Steve, ed. *Pop Music and the Press*. Philadelphia: Temple University Press, 2002.

Jones, Steve, and Martin Sorger. "Covering Music: A Brief History and Analysis of Album Cover Design." *Journal of Popular Music Studies*, 11–12 (1999–2000): 68–102.

Kaplan, E. Ann. *Rocking Around the Clock: Music Television, Postmodernism and Consumer Culture*. London: Methuen, 1987.

Keathley, Elizabeth. "Eminem's Murder Ballads." *Echo* 4, no. 2 (Fall 2002); available on-line at http://www.humnet.ucla.edu/echo/volume4-issue2/keathley/index.html.

Keightley, Keir. "Around the World: Musical Tourism and the Globalization of the Record Industry, 1946–66." Unpublished manuscript, 1998.

Keil, Charles. *Urban Blues*. Chicago: University of Chicago Press, 1966.

————, and Steven Feld. *Music Grooves: Essays and Dialogues*. Chicago: University of Chicago Press, 1994.

Kelley, Robin D. G. "Kickin' Reality, Kickin' Ballistics: 'Gangsta Rap' and Postindustrial Los Angeles." In Robin D. G. Kelley, *Race Rebels: Culture, Politics, and the Black Working Class*, 183–227. New York: Free Press, 1994.

Kopkind, Andrew. "Woodstock Nation." In *The Age of Rock 2: Sights and Sounds of the American Cultural Revolution*, ed. Jonathan Eisen, 312–18. New York: Random House, 1970. Originally published in *Hard Times* in 1969.

Kruse, Holly. "Subcultural Identity in Alternative Music Culture." *Popular Music* 12 (January 1993): 33–41.

Landau, Jon. "Rock and Art." *Rolling Stone*, July 20, 1968, 18–19.

Lipsitz, George. *Time Passages: Collective Memory and American Popular Culture.* Minneapolis: University of Minnesota Press, 1990.

Macan, Edward. *Rocking the Classics: English Progressive Rock and the Counterculture.* New York: Oxford University Press, 1997.

Magee, Jeffrey. "Before Louis: When Fletcher Henderson Was the 'Paul Whiteman of the Race.'" *American Music* 18 (Winter 2000): 391–425.

Mailer, Norman. "The White Negro: Superficial Reflections on the Hipster." *Dissent* 4 (Summer 1957): 276–93.

Malone, Bill. *Country Music U.S.A.* rev. and enlarged ed. Austin: University of Texas Press, 1985.

Manheim, James M. "B-side Sentimentalizer: 'Tennessee Waltz' in the History of Popular Music." *Musical Quarterly* 76 (Fall 1992): 37–56.

Manuel, Peter. *Caribbean Currents: Caribbean Music from Rumba to Reggae.* Philadelphia: Temple University Press, 1995.

Marcus, Greil. *Mystery Train: Images of America in Rock 'n' Roll Music.* 3rd rev. ed. New York: Plume, [1975] 1990.

————. *Dead Elvis: A Chronicle of a Cultural Obsession.* New York: Doubleday, 1991.

————. *Invisible Republic: Bob Dylan's Basement Tapes,* pp. 1–41. New York: Henry Holt, 1997.

Marsh, Dave. *The Heart of Rock and Soul: The 1001 Greatest Singles Ever Made.* New York: Da Capo Press, [1989] 1999.

————. "Live Through This." *Rock 'n' Roll Confidential* (May 1994): 1–8.

McClary, Susan. "Living to Tell: Madonna's Resurrection of the Fleshy." In Susan McClary, *Feminine Endings,* 148–66. Minneapolis: University of Minnesota Press, 1991.

McKeen, William, ed. *Rock and Roll Is Here to Stay: An Anthology.* New York: W. W. Norton, 2000.

McLeese, Don. "Anatomy of an Anti-Disco Riot." *In These Times* (August 29–September 4, 1979): 23.

McLeod, Kembrew. "The Politics and History of Hip-Hop Journalism." In *Pop Music and the Press,* ed. Steve Jones, 156–67. Philadelphia: Temple University Press, 2002.

McLuhan, Marshall. *Understanding Media: The Extensions of Man.* New York: Signet Books, 1964.

Mercer, Kobena. "Monster Metaphors: Notes on Michael Jackson's *Thriller.*" *Screen* 27, no. 1 (1986). Reprinted in Simon Frith, Andrew Goodwin, and Lawrence Grossberg, eds., *Sound and Vision: The Music Video Reader* (London and New York: Routledge, 1993), 93–108.

Middleton, Jason, and Roger Beebe. "The Racial Politics of Hybridity and 'Neo-Electism' Contemporary Popular Music." *Popular Music* 21 (May 2002): 159–72.

Middleton, Richard. "All Shook Up." In *The Elvis Reader: Texts and Sources on the King of Rock 'n' Roll,* ed. K. Quain, 3–12. New York: St. Martin's Press, 1992.

Modleski, Tania. *Feminism Without Women: Culture and Criticism in a "Postfeminist Age."* New York: Routledge, 1991.

Oliver, Paul. *Savannah Syncopators: African Retentions in the Blues.* New York: Stein and Day, 1970.

————. *Songsters and Saints: Vocal Traditions on Race Records.* Cambridge, England: Cambridge University Press, 1984.

Palmer, Robert. *Deep Blues.* New York: Penguin, [1981] 1985.

————. *Rock & Roll: An Unruly History.* New York: Harmony Books, 1995.

Pareles, Jon. "How Rap Moves to Television's Beat." *New York Times,* January 14, 1990, Sec. 2, 1–2.

Parsons, Michael. "Rolling Stones." In *The Age of Rock: Sounds of the American Cultural Revolution,* ed. Jonathon Eisen, 118–20. New York: Random House, 1970.

Peterson, Richard. *Creating Country Music: Fabricating Authenticity.* Chicago: University of Chicago Press, 1997.

————, and David G. Berger. "Cycles in Symbol Production: The Case of Popular Music." *American Sociological Review* 40 (1975). Reprinted in Simon Frith and Andrew Goodwin, eds., *On Record: Rock, Pop, and the Written Word* (New York: Pantheon, 1990), 140–59.

Post, Henry. "Sour Notes at the Hottest Disco." *Esquire* (June 20, 1978): 79–86.

Powers, Ann. "When Women Venture Forth." *New York Times,* October 9, 1994, 39.

Puterbaugh, Parke. "Anglomania: American Surrenders to the Brits–But Who Really Wins?" *Rolling Stone,* November 10, 1983, 31–32.

Ramsey, Guthrie P., Jr. *Race Music: Black Culture from Bebop to Hip-Hop.* Berkeley: University of Califoria Press, 2003.

Reynolds, Simon. *Generation Ecstasy: Into the World of Techno and Rave Culture.* New York: Routledge, [1998] 1999.

Roberts, John Storm. *The Latin Tinge: The Impact of Latin American Music on the United States.* 2nd ed. New York: Oxford University Press, [1979] 1999.

Rockwell, John. "The Artistic Success of Talking Heads." *New York Times*, September 11, 1977, D14, 16.

————. *All-American Music: Composition in the Late Twentieth Century.* New York: Vintage Books, 1984.

Rodgers, Jeffrey Pepper. "My Secret Place: The Guitar Odyssey of Joni Mitchell." In *The Joni Mitchell Companion: Four Decades of Commentary,* ed. Stacey Luftig, 219–30. New York: Schirmer Books, 2000.

Rodman, Gilbert. *Elvis After Elvis: The Posthumous Career of a Living Legend.* London: Routledge, 1996.

*The Rolling Stone Record Review.* By the editors of *Rolling Stone.* New York: Pocket Books, 1971.

*The Rolling Stone Record Review, Volume 2.* By the editors of *Rolling Stone.* New York: Pocket Books, 1974.

Rose, Tricia. *Black Noise: Rap Music and Black Culture in Contemporary America.* Hanover, N.H.: Wesleyan University Press and University Press of New England, 1994.

Rosenthal, David H. *Hard Bop: Jazz and Black Music, 1955–1965.* New York: Oxford University Press, 1992.

Ruhlmann, William. "Joni Mitchell: From Blue to Indigo." *Goldmine,* February 17, 1995; reprinted in *The Joni Mitchell Companion: Four Decades of Commentary,* ed. Stacey Luftig, 21–40. New York: Schirmer Books, 2000.

Rumble, John. "The Roots of Rock & Roll: Henry Glover of King Records." *Journal of Country Music* 14, no. 2 (1992): 30–42.

Ryan, John. *The Production of Culture in the Music Industry: The ASCAP-BMI Controversy.* Lanham, Md.: University Press of America, 1985.

Samuels, David. "The Rap on Rap: The 'Black Music' That Isn't Either." *The New Republic* (November 11, 1991): 24–29.

Sanjek, David. "One Size Does Not Fit All: The Precarious Position of the African American Entrepreneur in Post-WWII American Popular Music." *American Music* 15 (Winter 1997): 535–62.

Sanjek, Russell, and David Sanjek. *Pennies from Heaven: The American Popular Music Business in the Twentieth Century.* New York: Da Capo Press, 1996.

Savage, Jon. "Machine Soul: A History of Techno." *Village Voice Rock and Roll Quarterly* (Summer 1993): 19.

Schuller, Gunther. *The Swing Era: The Development of Jazz, 1930–1945.* New York: Oxford University Press, 1989.

Schwichtenberg, Cathy. *The Madonna Connection: Representational Politics, Subcultural Identities, and Cultural Theory.* Boulder, Colo.: Westview Press, 1993.

Shank, Barry. *Dissonant Identities: The Rock 'n' Roll Scene in Austin, Texas.* Hanover, N.H.: Wesleyan University Press and University Press of New England, 1994.

Shelton, Robert. "Bob Dylan: A Distinctive Folk-Song Stylist." *New York Times*, September 29, 1961. Reprinted in *Bob Dylan: The Early Years: A Retrospective,* ed. Craig McGregor, 17–18. New York: Da Capo Press, [1972] 1990.

————. "On Records: The Folk-Rock Rage," *New York Times*, January 30, 1966, 17–18.

Siegel, Jules. "A Teen-age Hymn to God," in *Rock and Roll Is Here to Stay: An Anthology*, ed. William McKeen, 387–99. New York: W. W. Norton and Company, 2000. First published in *Cheetah* (October 1967).

Slater, Jack. "A Sense of Wonder," *New York Times Magazine*, February 23, 1975, 18, 21–23, 26–32.

Smith, Jeff. *The Sounds of Commerce: Marketing Popular Film Music*. New York: Columbia University Press, 1998.

Smith, Paul, ed. *Madonnarama: Essays on Sex and Popular Culture*. Pittsburgh, PA: Cleis Press, 1993.

Sontag, Susan. "Notes on 'Camp.'" In Susan Sontag, *Against Interpretation and Other Essays*, 275–92. New York: Anchor Books, 1990. Originally published in 1964.

Tate, Greg. *Flyboy in the Buttermilk: Essays on Contemporary America*. New York: Fireside/Simon and Schuster, 1992.

————. Diatribe," *Village Voice*, September 3, 1996, 46.

Taylor, Timothy D. *Global Pop: World Music, World Markets*. New York: Routledge, 1997.

Thornton, Sarah. *Club Cultures: Music, Media and Subcultural Capital*. Hanover, N.H.: Wesleyan University Press and University Press of New England, 1996.

Toop, David. *Rap Attack 2: African Rap to Global Hip Hop*. London: Serpent's Tail, 1991.

Touré. "The Family Way: The Hiphop Crew as Center of the World." *Village Voice*, October 10, 1995, 49.

Townshend, Peter. Review of "The Who: *Meaty, Beaty, Big, and Bouncy*." *Rolling Stone*, December 7, 1971.

Trakin, Roy. "Avant Kindergarten [Sturm and Drone], *Soho Weekly News*, January 26, 1978, 31, 37.

Vincent, Rickey. *Funk: The Music, the People, and the Rhythm of the One*. New York: St. Martin's Griffin, 1996.

Vito, R. "The Chuck Berry Style: A Modern Rocker Pays Tribute to the Master." *Guitar Player* (June 1984): 72–75.

Waksman, Steve. *Instruments of Desire: The Electric Guitar and the Shaping of Musical Experience*. Cambridge, Mass.: Harvard University Press, 1999.

Wallace, Michele. "Michael Jackson, Black Modernisms and 'The Ecstasy of Communication." In Michele Wallace, *Invisibility Blues: From Pop to Theory* (London: Verso, 1990), 77–90.

Walser, Robert. *Running with the Devil: Power, Gender and Madness in Heavy Metal Music*. Hanover, N.H.: Wesleyan University Press and University Press of New England, 1993.

————. "Rhythm, Rhyme, and Rhetoric in the Music of Public Enemy." *Ethnomusicology* 39 (1995): 193–217.

————, ed. *Keeping Time: Readings in Jazz History*. New York: Oxford University Press, 1999.

Welch, Chris. "Jimmy Page, Part Three." *Melody Maker*, February 28, 1970, 10.

Wenner, Jann. *Lennon Remembers: The Rolling Stone Interviews*. New York: Popular Library, 1971.

Whitesell, Lloyd. "Harmonic Palette in Early Joni Mitchell." *Popular Music* 21 (May 2002): 173–94.

Wilder, Alec. *American Popular Song: The Great Innovators, 1900–1950*. New York: Oxford University Press, 1972.

Willis, Ellen. *Beginning to See the Light: Sex, Hope, and Rock-and-Roll*. Hanover, N.H.: Wesleyan University Press and University Press of New England, 1992.

Willis, Susan. "I Want the Black One: Is There a Place for Afro-American Culture in Commodity Culture?" In Susan Willis, *A Primer for Daily Life*, 108–32. London: Routledge, 1991.

Wolfe, Charles. "Presley and the Gospel Tradition." In *The Elvis Reader: Texts and Sources on the King of Rock 'n' Roll*, ed. K. Quain, 13–27. New York: St. Martin's Press, 1992.

Wolfe, Tom. *Electric Kool-Aid Acid Test*. New York: Farrar, Straus and Giroux, 1968.

Young, Charles M. "Rock Is Sick and Living in London: A Report on the Sex Pistols." *Rolling Stone*, October 20, 1977, 68–75.

Zabor, Rafi, and Vic Garbarini, "Wynton Vs. Herbie: The Purist and the Crossbreeder Duke It Out." *Musician* 77 (March 1985): 52–64. Reprinted in Robert Walser, ed., *Keeping Time: Readings in Jazz History*, 339–51. New York: Oxford University Press, 1999.

Zappa, Frank. "Statement to Congress, 19 September 1985." In *The Da Capo Book of Rock & Roll Writing*, ed. Clinton Heylin, 501–08. New York: Da Capo Press, [1992] 2000.

# INDEX

Within some of the longer entries, especially significant first-person statements are indicated in **bold**.